beyond
GLOBAL CRISIS

beyond
GLOBAL CRISIS

Remedies and Road Maps
by Daisaku Ikeda and
His Contemporaries

Terrence Edward Paupp

With a foreword by Olivier Urbain
and an afterword by Brian J. Foley

Transaction Publishers
New Brunswick (U.S.A.) and London (U.K.)

Library of Congress Catalog Number: 2011042480
ISBN: 978-1-4128-4616-5
Printed in the United States of America

Library of Congress Cataloging-in-Publication Data

Paupp, Terrence Edward.
    Beyond global crisis: remedies and road maps by Daisaku Ikeda and his contemporaries / Terrence Edward Paupp; with a foreword by Olivier Urbain.
        p. cm.
    Includes bibliographical references and index.
    ISBN 978-1-4128-4616-5 (acid-free paper)
    1. Conflict management—International cooperation. 2. Peace—International cooperation. 3. Human security—International cooperation. 4. Peace—Social aspects. 5. Human security—Social aspects. 6. United Nations—Reform. 7. Conflict management—Philosophy. 8. Ikeda, Daisaku—Political and social views. I. Title.
    JZ5601.P38   2012
    327.1′72—dc23
                                                          2011042480

For Richard Falk,
friend, colleague, international law scholar, and mentor

Contents

**Part III. Visualizing a Global Civilization of
Harmony and Interdependence in Concrete Terms**

Foreword

For many decades, Daisaku Ikeda has proposed solutions for world problems and built networks of solidarity across spiritual, geographical, cultural, and social boundaries. For more than six decades of activities for peace (1947–present), Ikeda has shown his capacity to weather crises at the local, national, and global levels when it comes to the development of the worldwide grassroots movement of which he is the leader, the Buddhist lay organization Soka Gakkai International (SGI), which has more than twelve million members worldwide. Moreover, the many institutions he has established in the field of peace, culture, and education are all part of a global network.

These networks all share the common characteristic of advancing the cause of peace and global human solidarity. In the present book, *Beyond Global Crisis*, the esteemed scholar Terrence E. Paupp has written a groundbreaking original new work bridging Eastern and Western thought, advancing a road map for the achievement of international peace. It is inclusive of Ikeda's philosophy and also the work of a variety of Western scholars and leaders who are introduced throughout this book as persons whom Paupp calls "contemporaries of Ikeda."

The first foundational work that systematizes and explains the central components of Ikeda's philosophy from the 1940s to the present was laid out in my book, *Daisaku Ikeda's Philosophy of Peace* (Urbain 2010). What was left unaddressed by my work is now taken to the next level by Paupp, who has published extensively on issues of governance, international law, and international relations (Paupp 2000, 2007, 2009). In *Beyond Global Crisis* we find Paupp addressing the challenges of how best to implement Ikeda's philosophy of peace and the road map that he has provided in the decades since the 1940s in the form of books, annual proposals to the United Nations, dialogues with world leaders and intellectuals, as well as editorials, speeches at universities and colleges, and in his various leadership roles as the head of SGI.

Yet this book is not merely seeking to be a tribute to Ikeda, but rather an appreciation and acknowledgment of his unique contributions to peace. We find, in chapters 1 through 8, that Paupp is engaged in presenting a scholarly work that unites the central tenets of Ikeda's philosophy of peace in a comparative and interdisciplinary approach with those of other thinkers of the nineteenth, twentieth, and twenty-first centuries. Further, in juxtaposition to this comparative analysis of thinkers and leaders, Paupp undertakes an explication of concrete issues that are global in scope and cross-cutting across civilizations, regions, and nations. Therefore, the result is one where we are able to see parallels to the challenges confronted by other great leaders and intellectuals. In their personal struggles and the resulting strategies that emerge from them we find a common ground for hope and action. That is because, in combination, Ikeda and many of his contemporaries are dedicated to the construction of a better world.

In this critical connection, Paupp presents Ikeda's philosophy as a workable guide to augment the various challenges presented by the intricacies of global governance. The aspects of global governance include institutions and issues. The institutions that are addressed range from the International Criminal Court to the United Nations, the International Monetary Fund to the World Bank. The issues range from nuclear abolition and strategies for nuclear disarmament to the interrelated problems of poverty, human rights, and climate change. In addressing these matters, Paupp introduces Ikeda's philosophy and peace proposals to the Western world. Ikeda's approach is centered on three interrelated conceptual pillars—(1) inner transformation, (2) dialogue, and (3) global citizenship leading to the construction of a more humane and peaceful global civilization. In my book on the foundations and structure of Ikeda's thought I have gone into great detail in explicating each of these three areas (Urbain 2010).

Paupp and I agree with Ikeda when he asserts that each individual human being is the starting place for the realization of peace. This is the central point of departure that connects the perspectives of Ikeda, Paupp, and my own. This perspective is premised on the idea that the only kind of individual who is truly capable of being an instrument of peace must have undergone a deep and profound transformation of heart and consciousness, mind and spirit. We see this dynamic in the lives of some of history's most effective peacemakers, such as Nelson Mandela, Martin Luther King Jr., and Robert F. Kennedy. In these examples we see what Ikeda refers to when he speaks of the "human revolution," by which he means a type of inner transformation (Urbain 2010). That is because the human revolution involves reaching a higher level of self-realization, which in turn, creates the inner and outer conditions for a constructive dialogue with others. When self-realized people engage in dialogue, they have the capacity for empathy, and it is this quality that opens the door for compassion. In turn, the exercise of this kind of compassion can lead to the transformation of the world. That is because the kind of dialogue that Ikeda has specified serves to lead to a new consciousness that can comprehend alternatives to the violence, injustices, and poverty of the status quo.

Hence, dialogue between self-realized people can help create the necessary conditions for a new kind of trajectory in human affairs and global history.

That is precisely what Paupp describes in his case study of the 1962 Cuban missile crisis when President John F. Kennedy and Nikita Khrushchev came to a peaceful resolution of the crisis. Shortly thereafter, Kennedy gave his "peace speech" at American University in June 1963, thereby opening the door for negotiations on a nuclear test ban treaty. By October 1963, a Limited Nuclear Test Ban Treaty had been signed by the United States, the Soviet Union, and Great Britain.

Concerning dialogue, Ikeda wrote:

> The real essence and practice of humanism is found in heartfelt, one-to-one dialogue. Be it summit diplomacy or the various interactions of private citizens in different lands, genuine dialogue has the kind of intensity described by the great twentieth-century humanist and philosopher Martin Buber (1878–1965) as an encounter "on the narrow ridge" in which the slightest inattention could result in a precipitous fall. Dialogue is indeed this kind of intense, high-risk encounter (Ikeda 2005-PP, 12).

I also see a direct link with Jürgen Habermas's philosophy of dialogue. On this matter, I wrote:

> Using Habermasian language, I want to assert that Ikeda's vision for a global civilization of interdependence and harmony includes a flourishing of the public sphere and a defense of humanity against the excesses of the administrative sphere, using dialogue as a vehicle for communicative rationality, in order to let deliberative democracy flourish, thereby strengthening the public sphere towards more peace and justice. Since the use of communicative rationality implies a constant effort to respect human life, in line with the Kantian imperative to always consider people as an end and never as a means, I think the Habermasian concepts explored here provide philosophical support to the thesis that inner transformation, dialogue and global citizenship form a coherent system leading to peace (Urbain 2010, 122–23).

Paupp and I agree that there are more than enough sources of encouragement to be found in the writings and actions of Ikeda and his contemporaries for humanity to move toward a more dialogical global society, beyond global crisis. This is critical if humanity is to be able to collectively progress to a more humane and inclusive global civilization. In his 1996 lecture at Columbia University entitled "Education toward Global Citizenship," Ikeda wrote:

> Over the past several decades, I have been privileged to meet and converse with many people from all walks of life, and I have given the matter some thought. Certainly, global citizenship is not determined

merely by the number of languages one speaks, or the number of countries to which one has traveled. I have many friends who could be considered quite ordinary citizens, but who possess an inner nobility; who have never traveled beyond their native place, yet who are genuinely concerned for the peace and prosperity of the world (Ikeda 2001b, 100).

Ikeda's ideas concerning global citizenship become more concrete in his annual peace proposals, which he has presented on January 26 each year since 1983. Ikeda does not provide a complete design for a future global civilization. He prefers to encourage individuals to develop courage, wisdom, and compassion, to refine their capacity for dialogue, and to flourish as global citizens concerned as much with their family members and neighbors as with global issues. What he does suggest is that the emergence of certain elements of a future global and more humane civilization has to be noticed and that their capacity to benefit humanity has to be examined and evaluated. Ikeda also supports the emergence of some of these structures in global society.

In *Beyond Global Crisis*, Paupp provides us with specifics. For example, he writes about nuclear abolition in the framework of the Nuremberg Principles. He proposes a "principle of hegemonic state accountability" based on the United Nations Charter and also on current calls for a global nuclear weapons convention dedicated to abolition. As Paupp acknowledges, this will also entail fundamental reforms of the UN Security Council and expanding the powers and scope of authority of the UN General Assembly. Similarly, on the challenges associated with climate change and global warming, Paupp identifies the need for the nations of the global North to enter into a serious dialogue with the nations of the global South in achieving a new planetary consensus on how best to deal with another global crisis—a crisis just as deadly dangerous as that of the potential for nuclear war.

Paupp's vision of the future of global relations perfectly concurs with Ikeda's vision on these very points. That is because in the twenty-first century, humanity needs to engage in a rethinking of the concept of what actually constitutes "human security." We can no longer think of security issues in strictly military terms, concerns with the "balance of power" between nations, or some kind of security that is purchased at the price of hegemony, the pursuit of empire, or the subordination of the human rights of people for the sake of the powerful being able to exploit the resources of the powerless. Rather, a new global civilization is emerging that can no longer afford the high costs associated with hegemony or empire. It is along these lines that Paupp is arguing that we are moving into a posthegemonic era. It will be characterized by a truly multicentric and multipolar world of regions as the most dominant trait for global governance.

Throughout this book, Paupp makes a persuasive case for asserting that we live in an age where the crumbling walls of US hegemony are giving way to a world of rising regions. On every continent, from Asia to Africa, from Europe to the Middle East, from India and China to Russia, from North America to Latin America, peoples and nations are becoming more open to a strategy and culture of peace that evolve through discovering a commonality of interests, the value of mutual cooperation, and the desirability of forging consensus. In this new century, the task will be to unite the ideal with the real and, in so doing, to finally transcend the limitations of the past. In this new endeavor, equipped with some of the proposed solutions and strategies that this book provides, it is hoped that humanity will collectively become engaged in remaking the character of global governance so that it is increasingly conducive to building a global culture of peace.

Honolulu, January 2012
Olivier Urbain
Director, Toda Institute
Author of *Daisaku Ikeda's Philosophy of Peace* (2010)

Acknowledgments

In the course of writing *Beyond Global Crisis*, I have found the process to be singularly unique. Rarely does an author have the opportunity and the challenge to engage in a dialogue between cultures, as I have had in this book. To find the bridges and common themes of concern on the great issues affecting the future of humanity actually being articulated with a sense of principled convergence in the writings and proposals of both East and West is truly remarkable. That is what engagement with the work of the Japanese peace scholar and activist Daisaku Ikeda has afforded. Further, the subject matter of the book has also permitted me to engage with writers and scholars who bridge the North–South divide—the historic division between the global South ("Third World") and the global North (industrialized nations of the "West").

In coming to terms with the implications of this global dialogue, I have been more than fortunate to have the benefit of the scholarship and friendship of Prof. Richard Falk. His distinguished career at Princeton University as an international law scholar and expert, in addition to his work with the United Nations, as well as his identification with progressive social movements and human rights efforts around the globe, has made him both an architect and an inspiration for thousands of people over many decades. His dozens of books and hundreds of articles have been a light and a beacon for those who, in the words of the poet Alfred Lord Tennyson, continue "to seek a newer world." I have been reading Richard's books and articles since 1980. It was not until I sent him the manuscript of my first major book (*for which he wrote the Foreword*) that I have had the joy of knowing him personally. In that regard, I am glad to say that I have been the beneficiary of his insights and expertise for over a decade as he has reviewed my work and contributed occasional editorial ideas on its improvement. To him, I remain indebted.

I am also very grateful to other international law scholars whose wisdom has contributed so much to the shaping of my thought and the approaches that I have taken throughout this book. At the top of the list, I feel the need to single out Prof. Brian Foley for praise and offer him my profound gratitude for the work he has done on the issue of United Nations Security Council reform. His views are well represented in this book. Like Richard Falk,

I believe that Brian Foley has helped to chart a path out of the darkness of our time. The amazing congruence of their work and proposals on the issue of United Nations Security Council reform, in combination with those of Ikeda and his contemporaries, is truly amazing.

On a personal note I want to express my gratitude to photojournalist Clyde Keller, whose photo entitled *"Spirit Place"* graces the cover of this book. During the course of writing this book, I appreciated being able to share the manuscript as it evolved with Clyde. In combination, his sharing of viewpoints about the manuscript, along with the pleasure of seeing so much of his wonderful photography, made this process more enjoyable. Clyde's photojournalistic accomplishments span the years from 1968 to the present times. My favorite examples of his work are the unequaled photos he took of the late senator from New York, Robert Francis Kennedy. Robert Kennedy has always been a personal hero of mine, and his idealism informs and inspires much of the spirit of this book in a way that complements the themes and proposed solutions that are being discussed.

Also, I cannot help but give my boundless praise and an expression of profound gratitude to Dr. Irving Louis Horowitz, the editorial director of Transaction Publishers. I am glad to say that this book has found its proper home with one of the world's truly preeminent publishers. I am honored to be associated with them and to enjoy the privilege of having *Beyond Global Crisis* published by them.

I also want to express my deep appreciation to the hardworking, dedicated, and visionary people at the Toda Institute for Global Peace and Policy Research. Their generous support of this project has made the journey worth the effort. In particular, I want to thank Dr. Hiroshi Morita for his support and belief in my abilities to bring this project to a successful completion. The Toda Institute is one of the preeminent scholarly and educational institutions in the world today that are dedicated to advancing the cause of peace.

Over the period of the last decade, I have been fortunate to have benefited from the research and work of The Lawyers Committee on Nuclear Policy, headquartered in New York. I am especially grateful to its executive director, Dr. John Burroughs, for his friendship and advice on the complexities of nuclear abolition and disarmament. Their influence is evident in various chapters throughout this book. In this regard, I have also benefited from the progressive activism and work of Mr. Bruce Gagnon, the director and policy coordinator for Global Network Against Weapons and Nuclear Power in Space.

Last, but not least, I want to express my thanks and eternal appreciation to my best friend, John Michael Thomas Baker. Through difficult times he has been always present, on the phone or in person, to remind me that my life and work have meaning for the world. He has also made me laugh with his good humor and his abilities as a gifted and upcoming actor in Los Angeles. I celebrate his career as much as he has celebrated mine.

In addition to Johnny, I also need to recognize my faithful golden retriever, Sparky, who is the epitome of a loving dog. My personal world is a better place because of him. Our collectively shared world is a better place because of all the individuals that I have had the privilege to acknowledge here.

Terrence E. Paupp
Los Angeles, California
September 12, 2011

Introduction

In his classic novel on the French Revolution, author Charles Dickens began *A Tale of Two Cities* with the observation that

> [i]t was the best of times, it was the worst of times, it was the age of wisdom, it was the age of foolishness, it was the epoch of belief, it was the epoch of incredulity, it was the season of Light, it was the season of darkness, it was the spring of hope, it was the winter of despair, we had everything before us, we had nothing before us, we were all going direct to Heaven, we were all going direct the other way—in short, the period was so far like the present period, that some of its noisiest authorities insisted on its being received, for good or for evil, in the superlative degree of comparison only.

In this book, *Beyond Global Crisis*, we can join with Dickens in his proclivity to speak of the extremes of our own time in the superlative. For the "global crisis" which we are addressing has its historical roots back into the nineteenth century in which Dickens wrote, became a series of global crises in the twentieth century, and manifests itself in a variety of planetary dimensions at the dawn of the twenty-first century.

In short, what Dickens described as a *"tale of two cities,"* we can look at in the twenty-first century as a *"tale of two worlds"*—one of those worlds is the one that we currently inhabit and is in the midst of a *"global crisis,"* while the other world is a newer world, a world that we have the capacity to envision and eventually actualize, achieve, and realize in the larger context of an emerging, sustainable, and peaceful global civilization. The volume entitled *Daisaku Ikeda's Philosophy of Peace: Dialogue, Transformation and Global Citizenship* (2010) is the first one systematizing the thoughts, writings, and actions for world peace of the contemporary Japanese spiritual leader. In this pioneering work, Olivier Urbain reveals how Daisaku Ikeda, the leader of the Soka Gakkai International (SGI), devoted his entire life to delivering a message of peace that allows each and every person to be part of a process toward a better world. What is offered in Urbain's systematization is a road map allowing each person to participate in the task of building a more peaceful global civilization through the combination of (1) innertransformation, (2) dialogue, and (3) a spirit of global citizenship.

Complementing the work of Ikeda and Urbain, and interconnected with it, are my voice and publications. My three previous books all address the empirical and normative problems associated with global governance in the late twentieth and early twenty-first centuries. Hence, the central components of Ikeda's philosophy of peace are juxtaposed to those of Ikeda's contemporaries through thematic discussions of how progressive proposals for a more peaceful world order can help humanity make the historic leap into a viable global civilization that is sustainable, justice-oriented, and centralized around peaceful solutions to global problems. In this regard, the themes of inclusion, participation, and distributive justice are all addressed from the perspectives of international law, political science, economics, and history, in my first major book, *Achieving Inclusionary Governance: Advancing Peace and Development in First and Third World Nations* (2000). The various problems posed to global peace and the challenge of building understandings between the world's different cultures, religions, and political systems are addressed in my second book, *Exodus from Empire: The Fall of the American Empire and the Rise of the Global Community* (2007). Finally, the end of US hegemony and the birth of a multicentric and multipolar world of regions are the prominent themes addressed in my most recent book, *The Future of Global Relations: Crumbling Walls, Rising Regions* (2009). Taken together, these works find common purpose and common voice with Ikeda and Urbain.

There are three distinct, but complementary, points of view in this book. First, the point of view of Daisaku Ikeda is reviewed through a textual analysis of his writings—from peace proposals to dialogues, from books to lectures and editorials. In this book, he is considered as a secular humanist philosopher who is inspired by Buddhist cosmology. Second, my point of view is best described as that of a secular humanist inspired by ecumenical Christianity with its emphasis on the universal message of peace, inclusion, and the ultimate unity and reconciliation of all peoples. My views are powerfully augmented by the existentialist views of Albert Camus, the theological and social justice perspectives in Latin American "liberation theology," the methodology and interdisciplinary approach of critical theory as embodied in the works of Herbert Marcuse, Erich Fromm, and the political legacy of Robert F. Kennedy. Third, the point of view of Olivier Urbain is also that of a secular humanist, inspired by Buddhist cosmology and, in particular, by Ikeda's writings. Urbain's understanding of Ikeda's philosophy is based on a typical European familiarity with the works of Victor Frankl, Jurgen Habermas, and cosmopolitans such as Daniele Archibugi and David Held.

Therefore, my task throughout this book is to critically and objectively describe the various dimensions of the global crisis. I shall do this by analyzing its components in the form of many different but interconnected crises—from nuclear weapons abolition to the dangers of global warming and climate change, from international lawlessness in the form of wars of aggression in violation of the Nuremberg Principles and the Charter of the United Nations to the need for reforming the United Nations and Security Council, from the challenge of global poverty and inequality to understanding that much of human conflict and environmental degradation is the direct consequence of these two realities. In combination, these crises are the most egregious elements of the current global crisis and constitute the most critical areas that humanity must deal with and seek to transcend. In short, throughout this book, I am embarking upon a journey that allows us to point toward solutions that will address the true nature of these various crises, challenges, and predicaments. By identifying various other road maps and remedies supplied by Ikeda and his contemporaries, it is hoped that viable solutions will emerge. In this regard, we also hope that readers will be enabled to discover and explain Ikeda's idea of how a universal consciousness—that resides as a potential in each of us—will be capable of transporting all of humanity *"beyond global crisis."*

In many crucial respects, one of the twentieth century's most influential and pivotal thinkers and a globally acknowledged advocate for world peace and peaceful solutions is Daisaku Ikeda. As mentioned earlier, the three pillars of Ikeda's philosophy of peace are (1) inner transformation, (2) dialogue, and (3) global citizenship. To begin with, it is critical to realize that, from Ikeda's perspective, the discovery of a universal consciousness that is contained as a potential in every person can only be realized by the effort, struggle, and will of the individual. It is what Ikeda calls the *human revolution.* It is a revolution that begins with the individual person, but its power and ramifications extend to the rest of humanity through *dialogue* and from dialogue to a shared sense of community among all people who perceive of themselves as *global citizens* with a sense of obligation to build *a peaceful global civilization.* The capacity to remake and transform global civilization is predicated upon the reconstitution of individuals who—through the power of *inner transformation*—come to the realization that we have the capacity to create within ourselves a new consciousness of what really matters, what is of real value, and how that is something we ultimately share in common with all peoples around the globe. This is the basis on which shared values and a shared global consensus can be articulated because, despite differences between cultures, civilizations, or nations, people with a transformed consciousness can see and conceptualize the world of global relations in a new and revolutionary manner.

In this regard, Ikeda suggests that it is through the power of *dialogue* with one another that we are able to provide one another with a new template on which we can rewrite our future so that it no longer mirrors the past or travels along the same trajectory of worn-out assumptions, age-old prejudices, or defunct dogmas and beliefs—such as the "inevitability of war," or the "fixed and unchangeable nature of human beings," or the enduring "wonders of our past accomplishments." When such a dialogue expands from local, national, and regional networks, we then witness the emergence of *global citizens* who think globally about global concerns. In this endeavor, Ikeda posits the idea that we are on the brink of achieving a more peaceful, humane, and inclusive *global civilization.*

Therefore, this book is dedicated to explaining how Ikeda and his contemporaries have provided us with remedies and road maps on how to transcend the mindsets, behaviors, and structures that have both contributed to and exacerbated the current "global crisis." It is with the purpose of articulating the values, practices, and policies for this renewed world that I have sought to bring together the voices of Daisaku Ikeda and his contemporaries. At its center, this book asks a very serious question: *Can innertransformation, dialogue, and global citizenship truly allow humanity to progress toward a more humane, inclusive, and harmonious global civilization despite the harsh realities of a world that is currently dominated by power struggles over resources, the exploitation of people by the national and international structures of capitalism (especially the neoliberal model), and in which billions of dollars are spent on armaments and war each year?* Closely aligned with this inquiry, we shall posit the following question as well: *Using Ikeda's proposals, as well as other road maps and remedies articulated by his contemporaries, can we really move 'Beyond Global Crisis'?*

In partial answer to the above-referenced questions I would suggest, for the sake of clarity, that by returning to Dickens's first paragraph in *A Tale of Two Cities*, I have a provisional answer to both questions. After Dickens employs his series of radical contrasts about 1789 as being "the best of times, the worst of times . . .," he concludes with the astute observation that "the period was so far like the present period" that it could be understood "in the *superlative* degree of comparison only." It is the use of the word *superlative* that we need to focus on here. *The Oxford English Dictionary* states that when used as either an adjective or adverb, it defines "*superlative*" as "expressing the highest or a very high degree of quality (e.g., bravest, most fiercely)," or as "an exaggerated; or excessive statement, comment or expression." Hence, when we contrast the ideas and themes of Ikeda, on the one hand, with an exposition of the true nature of the current global order, on the other, we are at that point of our analysis where a clearer understanding of the crisis emerges because we have revealed the superlative nature of the crisis—what makes the global crisis such a crisis and why it is so necessary to move beyond it.

Now, in the context of the title of this book, when speaking of moving *Beyond Global Crisis*, and analyzing it in all of its forms and dimensions, I also concurrently mean to imply that when I define, identify, and confront the true nature of this global crisis that—*with the road maps and remedies supplied by Ikeda and his contemporaries*—I wish to offer the reader a variety of road maps and remedies that will empower humanity to *supersede* this global crisis. The dictionary defines *supersede* as being able to "adopt or appoint another person or thing in place of," and to "set aside; cease to employ" and to "supplant, oust, take the place of, take over from, [or] substitute for." Therefore, as we progress through chapters 1 to 9, it is my hope that the reader will be able to (1) identify the outer boundaries of the global crisis; (2) take into account the intricacies of all of its dimensions as we discuss the major issue-areas that act as obstacles and roadblocks to achieving a more peaceful global civilization; (3) come to appreciate the interconnections Ikeda makes between inner transformation, dialogue, and global citizenship as complementing each other; and (4) come to understand that these interconnected elements of Ikeda's philosophy can be seen as human undertakings which are guided by a purpose to transform the existing order based on a set of shared values, new international structures, and a universally common purpose which, in combination, have the capacity to supersede the values and structures of the current order that are antithetical to the cause of peace and the advancement of both human and environmental well-being.

In Part I—Ikeda's Vision for Realizing a Global Civilization: The Power of Inner Transformation and Dialogue, there are two complementary chapters. Chapter 1 demonstrates why the global system does not allow for an unencumbered implementation of Ikeda's plans for peace. Both Ikeda and his contemporaries are cited together in order to explain the dysfunctional nature of the international system. In this analysis, international financial institutions such as the International Monetary Fund, the World Bank, and the World Trade Organization are identified as some of the main international obstacles to achieving peace. In this chapter and the ones to follow we shall juxtapose this reality to Ikeda's alternative vision which castigates the *"spirit of abstraction"* which allows for making humans and the resources of the environment little more than commodities to be exploited for profit in a global capitalist system that strips people of their dignity and disfigures both their individual and collective identity. Insofar as global civil society and/or international society can be understood as a "community of communities," Ikeda suggests that we need to invoke the idea of *"humanitarian competition"* so that we can construct an international environment that leads to *"win-win solutions"* and not a divided world of *"winners and losers."* Chapter 2 examines what we have called *the superlative* and from this perspective makes an assessment of where we are now and, in the alternative, what will be required to achieve a peaceful global civilization. At the most basic level, the chapter raises the question: *How do we move from a culture of violence to a culture of peace?* In large measure, the answer to this question is going to be ultimately predicated upon what we call our "identity" and how that identity is framed. Therefore, it is suggested that we look at Castells's argument that there are three possible ways to build one's identity in the world. First, there is the path of taking a *"legitimizing identity"* (agreeing with the status quo, not much in tune with Ikeda's philosophy). Second, there is the path called the *resisting identity* (which has a lot in common with Ikeda when he criticizes the lack of humanity in our global system). Third, there is the path of *"project identity"* (which is very much like what Ikeda is proposing—a new way of looking at the world that can offer peaceful and effective resistance to patterns of violence and domination). Makiguchi's concept of "humanitarian competition" is also presented as being conducive to a culture of peace. It also constitutes Ikeda's "third path." Those ideas find echoes in many other thinkers. From Ikeda's perspective, what is first required is a decision to work on one's inner transformation and then to develop a *"project identity"* by finding the best way toward global transformation. For Ikeda, the key to bridging the gap between one's identity and one's project for attaining global transformation is through dialogue. In the chapters that follow, Part II offers many other possibilities.

In Part II, chapters 3–5 are all under the rubric of how there are multiple pathways to move from the achievement of individual transformation to global transformation. Chapter 3 presents a case study of the 1962 Cuban missile crisis, which not only placed humanity on the nuclear precipice but also served as the epic event that transformed the consciousness of the leaders of the two leading nuclear weapons powers: President John F. Kennedy and Soviet Premier Nikita Khrushchev. Emerging from the crisis with a peaceful settlement, President Kennedy immediately proceeded to launch talks leading to the signing of the Limited Test Ban Treaty, which outlawed any further testing of nuclear weapons in the atmosphere. It was signed in early November 1963, only weeks before Kennedy's assassination in Dallas, Texas. While the treaty would significantly reduce the hazard to human health from radioactive fallout, it failed in its larger hopes of bringing an end to the Cold War and to the arms race. Yet it was followed by further arms control agreements leading ultimately toward the beginning of genuine nuclear disarmament. However, it failed to halt the dangers of nuclear weapons proliferation, which continue on into the twenty-first century.

Chapter 4 is about the power of self-transformation as the beginning of internal and external liberation. The argument that is presented emerges out of the nexus where Buddhism, liberation theology, and law are conjoined in a complementary manner to stand for the proposition that seeking genuine change in the external world is predicated upon genuine change in the internal world of a person's mind, spirit, and body. Insofar as antiquated modes of thought and behavior sustain the structural injustices of the world, Ikeda argues that the individual's own antiquated modes of thought, action, and behavior must first undergo a genuine transformation (*the human revolution*) before a true reformation of the world can be undertaken. In other words, the achievement of personal liberation must be understood as a necessary precedent to national, regional, and global liberation. To illustrate the point, the words and actions of Herbert Marcuse, Gustavo Gutierrez, Martin Luther

King, Rajni Kothari, and Robert F. Kennedy are brought to bear on the need to defeat egoism, ethnocentricity, and an all too comfortable reliance on technological advances as a substitute for building a more justice-oriented global order.

In this regard, chapter 4 addresses the power of moral courage and altruistic living as the transformative alternatives for people who seek to change a world that yields most painfully to change. Robert Kennedy's famous speech about the need to end the practice of racial apartheid in South Africa is such a call to embark upon individual and national transformation. Similarly, Gustavo Gutierrez argues that a radical change of unjust situations can really be brought about only by individual agents of change. Martin Luther King's call for civil and human rights is depicted as helping to open the doors of political power to Nelson Mandela, an agent of change whose own biography provides graphic evidence of Ikeda's principle of altruistic living in action. And in the spirit of Ikeda, we are reminded by Rajni Kothari that a proper concept of justice must foster respect for human diversity. This is essential and important for the sake of building a more just and peaceful global civilization so that whatever one does, individually or socially, while bound to be imperfect, is, nevertheless, undertaken as a form of respect for the dignity of persons. It is this self-critical awareness that makes central the dignity of persons which also restrains the exercise of power and the agents of power. That is because self-controlled individuals who use power must wield power in a manner that is consistent with showing respect for others and act with humility toward others.

Insofar as our current global order is controlled, managed, and dominated by an international hierarchy of unequal states and unequal powers, we find that it is an order which is guided by hegemonic states, international bankers, and financial practices that relegate the individual to the mercies of Western laissez-faire policies and the vicissitudes of the market. Ikeda and his contemporaries condemn these types of practices because they reflect the *"spirit of abstraction"*—both a mindset and mode of governance that places profits before people, wealth accumulation for the few before the preservation of the environment for the many, and glorifies the pursuit of private gain above the concept of *"universal humanity."* Yet it is only through recognizing our universal humanity that we are enabled to develop a spirit of tolerance and partnership. By ignoring the fact that we share a universal humanity with others who are deserving of dignity and respect, this failure of perception reflects the corrupting influence of a *hubris* (pride) that blinds the powerful to the need for and requirement of respecting—in theory and practice—the human rights of the weak, the vulnerable, and the excluded. Therefore, if we are to achieve a peaceful global civilization, it must be predicated upon inclusion, participation, and liberation from all exploitative, oppressive, and violent practices of domination.

Chapter 5 is an examination of the role of dialogue and dialogical mechanisms. Dialogue is presented as a central component in Ikeda's philosophy for building a global framework for deliberative democracy, human rights, and cultural pluralism. In fact, Ikeda has declared that *"dialogue can be called the Magna Carta of civilization."* This recognition is vital in a twenty-first-century era of interdependence, globalization, and the need for ever new structures of effective global governance. Only through the transformative potentiality of dialogue are we provided with an effective and peaceful means to engage in a constructive dialogue among civilizations which allows for peaceful coexistence. It is a process that begins with person-to-person dialogue, but it eventually is multiplied and extends outward to embrace our common humanity in a shared global culture. From this perspective, we are enabled to transcend Samuel Huntington's claim that we are historically trapped within the matrix of a *"clash of civilizations."* Rather, Ikeda and his contemporaries argue that we can transcend clash, violence, and terrorism by embracing cultural pluralism. This will entail leaving behind the dominant Western paradigm for world order by abandoning its culturally and intellectually circumscribed perspective. After all, civilizations exist in the plural and are pluralist because they coexist with each other within one civilization called "modernity." Within this shared world environment the role of dialogue is even more important because it creates a space for communication wherein we do more than merely "defend our position"—we can join together to discover truth. We can do so by discussing how we distinguish right from wrong, good from evil, and engage in a mutual critique. In the social ontology of our world community we come face-to-face with the requirement of mutual respect in the face of human diversity.

Chapter 5 provides the reader with a living model for the practice of these concepts in the form of the Association of Southeast Asian Nations (ASEAN). The principles by which ASEAN is guided are contained within the *Treaty of Amity and Cooperation*, adopted by ASEAN at its Bali summit in 1976. In keeping with the Asian tradition of seeking consensus, the treaty's central and overarching goal is *"to promote perpetual peace, everlasting amity and cooperation."* The treaty stipulates that relations between members should be guided by six basic principles—all of which center upon the renunciation of the threat or use of force, as well as an enduring commitment to maintaining effective cooperation among themselves in all matters of mutual concern. In this respect, Ikeda's formulation of the role of dialogue is given concrete expression. The way in which ASEAN conducts its business is predicated upon achieving a high degree of consultation and consensus. The very process of regional interactions is based upon discreteness, informality, consensus building, and nonconfrontational bargaining styles. The dynamic interplay of norms in the context of ASEAN provides us with substantive evidence of the value of Ikeda's proposals about the uses and significance of dialogue in advancing civilizational identities which can be supportive of peace processes at both the regional and global levels. I shall discuss this in further detail in chapter 7, which recounts how the UN and ASEAN have successfully influenced all other major regions in the world to adopt *nuclear weapons–free zones* (NWFZs), which are a precursor to achieving the dream of nuclear abolition and a nuclear weapons–free world. Chapter 6 concludes with a discussion about how patterns of regional and global change are transforming the world order and creating a system of multiple power centers and overlapping spheres of influence.

In Part III, the book is dedicated to visualizing what a global civilization of harmony would look like and examines how its emerging interdependence can be achieved in concrete terms. To this end, Part III employs insights from the field of international relations (IR), Richard Falk's model of *"humane governance,"* my model of *"inclusionary governance,"* and David Held's model of *"cosmopolitan governance."* In combination, these approaches set forth complementary strategies that embody the promise of realizing the converging theoretical and empirical elements of a peaceful global civilization. The convergence of these approaches and their fidelity to the principles and teachings of Ikeda also serves to underscore the fact that Ikeda's own work points us toward a new historical trajectory for humanity's future that envisions robust global cooperation among many interrelated networks of peoples and institutions—thereby revealing the fact that we all possess membership in a variety of communities. In this interconnected world, a consciousness of our interrelatedness and interdependence provides us with the power to remake the world and redefine the scope and power of global civilization itself.

Chapter 6 offers an analysis of the converging theoretical and empirical elements of global civilization. It does so by examining four main areas: IR, *humane governance, inclusionary governance*, and *cosmopolitan democracy*. The chapter begins with a reassessment of the nature of interstate law and the need to revisit international human rights and the *law of humanity*. The law of humanity is associated with the future and is therefore more a matter of potentiality than of either history or experience. Still, what is meant by "the law of humanity" is prefigured in the substance and theory of the international law of human rights. In other words, it constitutes the basis for the realization of Ikeda's concept of a peaceful global civilization because the law of humanity asserts that there already exists a "right to peace." While various states and their governments, as well as conservative academics, dispute the existence of a right to peace, this entire book asserts that it exists already in a variety of international legal documents and instruments—and has been specifically articulated and endorsed by the United Nations. Such a dispute should not be surprising insofar as there are still ongoing arguments about social welfare rights despite the fact that Article 28 of the Universal Declaration of Human rights declares that *"[e]veryone is entitled to a social and international order in which the rights and freedoms set forth in this Declaration can be fully realized."*

At present, the nation-state system itself is the primary structural reality that has been blocking the full realization of such a social and international order. Still trapped within the confines of the mindset called the "national interest" we find that some states, especially the most powerful states, have chosen to disregard the larger human interest of both their own people and the peoples of other nations in order to serve elite groups and elite interests located within their own domestic polity. In order to overcome this recalcitrance, chapter 6 prescribes the removal of these structural impediments by placing at the forefront of humanity's agenda for global change the principle of "human solidarity" and advancing the quest for what Richard Falk has termed the practice of *"moral globalization."* To that end, we reintroduce Ikeda's criticism of the *"spirit of abstraction"* and invoke James Rosenau's call for creating conditions for *"the emergence of a series of global consensuses"* that will allow for convergence around shared values.

It is for this reason that chapter 6 discusses the new emphasis on norms that can be found in current IR scholarship. The current trend in IR is to restore to equal balance the theoretical elements of IR inquiry with that of the empirical elements. To regain parity between these two approaches allows for greater insight into how best to resolve international problems and how best to restructure international relationships. This is necessarily the case insofar as theoretical assumptions often determine the contours of the field and inform even the most empirical research. By adopting this approach, we are able to point out that it becomes possible to shift our focus from a preoccupation with "state-centered security" to one of "human-centered security." This paradigmatic shift comports well with Ikeda's proposals for expanding the arsenal of peaceful channels through which we can advance human security for all people, thereby making the shift from a global culture of violence to the achievement of a peaceful global civilization. This shift entails all three tenets of Ikeda's philosophy of peace becoming fully operational: (1) an inner transformation of the consciousness of individuals; (2) the employment of dialogue to help unleash new insights and provide new understandings that can serve to build a sustainable consensus around shared values; and (3) more individuals and communities embracing their moral, ethical, and political obligation to humanity as a whole rather than the claims of a particular nation-state.

Hence, IR scholarship is depicted as a field of international political, social, and cultural inquiry that is concerned with more than just the subject of relations between states. It is an expanding field that now admits it should not take the core concerns of the most powerful states as the dominant issues for the discipline. Rather, the discipline of IR has to reject its current and historic privileging of a specific and culturally molded social scientific approach and replace it with one that accepts the proposition that there is a wide set of legitimate approaches to studying world politics. Chapter 6 proceeds to discuss alternative universal perspectives and principles through my lenses and those of Richard Falk, Joseph Stiglitz, Thomas Pogge, Alan Gewirth, and David Held. Taken together, they form a powerful critique of our current dysfunctional world order and agree with Ikeda as he recommends that we begin to think about moving out of our current global system insofar as it is a nonsynergic system. Hence, we must move instead toward developing a global culture and civilization that adopts a synergistic and participatory system that is truly conducive to sustaining a peaceful global civilization. For Ikeda, this means the need to adopt a *"spirit of fairness"*—also acknowledging that a true sense of fairness "must be derived from a universal spirit manifested on this higher plane." Despite their past reluctance to do so, governments must now confront the unpleasant realization that essential international institutions are facing imminent breakdown, largely because they are perceived as illegitimate, unjust, and unfair. In all of this, Ikeda detects that there is a global *"aspiration toward unity"* and that this can be easily juxtaposed against the current realities of *"division and sundering."* On this note, chapter 6 concludes with the promise of a better future predicated upon our coming to realize the converging theoretical and empirical elements of a peaceful global civilization.

Chapter 7 discusses the emerging pillars of a peaceful global civilization. These pillars are (1) nuclear disarmament, (2) United Nations reform, and (3) the emergence of the International Criminal Court (ICC). These emerging pillars constitute the foundation of an emerging peaceful global civilization insofar as they all promote dialogue about the inherent dignity of the person and the absolute sanctity of human life.

Hence, the purpose of dispensing with nuclear weapons and charting a global strategy for their abolition reinforces both the *"human right to peace"* and the right to a life of dignity, advancing the human welfare, and the protection of the environment, while, at the same time, redirecting national and international wealth from investments in armaments and the worldwide military–industrial complex toward the universal needs of people, the welfare of nations, and sustainability of the entire global community.

The purpose of UN reform is focused on two primary considerations: (1) the need to expand the membership of the Security Council and to ensure that the number of seats available on it are revolving and that the veto power of the current leading nuclear weapons states is removed and; (2) additionally, the focus of UN reform on actualizing Ikeda's proposal to create two separate and distinct United Nations vis-à-vis an Environmental Security Council. The logic for such a change and the practical necessity of such a change is found in the fact that dividing the UN into two strengthened and independent bodies—*one concerned with peacekeeping and the other concerned with problems such as environmental global governance and human rights*—would help each nation in the task of readjusting its self-chosen priorities to more perfectly mirror the ideals that lay behind *"humanitarian competition."* In other words, the "national interest" (as *a vestige of a system of sovereignty and global inequality*) would be replaced by the "global interest" (*which serves all humanity and actualizes the ideal of the "sovereign equality" of all states*).

Finally, the emergence of the ICC stands for the proposition that our current system of global hierarchy and the lack of *"accountability"* among nuclear weapons states and the world's leading hegemonic state no longer serve the global human interest—if they ever did. Therefore, the time has come—in the first decades of the twenty-first century—to invoke the full weight and purpose of the Nuremberg Principles and the UN Charter by adopting what I call the *principle of hegemonic state accountability* (PHSA). No longer should a hegemonic state's national and/or geopolitical agenda be imposed on the rest of humankind to the exclusion of all other standards of international law—specifically those standards that act as a barrier against the use of aggression, force, or threat of force, and the possibility of war (wars of preemption, wars of choice, and wars of necessity). If we are to say that war should no longer be a legitimate arm of statecraft, then it follows that it must be outlawed. In short, the PHSA seeks to make the preservation of peace and the accountability of state action in international affairs throughout the global commonwealth its central concern. To that end, the PHSA represents both a call and a demand that the United Nations, the ICC, and the nuclear weapons states remain, at all times, accountable to the line that divides legitimate self-defense from aggression. In this regard, the UN, the ICC, and the goal of nuclear weapons abolition all serve to actualize the principle of the *sovereign equality* of all nations and the rights of the people within them. Therefore, in the words of the *Preamble of the Rome Statute of the International Criminal Court,* "[t]he States Parties to this Statute . . . Affirming that the most serious crimes of concern to the international community as a whole must not go unpunished and that their effective prosecution must be ensured by taking measures at the national level and by enhancing international cooperation, [are] Determined to put an end to immunity for the perpetrators of these crimes and thus to contribute to the prevention of such crimes." (See the full text of the *Preamble of the Rome Statute of the International Criminal Court* in the Appendix of this book.)

Chapter 7 discusses the imperative of nuclear weapons abolition in juxtaposition to the Nuremberg Principles, the substantive prohibitions found in the Nuremberg Charter (for crimes against peace, war crimes, and crimes against humanity), the PHSA, the 1996-Advisory Opinion of the International Court of Justice, and the mandates of the UN Charter with respect to the threat and use of force. The chapter also undertakes to explain both the rationale and the necessity for advancing prospects for undertaking a global nuclear weapons convention (NWC). The NWC initiative has been suggested as something worthy of global advocacy since its foundation in 1993 by the International Network of Engineers and Scientists Against Proliferation. The origin of this approach to nuclear weapons abolition was first outlined in the Delhi Declarations of 1978 and was subsequently renamed as a *Nuclear Weapons– Free World*. Now, in the late twentieth and early twenty-first centuries it has reemerged as a global call for undertaking a NWC.

Such an undertaking is especially urgent given the fact that Articles 42 and 51 of the UN Charter (the only articles that deal with the actual use of armed force) can be effectively circumvented by the leading nuclear weapons states. This fact places all humanity at risk. The circumvention of Articles 42 and 51 by the Bush-II administration during its invasion and occupation of Iraq since 2003 also lends urgency and credibility to this proposal. The unilateral actions of hegemonic states or leading nuclear weapons states need to be replaced by multilateral accountability. Otherwise, the very foundations of the pillars for a peaceful global civilization will be critically undermined, if not altogether destroyed. Therefore, the negation of the principles behind Articles 42 and 51 set back the advancement of the human condition, especially where that negation is by a power that wields special influence and authority in the community of nations by virtue of its hegemony and its monopoly over the instruments of violence and destruction. Hence, if we are to effectively implement the PHSA and give practical credence to the ultimate purpose of the UN Charter, the Nuremberg Principles, and the *Preamble of the Rome Statute of the International Criminal Court*, it is imperative that nuclear weapons and nuclear weapons states be brought under international control and made accountable to the entire human race.

Chapter 7 also further addresses the question of the validity of the doctrine of *"humanitarian intervention"* and finds that the legal basis for this doctrine is dubious at best. The invocation of this doctrine by the United States and NATO in Kosovo, Iraq, and Afghanistan has created an institutional crisis at the UN regarding the unauthorized use of force. The institutional integrity of the Security Council has been undermined by these undertakings while, at the same time, the ICC has been systematically blocked from fulfilling its mandate and role in bringing war crimes and war criminals to justice. These are serious allegations. Yet these examples serve to showcase the consequences of abandoning a law-oriented approach to foreign policy and world order. These examples also serve to illustrate how the Nuremberg Principles have been undermined by the pursuit of geopolitical calculations of a hegemonic state and its allies. Insofar as the Nuremberg approach to international accountability for those who act on behalf of sovereign states must be respected if humanity is to be able to support the unconditional repudiation of aggressive war, it follows that both the UN and the ICC need to be greatly empowered in order that they can act as an effective bulwark against such violations of international law in the future. If this is not possible, then the prospects for realizing a peaceful global civilization are severely diminished, if not altogether compromised. Therefore, this chapter argues that the PHSA, which takes all of these considerations and issues into account, ought to be embraced by the UN, the ICC, and the entire global community as the most direct way to not only demand but also enforce accountability.

To that end, chapter 7 reexamines the basis of what constitutes *human security*. It does so by invoking the concept of an expanding circle of human solidarity. Great attention and detail are given as to how *confidence-building measures* (CBMs) can serve to effectuate the expansion of a circle of human solidarity—moving from the regional level to the global level. In so doing, these considerations fit comfortably with Ikeda's concept of how to practice *humanitarian competition* as a means through which a flexible framework is created that allows different cultures to cooperate, thereby serving to advance the creation of new structures for global governance that are more democratic and accountable to the peoples of the world. As such, these CBMs and newly emerging regional orders may be seen as constitutive of a global civilization of peace. While they maintain a reasonable amount of sovereignty for national governments, they also provide a new emphasis upon human security, which expands the circle of human solidarity by ensuring the participation of all individuals and groups. Hence, these changes in policy, practice, and orientation open the door for realizing Falk's concept of *humane governance* and my concept of *inclusionary governance*. Taken together, they buttress Ikeda's proposal for a *universal declaration for the renunciation of war*.

In turn, these new undertakings toward peace also provide greater clout and influence to the PHSA, the strengthening of treaty regimes that advance the cause of peace, and reinforce the case for a NWC. We have already established how a regime of CBMs has been effectively invoked to create NWFZs under the auspices of the UN and the work of ASEAN. In fact, the UN and its agencies have been at the center of efforts designed to advance, promote, and support the regional nuclear-free zone concept. The NWFZ concept is one rung in the regional confidence-building ladder that needs to be erected in the remaining crisis regions of the world, with zone establishment integrated into a wider global agenda for peace that includes arms control, nonproliferation, disarmament, security and political measures that need to be negotiated at both the regional and global levels. This strategy is fully aligned with Ikeda's 1999 peace proposal wherein he notes, "*To make the new millennium an age of peace and hope, we must explore the means of deinstitutionalizing war.*" To that end, chapter 7 explains, explicates, and enumerates those means. Ultimately, however, the abolition of nuclear weapons, the renunciation of war, and the accountability of hegemonic states in conjunction with the leading nuclear weapons states will have to be predicated upon the degree to which a genuine *human revolution* takes place in the hearts and minds of individuals, thereby opening the door for a *nuclear revolution* and the dawn of a peaceful global civilization.

Chapter 8 undertakes an examination of the challenges presented by climate change. It also reintroduces some of the same considerations that were previously addressed in chapter 7 with respect to the need to expand the circle of human solidarity so that the current *climate of mistrust* between the global North and the global South can be transformed into a *climate of human solidarity*. As with the nuclear weapons threat, we discover that the threat of global warming and the realities of climate change are largely the result of human choices, human actions, and the all too human addiction to what Ikeda, quoting Gabriel Marcel, has called the *"spirit of abstraction."* Insofar as people are bound up and guided by social structures that are subservient to profit-making and greed, they are diverted away from peaceful pursuits and the desire for justice between human beings and between person and planet. Hence, the ecological crisis and the nuclear weapons threat share a common denominator. The nature of both crises and both threats emerges out of a consciousness that is addicted to a cultural, economic, and political global hierarchy that serves the interests of elites—interests that are antithetical to meeting the needs and aspirations of humanity as a whole. That is because the common denominator for war and environmental degradation involves the exploitation of resources (material and human), the violent displacement of people from their right to enjoy their possessions and share in the bounty of the natural environment, and the refusal of the powerful to acknowledge the interdependence of all living things. Hence, just as nuclear weapons are a fundamental evil that cannot resolve in any way the complex of global issues, but only exacerbate them, so too the degradation of nature is a fundamental evil that can only reinforce human poverty, continue policies and practices that make the environment less inhabitable, and leave us with a growing and expanding "ecological debt."

In many ways, both the global North and the global South have clearly failed to understand the imperatives associated with the growing interdependence of humankind. What is required is a new consciousness that reunites the reality of human needs with human ecology. At the epicenter of this problem are the antiecological tendencies inherent to capitalism and the problems that emerge as a consequence of this type of socioeconomic organization. The ideology of growth, the reality of global inequality, and the environmental crisis are all linked. The very interconnectedness of these three elements serves to identify the magnitude of the problem and also points to the vastness and seeming intractability of this challenge. Given this analysis, it should be clear as to why Ikeda's condemnation of the *"spirit of abstraction,"* as well as his prescription of *"humanitarian competition,"* is a prescient alternative to the status quo. That is because the components of a Darwinian, competitive, and predatory behavior—as exemplified in the neoliberal model of capitalist practice—has so plundered both person and planet under the banner of privatization and profit that corporations have left the planet's environment in crisis.

Chapter 8 argues that, in the spirit of Ikeda, the best way to advance harmony, coexistence, and coprosperity among the nations of the world (especially between those of North and South) would be through applying the Buddhist principle of *"esho funi"*—that sees the self and "the Other" (the self and the environment) as being inseparably and cooperatively interconnected. In this task it will be necessary to centralize the role of dialogue in overcoming the distrust and mistrust between the peoples of the global North and the global South. In the aftermath of the 1970s debacle over the question of whether the South would be treated cooperatively by the North in its desire to establish a new international economic order (NIEO), the relationship between North and South has been characterized as "a model of North–South (non-) cooperation." It is only recently that scholars have turned their attention to the largely understudied factor of the level of "trust" among developed and developing nations. The level of trust is now understood as being critical to explaining the failure of the NIEO debate and what is needed now so that the same mistakes are not replicated in current dialogues about how to deal with climate change, global warming, and the factors that contribute to environmental degradation.

Further, chapter 8 presents the views of many of Ikeda's contemporaries—including Mahbub ul Haq, J. Timmons Roberts, Bradley C. Parks, and Robert Johansen to explain the dynamics associated with the restoration of trust and the need to use a value-centered approach in addressing the environmental crisis. In this regard, a value-centered strategy leads to the adoption of a value framework that can be deliberately constructed so as to reflect planetary rather than strictly national concerns. Such an approach to the planet's environmental challenges and to the dialogues associated with them also avoids the trap of looking at IR from a parochial nation-state view. This is important insofar as it is a strategy that dovetails with Ikeda's own emphasis on the need to transcend national particularities and instead to adopt a worldview worth of global citizens. Hence, by being able to navigate a global dialogue beyond the shoals of the state-centric framework of global relations, Ikeda posits the idea that we can attain practical remedies by attaining a more inclusive worldview of everyone's needs, interests, and concerns. This is the antidote to distortion—the distortion of perceptions and of policies. Further, such an achievement is made possible, in no small measure, by the application of the concept of *"humanitarian competition"* to the resolution of the global environmental crisis because it is a concept that encourages changes in behavior at both the individual and societal levels. By so doing, it also aligns our focus with a concern for others by acknowledging that what benefits others, in the final analysis, benefits us as well. The entire planet enters a win–win scenario.

The chapter concludes with a brief overview of the great global accomplishments of the 1970s through 2002. From this historical review of the record the chapter addresses the nature of the unfinished global agenda for environmental transformation. This discussion includes how current visions for planetary renewal are unfolding under the rubric of regionalism, as exemplified by the experience of ASEAN. In so doing, the chapter reveals how a serious and trustworthy dialogue between the world's peoples can also contribute to a peaceful close to the geopolitical era of hegemonic dominance as an end in itself and reveal the sociopolitical, socioeconomic, and environmental benefits arising from a repudiation of past practices derived from a history of colonial and imperial exploitation. Regionalism has, as I have argued, become the basis for a new multicentric world of *"rising regions"* that centralizes the interdependent values of mutual cooperation, respect for the environment, and a renunciation of the use of force or threat of force. Insofar as Asian/Pacific regionalism resists any renewal of Western hegemonic projects, it also offers the West an opportunity to rethink its approach to global governance as a steward of the environment working cooperatively with the rest of the world. In this regard, the chapter identifies some of the key strengths of ASEAN's environmental policies and differentiates its approach from that of the more formalistic and parliamentary decision-making systems found in Europe. In so doing, we are able to make the case that regional environmental governance represents an indispensable link between, and complement to, national and global initiatives. This is vitally important because sustainability will depend on taking into present account the needs of future generations and this includes giving greater weight and attention to the management of resources and the very foundations of life that are fundamentally supportive of both individual and collective human dignity.

Part I

Ikeda's Vision for Realizing
a Global Civilization:
The Power of Inner
Transformation and Dialogue

1

The Global Crisis through the Lens of Ikeda and His Contemporaries

In the introduction, the importance of Daisaku Ikeda's philosophy of peace in the context of the current global crisis was made clear. To begin this chapter, perhaps the best place to start is with reference to a commitment Ikeda made in 1947 when he met Josei Toda for the first time. After meeting Toda, Ikeda dedicated his life to the realization of a peaceful world, based on the belief "that people can generate something positive, productive and useful for the peace and happiness of humankind by creating value and transforming reality" (Urbain 2010, 28).

Ikeda's vision emerged out of the trauma of World War II. The defeat of Japan, coupled with the first use of the atomic bomb on Hiroshima and Nagasaki, was horrific enough (Bix 2000; Dower 1986, 1999; Hasegawa 2005; Totani 2008). But even prior to these events, a historical review of the pre–World War II period in Japan reveals that the institutional choices of Japan's Buddhist leaders toward their country's expansionist policies allowed for the emergence of what came to be known as the *imperial way Buddhism* (koda Bukkyo). It was a codification of previous positions—"[s]tated in Buddhist terms, imperial way Buddhism represented the total and unequivocal subjugation of the Law of the Buddha to the Law of the Sovereign. In political terms, it meant subjugation of institutional Buddhism to the state and its policies" (Victoria 2006, 79). It was in this environment that Josei Toda, a disciple of Tsunesaburo Makiguchi, opposed the Japanese military government and was imprisoned with Makiguchi. Together they had formed an educational/religious organization known as Soka Kyoiku Gakkai (Value-Creating Educational Society). It was beginning to become a social movement on the eve of the Second World War insofar as its teachings reflected a "new" school of thought and action. Whereas "the 'old' schools, already a part of the establishment, were supported mainly by the aristocrats and geared above all toward *chingo kokka* (protection of the state), the new Buddhism addressed itself to the individual or, in a sense, personal needs for salvation" (Tamaru 2000, 19). Together with his own mentor, Toda refused to have the Soka Kyoiku Gakkai submit to the militaristic propaganda of Japan's government and fought to keep Buddhism where it should be—at the service of the people. Both Makiguchi and Toda were jailed in 1943. Makiguchi died in jail in 1944 and Toda survived, rebuilding the organization in 1945 and renaming it Soka Gakkai.

The refusal to unequivocally support a militaristic government would be a pivotal and determinative decision not only for Toda and the Soka Gakkai but for Ikeda as well. This was necessarily the case insofar as "the difficulties experienced by his mentor who had to cope with ill-health and financial ruin while rebuilding a grassroots movement from scratch, provided strict and valuable training for Ikeda's continued growth as a peace worker and philosopher" (Urbain 2010, 29). Specifically, this meant that, like Toda, Ikeda's work and philosophy were attuned to following a path that was devoted to a life of determined value creation for peace. In a dialogue with Prof. Harvey Cox about modern spirituality, Ikeda asserted, "My own conviction is that, as long as we live, we must move forward, always creating new values" (Cox and Ikeda 2009, 90).

It is a conviction that was forged by meeting and studying under Toda from 1947 through 1958, the year of Toda's death. The implications emanating from this relationship cannot be overstated insofar as Ikeda regarded meeting Toda as the most important event in his life (Urbain 2010, 21–22). When understood in this context, "with hindsight it can be said that Ikeda's focus on the steady sharing of the peace-enhancing principles of Buddhism has enabled him to bring consistency and coherence to his leadership and to his philosophy of peace" (Urbain 2010, 28). Nowhere is this more evident than in the three main elements of Ikeda's philosophy of peace—(1) inner transformation, (2) dialogue, and (3) global citizenship. These are the central elements of Ikeda's strategy of peace, which began to be developed out of the August 14, 1947, meeting with Toda and all of their subsequent interactions.

These three central elements of Ikeda's philosophy should also, in part, be understood as part of the socioeconomic and sociopolitical transformation of Asia itself in the aftermath of the Second World War. New religious movements arose out the ashes of the war in an attempt to address the questions and problems that affected people in industrializing and postindustrial societies worldwide. In point of fact, "these issues include peace and war, a declining environment, conditions at work, family relations, matters of individual health, psychological well-being, and prosperity" (Metraux 2000, 403). Within this historical matrix of commonly held concerns, "when other East and Southeast Asian cultures experienced parallel forces of urbanization and industrialization, many people felt a need for religions responsive to their circumstances. Their new lives forced a break with the cultures, religions, and traditions that had held fast for thousands of years. There is increased emphasis on the role of the individual and the importance of individual initiative" (Metraux 2000, 404).

The advent of World War II, as well as its immediate aftermath, serves to provide not merely a history lesson but rather an insight into how war has long-reaching effects that affect the consciousness of individuals. War and its legacies reveal much more than the interplay between military, diplomatic, and economic forces. The phenomenon of war is a social enterprise that transforms entire societies as well as the mood, aspirations, and consciousness of the individuals within them. In this regard, historian Gabriel Kolko astutely notes, "Modern wars retain, as before, their traditional military and diplomatic dimensions, but *their outcomes are also defined increasingly in the changes they provoke in individual and national consciousness. This additional change obligates us to give far more consideration to a war's impact on social systems in the largest sense—their economies, the new moods they encourage among the people, and changing political and class structures*" (Kolko 1990, 627) (italics added).

The limits and boundaries of war as a means to effectuate certain desired results have become increasingly evident over time. From generation to generation, culture to culture, the use of war as a means to bring about certain kinds of results in the international socioeconomic hierarchy (usually by political and economic elites) has been proven to be ineffective and counterproductive in a host of ways. Yet even beyond this realization, we can and should expand our analysis of war so as to incorporate other considerations and dimensions of its failures and inadequacies to achieve a just and humane result so that we can more clearly formulate precise alternatives to it. This is what Ikeda has done. In the aftermath of the events of September 11, 2001, Ikeda wrote thus:

> Unless we can achieve a fundamental transformation within our own lives, so that we are able to perceive our intimate connection with all our fellow human beings and feel their suffering as our own, we will never be free of conflict and war. In this sense, I feel that a 'hard power' approach, one that relies on military might, will not lead to a long-term, fundamental resolution. I believe that dialogue holds the key to any lasting solution. Now, more than ever, we must reach out in a further effort to understand each other and engage in genuine dialogue. *Words spoken from the heart have the power to change a person's life. They can even melt the icy walls of mistrust that separate peoples and nations. We must expand our efforts to promote dialogue between and among civilizations.* (Ikeda 2001c; italics added.)

A Philosophy of Peace Forged out of the Fires of War

To begin with, Ikeda felt that he had been lied to by the authors of Japan's war propaganda. Also, since Toda had spent two years in jail because of his convictions in opposition to such propaganda and the militaristic government behind it, Ikeda found a convincing example of the power of inner transformation and dialogue. After all, in their first and subsequent meetings, Ikeda discovered Toda's capacity to use language and logic to bring out the best in others. In turn, this inspired Ikeda to develop his idea of and capacity for global citizenship (Urbain 2010, 62). Central to this strategy is Ikeda's belief that "a full engagement towards the threefold approach of inner-transformation, dialogue, and global citizenship does require an awareness of the situation of the world and of the actual suffering of millions of people" (Urbain 2010, 200).

To fully comprehend the development of this consciousness of global citizenship for Ikeda, it is necessary to return to the influence of one of Ikeda's intellectual mentors, Makiguchi.[1] The writings of Tsunesaburo Makiguchi have remained meaningful to Ikeda because of his preoccupation with human-scale, self-reliant local communities. The idea is that individuals can really experience the fullness of their potential only through intimate, caring, reciprocal relationships with other humans in community—especially in the early stages of life but in some degree at all stages (Bethel 2000, 51). In Makiguchi's words—in what was to become a central part of Ikeda's perspective as well—

> it is our nature as human beings to forge societies. It is through association in society that we can provide not only for our basic needs and security, but for everything that makes our lives fulfilling and rewarding. This realization leads to the universalization of sympathetic feelings that were initially toward a specific individual or object. Growing awareness of our indebtedness to our society gives rise to feelings of appreciation and a sense of social responsibility within us. Beginning in our very personal relationships . . . [O]ur sympathetic concern and appreciation expands to include the larger society and, ultimately, the whole world. (Makiguchi 1971, 56)

A large part of Makiguchi's preoccupation with the human community at every level—local, national, and global—was a product of his being able to foresee the ultimate ecological possibility toward which his country's headlong rush to embrace American-style industrialism would lead. In this crucial respect, "that vision of an ecologically devastated Japan galvanized Makiguchi to undertake his first major work, *Jinsei chirigaku* ("*A Geography of Human Life*"), written during the final decade of the nineteenth century and published in 1903" (Bethel 2000, 48). During the last half of the twentieth century, we now have the benefit of history to see that the single-minded pursuit of profit by the world's industrial elite, led by the United States and Japan, has brought the environmental health of the planet into a state of critical condition (Bethel 2000, 47).

It is for this reason that, throughout this book, I have devoted as much attention as I have to discussing the role of dominant Western institutions such as the World Bank, IMF, the WTO, and the global military–industrial complex as being antithetical to an attitude of compassion for the actual suffering of millions of people—as well as the environmental sustainability of planet earth as well. While Ikeda himself never mounted a frontal attack against these institutions, *I*, on the other hand, have done so because they are the institutions that figure so predominantly in the violations of those principles that Ikeda has been seeking to advance. Correspondingly, it is because of the salience of Ikeda's prescription for peaceful change—using his threefold approach (inner transformation, dialogue, global citizens)—that we have devoted as much attention as we have throughout this book to the constructive roles of the United Nations, the ICC, social and scientific movements to save the environment due to climate change as well as unregulated pollution, and the legacy of legal rulings by international courts dedicated to the abolition of nuclear weapons.

In all of these issue areas the role of SGI alone has effectively provided a strong organizational base in virtually every Asian country. In its long and distinguished history, the Soka Gakkai[2] strongly opposed the Japanese war effort of the 1930s and 1940s. As a result, its leaders at the time, Tsunesaburo Makiguchi and Josei Toda, were imprisoned when they refused to cooperate with government authorities. Its teachings have focused on the twin concepts of karma and responsibility for one's own actions (Metraux 2000, 406). While its Buddhist identity is central to its philosophical self-understanding, SGI leaders "stress that Buddhism is not for those people who like to be told how to order their lives, who look constantly for guidance from an outside authority, whether in the form of a priest, scripture, or ritual. Throughout the Gakkai's teachings, along with the insistence on a balanced life and common sense, there is a stated obligation for each person to think things out for himself, to make up his own mind and to make his own decisions. The doctrine of karma requires each believer to be responsible for his own salvation" (ibid., 406).

Giving dual attention to these issues and institutions is important insofar as the reality of the situation is that Ikeda's idealism and strategy for peace and human happiness are constantly blocked and thwarted by entrenched private interests and structural forces of injustice. Unlike Ikeda himself, we would single out for criticism and critique because institutions such as the World Bank, IMF, WTO, the global military–industrial complex, as well as the priorities that guide them, are disconnected from the lives and well-being of billions of people (Chossudovsky 2003). Further, from my interpretation of Ikeda' work and our understanding of how his principles could be applied in bringing about a transformation of the current global crisis, I assert that these particular institutions and the priorities that guide them are too narrowly attuned to utilitarian calculations. Because of their utilitarian focus in the service of profit-driven capitalism and their lack of democratic accountability, they resist dialogue with others and their dissenting views. Hence, caught in a utilitarian vacuum, these institutions have pursued a narrowly designed "*Washington Consensus*" that promised the alleged benefits of privatization, deregulation, openness to foreign direct investment, a competitive exchange rate, fiscal discipline, lower taxes, and smaller government. Yet according to recent scholarship on the issue, we now find that "over the years of neo-liberal hegemony growth has slowed, poverty has increased, and economic and financial crises have plagued most countries of the world economy. The data on all of this are overwhelming . . . . In its unannounced goal it has increased the dominance of transnational corporations, international financiers, and sectors of local elites" (Tabb 2004, 3).

This neoliberal hegemony of the nations of the North over the nations of the global South is more than just an issue of economics, however, for it exposes the real reasons for a growing "democratic deficit" both within and between nations. This deficit has real-life consequences for individuals, the quality of citizenship, as well as moral and ethical questions about the effects of the foreign policies of rich nations on poor and "lesser developed countries." On this point, philosophy professor and human rights advocate Thomas Pogge notes the following:

> There is a serious democratic deficit . . . in the affluent countries, whose citizens have not approved, and for the most part do not even understand, very important foreign policies and international practices that are conducted and upheld in their name . . . . Democracy involves the fulfillment not only of important rights, but also of important responsibilities of citizens. To the extent that citizens abandon their responsibility to control the power that is exercised in their name, their country is less than fully democratic. Most citizens of the affluent states are abandoning this responsibility insofar as they choose to understand very little about how vast quantities of imported resources they consume are acquired and about the impact that the terms of such acquisitions have in the countries where these resources originate. (Pogge 2002, 166)

In addressing this same issue one year after the 2003 US invasion and occupation of Iraq, Richard Falk noted, "The pathological dualism of America's global role persists, creating a confusingly symbiotic link between self-righteous protective claims based on confusing admixtures of defensive necessity, idealistic endorsements of democracy and freedom, and a greedy geopolitics that seeks to sustain military, economic, and cultural dominance into the indefinite future. Such an undertaking of global empire confronts the entire world with the horrifying choice of devastating violence or humiliating submission, while marking a transition for America from a dominant political

7

tradition based on republicanism to one premised on empire" (Falk 2004b, 44). I would argue that this same pathological dualism is reminiscent of the period of the 1930s and early 1940s when the possibilities for conflict in the US–Japan relationship escalated with the tragic consequence that war came to dominate the possibilities for cooperation. As economist Jonathan Marshall has noted, "The economic stress of the Great Depression germinated seeds of rivalry. The growing political gulf between Japan's strange blend of modernism, militarism, and feudalism, on the one hand, and the Roosevelt administration's Wilsonian liberalism, on the other, was put into sharp focus by the China Incident, Japan's brutal attempt at conquest of the Asian mainland. In this poisoned atmosphere, policymakers on both sides of the Pacific viewed economic competition as a form of economic attack—and economic attack in turn as a threat to national security" (Marshall 1995, 175). Extending this analysis further, historian Gabriel Kolko suggests that in order to transcend a repetition of the march to war experienced by Japan and the US in the 1930s and 1940s, we must reflect and dialogue with one another about the true meaning of that period. Kolko asserts, "By understanding the meaning of that period we comprehend our own decade in microcosm and the challenges we face in breaking the paralyzing grip of a thirty-year-old crisis in international relations over the future of all mankind. In viewing the genesis of the challenge of our time we hold a mirror to ourselves, the problems we confront, and the source of our malaise" (Kolko 1990, 9). These are the reflections of historians on an era of war that Ikeda lived through. So it should be kept in mind that Ikeda's reactions to these events may be somewhat different, thereby supplying him with a qualitatively different focus. But the objective historical realities identified by the writers of history cannot be ignored.

Reflecting on these historical dynamics, Ikeda would argue that there is one major discovery that should be noted—and that is the duties of citizens to be self-aware and involved participants in the life of the larger society and world of which they are a part. For without personal participation there is no real check on political leaders to abstain from power grabs, aggressive behavior, and the temptation to engage their nations in war and violence for less than noble purposes. Further, it is unfortunate that personal apathy has so often translated into public apathy. That is because the quality of the relationship between the society at large and its individual members will be largely determinative in deciding whether human life on planet earth leads to more inclusive and humane forms of governance or, in the alternative, whether the old patterns of exclusion, exploitation, and deprivation will continue to move individuals and nations in the same direction. If we are to achieve a more rational organization of our national and international society, eventually leading toward the realization of a more peaceful global civilization, then it will be necessary to implement the kind of integrated threefold strategy advocated by Ikeda—beginning with the inner transformation of the person, the engagement of people in honest, truthful, and evolving patterns of dialogue with one another, and culminating with a shared dedication to building a peaceful global civilization that makes war, poverty, and environmental degradation obsolete. As historian Gabriel Kolko has astutely observed, ". . . the basic premise that while society owes everyone a reasonable material minimum, individuals in turn also have a constant duty to weave significant networks of social cooperation and interaction, is no less vital. A dedication to personal participation is also an essential precondition for the control of political leaders, which cannot be attained where there is a large measure of apathy among those who share the same nominal goals. Social responsibility that operates reciprocally between a society and its members has hardly been considered in the general socialist literature, but it remains a precondition for the emergence of a more rational human organization, and above all truly radical politics based on changing both societies and people—and thereby the world" (Kolko 1994, 483).

Without the benefit of honest and truthful dialogue we find that the forces behind the neoliberal economic model pursued a utilitarian course of action that served their private and hidden agendas while bankrupting most of humankind of the chance to have decent lives and happiness. Had a different set of priorities, goals, and strategies been in place, a different outcome for a more just and peaceful world could have been the result. In the alternative, a more democratic dialogue dedicated to building understanding and a shared consensus on common values and goals would give all people—even the currently excluded and marginalized—a way in which their views could be taken into account and made a part of a more global solution to these problems. In Ikeda's view, as extrapolated upon by Olivier Urbain, that "unconcerned by utilitarian calculations concerning the potential benefits to be reaped by specific dialogical efforts" we find that "holding dialogues is like planting seeds" because such an undertaking will "inevitably produce positive, yet undefined, results" (Urbain 2010, 141).

The Liberating Power of Dialogue and Discourse

In Ikeda's formulation, in an editorial written for the *Japan Times*, Ikeda noted, "Dialogue starts by clearly recognizing the positions and interests of the respective parties and then carefully identifying the obstacles to progress, patiently working to remove and resolve each of these. It is the ultimate constructive undertaking of the human spirit. And it is for just this reason that conflict resolution through dialogue—unlike military force whose essence is destruction—holds the promise of a genuine and lasting solution" (Ikeda [2007] 2008, 78). Through the use of this approach we discover that Ikeda strategically avoids imposing a particular model upon the parties to the dialogue. Unlike the philosopher John Rawls, who concentrated on identifying what constitutes perfectly just social arrangements, Ikeda works from the opposite direction. Ikeda relies on dialogue between people and groups to establish a consensus about common values and shared interests as the best way to mitigate the drift toward conflict and war, or what should be the organizing principles of a peaceful and just global civilization. Thus, Ikeda's approach is radically different from the social contract approach invoked by Rawls, who took the characterization of "just institutions" to be the principal—and often the only identified—task of the theory of justice.

By centralizing the role of dialogue and the way in which it is conducted, I find that Ikeda can use the avenue of rational discourse to greater advantage in arriving at "just solutions" to common problems. Again, it should be emphasized that this is a radically different approach from the way in which Rawls centralizes his thought and focus on the characteristics of just institutions—a priori—as though they were preordained. In contrast, Ikeda centralizes his focus on the dynamics of discourse and dialogue as that place in the human experience that is always open to value creation and free expression between parties who may—at the start of a discussion or dispute—be locked into what seems to be unwavering positions but who, at the end of the dialogic encounter, find themselves as having moved to common ground and common understandings by virtue of what Jurgen Habermas has called "communicative rationality" (Habermas 1984). In this crucial regard, the communicative use of rationality serves the dialogic encounter well because it is "one essential component of Ikeda's vision for a new global civilization which is a resolutely dialogical project" (Urbain 2010, 121).

Similarly, Amartya Sen, the Nobel Prize–winning Harvard economist and philosopher, departs from much of the recent philosophical discourse on the idea of justice, usefully drawing not only on Western philosophy but also on the wisdom of ancient Asian thinkers. Sen also rejects the social-contract approach to justice in favor of a results-based one that relies on an understanding of generally acknowledged injustices—without attempting to design a perfectly just society, as the social-contract approach typically does. Also, he accepts the idea that there may be many different but equally legitimate views of what is just or unjust in particular cases. Instead of trying to adjudicate definitely among them, Sen encourages reasoned discourse about the different ethical principles involved. This discourse becomes an important element in moving toward a more just society (Sen 2009).

So it is with Ikeda. His "Buddhist diagnosis goes to the very heart of the matter, and therefore leaves specific analysis and diagnosis to others . . . . Using the examples of Gandhi and Havel, Ikeda makes clear that a serious commitment to human happiness will allow one to create value without dwelling too much on diagnoses and prognoses" (Urbain 2010, 200). According to Ikeda, by centralizing "an unconditional, indestructible faith in humanity, a faith born of justice, nonviolence and penetrating self-observation" we can move beyond relativism (Ikeda and Galtung 1995, 56). Hence, operating within the boundaries of this moral universe, it is possible to guide people toward inner transformation, engagement in constructive dialogue and discourse, thereby facilitating the movement toward a more peaceful global civilization.

The genius of both Sen and Ikeda is that their respective approaches to building a more just world and global civilization lie in the fact that they look beyond the particularity of the various strategies, designs, diagnoses, and prognoses for implementing a more just world and global civilization. Rather, they both transcend the relativism associated with what we could call "the game of particularity." Instead, they seek to focus on what are "universally shared understandings" about justice, human dignity, and peace among all peoples. These "universally shared understandings" emerge out of peoples' engagement with one another in dialogue and discourse. Through this engagement with one another, peoples from different cultures, backgrounds, and belief systems are enabled to transcend the particularity of their own viewpoint by jointly engaging with each other in the task of facilitating the movement toward a more peaceful global civilization. This movement is made possible by virtue of the fact that the foundation for it is an unconditional and indestructible faith in humanity itself. As long as humanity demonstrates that it retains a willingness to engage in dialogue and discourse, then the power of nonviolence is enhanced along with the capacity for penetrating self-observation.

In Ikeda's formulation, the power of self-observation leads to inner transformation. Engaged and reflective individuals have the capacity to re-create themselves and, in so doing, are thereby empowered to engage in higher levels of dialogues and discourse with other people who have benefited from a similar process. What this ultimately means is that the process of transformation at the individual level makes possible the conditions for moving beyond particularity and the ideologies of the past—both personal and collective. Particularity is replaced by a process of value creation. In this process, more universally shared values emerge through discourse and dialogue that are capable of sustaining a global consensus. For example, the desire for justice and a corresponding desire for nonviolent solutions to human problems become emblematic of organizations such as the United Nations. The UN Charter itself is evidence of the kind of product of shared values that people are capable of articulating through shared discourse matched to faith in humanity's eventual capacity to realize justice on a universal scale.

In Sen's formulation, he notes that "[w]hat moves us, reasonably enough, is not the realization that the world falls short of being completely just—which few of us expect—but that there are clearly remediable injustices around us which we want to eliminate" (Sen 2009, vii). But before the discourse about the need to remove injustices can begin, it is required that individuals form and formulate their own existential understanding of what is to be opposed and what should be affirmed in their own lives and lived experiences. Ikeda's own formulation is replete with life-affirming principles, but does not contain a comprehensive list of what should be opposed—except greed, anger and foolishness, lack of dialogue, and violence-prone nationalism. On the other hand, Sen believes that individuals need to formulate their own existential understanding of what needs to be declared as a source of injustice and, therefore, should be opposed. In Sen's view, this is "evident enough in our day-to-day life, with inequities or subjugations from which we may suffer and which we have good reason to resent, but it also applies to more widespread diagnoses of injustice in the wider world in which we live" (Sen 2009, vii). Then, from individual experience and transformation it becomes possible and necessary to engage in discourse with others on how best to achieve a resolution of these injustices. So, from the particularity of our own experience of individuals suffering the pangs of injustice—to the realization that this need not be the case—we can move toward a perception of what may become a principle that can ultimately be universally acknowledged in the world: *that certain forms of injustice must be brought to an end for the sake of the greater good*. According to Sen, "It is fair to assume that Parisians would not have stormed the Bastille, Gandhi would not have challenged the empire on which the sun used not to set, Martin Luther King would not have fought white supremacy in 'the land of the free and home of the brave', without their sense of manifest injustices that could be overcome. They were not trying to achieve a perfectly just world (even if there were any agreements on what that would be like), but they did want to remove clear injustices to the extent that they could" (Sen 2009, vii).

In Ikeda's formulation on this issue, we discover that "Ikeda emphasizes once more that the goal of dialogue, the purpose of using language, reason, meaning and idea to communicate, should first and foremost be to enhance our common humanity, not to obtain some advantage" (Urbain 2010, 121). In an editorial written for the *Japan Times* entitled "Embracing the Future", Ikeda states, "From my own experience of having engaged in dialogue with many people from a wide range of political, religious, ethnic and cultural backgrounds, I am equally convinced that when we speak frankly on the basis of our common humanity it is always possible to see our way to the next step forward" (Ikeda [2007] 2008, 79). So, beginning with the particularity of the experience of the individual, we can eventually extrapolate that experience beyond the boundaries and particularities of a wide range of political, religious, ethnic, and cultural backgrounds. It is our shared common humanity which provides the foundation for beginning a transformative discourse with one another. And out of that discourse, there may arise an opportunity to build a more just global civilization. In the same *Japan Times* editorial Ikeda wrote the following:

> Today we confront the unique opportunity to begin building a new civilization—one based on a consistent commitment to dialogue on

all levels. The vital, vibrant currents of dialogue have the capacity to shake even the most stubborn allegiance to the use of force. Dialogue is not limited to the exchange of pleasantries, but includes the sharing of sharply differing perspectives. Courage and endurance are essential if we want to continue the painstaking work of loosening the knots of attachment that bind people to a particular point of view. The impact of this kind of humanistic diplomacy can move history in a new direction. In a world of richly diverse cultures, we cannot afford a regression to shuttered isolationism. It is crucial to revive the spirit of dialogue and to unleash a creative search for peaceful coexistence. To have faith in the promise of dialogue is to believe in the promise of humanity. (Ikeda [2007] 2008, 81–82)

Building a more just and peaceful global civilization, as Ikeda has suggested in the above-cited editorial, will require us to acknowledge a series of interrelated points with respect to the liberating power of dialogue. They are as follows:

1. First, dialogue can be more powerful than the use of force.
2. Second, dialogue presupposes and includes the sharing of sharply differing perspectives.
3. Third, we must loosen the "knots of attachment" that bind people to a particular point of view.
4. Fourth, the process of loosening the knots of attachment may be understood as a kind of "humanistic diplomacy" that can move history itself in a new direction. Hence, we are not the captives of some kind of preordained fate.
5. Fifth, shuttered isolationism is the antithesis of discourse and the greatest threat to peace.
6. Sixth, restoring dialogue to a place of centrality in our consciousness, politics, and discourse with others is to unleash a creative search for peaceful coexistence.
7. Seventh, maintaining faith in the promise of dialogue is of utmost importance in demonstrating our belief in the promise of humanity.

These seven points happen to perfectly correspond with Sen's own prescription for creating a more just world, meeting the requirements for global democracy and engaging in global reasoning through an enhanced global dialogue. Insofar as both Sen and Ikeda are dedicated to a shared vision of how to effectively lay the groundwork for a peaceful and just global civilization through dialogue, it is interesting to observe how they both have recognized the dynamics of a participatory process that dialogue opens up for people on a global scale. Sen notes, "Giving serious consideration to distinct and contrary arguments and analysis coming from different quarters is a participatory process that has much in common with the working of democracy through public reasoning . . . . The two of course are not the same, since democracy is concerned with a political assessment—leading us (in this interpretation) to 'government by discussion'—whereas undertaking non-centered and non-parochial scrutiny through paying attention to distant perspectives may be largely motivated by the demands of objectivity" (Sen 2009, 408).

In this regard, both Ikeda and Sen share a fundamental commitment to the primacy of giving great weight to the "demands of objectivity" insofar as the capacity for objectivity helps one to listen to the other, to the unfamiliar, and thereby create the conditions for a genuine exchange of ideas, feelings, and aspirations. On this matter, Sen observes that "it can be asked, in this context, what the implications of these recognitions are for the demands of global justice and also for the nature and requirements of global democracy" (Sen 2009, 408).

The Demands of Global Justice and the Requirements of Global Democracy

From Ikeda's perspective, the function and workings of the United Nations as a multinational structure underscore its importance in furthering both the demands of global justice and helping to structure the requirements of global democracy. This institutional mechanism is also a forum for discourse and giving due attention to the normative power of international law in a multinational framework. So, Ikeda concludes that "since justice is often in the eye of the beholder, international law, which operates within a multinational framework, is our most rational recourse. In his *Republic*, Plato said that 'justice' benefits the strong; it is now time to put an end to this millennia-old idea that might equals right. The most rational way to do so is to work out a multinational system of international law" (Ikeda and Diez-Hochleitner 2008, 67). This perspective reopens the door for a reconsideration of the possibilities for global democracy as something that is currently attainable. It becomes attainable, Sen and Ikeda would argue, because of the force of public reasoning. In Sen's formulation, he acknowledges that "the point is often made, with evident plausibility that, for the foreseeable future, is really impossible to have a global state, and therefore *a fortiori* a global democratic state. This is indeed so, and yet if democracy is seen in terms of public reasoning, then the practice of global democracy need not be put in indefinite cold storage. Voices that can make a difference come from several sources, including global institutions as well as less formal communications and exchanges" (Sen 2009, 408).

The central problem that remains is the degree to which previously marginalized and excluded voices will be given a place at the table. I call this the challenge of "achieving inclusionary governance" (Paupp 2000). For the reality is that even in formally democratic states, the degree to which major classes, parties, and interests are actually heard and involved in the deliberations of governance—which includes issues of distribution—remains marginalized and excluded. At the international level this problem is compounded. Therefore, if we are to achieve greater degrees of inclusion at the international level between nations that allow for discourse and deliberations on eminently discussable issues, Sen argues that "there also remains the need to go beyond voices coming from countries with recent economic success (including, in different ways, China, Brazil, India and others), which speak more forcefully now, but often do not represent the concerns and views of people in countries with lesser economic stride (including much of Africa and parts of Latin America). There is also the need, in any country, to go beyond the voices of governments, military leaders, business tycoons and others in commanding positions, who tend to get an easy hearing across borders, and to pay attention to the civil societies and less powerful people in different countries around the world" (Sen 2009, 409). While Ikeda would not single out the name and rank of these powerful people, he would oppose on general principle the ideas they are expressing as being antithetical to the welfare of their own people. This is a central point for both Sen and Ikeda. Both of them recognize that dialogue and discourse must be inclusive of all publics—and not just the economically privileged sectors and elites of the world.

A good example of this need to hear all voices and concerns on important national and international issues can be seen in the context of the challenge of nuclear nonproliferation. In April 2004 the UN Security Council unanimously passed Resolution 1540, mandating that all member states implement a rigorous set of controls to prevent the proliferation of nuclear, biological, and chemical weapons. The response by governments to 1540 has helped to strengthen global nonproliferation standards. Yet,

> despite these efforts, the urgency of implementing 1540 in capitals around the world has not been commensurate with the threat.... The sluggish implementation of 1540 has become a question of resources and priorities ... the vast majority of UN members are plagued with an array of threats to security and well-being of their people that seem to have little to do with the proliferation of advanced weapons and technologies. Implementation of 1540 thus ranks low on their long list of government priorities. In Western capitals panicked by the growing nexus between technology proliferation and the rise of catastrophic terrorism, it is easy to lose sight of this realization—in the Global South, where more than a billion people live on less than $1 a day, one illness, one unlucky encounter with a drug or small arms trafficker, one hurricane, or one month of poor rainfall can mean death. It is unreasonable and even immoral to expect their governments to divert scarce resources from public health, education, or infrastructure development to meet the seemingly distant threat of WMD proliferation. (Finlay 2009, 9)

It is for these reasons that the rich nations can secure nuclear materials by meeting developing world needs. Therefore, "when viewed expansively, UNSCR 1540 can be a complementary rather than competing priority for developing world governments. For instance, the technical assistance needed to detect and interdict weapons of mass destruction is equally critical to natural disaster response. The ability to prosecute potential weapons smugglers requires a well-trained police force and functioning judiciary—traits equally critical to the rule of law" (Finlay 2009, 9).

What are the implications of all of this for global democracy and global justice? The implications are manifold. To return to Ikeda's emphasis upon the centrality of dialogue as necessary to building a peaceful global civilization, we need to realize that the nature of global relations has to move toward what I have called "inclusionary governance" for the accommodation of the needs and interests and well-being of the previously excluded and marginalized peoples of the planet (Paupp 2000). In this regard, Sen has explicitly noted, "The distribution of the benefits of global relations depends not only on domestic policies, but also on a variety of international social arrangements, including trade agreements, patent laws, global health initiatives, international educational provisions, facilities for technological dissemination, ecological and environmental restraint, treatment of accumulated debts (often incurred by irresponsible military rulers of the past), and the restraining of conflicts and local wars. These are all eminently discussable issues which could be fruitful subjects for a global dialogue, including criticisms coming from as far as well as near" (Sen 2009, 409). While Sen has identified the culprits of this injustice, Ikeda would not do so. Ikeda believes that it is more important to identify specific wrongs than specific people.

In the spirit of Ikeda, Sen has proposed the centrality of a global dialogue in the shaping of a new and more peaceful global civilization. One of its characteristics is that it must become more inclusionary, as I have argued (Paupp 2000). By becoming more inclusionary, the very nature of global culture can be transformed into what Richard Falk has called "humane governance" and what David Held has termed "cosmopolitan governance" (Falk 1995; Held 1995). For Ikeda, the idea of inclusionary governance was first best expressed by Toda. Ikeda has often stressed the point that "Josei Toda advocated the idea of the global family at a time when the tensions of the Cold War were intensifying, and few paid attention to his ideas. At best, they were dismissed as unrealistic reveries. But today, this idea has finally entered the public consciousness as '*transnationalism*,' which has become a key concept in explaining and predicting the future direction of global affairs" (Ikeda 2001a, 65).

Transnationalism and the Transformation of People's Thinking

What I will argue throughout this book is that the idea of *transnationalism* must involve more than just a process of dialogue, insofar as the process of dialogue should lead to some positive outcome for the greatest number of the world's peoples in the structural sphere of human activity and organization. While we cannot predict the exact nature of this structural change, what is clear is that institutions and institutional arrangements defensive of the status quo will not be up to the task of such fundamental changes. That is because the status quo is at odds with the kinds of change that these new forums of dialogue are and will be demanding. Nowhere is this reality more evident on a global basis than in the area of peace and security. That is because "in the existing global order, interstate rivalries are settled ultimately through military competition, including the threat and use of military force" (Pogge 2002, 181). It follows, therefore, that

> it is unlikely that national control over weapons of mass destruction can be abolished within the existing world order—through a disarmament program that depends upon the voluntary acceptance and compliance of each and every national government, for example (. . .) Nonproliferation and gradual abolition of weapons of mass destruction presuppose a substantial centralization of authority and power at the global level—in violation of the prevalent idea of state sovereignty. Such centralization can best be accomplished in the context of a multilayered global order . . . . If such global institutional reform process also reduced repression and economic injustice, its disarmament component might well win broad support from peoples and governments—provided it increases the security of all on fair terms that are effectively adjudicated and enforced. The attempt to advance disarmament in this way would in any case be far less dangerous than continuing the status-quo. (Pogge 2002, 182)

For Ikeda, the place to begin the process with a comprehensive nuclear disarmament program is in the transformation of people's thinking: "Human hands produced nuclear weapons and weaponry systems, and human hands should be able to reduce and eliminate them" (Ikeda 2001a, 199). A similar perspective is offered in the work of Philip Allott:

> Each of us lives at the imperceptible intersection between our private mind and the public minds of the societies to which we belong. It follows that the way we understand human society and the way we understand the human mind are two aspects of a single process of human self-knowing. It follows also that the task of remaking our idea of humanity contains two projects—reconceiving human society and reconceiving the human mind. We have done it before. We can do it again. The human mind has made the old human world in which we are obliged to live. The human mind must make a new human world in which we would want to live. (Allott 2002, 137–38)

What Allott has presented us with is a dialectical proposition. We could analogize it to the "mind–body" relationship. Whatever the mind thinks has the capacity to make the body healthy or sick. Similarly, the minds of individuals produce ideas that are either supportive of the belief systems and ideologies that support the status quo or, in the alternative, conceptualize a utopian alternative. I use the term *utopian* to imply not something that is unrealistic but rather something that has yet to be born within the matrix of our current history, even though it can be imagined in the mind's eye. As Karl Mannheim astutely noted, "We should not conclude . . . that the function of history is to furnish a record of what man is not, but rather we should regard it as the matrix within which man's essential nature is expressed" (Mannheim 1936, 92). The history of humankind largely records how vast swaths of time, experience, and belief have become hostage to the ideologies of church and state (Burleigh 2005). Instead of helping people to liberate themselves from various forms of false consciousness, religious and political power structures have too often served to obfuscate the path of inner transformation that leads to truth and, instead, insisted on adherence and obedience to their own dogmatic and ideological formulations. In fact, a review of the history of nineteenth- and twentieth-century world history reveals the fact that successive totalitarian leaders coveted and mimicked the hierarchy, rites, and ritual of the churches in the desire to return to the day when ruler and deity were one (Burleigh 2007).

From a sociological point of view, Karl Mannheim described how this practice relied on the "force of the traditional modes of thought and conceptions of life" but proved to be incapable of allowing "for the accommodation of action and thought to a new and changed situation and in the end actually obscures and prevents this adjustment and transformation of man" (Mannheim 1936, 95). This path leads away from the kind of inner transformation of which Toda and Ikeda have spoken and written. In place of inner transformation we find that "antiquated and inapplicable norms, modes of thought, and theories are likely to degenerate into ideologies whose function it is to conceal the actual meaning of conduct rather than to reveal it" (Mannheim 1936, 95). To have arrived at a point of history in such a predicament is to foreclose on human possibility and the promise of a transformed people engaged in a transformative politics. To fall prey to the claims of old ideologies is to open the door to personal and collective despair. That is because "a despairing humanity is not merely an unhappy humanity, it is an ugly humanity, ugly in its own easy way—dwarfed, diminished, stunted and self-loathing. These are the buried sources of world war and despotic collectivism, of scapegoat hatred and exploitation . . . . Out of despair, people rush to the counterfeit community of the totalitarian state. Out of despair, they invent themselves fantastic enemies that must be punished for their own failure. Out of despair, they grow burdened with moral embarrassment for themselves, until they must at last despise and crucify the good which they are helpless to achieve. And that is the final measure of damnation: to hate the good precisely because we know it is good and know that its beauty calls our whole being into question" (Roszak 1973, xxii–xxiii).

Ikeda has offered a philosophy of peace that, according to Urbain, is structured in such a way that its three major elements interact with one another to produce a new kind of person through inner transformation and, in so doing, produce a newer world—a world capable of sustaining and advancing a peaceful global civilization. In this crucial regard, the linkages between inner transformation, dialogue, and global citizenship are the critical components for building a peaceful global civilization (Urbain 2010, 185). For Ikeda, the inner transformation of the individual is a necessary prerequisite to having a chance to begin the process of engaging in a transformative dialogue with other people. Out of dialogue and shared discourse, common values can emerge that are supportive of the cognitive and spiritual lives of individuals, which, in turn, supply supportive mechanisms for taking the next steps toward building a more peaceful national and international order. If inner transformation is to be also understood as what Allott refers to as "*reconceiving the human mind*," then there is a direct linkage to Ikeda's formulation which places a primary focus on individual transformation as being the foundational achievement for the kind of dialogue that is necessary to produce a more peaceful global civilization.

The inner transformation of the individual is the necessary and essential starting point for the journey to peace because that is where we find the human-historical possibility of transcendence. To transcend the despair of our souls, our sense of alienation, our susceptibility to the claims of old ideologies and prejudices, we must rediscover that which is most sacred—the life within us and the nature about us. Until the discovery and experience of transcendence are made manifest within us "there will seem to us no 'realistic' future other than more of the same . . . . That is why the politics of our time must reopen the metaphysical issues which science and sound logic have for the last two centuries been pleased to regard as closed. For to expound upon social priorities or the quality of life without confronting those issues is the very folly of alienation" (Roszak 1973, 420). It is for this very reason that Ikeda has specifically rejected the notion that the starting point for change is some kind of external political revolution. No, because the source of our despair and alienation is first and foremost an internally experienced reality that manifests itself in the external world, it follows that only through a process of inner transformation can we be empowered to achieve an experience of being in the world that is no longer subject to the alienating force of despair and the existential crisis brought by a sense of alienation.

The same attention to inner transformation that animates Ikeda's philosophy of peace is forcefully present in the writings of Richard Falk. Like Ikeda,

Falk envisions the process of inner transformation as not initiated by dogma or driven by it. Rather, like Ikeda, Falk is an advocate of a particular kind of spiritual practice that transcends both the acceptance of dogma and the mandates of institutional authorities. Falk speaks of persons who undertake this kind of spiritual practice as *"citizen pilgrims."* The definition that Falk supplies is as follows: "The citizen pilgrim abandons neither suffering nor hope, insisting that inner healing is as 'political' as elections and tribunals, and believing that a *total* disengagement from the debates of the moment may be the necessary precondition for liberating the moral imagination, opening wide spaces in the mind and heart that are receptive to drastic change, as well as being responsive to calls for justice and relief that will inform a genuinely transformative politics" (Falk 2009, 204). The nature of such a transformative politics is guided by the process of liberating the moral imagination of people, and this is the main reason why Ikeda insists on the primary necessity of embarking upon inner transformation. The reason for establishing the primacy of inner transformation in the peace process is so that the citizen pilgrim can personally realize the fact that "if the heavenly city is to be built on this earth then human finitude has to be taken into account. In this sense the citizen pilgrim is inevitably drawn back to religious belief, or at least to spiritual practice, but not in any sense that implies an acceptance of dogma or institutional authority. This religious renewal is carried on individually, and needs to be distinguished from the religious resurgence that is leading traditional religions in many circumstances to seek and gain political influence, and pose threat to the moderation and ethos of tolerance that were such important signifiers of modernity" (Falk 2009, 205) (italics added). This is the necessary configuration for a genuinely transformative politics insofar as it is only through this individually focused process that despair, alienation, and mistrust can be overcome at the deepest levels of the human being and human experience.

After all, despair, alienation, and mistrust are those very qualities that make wars possible and reliance upon the weapons of war inevitable. However, to place one's trust in weapons is to worship the proverbial golden calf, a false god. This is especially the case with respect to nuclear weapons. Following the intellectual example of Toda, we find in the writings of Ikeda that the abolition of nuclear weapons is one of his top priorities. It is not only the capacity of nuclear weapons to bring all life on planet earth to an end should they ever be used, but it is their current pollution of the human mind that has the simultaneous effect of destroying the human spirit. In this critical respect, "the theory of deterrence that lies at the heart of the presence of nuclear weapons is part of a culture of fear and mistrust pervading international society" (Urbain 2010, 168). It is for this precise reason that Toda called these weapons "absolute evil" and called for their abolition. As Ikeda emphatically asserts, we discover that "trust in nuclear arms is a negation of trust in humanity. The more people trust in arms, the less they trust in one another. Ceasing to put their trust in arms is the only way to cultivate mutual trust among peoples" (Ikeda 2001a, 187).

Trust is the necessary first step toward building an inclusive global civilization. Such an undertaking must, in Ikeda's view, be premised on the willingness of people "to build tolerant and enduring links" (Ikeda 2001a, 132). In Ikeda's 1991 peace proposal, he sets forth specific criteria as a way to monitor progress toward a peaceful global civilization. He cites Arthur Kaufmann's six prerequisites to build a peace compatible with justice as a good example:

> First is the principle of equality. Based on recognition of the fundamental sanctity of life, it guarantees dignity equally to all individuals. Among nations, it assures equal opportunity and equal respect in economic and cultural relations. The second prerequisite is "the golden rule" as expressed in the Bible: "Do unto others as you would have them do unto you." But Prof. Kaufmann translates the rule into an ethical principle and expands on it to include the negative proposition, "Don't do unto others what you would not have them do unto you." The categorical imperative is the third prerequisite, following Immanuel Kant's famous aphorism, "Act only that maxim through which you can at the same time will that it should become a universal law." The fourth is the principle of fairness. As in sports where playing on a level field is the basic rule, in international relations all countries must be entitled to the same advantages and subject to the same disadvantages. The fifth is the principle of responsibility. No action should be taken the consequences of which might destroy, endanger or degrade people's lives or the environment in which they live, now or in the future. The sixth is the principle of tolerance. Even if your neighbor's thoughts run counter to your own interests, you should respect them. (Ikeda 1991)

I argue that all six of these points serve to reveal the moral, political, and economic inadequacy of the current status quo in global relations. Take, for example, the negative proposition: "Don't do unto others what you would not have them do unto you." Thomas Pogge has elaborated on this principle by observing, "By continuing to support the current global order and the national policies that shape and sustain it without taking compensating action toward institutional reform or shielding its victims, we share a negative responsibility for the undue harms they foreseeably produce" (Pogge 2002, 144). Similarly, when we speak of the criterion of equality or the criterion of the "golden rule" or the categorical imperative or the criterion of fairness or the criterion of responsibility or the principle of tolerance—all these criteria are elements of the same phenomenon. They all point to the ways in which we can avoid inflicting human misery or, by ignoring their implications and ethical demands, impose human misery on millions (if not billions) of people. Again, Pogge has expressed the reality quite well in noting, "Current policies of the rich countries and the global order they impose greatly contribute to poverty and unfulfilled human rights in the poor countries and thereby inflict severe undue harms on many. These harms could be drastically reduced through even relatively minor international reforms" (Pogge 2002, 144). When we fail to admit these wrongs and then fail to correct them, "we are violating a negative duty of justice insofar as we contribute to (and fail to mitigate) the harms it reproduces and insofar as we resist suitable reforms" (Pogge 2002, 210).

Similarly, Ramesh Thakur, vice rector of the United Nations University, Tokyo, and head of its peace and governance program, wrote in 2002 that "as the sun rises on the new century and illumines some of the darker legacies of the last one, we should engage in sober reflection and somber introspection. It is simply not acceptable that (1) at a time of unprecedented economic prosperity and stock market booms in some parts of the world, millions of people should continue to be condemned to a life of poverty, illiteracy, and ill health; (2) the combined GDP of the 48 least developed countries should be less than the assets of the world's three richest people; (3) the annual income of 2.5 billion—47 percent—of the world's poorest people should be less than that of the richest 225 [people on the planet]" (Thakur 2002, 284). Thakur wrote these words six years before the 2008 financial meltdown on Wall Street when the stock and housing bubbles wrecked havoc on not only the US economy but the entire global economy (Baker 2009; Foster and Magdoff 2009; Panitch and Konings 2009; Stiglitz 2010).

Since 2008, the situation of the world's poor and middle classes has worsened dramatically. What this situation reveals is the fact that all of humanity is faced with a multidimensional crisis. It is not merely a crisis of economics and economic theory, although it has economic components. It is not merely a political problem both within and between nations, although political issues seem to predominate in most discussions and debates. The reality is that it represents a convergence of challenges and problems from many different sources: economic, ethical, political, sociological, psychological, and philosophical.

In this profound sense, Ikeda's perspective on Toda's idea of transnationalism is even more significant in the aftermath of the events of 2008, for the entire global family has now been consciously exposed to the vicissitudes of an unrestrained and unregulated capitalism drive by greed—perhaps the lowest form of human consciousness. From a different perspective, in accordance with Toda's legacy and Ikeda's vision of transnationalism, it is possible now to argue that human history has reached a turning point where in the midst of massive dehumanization and misery there may be a corresponding opportunity for humans to engage in a process of rehumanizing their world by expanding the definition of the word *wealth* in conjunction with improving the quality of human consciousness itself. If, as Ikeda has suggested, the focus on inner transformation is the beginning of wisdom on the path to peace, then it follows that as conscious members of self-perfecting societies we can begin to make fundamental changes in ourselves and our own society in accordance with this new emphasis on what really constitutes genuine wealth for ourselves and one another. Such a deepened and expanded consciousness of wealth can have dramatic repercussions for the whole of humanity, which—understood as the international society of the whole of humanity—is the *"society of all societies."*

In the spirit of Ikeda, to speak of the society of all societies is to speak of what truly defines and constitutes transnationalism. In the words of Philip Allott,

> The millennial challenge, and the re-humanizing opportunity, is to maximize the wealth of nations in the widest possible definition of the word *wealth*. At long last, we must make the benefits of human socializing for all human beings exceed its costs, actualizing the human potentialities which we have discovered within ourselves. To meet this challenge we must undertake to improve the quality of human consciousness, not only our consciousness as members of self-perfecting societies but also our personal consciousness as self-perfecting human beings. It is a challenge for every form of human society and, above all, for the international society of the whole human race, the society of all societies. (Allott 2002, 143–44)

How the Bandung Conference Inaugurated a New Global Consciousness

Our recent twentieth-century world history reveals glimpses of a consciousness of the society of all societies on its way to global recognition. Glimpses of this consciousness emerged in the April 1955 inaugural Asian–African Conference—more popularly known as the Bandung Conference. Its fiftieth anniversary was recently celebrated in April 2005 with a second gathering in Bandung and Jakarta, Indonesia. It was originally described by President Sukarno of Indonesia as "the first intercontinental conference of colored peoples in the history of mankind." Meeting in Bamako on January 18, 2006, on the eve of the opening of the Polycentric World Social Forum, the participants of this special day dedicated to the fiftieth anniversary of the Bandung Conference sought to express the need to define other development objectives, to create harmony in societies by abolishing exploitation by class, gender, race, and caste—thereby showing the way to a new balance of power between the rich North and the developing Global South. Emerging from this conference, the Bamako Appeal "seeks to promote the principle of the right of everyone to enjoy a full life, put forward the broad outlines of a collective life of peace, justice, and diversity, and advance ways of achieving these objectives at the local level and at the level of humanity as a whole" (Amin 2008, 107).

In broad and general terms these principles are the same principles at play in Ikeda's formulation for building a more peaceful global civilization. The primary difference between the two approaches lies in the degree of specificity with which they apply these principles. For example, while Ikeda denounces militarism, he does not explicitly single out the United States for this criticism insofar as he sees it endemic to many other nations. In contrast, the Bamako Appeal, constructed around broad themes discussed in committees, expresses its more explicit commitment to (1) construct an internationalism that joins the peoples of the South and North who are ravaged by the dictatorship of financial markets and the uncontrolled global expansion of transnational corporations; (2) construct the solidarity of the peoples of Asia, Africa, Europe, and the Americas confronted with the challenges of development in the twenty-first century; and (3) construct a political, economic, and cultural consensus that is an alternative to neoliberal and militarized globalization and the hegemony of the United States and its allies (Amin 2008, 108).

In both Ikeda's formulation for global change by peaceful means and that of the participants at Bandung and Bamako, the common underlying theme which presents itself is that there seems to be an intersection between the processes of transnationalism and the transformation of people's thinking. At the center of that intersection is the discovery of the importance of deliberative politics. To that end, our recognition of the value of dialogue over coercion and confrontation presents itself as the best avenue to travel the pathway of transnationalism in the twenty-first century. As such, it is a discovery that brings out the value and heightened significance of Toda and Ikeda as beacons of light in a time darkened by war and the threat of war. For if people from different backgrounds, cultures, and experiences can forge a consensus on values and agendas, then the nature of problem-solving itself will be transformed in ways that make solutions truly universal and transnational.

In reflecting on the historical significance of Bandung, we discover that some scholars have written about the conference not only in terms of the political economy of international relations but also in terms of it as having sown the seeds for *"re-visioning"* international society (Nesadurai 2008, 68). The 1955 conference took place in a period when European colonialism was coming to an end throughout the Third World. The newly claimed juridical sovereignty and emerging identity of many newly formed Third World nations were ascendant. In this atmosphere, interstate politics rather than economics was the central focus of high-level talks at the conference. It was an era throughout the global South that embodied the essence of the "Bandung Spirit." This spirit largely defined the period of 1955–75. This period was an integral part of the Bandung era. It has also been referred to as the period of

Third Worldism because calls for a *new international economic order* came to predominate throughout the developing world.

Increasingly, calls for economic justice came to characterize the so-called North–South dialogue. What is important to note, however, is how the nature of that dialogue has changed with the passage of time. Specifically, it has been suggested that we have discovered, following Jurgen Habermas's theory of communicative action, "the Bandung principle that endorses that dialogue over coercion and confrontation may be the best option to reach consensus on values and agendas, and in problem-solving" (Nesadurai 2008, 70). The centrality of dialogue as the most effective means to achieve a peaceful resolution of differences between peoples, cultures, and nations is what connects Ikeda's philosophy of peace with the central message of the Bandung principle. Hence, this discovery about the real legacy of the Bandung Conference makes it possible to consider Ikeda's approach to the achievement of peace as a reflection upon modern history, as well as current discourses and discussions about how to best proceed in the field of global relations. In this regard, we find that "in the end, Bandung's lasting legacy for a plural world—yet one that is fast integrating—could well be its endorsement of deliberative politics" (Nesadurai 2008, 70).

Discourse and deliberation are also at the heart of Ikeda's strategy of peace. The spirit behind this particular kind of discourse and deliberation is special insofar as it has the capacity to animate people to act from the heart as opposed to some kind of selfish calculation. Therefore, when we speak of the special nature of discourse and deliberation as being capable of sustaining a genuinely held commitment to the peaceful resolution of differences, we are also beginning to speak of a transformative politics that is uniquely characterized by a community of persons in dialogue who are emotionally, intellectually, and morally attuned to the expression of a new identity—an identity that is capable of addressing global problems and challenges that are planetary in scope. This is vitally important for the sake of a transformative politics dedicated to the realization of peace, for, as Richard Falk has observed, "[u]ntil citizenship is embedded in a community that binds at the level of emotion, it will not lead to the construction of a new identity capable of addressing challenges of planetary scope" (Falk 2009, 203). Such a community could effectively combat world poverty and underdevelopment, could sustain a long-term moral commitment to the eradication of our habitual reliance on weapons of war as the chief means through which we solve disputes, and could lead to more people seeking justice in an increasingly justice-oriented world.

Unfortunately, the decade of the 1980s saw a shift away from collective efforts to relieve world poverty and underdevelopment (McMahan 1985). In my view, it can be argued that the ascendancy of the right wing in the United States, under the leadership of President Ronald Reagan, saw a decade in which US foreign policy was dedicated to the rollback of gains made by the Third World in the 1960s and 1970s (Paupp 2007; see also Bello 2005, 1–11; Kozul-Wright and Rayment 2007, 209–65). In place of dialogue and deliberative politics came the heyday of free-market fundamentalism, as embodied in the work of the Chicago School of Economics under the guidance of Milton Friedman. It was postulated that the liberalization of markets, the retrenchment and retreat of the state from the "commanding heights" of economic decision-making, coupled with deregulation and privatization, would be both the necessary and sufficient conditions for development in the Global South (Yergin and Stanislaw 1998). In reality, it was an ideological mask designed to camouflage the nature of a world where states do not confront each other as economic equals and where agenda-setting and rule-writing in global organizations have been governed by unfair practices. In my view, this is most evident in the documented predatory practices of the IMF, the World Bank, the General Agreement on Tariffs and Trade (later to be replaced in 1995 by the WTO), and the role of US-based multinational corporations (Paupp 2007, 2009; see also Petras and Veltmeyer 2007).

In Reagan's formulation the *magic of the market* would bring prosperity to all, while in leading US academic and policy circles it was decided that underdevelopment was directly caused by poor policy choices and inefficient or corrupt governments, rather than structural barriers in the international political economy. In reality the destructive dimensions of capitalist accumulation through commodification and privatization have affected all aspects of human existence. They have produced "a threefold destruction of the individual, nature and whole peoples" (Amin 2003, 154–58). In the final analysis, "these new views helped undermine whatever consensus, especially its moral claims for collective approaches to addressing underdevelopment and poverty and the obligation of rich states to help poor states" (Nesadurai 2008, 91). These realities are part of the history of the late 1970s and early 1980s. However, they are also realities that have morphed over time in such a manner that the early history of the twenty-first century is already marred by the legacy of decisions made in those days. For example, Michael Klare has grimly noted the following:

> If poverty alleviation is not a likely outcome of major foreign resource projects, the prospects are no better for the alleviation of internal violence. By increasing the flow of illicit wealth to elites that collect the "rents" form oil, gas, and mineral production, such projects inevitably fuel resentment—and, in many cases, rebellion or violent attack—from those who feel unjustly deprived of any benefits. Adding to the prospective flames, the leading energy-consuming nations have tried to protect access to vital materials by providing arms and military training to the armed forces of their primary suppliers, thereby encouraging the rulers of these countries to rely on brute

force rather than compromise and inclusion when dealing with any group that seeks a greater share of oil or mineral revenues. More often than not, this guarantees an endless succession of coups at the top and revolts, ethnic upheavals, and gang wars below. (Klare 2008, 176)

Given the intractable opposition of the United States, as a hegemonic power, to allow any fundamental change in its status as the most dominant power in the international hierarchy of states, I have noted that "[t]he architects of the US Global empire have historically resisted the pursuit of genuine national development in the global South insofar as it would bring an end to virtual US domination. Yet, if the nations of the South are to build an effective Global Community in which they are no longer vulnerable to the exigencies of empire, it will be necessary for them to create effective South–South linkages that empower their drive for independence from the US Global Empire" (Paupp 2007, 275). The need for the active development of such linkages constitutes what I call a "counterhegemonic alliance" to the power and institutions of Western dominance and exploitation. I write, "A viable twenty-first century counter-hegemonic alliance must comprise both national and international social forces and social movements. Between its national and international constituencies, a viable twenty-first century counter-hegemonic alliance must have the capacity to agree upon a common set of principles, practices and policies" (Paupp 2007, 311). What is identified as emerging from this counterhegemonic alliance is a world of rising regions whose development and trajectory are characterized by an adherence to the basic principles from the Bandung Conference's final communiqué. These principles include respect for human rights and the Charter of the United Nations, refraining from acts or threats of aggression or the use of force against the territorial integrity or political independence of any country, as well as the settlement of all international disputes, by peaceful means, such as negotiation, conciliation, arbitration of judicial settlement as well as other peaceful means of the parties' own choice, in conformity with the Charter of the United Nations (Paupp 2007, 311).

By returning our attention to regulating state conduct and international affairs with reference to the UN Charter, we are returned to a fundamental premise of Ikeda's own emphasis on the structural and institutional components of peace. Ikeda has endorsed the UN as one the leading international bodies capable of sustaining the kind of dialogue and conciliation that is necessary not only to maintaining the peace but to extending the promise of peace and human rights to all humankind. In this regard, we are also returned to the way in which the Bandung Conference reenvisioned international society. First, the conference's call for "equitable representation in international decision-making for the new members of the now expanding international society of states was essentially a call to take seriously the issue of international justice, particularly that of procedural justice in the management of world affairs (. . .). Bandung participants also articulated a set of principles for inter-state engagement that emphasized dialogue and accommodation, collective and peaceful problem-solving, and the search for consensus or compromise that they saw as more suited to the expanding and increasingly plural international society of states, therefore rejecting power politics and coercion as the basis for international relations (. . .). These alternative principles for international society remain salient in the twenty-first century" (Nesadurai 2008, 93). These alternative principles are also evident in Ikeda's work. Ikeda has harmonized the relationship between inner transformation and the role of dialogue in creating the conditions for peace. As Urbain notes, "Whereas for Ikeda inner transformation is the starting point of endeavors toward peace, dialogue is the indispensable axis around which the system of his philosophy of peace revolves . . . . Equipped with the capacity for both inner transformation and meaningful dialogue, according to Ikeda, people of all backgrounds and walks of life can discuss issues concerning their lives at the local, national and global levels, enhance deliberative and participatory democracy and widen the political space of their societies, a major ingredient for peace and stability" (Urbain 2010, 225–26).

This strategy of dialogue at the local, national, and global levels has more salience and relevance in a twenty-first-century world that is increasingly moving toward a multicentric set of global relations between rising regions. As the ideology of regionalism and the processes of regionalization continue to expand, the future of global relations will increasingly be characterized by greater mutual cooperation and respect between people engaged in a global dialogue, in conjunction with global trade, and dedicated to a global politics that in principle adheres to finding common solutions to common problems (Paupp 2009). We see this process already being undertaken as China invests in Africa to help build the continent's infrastructure (as well as supply China with needed sources of energy), as Russia is increasingly engaged with Latin American nations in building new alliances and creating new avenues for investment, and as the European Union reaches out to the entire global South in efforts to advance the process of regionalization. In all of these endeavors a more cosmopolitan world is rising. Yet an objective view of the current twenty-first-century situation also reveals that "if we continue to extract and consume the planet's vital resources in the same improvident fashion as in the past, we will, sooner or later, transform the earth into a barely hospitable scene of desolation. And if the leaders of today's Great Powers behave like those of previous epochs—relying on military instruments to achieve their primary objectives—we will witness unending crisis and conflict over what remains of value on our barren wasteland" (Klare 2008, 261).

Having arrived at this point of discussion with respect to introducing some of Ikeda's most relevant principles for moving toward peace and a peaceful global civilization, in juxtaposition to the problem and challenge of *structural powerlessness* among people suffering from poverty and social hardship, environmental degradation and resource depletion, we need to turn our attention to an attendant problem. Simply put, the problem is, *How do we overcome the structural powerlessness of people in a global order that systematically works against their basic interests?* It is hoped that by addressing this question directly it may be possible to clarify the ways in which Ikeda's approach to building a more peaceful global civilization can be practically realized.

Transnationalism as a Means to Overcome Structural Powerlessness

A new, comprehensive, and more precise understanding of our structural powerlessness, both within and between nations, needs to be put forward. That is because, from a Marxian viewpoint, the current global order of domination systematically works against the basic interests of the majority of humankind. Given this undemocratic and/or antidemocratic outcome, it would seem that the time has come for a sincere and objective reexamination of the structural forces that work against the dignity of the person, as well as the collective dignity of groups, cultures, and social classes at every level—local, national, international, and regional (Paupp 2007, 2009).

As long as individuals remain locked into a dehumanizing status quo and do not possess the tools necessary to liberate themselves from this bondage, or even to acknowledge it as bondage, the current order of dehumanization, emotional and political slavery, socioeconomic exploitation and inequality will remain in place. Therefore, the challenge of the twenty-first century is to find that place within the human experience and collective consciousness for an oppositional politics to arise against this current set of arrangements. At this point of the discussion we can, in good conscience, blend the Marcusian formulation of the problem with Ikeda's principles of peace. From the perspective of Ikeda, the kind of transformational politics he advocates, starting with the individual will, by definition, automatically becomes oppositional to this order of dehumanization. For Ikeda, the starting place for transformation is found within the hearts and minds of individual human beings who can come to recognize the one-dimensionality of their existence, as well as those oppressive systems of domination that have made them into the stereotypical figure of the *"one-dimensional man"*—a description first put forward by the German philosopher Herbert Marcuse.

According to Douglas Kellner, we discover that *"One-Dimensional Man* raises the specter of the closing-off, or 'atrophying,' of the very possibilities of radical social change or human emancipation"* (Kellner 1991, xxix). In this world, "Marcuse depicts a situation in which there are no revolutionary classes or groups to militate for radical social change and in which individuals are integrated into the existing society, content with their lot and unable to perceive possibilities for a happier and freer life" (Kellner 1991, xxix). Using a combination of perspectives derived from Marxian theory, the critical theory of the Frankfurt School, French social theory, and American social science, Marcuse presents us with a critical theory of the present age. In this theory, "his argument is that the system's much lauded economic, political, and social freedoms, formerly a source of social progress, lose their progressive function and become subtle instruments of domination which serve to keep individuals in bondage to the system that they strengthen and perpetuate. For example, economic freedom to sell one's labor power in order to compete on the labor markets submits the individual to the slavery of an irrational economic system; political freedom to vote for generally indistinguishable representatives of the same system is but a delusive ratification of a non-democratic political system; intellectual freedom of expression is ineffectual when the media either co-opt and defuse, or distort and suppress, oppositional ideas, and when the image-makers shape public opinion so that it is hostile or immune to oppositional thought and action" (Kellner 1991, xxxi).

According to Marcuse, we discover that oppositional thought and action are precluded by the logic of capitalism itself, for he asserts, "Even the most highly organized capitalism retains the social need for private appropriation and distribution of profit as the regulator of the economy. That is, it continues to link the realization of the general interest to that of particular vested interests" (Marcuse 1964, 53). In Marcuse's view, however, we find that communism fares no better than capitalism in this regard because, in both cases, both of these systems are engaged in a "struggle against a form of life which would dissolve the basis for domination" (Marcuse 1964, 55). The forces of domination (regardless of their ideological label) feed like vampires off people who are subjected to an entire range of oppressive structures that are lorded over by special interests and elites whose primary purpose is to maintain their hegemonic control of all human thought and action. It is because of the nature of this mind-set bent on the maintenance of elite primacy to the exclusion of all other values that Marcuse astutely notes that "the facile historical parallel with the barbarians threatening the empire of civilization prejudges the issue—the second period of barbarism may well be the continued empire of civilization itself" (Marcuse 1964, 257). The civilization of which he speaks is "the closed operational universe of advanced industrial civilization with its terrifying harmony of freedom and oppression, productivity and destruction, growth and regression [which] is pre-designed in this idea of Reason[3] as a specific historical project" (Marcuse 1964, 124).

The nature of this kind of civilization has resulted in a situation where, according to Douglas Kellner, "[e]conomic planning in the state, automatization in the economy, the rationalization of culture in the mass media, and the increased bureaucratization of all modes of social, political, and economic life has created a 'totally administered society'[4] that was resulting in 'the decline of the individual.' By the 1950s, Marcuse thus perceived that the unparalleled affluence of the consumer society and the apparatus of planning and management in advanced capitalism had produced new forms of social administration and a 'society without opposition' that threatened individuality and that closed off possibilities of radical social change" (Kellner 1991, xxv). Similarly, in his 2007 peace proposal, Ikeda noted, "Without the qualitative elevation of individual human beings, neither social transformation nor the creation of a more positive society is possible" (Ikeda 2007-PP, 25). It is for this same reason that Richard Falk, in his description of the citizen pilgrim cautions that "the citizen pilgrim departs from this world of contending ideas of 'world citizen,' sensing that none can produce that 'heavenly country' to which s/he aspires, but not in order to escape by wishful thinking (advocate of world federalism) or self-indulgence (new age escapism). The citizen pilgrim does not pretend that the promised land is at hand (the happy corporate globalist) or to suppose that an American victory in the holy war now raging in Iraq and elsewhere will lead to the happy unification of the entire world (the global imperialist disguised as missionary for democracy)" (Falk 2009, 204).

What Marcuse, Ikeda, and Falk all seem to share in common is twofold: (1) a recognition that many of the current structures of human civilization are actually cages of bondage for the human spirit that stifle the spirit of peace while inflaming warlike sentiments without reflection or reason or dialogue; (2) a recognition that the individual will need to take a step back, look at the overall picture, and temporarily disengage from the narrowly tailored debates of the moment in order to find the freedom to engage in a form of inner transformation that will empower them to advance beyond the status quo and to embrace instead the calls for justice that will eventually come to inform a truly transformative politics on a transnational basis. The recognition of these two dynamics of our current history will provide the beginning of a path toward overcoming humankind's current state of structural powerlessness and the experience of inward imprisonment born of "*one-dimensionality*."

Replacing both structural powerlessness and narrowly tailored debates, we can, according to Ikeda and Falk, recognize that "the dialogic way is open to exploration and discovery, as humans are genetically enabled to shape their future by learning, adapting, reciprocating, renouncing, dreaming, and encompassing. Dialogues undertaken in such a spirit allow us to experience 'the other' without a sense of strangeness and fear, dysfunctional attitudes that so often reflect the discontents of the militarized, unheavenly city that the citizen pilgrim has long ago abandoned because of its negative foreclosure of human destiny, its essential hopelessness regarding human potential with respect to community-building and creative forms of humane governance" (Falk 2009, 206).

The dialogic way also characterizes the work of the German philosopher Jurgen Habermas. Instead of using the term *dialogue* Habermas employs the concept of "communicative rationality." For all practical purposes, we should note that Ikeda's use of the terms *discourse* and *dialogue* has virtually the same import as Habermas's use of the concept and term *communicative rationality*. The central point to be made here is that "Habermas's concept of communicative rationality is useful when attempting to explain why rational discourse can still be used successfully as a tool for dialogue between people of different backgrounds despite the catastrophic tragedies and disappointments of the twentieth and early twenty-first centuries" (Urbain 2010, 121). With regard to how rational discourse can be used to enable the growth and maturation of deliberative democracy, it has also been noted that "the kind of deliberative democracy Habermas has in mind, which is based on a communicative use of rationality, is one essential component of Ikeda's vision for a new global civilization, which is a resolutely dialogical project" (Urbain 2010, 121). This is an important element for us as we seek to explicate Ikeda's strategy for peace in the sense that it allows us to achieve a new level of analysis as we seek to confront and to remove the structural powerlessness of people around the globe.

On the global level we have come to comprehend the reality of a system wherein "poverty, human misery, and social hardship are more than ever expressions of '*structural powerlessness*' . . . of people in a global economic order that systematically works against their basic interests" (Wettstein 2009, 113; italics added). This system has largely been the construction of a neoliberal agenda based on the neoliberal economic model that was born out of the Chicago School of Economics. According to Michel Chossudovsky, "The powers behind this system are those of the global banks and financial institutions, the military–industrial complex, the oil and energy giants, the biotech–pharmaceutical conglomerates and the powerful media and communications giants, which fabricate the news and overtly distort the course of world events" (Chossudovsky 2005, 127). From the perspective of Dr. Paul Farmer, professor of medical anthropology at Harvard Medical School and founding director of Partners in Health, the effects of global structures producing inequality are such that "although the pathogenic effects of such inequality per se are now recognized, many governments, including that of the United States, do little to redress inequalities in health, while others are largely powerless to address such inequity. The reasons for failure are many and varied, but even optimists allow that human rights charters and covenants have not brought an end to—and may not even have slowed—egregious abuses, however they are defined. States large and small—but especially large ones, since their reach is transnational—violate civil, economic, and social rights; and inequality both prompts and covers these violations" (Farmer 2003, 222).

This insight by Dr. Farmer leads us to despair of the real-world possibilities for the salutary role of even human rights charters and covenants. Yet this fact also forces us to inquire further about the true nature of the structural forces and the supportive consciousness behind it that allows for the continuation of such massive violations of rights. On this point, Florian Wettstein, assistant professor in the Department of Ethics and Business Law at the University of St. Thomas, has noted, "If human deprivations are the symptoms of structural powerlessness (. . .) then the practical focus on human development must be the powerful particular interests that dominate and distort those structures. The flip side of powerlessness and dependency of some is control and domination by others. Thus a key insight about human development is that it must aim at the transformation of global structures with the intent of realizing people's rights instead of serving the particular interests of their dominant participants" (Wettstein 2009, 113; italics added).

Taking into account the true nature of the global challenge to human rights, we discover that a more precise enumeration of the combined effect of these structures and institutions, leading to a condition of structural powerlessness, "suggests that the agenda of neo-liberal globalization consists of four fundamental global policies: (1) protection of the interests of capital and expansion of the processes of capital accumulation on a world scale; (2) a tendency toward homogenization of state policies to render them instrumental to the protection of capital and the process of capital accumulation on a world scale, via a new 'market ideology'; (3) the formation and expansion of a new tier of transnationalized institutional authority above the state's, which has the aim and purpose of re-articulating states to the purposes of facilitating global capital accumulation; and (4) the political exclusion of dissident social forces from the arena of state policy-making, in order to de-socialize the subject and insulate the neo-liberal state form against the societies over which they preside, thus facilitating the socialization of risk on behalf of capital" (Gills 2000, 4). These points all constitute a process that has been labeled by Richard Falk as "*globalization from above*" (Falk 1999, 46–56).

In juxtaposition to this above-cited formulation we also have what has been labeled as "*globalization from below*," which is the normative thrust of resistance to the neoliberal project and the forms of structural violence that it has spawned. Five specific examples of this resistance are as follows: "(1) the rights of individuals, families and communities to employment, welfare, and social stability and social justice; (2) the right of labor, whether in the informal or formal sectors, unionized or non-unionized, to resist unemployment, austerity measures, dislocation and immiseration; (3) the right of the poor, dispossessed and marginalized, wherever they exist, to resist the imposition of poverty and the intensification of social polarization; (4) the right of people to reclaim and deploy government (state power) in their own defense, at all levels from local, national, and regional to global, and whether through radical, revolutionary or reformist forms; and (5) the right of all people to establish social solidarities and autonomous forms of social organization outside the state and the market; and finally the right to imagine 'post-globalization' and realize alternative modes of human development" (Gills 2000, 7). All of these forms of resistance are being undertaken by those on the "underside of history." It is those on the underside of history who are engaging in their version of *"globalization from below,"* insofar as they are people supportive of the protection and expansion of human dignity and human rights. As such, they have compatriots in every corner of the globe insofar as these various forms of resistance characterize new expressions of *"transnationalism"* or what has been termed a global *"counter-hegemonic alliance"* against US-led hegemony, neo-liberalism, and empire (Paupp 2007, 2009).

From the perspective of Habermas, it is clear that "the public sphere is under constant threat of being colonized by the administrative system. Communicative action theory can be used to protect society against dehumanization, to protect the public sphere against the inhumane struggle for power that often characterizes the administrative sphere" (Urbain 2010, 121). On this very issue Habermas has written, "Many different occasions for discontent and protest arise wherever a one-sided process of modernization, guided by criteria of economic and administrative rationality, invades domains of life which are centered on the task of cultural transmission, social integration, socialization and education, domains oriented towards quite *different* criteria, namely towards those of communicative rationality" (Habermas [1980] 2007, 365).

Resistance to structural powerlessness is also constitutive of examples of broad-based resistance to various forms of structural violence and direct violence. By adopting strategies of peace, thereby resisting any further participation in or support for the policies of *globalization from above,* I shall argue that this phenomenon constitutes a conscious adoption of peace as a value in both the lives of individuals and in the conduct of global affairs. Yet it can also be argued that it is even more than just a value in and of itself. Choosing the value of peace constitutes what has been called a *"synthesis value."* It is a "synthesis value because, *if* violence is defined as everything that militates against a human's full development, and if the humanist conception of society entails the maximization of such values as social justice, economic welfare, participation, ecological balance, national autonomy, and cultural pluralism in order to make that development possible, *then* any act, process, structure, or institution that is inimical to these values will be inimical to peace" (Lagos and Godoy 1977, 129; italics added). In this crucial respect, "a nation whose international and national policies maximize the peace value will be one that does away with all forms of violence, direct and structural, external and internal,"—as exemplified by Table 1.1.

Table 1.1   Forms and Dimensions of Violence[a]

Forms of violence	Dimensions of violence	Acts, structures, institutions, and processes
Direct	External (international)	War, preparation for war, trade in armaments, military alliances
	Internal (international)	Acts of repression
Structural	External (international)	Domination-dependence systems, colonialism or neocolonialism, imperialism
	Internal (international)	Economic-exploitation systems; social, economic, political, and cultural; structures productive of alienation; absence of participation

Source: Gustavo Lagos and Horacio H. Godoy, *Revolution of Being: A Latin American View of the Future*. New York: Free Press, 1977, p. 130.
[a]See also Johan Galtung, *Peace by Peaceful Means* (1996).

The global impact of peace as a synthesis value on the course of global relations and the maintenance of those forces that benefit from the condition of structural powerlessness is enormous. If we come to appreciate the true nature and definition of this conceptualization of peace, then Ikeda's notion of global citizenship,[5] which I translate here as transnationalism, becomes even more radical. It becomes more radical because it has the capacity to directly threaten the continued domination of those dominant interests who have unjustly benefited from these kinds of oppressive, exploitative, and degrading policies and practices. In short, the articulation of this particular conceptualization of peace now places the attainment of and respect for human dignity at the center of both our personal lives and our socioeconomic and sociopolitical agenda.

This conceptualization of peace—as a synthesis value—empowers us to cross the boundaries of our previously self-imposed limitations, both personal and political, for, as a synthesis value, we discover the power of peace can offset the powers of structural violence by laying claim to the loyalty, consciousness, and commitment of people around the globe, irrespective of cultural, ideological, or religious orientations. Peace as a synthesis value allows for the transnationalism of human rights to be made manifest as a realizable goal that not only brings humanity to a higher level of being but, at the same time, delegitimizes, dislocates, and disempowers those forces of structural violence and structural domination that have been responsible for keeping in place the one-dimensionality of what we have identified as structural powerlessness. Therefore, to find a path to personal and collective freedom from violence that is immediately accessible to call creates for us in the midst of history a revolutionary opportunity to remake our lives and human history itself. It is a transformative politics that is being undertaken by a transformed people.

All future actions that are undertaken in this spirit will be, by definition, transformative and transforming. The promise of a *"new heaven and a new earth"* now are re-moved from the realm of utopian thinking and placed in the matrix of our current historical *praxis* (a specific time, place, and situation). By breaking into our historical present, then, this synthesis value of peace itself is transformed into an *"ethical ought."* The old Kantian formulation about treating people as ends in themselves and not as means to some other end now, in this historical moment, becomes attainable because we, in light of the strength of the arguments of all the aforementioned authors cited herein, have declared that it is not only attainable but *"ought to be."* In this regard, Ikeda himself stressed the importance of the virtues of courage, wisdom, and compassion in his 1996 lecture at Columbia University entitled "Education for Global Citizenship": "I think that I can state with confidence that the following are essential elements of global citizenship[:] (1) The wisdom to perceive the interconnectedness of all life and living; (2) The courage not to fear or deny difference; but to respect and strive to understand people of different cultures, and to grow from encounters with them; (3) The compassion to maintain an imaginative empathy that reaches beyond one's immediate surroundings and extends to those suffering in distant places. The all-encompassing interrelatedness that forms the core of the Buddhist worldview can provide a basis, I feel, for the concrete realization of these qualities of wisdom, courage, and compassion (Ikeda 2001b, 100–01). So, while Ikeda has left the working out of the concrete realization of these qualities to others, he has still provided us with a necessary roadmap on how to bring about the realization of a more peaceful global civilization. In this regard, it may be truly said that if you know where you are going, almost any road, arguably, will get you there.

Notes

1. As mentioned in the Introduction, Ikeda and Makiguchi never met in person; it is through Toda that Ikeda has come to know Makiguchi's teachings.
2. The Soka Gakkai was first called Soka Kyoiku Gakkai from 1930 to 1945.
3. Habermas has made a distinction between instrumental/purposive rationality and communicative rationality, condemning the first one, but not the entirety of the concept of Reason, like Marcuse does.
4. Habermas also criticizes the negative sides of the administrative sphere in opposition to the public sphere.
5. Josei Toda had used the term *Chikyu Minzoku Shugi*, which can be translated as "global nationalism" or "one-worldism." This corresponds to what Ikeda calls "global citizenship."

2

Where We Are Now—and What Is Required to Achieve a Peaceful Global Civilization

Even when a sheer rock face looms before us, we should refuse to be disheartened, but instead continue the patient search for a way forward. In this sense, what is most strongly required of us is the imagination that can appreciate the present crisis as an opportunity to fundamentally transform the direction of history.

—Daisaku Ikeda
(2010 peace proposal, "Toward a New Era of Value Creation")

The current state of global relations is in a state of global crisis. There are a variety of sources from which a crisis of this kind of magnitude arose. Some key examples include the aggressive and exploitative practices of the US global empire. In the twin areas of war and financial sector dominance, the United States has held a virtual monopoly on the use of force and the employment of military violence—as exemplified by the illegal invasion and occupation of Iraq since 2003, Afghanistan since 2001, and its planned war of aggression against Iran (Chossudovsky 2005, 114–24; Mittelman 2010).

Further, the US global empire is also an empire of capital. Its financial sector has set in motion a series of crises that have consumed the attention of Wall Street, US Treasury, and the world at large as a global recession has nearly led humanity into the abyss of a worldwide depression after the events of 2008. Yet the roots of the crisis may be traced back much further to the Clinton years. Under the Financial Modernization Act adopted in November 1999, US lawmakers had set the stage for a sweeping deregulation of the US banking system. Under new rules that were approved by the US Senate and approved by President Clinton, the legislation repealed the Glass-Stegall Act of 1933, a pillar of Franklin Roosevelt's New Deal. As a result of this new legislation, "[e]ffective control over the entire US financial services industry . . . had been transferred to a handful of financial conglomerates—which are also the creditors and shareholders of high tech companies, the defense industry, major oil and mining consortia, etc." (Chossudovsky 2003, 315–16; 2005, 114–34; Hudson 2005). While these events have been unfolding, financial and political elites in the United States have sought to maintain US hegemony and US global primacy at any cost, irrespective of the established constraints of international law and the consensus of the global community (Paupp 2007, 2009).

In the admixture of a campaign of US-sponsored global wars in combination with the power of international finance—including the IMF, the World Bank, and the WTO—we find that the ravages of these combined forces have worsened the plight of all humanity by any moral or statistical measure. Whether we examine widening gulfs of inequality both within and between nations, the rise in the numbers of people trapped in poverty, or the growing waste of planning and preparation for wars of aggression in the name of fighting terror, the bottom line is that we have arrived at an historical tipping point. When viewed from this perspective, Prof. James Mittelman has suggested that "[t]aken together, these measures offer an opportunity to step up and reshape the kinds of societies we will live in after the wars and bailouts of the early part of this millennium. After all, what are those efforts really for? To return to prior ways of political and economic life? Or are they an occasion to help reorient world order?" (Mittelman 2010, 203). This chapter is dedicated not only to examine where we are but also to inquire about where we are going. For us, that inquiry involves a most fundamental question: Can we transform a culture of violence into a culture of peace?

By juxtaposing the philosophy and views of Ikeda and his contemporaries with the nature of the current crisis and the sources from which it sprang, it is my hope that I can set forth both an understanding and an agenda that effectively addresses the challenge of how to reclaim our lives and our global civilization from violence. In so doing, I also seek to provide concrete insights, proposals, and solutions to the question of how we might best go about creating a more peaceful global civilization.

Transforming a Culture of Violence into a Culture of Peace

The theoretical, philosophical, and practical divide that exists between capitalism's twenty-first-century vision and the vision of Ikeda for achieving a peaceful global civilization could not be greater. On the one hand, there is the vision of a world under the rule of capitalism's financial sector dominance, combined with the military arm of US hegemony (Paupp 2007, 2009). On the other hand, there is the vision of a world characterized by *"an expanding network of human solidarity"* as *"the true path to peace"* (Ikeda 2009-PP, 12). In Ikeda's view, this network is premised on a number of interactive elements. The first element is grounded in *"perspectives and principles"* which Ikeda refers to as *"inner universality"* which *"can only be developed from within"* (Ikeda 2009-PP, 10). Intertwined with this inner universality is the power of dialogue which *"presents infinite possibilities"* insofar as it is *"a challenge that can be taken up by anyone—anytime—in order to realize the transformation from a culture of violence to a culture of peace"* (Ikeda 2009-PP, 24). In other words, through the dynamic between inner transformation and dialogue, Ikeda postulates that we have the capacity to become global citizens and, through the exercise of that citizenship, are capable of birthing into existence a peaceful global civilization. It is a vision that replaces the profit motive and the use of force with the transformative dynamic of changed consciousness and an interactive dialogue dedicated to building mutual respect, cooperation, and advancing human dignity.

In essence, in light of the analysis presented above, one could not find two worldviews more diametrically opposed. This is important to recognize, for when we use the term *diametrically opposed,* we could also use the term *dialectically opposed* or even *dialogically opposed* insofar as there are two opposing logics before us that place human experience, identity, and purpose on two radically different historical trajectories. In the case of the global capitalist system, under the auspices of the US empire, an agenda of violence and exploitation is written into its DNA. For example, Manuel Castells, a professor of sociology at the University of California, Berkeley, notes, "Instead of understanding the new world, and finding new ways of dealing with its issues, the US decided to use its military superiority, based on technological excellence, thus on its advance in the technological revolution, *to adapt the world to itself, to its interests, to its ways of thinking and being,* rather than the other way round" (Castells 2004, xviii; italics added). Similarly, Walden Bello notes, "Once, in the era of decolonization, the promise of economic development along lines that would enhance national independence excited the non-industrialized countries. But it ran up against the desire of the United States to incorporate the newly independent economies as subordinate elements in the global capitalist system" (Bello 2005, 153). Hence, by virtue of this decision to impose a form of globalization "from above" in the name of neoliberal economics, the US empire effectively foreclosed on alternative paths for human development and alternative individual and cultural identities. This same decision, in turn, effectively foreclosed upon the realization of socioeconomic and sociopolitical values that would be supportive of human rights and dignity. That is the reason why Gustavo Lagos argued, "It would be illusory and hypocritical to talk of the integral development of man, to issue declarations in favor of democracy and human rights, unless at the same time socioeconomic and political structures are changed in such a way as to permit the implementation of the values in question" (Lagos 1975, 80).

Given the realities of the current system of global domination under the US empire and the power of global capitalism, the challenge for people to develop an alternative model of being, of life, of action, will require a definitive substitution of values. The values that have guided and defined the imperial culture of global capitalism and militarism cannot be blindly adopted by the people of the global South without the danger that they will be subsumed up under these very same values. Therefore, as a Chilean, Lagos argues, "Our nation must learn from the developed countries to avoid stumbling into the same pitfalls as they. It is absolutely essential that our creative endeavor should be directed towards the formulation of genuinely Latin American solutions. Hence, there is no point in persisting in a race for development that takes no account of the values inherent in a developed society" (Lagos 1975, 78).

Similarly, Ikeda rejects the idea that our human identity should be forced upon us by some external power that seeks to exercise domination over our lives, thoughts, and self-knowledge. Rather, Ikeda sets forth the proposition that rather than adapting to an empire of elite-sanctioned ideas and identities, in the alternative, we tap into our own potential for inner transformation, thereby discovering our common humanity and common global citizenship with one another. Rather than exploit artificial differences that can lead to violence, it is better to seek out our commonality and discover the power of consensus. For example, Ikeda speaks of *"perspectives and principles that con-stitute what I refer to as 'inner universality'. . . . The truly important questions are always those close at hand, in our tangible and immediate circumstances"* (Ikeda 2009-PP, 10). The prospects for achieving a peaceful global civilization are greater at this point because when we *"set out from our immediate and concrete realities"* we are automatically engaged in *"an expanding network of human solidarity"* which, according to Ikeda, *"is the true path to peace"* (Ikeda 2009-PP, 12).

In short, what we are presented with here is the fundamental difference between our adapting to a system of external domination versus our embrace of a journey of inner exploration and inner transformation that can lead us to a sense of solidarity with others as our shared perspectives and principles create an "inner universality" between people of all cultures and backgrounds who are not only capable of being global citizens but can also reject a culture of violence and militarism because they choose to create a culture of peace. In this regard, Ikeda promises us that *"[i]f we search beyond the arbitrary, surface labels and engage with each other as individuals in dialogue, generating spontaneous and intense interactions of heart and mind, we will be able to give rise to the 'deeper, slower movements' which Toynbee considered to ultimately shape human history"* (Ikeda 2009-PP, 25). Given this perspective, it can be argued that a great number of the arbitrary, surface labels with which people are encumbered by actually arise out of a false sense of identity.

If we appreciate the idea that identity, from a sociological perspective, is a social construction forged by existing power relationships, then we can also face the reality of how a global empire of military, economic, and cultural dominance has constructed not only our current world but also false identities, which, in turn, have served to create our current global crisis. For example, the rallying cry in the so-called *war on terror* has been *"the West versus the Rest."* This *us/them* dichotomy not only has been destructive of possibilities for true dialogue between people but has also postulated the thesis that there is an inevitable and inexorable *clash of civilizations*. Hence, since 2001 the current global crisis has manifested itself in terms of what could be referred to as an identity crisis.

Overcoming Our "Identity Crisis"

From the perspective of Castells, "Identity is people's source of meaning and experience" (Castells 2004, 6). He also notes, "It is easy to agree on the fact that, from a sociological perspective, all identities are constructed . . . . Since the social construction of identity always takes place in a context marked by power relationships, I propose a distinction between three forms and origins of identity building: (1) *Legitimizing identity*: introduced by the dominant institutions of society to extend and rationalize their domination vis-à-vis social actors . . . . (2) *Resistance identity*: generated by those actors who are in positions/conditions devalued and/or stigmatized by the logic of domination, thus building trenches of resistance and survival on the basis of principles different from, or opposed to, those permeating the institutions of society . . . . (3) *Project identity*: when social actors, on the basis of whatever cultural materials are available to them, build a new identity that redefines their position in society and, by so doing, seek the transformation of overall social structure . . . ." (Castells 2004, 7–8; italics in original).

We can easily appreciate how Castells's schema on the three forms and origins of identity building actually fit well with an analysis of Ikeda's vision for a more peaceful global civilization. *First*, it seems evident that in the form of identity-building called *"legitimizing identity"* we find an account of the practices and perspectives characteristic of those who seek to maintain a status quo that is antithetical to peace. That is because its main function and purpose of a legitimizing identity in the value structure of a global system of military and economic domination is to guard and maintain the idea that the use of force and the legitimacy of violence can be viewed as an acceptable means to maintain an unjust status quo. The actual cost of maintaining such a status quo of power results in an ideological justification of actions that are designed to enforce the domination of the West over and above the rest of humanity. Such a value structure and policy are antithetical to the advancement of peace insofar as they ultimately require the use of force and violence to attain compliance through coercion. Such a policy has negative effects because it is also conducive to producing greater socioeconomic inequalities both within and between nations. The significance of this observation cannot be overstated insofar as it serves to reveal the actual functioning of the US empire as an enterprise that is largely dedicated to a narrowly circumscribed concept of what is required to maintain its global hegemony, which is often cast in terms of the defense of the *national interest*. The problem lies in the fact that the current distribution of power is primarily devoted to the perpetuation of a system in which the most powerful countries maintain privileged positions at the expense of weak and poor societies. According to Robert Johansen, we find, "[t]his arrangement of power and authority denies further realization of global justice and basic human rights. Not only is the denial of justice undesirable in itself, it also contributes to the difficulty and detracts from the desirability of maintaining peace. Thus, the present distribution of power threatens both the quality of life for a substantial number of co-inhabitants of the globe and ultimately the survival of human civilization" (Johansen 1980, 14).

Second, in Castells's schema wherein he defines "*resistance identity*" we also discover a vivid account of the effects of marginalization and social exclusion suffered by those who have been stigmatized by the logic of domination. The US empire has clearly had a negative effect on the people and states that it has colonized, occupied, and invaded. In response, those who have chosen to resist the logic of domination have built trenches of resistance and survival against the brutal invasion of their lives by military force, economic coercion, or both. In light of these circumstances, it should not be surprising that people who have been so negatively affected by imperialism, empire, and domination should choose to adopt a resistance identity in order that they might reclaim ownership of their own lives. After all, since the decade of the 1980s, the US-sponsored neoliberal economic model has effectively crippled the nations of East Asia, Argentina, Russia, Iraq, and Eastern Europe. In the case of Latin America, Prof. William I. Robinson has noted, "As transnational capital achieved hegemony, the new transnationally oriented dominant groups (1) achieved a more direct control over the state; (2) expelled popular classes from ruling coalitions as the doors of the neoliberal state slammed shut; (3) reoriented the state from developmentalist to neoliberal; and (4) shifted its function from promoting previous national models to promoting the transnational model of accumulation" (Robinson 2008, 183).

Of course all of these efforts by the managers of the US empire have been undertakings that have sought ideological justification in reference to ideas such as the pursuit of the "*national interest*," "*democracy promotion*," or "*the cause of freedom*." In the alternative, Ikeda has been critical of global pursuits dedicated to a narrowly defined national interest. Urbain has argued that ". . . Ikeda's peace proposals contain most of his ideas on global citizenship and on the way to make progress toward a better world by overcoming narrow interests" (Urbain 2010, 145). Such a perspective fits well with Ikeda's renewal of the concept of humanitarian competition, as well as SGI's activities for coalition building. This perspective on coalition building also fits well with my prediction that the future of global relations will be increasingly defined by a world of "rising regions" in a posthegemonic international order (Paupp 2009).

My perspective on the future trajectory of global relations is shared by Walden Bello, who notes, "Regional economic collaborations among Third World countries—or, in the parlance of development economics, 'South-South cooperation'—are the wave of the future" (Bello 2005, 212). Already the positive effects of regional economic collaboration have become evident in not only advancing cooperation between people but also advancing the cause of human rights. The historical trends that have emerged in the last half century toward regionalism (*as an ideology*) and regionalization (*as a process*) disclose to us an amazing predictive power about where the human future could possibly move. The global trends toward regionalism are beginning to define a new pattern of global identities which are being concretely manifested in the creation of regional human rights procedures and institutions. Prof. Dinah Shelton has noted, "Over the past half century, regional human rights procedures and institutions have evolved perhaps to an even greater extent than have substantive human rights guarantees. The major changes have been accomplished by amending the basic legal instruments, but other innovations have emerged as regional human rights bodies have made use of their express and implied powers" (Shelton 2008, 491).

Examples can be cited in the European system where the European Convention on Human Rights has often served as a model for other nations seeking to embark on their patterns of experimentation. The Inter-American system has evolved through the Organization of American States (OAS). The fifth meeting of consultation of ministers of foreign affairs of the OAS authorized by resolution the establishment of an Inter-American Commission on Human Rights in 1959. The African system has evolved in conjunction with the African Charter on Human and People's Rights. Article 30 provides for a commission, established within the institutional framework of the African Union, "to promote human and people's rights and ensure their protection in Africa" (Shelton 2008, 493–552).

This record of accomplishment demonstrates, if nothing else, the importance of dialogue in building bridges between people in order to effectuate a more humane and inclusive world. In this regard, Ikeda's wisdom about the centrality of dialogue in advancing the cause of a more peaceful global civilization resonates with history and experience. These regional advances all underscore the transformative power of dialogue to create a new appreciation of human possibility. Given the importance of this approach to building a more humane global civilization, it is useful to recall a proposition that Ikeda noted in his 1989 peace proposal: "To abandon dialogue is in fact to abandon being human" (Ikeda 1989-PP, 5). The centrality of Ikeda's emphasis on dialogue connects well with Castells's concept of "*resistance identity*" insofar as new identities that emerge from the experience of resistance to oppression and injustice can gather strength as human networks become thicker and more conversant with one another. We can see this process at work in the global

43

South—specifically in the case of southern Africa and surrounding regions. We discover that

> While regional social movements remain relatively weaker than in South Africa, this does not mean that the status quo cannot change over time. South Africa is already showing signs of an increasing groundswell of social movement activity, even among those understood as being more marginalized, and it is only a matter of time before this begins to manifest more regionally. Ironically, it appears the more globalization processes and networks become thicker, the more sustained the level of civil society participation and resistance becomes. In the long run, this will definitely be a positive, if not *the* positive consequence of globalization in the South. (Thompson 2007, 132; italics in the original)

This account of Africa's recent history demonstrates the importance of civil society as a much-needed forum for dialogue, identity formation, and clarification, for in the human exchanges between individuals throughout the civil society there comes about a critical mass of energy and consciousness directed toward more humane alternatives to the status quo. The transformative power of an engaged civil society should not be underestimated when it comes to our view about how much the world we live in can be changed. This is especially the case when we understand discourse and dialogue throughout civil society can bring about a wider range of participation from those previously marginalized and excluded (Paupp 2000). Their discourse and their dialogue emerge from the process of globalization *"from below."* As such, they are alienated from the dynamics of a US-led globalization project *"from above."* This is what separates the two realities about the discourse of globalization as an historical project. We discover that "elite discourse is framed around globalization as the spread of freedom: a perspective uniquely strong in the US and an echo of Britain's imperial past when the civilizing mission of Empire was a dominant discourse. And just as Empire meant British leadership in the 19th century so globalization means US leadership in the early 21st century from a US elite perspective" (Bowles and Veltmeyer 2007, 208).

In other words, dialogues that take place in the context of globalization *from below* can reach a common consensus about a human future that is radically different from those dialogues that take place from the perspective of globalization *from above*. Insofar as the socioeconomic and sociopolitical project of those guiding globalization *from above* has consistently resulted in the violation of human rights without remedy, the practice of economic exploitation without recourse or remedies, it follows that an identity of resistance to the status quo is the best hope for the transformation of history *from below* so that the marginalized, dispossessed, and excluded of the globe can finally advocate and achieve an alternative global civilization that is dedicated to the maintenance of peace and the end of aggrandizement, aggression, and the endless drive for acquisition.

Third, in Castells's schema wherein he defines "*project identity*" we find a description of what happens when social actors seek to build a new identity that redefines their position in society and, in undertaking this task, engage in dialogue leading to the transformation of the overall social structure. This paradigm is perhaps the closest to what Ikeda has in mind when he speaks and writes of the idea of "*humanitarian competition.*" In his 2009 peace proposal entitled "Toward Humanitarian Competition: A New Current in History," Ikeda renewed Makiguchi's call for us to set our sights on the goal of engaging in what he termed *humanitarian competition*. Makiguchi describes humanitarian competition as follows: "*To achieve the goals that would otherwise be pursued by military or political force through the intangible power that naturally exerts a moral influence; in other words, to be respected rather than feared*" (Ikeda 2009-PP, 7–8; italics added).

Ikeda rejects the logic that lies behind the pursuit of the "*national interest*" because it violates the principle of human solidarity, it fails to promote peace, and it often leads to negative interactions between states. In his 2008 peace proposal, Ikeda again emphasized the importance of Makiguchi's concept of humanitarian competition, as well as its contemporary use and relevance, noting, "In a book published in 1903, Tsunesaburo Makiguchi called for '*humanitarian competition*' among states. This was a vision of an international order in which the world's diverse states strive to positively influence each other, to coexist and flourish together rather than pursuing narrowly defined national interests" (Ikeda 2008-PP, 21; italics added). In place of a narrowly defined national interest approach to global relations, Ikeda has stressed common themes that could serve as foci for an organized global solidarity around issues and values such as human rights, nuclear disarmament, and environmental problems (Urbain 2010, 167). Similarly, Robert Johansen notes, "If one chooses to depart from traditional definitions of the national interest, one is not less scientific or less empirically oriented than the defenders of traditional definitions. An untraditional orientation may simply mean that one endorses a slightly rearranged hierarchy of values" (Johansen 1980, 20). In this regard, we can make the case that Ikeda's concept of humanitarian competition represents such a rearranged hierarchy of values. As such, the placement of the concept of humanitarian competition at the center of Ikeda's philosophy of peace and plan for a more peaceful global civilization represents a new hierarchy of values that transcends the limitations and ethical dilemmas presented by the ongoing priority given to the concept of advancing the national interest.

In no uncertain terms, Ikeda has declared, "I am fully convinced that the time has now arrived, a hundred years after it was originally proposed, for us to turn our attention to *humanitarian competition* as a guiding principle for the new era" (Ikeda 2009-PP, 7–8; italics added). The transcendent and transformative power of the concept and practice of humanitarian competition fits well with Castells's definition of *"project identity."* That is because project identity allows social actors to build a new identity that redefines their place in society. The opportunities that are unlocked by this new identity allow for the larger transformation of the overall social structure. These opportunities exist at all levels of social life and governance, from the local to the national, from the national to the regional, and from the national to international life.

We can see this dynamic at work in the historical experience of South Africa in the 1990s, as it moved in the direction of becoming a postapartheid society. Nelson Mandela and F. W. de Klerk were able to open up new avenues of dialogue which allowed for the emergence and discovery of a common interest. The version of a common interest that they created together allowed for a core of moderation to arise in a society divided by race and ethnicity. By forging a truly human identity through deracializing the apartheid state and placing the nation on an inclusive path by adopting a democratization pact, it became possible for both sides to mitigate the forces of extremism. This process allowed for the discovery of a more moderate center in which the politics of accommodation could unleash creative processes that resulted in the building of a new set of political institutions that were more attuned to the dynamics of new forms of consciousness, identity, and discourse. The net result was the achievement of what has been called *inclusionary governance* (Paupp 2000).

The replacement of an exclusionary apartheid regime with an inclusive and democratized state allowed for the emergence of a civil society, a state, and a culture that became empowered enough to embrace and endorse a politics of consent born of moderation. Timothy Sisk has noted thus:

> In the wake of the polarized politics of apartheid, a common interest in deracializing the state emerged, which avoided the politics of ethnicity and reinforced the small core of moderation that arose in this deeply divided society. Beginning with the democratization pact, and perhaps fully realized by a new set of political institutions, the politics of extremism could be delinked from the state through a set of institutions chosen precisely because they had the effect of promoting a political system that rewards moderation. In the wake of an exclusive, unilaterally dictated political system, the parties converged on a system that is fundamentally inclusive and incorporates codetermined decision making. Most important, this was achieved on the basis of consent grounded in the interests of the moderate parties, who began to discover, in pursuit of their goals, what constitutes fairness in their own milieu. (Sisk 1994, 274).

Identifying the Creative Elements of a Humane Global Civilization

The example of South Africa's transformation from an apartheid state of racial segregation into a democratic and multiracial nation serves to illustrate how moving away from unilateral decision-making and unilaterally imposed value structures opened the door to a more creative, inclusive, and consensual future. In many ways, what happened to South Africa in the early 1990s serves as a template for how we can begin to think about the creation of a new kind of global civilization that is born of consensus, leads toward cultural convergence, and maintains a flexible framework. According to Timothy Sisk, we discover that "[n]egotiation in South Africa entailed redefining the new rules of the political game for both the transition and the new political order. Driving negotiation forward to settlement was the central lesson of conflict in deeply divided South Africa as it entered the post-apartheid era: no single actor could unilaterally impose its rule preferences on others, given the balance of power" (Sisk 1994, 284). In other words, the situation was such that all social actors, all people in South Africa's society emerged as victors from this process.

According to Urbain, "Makiguchi wrote only about competition between nations, but this concept can be broadened to include humanitarian competition between all actors in society: economic, financial, political, administrative or educational. Ikeda mentions Mandela and de Klerk as excellent examples of leaders who desired to create a society in which all people are victors (1996-PP), and I believe this idea was one of the keys to the rebuilding of post-apartheid South Africa. Instead of the win/lose options of traditional competition, Ikeda proposes the win/win solutions of humanitarian competition, with groups vying with each other to show the greatest proof of humane behavior" (Urbain 2010, 163). In other words, the concern of the parties switches from a desire to dominate others toward a realization of the importance of two other radically different ideas that emerge out of Ikeda's peace proposals: *"inner universalism"* (1989-PP) and *"interconnectedness".* Each of these ideas may be interpreted, from Ikeda's perspective, as being the central mechanisms for producing an inclusive global civilization. An elaboration of these two core ideas is as follows: (1) protecting the dignity of each and every human being by affirming their potential—an idea that is at the basis of the concepts of inner transformation and human revolution. This constitutes the idea of what Ikeda calls inner universalism. It is an idea that ". . . counteracts both the imposed-from-without, one-size-fits-all universalism of Western models (such as economic globalization) . . ." and (2) realizing our interconnectedness. On this point, it is essential to realize that "[i]nterconnectedness is a fundamental Buddhist concept" that affirms "that people cannot live in isolation, and therefore need to reach out to each other, using different means of communication including dialogue" (Urbain 2010, 162).

Now, applying these lessons and concepts to the task of building a more humane and inclusive global civilization, we are returned to the fundamental realization that the values and framework for this undertaking should not be imposed *from above*—whether in the name of globalization, whether in pursuit of a particular economic model, or in the name of a particular culture's unilateral selection of values. Rather, as Urbain reminds us, "It is . . . essential to understand that the kind of global civilization Ikeda has in mind is more like a flexible framework than a set of cultural practices to be imposed on the world" (Urbain 2010, 160). So the future global civilization Ikeda envisions must first and foremost be inclusive and allow all cultures to flourish. In Ikeda's words, "One necessary aspect of a culture of peace is that it must provide a basis on which a plurality of cultural traditions can creatively interact, learning and appropriating from one another toward the dream of a genuinely inclusive global civilization" (Ikeda 2001a, 108).

In much the same spirit, African scholar and author, Ali A. Mazrui, speaking as a member of the *World Order Models Project*, observed the following:

> Our perspective on world order puts a special premium on cultural convergence, partly derived from the conviction that *a shared pool of values constitutes consensus*. The reform of the world in the direction of greater social justice, enhanced economic welfare, and diminishing prospects for violence requires human consensus behind some core values. The world of tomorrow can either be tamed through outright force or through shared values. And the shared values are what constitutes cultural convergence. (Mazrui 1976, 65; italics added)

To arrive at a place in African history where there will be "a shared pool of values," it has been asserted that "Africa will remain in its multilevel crisis until a comprehensive solution producing stable conditions for development is *found from within* . . . . We should understand that African leadership cannot claim legitimacy without courageously confronting the plight of the African peoples and their urgent quest for the universal ideals of human dignity" (Abegunrin 2009, 201; italics added).

In conjunction with Mazrui's perspective, it should also be noted that Ikeda's philosophical devotion to three central themes remains operative in the task of guiding us through the creative processes that can lead to the building of this global civilization. The three central themes are *global citizenship*, *humanitarian competition*, and *global civilization*. What this means is that "Ikeda's vision for a global civilization can be described as a platform, a set of dialogical mechanisms, a framework allowing people of different backgrounds and ideologies to participate together in the construction of a better world" (Urbain 2010, 161). To that end, acknowledging the significance and power of the ideas of inner universalism and interconnectedness serves to reunite us with a recognition of our common humanity, our common needs, and our common aspirations for a better world. In that regard, we will be forced to reinterpret and to reformulate our past definitions and assumptions about what really constitutes human development in a world that has been bitterly divided by the habits of exclusionary forms of governance, the suppression of civil society, and the exploitation of the dispossessed. Therefore, if the practical and concrete implementations of Ikeda's ideas about the meaning of inner universalism and interconnectedness are to have meaningful application, then the concepts of human rights and the task of development need to be united in practice.

The practice of these principles is highly participatory. Communities, civil society, minorities, and the economically and politically excluded must all be engaged in forging a developmental agenda that is faithful to their identities and respectful of their heritage. Only in this way can the meaning of inner universalism be experienced and the dynamics of interconnectedness unleashed. To that end, it has been argued that

[a] key component of a rights-based approach to development is the idea that poverty means more than people lacking income. It also means that they lack control over their lives. Accordingly, development initiatives should have a high degree of participation, including from representatives of affected communities, civil society, minorities, indigenous peoples, women, and other groups likely to be overlooked with traditional forms of consultation. Development should be based on *inclusive processes*, rather than externally conceived "quick fixes," and imported technical models. (Manby 2004, 1003; italics added)

For the entirety of the twentieth century, the people of the Third World—the global South—have had Western models of development imposed upon them. The results have usually not been good for the majority in the global South. Denis Goulet, a progressive leader and author in the field of development, has noted, "Genuine development means the construction by a human society of its own history, its own destiny, its own universe of meanings. The special challenge facing developing societies is that they are obliged to work out their destiny in conditions which subject them to the many destructive influences operating under the banners of modernization, development, or progress" (Goulet 2006, 135). Given the historical experiences of the people of the global South, it should be acknowledged that "[e]very human society has its own rationality system. And, contrary to the general assumption, rationality is not synonymous with modern technology or scientific method. Many attitudes and actions which some might consider to be irrational, superstitious or uncritical are, when properly understood in their true context, fully rational" (Goulet 2006, 136). It is for that reason that the people of the global South need to establish not only new South–South relationships in order to advance the quality of their own lives and regional projects but also a new relationship with the dominant Northern Hemisphere. This is especially true given the negative effects of the military intervention of the US empire into their nations in violation of international law and the negative effects of US-dominated economic institutions such as the World Bank, the IMF, and the WTO (Bush 2007; Chossudovsky 2003; Khalidi 2009; Paupp 2007, 2009).

This is the situation that has led to the current global crisis. In order to move *beyond global crisis*, it is critical to realize the dynamic economic component that has been driving millions of people into both poverty and war. Kolko has described the problem and its eventual solution quite accurately when she asks this:

> *[H]ow much "creative destruction" can the world endure before it generates political struggle, which in the past too often led to war?* Technology has escalated the dangers inherent in capitalist crisis, because its new changes have the potential to create consequences far more serious for humanity than any in previous epochs or crises . . . . Objectively, the world system is integrated and reform is not possible in a national context . . . *who is to pay for the restructuring of the world economy, in the Lesser Developed Countries, in the OCED states, and in the Centrally Planned Economies?* It is a rhetorical question. *The answer is those who always pay and always will until the structure of power relations is changed and until the systemic features of capitalism are eliminated.* (Kolko 1988, 348; italics added)

In response to these realities, Mazrui has persuasively argued that

> Third World transnationalism requires not only a new relationship among Third World countries but also a new relationship between the Third World and the dominant northern hemisphere. *What should the nations of Asia, Africa, and Latin America do in the face of the continuing hegemony of the northern hemisphere? How is the economic and political dependency to be broken? An important school of thought in the Third World has opted for the strategy of disengagement.* Under this strategy the Third World countries should seek to explore the maximum possibilities of self-reliance. (Mazrui 1976, 319; italics added)

For all these reasons, Mazrui concludes, "The doctrine of *disengagement,* as defined and elaborated upon in the Third World, has placed special emphasis on the need for at least partial disengagement from the international capitalist system. The reasoning is to the effect that the international system of trade and investment is for the time being so structured that full integration of a Third World country within it cannot but lead to exploitation" (Mazrui 1976, 319; italics in the original).

Similarly, professor of International Relations and African Studies, Olayi-wola Abegunrin, has noted, "Africans have been studying Western culture and practicing the Western system for decades in the hope of stimulating its development. However, what are the results—dependency, poverty, miseries, mismanagement, and corruption? We need a new approach and look to the Eastern World, and not just the Asian Tigers but China and India as well. It is time that Africa diversified the cultural models it has adopted for development lessons" (Abegunrin 2009, 200). This dynamic is already at work as China's rise in world affairs begins to surpass the "crumbling walls" of US hegemony (Paupp 2009). China's history is now in the process of coming full circle insofar as "[h]aving inherited from its revolutionary heritage a genuine conviction that the future of the world still lies with the less-developed countries, China's renewed economic commitment to that proposition . . . seems to have shaped a new global dynamic. Like the United States after World War II, China in the wake of the 2008–09 global financial crisis has been stepping up with its 'deep pockets' to claim a unique status not as traditional 'great power' but as benefactor and leader of the developing world" (Dittmer 2010, 227). This is not merely a commentary on the perspectives and policies of the Chinese in the twenty-first century; it is also in harmony with the evolving perspectives and policies of the people of Africa. In this regard, it has been asserted that ". . . African leaders should take serious leading roles in strengthening their cooperation with the rest of the developing nations, in order to enhance the bargaining power of the African states as well as expand political, economic, and cultural relations as well as trade and investment among themselves and the developing world, particularly the South-South regions . . . . The twenty-first century should not mimic the twentieth century" (Abegunrin 2009, 202).

In order that the twenty-first century not mimic the twentieth century, Latin American author and professor of international relations Gustavo Lagos proposed eleven principles capable of advancing values that reflect what he calls "the essential dimensions of the revolution of being." The fidelity of these principles to those already enunciated (above) by Ikeda is remarkable. For they share a common commitment to the liberation of individuals and communities from the old models of both capitalism and socialism. Even though it might seem anachronistic to mention socialism as a global model almost two decades after the demise of the Soviet Union, the point here is the emphasis on the humanistic values which should underlie all systems—capitalism, socialism, or any other model. Lagos's principles (values) share one common denominator—they are genuine consensus values that can be shared by all people, regardless of culture, ideology, or political persuasion, who genuinely seek to participate in the achievement of a peaceful global civilization. Table 2.1 lists these eleven principles.

Table 2.1   Values of the "Revolution of Being" and Characteristics That Give Expression to the Values

1. Multidimensional man (versus the one-dimensional man of capitalist and socialist societies, the former being alienated mainly from the base, the latter mainly from the superstructure)

2. Community spirit guided by an ethic of solidarity (versus the rampant individualism of capitalist societies and the grim collectivism of socialist societies)

3. Work for the benefit of man (versus work for the benefit of the corporation or the state)

4. Tendency toward rationality in consumption oriented to being more rather than having more (versus the tendencies toward unlimited production of goods in socialist societies and toward unlimited consumption in capitalist societies)

5. Liberating pedagogy oriented to the construction of the world: teaching–learning society (versus pedagogy oriented to the installation of the socialist system and pedagogy designed to preserve the status quo or establishment of the capitalist societies)

6. Dialogic society: dialogue between generations, social groups, ideologies, civilizations (versus the nondialogic societies of the socialist countries and the limited dialogue of capitalist societies)

7. Tendencies toward equalitarian income distribution (versus tendencies toward equal distribution limited by the emergence of a new class in socialist societies and wide disparities in income distribution in capitalist societies)

8. Participation of all sectors of society (versus marginality of sectors not belonging to the new class in socialist societies and existence of numerous marginal sectors in capitalist societies)

9. Rationality oriented toward the integral development of man and subordination of economic growth to this goal (versus rationality oriented toward the attainment of economic growth that dominates both capitalist and socialist societies)

10. Rationality oriented toward integration with other national societies with a view to maximizing peace, economic welfare, and social justice at the world level (versus rationality enclosed within the framework of the national society in the capitalist countries and rationality oriented toward the ideological, political, and economic conquest of other national societies in socialist countries)

11. Limitation of sovereignty by practical implementation of cooperation and solidarity at the world level (versus unlimited conception of sovereignty, except for satellite countries, prevailing in both capitalist and socialist societies)

Source: Gustavo Lagos, "*The Revolution of Being*," in *On the Creation of a Just World Order: Preferred Worlds for the 1990s,* edited by Saul H. Mendlovitz. New York: The Free Press, 1975, pp. 81–82.

We can concur with Mazrui that the *doctrine of disengagement* from such a system is reasonable insofar as the dominant power in the current international system has systematically used military force and violence, in violation of international law, simply to further its own geopolitical advantage and to maintain its hegemony over the world's economic system (George 2000, 27–35; Johansen 1980; Marichal 2008, 90–113; Paupp 2009). In the course of that effort the US empire has subjected the people of the globe to an inhumane value structure that places economic profit above people, allows multinational firms, corporations, and banks to exploit millions of people, and has denied the realization of basic human rights to millions of others in violation of its own rhetoric about human rights and democracy (Blum 2000, 2004; Boggs 2000; Chomsky 1991, 2006; Kolko 1988; Mittelman 2000; Prashad 2007a; Scott 2007). Given this gap between rhetoric and reality, it is possible for us to outline the true nature of the global crisis that we now confront. Given the directions, policies, and practices embraced by the US empire, its allies, and affiliates, we now turn to a discussion of the sources of the current global crisis.

Sources of the Current Global Crisis

The current global crisis is multifaceted, but a large part of the explanation for it is found in the operational logic and self-authenticating law of the US empire itself. In its efforts to maintain global hegemony within an ever-precarious global hierarchy of power we now can discover the existence of a new reality in the conduct of international relations: the US empire has produced its own version of law to govern its practices and that law is at odds with and in violation of established principles of international law. It is the law of the empire—"empire's law." Prof. Amy Bartholomew notes the following:

> Empire's law . . . is more than the sum of individual legal assertions which have come to gain prominence. It is instead an assertion of a constitutional superiority backed by the power of violence. Empire's law overrides all other legal orders, in fact. This new constellation asserts the following: (1) Within the empire, all laws are not equal; (2) There is no international law deriving from the UN Charter that can be interpreted as applying to prevent the US (as empire's politico-military center) from undertaking unilateral action to maintain or establish the global political conditions necessary for the proper functioning of empire's activities; (3) All international laws supporting empire's fundamental interest in the unrestrained movement of capital across territorial boundaries shall be inviolable, and shall be enforced through international enforcement agencies; (4) All laws at the national or sub-national levels that aim to preserve and protect the political, economic and cultural needs of empire shall be inviolable, and must be respected through effective enforcement of

the relevant authorities; (5) All laws that seek to preserve national or sub-national self-determination in matters pertaining to the conduct of empire's activities are repugnant to the idea of empire's law and shall thereby be non-enforceable by reason of unlawfulness, and shall instead be subject to harmonization to facilitate the smooth progress of empire's activities. (Bartholomew 2006, 314)

Taken together, these five characteristics of the empire's law serve as both a summation and critique of the foreign policy and legal position of the United States since 2001. In establishing the *"self-authenticating law of the US Empire"* we discover that the imperial reign of President George W. Bush unleashed an endorsement of the doctrine of "preemptive war," embraced the practice of torture and secret detention in violation of the Geneva Conventions, and guided the belief of the Bush administration's legal team that they needed to evade international law. Prof. Mary E. O'Connell noted, "They did not simply ignore international law; they attempted to circumvent it" (O'Connell 2008, 1).

The legal advice that the Bush administration received from its ideologically sanctioned lawyers, such as John Yoo, constituted an unprecedented reinterpretation of the US Constitution that eviscerated its clear meanings and statements about the US war power (Yoo 2005, 2006, 2009). Throughout the tortured paths of neoconservative legal reasoning, Yoo set forth the legal theory of the *"unitary executive."* In a clear renunciation of historical experience and legal precedent, the theory of the unitary executive sought to justify all presidential war-making power as being already subsumed up under the president's title as *"Commander in Chief"* (Savage 2007, 64, 124–25, 234, 240, 256, 271, 273, 282, 305; Schwarz and Huq 2007, 156–60, 161, 178; Wolin 2008, 105). In reality, as set forth by Yoo, the entire smokescreen of tortured legal arguments and omissions was primarily designed to facilitate the smooth progress of the empire's activities (Ball 2007; Crenson and Ginsberg 2007; Fisher 2008; Irons 2005).

In this endeavor, Yoo's attack on the both US Constitutional law regarding war and the prohibitions of international law was supplemented by the efforts of other American academics, including Jack Goldsmith and his former colleague at the University of Chicago, Eric Posner. Goldsmith and Posner produced a book entitled *The Limits of International Law*. In the book they unequivocally claim, "The morality or immorality of international law is exhausted by its content; international legality does not impose any moral obligations" (Goldsmith and Posner 2005, 197). Relying on the methodology of *"rational choice theory,"* Goldsmith and Posner claimed that "international law serves more as a set of guidelines than a set of legal obligations. It can help states coordinate their pursuit of self-interest but has no independent pull to compliance; it does not constrain the pursuit of self-interest" (O'Connell 2008, 2).

Based on this interpretation of Goldsmith and Posner's thesis, O'Connell argues, "The Goldsmith–Posner book provides any interested legal advisor with an apparent basis upon which to question the binding power of international law" (O'Connell 2008, 3). Her observation serves to identity the dangers and weaknesses endemic to the Goldsmith–Posner thesis insofar as its methodology of "rational choice" is actually connected up to the imperial purposes of the US empire itself. This is necessarily the case because the concepts of "superpower," "empire," and "globalization" all have one thing in common:

> . . . all presupposed and depend upon inequalities of power while maintaining the illusion that somehow those inequalities are not retrojected into the homeland . . . . In fact, empire and Superpower undermine and implicitly oppose two presumable fundamental principles of American political ideology: that the Constitution provides the standard for a government of limited powers, and that American governance and politics are democratic. Despite the incongruity and inherent tensions between unlimited global hegemony and constitutionally limited domestic power, between arbitrarily projected power abroad (unilateralism, preemptive war) and democratic power responsible to the citizenry at home, *the implications of Superpower, imperial power, and globalizing capital for democracy and constitutionalism have not been publicly confronted* . . . . On the contrary, the defenders and practitioners of these extraordinary forms of power process to be employing Superpower to force the values of American democracy and the institutions of the free market upon the world. (Wolin 2008, 237; italics added)

By failing to confront the implications arising out of the imperial impulse to impose the agenda of the US empire on the rest of the world, both the efficacy of international law and that of the US Constitution itself are left in a vulnerable state of affairs. This conclusion has even greater salience when we turn our attention to Erich Posner's follow-up book entitled *The Perils of Global Legalism* (Posner 2009).

In the spirit of the first book, Posner's new book makes a spirited attack on "excessive faith in the efficacy of international law." In making his case, Posner focuses on the thinking of American and European legal intellectuals who see international law as normatively good for the world regardless of whether it serves specific state interests. Posner states, "The rule of law at the international level . . . is in tension with the state system. In the absence of a world government, powerful states have little reason to comply with the rules they agree to, except when doing so remains in their interest. Rather than being universal, applying to all equally, as domestic law does, international law consists of the rules that emerge from discrete bargains between different states and is vulnerable to shifts in the balance of power" (Posner 2009, 80).

Given the inherent logic of this interpretation, Posner sees global legalism as utopian because it is built on unsustainable premises about human nature and the practicality of transferring domestic legal traditions to the international level.

But in a world of shared values and common problems, it should not be surprising that many states want to build global systems of laws and institutions that go far beyond Posner's minimalist vision. For example, we can explore how international constitutionalism at the United Nations, European Union, the WTO, and other sites of global governance affects the practice of an institutionalized system of cooperation (Dunoff and Trachtman 2009). Already, the dynamics of tolerance and coexistence have helped to generate an institutionalized system of cooperation that is embodied and memorialized in international treaties. Contrary to Posner's minimalist views and his interpretations about the sustainability of premises about human nature, an examination of international institutions, treaties, and the membership of nations in this treaty structure, we discover that there is stronger evidence for the proposition that humanity has already developed a near-universal organization of global human society through treaties. Prof. Thomas M. Franck notes, "International institutions, with a few minor exceptions, are firmly grounded in treaties that establish their objectives, conditions of membership, and international and external operational parameters. These treaties are binding on their party members and, perhaps—in the instance of near-universal organization—also on nonmembers" (Franck 2009, xi).

Even in the current situation of global relations—which is characterized by a hierarchical order—there are incentives for dominant states to still seek approval for the kind of rule structure that they wish to impose on the world. Prof. David Lake notes, "Dominant states benefit from setting the rules of political order in ways that reflect their interests or advantage themselves in particular ways, subject to the constraint that these rules must be accepted by a sufficient number of subordinates to gain legitimacy. Their ability to enforce these rules, in turn, is enhanced by the legitimacy and support they are accorded. Rather than continuously coercing others into abiding by their will, it is far cheaper and more efficient for dominant states if subordinates comply with rules regarded as rightful and appropriate" (Lake 2009, 9). In other words, even the imperial project of the US empire is limited in projecting its hegemony insofar as there is no sustainable or supportive global consensus for its project. In the absence of a general global consensus, the US empire cannot impose its imperial will on the world without the good opinion and support of those to whom it seeks to dictate its rules, policies, and priorities. That is because an objective examination of how power must be practiced in the world to be effective reveals that "[m]uch as some might wish otherwise, legitimacy originates in the opinion of subordinates. Authority is conferred upon the ruler by the ruled. Rulers—dominant states included—are not free to define for themselves what actions are or are not legitimate. Regardless of its extraordinary coercive capabilities, which seduced many into thinking the country could and should shape its destiny and the world's single-handedly, the United States must again learn to listen and then to act within the bounds of what is acceptable to its subordinates" (Lake 2009, 189).

Seizing Opportunities for Building a Peaceful Global Civilization

And so it is that we are confronted with two polar opposites in adjudicating upon global relations: the actual power and force of international law, and the possibilities for building a more peaceful and humane global civilization. On the one hand, we have been presented with a picture a global civilization whose predominant characteristics are defined by war, clash, and self-interest. On the other hand, we have a picture of global civilization that is characterized by mutual respect, cooperation, and plurality. Which of these two possibilities will become our global future?

In response to these contending views, Prof. Peter Katzenstein suggests the following:

> Civilizations exist in the plural. They coexist with each other within one civilization of modernity, or what we often call today a global world. Civilizations are pluralist. Their internal pluralism results from multiple traditions and vigorous debates and disagreements. This is not to deny that, in specific political units existing within civilizations—states, polities, or empires—pluralism can give way to unity as political and discursive coalitions succeed in imposing a singular view and set of core values over alternatives. Since civilizations are relatively loose systems and encompassing across both space and time, however, such unity tends to be the exception, not the rule. The existence of plural and pluralist civilizations is reflected in transcivilizational engagements, intercivilizational encounters, and civilizational clashes" (Katzenstein 2010, 1).

Yet for all of these aforementioned differences and the ways in which we can categorize those differences, the fact remains that "[c]ivilizations are most similar not in their cultural coherence and isolation or tendency toward clash but in their pluralist differences, in their plurality, and in their encounters and engagements" (Katzenstein 2010, 38).

Katzenstein's description of the world's civilizations is probably one that best fits with Ikeda's proposition that "win/win solutions" are what is most needed in our quest to build a peaceful global civilization. That is because, given the pluralist differences of the civilizations, Ikeda would argue that win/win solutions will most readily emerge from engaging in humanitarian competition—where groups compete with each other to show the greatest proof of humane behavior. This goal is precisely what has led Ikeda to find what he calls a *"third path."* In the aftermath of the post–Cold War failure to bring about a peaceful world system, Ikeda stated, "What we should pursue, therefore, is not a world order based on the universalization of certain specific values (as in Francis Fukuyama's *The End of History and the Last Man*) or one which sees cultures in ceaseless conflict (as in Samuel Huntington's *The Clash of Civilizations and the Remaking of the World Order*). Rather, we must seek the 'third path,' a global civilization whose core values are tolerance and coexistence" (Ikeda 2001a, 124).

Throughout this book, I will argue that this conception of the core values of tolerance and coexistence represents a central component of Ikeda's path to building a peaceful and humane global civilization, for, at its core, Ikeda's concept and application of the third path avoid the tendencies toward war and conflict that emerge from the *"clash thesis"* while, at the same time, the third path also avoids the tendencies toward inaction and a self-satisfied paralysis present in *"the end of history"* thesis. In this critical respect, the approach of the third path allows for the full integration of Ikeda's major principles to be put into action simultaneously—inner transformation creates the necessary conditions to realize a new consciousness for humane forms of discourse. In turn, new forms of humane discourse allow for the kinds of interactions between individuals, nations, and civilizations to embark on a third path toward building a peaceful global civilization that respects differences because it also acknowledges the plurality and diversity of the world's peoples and their civilizations. As such, the core values of Ikeda's third path are—of necessity—tolerance and coexistence.

As surprising as it may appear at first glance, we will argue that humanity has already embarked upon the third path. In the aftermath of the 1962 Cuban missile crisis, President John F. Kennedy embarked upon a strategy of peace with the leaders of the Soviet Union that centralizes the importance of Ikeda's emphasis upon tolerance and coexistence. All one has to do is to read President Kennedy's groundbreaking June 1963 speech announcing his intention to embark with Great Britain and Russia toward the ratification of a nuclear test ban treaty, delivered during commencement ceremonies at American University. The concept of détente or "peaceful coexistence" was at the heart of his argument as to why the ratification of his proposed nuclear test ban treaty was vital to the achievement of world peace. In this regard, an entirely new foreign policy was beginning to evolve for the United States and the rest of the world. Kennedy had begun to embark on his own third path—attempting to lead the world out of the destructive, dangerous, and internecine struggles of the Cold War. What effectively brought to an end the continued progression of this vision was his assassination on November 22, 1963.

In the years after his death in Dallas historians would record a pattern of continuing investments in the weapons of war, including nuclear stockpiles.

Yet the limitations associated with these forms of terror, weapons systems, and nuclear threat have started to become clear to even the managers of the US empire and its ruling primacy coalition (Paupp 2009). That is because, in the final analysis, self-interest must eventually be tempered by the general interest. In this critical regard, Prof. David Lake notes the following:

> Dominant states seek legitimacy and do not attempt to reap all the fruits of their coercive abilities. Under anarchy, the powerful are expected to exploit the weak. As Thucydides observed, international politics is not conditioned on rights or justice, but "the strong do what they have the power to do and the weak accept what they have to accept." In actuality, however, dominant states forsake self-aggrandizing policies and seek to build up others in order to expand or preserve their own legitimacy. To acquire authority, it is essential that self-interest be tempered by actions in the general interest. And to credibly commit not to abuse the authority they have been granted, dominant states will tie their own hands or, in John Ikenberry's phrase, "self-limit" their power. (Lake 2009, 177)

This self-limitation of US power in international affairs is precisely what President Kennedy sought to undertake in the aftermath of the 1962 Cuban missile crisis. James W. Douglass recounts this:

> JFK's decision to withdraw from Vietnam was part of the larger strategy of peace that he and Nikita Khrushchev had become mutually committed to . . . . Thomas Merton had seen it all coming. He had said prophetically in a Cold War letter that if President Kennedy broke through to a deeper, more universal humanity, he would before long be 'marked out for assassination.' Kennedy agreed . . . . After vetoing the introduction of US troops at the Bay of Pigs, he resisted the Joint Chiefs' even more intense pressures to bomb and invade Cuba in the October 1962 Cuban missile crisis . . . . As Merton had hoped, Kennedy was breaking through to a deeper humanity—and to its fatal consequences. (Douglass 2008, 94)

So while Kennedy sought to place a self-limitation on the exercise of US power in the world, the military–industrial complex would not allow him to continue on his strategy of peace. His assassination signified that "the powers that be" within the military–industrial complex would allow no deviation from their adherence to the doctrines of militarism, financial profit for the few, and the hegemonic enslavement of the world's people under the umbrella of nuclear threat and direct military intervention.

Neither were his successors allowed to place US foreign policy on a self-limiting course with respect to planning and preparation for wars of intervention and aggression. Therefore, the fact that this self-limitation was not allowed to continue in the aftermath of his assassination seems to substantiate the claim that dominant elite sectors of the US empire disagreed with Kennedy's embrace of the core values of self-restraint, tolerance, and coexistence. In its place, the US primacy coalition constructed what has been termed *empire's law* (Bartholomew 2006). Its purpose has been to subordinate all other nations to the imperial dictates of what can only be described as a totalitarian credo. It is exemplified in a statement made by a high-level Bush II administration official who stated, "We're an empire now, we create our own reality. And while you're studying that reality—judiciously as you will—we'll act again, creating other new realities, which you can study, too, and that's how things will sort out. We're history's actors . . . and you, all of your, will be left to study what we do" (Wolin 2008, 3).

What this totalitarian credo embodies, at the deepest levels of human existence, is what Thomas Merton termed *the Unspeakable*. Writing in 1965, Merton asserted, "One of the awful facts of our age is the evidence that [the world] is stricken, stricken to the very core of its being by the presence of the Unspeakable" (Douglass 2008, xv). It is a quality that lurks in the words of the Bush-II administration (cited above) regarding the US empire and how it really functions. The definition of *the Unspeakable* is "an evil whose depth and deceit seemed to go beyond the capacity of words to describe. . . . When we become more deeply human . . . the wellspring of our compassion moves us to confront the Unspeakable. Merton was pointing to a kind of systemic evil that defies speech. For Merton, the Unspeakable was, at bottom, a void: 'It is the void that contradicts everything that is spoken even before the words are said; the void that gets into the language of public and official declarations at the very moment when they are pronounced, and makes them ring dead with the hollowness of the abyss.'" (Douglass 2008, xv)

In the decades since Kennedy's death, the people of the world have been forced to engage in various forms of resistance to imperial rule. Their resistance is, in part, born of Thomas Merton's warning in 1966 that "[t]hose who are at present so eager to be reconciled with the world at any price must take care not to be reconciled with it under this particular aspects: *as the nest of the Unspeakable*. This is what too few are willing to see" (Merton 1966, 5; italics in the original). Part of the current global resistance to the US empire has been aimed at opposing what has been called empire's law. In place of this law it has been argued that

> *[a] people's law perspective of resistance against empire's rule would begin with a series of demystifications necessary as a first act of repudiation:*
>
> (1) *Despite attempts to claim the opposite, there exists no inviolable right, on the part of the powerful, to govern, rule, order, the weak.*

(2) Regardless of the ideological claims being advanced, there exists no unified civilizational consensus on the naturalness of a corporate-dominated, militaristic imperialism as comprising the common values, truths, visions of human futures that prescribe a universal course for humanity's social evolution.

(3) Notwithstanding attempts to convince otherwise, there exists no pre-ordained rationale for, eternal truth of, inevitability regarding forms of socially constructed orders that form the institutions of governance, including the form of 'law.'" (Bartholomew 2006, 319; italics added)

It is important to note that "*a people's law perspective of resistance*" begins with the inner process of "*demystification*." This relates directly to Ikeda's concept of inner transformation because inner transformation leads individuals to a point wherein they can see the world and themselves clearly—with the influence of imposed illusions and socially sanctioned mystifications. To be in a "demystified" state is to have broken free of the illusions that others share, a tolerance of the injustices imposed by the dominant power structure, and begin to engage in a dialogue of liberation with other human beings who also seek freedom from the bondage of their oppressions, the scourge of war, and the mindlessness of power when it enforces unjust conditions upon innocent people.

A people's law of resistance to the claims and assertions of empire's law represents a global opposition to having the national interest of a global superpower imposed from above. Therefore, we can argue that a people's law of resistance, which emerges "*from the bottom up*," would embrace and embody a law of human rights that was truly reflective of the plurality of civilizations that make up our global civilization. In this critical sense, we can extrapolate from Bartholomew's reasoning about empire's law to the important role of human rights law and argue, according to Stephen Gardbaum, that "...there is no single international human rights system but regional and global ones that overlap and interact in complex ways; and (2) there is no single international legal source of human rights law, and many of the sources also overlap. So although the most common method of legalizing human rights has been international treaties, some human rights laws—including many rights also incorporated into treaties—have their source in custom and, arguably, *also in general principles*" (Gardbaum 2009, 239–40; italics added). Therefore, when human rights principles speak of the right to "*freedom of association*" they are principles that seek to protect the sanctity of dialogue between people—a key concept in Ikeda's philosophy of peace because of the inherent capacity within the dialogic process to advance understandings between people of different backgrounds, thereby contributing to the ultimate realization of a more peaceful global civilization.

From the perspective of Ikeda, what this *"bottom up"* human rights law and consciousness also represents is the phenomenon of what transpires when the values of tolerance and coexistence are at work. If we are to ever transcend and move away from *"the Unspeakable"* and the *"hollowness of the abyss,"* then it will be necessary to take up the cause of peace where legal treaties and conventions have left off. Ikeda's 2010 peace proposal is entitled "Toward a New Era of Value Creation." At its core, Ikeda seeks to underscore the vital importance of humanity moving toward a world without nuclear weapons. To that end, Ikeda proposes "expanding frameworks for the non-use of nuclear weapons" such as "the establishment of nuclear-weapon-free zones (NWFZ)" as an essential first step toward disarmament and the nonuse of nuclear weapons because, historically, NWFZs have "represented an effort to fill the gap in the legal framework left by the absence of any treaty or convention providing a blanket prohibition against the use of nuclear weapons" (Ikeda 2010-PP). The treaty on the nonproliferation of nuclear weapons (NPT) has not been acted upon to remove the nuclear weapons threat because "[a]lthough the preamble to the NPT, which entered into force forty years ago, calls on signatories to 'make every effort to avert the danger of such a war and to take measures to safeguard the security of peoples,' it is clear that the nuclear-weapon states have not fulfilled that obligation" (Ikeda 2010-PP). From this proposal he moves to his second proposal, which regards "establishing norms that make explicit the illegality of the use of nuclear weapons" (Ikeda 2010-PP). Taken together, these two proposals reflect the practical and normative dimensions of Ikeda's quest to confront the dynamics of *the Unspeakable* and to lay the foundations for a more humane global civilization.

Hence, in combination with *the people's law of resistance*, which relies on human rights claims, Ikeda's proposal seek to redirect the course of human history away from its technological ability and proclivity to engage in planetary suicide. In large measure, his efforts and proposals dedicated to making nuclear weapons illegal connect directly to his other core concerns regarding the implementation and practice of human rights, insofar as the destruction of life on this planet by nuclear war would constitute the ultimate denial of human rights. Therefore, Ikeda's emphasis on nuclear weapons abolition extends toward the challenge of creating *an era of human dignity* which would reflect the universal core consciousness of humanity in its aspiration to achieve a more fair, just, and equitable world by allowing for regional and global dynamics to create an atmosphere for mutual tolerance and the achievement of peaceful coexistence. Such a path is reflective of Ikeda's third path because it represents the creation of an historical opening for global peace and consensus, irrespective of the power claims of empire's law.

Empire's law has already set out to destroy the aspirations and historical project of the global South (Third World) to develop its own resources. Now, in the early twenty-first century, it is time for the global South to be free of exploitation by the nations of the northern hemisphere. Given the history of the twentieth century, the search for a nonexploitative twenty-first century is essential to our ability to give birth to a more humane global civilization. On this matter, Vijay Prashad has observed about the era of decolonization, during the decades of 1950s and 1960s:

> The central concept for the new nations was the Third World. For them, the Third World was not a place; it was a project . . . . Politically they wanted more planetary democracy. No more serfs of their colonial masters, they wanted to have a voice and power on the world stage . . . . Today the Third World project is no longer. It was not a failure, for that implies it was doomed from the start. No, it was assassinated. (Prashad 2007b, 7)

In September 2007 at a meeting of the Non-Aligned Movement in Havana, the call was again made to evoke the history of the Third World by calling for the construction of a global project directed to the requirements of our time. In much the same spirit, Ikeda's 2010 peace proposal discusses ". . . steps toward the resolution of the structural distortions of global society that threaten human dignity and have been brought to the fore by the current economic crisis" (Ikeda 2010-PP). Similarly, Prahsad has argued that "[t]he Third World awaits such a resurrection, not as nostalgia but as a project that matches our contemporary dilemmas" (Prashad 2007b, 8).

Conclusion

The structural distortions of which Ikeda speaks date back to the nineteenth century when the European nations embarked upon their colonial adventures into Asia, Africa, the Middle East, and Latin America. Historians later termed the era of these colonial endeavors the *age of imperialism* or the *age of empires* (Hobsbawm 1987). At the dawn of the early twentieth century, in the aftermath of World War I, the Paris Peace Conference of 1919 provided a forum in which the colonized nations of the Third World spoke out for the principles of self-determination. In so doing, they expressed the first global rebellion against European domination and embarked upon a path of what historian Erez Manela calls *anticolonial nationalism*. Manela notes the following:

> The Versailles peace is often seen as heralding the apex of imperial expansion, and indeed the empires of the victorious powers, especially the British, French, and Japanese, made significant territorial gains in the wake of the war. Empires, however, cannot survive on territorial control alone. It requires accommodation and legitimacy, at least among a portion of the populations in both the metropole and the periphery. The adoption of the language of self-determination

by colonial nationalists, as well as by anti-imperialists in the metropole, weakened these underlying supports of the imperial edifice. (Manela 2007, 11)

At the Paris Peace Conference of 1919, President Woodrow Wilson, in his Fourteen Points, had called for "a free, open-minded, and absolutely impartial adjustment of all colonial claims," giving equal weight to the opinions of the colonized peoples and the colonial powers. Among those nations paying attention to Wilson's words and actions were the nationalist leaders of four non-Western societies—Egypt, India, China, and Korea. That spring, Wilson's words would help ignite political upheavals in all four of these countries. In looking back at this period, Manela has invoked the image of *"the Wilsonian moment"* in order to depict the broader context of a series of global actions taken in reference to a new international consciousness that challenged the existing international order. Manela notes, "Framing the Wilsonian moment in the colonial world as an international and transnational event is not merely an analytical device or an expression of a particular historical method. Rather, it reflects the perceptions and actions of historical actors at the time, and much of what they saw and did at that time is rendered incomprehensible, even invisible outside of that framework. The moment was inherently international in that it played out in an arena defined by the interactions between sovereign nation-states and in which such states were the primary actors" (Manela 2007, 222).

The experience of the Wilsonian moment reverberated through the ensuing decades. It was felt and experienced in the aftermath of World War II as the nations of the Third World struggled to toss off the last vestiges of colonialism and used the newly formed United Nations to articulate their sovereign claims. From the late 1940s through the 1950s and on into the 1960s these Third World nations sought to find their own self-defined place under the sun. In so doing, a new dawn within the field of international relations came and with it the birth of the Non-Aligned Nations Movement (NAM) and calls from the global South for a new international economic order (NIEO). Newly emerging nations did not want to escape the prison of colonialism merely to be entrapped in the Cold War geopolitical struggles of the Soviet Union and the United States for *spheres of influence*. The nature of this struggle and its ramifications has had profound implications for every part of the global South, but especially in the Middle East, where the Western powers sought to dominate the region by whatever means necessary. There was and there still remains a sustained campaign to dominate the region irrespective of the human cost of the policies in place to preserve "Western interests" or formulated in the name of bringing civilization, democracy, or freedom to the region (Salt 2008). In response to these interventions, policies, and pressures, these newly independent Third World nations sought to embark upon a path of nonalignment—devoid of the pressures of alliance with either of the superpowers (Arnold 2006). Hence, in the midst of Cold War realities, the NAM sought to engage in both a global deliberative project that would create the socioeconomic and sociopolitical space for their own developmental paths and projects within a truly pluralistic international context—a context that would allow for South–South cooperation, the search for compromise, and the task of unraveling complex notions of justice through processes of substantive dialogues (Cox 1979; Singham 1977).

The NAM was founded six years after Bandung—in Belgrade, Yugoslavia, in 1961. It was at a summit that was under the chairmanship of Marshall Tito. In fact, Tito, Nehru, and Nasser are considered to be the founding fathers of the movement (Adebajo 2008, 111). A total of twenty-five Arab, Asian, and African countries attended the summit. A highlight of the summit was the condemnation of "imperialism" in the Middle East and support for the Arabs in Palestine. Most, but not all, NAM members are part of the group of seventy-seven developing countries set up in June 1964 in the context of the first UN Conference on Trade and Development. It is known under the abbreviation UNCTAD. Unfortunately for the cause of the NAM and Third World development, UNCTAD's progressive role as a force for global economic justice and human rights has been largely obliterated by the rise of the WTO. This was not accidental. According to Asbjorn Eide,

> That WTO differs significantly from UNCTAD appears already from its name: the 'W' stands for 'World,' as opposed to the 'UN' (United Nations) in UNCTAD. This was deliberate: the major industrial countries did not want the trade organization to be a part of the UN system. Secondly, while the 'TAD' in UNCTAD stands for 'Trade and Development,' the 'T' in WTO stands only for 'Trade,' excluding the 'D' for 'Development.' Neither in name nor in practice is the WTO a development organization. (Eide 2006, 233; Jackson 1983; Sauvant and Hasenpflug 1977)

The United States, acting through the IMF and World Bank, sought to serve for the interests of US and European multinational corporate firms more than to respect the needs and aspirations of the people of the global South. Such an outcome became more than apparent during the Reagan/Thatcher era of the 1980s. It was an era that led to the emergence of the Washington Consensus. Reflecting the neoliberal economic model and agenda, the concrete measures that the Washington Consensus proclaimed involved (1) the privatization of public enterprises, (2) the deregulation of the economy, (3) liberalization of trade and industry, (4) massive tax cuts for the rich, (5) the strict control of labor, (6) the reduction of public expenditures—particularly social spending, (7) the downsizing of government, (8) the expansion of international markets, and (9) the removal of controls on global financial flows. All these policies were in direct contradiction with the priorities of the NAM and the global South's desire to create a NIEO (Sauvant and Hasenpflug 1977).

According to Walden Bello, the logic behind the Washington Consensus results from the fact that "[m]omentarily, in the 1970s, left-wing and right-wing elites—in Mexico, Cuba, Indonesia, Brazil, Iraq—united under the ideology of the New International Economic Order (NIEO), which proposed a substantial redistribution of wealth and power from the North to the South" (Bello 2005, 8). As far as the global South is concerned, Bello notes, ". . . the founding of the WTO and the acceleration of corporate-driven globalization marked a retreat from efforts at independent national development dating back to the 1970s" (Bello 2005, 132). In practical terms what this means is that ". . . there is a conflict between the major economies of the North and the developing countries of the South, where most of the world's marginalized people, some three billion, are located. *More and more, this complex struggle defines the age we live in*" (Bello 2005, 8; italics added). In examining the true nature of this complex struggle, Charles S. Maier has asked a series of pointed questions: "Will we have the wisdom to prove to the rest of the world—friends, skeptical onlookers, even possible adversaries—that we are not just preoccupied with power for power's sake? Or might we decide that no state can exercise empire without an inevitable and unacceptable cost in terms of violence and its own institutional corruption? Are atrocities just the exception or an almost inevitable consequence of imperial behavior?" (Maier 2006, 14). These are just a few of the seminal questions that we must ask as we move in the direction of what Ikeda calls "a new era of value creation" (Ikeda 2010-PP).

Michael Hudson notes thus:

> It seems absurd to call the present system's high taxes and public guarantees to foreign bondholders "free enterprise." Under these conditions "market fundamentalism" becomes a euphemism for financial dominance over governments. It is merely another form of centralized planning, not the absence of planning. It is planning to impose dependency, not self-reliance. A more equitable and peaceful world order would reverse today's trend of turning planning power over to financial institutions. (Hudson 2005, xxx)

Therefore, when we look at Ikeda's call for the creation of an era of human dignity—an era that would enable humanity to move toward "the resolution of the structural distortions of global society that threaten human dignity and have been brought to the fore by the current economic crisis" (Ikeda 2010-PP, 13), we are looking very seriously at the kind of transformation that Michael Hudson has suggested as a precondition for a more equitable and peaceful world order.

Historian L. S. Stavrianos in his 1981 book, *Global Rift: The Third World Comes of Age*, sternly warned, "The world of the late twentieth century can ill afford superpower *realpolitik* that ends up as crackpot realism. The need is to recognize and to address the interdependent problems of overdevelopment as well as underdevelopment. And this requires a common vision relevant to the unprecedented peril and unprecedented promise now confronting all humanity" (Stavrianos 1981, 814; italics in the original). We are relearning the truth that self-interest must be tempered by the general interest. Coexistence and tolerance must be rediscovered in our own time as governing principles for the planet. In short, embarking upon Ikeda's third path represents the end of illusions and a radically demystified understanding of power.

Part II

From Individual to Global Transformation: Multiple Pathways

3

Case Study—The Inner Transformation of JFK and the End of the Cold War

"As weapons have grown more destructive and national states more confident of their sovereign rights, large-scale, indiscriminate slaughter has become a commonplace of war. A backward look at the development of modern warfare makes apparent the extent to which human beings have become subservient to the weapons they have created. To alter this situation, each individual must strive to attain wisdom and enlightenment. We must do all we can to hasten the arrival of the day when the enlightened commonality of the human race assumes the lead in the work of preserving peace."

—Daisaku Ikeda
(Ikeda 2009a, 90)

"President Kennedy humanized politics; transcending the power ethic, he believed in the power of conscience. He told us that pessimistically considering peace impossible and unreal is defeatist, that man can be as big as he wants, and that no problem of human destiny is beyond human beings' capacity to solve it. Like a fresh breath of hope in leaderless times, his words encourage us in our struggle for peace."

—Daisaku Ikeda
(Ikeda 2008-PP, 74)

"Norman Cousins is another figure who made an enormous contribution to furthering East–West relations during the Cold War. In my published dialogues with him, Mr. Cousins described his role in serving as US President John F. Kennedy's personal envoy to Moscow to meet with Premier Nikita Khrushchev. Mr. Cousins had an underlying faith in the possibilities of the human heart, and most important of his convictions was the view that a true understanding of others comes about through mutual cooperation."

—Daisaku Ikeda
(Ikeda 2007-PP, 7–8)

70

"The future fate of our planet depends in large measure on the extent to which we can strengthen and expand human abilities to engage in dialogue. If, as the Spanish philosopher Ortega y Gasset said, violence is the Magna Carta of barbarism, dialogue can be called the Magna Carta of civilization."

—Daisaku Ikeda
(Ikeda 2009-PP, 117)

The challenge of nuclear weapons in the twentieth and twenty-first centuries confronts us, in the most dramatic terms, with the power ethic. The invention, production, and maintenance of these weapons have provided us with a history of tragedy, confrontation, and coming to the brink of planetary annihilation. From the dropping of the atomic bomb on the Japanese cities of Hiroshima and Nagasaki in 1945 to the Cuban missile crisis of 1962, the first decade and a half of the bomb's existence served to demonstrate the dangerous finality it threatened for all life on planet earth. In recognition of these realities both US President John F. Kennedy and the Soviet Premier Nikita Khrushchev would begin to make an unprecedented turn in the conduct of their nation's foreign policy with respect to the deployment and use of nuclear weapons. In so doing, the years between 1962 and 1963 would become years of transformation and renewal for both leaders. By the close of 1963, the United States, the Soviet Union, and Great Britain would sign and ratify the first nuclear test ban treaty. Its signing marked a turn toward peace in the Cold War and represented the twentieth century's first major effort to step back from the brink of nuclear catastrophe (Oliver 1998; Seaborg 1981).

By avoiding the holocaust of nuclear war during the 1962 Cuban missile crisis, Kennedy and Khrushchev were able to embark on a path toward peace. By the end of 1963, this new path culminated in the signing and ratification of the Nuclear Test Ban Treaty. In retracing the history of this era, we are able to reencounter the possibilities that they envisioned for their respective countries to live in a relationship of peaceful coexistence. Upon reflection, their efforts have provided us with a historical paradigm with ongoing relevance for the challenges we face in our own day and generation with regard to the control and eventual abolition of nuclear weapons. In this respect, our review of the record from 1962 to 1963 presents us with a story of transformational change at many levels—psychological, ethical, political, decision-making, and policy. In short, the changes brought about by the Kennedy/Khrushchev interactions, dialogues, and foreign policy decisions serve to reveal to us the historical promise that such changes held for the rest of humanity that has continued to live under a nuclear sword of Damocles.

This chapter offers a case study of this short-lived era as evidence that Ikeda's own views on the possibilities for the control and abolition of nuclear weapons are not only necessary but fundamental for the achievement of a peaceful global civilization. Hence, to that end, this chapter will focus primarily on how issues of war and peace—*especially with regard to the nuclear weapons issue*—were dealt with during the thousand days of John F. Kennedy's presidency.[1] For many reasons, this period stands out as a unique case study and presents us with an unprecedented lesson with regard to the power of transformational consciousness, new ways to approach a viable strategy for peace, and how the role of enlightened leaders in a time of crisis can help to change history's path and ultimate direction.

In particular, this chapter will seek to explicate the events surrounding those thirteen days in October 1962 when the world was forced to the brink of the nuclear precipice as the United States and the Soviet Union deliberated over what was to be done with respect to the introduction of Russian missiles into Cuba. Yet the full complexity of this story embraces what came before as well as what came after. The first months of 1961 frame the beginning of the story with the US invasion of Cuba at the Bay of Pigs and nuclear tensions over the fate of West Berlin. It would be in response to the US invasion of Cuba in early 1961 that the groundwork was laid for the introduction of Russian missiles into Cuba in 1962 insofar as both Russia and Cuba feared that the United States might once again try to invade Cuba and overthrow the Castro regime. However, the way in which the crisis was handled led not only to the avoidance of war—a victory for both the United States and the USSR—but to a victory for all humankind. It was a victory for all concerned because it represented a psychological and strategic turn in the conduct of the Cold War from a policy of confrontation to one of cooperation leading to détente. Hence, from the resolution of the crisis to the signing of the 1963 Test Ban Treaty, we shall trace the changes in both policies and perspectives contemplated by President John F. Kennedy and Soviet Premier Nikita Khrushchev. Their decisions, deliberations, and policy changes with regard to nuclear weapons, as well as their approach to each nation's geopolitical relations, will be examined with respect to a number of interrelated aspects.

First, the inner transformation of consciousness that Kennedy and Khrushchev experienced, which led to higher levels of serious dialogue about the control and use of nuclear weapons, will be examined. For both men, the processes associated with their respective inner transformation began much earlier than the Cuban missile crisis itself, yet their continuing inner growth led them toward a point of inner preparation that was essential for their decision-making processes during those harrowing thirteen days in October 1962. The general lesson from that experience is that all of us have the capacity to undergo significant transformations in our own lives and the lives of those we affect. Therefore, as we become active "global citizens" in the quest for peace, we can also be transformative agents upon those in positions of social, political, and economic power to rethink and to rework their paradigms about global relations, about the future of humanity, and about the need to move toward the eventual abolition of nuclear weapons.

In keeping with Ikeda's emphasis upon the primacy of *inner transformation as foundational to world peace*, our examination of the thought processes and responses of Kennedy and Khrushchev—as individuals—serves as a necessary template for appreciating the dynamic of inner transformation as a necessary precondition to bringing about changes in the realization of new policies through heart-to-heart dialogue, the power of a transcendent and universal vision for world peace, and the achievement of a transformed world through mutual cooperation.

Second, the nature of US–Soviet *dialogue and negotiations* that finally culminated in the signing of the 1963 Test Ban Treaty will be offered as evidence of a fundamental change in US–Soviet relations and world history. When viewed in this light, we will finally discover that through a process of dialogue between Kennedy and Khrushchev both the US and Soviet approach to containing and constraining the use and proliferation of nuclear weapons would be transformed. Through their dialogic approach to crises and their resolution we will discover that the process of working toward achieving peaceful outcomes that could have turned into war would be transformed by eliminating, at least in part, the role of ideology as the predominant guide to policymaking. Further, the elimination of ideologies allows people to clear their minds of false assumptions and dogmatic certainties about the world that we inhabit and our capacity to change and alter its practices, institutions, and guiding values. In this task, the nature of our communications will be altered as our categories of thought are seen as fluid, alterable, and subject to inspection and criticism. As such, Ikeda's emphasis upon dialogue as a necessary component of peaceful change will be confirmed as essential for undertaking peaceful changes in global relations. The power of dialogue, in this context, will also show how the ethic of power can be transformed and rechanneled into more peaceful expressions. This is especially the case when we come to the realization that engagement in dialogue—which emanates from the inner transformation of individuals—can ultimately become the transformative avenue over which gulfs of misunderstanding can be bridged. Commenting on this phenomenon in his memoirs, Khrushchev himself said of the "Caribbean crisis" that

> [i]t was a very interesting and highly instructive series of events. It seemed as though the two most powerful countries in the world were about to butt heads. It seemed as though a military denoue-ment was unavoidable. We actually had our strategic missiles ready to be launched, while the United States had surrounded the island of Cuba with naval vessels and had concentrated its infantry and air force. But we showed that *if we were guided by rational aims and the desire not to allow a war to happen, the disputed questions could be resolved by compromise and it was possible to find such a compromise. Reason prevailed.* (Khrushchev 2007, 356; italics added)

Third, beginning with Kennedy's *peace speech* at American University (June 1963) and culminating with the late 1963 ratification and signing of the Test Ban Treaty, we shall discover that a jointly conceived strategy of peace was successfully embarked upon the leaders of the United States and the Soviet Union at the height of the Cold War. In this regard, we shall discover that a new concept of what it means to be a "global citizen" was starting to emerge. It was developing in a way that comports with Ikeda's linkage of the phenomenon of inner transformation, the power of dialogue and mutual cooperation, and the vision of a global society of self-conscious global citizens seeking to build a peaceful global civilization. On this matter, one merely has to consult the memoirs of Nikita Khrushchev to see this linkage emerge through his personal reflections on the period of the 1960s. In his memoirs, Khrushchev remained committed to the ideas of Marxism–Leninism, but he also actively acknowledged the centrality of the principle of *peaceful coexistence* because it was a practice that allowed for *"reciprocal contacts and exchanges of opinion."* In this regard, Khrushchev conceded thus:

> This is useful for socialist countries. Much can be obtained from the capitalists. We still do many things worse than they do. They have more experience and knowledge. Even after several decades, after we have built up a huge army of educated people, we still have to take a good look at what is going on in the capitalist world, so as to transfer everything useful into our socialist context. (Khrushchev 2007, 255)

Similarly, Kennedy noted the following in his June 10, 1963, speech at American University:

> Some say that it is useless to speak of world peace or world law or world disarmament—and that it will be useless until the leaders of the Soviet Union adopt a more enlightened attitude. I hope they do. I believe we can help them do it. But I also believe that we must reexamine our own attitudes—as individuals and as a Nation—for our attitude is as essential as theirs. And every graduate of this school, *every thoughtful citizen who despairs of war and wishes to bring peace, should begin by looking inward—by examining his own attitude toward the possibilities of peace, toward the Soviet Union, toward the course of the Cold War and toward freedom and peace here at home.* (Kennedy 1963; italics added)

In meeting this challenge, Kennedy closed his address by asking his audience to balance the national interest along with safeguarding the larger human interest. With this admonition, Kennedy effectively transcended the narrow nationalism that characterized the thought processes of not only his own national security bureaucracy but also the right-wing extremists, and all those who remained intellectually captured in the prison of conventional Cold War logic. Kennedy stated the following:

> *While we proceed to safeguard our national interests, let us also safeguard human interests. And the elimination of war and arms is clearly in the interest of both.* No treaty, however much it may be to the advantage of all, however tightly it may be worded, can provide absolute security against the risks of deception and evasion. But it can—if it is sufficiently effective in its enforcement, and if it is sufficiently in the interests of its signers—offer far more security and fewer risks than an unabated, uncontrolled, and unpredictable arms race. (Kennedy 1964; italics added)

What Kennedy offered in his American University speech was nothing less than what international relations scholars have termed *rapprochement*. According to the definition of the term offered by Prof. Charles Kupchan, we find this:

> *Rapprochement entails a standing down, a move away from armed rivalry to a relationship characterized by mutual expectations of peaceful coexistence.* The parties in question no longer perceive each other as posing a geopolitical threat and come to see one another as benign polities. They do not, however, seek to generate an articulated set of rules and norms to guide their behavior, nor do they come to embrace a shared or common identity. In this sense, the parties succeed in eliminating geopolitical rivalry and entering a nascent type of international society, but they then live comfortably alongside each other rather than seeking to expand and deepen the social character of their relations. The states in question define their interests individually, but these interests are deemed to be congruent. They maintain separate identities but those identities are compatible rather than oppositional. (Kupchan 2010, 30; italics added)

In the aftermath of the 1962 Cuban missile crisis, reflecting upon the nature of the separate identities embodied in the socialist system versus the capitalist system, Khrushchev's own memoirs addresses this anomaly by noting thus:

> We solved the crisis by peaceful means when it could have broken out into a war. I think that in the end it was we who won, but the Americans won because there was no war. Similar crises may develop in the future, because two opposing social systems exist in the world, the socialist system and the capitalist system based on private ownership, private capital. These systems are antagonistic, and that must be kept in mind. (Khrushchev 2007, 352)

In light of these aforementioned events, this chapter shall demonstrate that a historical shift took place between 1961 and 1963 which signaled the beginning of a new era for all humankind and the start of a dramatic alteration of geopolitical calculations that gave impetus to a possible end to the Cold War itself. Were it not for the assassination of President Kennedy in November 1963, the evidence we shall present offers a compelling case that the Cold War could have been brought to an end much sooner than the year of 1989.

Providing the Context—Cold War Doctrines versus Kennedy's *"Strategy of Peace"*

The Cold War began as soon as World War II ended. In large measure, the Cold War grew out of a mind-set of geopolitical strategic thinking that assumed the Soviet Union would be an adversary and competitor for global dominance once the Axis powers of Germany, Japan, and Italy had been subdued. In this struggle, the newly formed US National Security State officially formed the Central Intelligence Agency (CIA) in 1948 in order to deal with the "communist threat." Alan Dulles, the first director of the CIA, recruited ex–Nazi intelligence officers to serve in the CIA due to their familiarity with the Soviets after having fought Nazi Germany since 1942 on the infamous "eastern front" (Simpson 1988). Also, the decision by President Truman to use the atomic bomb on Japan was designed not merely to end the Second World War but also to send a message to Soviet leader Joseph Stalin about the imprudence of attempting to extend his nation's territorial gains beyond those seized by the Russians in the course of ending the war in Europe. Historian Arnold Offner has suggested that "Truman's parochialism also caused him to disregard contrary views, to engage in simplistic analogizing, to show little ability to comprehend the basis for other nations' policies and to demonize those leaders or nations who would not bend to the will of the US. Consequently, his foreign policy leadership intensified Soviet–American conflict, hastened division of Europe, and brought tragic intervention in Asian civil wars and a generation of Sino-American enmity" (Offner 2002, xii). A general consensus on this point has emerged among historians since 1945 as they have reviewed the archives of the United States and Great Britain with respect to foreign policy priorities and assumptions. It is because of these geopolitical calculations that US foreign policy has remained hostage to the whims of American leadership as it has continuously sought to maintain and even advance US hegemony rather than enforce and honor the mandates of international law. As Richard Falk has noted, "International law is likely to remain subordinate to geopolitics for some time to come, and thus the quality of global security is shaped to a considerable extent by the priorities and prudence of the leading political actor at a given historical interval" (Falk 2008c, 23).

Falk's observation about leadership in the nuclear age and questions about the force of international law being subordinate to geopolitics form the crucible for our analysis of President John F. Kennedy's actions. John Kennedy was different from most if not all American presidents in the nuclear age (Nash 1999, 120–40). Historian Philip Nash noted ". . . Kennedy's reliance on non-nuclear 'assets' overshadowed his reliance on nuclear weapons, just as his nuclear restraint eclipsed any nuclear recklessness" (Nash 1999, 140). For example, he was not lured into engaging in the hegemonic temptation offered by the American National Security State to engage in "nuclear first-use." The preemptive first-use of nuclear weapons, long the foundation of America's nuclear strategy, was not the carefully reasoned response to a growing Soviet conventional threat. Rather, the historical record demonstrates that

> Since 1954, it has been the declaratory policy of the United States to use nuclear weapons *first*. It was a policy the Eisenhower administration drafted for its NATO allies, making it the *soi-disant* centerpiece of the alliance's military security throughout the Cold War. Even after its 1991 and 1999 strategic concepts addressed new concerns about regional stability and state-building, first-use was untouchable. It is the most enduring statement of the Western alliance. (Johnston 2005, 1; italics in original)

In fact, we discover that "President George W. Bush's resuscitation of 'preemption'. . . is not, then, a wholly unprecedented departure from American strategic thinking: striking first in anticipation of a threat was at the heart of American Cold War strategic doctrine" (Johnston 2005, 1).

References to "first-use," may be understood as part of a largely uninterrupted doctrine (Bunn and Chyba 2006; Doyle 2008; Ellsberg 2009; Keller and Mitchell 2006; Nichols 2008). It is only in the presidential decisions of John F. Kennedy that this doctrine was opposed, deemed unacceptable, and a more diplomatic approach taken in international affairs—especially with regard to the treatment of adversaries. Had Kennedy followed the logic of the doctrine of first use, the conclusion of the 1962 Cuban missile crisis may well have been the end of human history and the end of all life on this planet as we know it. Kennedy's prescription for leadership in the Cold War might well have been taken from a book by the British strategist Basil Liddell Hart, which he reviewed in 1960: "Keep strong, if possible. In any case, keep cool. Have unlimited patience. Never corner an opponent, and always assist him to save his face. Put yourself in his shoes—so as to see things through his eyes. Avoid self-righteousness like the devil—nothing is so blinding."[2] Commenting on this perspective and Kennedy's response to it, Lawrence Freedman noted the following:

> Advice such as this put a premium on an ability to read a crisis—the sources of its urgency, the interests of those involved, and the

options available to them. It required a readiness to focus hard on primary interests, if necessary letting the secondary go, and developing military options carrying a minimal risk of escalating in a catastrophic war. Forms of activity that signaled resolve without recklessness were required. All this led under Kennedy to what became known as graduated or flexible response, moving forward in crises one step at a time, raising at each stage the pressure on opponents, probing their will, exploring opportunities for a settlement even while preparing to up the ante. It was his method when dealing with awkward clients as much as with dangerous adversaries. It was a method that came naturally to Kennedy the politician, but it was reinforced by his conviction that it was the only way to manage the cold war. (Freedman 2000, 9)

John Kennedy's management of the Cold War was typified by his aversion to taking any reckless chances with nuclear weapons. While the Joint Chiefs of Staff and the bureaucracy of the US National Security State did not fear contemplating the use of nuclear weapons, the record is clear that Kennedy acknowledged the dangers associated with the willingness of his bureaucracy to employ these weapons regardless of the larger political and moral context that such an unrestrained use would signify. For example, "Kennedy in 1961 had shied away from war on Laos as soon as he realized that the United States would be outnumbered on the ground and that the military would count on nuclear weapons to redress the balance. He had also avoided war over the far more critical issue of Cuba partly because of the fear of nuclear escalation" (Kaiser 2000, 378). Tragically, the same cannot be said of either the Johnson or Nixon administrations. According to historian David Kaiser, "The extent to which the Johnson and Nixon administrations actually considered the use of nuclear weapons during the Vietnam War remains an important topic for future investigation" (Kaiser 2000, 433).

What is not such a mystery, as least since the late 1980s, is that "a few scholars have established that a key turning point in US Cold War policy occurred during the Korean War and that this was directly attributable to the achievement by the United States of clear-cut dominance over the Soviet Union in strategic weapons. . . Once it became clear that the Soviet Union could not provide a counterweight to US military power, the United States had a new freedom of action, which translated into more aggressive and interventionist policies. The US path to a major land war in South Vietnam was closely related to this new global distribution of power" (Porter 2005, 1). On this point, it has been noted, "The problem for the American imperialists was . . . that America was already fast becoming something more than one among many: in terms of its economic and military power, it did not need to conform or take on a role that, in ideological terms, was foreign to it. Rather than being *one* imperial power, the United States was fast becoming the protector and balancer of a capitalist world system" (Westad 2005, 15). Given this historical trajectory, we discover that "[t]he Cold War provided an extreme answer to a question that had been at the center of US foreign policy since the late eighteenth century—in what situations should ideological sympathies be followed by intervention? The extension of the Cold War into the Third World was defined by the answer: *everywhere* where Communism could be construed as a threat" (Westad 2005, 38; italics in original). As early as the Truman administration, concerning the anti-Communist impulse in US foreign policy, the historical record shows that "[t]he Soviet danger and the growing importance of Gaullist France in international context pushed the American government to recognize French sovereignty over Indochina in 1945 . . . Secretary of State Dean Acheson clearly affirmed that the United States did not oppose the return of France to Indochina, and the chief of the OSS,[3] William Donovan, stated that it was necessary to maintain the European colonial empires in the face of communism" (Brocheux and Hemery 2009, 353; Lawrence 2005, 100; Morgan 2010, 97; Tonnesson 2010, 17).

John Kennedy's views on European colonialism were diametrically opposed to those who sought accommodation to colonial programs and policies for the sake of "opposing communism" and the "geopolitical pressures" of the Cold War. On July 2, 1957, Senator John Kennedy, speaking on the floor of the US Senate, condemned French policies with respect to its conduct of colonial wars in Algeria and throughout North Africa. Kennedy emphatically stated that "the war in Algeria has steadily drained the manpower, the resources, and the spirit of one of our oldest and most important allies—a nation whose strength is vital to the Free World . . . No matter how complex the problems posed by the Algerian issue may be, the record of the United States in this case is, as elsewhere, a retreat from the principles of independence and anti-colonialism, regardless of what diplomatic niceties, legal technicalities, or even strategic considerations are offered in its defense" (Kennedy 1961, 99–100). In fact, Kennedy rejected the Cold War logic of Washington in its assumption that the support of French colonialism—in either Algeria or Indochina—would automatically prevent these nations from joining in an alliance with either the Soviet Union or China. In the same speech, Kennedy stated, "Fortunately for the United States and France, and in spite of—not because of—our past records, neither Tunisia nor Morocco has a natural proclivity toward either Moscow, Peking or Cairo today . . . But it is apparent, nevertheless, that the latter constitute possible alternate magnets if the Western nations become too parental or tyrannical" (Kennedy 1961, 104). He concluded his remarks with an appeal to democratic principles and ideals, as he observed, "The United States must be prepared to lend all efforts to . . . a settlement, and to assist in the economic problems which flow from it. This is not a burden which we lightly or gladly assume. But our efforts in no other endeavor are more important in terms of once again seizing the initiative in foreign affairs, demonstrating our adherence to the principles of national independence and winning the respect of those long suspicious of our negative and vacillating record on colonial issues" (Kennedy 1961, 110). A few days later, on the floor of the US Senate, Kennedy put the issue of Algeria in even more stark terms when he warned leaders throughout the West that "[t]he world-wide struggle against imperialism, the sweep of nationalism, is the most potent factor in foreign affairs today" (Kennedy 1961, 112).

Driven by the irrationalities of Cold War doctrines, assumptions, preconceived opinions, and fundamentalisms about the true nature of the competition between the United States and the Soviet Union, the hardliners and the hawks on both sides of the Iron Curtain were inclined to allow their subjective fears and ideological extremism to supplant the processes associated with critical thought, moral reasoning, and an enlightened willingness to question the prevailing tenets of military and strategic thinking. Nowhere was this reality more apparent and dangerous than with respect to the nuclear strategy of the United States in its conduct of the Cold War. Once again, irrational fears about the spread of communism created a strategic paranoia among elites within the American primacy coalition. In the case of the US National Security bureaucracy versus President Kennedy, historians have revealed that "Kennedy would have been happier if he could have disavowed a first-strike strategy... but without a continuing commitment to '*first strike*,' Washington feared Franco-German abandonment of NATO, a negotiated compromise with the Soviet Union, and the neutralization of Europe, which would 'have left the United States alone to face the whole communist problem.' Nevertheless, Kennedy urged McNamara publicly to '*repeat to the point of boredom*' that we would use nuclear weapons *only* in response to a major attack on the US or the allies; that *we were not contemplating preventive war*; and the Europeans should not believe that by firing off their own nuclear weapons they would drag the United States into a war, that we would withdraw our commitment to NATO first" (Dallek 2003, 346–47; italics added).

This is an important reality to grasp. As we set out to explain the Cold War context which pitted the US National Security State, on the one hand, against the strategy of peace that John Kennedy was attempting to pursue, on the other, we find that Kennedy's approach of restraint in foreign affairs came into constant conflict with the unrestrained commitment of the US National Security State to impose global hegemony on the rest of the world. While the hardliners and hawks always moved in a quasi-automatic manner toward military solutions, Kennedy sought out the paths of diplomacy, dialogue, and compromise. Hence, Kennedy's approach was antithetical to the dominant logic of the National Security State and its bureaucrats. As historian Gareth Porter has noted, "What has been missing from the story of the Kennedy administration's Vietnam policy is the intense pressure brought to bear on

Kennedy by the national security bureaucracy to use military force in Laos and Vietnam. That pressure, from both military and civilian advisors, clashed with Kennedy's own political instincts and created an unprecedented political struggle between the president and his advisors over a major issue of war and peace" (Porter 2005, 141). It was a fundamental philosophical difference that pre-dated Kennedy's ascension to the presidency.

As a senator, speaking in Portland, Oregon, on August 1, 1959, Kennedy actively criticized those who opposed a test ban treaty on nuclear weapons testing: "There is no serious scientific barrier to international agreement—despite increasing difficulties in problems of inspection and implementation." Therefore, he maintained, "The only difficult barriers now are political and diplomatic" (Kennedy 1961, 51). On December 11, 1959, speaking on the larger issue of disarmament, Kennedy noted the following:

> Disarmament talks historically fail when nations refuse to trust each other's intentions enough to take the first step. Even the first step must be subject to adequate inspection and enforcement. But this, too, requires a minimum of trust ... In this search for beginnings we must bring into play the imagination which our fears have in recent years paralyzed ... So far we have lacked the vision to present a comprehensive program for the development of a world community under law and we have lacked the courage to try small beginnings... It is time to stop reacting to our adversary's moves, and to start acting like the bold, hopeful, inventive people that we were born to be, ready to build and begin anew, ready to make a reality of man's oldest dream, world peace. (Kennedy 1961, 54–56)

By the time Kennedy was elevated to the presidency the reluctance of the national security bureaucracy to embrace his ideas was still rigidly in place. On every major foreign policy issue—from the Nuclear Test Ban Treaty to US intervention in Vietnam—it would appear that the entire US national security apparatus was organized against any serious presidential moves toward peace and a lessening of Cold War tensions. In this regard, Kennedy stood virtually alone in his efforts to seek ratification for a nuclear test ban treaty, in advocating withdrawal from Vietnam, and in moving toward a policy of détente and peaceful coexistence with the Soviet Union. Tragically, it has been noted, "The assassination of John F. Kennedy and the entrance of a new president into the White House dramatically increased the distorting effects of the aggressive role of national security advisors on Vietnam policy" (Porter 2005, 266). Similarly, Peter Dale Scott noted that, in the aftermath of Kennedy's assassination, ". . . an entire Cold War status quo in Washington was preserved along with Lyndon Johnson . . . It was this power base for the Vietnam War whose power was preserved by the assassination; and key elements of it survived to play a similar, equally hidden, role in Watergate" (Scott 1993, 223).

Looking at these events in retrospect, an examination of the historical record demonstrates "how Vietnam had . . . overshadowed all the issues which in the Kennedy administration had enjoyed a vastly higher priority—and how the decision to pursue the war with maximum American objectives had deprived Washington of significant diplomatic opportunities" (Kaiser 2000, 469). Whereas Kennedy had always sought diplomatic solutions through dialogue and negotiation, we discover that those who succeeded him in power usually cut off the possibilities for both dialogue and diplomacy. What we find in the historical record of the Kennedy years is the fact that there was a hidden struggle over peace diplomacy in the bureaucracy of the US government itself. Hence, "The one thing on which past accounts of Kennedy's Vietnam policy have agreed is that Kennedy rejected the idea of any negotiated settlement on Vietnam. The evidence now shows, however, that Kennedy maneuvered to ensure that he would have someone in the lead position in the bureaucracy on Vietnam policy who could be expected to pursue a diplomatic option on Vietnam, and that he tried to open secret diplomatic channels with North Vietnam or China. And when those efforts were blocked, he switched policy makers yet again to maintain the option of negotiating the neutralization of South Vietnam" (Porter 2005, 153–54). For example, we find that instead of helping Kennedy draw Moscow into a diplomatic track on the problems associated with America's presence in Vietnam, Kennedy's diplomatic representative, Averell Harriman, lost no time on communicating to the Russians in Geneva that the administration was not interested in negotiation (Porter 2005, 154). As a result of this obstructionism to Kennedy's orders, the record shows that, in March 1963, Kennedy replaced Harriman as assistant secretary of state with Roger Hilsman, whom he could expect to be far more responsive to his wishes on Vietnam policy (Porter 2005, 164). Yet even after Hilsman became Kennedy's aide on Vietnam, the historical record shows that the CIA's Saigon maneuvers set back Kennedy's hope to neutralize Vietnam in parallel to Laos (Douglass 2008, 343).

The bureaucratic struggle over going to war or, in the alternative, arriving at a negotiated settlement on Vietnam continued right up until Kennedy's assassination. In the aftermath of his death, Kennedy's Vietnam policies for negotiations with North Vietnam and an immediate withdrawal from South Vietnam were reversed within days (Scott 1993, 24–37). As a direct consequence of Kennedy's assassination, negotiation with North Vietnam ended as a strategy of the US government. The hawks had won. Yet their legacy would turn out to be a dismal defeat for the United States in Vietnam once the diplomatic door had been slammed shut by Lyndon Johnson and the Cold War contingent that he represented. According to historian Gareth Porter, "By rejecting diplomatic negotiation, the United States threw away most of its actual ability to shape the political outcome in South Vietnam through a combination of threat, restraint, and knowing what concessions it could extract from Hanoi, short of giving up the ultimate possibility of reunification. Paradoxically, by attempting to press its advantage too far—and especially by engaging in systematic bombing of North Vietnam while blocking the possibility of diplomatic compromise—the United States sacrificed its considerable influence over Hanoi's choices" (Porter 2005, 274).

The same basic problem attended every discussion on every foreign policy issue during the Kennedy years. From the Cold War problems over the sovereign status of West Berlin to the Bay of Pigs, from the Cuban missile crisis to reaching agreement on a nuclear test ban treaty with the Soviets, from Laos to Vietnam, Kennedy was at odds with the Cold War mind-set of the hardliners and hawks who viewed the world through the prism of war, the idea of employing a nuclear "fist strike," and a Cold War paradigm that centered on military solutions to each and every challenge. In this highly charged ideological environment, Kennedy's calls for peace were, more often than not, interpreted by his enemies and adversaries as an expression of weakness (Reeves 1993, 184). In the Pentagon, the joint chiefs of staff regarded Kennedy's refusal to endorse their first-strike mandate as nothing short of treason (Douglass 2008, 30).

The leadership in both the Pentagon and the CIA viewed Kennedy's peace-oriented policies as the initial stages of a Communist victory. As such, they viewed Kennedy as a traitor to the United States because they thought it was Kennedy—not themselves—who had gone off the deep end (Douglass 2008, 98). In sum, we can say that Kennedy was at war with those, both in and out of government, who represented the views of the American primacy coalition. This elite coalition wanted to "win" the Cold War through war. The American primacy coalition was dedicated to the furtherance and extension of US hegemony. Kennedy's response was to leave them out of the decision-making process that he was committed to so that his peace initiatives would not be fatally sabotaged. Therefore, the record shows that

> By leaving the Pentagon and the CIA out of the Vietnam loop, he wasn't fooling them. They knew he planned to withdraw from Vietnam. They also knew they'd been left out of other key decisions. At precisely the same time, the early summer of 1963, besides side-stepping the Pentagon and CIA on Vietnam, the president had also left them out of consultations for his American University address and the test ban treaty. The reason was simple. Kennedy knew the military-intelligence elite were opposed to all his efforts to end the Cold War. They wanted to win it. (Douglass 2008, 162)

In this environment, Pope John XXIII enlisted Norman Cousins—editor of the liberal magazine *Saturday Review* and a longtime peace activist, to serve as an informal emissary between the Vatican, Washington, and Moscow. Kennedy readily agreed to discuss strategy with the amateur diplomat. Cousin's role assumed an even more conspicuous importance in the aftermath of the 1962 Cuban missile crisis. In early 1963, he reported to Kennedy. Kennedy's responses are insightful about the real challenges that he and Khrushchev faced in dealing with the Cold War warriors and hawks of their respective nations. In this regard, Cousins discovered that

> While Khrushchev clearly desired diplomatic progress . . . the Russian leader also stressed that he was under intense political pressure to maintain a militant Cold War stance. This prompted a revealing reply from Kennedy. *'One of the ironic things about this entire situation is that Mr. Khrushchev and I occupy approximately the same political positions inside our governments,'* the president observed. *'He would like to prevent a nuclear war but is under severe pressure from his hard-line crowd, which interprets every move in that direction as appeasement. I've got similar problems. Meanwhile, the lack of progress in reaching agreements between our two countries gives strength to the hard-line boys in both with the result that the hard-liners in the Soviet Union and the United States feed on one another, each using the actions of the other to justify its own position.'* When Cousins suggested that Kennedy blast through the impasse with 'a breathtaking new approach, calling for an end to the Cold War and a fresh start in American–Russian relationships,' Kennedy was intrigued. (Talbot 2007, 207–09; italics added)

In response, the hardliners in the United States did what they could to disrupt the new direction. On this matter, James W. Douglass noted, "To the discouragement of both Kennedy and Khrushchev, the later winter and early spring of 1963 marked a cooling off of their dialogue. Their distancing was accomplished partly by militant Cold War forces in the US government. From Cuba to Vietnam, the CIA was systematically undermining Kennedy's peace initiatives and antagonizing Khrushchev" (Douglass 2008, 342). Prof. Robert Jay Lifton described the mind-set of these militant forces as one that has been trapped within a *"superpower syndrome."* Lifton explains, "By that term I mean a national mindset—put forward strongly by a tight-knit leadership group—that takes on a sense of omnipotence, of unique standing in the world that grants it the right to hold sway over all other nations" (Lifton 2003, 3). This syndrome has directly affected our collective ability to deal realistically with the threat of nuclear weapons and the still looming danger of nuclear war or accident. According to Lifton, we discover that "[t]he absence of nuclear fear, then, meant that we lacked appropriate feelings about the actual threat we faced. Unfortunately, that psychological dysfunction contributed greatly to the American failure to take advantage of a unique post–Cold War opportunity for radical worldwide denuclearization" (Lifton 2003, 185). This lost post–Cold War opportunity stands alongside a long historical trajectory of lost opportunities for peace during the entire sweep of the Cold War era as well.

Opposition to any kind of Cold War peace initiatives during Kennedy's thousand days in the White House characterized his entire presidency. It was Kennedy's ongoing struggle with Washington's Cold War establishment and the corporate interests that it represented which characterized the true nature of his battle with domestic US elites and institutional forces (Gibson 1994). It was a battle that typified the true nature of a constant threat to Kennedy's leadership at every turn. Even during the course of the 1962 Cuban missile crisis this dynamic was evident. According to David Talbot, "In his memoirs, Nikita Khrushchev offered a startling account of Robert F. Kennedy's emotional conversations with Dobrynin, in which Kennedy stressed how fragile his brother's rule was becoming as the crisis dragged on. It was not the first time in the Kennedy presidency that Bobby had communicated this alarming message to the Russians. But in this high-stakes moment, Kennedy's plea struck Khrushchev as especially urgent" (Talbot 2007, 170–71). It was for this reason that, as president, "Kennedy felt it important to hear Khrushchev explain Soviet policy in his own terms. Following the Bay of Pigs disaster, Kennedy 'did not trust the conclusions of his own advisors'" (Fursenko and Naftali 1997, 127).

Kennedy's real distrust of certain individuals in the US government's Cold War bureaucracy had been with those located primarily in the Pentagon and the CIA. Among the members of the Pentagon's top brass in the Joint Chiefs of Staff, Kennedy held Strategic Air Command Air Force General Curtis LeMay in particular contempt. The feeling was mutual. In 1961, Kennedy had come under increasing pressure from both military and intelligence officials to consider launching a preemptive nuclear first-strike against the Soviet Union. They informed Kennedy that the United States enjoyed a growing lead in land-based nuclear missiles. They warned Kennedy that this "window" of nuclear superiority would eventually close as Soviet nuclear weapons production began to catch up. However, while the "window" remained open, there were those like General LeMay who sought to turn Washington into "a hothouse of militaristic fever" (Talbot 2007, 68). Refusing to be subjected to the continuous battering and complaints of these right-wing militarists, one historian of the era wrote, "Walking out on generals was a Kennedy specialty. 'The uniforms' seemed incapable of listening or understanding, and they could not stop once they swung into canned briefings, not even to take questions from their Commander-in-Chief" (Reeves 1993, 182).

In retrospect, it is clear that the vital importance of direct talks, as well as back-channel communications, combined with a consistent dialogue between Kennedy and Khrushchev, proved to be a determining factor in the peaceful resolution of the 1962 Cuban crisis as well as making progress toward the achievement of the 1963 Test Ban Treaty (Beschloss 1991; Stern 2003). Their dialogue began in earnest in a state of nuclear peril during the Cuban missile crisis. Reflecting on that dialogue and Kennedy's character during that period, Khrushchev wrote in his memoirs that

> [he] showed soberness of mind; he didn't allow himself to be frightened, nor did he allow himself to become intoxicated with the military might of the United States; he didn't decide to go for broke. It doesn't take great intelligence to start a war. But he displayed civic courage, the courage of a statesman. He was not afraid of being condemned from the right. And peace won out. That is what I wanted to say. I think that the correct understanding of each other's positions, which is what we based ourselves on, was the only rational way to proceed in the situation that existed then. (Khrushchev 2007, 356)

Once both sides determined that a nuclear war was unthinkable due to their mutual vulnerability (*mutually assured destruction*), it then became possible for a new beginning to be made in the US/USSR relationship in the aftermath of the crisis. The crisis was largely resolved by the United States accommodating Khrushchev by removing Jupiter nuclear missiles from Turkey and Italy, while in turn, the USSR removed its missiles from Cuba. These acts, in turn, led to acts of mutual restraint and allowed a pattern of negotiations to move forward toward the conclusion and signing of a nuclear test ban treaty in late 1963. In broad terms, Charles Kupchan has argued that, "the trading of individual acts of accommodation gives way to the practice of reciprocal restraint. Concessions are no longer bolts from the blue—risky gambits aimed at sending benign signals and probing the others' intentions. Rather, both parties readily practice accommodation and expect reciprocity; cautious testing gives way to a purposeful effort to dampen rivalry and advance reconciliation" (Kupchan 2010, 41).

To fully appreciate Kennedy's inner transformation and the transformative purposes that drove his anti-Cold War policies, it is important to review the nature of the dialogues between Norman Cousins and Kennedy as they discussed Khrushchev's own inner transformation after the 1962 Cuban missile crisis and in response to Kennedy's breakthrough peace speech at American University in June 1963. To begin with, Norman Cousins was acutely aware of one of the best-known axioms on human behavior: "*Power tends to corrupts; absolute power corrupts absolutely.*" In his 1987 book, *The Pathology of Power*, Cousins wrote thus: "Connected to the tendency of power to corrupt are yet other tendencies that emerge from the pages of the historians: (1) The tendency of power to drive intelligence underground; (2) The tendency of power to become a theology, admitting no other gods before it; (3) The tendency of power to distort and damage the traditions and institutions it was designed to protect; (4) The tendency of power to create a language of its own, making other forms of communication incoherent and irrelevant; (5) The tendency of power to spawn imitators, leading to volatile competition; (6) The tendency of power to set the stage for its own use" (Cousins 1987, 23–24).

The net effect of all of these tendencies is that

> We exist in two different worlds but we pay a price for it. Decisions may be made on the level of old-world thinking but the consequences take place in the new. A nation that is guided primarily by traditional ideas of self-interest may quickly discover it will lose its principal power. For workable power in the new world is measured by the leadership a nation is able to exert among the large majority of the peoples on earth, by its moral standing, by its ability to recognize new realities, by its desire not to use force but to control it. (Cousins 1987, 198)

These observations for "*workable power*" in a new world of human consciousness that has transcended a narrow focus on the national interest may also be seen as a commentary on President Kennedy's *strategy of peace*, as well as Ikeda's approach to building a more peaceful global civilization through humanitarian competition.

In the closing sentences of Kennedy's peace speech at American University, on June 10, 1963, Americans, Kennedy declared, were ready to ". . . do our part to build a world of peace where the weak are safe and the strong are just. We are not helpless before that task or hopeless of its success. Confident and unafraid, we labor on—not towards a strategy of annihilation but toward a strategy of peace." Commenting on the concluding words of the speech, it has been noted, "The last three words of Kennedy's address are significant, for they connect the message he now proclaimed with the ideas he had advanced in the past. *The Strategy of Peace* had been the title of a collected volume of Kennedy's pre-presidential speeches on foreign policy published in 1960. To Walt Rostow, there was indeed 'great consistency' between the pronouncements of Kennedy's early career and his politics as a mature president: 'Kennedy, from beginning to end, pressed across the din of confrontation toward reconciliation with Moscow on the nuclear question'" (Oliver 1998, 186).

In assessing the net effect of the above-cited tendencies of power, Cousins has actually outlined many of the central insights that guided the thought processes and decision-making of President Kennedy. In so doing, Cousins has also outlined some of the central ideas that have guided Ikeda's own work and prescriptions regarding the renunciation of force, the need to work for the abolition of nuclear weapons, and the practical requirements for the building of an effective international legal framework to augment the cause of peace. Additionally, Ikeda's formulation for employing "workable power" in the service of all humanity involves controlling the proliferation of nuclear weapons in conjunction with enforcing legal and moral prohibitions against their use.

In previous chapters, I have addressed Ikeda's conception of humanitarian competition as a way in which nations can challenge each other to a peace race—seeking to reward those acts and policies that advance the welfare and well-being of all humankind as humanity steadily progresses toward building a more peaceful global civilization. Similarly, in harmony with Ikeda's conception of humanitarian competition, Cousins affirmed the fact that we cannot do away with competing ideologies, but we can begin to find new ways that allow for a competition between ideologies that does not lead to war. Writing on the eve of the end of the Cold War in 1987, Cousins noted, "Living in this new world does not mean we ignore the existence of threatening ideologies. It simply means we have to fashion new ways of competing with those ideologies. For Americans and Soviets, it means they can challenge each other to the most important competition of all—*a competition in service to the human community*" (Cousins 1987, 198; italics added). It is to this challenge that we now turn. In so doing, we shall examine the idea of how enemies become friends.

How Enemies Become Friends—The Sources of a Stable Peace

In 2010, Charles Kupchan, professor of international affairs at Georgetown University, produced a book entitled *How Enemies Become Friends: The Sources of Stable Peace*. He argues that "[s]table peace emerges through a sequential process that cuts across long-standing theoretical divides" (Kupchan 2010, 35). In outlining the process that leads to a stable peace, he begins with a realist perspective in arguing that "[s]trategic necessity induces a state faced with an unmanageable array of threats to seek to befriend an existing adversary; resource constraints make accommodation and cooptation preferable to balancing and confrontation . . . A constructivist perspective best explains the final stage of the process. Changes in political discourse and identity erode the self-other distinctions that are at the foundation of geopolitical competition" (Kupchan 2010, 35).

Both the realist emphasis upon "strategic necessity" and the constructivist perspective on the effects of "changes in political discourse and identity" serve to explain the dynamics at work between the United States and USSR in the 1962 missile crisis and its aftermath. Also, both the realist and constructivist perspectives on the elements of discourse and identity serve to augment and support Ikeda's approach to peace and reconciliation. Therefore, we intend to take Kucphan's typology and the sequential process he identifies (*consisting of four distinct phases*) to explain the dynamics at work in the Cuban missile crisis and the subsequent changes in policies and perspectives between the United States and USSR that culminated in the signing of the 1963 Test Ban Treaty. In taking this approach, we shall also juxtapose key excerpts from

President Kennedy's June 10, 1963, speech at American University with each of these phases in order to offer a historical illustration of how the theory of moving toward a stable peace was undertaken by Kennedy. In so doing, we seek to illuminate the viability of Ikeda's approach to peace against the backdrop of a key moment in the Cold War.

According to Kupchan, we find that in the movement toward stable peace

> Phase one consists of *unilateral accommodation*. One party makes an initial concession to the other as an opening gesture of good will. It is then up to the target state to reciprocate with its own act of accommodation. During these opening concessions, the parties seek to discern the *intent* behind such moves and begin to entertain *hope* that they are dealing with a potential partner rather than an implacable adversary. (Kupchan 2010, 35; italics in the original)

During the Cuban missile crisis, President Kennedy made the first moves toward accommodation and a de-escalation of the crisis by suggesting to Khrushchev (*through a back channel between Robert Kennedy and a Russian emissary*) that a good faith removal of US missiles from Turkey and Italy would be undertaken once the Soviets had removed their missiles from Cuba. What this secret bargain between Kennedy and Khrushchev accomplished was manifold. President Kennedy made an opening gesture of good will by giving Khrushchev a promise that he could take back to the Central Committee of the Communist Party which gave something of value to the Soviets. This allowed the Soviets to save face and not be humiliated or feel that they had been backed against a wall with nothing to show for their efforts. Yet even more important, Kennedy gave the Russians a firm unilateral pledge that the United States would never again seek to invade Cuba by force (*as happened in 1961 at the Bay of Pigs*). This pledge, therefore, removed the original rationale for the placement of Russian missiles in Cuba (*as a deterrent to any future potential invasion of Cuba by the United States or its allies*). Throughout this process, by making their respective concessions, both parties were able to effectively gauge each other's intent regarding these proposed moves. Insofar as these concessions did not disrupt the balance of power and/or any other relevant geopolitical considerations—at that historical moment—both parties could undertake this exchange of promises in good faith. Further, these acts were reciprocal in nature so that both sides saw that their hopes for dealing with a potential partner were justified in defusing the dangers of war under immense Cold War pressures.

At the beginning of President Kennedy's speech at American University on June 10, 1963, he began by addressing our attitudes toward peace as a real possibility and then proceeded to characterize it as "a process—a way of solving problem." In explaining how this process has worked throughout history, Kennedy made it clear that "enmities between nations, as between individuals, do not last forever" and, because changes in relations between nations and neighbors are inevitable, it follows that peace "need not be impractical, and war need not be inevitable." In short, Kennedy was making the case that the USSR was not an implacable adversary. He sought to humanize, not demonize, the Russian people with his rhetoric. In full context, these ideas were presented by Kennedy as follows:

> First, let us examine our attitude toward peace itself. Too many of us think it is impossible. Too many think it is unreal. But that is a dangerous defeatist belief. It leads to the conclusion that war is inevitable—that mankind is doomed—that we are gripped by forces we cannot control. We need not accept that view. Our problems are manmade—therefore they can be solved by man . . . No problem of human destiny is beyond human beings. Man's reason and strength have often solved the seemingly unsolvable—and we believe they can do it again . . . There is no single, simple key to this peace—no grand or magic formula to be adopted by one or two powers. Genuine peace must be the product of many nations, the sum of many acts. It must be dynamic, not static, changing to meet the challenge of each new generation. For peace is a process—a way of solving problems. (Kennedy 1964, 460–61)

Having argued that (1) peace is attainable; (2) the achievement of peace is a real possibility; (3) peace is the product of many nations and many acts; (4) peace is dynamic, not static; and (5) peace is a process in the sense that it is an actual way of solving problems, Kennedy also goes on to admit that there will still be "quarrels and conflicting interests." However, if we agree to "live together in mutual tolerance" and submit our disputes to "a just and peaceful settlement," then we will discover that "war need not be inevitable." As with Ikeda's arguments in an editorial written for the *Japan Times* entitled "Embracing the Future," Ikeda noted, "From my own experience of having engaged in dialogue with many people from a wide range of political, religious, ethnic and cultural backgrounds, I am equally convinced that when we speak frankly on the basis of our common humanity it is always possible to see our way to the next step forward" (Ikeda [2007] 2008, 79). This was demonstrably true of Kennedy as well. In full context, Kennedy argued that

> There is no single, simple key to this peace—no grand or magic formula to be adopted by one or two powers. Genuine peace must be the product of many nations, the sum of many acts. It must be dynamic, not static, changing to meet the challenge of each new generation. For peace is a process—a way of solving problems. With such a peace, there will still be quarrels and conflicting interests, as

there are within families and nations. World peace, like community peace, does not require that each man love his neighbor—it requires only that they live together in mutual tolerance, submitting their disputes to a just and peaceful settlement. And history teaches us that enmities between nations, as between individuals, do not last forever. However fixed our likes and dislikes may seem the tide of time and events will often bring surprising changes in the relations between nations and neighbors. So, let us persevere. Peace need not be impracticable, and war need not be inevitable. By defining our goal more clearly, by making it seem more manageable and less remote, we can help all people to see it, to draw hope from it and to move irresistibly toward it. (Kennedy 1964, 461)

According to Kupchan, we find that in the movement toward a stable peace, [p]hase two entails *reciprocal restraint.* Expectations of reciprocity promote successive rounds of mutual accommodation. The parties evaluate one another's broader *motivation*, not just their narrow intent with respect to specific concessions. Hope gives way to mutual *confidence* that rivalry can be averted and that repeated acts of mutual accommodation can lead to peace and possibly, programmatic cooperation. (Kupchan 2010, 35; italics in the original)

In Kennedy's speech at American University, his approach to addressing reciprocal restraint was premised on our need to reexamine our attitude toward the Soviet Union. In the course of that reexamination within ourselves it should be possible for us to come to realize that we have not only an interest in avoiding war but also shared interests to combating "ignorance, poverty, and disease." While these shared interests do not wipe away all our differences, our shared focus on these issues can lead to repeated acts of mutual accommodation as we address "our common interests."

In addressing our common interests, we can engage in what Kupchan has called "*programmatic cooperation.*" Similarly, Ikeda has written of the process of loosening the "*knots of attachment*" by engaging in a kind of "*humanistic diplomacy*" (*Japan Times* [2007] 2008) that can actually move history itself in a new direction. Hence, we need not view ourselves as the captives of some kind of preordained fate. Such a view was at the heart of Kennedy's speech and purpose at American University. He believed that the greatest obstacle to peace with the USSR was to continue to engage in shuttered isolationism because it is not only the antithesis of discourse but also a threat to peace itself. Taking into consideration the larger context of the Cold War and the dynamics of international relations, Kennedy argued that "*suspicion on one side breeds suspicion on the other*" and "*new weapons beget new counter-weapons.*" Hence, if we are to transcend "*a vicious and dangerous cycle*" that could lead to war, then we must become engaged instead in constructive dialogue or committed to what Ikeda has called humanistic diplomacy, as well as become active participants in humanitarian competition. These concepts from Ikeda are both good examples of where opposing parties can begin to engage one another in acts of mutual accommodation. Only in this manner, Ikeda would argue, can we effectively begin to change our focus and our identities from being trapped within old paradigms about "the other."

In his book on stable peace, Kenneth Boulding recognized the importance of iterative acts of mutual accommodation, labeling such behavior as graduated and reciprocated initiative in tension reduction (GRIT). Boulding writes, "The GRIT process begins by some rather specific, perhaps even dramatic, statement or act directed at a potential enemy (like Sadat's 1977 visit to Israel), intended to be reassuring . . . If the potential enemy responds, then a third act by the first party, a fourth by the second party, and so on provides the foundation for a peace dynamic" (Boulding 1978, 112–13). Such a dramatic statement was made by Kennedy on June 10, 1963, when he called upon the Soviet Union and Great Britain to join with the United States in completing negotiations leading to the signing of a nuclear test ban treaty.

By taking this new path, as outlined in the GRIT process, we can leave behind our unreasonable fears associated with what is in the category of the unknown. Instead of being trapped on the trajectory of the past, the GRIT approach allowed for the adoption of a new path that would allow the United States, the USSR, and all humanity to embrace with a strong reasonable confidence a renewed hope and promise for establishing a viable foundation for "peaceful coexistence." Such an accomplishment would, as Kennedy knew, open the door for the host of benefits which would flow from creating the conditions for détente and rapprochement. The relationship between the United States and the USSR could, at last, be transformed from permanent armed rivalry to one that would be characterized by mutual expectations of peaceful coexistence. While the separate identities of the United States and USSR would remain intact, their identities would increasingly be seen as compatible rather than oppositional. Such a change in focus would, in Kennedy's view, give all concerned the capacity to see and to appreciate the fact that *"we can help make the world safe for diversity."* In so doing, we can begin to rediscover our common humanity. In full context, Kennedy argued thus:

> Second: Let us reexamine our attitude toward the Soviet Union . . . Today, should total war ever break out again—no matter how— our two countries would become the primary targets. It is an ironic but accurate fact that the two strongest powers are the two in the most danger of devastation. All we have built, all that we have worked for, would be destroyed in the first 24 hours. And even in the [C]old [W]ar, which brings burdens and dangers to so many countries, including this Nation's closest allies—our two countries bear the heaviest burdens. For we are both devoting massive sums of money to weapons that could be better devoted

to combat ignorance, poverty, and disease. We are both caught up in a vicious and dangerous cycle, in which suspicion on one side breeds suspicion on the other, and new weapons beget counter-weapons. In short, both the United States and its allies, and the Soviet Union and its allies, have a mutually deep interest in a just and genuine peace and in halting the arms race. . . . So, let us not be blind to our differences—but let us also direct attention to our common interests and to the means by which those differences can be resolved. And if we cannot end now our differences, at least we can help make the world safe for diversity. For, in the final analysis, our most basic common link is that we all inhabit this small planet. We all breathe the same air. We all cherish our children's futures. And we are all mortal. (Kennedy 1964, 461–62)

According to Kupchan, we find that in the movement toward a stable peace, "[p]hase three consists of *social integration*. As the polities in question interact with increasing frequency and intensity, they come to attribute benign qualities to one another's *political character*. Confidence builds, giving way to a sense of mutual *trust*" (Kupchan 2010, 35–36; italics in the original). In this third phase, "Reciprocal restraint, the gradual winding down of geopolitical competition, and the mutual attribution of benign motivation clear the way for the intensification of direct contact between the reconciling societies. In contrast to the first two phases, when governing elites are the primacy agents driving forward the process of reconciliation, the third phase entails the involvement of bureaucracies, private firms, and mobilized citizens" (Kupchan 2010, 46).

In Kennedy's peace speech his third major point addressed his commitment to end the Cold War. With this specific goal in mind, he speaks of a search for solutions to ending the Cold War that would require not only hope but also a practical way to conduct US foreign policy so that there could finally be a winding down of geopolitical competition: "We must conduct our affairs in such a way that it becomes in the Communist's interests to agree on a genuine peace." To that end, Kennedy argued thus:

Our interests converge . . . not only in defending the frontiers of freedom, but in pursuing the paths of peace. It is our hope—and for the purposes of allied policies, to convince the Soviet Union that she, too, should let each nation choose its own future, so long as that choice does not interfere with the choices of others . . . This will require a new effort to achieve world law—a new context for world discussions. It will require increased understanding between the Soviets and ourselves. And increased understanding will require increased contact and communication . . . The pursuit of disarmament has been an effort of this Government since the 1920s. It has been urgently sought by the past three administrations. And however dim the prospects may be today, we intend to continue this effort—to continue it in order that all countries, including our own, can better grasp what the problems and possibilities of disarmament are. The one major area of these negotiations where the end is in sight, yet where a fresh start is badly needed, is in a treaty to outlaw nuclear tests. (Kennedy 1964, 463)

It is important to note that Kennedy's call to end the Cold War begins with a call to embrace the possibilities of disarmament. In articulating this new paradigm, Kennedy sets himself at odds with the military–industrial complex of his own nation and that of the European allies, as well as that of the USSR. Kennedy's call to negotiations over a test ban treaty with a focus on nonproliferation is a call to reason, not a call to arms. Hence, he and Khrushchev had embraced reciprocal restraint both during and in the immediate aftermath of the 1962 Cuban missile crisis. They now were both committed to creating a new political narrative for peaceful relations not only between themselves but also with every other nation on earth. In this new context for international relations, historians have discovered that "[t]he two superpowers explored cooperation on nonproliferation, as well as test ban, in the wake of the Caribbean confrontation. The desire to avoid a repeat crisis added momentum to efforts to create a Latin American denuclearized zone.... The new US–Soviet dialogue flowed through multiple channels. Kennedy seemed intent on exploiting every opportunity for a test ban or nonproliferation agreement" (Maddock 2010, 198).

However, Kennedy's efforts to advance toward the ratification and signing of a comprehensive test-ban treaty, with a strong focus on nuclear nonproliferation, were constantly hampered domestically by elite members of the US primacy coalition, who wanted to maintain their version of US hegemony—even risking a nuclear war if necessary to further their hegemonic fantasies. In this troubled environment "[t]he nuclear nationalists tried to appear reasonable by saying that they did not oppose the idea of a treaty, only the language of the Kennedy proposals. But the crux of their critiques suggested that any agreement would be foolish because Moscow could not be trusted" (Maddock 2010, 208). In response, Kennedy "... had advised his subordinates to get off the defensive and strike back at test ban opponents" (Maddock 2010, 209). In the course of Kennedy's principled struggle for peace, typified by the American University speech, we discover that "[w]hile the president's peace speech did convey to the Soviets a desire for agreement, it also used the bully pulpit in an attempt to defang hard-line American Cold warriors and create a congressional climate more hospitable to a comprehensive test ban treaty" (Maddock 2010, 209).

In the end, "Kennedy reluctantly resigned himself to achieving only a limited test-ban treaty—a major concession in light of his labeling nonproliferation the primary focus of the negotiations prior to the conference"

(Maddock 2010, 213). But in the American University speech, prior to the conference, Kennedy firmly stated the following:

> I'm taking this opportunity . . . to announce two important decisions . . . First, Chairman Khrushchev, Prime Minister Macmillan, and I have agreed that high-level discussions will shortly begin in Moscow looking toward early agreement on a comprehensive test ban treaty. *Our hopes must be tempered with the caution of history—but with our hopes go the hopes of all mankind.* Second: To make clear our good faith and solemn convictions on the matter, I now declare that the United States does not propose to conduct nuclear tests in the atmosphere so long as other states do not do so. We will not be the first to resume. Such a declaration is no substitute for a formal binding treaty, but I hope it will help us achieve one. Nor would such a treaty be a substitute for disarmament, but I hope it will help us achieve it. (Kennedy 1964, 464–65; italics added)

According to Kupchan, we find that in the movement toward a stable peace, "[t]he final phase consists of the *generation of new political narratives.* Using the discourse of community as a vehicle, the polities in question embrace a compatible, shared, or common *identity* and expectations of peaceful relations come to have a taken-for-granted quality, producing a sense of social *solidarity*" (Kupchan 2010, 36; italics in the original). Kennedy embraced a universal discourse that transcended nationalism, and a narrow focus on an ever-shifting conception was what was "in the national interest." Instead, Kennedy adopted a form of discourse of community that was, in the last analysis, addressed to the world community and offered on behalf of the global commons. After all, Kennedy had a choice to make between "whether he would be a politician or a statesman" (Leaming 2006, 425). With the opportunity for a test ban treaty, Kennedy was afforded a moment of great historical magnitude. On the one hand, he could have been swayed by critics and opposition to the test ban. One the other hand, Kennedy could respond to the call of duty and take up Winston Churchill's mantle and ". . . move for the critical first agreement with the Soviets that had eluded Churchill himself" (Leaming 2006, 427). In the end, he chose to do great things and claim his place in history.

In employing the discourse of community, embracing a common identity with all those living under nuclear threat, in advancing the idea that the United States and USSR could evolve toward peaceful expectations which would produce a sense of social solidarity both within and between their two countries, Kennedy rejected the dominant dogmas of the Cold War in favor of turning the page of history in the direction of a new chapter in US, Soviet, and global relations. The closing paragraph of Kennedy's speech at American University contains all of these elements. Kennedy's last words in this speech were as follows:

The United States, as the world knows, will never start a war. We do not want a war. We do not now expect a war. *This generation of Americans has already had enough—more than enough—of war and hate and oppression.* We shall be prepared if others wish it. We shall be alert to try to stop it. But *we shall also do our part to build a world of peace where the weak are safe and the strong are just.* We are not helpless before that task or hopeless of its success. *Confident and unafraid, we must labor on—not toward a strategy of annihilation but toward a strategy of peace.* (Kennedy 1964, 464; italics added)

Reviewing the history of the time from when Kennedy delivered this speech to the time of its ratification and signing in late 1963, historians have arrived at a general consensus on the importance of Kennedy's efforts and success. One historian summed it up well when he wrote thus:

Kennedy had entered office committed to halting the spread of nuclear weapons. But alliance politics, Soviet defensiveness, political cautiousness, administrative ineptness, bureaucratic resistance, and domestic politics prevented him from concluding a nonproliferation agreement during his brief presidency. Many analysts and Kennedy administration policymakers have legitimately touted the Limited Test Ban Treaty (LTBT) as a significant first step toward the solution of multiple Cold War problems and conflicts, including proliferation. But it also represented the last time two superpowers could conclude an agreement bilaterally with any hope of the rest of the world acceding to it. (Maddock 2010, 215)

To explain the Kennedy legacy on the 1963 Limited Test-Ban Treaty even more starkly, James W. Douglass has offered this final assessment: "These now forgotten winds of change in which John Kennedy had set sail in 1963 put him in the position of becoming a peacemaker while still commanding a military force with the capacity to destroy the world many times over. He was trapped in a contradiction between the mandate of peace in his American University address and the continuing Cold War dogmas of his national security state" (Douglass 2008, 95).

Many years later in an interview with the French journalist Ignacio Ramonet, Cuba's president—Fidel Castro—was asked, "Despite the crisis in October, the so-called Cuban missile crisis, you still maintain a positive opinion of Kennedy." Castro responded thus:

The crisis gave Kennedy added stature, authority—he showed he had the ability to come up with an effective response. If we'd taken part in the negotiations, we'd have done so in, let's say, a conservative way . . . A dialogue might have begun, an exchange of impressions and points of view that might have allowed us to avoid many of the problems that our two countries have had since then. Irrespective of what happened, in judging Kennedy's policies I have to consider the times we were living in, what doctrines prevailed, what disturbance must have been caused by a government ninety miles from the United States that declared itself to be a socialist revolution—and declared itself Socialist on its own, because the Soviets didn't give us one penny for the revolution, or one rifle. In January 1959 I didn't know a single Soviet or the leaders. (Castro and Ramonet 2007, 288)

What Castro describes here confirms what a general consensus of modern historians have written about Kennedy and his handling of the Cuban missile crisis, as well as its aftermath. Castro's description of the dynamics of the crisis also supports Ikeda's prescription for an effective dialogue—capable of leading toward new forms of humanistic diplomacy, an end to shuttered isolationism, and the search for peaceful coexistence. In a *Japan Times* editorial, Ikeda wrote the following:

> Dialogue is not limited to the exchange of pleasantries, but includes the sharing of sharply differing perspectives. Courage and endurance are essential if we want to continue the painstaking work of loosening the knots of attachment that bind people to a particular point of view. The impact of this kind of humanistic diplomacy can move history in a new direction. In a world of richly diverse cultures, we cannot afford a regression to shuttered isolationism. It is crucial to revive the spirit of dialogue and to unleash a creative search for peaceful coexistence. (Ikeda [2007] 2008, 81–82)

There is no better epitaph to the 1962 Cuban missile crisis and the eventual signing of the 1963 Limited Test-Ban Treaty than this observation by Ikeda.

Ideology, Hegemony, and the Nuclear Weapons Dilemma

It may be a surprise to many people that their attachments to their political beliefs (ideology) and the dominant form in which it expresses itself (hegemony and/or empire, nationalism and/or militarism), augmented and supported by developments in technology (associated with technique, productivity, and unregulated capital accumulation), have created a prison for all humanity. Yet the fact is that humanity is imprisoned by these attachments. These attachments have created a global prison. This global prison denies freedom to all who toil within it. According to the German theologian, Paul Tillich, we find that

> We do not experience un-freedom as dehumanizing because we are deprived of definite possibilities but because we are no longer able to react as whole persons. And this is the reason *the struggle for freedom*

97

is a struggle for man himself and not for something belonging to man. He who is no longer able to act from centeredness, from wholeness, whence all elements of his being join in an ultimate decision, has ceased to be man in the true sense of the word. He is dehumanized; and it is very important that we understand clearly that the concept of dehumanization derives from this phenomenon of un-freedom. (Tillich 1971, 127; italics added)

Our global condition in the "modern world" of the twentieth and early twenty-first centuries is largely one of unfreedom. It is born of what Jacques Ellul has called an "illusion" because "it is an illusion—unfortunately very widespread—to think that because we have broken through the prohibitions, taboos, and rites that bound primitive man, we have become free. We are conditioned by something new: technological civilization" (Ellul 1964, xxix). Hence, the nuclear taboo is negated by developments in an evolving nuclear technology that might make, in the minds of some people, a "first strike" feasible. This would be a decision made at the highest levels of the state. Yet that does not mean that those who occupy the decision-making seats in the state are really free to make that determination based upon moral imperatives or even political realities. Rather, we discover that "[i]n the same way that military machines condition strategy, organizational and other techniques condition the structure of the modern state.... Technique puts the question, not whether a state form is more just, but whether it permits more efficient utilization of techniques. The state is no longer caught between political reality and moral theories and imperatives" (Ellul 1964, 277).

In the age of nuclear weapons, the threat of nuclear holocaust has remained an all too likely prospect given the propensity of the nuclear power brokers—the *"wizards of Armageddon"*—in order to maintain and extend their hegemonic control and influence throughout the world (Kaplan 1983; Nolan 1989). Take, for example, the geopolitical situation in Vietnam in the mid-1950s. Historians have discovered that "... in spite of France's refusal in 1954 to accept the Eisenhower administration's offer of two nuclear weapons to break the decisive Viet Minh siege at Dien Bien Phu, the United States' 'commanding nuclear superiority' framed its efforts to add Indochina to its empire from the negotiation of the Geneva Accords through the Johnson administration's massive escalation of the war in 1965" (Gerson 2007, 131). Rejecting the stigma that shadowed nuclear weapons in the 1950s, US Secretary of State John Foster Dulles declared, "In the past higher civilizations have always maintained their place against lower civilizations by devising more effective weapons." This statement reflects not only an attitude of racism but a quality of the imperial mind-set as well. Recent scholarship has definitively established that the ideologies of race and empire were integral to both European and American expansion. Prof. Thomas McCarthy asserts, "Racism and imperialism have been basic features of the modern world order from the start. They have often appeared together: colonial regimes were usually racially organized, and racist beliefs and practices usually flourished in colonial contexts. And they have also been conceptually linked in various ways: in particular, both racial and imperial thought have drawn heavily upon developmental schemes, in which designated groups have been represented not only as racially distinct but also as occupying different stages of development, with their degree of advancement often being understood to depend on their race and to warrant various forms of hierarchical relations" (McCarthy 2009, 1).

We see this hierarchical structuring present in the arena of nuclear weapons possession and proliferation as well. Emerging from this racist-imperial mind-set, it is possible to identify a deep-seated ideology that infused US nuclear policy in general and US nonproliferation policy in particular during the Cold War and beyond. According to Prof. Shane Maddock, it is manifestly clear that

> The primacy tenets remained consistent from the beginning of the nuclear age—some states could be trusted with nuclear weapons and some could not. *An atomic hierarchy emerged, first in the imagination of US policymakers, then in political reality, that mirrored power inequities in the global system.* This nuclear regime positioned Washington at the top, followed by its NATO allies and, later, Israel, with the post-colonial world consigned to the bottom. *An Indian diplomat rightly labeled the system 'nuclear apartheid.'* (Maddock 2010, 1; italics added)

In following this logic out from theory into practice, we discover that "[t]he end result was a foreign policy that referenced democratic ideals to advance US hegemonic power as a nuclear policy that falsely presumed American moral and political guardianship over atomic technology. Both ultimately undercut the professed US goal of nuclear containment" (Maddock 2010, 2). In this context "[n]ational security and hegemonic goals were used to justify selective proliferation—the controlled spread of US-owned nuclear weapons to trusted allies in order to offset the military strength of the Soviet Union and its Eastern European clients" (Maddock 2010, 3).

In reviewing this legacy it is clear that a number of dynamic elements were at work simultaneously—everything from Ellul's depiction of the role of technique as determinative in a technological civilization to the combined role of the ideologies of racism and imperialism, as outlined by McCarthy. Hence, "The misguided faith in American supremacy in nuclear physics resulted in the wrongheaded policy of selective proliferation in the military and civilian fields. Such an approach served only to speed the acquisition of nuclear weapons by India, South Africa, and Pakistan. When Moscow responded with nuclear aid of its own, China accelerated its nuclear program" (Maddock 2010, 297). The final irony was that "the quest for perpetual hegemony sustained by nuclear weapons proved self-defeating. The Cold War arms race drained the treasuries of both Washington and Moscow, while the former Axis powers, Germany and Japan, refrained from nuclear militarism and thrived economically" (Maddock 2010, 298; Odom, 1998). Detailed studies emerged in the early 1990s, which demonstrated how Cold War technologies had distorted and drained the American economy, displaced workers, and weakened the ability of the United States to compete in world markets (Markusen and Yudken 1992). Further, the costs to the former Soviet Union have been documented by various authors in the early to middle 1990s and have corroborated the idea that "we all lost the Cold War" (Gaddy 1996; Lebow and Stein 1994).

As early as 1986, one author produced an authoritative and documented study that showed how the Reagan administration had falsely claimed that the Soviets held a margin of "superiority" in order to justify higher levels of Pentagon spending throughout the decade of the 1980s. These false claims were exposed in the appendices of the book, which compared not only the number of weapons in opposing arsenals but also the most significant limitations and capabilities of these weapons. This study served to provide a qualitative as well as quantitative assessment of the military balance which exposed the lies, deceit, and bankruptcy (literally and figuratively) of the US military buildup of the 1980s (Gervasi 1986). In addition, the role of the NAM (*as discussed in previous chapters*) refused to embrace either the American or Soviet bloc in the Cold War, thereby weakening the capacity of both the United States and USSR to achieve a long sought-after superpower hegemony. As a result of these choices, the nonproliferation treaty (NPT) "... emerged as an empty pledge not to sin, enforced by sinners. The United States and the Soviet Union refused to recognize that the only basis for a stable and enforceable agreement rested on mutual respect and sacrifice" (Maddock 2010, 298–99).

Moving Beyond Hegemony and Toward Mutual Respect

If mutual respect and self-restraint are to be actualized in practice, both Toda and Ikeda stand for the proposition that what is really needed is a new concept of what constitutes genuine *human security*. What this ultimately means is that human security must be conceptually separated and differentiated from military security. In this regard, the scope and depth of human security is much broader than that of military strategists who only look at a narrowly tailored view of the national interest and/or geopolitical calculations designed to maintain and extend hegemonic practices (Paupp 2009, 110–11). Therefore, the concept of human security "... first mentioned by Ikeda in the

1995 peace proposal can be considered as one way to translate the concept of the fundamental worth of each human being, or inner universalism, into a concrete form" (Urbain 2010, 162). According to Olivier Urbain, "Without denying the functional importance of nations, proponents of human security try to place the emphasis on human beings rather than on states . . . The key point is to develop frameworks allowing for the protection of people . . . frameworks which can include, but also go above and beyond, preoccupations with national security" (Urbain 2010, 162). Both Toda and Ikeda derive their idea for such frameworks from Toda's colleague and mentor Makiguchi. It was Makiguchi in 1903 who called for engagement in humanitarian competition in order "[t]o achieve the goals that would otherwise be pursued by military or political force through the intangible power that naturally exerts a moral influence; in other words, to be respected rather than feared" (Makiguchi [1903] 1983, 399).

Examples of the kind of frameworks for human security that Ikeda envisions range from the formation of an international nuclear disarmament agency, within the United Nations itself, to the establishment of a universal declaration for the renunciation of war, to be adopted by the United Nations. By centralizing the United Nations in this process, Ikeda has embarked upon a more democratic vision for the United Nations that would lead to significant reform and restructuring of the UN itself. To that end, Ikeda has called for the UN to become a place where the interests of people—not just nation-states— are represented in what would be a UN People's Assembly. Ikeda presented this idea in 1997, 2000, and 2001. Finally, he has also urged that there be a fundamental change with respect to the role played by the UN Security Council. The solution he seeks is to have the United Nations engage in a disempowerment of the Security Council in relationship to a more empowered and vibrant United Nations General Assembly (UNGA). Why? According to Urbain, we find that from Ikeda's perspective "[o]ne of the main obstacles preventing the UN from becoming a true parliament of humanity is the veto power of the five permanent members of the UN Security Council. Ikeda has repeatedly criticized this flaw (1991) and in 1992 he mentioned Galtung's proposal for dividing the UNGA into lower and upper houses" (Urbain 2010, 174). In Ikeda's own words, "[W]e must conclude that the current state of the United Nations—with the Security Council in a position of pre-eminence and the General Assembly playing a subordinate role—is undesirable. If we are to enhance the qualities of what *should become a parliament of humanity*, I believe we should do all we can to strengthen and further the power of the General Assembly (Ikeda 1995-PP, 24; italics added).

I have argued that the reason this has not yet happened is because of both the hierarchical ordering of the global system of power relations and the attempt of the United States to maintain its hegemonic position in relationship to its allies (Paupp 2007, 2009). Therefore, by arguing that the UN should be reformed along the lines suggested by Ikeda is to also argue that the current international order of global relations based on US hegemony and international hierarchies must come to an end. From my perspective, such a change in the role of the United Nations and its institutional framework would be a positive move in the tasks of doing a better job than the Security Council has done in monitoring the use of force and reducing wars, halting illegal interventions into the sovereign affairs of other states, and be more helpful in the work of nuclear disarmament programs leading toward the eventual abolition of nuclear weapons (Paupp 2009, 232–39). Hence, the kind of UN reform envisioned by Ikeda is a pivot point for the cause of peace. This is especially significant when one considers the fact that the Security Council's five permanent members—China, France, Russia, the United Kingdom, and the United States—account for nearly 30 percent of the world's population and more than 40 percent of global economic output. In military affairs, their dominance is even more overwhelming. They control more than 26,000 nuclear warheads—which is 99 percent of all those in existence (Bosco 2009, 3).

This nuclear monopoly has created a situation that sanctifies the bomb and the wielders of that force as the ultimate power brokers. Their competition for power and the maintenance of their power has put the welfare of the entire global commons at risk. It has also freeze-framed into place an unequal hierarchy of economic, political, and military predominance among Security Council members that is antithetical to the advance of peace and the control of nuclear weapons. In this regard, it is clear from the vantage point of the excluded majority of people on this planet that *"the privileged powers must exchange their tiered system of inequality for one based on the principles of openness and democratic ideals that have characterized nonproliferation endeavors at their best. Such an approach necessitates that US and Russian policymakers, along with other international forces, dedicate themselves to a truly transnational effort based on mutual and balanced sacrifice both in disarmament and the economic realm.* Rather than tending to individual plots the nuclear powers must return to the global commons; only by shifting from competition to cooperation can proliferation be curtailed" (Maddock 2010, 299; italics added). This distinction between competition versus cooperation is an important one to make. The reason being that "[t]he persistence of a hegemonic version of American ideology and culture, rooted in beliefs about American exceptionalism, race, gender, and technological utopianism, has continued to spawn nonproliferation failures" (Maddock 2010, 300).

This prescription for controlling and eliminating the nuclear weapons threat comports well with Ikeda's concept of humanitarian competition wherein cooperation for the general welfare surpasses selfish preoccupations with a narrowly defined national interest. Also, it is a prescription that focuses on the welfare of the global commons so that all of those who have been excluded from distributional justice and socioeconomic rights can have, at last, access to basic human needs and can begin to actualize their internationally recognized human rights. Whatever sacrifices these five great powers of the UN Security Council eventually make will ultimately remake the global commons by virtue of what will have to be a truly transnational effort. According to John Burroughs, the executive director of the Lawyers' Committee on Nuclear Policy, "The United States should work to develop a pluralist international system managed through norms and regimes and improve and utilize the United Nations and other tools for the prevention of war" (Burroughs 2007, 126). This view is in keeping with the major findings of the Weapons of Mass Destruction Commission of 2006, insofar as ". . . US military and nuclear superiority is not a safe or moral strategy. In particular, absent far-reaching disarmament measures there is no escape from the unprecedented and unspeakable risks posed by nuclear weapons" (Burroughs 2007, 126). This prescription is in concert with Ikeda's 1997 peace proposal in which he "expressed his approval of the 1996 ICJ (International Court of Justice) advisory opinion, siding with those who interpret it as a declaration of illegality; namely that the use or threat of nuclear weapons was against international law. He did so again in 1998, and in 1999 added that the use of nuclear weapons and WMD should fall under the competence of the ICC (International Criminal Court)" (Urbain 2010, 170).

If we are committed to building a new global civilization, then we have to hit the reset button at the UN by embarking upon a fundamental reform of the institutional arrangements at the UN itself in order to end what amounts to a great power monopoly of the UN Security Council, the future of humanity and issues of war and peace (Bjola 2009; Bosco 2009; Lowe et al. 2008a; Malone 2004; Moore and Morrison 2000; Ramcharan 2008; Sriram and Wermester 2003). On this matter, Prof. David Lake has noted, "Potentially subordinate states have intentionally promoted the liberal principle of human equality to de-legitimate direct 'foreign' rule. European empires were long based, even justified, on a norm of racial inequality . . . With the principle of human equality central to political structures in the dominant states, especially with the advent of democratization, and to relations between states themselves, when subordinate peoples began denouncing empire on the ground that it violated the equality of all humans, they were pushing on a door already opened by prior and broadly accepted liberal principles" (Lake 2009, 37).

This liberal principle of human equality has been actively embraced by the majority of the human race since the beginning of the twentieth century. It was first loudly articulated at the end of World War I at the Versailles Peace Conference in 1919 by peoples from every corner of the Third World, who were held in political bondage by the European colonial powers. Their claims to human equality, under the banner of the principle of "sovereignty" echoed the rhetoric of the president of the United States, Woodrow Wilson, who had recently emerged in the international arena as a champion of the right of all peoples to self-determination. Given this history, it is clear that Ikeda's claim that a strengthened and reimagined UNGA is needed in order to offset the imperial and hegemonic control of the reigning permanent members on the UN Security Council constitutes not only a reasonable proposal but also a historical demand that has remained unanswered for almost one hundred years. In this regard, historian Erez Manela has noted of the Versailles Conference of 1919 that "[t]he Western powers in Paris ignored the demands and aspirations of non-Western peoples, but their struggles for sovereignty, equality, and dignity as independent actors in international society continued. The Wilsonian moment marked the beginning of the end of the imperial order in international affairs, precipitating the crisis of empire that followed the war and laying the foundations for the eventual triumph of an international order in which the model of the sovereign, self-determining nation-state spread over the entire globe" (Manela 2007, 225).

Yet while the peoples of the Third World threw off the shackles of European colonialism, they have yet to cast off the chains of socioeconomic bondage and superpower intervention into their sovereign affairs, which has too often been undertaken by American and European powers irrespective of the protections endowed on them by international law and international state practice. Hence, the promise and protections embodied in the UN Charter have yet to be fully realized for the majority of the human race. Central to the realization of this promise is the actualization of Ikeda's institutional reform proposals for the strengthening of a UNGA in order to offset the hegemonic dictates of the leading powers who sit as permanent members in the UN Security Council. Just as the anticolonial movements of 1919 and succeeding years embraced the language of self-determination and human equality, so too this generation needs to embrace antihegemonic movements and construct counterhegemonic alliances to the current monopoly of global power relations (Paupp 2007).

Proposals for amendment of the Security Council have already been many and varied. Prof. Daniel Joyner has noted, "One set of proposals for changing the size and membership was made by the 2004 High-Level Panel Report. *The Panel concluded that a decision to enlarge the Security Council's membership was 'a necessity,' and that it should be guided primarily by principles of increased democratic representation of UN members, particularly from the developing world, and of accountability in decision-making.* Realization of these principles, it is argued, was necessary for the Council to be seen as a legitimate, credible body in taking decisions regarding international uses of force" (Joyner 2009, 343; italics added). In the spirit of Ikeda, the principles enunciated by the panel report centralized the need for greater democratization with regard to obtaining greater representation from the developing world. Such a change would be a practical expression of what I have called inclusionary governance in an international setting of great institutional magnitude (Paupp 2000). Yet Ikeda's formulation transcends the idea of merely tinkering with the Security Council in isolation from the rest of the UN apparatus and institutional structures. In the aftermath of the US invasion and occupation of Iraq the need for such legitimacy regarding the UN Security Council was even more obvious. However, it is significant to note that Ikeda's proposals regarding the need to counterbalance the influence of the Security Council with a strengthened, democratized, and more influential UNGA take the discussion about greater democratic representation in the UN and with respect to UN reform to a higher level.

The main point of this discussion is to consider how best to make international law an actionable force in restraining the use of force for merely geopolitical ends by a hegemonic state and other great powers. In other words, for the sake of developing a just and peaceful international order there needs to come into existence some international legal principle, accompanied by institutional means and mechanisms—developed within the institutional matrix of the United Nations—that can give credence to what I have called the principle of hegemonic state accountability (PHSA) (Paupp 2009, 184–87, 193–205). The actual wording of the PHSA is as follows:

> It shall be the goal of the entire international community to bring about an end to hegemonic practices of any nation or group of nations. In this regard, hegemonic practices shall be defined as any policies or actions undertaken in furtherance of (unlawful) acts that are undertaken for the sole purpose of achieving hegemonic dominance in world affairs. Additionally, *if* the primary purpose of the State's conduct (and behavior) is specifically undertaken in furtherance of a Hegemonic State's national and/or geopolitical agenda to the exclusion of all other standards of international law and it subsequently undertakes actions that may be considered acts of aggression that violate established principles, practices, and obligations governing State action in world affairs, *then* the Hegemonic State shall be deemed to have engaged in unlawful acts against the international community and must be held accountable for those acts under the applicable standards of what constitutes the boundaries of acceptable State conduct in international law. (Paupp 2009, 184; italics in the original)

At the start of the twenty-first century, the challenge presented to the world by the unconstrained forces of American hegemony in reference to the demands of international law has been summed up well by Prof. Richard Falk, who notes the following:

> This focus on American behavior obscures the larger framework of argument. It has become a requirement of constitutional democracy

in the twenty-first century for a government's foreign policy, as well as its domestic behavior, to be conducted in a manner consistent with the discipline of international law. In a globalizing world the extension of law to international activity almost always serves the national interest of even powerful states. The constraints of international law keep the leaders of democratic states from undertaking dangerous and costly geopolitical ventures that would not be supported by an informed citizenry. The refusal of one state, particularly if it is seen to be a leading state, to abide by international law creates a precedent that gives other states a reciprocal right, as well as political encouragement, to violate their legal obligations. (Falk 2008c, 22–23)

Therefore, it should be no great surprise that the nation-state of Iran, itself a signatory to the NPT, embarked upon the development of a nuclear weapons program in the immediate aftermath of the illegal US invasion and occupation of Iraq (Hymans 2006; Joyner 2009; Smith 2006; Solingen 2007). On this very point, Fidel Castro has argued, "*No one* should have the right to produce nuclear weapons, much less the privileged right demanded by imperialism to impose its hegemonic domination [on the world] and take away the Third World's natural resources and raw materials . . . More and more nations have less and less to fear, more and more nations will rebel, and the empire will not be able to uphold the disgraceful and despicable system it is now upholding. One day Salvador Allende talked about 'sooner or later'—well, I think that sooner or later that empire will no longer be lord and master of the world" (Castro 2007, 395; italics in the original).

Similarly, it is important to recognize that, ". . . as Robert Gilpin has noted, 'no state has ever completely controlled an international system,' and thus hegemony is a relative, not an absolute concept . . . Implicit in Gilpin's observation that hegemony is a relative concept is a subtle, but important, point: although the United States is an extra-regional hegemon, it is not what students of international politics once called a 'universal empire.' The United States is not omnipotent" (Layne 2006, 4). In much the same vein of interpretation, Prof. David Lake admonishes us to realize that

Much as some might wish it otherwise, legitimacy originates in the opinion of subordinates. Authority is conferred upon the ruler by the ruled. Rulers—dominant states included—are not free to define for themselves what actions are or are not legitimate. Regardless of its extraordinary coercive capabilities, which seduced many into thinking the country could and should shape its destiny and the world's single-handedly, the United States must learn to listen and then act within the bounds of what is acceptable to its subordinates. Otherwise, it will nonetheless be defined by others as an imperialist power, and its authority . . . will be rejected by those over whom it would rule. (Lake 2009, 188–89)

The problem that the world currently confronts is one where the elites of the American primacy coalition are living in an illusion about their hegemonic project insofar as they have succumbed to a rejection of the traditional realist viewpoint of international relations and instead engaged in their own folly and unilateralist ambitions as the final arbiter and determinant of US foreign policy (Hixson 2008; Scoblic 2008). In this respect, Prof. Christopher Layne has noted, "[A] hegemonic United States would be tempted to equate its own preferences with justice, and be just as likely as other powerful states to use its power unwisely . . . For the present, at least, there is no counterbalancing power that can compel the United States to forsake its pursuit of hegemony. Thus, the United States must follow a policy of self-restraint if it is to avoid hegemony's adverse geopolitical and domestic consequences" (Layne 2006, 204). Yet as Falk has noted, "The bad American example should not confuse political leaders around the world. It will be beneficial for the peoples of the world to strengthen the global rule of law, and to encourage a pedagogy of peace and security that emphasizes that respect for international law is an indispensable (element) to achieving a peaceful, equitable, and sustainable world order. . . . The world is now far too morally sensitive and politically integrated to ignore or tolerate the commission of Crimes Against Peace or Crimes Against Humanity" (Falk 2008c, 23). Put another way, senior lecturer in politics at the University of New South Wales, Brett Bowden, has observed, "The supposedly exclusively Western idea of democracy is just one key example of how ideas or values that are thought to originate in or 'belong' to one particular civilization or people are in fact shared across civilizations . . . In essence, John Donne's phrase, 'No man is an island, entire of itself,' applies equally as much to any civilization—Western civilization and civilizations of the East included" (Bowden 2009, 223–24). Ikeda would agree with this assessment. Further, it is an assessment that serves to resuscitate the Third World's cries for human equality, human dignity, and self-determination in a new century.

Since 1919, the Third World has represented an idea—a project—to recreate the world for the sake of human dignity, cultural dignity, and the construction of democratic institutions (Lake and Reynolds 2008). To that end, Ikeda's idea about the global need to reclaim the United Nations through an empowered UNGA represents a structurally creative initiative that is capable of articulating and sustaining a genuinely humane, inclusive, and cosmopolitan vision for the future. Hence, Ikeda's concept is central to the remaking of world order so that it becomes a world order that is more a reflection of the needs and aspirations of all humanity and not a select few. In his *People's History of the Third World*, Prof. Vijay Prashad has persuasively argued, "The limitations of IMF-driven globalization and . . . traditionalism provoke mass movements across the planet. The battles for land rights and water rights, for cultural dignity and economic parity, for women's rights and indigenous rights, for the construction of democratic institutions and responsive states—these are legion in every country, on every continent. It is from these many creative initiatives that a genuine agenda for the future will arise" (Prashad 2007a, 281). In this effort, Ikeda's proposal for an empowered UNGA is central to the realization of these creative initiatives. Hence, a genuinely broad-based, inclusive, and democratic global order can eventually emerge from our global civil society. It will not be the product of guns, bullets, or weapons of mass destruction. Rather, it will be a peaceful global civilization that emerges from the civilized and compassionate efforts of all those who seek to promote human dignity and human equality as the central values for a peaceful global order.

The Legacy of JFK and the Twenty-First Century

Looking back on the early 1960s is instructive and vital for all global citizens at the beginning of the twenty-first century. President Kennedy's resolution of the Cuban missile crisis of 1962 was a turning point in his presidency and in the course of the Cold War. As we have demonstrated through a review of the historical record, Kennedy and his counterpart, Nikita Khrushchev, survived the crisis by transforming their consciousness and perceptions about how two superpowers should and would conduct their great power competition. Their resolution of this question provided the definitive answer—the need to move toward nuclear weapons abolition. To that end, they jointly embarked upon a path leading to détente, the signing of a limited test-ban treaty, and the beginning of efforts to deal with the need to establish nuclear weapons–free zones as well as efforts to strengthen the nuclear nonproliferation regime.

How did such a radical change in consciousness take place? One explanation has been offered by Irving Janis, a professor of psychology at Yale University in the 1980s. When people come together to solve a problem or resolve an issue that is in dispute, there is a lot of "peer pressure" to arrive at the same conclusion—based on previous experience and assumptions. In other words, rather than objectively dealing with the new situation as it really is, there is the temptation to suspend critical thought and reflexively adopt the more familiar paradigm of the past. Janis developed the term *Groupthink* to describe a process that takes over when decision-making bodies agree for the sake of agreeing and abandon their critical judgment. He recounts how the decision-making process that led to the Bay of Pigs disaster in 1961 was *not* replicated by the same decision-makers in 1962 during the Cuban missile crisis. Janis recounts how Kennedy's private executive committee's deliberations during the 1962 Cuban missile crisis are *"at the opposite pole from the symptoms of groupthink"* (Janis 1983, 157; italics added).

Janis notes the following:

> President Kennedy and others in the committee were frequently frustrated and sometimes exasperated by the group's failure to

arrive at a stable consensus as the members vigilantly appraised and reappraised the risks. They had to undergo the unpleasant experience of hearing their pet ideas critically pulled to pieces, and the acute distress of being reminded that their collective judgments could be wrong . . . The key members of the Executive Committee who so successfully avoided succumbing to groupthink tendencies . . . were the same individuals who had formed the nucleus of the group that eighteen months earlier had shown all the symptoms of groupthink when planning the Bay of Pigs invasion. The members of the Executive Committee who had not been involved in the Bay of Pigs decision differed little in intelligence, experience, outlook, and personality from those they replaced. This implies that groupthink is not simply a matter of a fixed attribute of a group, nor is it a question of the types of personalities that happen to be dominant within the group."

Given this analysis, Janis concludes by noting, "If the same committee members who groupthink tendencies in making a decision at one time and not at another, the determining factors must lie in the circumstances of their deliberations, not in the fixed attributes of the individuals who make up the group. The determining factors therefore seem to be variables that can be changed and lead to new and more productive norms" (Janis 1983, 157–58).

Today, at the dawn of the twenty-first century, humankind needs to recognize that there are variables in the current "nuclear equation" that need to be changed so that we may move toward an embrace of new and more productive norms. Ikeda has suggested, "We need those who have heretofore advocated nuclear deterrence to now earnestly consider the risk of continuing with the current non-proliferation regime, with all its weaknesses, versus the risk of putting in place a non-nuclear system. Clearly, without effort toward nuclear abolition, the current non-proliferation regime will sooner or later reach an impasse" (Ikeda and Krieger 2002, 81). In light of the current dispute between Iran and the United States, it may be that such an impasse has already been reached. The point is that old, worn-out, and unworkable dogmas and doctrines need to be jettisoned so that humankind can reach a new historical plateau that is more hospitable to the realization of peace between peoples and nations.

In all these endeavors, President Kennedy provides us with an example of a leader who had chosen to take the first step away from the decades-long American commitment to the dogmas of Cold War confrontation and "first use". Even more fundamentally, he made a radical left turn in terms of US policy. He did not uncritically accept the status quo. Instead, Kennedy renounced these confrontational and provocative policies because he had decided that the cost of keeping and continuing US hegemony under the auspices of a militarized US global empire was counterproductive. From

Kennedy's perspective, the prospect of an ever-extending *Pax America—* *"imposed on the world by American weapons of war"*—signaled a failure of reason and embraced insanity in the nuclear age. In this sense, Kennedy had articulated what I have called the principle of hegemonic state accountability (Paupp 2009). Kennedy recognized the actual criminality of a superpower's military force threatening the very existence of all humankind.

Both Kennedy and Khrushchev, therefore, had concluded that the old path was not only dangerous but also counterproductive to a lessening of Cold War tensions, to the welfare of the people of the entire world, and to the long-term prospects for peace on earth. Hence, we discover in his June 1963 speech at American University that Kennedy both asked and answered the most fundamental question of the Cold War period:

> What kind of peace do I mean? What kind of peace do we seek? Not a *Pax Americana* enforced on the world by American weapons of war. Not the peace of the grave or the security of the slave. I am talking about genuine peace, the kind of peace that makes life on earth worth living, the kind that enables men and nations to grow and to hope and to build a better life for their children—not merely peace for Americans but peace for all men and women—not merely peace in our time but peace for all time. (Kennedy 1964; italics added)

Just two years after Kennedy made this pronouncement, his former deputy director of political research in the US Arms Control and Disarmament Agency, Richard Barnet, wrote, "Disarmament has seemed so fundamentally at odds with the hard facts of a divided world that it is widely regarded as a utopian solution. The question is, however, whether disarmament is any more utopian a means of preserving peace than the mechanism of deterrence on which we have put such great reliance." Barnet concluded by noting that "[t]he success of each appears to require a basic change in existing patterns of behavior" (Barnet 1965, 55). In other words, the Cold War doctrine of deterrence as a means to maintain the peace was just as *utopian* as calls for disarmament. Therefore, as rational and reasonable human beings, it is proper and necessary for us to question the assumptions upon which we act, formulate our worldview, and pursue our policies. At that moment when we begin to question our assumptions and to seriously interrogate the validity of our doctrines, it is at that point that we can start to recognize errors contained in our most closely held beliefs, policies, and dogmas. This is what happened to both Kennedy and Khrushchev during and after the Cuban missile crisis.

By 1965, it had become clear that Kennedy's and Khrushchev's newly chosen path toward détente signaled a change that was not only clear evidence of a radical change of consciousness within individual leaders, but also represented a radical change in Great Power behaviors. Such a change in behavior and policies, linked to values that actively served the promotion of peaceful pursuits between the superpowers, would eventually mean a reduction in profits and power for the men who ran the military–industrial complex. It had become clear that the transformative embrace of policies dedicated to peace served to launch both Kennedy and Khrushchev on a new trajectory. Ultimately, it was nothing less than a new historical trajectory for social change at both the national and international levels. As an advocate for peace, Kennedy had become a real threat to the global military–industrial complex. In this context, it is no mystery as to why certain governmental and financial elites, as well as military industrialists, wanted him removed from office—even if that involved the president's assassination. After all, the prospect of a *warless world* would leave the CIA, the Pentagon, military industrialists, and weapons dealers with less and less business (Groden and Livingstone 1989; Hepburn 2002; Joseph 1981; Markusen et al. 1991; Oglesby 1976; Prouty 1992; Sale 1976). In this arena, Kennedy was moving very rapidly toward achieving a new international consensus for peace. He had become a dangerous man to the business of war-making and to the war-makers, those military-industrialists whose business and livelihoods depended on their ability to thrive as "merchants of death."

In 1966, Richard Falk expanded upon Barnet's arguments by addressing the idea of a warless world. As utopian as a warless world may seem to some, Falk observed that "the task of eliminating force includes, but exceeds, the problems of controlling processes of national coercion; it is essential to find alternative ways to legislate changes in national communities, even in the face of resistance to these changes by domestic governmental elites. Partly this broadening of the goal of a *warless world* to encompass institutions of social change responds to the need for securing the peace in a disarming world . . . The job of social change is to devise alternatives to force, especially when social objectives accord sufficiently with values that are widely shared to allow us to assert *the presence of an international consensus*" (Falk 1966, 173; italics added). In other words, by linking the values associated with the achievement of world peace to clearly defined social objectives we then have the opportunity to realize genuine social change on a global basis. In this regard, Ikeda's idea of a peaceful global civilization becomes more attainable as the processes of social change—and values reflective of peaceful pursuits—allow human beings to embrace what can be shared by all—an international consensus. Such a consensus is accelerated when people move out of *Groupthink*.

Such a consensus was emerging by the close of 1963. Kennedy had already set a new course. In fact, Kennedy clearly and unequivocally stated as much at the start of his American University speech, on June 10, 1963:

> I speak of peace because of the new face of war. Total war makes no sense in an age when great powers can maintain large and relatively

invulnerable nuclear forces and refuse to surrender without resort to those forces. It makes no sense in an age when a single nuclear weapon contains almost ten times the explosive force delivered by all of the allied air forces in the Second World War. It makes no sense in an age when the deadly poisons produced by a nuclear exchange would be carried by wind and water and soil and seed to the far corners of the globe and to generations yet unborn . . . I speak of peace, therefore, as the necessary rational end of rational men. I realize that the pursuit of peace is not as dramatic as the pursuit of war—but there is no more urgent task. (Kennedy 1964)

Notes

1. Ikeda and Kennedy never met in person, but a meeting had been planned for February 1963 at Kennedy's request. The meeting had to be cancelled due to pressure by an influential politician from Japan's ruling party. Details of this episode can be found in novelized form in *The New Human Revolution*, Vol. 7, pp. 85–87, 174, 196, 287–89, 292–96 (Ikeda 2001–7).
2. Liddell Hart, Deterrent or Defense, 247–48. Kennedy's review of Liddell Hart appeared in *Saturday Evening Post*, September 3, 1960. Quoted in Arthur Schlesinger, *A Thousand Days: John F. Kennedy in the White House*, New York: Fawcett, 1965, p. 110.
3. The OSS is the Office of Strategic Services.

4

The Power of Self-Transformation as the Beginning of Internal and External Liberation: The Nexus of Buddhism, Liberation Theology, and Law

"Whereas science begins with a reformation of the external world, Buddhism starts with reforming the inner human world—what we call the human revolution[1]—*and moves on to society. If we want to halt the excesses of science and technology and save humanity from the crises confronting contemporary civilization we can no longer merely treat the symptoms."*

—Daisaku Ikeda
(Ikeda 2001a, 107)

"The life and preaching of Jesus postulate the unceasing search for a new kind of man in a qualitatively different society."

—Gustavo Gutierrez
(Gutierrez 1973, 231)

"[T]he emancipation of the senses must accompany the emancipation of consciousness, thus involving the totality *of human existence. The individuals themselves must change in their very instincts and sensibilities if they are to build, in association, a* qualitatively different society."

—Herbert Marcuse
(Marcuse 1972, 74)

"The Third World ought not to be content to define itself in terms of values which have preceded it. On the contrary, the underdeveloped countries ought to do their utmost to find their own particular values and methods and a style which shall be particular to them."

—Frantz Fanon
(Fanon 1968, 99)

*"Each time a man stands up for an ideal, or acts to improve the lot
of others, or strikes out against injustice, he sends forth a tiny ripple
of hope, and crossing each other from a million different centers of
energy and daring those ripples build a current that can sweep down
the mightiest walls of oppression and resistance."*

—Robert F. Kennedy
(Kennedy 1993, 244)

The power of self-transformation is the power to remake individuals and
to transform the world. This power has been recognized since the time of
Aristotle, the founder of virtue ethics. In the Aristotelian formulation of virtue
ethics, we discover that human qualities such as justice, charity, and generosity
are dispositions to act in ways that benefit both the person possessing them
and that person's society (Timmons 2002). This relationship constitutes the
dialectic of what Ikeda has called the *human revolution*. Contained within
virtue ethics are the ingredients that transform the individual person, while
simultaneously providing a new historical trajectory for creating a more
peaceful global civilization. According to Urbain, we find, "Virtue ethics
considers character as the main driving force in attempts to lead the good
life. This type of ethics recommends the development of human qualities
such as *arête* (excellence), *phronesis* (wisdom) and *eudaimonia* (flourishing). I
believe that there are strong links between Aristotle's virtue ethics and Ikeda's
emphasis on inner transformation and human revolution" (Urbain 2010, 101).
In Ikeda's own words, there is the following observation: "What can bring
about change in character? In Buddhist practice, cultivating the awareness
of one's 'life-condition' and making a diligent, constant effort to elevate that
condition constitute self-mastery, the practice of '*human revolution*'" (Ikeda
2001a, 33; italics added). The ramifications of this insight are the subject of
this chapter. Hence, this chapter will address the interconnections between
the human revolution and inner transformation, altruistic living and humanitarian competition, the relationship that exists between self-transformation
and societal transformation, as well as the way in which freedom from greed,
illusion, and selfishness opens the gateway to the possibility of achieving a
peaceful global civilization.

The recognition of the need for the practice of human revolution points toward that nexus where persons undergoing such a change not only transform
themselves but transform the very society of which they are a part. In this
manner, a change in focus and priorities—at the personal and global levels—is
predicated upon the efforts of individuals dedicated to changing themselves in
correspondence with values and virtues that bring into harmony the internal
and external worlds. The historical record and current reality of global crisis
are manifest all around us. The continuing presence of war throughout the
world is not only a product of the search for profit-maximization by weapons

dealers and the desire of those in power to hold on to it at any cost but also a product of the political and sociobiological reality. The foundations for this current state of affairs are directly connected to antiquated modes of thought and conduct that have produced and reproduced a paradigm from which most people have yet to free themselves from. Therefore, if we are to move beyond global crisis, it is imperative to recognize its roots.

Insofar as humanity is too often guided by following the repetitive norms and practices from the past, Ikeda and a few of his contemporaries have identified the source of this global crisis as largely arising from a preoccupation with past modes of thought that are grounded in illusion and not in reality, the product of greed rather than generosity, an expression of selfish and egotistical pursuits that suppress the countless possibilities for a peaceful global civilization that is associated with the principles of altruistic living. The current global crisis continues to mutate exponentially because too many individuals have proceeded to live their lives through the narrow prism of an uncritical adoption of past practices and assumptions. In this sense, our current era reflects a critical lack of humanity that is not only identifiable in lives devoid of any real spiritual content but chained to warped thought patterns supportive of racism, militarism, and social injustice. At bottom, however, all of these difficulties may be traced back to serious defects in the thought processes and conceptual universe of individuals. Hence, if humanity is to ever overcome this ceaseless cycle of violence, affronts to human dignity, and the collapse of the values and the compromised legalities that structure our global human rights regime, then the starting place must be within individual frameworks of meaning, of closely held concepts, and our overarching worldview. In this critical regard, in his last published book, Martin Luther King asserted, "We must rapidly begin the shift from a 'thing'-oriented society to a 'person'-oriented society. When machines and computers, profit motives and property rights are considered more important than people, the giant triplets of racism, materialism and militarism are incapable of being conquered. A civilization can flounder as readily in the face of moral and spiritual bankruptcy as it can through financial bankruptcy" (King 1968, 216).

A "thing-oriented society" that glorifies money, selfish ambition, and currency above all else eventually turns people into little more than abstract concepts. Under these circumstances, when people are viewed as mere abstractions, they become expendable. So when the United States admits that it has allowed over forty million of its citizens to go without healthcare, then that fact becomes more of a statistic than a moral call to action to right a wrong. When predatory financial lenders devastate the nation's real estate market and Wall Street firms falsify the true value of mortgages and repackage bad loans, then we discover that the "powers-that-be" want to retain the deregulated market environment of moral ambivalence in which they operated so that they can proceed with "business as usual." What the "subprime" mortgage crisis has revealed is that ". . . little sense can be made of the crisis without a clear understanding of its roots in the domestic dimensions of American empire, i.e., of the networks of financialized power through which the working class and the middle class have been subjected to a regime of debt and discipline" (Panitch et al. 2009b, 263).

Given the human dimensions of the financial crisis for both the working and middle classes of the US—not to mention the world as a whole—it has been argued that "[i]t would be a tragedy if a far more ambitious goal than making financial capital more prudent did not now come back on the agenda. What is needed is to go beyond this so as to probe—intellectually and culturally as well as politically—whether this crisis could provide a historic opening for the renewal of the kind of radical perspective that advances a systemic alternative to global capitalism" (Panitch et al. 2009b, 292). What has also been exposed in this crisis is the inadequacy of democratic institutions to tackle these economic challenges and the threat they pose to the maintenance of a free society (Posner 2010). Hence, what is at stake is the question of not only how to create a prosperous economy but how to create a moral society for the future (Stiglitz 2010). Part of the answer to the structural crisis is to reconfigure the megabanks from being "too big to fail" to a situation where they are "small enough to fail" (Johnson and Kwak 2010). Yet beyond the structural crisis is the unresolved moral crisis of this system that has caught up millions of people in "the spirit of abstraction." When the spirit of abstraction begins to become predominant in a society, it is at that point that people in key decision-making roles often try to justify the fact that they are devoid of their humanity, or simply want to continue on the same path by working without remorse or reflection at the practice of divesting all concerned of their humanity through greed, exploitation, and theft. This is the situation of what Ikeda has termed *the runaway avarice of present-day capitalism* (Ikeda 2009-PP, 1; italics added).

In Ikeda's view, "as soon as people are transformed into abstract concepts, they can be treated as valueless and inferior, even as something harmful to be eradicated. People, in the fullness of their humanity, no longer exist" (Ikeda 2009-PP, 3). That is a problem that even affects human rights discourse. As we will discover in this chapter, there has been a sharp bifurcation in human rights laws, covenants, and policies at both the national and international levels since 1945. This is directly related to the West's purposeful decision to separate the enforcement of political and civil rights protections from the achievement and realization of socioeconomic rights. As a result, both in the West and throughout the global South, people have been reduced to an abstraction (to use Ikeda's phrase) because they have been relegated to a position of lesser concern than that of economic profit and the superiority of the marketplace. Human rights and human dignity have been left exposed to the vagaries of politics and the strength of social movements and nonviolent action dedicated to the realization of people's socioeconomic rights and well-being. Given the nature of this ongoing struggle, Makiguchi's concept of humanitarian competition, taken up by Ikeda, now takes on a new significance, insofar as the realization of human dignity, rights, and well-being in the twenty-first century is predicated upon the efforts of all people to move beyond the limiting and limited legal concepts of "sovereignty," the "freedom of the market," and "hegemonic domination" to embrace new forms of accountability to human beings as human beings. Yet to accept, embrace, and act on the realization and the achievement of these rights will necessitate a change in consciousness, culture, and a refocusing of priorities on more humane and inclusive values. Hence, the need for what Ikeda calls the human revolution becomes transparent. It is to this concept that we now turn.

Discovering "the Human Revolution" in the *"Fierce Urgency of Now"*

In 1968, Dr. Martin Luther King spoke of the *fierce urgency of now*. King purposefully invoked this language as a way of identifying the immediate need to make a critical decision before time runs out, before the entrenched patterns of procrastination deny people a chance to change course, as well as to change their own character. A little over a century earlier, Henry David Thoreau voiced his criticisms of modern culture in an essay entitled "Life without Principle" (1861). He says this:

> Let us consider the way in which we spend our lives. This world is a place of business. What an infinite bustle! I am awakened almost every night by the panting of the locomotive. It interrupts my dreams. There is no Sabbath ... Do we call this the land of the free? What is it to be free from King George and continue to be slaves to the King of Prejudice? What is it to be born free and not to live free? What is the value of any political freedom, but as a means to moral freedom? (Thoreau 1947, 631–55)

The need for the practice of Ikeda's concept of human revolution was equally apparent in 1897, when one of the most penetrating diagnoses of capitalist culture in the nineteenth century was made by the sociologist E. Durkheim, who was neither a political nor a religious radical: According to Eric Fromm, Durkheim "... states that in modern industrial society the individual and the group have ceased to function satisfactorily; they live in a condition of 'anomie', that is, a lack of meaningful and structuralized social life; that the individual follows more and more '*a restless movement, a planless self-development, an aim of living which has no criterion of value in which happiness lies always in the future, and never in any present achievement*.' The ambition of man, having the whole world for his customer, becomes unlimited, and he is filled with disgust, with the *'futility of endless pursuit'*" (Fromm 1965, 191; italics added). In this example—as well as many other

117

examples from which Fromm cites—the common denominator that emerges from this critique of the effects of capitalism on the human personality is *the phenomenon of alienation*. The reality of internal alienation points toward the corresponding reality of external alienation. Fromm writes thus:

> By alienation is meant a mode of experience in which the person experiences himself as an alien. He has become, one might say, estranged from himself. He does not experience himself as the center of his world, as the creator of his own acts—but his acts and their consequences have become his masters, whom he obeys, or whom he may even worship. *The alienated person is out of touch with himself as he is out of touch with any other person.* He, like the others, is experienced as things are experienced; with the senses and with common sense, but at the same time without being related to oneself and to the world outside productively. (Fromm 1965, 111; italics added)

In order to begin the process of reversing the negative effects of this alienation, Ikeda refers to an axiom in the Buddhist scriptures that can be formulated as follows: *"You are your own master."* To realize this liberating truth, Ikeda notes that it is necessary for us

> . . . to live independently, true to ourselves and unswayed by others. The *'self'* referred to here is not the Buddhist *'lesser self,'* caught up in the snares of egoism. Rather, it is the *'greater self,'* fused with the life of the universe through which cause and effect intertwine over the infinite reaches of space and time. The greater, cosmic self is related to the unifying and integrating *'self'* that Jung perceived in the depths of the ego. It is also similar to Ralph Waldo Emerson's 'universal beauty, to which every part and particle is equally related; the eternal One.' *I am firmly convinced that a large-scale awakening to the greater self will lead to a world of creative coexistence in the coming century. . . . The greater self of Mahayana Buddhism is another way of expressing the expansiveness of character that embraces the sufferings of all people as one's own.* (Ikeda 2001a, 35–36; italics added)

These statements by Ikeda serve to show the profound relevance of his call for the inner transformation of the individual within the human revolution.

In a similar fashion, Martin Luther King identified the need for individuals to engage their efforts and energies toward inner transformation. King observed the following:

> *Every man lives in two realms, the internal and the external. The internal is that realm of spiritual ends expressed in art, literature,*

morals and religion. The external is that complex of devices, techniques, mechanisms and instrumentalities by means of which we live. *Our problem today is that we have allowed the internal to become lost in the external. We have allowed the means by which we live to outdistance the ends for which we live. So much of modern life can be summarized in that suggestive phrase of Thoreau: 'Improved means to an unimproved end.'* This is the serious predicament, the deep and haunting problem, confronting modern man. Enlarged material powers spell enlarged peril if there is not proportionate growth of the soul. When the external of man's nature subjugates the internal, dark storm clouds begin to form. (King 1968, 200; italics added)

Given the sweeping nature of King's radical diagnosis of what ailed American society, it is clear why his message upset and threatened the US elite and the bulk of the American establishment. Like the liberation theologians of Latin America, Martin King had placed himself in opposition to what amounted to a colonial establishment that sought to colonize people's minds, money, and memory. It is for this reason that "[f]rom the moment that he formally opposed the [Vietnam] war, followed by his commitment to the Poor People's Campaign, Martin King began a fateful struggle against another type of colonial domination and another colonialist master. This enemy would emerge as the most powerful force ever to span the globe. During the last year of his life, he became locked in a deadly struggle with the behemoth of transnational corporate colonialism and the awesome power of its steward state, the United States of America" (Pepper 2003, 179). In light of these harsh realities, King argued that a new man, a new personality had to be brought forth who would embrace the brotherhood and sisterhood of all. He called on people to be, as he put it, "maladjusted." Because of certain values and practices of the existing order, especially the growth of militarism, he was proud to be *maladjusted* and "he called upon all people to become *maladjusted*. He said he refused to adjust to a socioeconomic order which deprived the many of necessities and allowed luxuries for the few. *He refused to adjust to the madness of militarism and the self-perpetuating use of violence in the development of the American empire.* He refused to adjust to an economic system in which people had become objects—things used in the pursuit of riches by others and disposed of when no longer needed" (Pepper 2003, 172; italics added).

Both Ikeda and King speak of the wrongness of reducing people to objects—mere things within a capitalist system of greed, exploitation, and selfishness. On the world stage, both Ikeda and King speak of the need for realizing *"creative coexistence"* (*as well as nonviolent coexistence*). Additionally, both Ikeda and King call for the realization of a greater self that will be capable of embracing the suffering of all people as one's own. King stated thus:

119

We can no longer afford to worship the God of hate or bow before the altar of retaliation. The oceans of history are made turbulent by the ever-rising tides of hate. History is cluttered with the wreckage of nations and individuals who pursued this self-defeating path of hate. . . . We are now faced with the fact that tomorrow is today. *We are confronted with the fierce urgency of now . . . We still have a choice today: nonviolent coexistence or violent co-annihilation. This may well be mankind's last change to choose between chaos and community.* (King 1968, 222–23; italics added)

Ikeda chooses to seek the realization of community through a transformative process that starts with taking command of our own lives, accepting personal responsibility for our lives and conduct, so that we do not fall into the egotistic trap of seeking to impose our selfish will on others. Hence, Ikeda states, *"If we are in sufficient command of ourselves we will not feel compelled to impose our own values upon others nor to trample upon the customs and values they hold dear"* (Ikeda 2001a, 37; italics added).

In this regard, Ikeda shares much in common with Enlightenment thinkers such as Immanuel Kant, who attacked European imperialism as manifestly unjust. Kant's cosmopolitan worldview collided with imperialist thought, which gave no attention to matters of human agency, human rights, human suffering, or human freedom. It was for this reason that "Kant criticized European imperialism and defended non-European peoples against what he viewed as the destructive powers that were being exercised by imperial trading companies, explorers, and other imperial travelers whose violent conquests of foreign lands and peoples transgressed the fundamental right of hospitality shared by all humans. Cosmopolitan right emerges as fullest expression of what Kant identifies as the one 'innate right of humanity,' the right to a distinctively human freedom (cultural agency) that all humans possess by virtue of their humanity" (Muthu 2003, 172–73).

In reviewing Kant's philosophy, we discover that "[i]n discussing ends that are also duties, Kant lists two kinds: promoting one's own (not others') perfection . . . and the happiness of others, for instance, by improving social and political conditions or through individual acts of kindness and beneficence" (Muthu 2003, 176). Further, just as Ikeda rejects the temptation to impose our own values upon others, so too, ". . . when applied to groups of humans, Kant's argument against attempting to perfect others and the wide latitude that he recommends individuals should have to determine their own lives will inform some of his anti-imperialist arguments" (Muthu 2003, 177). In the final analysis, Kant argues that what makes us incommensurably different relates fundamentally to what defines us as human.

Given this analysis, it becomes clear that Kant sees a correspondence between individuality and diversity. These realities are not mutually exclusive.

Rather, it is by seeing diversity and plurality as the flipside of individuality that one is allowed to discover a relationship that is highly complementary. If the very fact of difference is what defines us as being human, then the very fact of our plurality should point us toward the recognition of our shared humanity. To fail to see this reality accounts to explain why "the defenders of empire, in their quest to justify the profitable destruction and conquest of foreign societies," wind up actively denying human plurality, for if the defenders of empire were to admit that the fact of human plurality is what defines us as human, then they would be forced to concede this as evidence of our shared humanity (Muthu 2003, 209). Such an admission would undermine the imperial project. The practice of empire and its ideological justifications would eventually be left without ideological support. This is exactly what would happen by the middle of the twentieth century with the success of the anticolonial and antiapartheid struggles that liberated millions from oppressive conditions (Falk 2009, 3).

Discovering the *"True Self"* in Buddhism and Liberation Theology

Erich Fromm, the great humanist, writer, and scholar, like Ikeda, acknowledged the limitations of seeking change in just one arena of human endeavor. Every aspect of human life and effort should be constructed in accordance with the full spectrum of the needs of the person. Fromm argues that for change to be effective, it needs to be nothing less than comprehensive, holistic, and all-encompassing in scope: "No change must be brought about by force—it must be a simultaneous one in the economic, political and cultural spheres. Changes restricted to *one* sphere are destructive of every change. . . . Man can protect himself from the consequences of his own madness only by creating a sane society which conforms with the needs of man, needs which are rooted in the very conditions of his existence" (Fromm 1965, 314; italics in original). The nature of the "sane society" is predicated upon the individual person's ability to establish a sense of unity within themselves insofar as "[t] he existential split in man would be unbearable could he not establish a sense of unity within himself and with the natural and human world outside. But there are many ways of reestablishing unity" (Fromm 1975, 262). In Fromm's view, *"[g]reat as the differences are between Taoism, Buddhism, prophetic Judaism, and the Christianity of the Gospels, these religions had one common goal: to arrive at the experience of oneness, not by regressing to animal existence, but by becoming fully human—oneness within man, oneness between man and nature, and oneness between man and other men"* (Fromm 1975, 263; italics added).

For Ikeda, the experience of oneness at all of these levels must begin with the recognition of the need for self-control in conjunction with respect for all humanity. Ikeda notes the following:

In the Lotus Sutra, there is a bodhisattva named *Never Disparaging*. This bodhisattva believed that since all humans possess the Buddha nature, none could be despised; that all life, all humanity, had to be accorded the highest respect. . . . In the Lotus Sutra, the story of the Bodhisattva *Never Disparaging* is a parable of the ultimate in Buddhist discipline. It is also akin to Plato's contention that we must control our 'rational part' and illustrates the importance of self-control as a universal virtue of all humankind and the primary requirement for a world without war. (Ikeda 2001a, 37–38; italics added)

In other words, change in ourselves leads to change in the external world due to the comprehensive nature of the approach to change that is endorsed by both Fromm and Ikeda.

A world without war is predicated upon individuals realizing how to control their "rational part" so that self-control results. Self-control makes this journey toward peace possible insofar as such self-control frees the rational part of their mind to become detached from that which is an illusion, of nonimportance, and the source of conflict. In Ikeda's own words, we discover that *"[d]etachment from the transient and illusory is one mark of character, which is another name for human wholeness or completeness. The principles to which I have been referring are not just abstractions but something that must be sought inwardly by people striving to grow in character"* (Ikeda 2001a, 32; italics added).

Ikeda is making the point that as individuals grow in character they embark upon a path leading toward wholeness and completeness which, in turn, allows them to connect with other people and the rest of the world in a new way. Their detachment from illusory ways of perceiving themselves and their world opens up spiritual and intellectual channels for being attached to the world of truth, mutual interdependence, and a sense of interrelatedness with others and nature. This new way of making a connection with other people invariably—and almost automatically—allows for the connection to be made with a newer world. That is because our newfound ability to see this newer connection allows us to see that this newer world embodies truths and realities that are permanent, enduring, and meaningful. Hence, we discover that the remade consciousness of individuals who have undergone character transformation through the processes of the human revolution are the ones who make possible the recognition and reality of a world that is now self-conscious about the reality of our mutual interdependence. A spiritual richness informs the perceptions of those who have undertaken the path toward personal wholeness and completeness. This same spiritual richness constitutes the foundation for a qualitatively newer world that is guided by the fundamental premise: *"Nothing exists in isolation.* Modern cosmology, the results of ecological study, and also the Buddhist doctrine of dependent origination all teach us this. We live in a system of interrelations with other humans, nations, societies and the natural world. Human spiritual poverty spews forth in war and environmental pollution, which disrupts these relations" (Ikeda and Krieger 2002, 111; italics added). Therefore, we can conclude from Ikeda's formulation that spiritual poverty is overcome when we recognize our place in *a system of interrelations with other human, nations, societies and the natural world*" because, in the final analysis, "*[t]he whole world depends on mutual interdependence*" (Ikeda and Krieger 2002, 111).

Ikeda also addresses the issue of human wholeness or completeness in the context of dialogue and tolerance. Within the framework of dialogue, Ikeda notes, we see that language, dialogue, and cultural tradition all emerge and converge to help humans sustain their long sought-after completeness. He writes thus:

> *Only within the open space created by dialogue, whether conducted with our neighbors, with history, with nature or the cosmos, can human wholeness be sustained.* The closed silence of the disengaged can only become the site of spiritual suicide. We are not born human in any but a biological sense; we can only learn to know ourselves and others and thus be trained in the ways of being human. We do this by immersion in the ocean of language and dialogue led by the springs of cultural tradition. (Ikeda 2001a, 41–42; italics added)

Similarly, Prof. Thomas M. Frank in his book *The Empowered Self: Law and Society in the Age of Individualism* has identified the dynamics of dialogue and social interaction as the underlying factors contributing to the evolution and development of a truly global civil society. He states "[t]hat society features growing, interactive transnational factions, *passionate global value-and-policy discourses*, and emerging public and private transactional networks: in short, *a community of communities* is emerging in which, for the first time, individuals are comparatively free to choose the multiple components of their identities and to choose their affinities" (Franck 1999, 100; italics added). The roots of this historic achievement go back to the mid-eighteenth century when Kant's disciple Friedrich Schiller (1759–1805) sought to dramatize his mentor's idea of "*Weltburgertum*" (world citizenry), adding "*allgemeine Menschenliebe*" (general love of humanity) as the personal loyalty most appropriate to the emerging post-Enlightenment civilization. What is new in all of this is not the idea of world citizenship, but rather the birth of a notion that identity "... whatever its manifestation, is a personal attribute" and that "... an individual's identity is increasingly self-chosen, rather than being imposed by accident of birth or some liege lord's fiat. New is the dawning of a spirit of individual assertiveness: a refusal to accept, as absolutely determinative, the identities traditionally handed out to persons by those claiming to be ordained by God, history, or the law to tell us who we are" (Franck 1999, 60).

Many different manifestations of this phenomenon from the early twentieth century onward can be seen on every continent throughout the globe. Take, for example, the pronouncements from Latin American liberation theologians in the 1960s and 1970s. Most prominent among them is Gustavo Gutierrez, who in his book *A Theology of Liberation: History, Politics and Salvation* declared, "To characterize the situation of the poor countries as dominated and oppressed leads one to speak of economic, social, and political liberation. But we are dealing here with a much more integral and profound understanding of human existence and its historical future. *A broad and deep aspiration for liberation inflames the history of mankind in our day, liberation from all that limits or keeps man from self-fulfillment, liberation from all impediments to the exercise of his freedom*" (Gutierrez 1973, 27; italics added). When viewed panoramically, in all of its varied dimensions, we discover that "[t]he theology of liberation attempts to reflect on the experience and meaning of the faith based on the commitment to abolish injustice and to build a new society: this theology must be verified by the practice of that commitment, by active, effective participation in the struggle which the exploited social classes have undertaken against their oppressors. *Liberation from every form of exploitation, the possibility of a more human and more dignified life, the creation of a new man—all pass through this struggle*" (Gutierrez 1973, 307; italics added).

It is not surprising that Gutierrez remains so emphatic about the nature of the liberation that Latin Americans are seeking (Paupp 1978). After all, the claims of Third World nations for the recognition of their sovereignty, equality, and dignity date back to the Paris Peace Conference of 1919. It was at that conference that the Western powers ". . . ignored the demands and aspirations of non-Western peoples, but their struggles for sovereignty, equality, and dignity *as independent actors in international society* continued" (Manela 2007, 225; italics added). Despite Western resistance to the Third World's claims to freedom from colonialism, violations of human dignity and rights around the world, as well as the white establishment's support of imperialist policies, historians would eventually come to recognize and record the fact that "[t]heir struggles for recognition as fully sovereign actors in international society would shape the history of the succeeding decades" (Manela 2007, 225). This reality was made manifest in the case of South Africa's struggle against the white racist regime of apartheid. While there was, of course, tremendous domestic resistance to the apartheid government, there was a corresponding growth of global consciousness regarding the unjust state of affairs that predominated in all of South Africa's apartheid structures, institutions, and governing practices. This consciousness of injustice led to moral outrage and disapproval around the globe. Hence, the reality of the situation is that "[t] he apartheid regime was not in fact decisively defeated on the battlefield or driven from power by a successful domestic insurrection. The armed struggle of the African National Congress (ANC) served to remind the world that blacks were determined to be liberated from white oppression, but it was the moral disapproval of much of humanity that destroyed the morale and self-confidence of South Africa's ruling whites, and the increasingly effective economic sanctions that persuaded its business community and those in the government whom they influenced that apartheid had no future" (Fredrickson 1995, 275).

It is important to note that the real spark for change in South Africa came from the entire global community and not just from the West. Despite the argument that the United States and Great Britain led the way on developing human rights principles and casting them into a covenant at the first meetings of the United Nations in 1945, the historical record is quite different. Far from being some great source for the realization of human rights or the articulation of human rights principles, the historical record shows that the West was too deeply immersed in its projects of imperialism and colonialism to ever seriously entertain the calls from Third World nations to advance a concrete human rights agenda with real substance. Prof. Vijay Prashad notes, "Between the 1950s and the 1970s, the Third World formed a unique political force outside the atomic face-off between the United States—United Kingdom—France and the USSR. Filled with tactical and strategic disagreements on how to deal with colonialism and imperialism, the Third World nonetheless had a core political program around the values of disarmament, national sovereignty, economic integrity, and cultural diversity" (Prashad 2007a, 113–14). Now, juxtapose this consciousness to that of the United States with regard to its preoccupation with "American exceptionalism." Prof. David Forsythe has noted, "American exceptionalism as a cultural phenomenon is broadly and especially evident in US approaches to internationally recognized human rights. The United States preaches universalism, but it practices national particularity and cultural relativism" (Forsythe 2004, 62). Ikeda is painfully aware of the dangers inherent in cultural relativism. That is precisely why he addresses the issue directly. Ikeda writes, "Passive cultural relativism does not offer a viable alternative to the highhandedness of cultural imperialism. *One necessary aspect of a culture of peace is that it must provide a basis on which a plurality of cultural traditions can creatively interact, learning and appropriating from one another toward the dream of a genuinely inclusive global civilization.* Without this kind of overarching goal, we risk being inadequately equipped to meet the challenges of globalization or, worse, of lapsing into a cynical paralysis" (Ikeda 2001a, 107–08; italics added).

When coupled with West's late twentieth-century practice of globalization, there has been a heightened insensitivity to human rights concerns. Richard Falk has observed the following:

> Economic globalization . . . weakens the overall capacity and will of governments to address human wrongs either within their own society or elsewhere. Furthermore, by undercutting the basis for supporting most categories of global public goods, economic globalization also weaken the resource base of those international institutions with a mandate to alleviate human suffering. Such tendencies are currently abetted by an ideological climate that does not mount significant resistance on behalf of those being most acutely victimized by the discipline of global capital. For these reasons, it seems appropriate to link economic globalization with a high threshold of tolerance for human wrongs, at least for now. (Falk 2000b, 185)

This kind of tolerance for human wrongs constituted a pattern of neglect and indifference that was evident since the founding of the state system itself. Richard Falk commented on this phenomenon in 1981, long before the trends associated with globalization were even an asterisk on the horizon of history. Falk stated, "Juridical equality has been up against the geopolitical reality of gross inequality since the inception of the states system . . . *The colonial system, assimilated into the world legal order with different degrees of formality in the nineteenth century, upheld imperial patterns of control*" (Falk 1981, 38; italics added). The tragedy of this system for millions if not billions of people is that "[i]n essence there is no such thing as quality in international life on the level of states, no matter how much equality is achieved on the level of persons" (Falk 1981, 39).

International relations scholar Paul Keal has addressed this matter from the perspective of the European conquest of the Third World and the question of what actually happened to the rights of indigenous peoples in this expansion of Europe's colonial powers. Keal has come to the conclusion that individual rights were rights limited to those who were citizens of the European states. We discover that it was the European states themselves that defined and controlled membership of the society of states. Therefore, Keal concludes that "[i]t is a view that does not address the indigenous and other non-European people who were not included in the society of states defined by the international law of Europe . . . the expansion of Europe resulted in a progressive erosion and denial of the rights of indigenous people" (Keal 2003, 35). It is probably for that precise reason that Keal subtitled his study "*the moral backwardness of international society.*"

Hence, both Europe and the United States should be seen as Western powers that have taken turns at playing a hegemonic role in the Third World—and this includes what has been done with the concept of "development." Some scholars have maintained, "Development has always been a hegemonic idea in that it has always been clear about who needs to be developed, who will do the 'developing,' how and in which direction" (Rajagopal 2008, 71).

In light of the direction that history has taken, we may conclude that *"[g]iven the centrality of colonialism and development in producing the architecture of modern international law, and their impact on substantive areas of law, a critical approach to international law must begin by closely interrogating the meaning, purpose, goals and means of development itself"* (Rajagopal 2008, 76; italics added).

A review of the historical record of the West in the nineteenth through the twentieth centuries supplies evidence of Western complicity in genocide, resource exploitation, violations of the sovereign rights of nations and peoples, as well as the denial of human rights and dignity on a massive scale (Jones 2004). It is for this reason that Prof. David Abernethy has counseled students of Europe's overseas empires to recall that

> Among the most reprehensible aspects of colonialism . . . were its deliberate, systematic, and sustained assaults on human dignity. The assertions of cultural and racial superiority accompanying European rule had devastating effects on the self-respect of many people . . . The imperial project consumed the lives of millions of human beings and blighted the lives of millions more. Its worst aspects—the transatlantic slave trade, plantation slavery, forced labor, sexual exploitation—should not be forgotten or excused. (Abernethy 2000, 406)

Yet even in the twenty-first century, the nightmare of racism and its connection to various forms of colonialism still resides in the hearts of individuals who benefit from systems supportive of the maintenance of hierarchy and hegemony. In the words of Prof. Howard Winant, "The disruption of the old world racial system during and after the post–World War II racial break has given rise to a 'new world racial system' characterized not by racial domination, but instead by racial hegemony. This new system can maintain white supremacy better than the old one could. This system of racial hegemony can present itself as color-blind and multicultural, not to mention meritocratic, egalitarian, and differentialist, all while restricting immigration, exporting industry (and pollution) to the low-waged South, and doing away with the welfare state in the North" (Winant 2001, 309).

When viewed against this historical backdrop, the struggles against colonialism and imperialism—and for liberation—are not only decades in the making, but centuries in the making. Stories of resistance and liberation struggles represent part of an ongoing theme of liberation that stretches throughout human history. Going back to the history of ancient Egypt, as recounted in the Bible's *Book of Exodus*, we discover how the reality of oppression, slavery, and exploitation led to a great encounter between the consciousness of the powerful oppressor and the consciousness of the oppressed (Paupp 1978). With regard to this particular encounter, Gutierrez emphatically declares that "[t]he Exodus experience is paradigmatic. It remains vital and contemporary due to similar historical experiences which the People of God undergo . . . it is characterized 'by the twofold sign of the overriding will of God and the free and conscious assent of men'" (Gutierrez 1973, 159).

From the standpoint of liberation theology the Exodus event remains important because, as far as liberation theology is concerned, "[t]his is a theology which does not stop reflecting on the world, but rather tries to be part of the process through which the world is transformed. It is a theology which is open—in the protest against trampled human dignity, in the struggle against the plunder of the vast majority of people, in liberating love, and in the building of a new, just, and fraternal society"(Gutierrez 1973, 15). In this task, Gutierrez reaffirms the idea that "[t]he concept of political liberation—with economic roots—recalls the conflictual aspects of the historical current of humanity. In this current there is not only an effort to know and dominate nature. There is also a situation—*which both affects and is affected by this current*—of misery and despoliation of the fruit of man's work, the result of the exploitation of man by man; there is a confrontation between social classes and, therefore, a struggle for liberation from oppressive structures which hinder man from living with dignity and assuming his own destiny" (Gutierrez 1973, 174; italics added).

As true and as valid as these insights remain for us in the twenty-first century, Ikeda reminds us that we must expand our thoughts and our understanding beyond the realm of the political insofar as there are deeper issues of cultural identity that are at work which go far beyond ". . . the more superficial layers of political definitions and concerns." Given this understanding, Ikeda counsels us to come to realize that

> if we are overly entangled in the national dimension, it is easy to lose sight of the fact that national identities are often deliberate constructs created for political ends. The great danger, of course, lies in falling into the trap of viewing them as unchanging entities or essences with an absolute ontological standing . . . We must never lose sight of the fact that, however much globalization and communication technology may advance, people still count. *The individual—the character of each individual—is decisively the creator and protagonist of culture.* (Ikeda 2001a, 109–10; italics added)

The Power of Moral Courage and Altruistic Living

In the mid-twentieth century, while reflecting on the revolutionary tide sweeping the Third World, but Latin America in particular, Robert Kennedy noted the following:

> Around the world—from the Straits of Magellan to the Straits of Malacca, from the Nile Delta to the Amazon basin, in Jaipur and

Johannesberg—the dispossessed people of the world are demanding their place in the sun. For uncounted centuries, they have lived with hardships, with hunger and disease and fear. For the last four centuries, they have lived under the political, economic, and military domination of the West. We have shown them that a better life is possible. We have not done enough to make it a reality. A revolution is now in progress. It is a revolution for individual dignity, in societies where the individual has been submerged in a desperate mass . . . This revolution is directed against *us*—against the one-third of the world that diets while others starve; against a nation that buys 8-million new cars a year while most of the world goes without shoes; against developed nations which spend over 100-billion dollars on armaments while the poor countries cannot obtain the 10 to 15 billion dollars of investment capital they need just to keep pace with their expanding populations. (Kennedy 1968a,b, 423–24; italics in original)

The practical nature of the challenge unleashed by this struggle for human liberation and freedom is dramatically depicted in the dialectical problem posed by personal rebellion, on the one hand, and political rebellion, on the other. As framed by Herbert Marcuse, the challenge may be stated as follows: "The new individualism raises the problem of the relation between personal and political rebellion, private liberation and social revolution. The inevitable antagonism, the tension between these two, easily collapses into an immediate identification, destroying the potential in both of them. True, no qualitative social change, no socialism, is possible without the emergence of a new rationality *and sensibility* in the individuals themselves: no radical social change without a radical change of the individual agents of change" (Marcuse 1972, 48; italics in original).

Both Gutierrez and Kennedy recognized the reality that a radical change of unjust situations of oppression and exploitation could really only be brought about by individual agents of change—individuals with a transformed consciousness which would be capable of transforming a corrupt world. This was especially the case with regard to taking on the challenge of poverty in the ghettos of both the United States and Latin America (Paupp 1988; Schmitt 2010). It is for this precise reason that Marcuse's emphasis on the need to approach qualitative social change through the prism of an emerging "sensibility" in the individuals themselves also represents a central tenet of Ikeda's own views on this matter from the standpoint of "altruistic living." After all, as Gutierrez, Marcuse, and Kennedy acknowledged, a corrupt world of oppression, violence, and war was largely the product of greed, selfishness, and a lack of empathy for the suffering of others. What would be required is a new consciousness of identification with others that might lead to altruistic acts of compassion, love, and a commitment to social justice. In this regard, Ikeda writes the following:

Nichiren spoke of earthly desires being used as fuel for the flame of wisdom. Buddhism teaches the converting of personal ambitions and desires, even base ones, into good traits like wisdom through altruistic living. A Buddhist doctrine that earthly desires *are* enlightenment indicates that greed, anger (violence) and egocentricism can be transformed into altruistic traits like compassion, trust and nonviolence. The underlying delusions that drive our desires (. . .) can be essentially transformed in a way that changes selfishness into altruism, violence into nonviolence and suspicion into trust. (Ikeda and Krieger 2002, 108; italics in original).

Perhaps one of the most dramatic modern examples of this phenomenon is the fall of the white apartheid regime of South Africa. As already mentioned, it was a racist regime that was to be torn down largely due to the moral opposition of the entire international community and pressures exerted by international economic sanctions in the 1980s. But two decades before that event, Martin Luther King had already made the argument that US reluctance to engage with the regime for the sake of maintaining a Cold War ally in its anti-Communist crusade was morally indefensible. Further, King laid out a vision of the divestment and sanctions movement that was to follow over the next two decades. In philosophical bond with the approach of nonviolence, King asked, "Have we the power to be more than peevish with South Africa?" He continued, "To list the extensive economic relations of the great powers with South Africa is to suggest a potent non-violent path . . . a massive international boycott." According to historian Robert Massie, we discover that

> [f]or King the two struggles—for civil rights in the United States and for political freedom—were intimately connected. [King stated] "In this period when the American Negro is giving moral leadership and inspiration to his own nation, he must find the resources to aid his suffering brothers in his ancestral homeland," King insisted. "Nor is this a one-way street. The civil rights movement in the United States has derived immense inspiration from the successful struggles of those Africans who have attained freedom in their own nations." (Massie 1997, 193–94)

These statements by King reflect the spirit of altruism in its most profound and universal form.

For individuals to be inspired to follow the path to altruistic living, concrete goals showing what direction to take can be beneficial. Martin King provided such a goal when he spoke of the struggle for human rights in South Africa in conjunction with his speeches on civil rights in America. King called upon people to embrace the demands of moral leadership by being willing to identify with the suffering of others in another country—their brethren in their ancestral homeland. This is where Marcuse's discussion about political rebellion and social revolution has its most profound relevance. Insofar as the inevitable antagonism between private liberation and social revolution needs to be overcome in order to avoid a destruction of the potential in each, it is clear that people require what Erich Fromm has called *a frame of orientation* (Fromm 1975, 260). The need for a frame of orientation for action is necessary because

> a map is not enough as a guide for action; man also needs a goal that tells him where to go . . . He needs such an object of devotion for a number of reasons. The object integrates his energies in one direction. It elevates him beyond his isolated existence, with all its doubt and insecurity, and gives meaning to life. In being devoted to a goal beyond his isolated ego, he transcends himself and leaves *the prison of absolute egocentricity.* (Fromm 1975, 260; italics added)

In a footnote to this sentence, Fromm emphasizes that "*[t]there is a need to transcend one's self-centered, narcissistic, isolated position to one of being related to others, of openness to the world, escaping the hell of self-centeredness and hence self-imprisonment.* Religious systems like Buddhism have postulated this kind of transcendence without any reference to a god or superhuman power" (Fromm 1975, 260; italics added).

What Fromm has identified here in reference to the individual person's need to escape *self-imprisonment* is directly related to Ikeda's discussion about the need to adopt and to incorporate into one's being the style and elements of what constitute the components of altruistic living, because that is the pathway to compassion. Without compassion at work inside the souls of people who are seeking to be the agents of social change we discover that the possibility for achieving genuine social change itself is compromised and will collapse. So the reality is—regardless of how intellectually brilliant we are, regardless of how ideologically committed we are to social change—the fact remains that we cannot allow ourselves to be so preoccupied with our own self-centered agendas, social status and position, or selfish priorities that we fail to feel empathy and compassion for others. Only through altruistic acts that engender compassion will it be possible to undertake the path of transcendence that leads out of our own egocentric prisons and, at the same time, makes it possible for us to effectively work toward the transcendence of social structures of oppression that deny liberation, freedom, and human dignity to our fellow human beings.

In rendering this insight in more accessible and understandable terms, Ikeda relates a story in which

> [t]he founder of Buddhism, Shakyamuni, once severely scolded some brilliant disciples. They had heard many teachings and understood

basic principles, and they concentrated exclusively on their own attainment of enlightenment. He told them that just as a split stone cannot be rejoined and parched grain can never germinate, so they would never attain Buddhahood. The reason for their scolding was this: *Although the disciples in question were of superior ability and exerted great influence on others, they performed no altruistic acts and were in danger of cloistering themselves within their own egos.* Shakyamuni was attuned to the danger of people who, though intellectually superior, lack compassion. (Ikeda and Krieger 2002, 109; italics added)

From the perspective of Robert Kennedy, what is at the heart and center of altruistic acts is "moral courage." The problem is that all too few ". . . are willing to brave the disapproval of their fellows, the censure of their colleagues, the wrath of their society. *Moral courage is a rarer commodity than bravery in battle or great intelligence.* Yet it is the one essential, vital quality of those who seek to change a world which yields most painfully to change" (Kennedy 1993, 244; italics added).

On June 6, 1966, in his speech at the University of Cape Town, South Africa, Robert Kennedy delivered a *"Day of Affirmation"* message that contained deep insights, references to eternal values, and humanistic priorities which are clearly complementary to those cited by Ikeda. Both Kennedy and Ikeda often noted that the need to recognize the presence of unenlightened attitudes is essential if we are to transcend the injustices, suffering, and unnecessary pain of both history and our own time. That is because the power and presence of unenlightened attitudes within individuals only serve to further reinforce and support the externalized powers of oppression, structural violence, militarism, and exploitation. At the time when South Africa was still dominated by a political, social, and economic system of racial apartheid and, in the midst of those who benefited from this exploitative arrangement, the principled and visionary words of Robert Kennedy declared thus:

> Each nation has different obstacles and different goals, shaped by the vagaries of history and experience. Yet as I talk to young people around the world I am impressed not by the diversity but by the closeness of their goals, their desires and their concerns and their hope for the future. There is discrimination in New York, the racial inequality of apartheid in South Africa, and serfdom in the mountains of Peru. People starve in the streets of India, a former Prime Minister is executed in the Congo, intellectuals go to jail in Russia, and thousands are slaughtered in Indonesia; wealth is lavished on armaments everywhere in the world. *These are differing evils; but they are the common works of man. They reflect the imperfections of human justice, the inadequacy of human compassion, the defectiveness of our sensibility toward the sufferings of our fellows; they mark*

the limit of our ability to use knowledge for the well-being of our fellow human beings around the world. And therefore they call upon common qualities of conscience and indignation, a shared determination to wipe away the unnecessary sufferings of our fellow human beings at home and around the world. (Kennedy 1993, 141; italics added)

Here, in the most graphic terms, Kennedy supplies the nexus between inner transformation and the path toward social change for the realization of social justice. When the realities of social injustice finally ignite our conscience and indignation, we discover our human capacity to empathize with those who suffer and, at the same time, are moved to do something about a situation of injustice that has led to such unnecessary suffering. At that juncture, it becomes possible for us to undertake what Ikeda calls altruistic living. In this particular manifestation of altruism, as annunciated by Robert Kennedy, we find that the personal dimension combines and engages interactively with the social dimension in order to undertake the twin tasks of personal and political liberation from oppressive practices, structures, and policies. In this task, Kennedy realized the tides of human history could not be reversed in order to keep a corrupt status quo in place. Therefore, to those who clung to the hope that change could be suppressed, the status quo maintained, Kennedy said the following:

> We must recognize that the young in many areas of the world today are in the midst of a revolution against the status-quo. They are not going to accept platitudes and generalities. Their anger has been turned on the systems which have allowed poverty, illiteracy and oppression to flourish for centuries. And we must recognize one simple fact: that they will prevail. They will achieve their idealistic goals one way or the other. If they have to pull governments tumbling down over their heads, they will do it. But they are going to win their share of a better and cleaner world. (Kennedy 1968a,b, 425)

Moving Beyond Illusion, Egotism, the Market and toward Social Justice

Since Kennedy delivered those words, the world has been dramatically altered. The revolution that he was watching unfold in the mid-1960s has taken many radical turns as history has moved into the twenty-first century. Both within the US and around the world, revolutionary change and unexpected turns of fortunes and events have defined our recent global history. To begin with, since Kennedy's time, the Berlin Wall fell in 1990, signaling an end to the Cold War. The ideological struggle with communism ended an almost fifty-year global competition between two superpowers with the Third World caught in the middle. By 1990 the winds of change had also swept South Africa. By 1996 the white apartheid regime of South Africa had been peacefully replaced by elections that made Nelson Mandela the country's first black president. Similarly, in 2008, the United States itself elected its first black president in the person of Barack Obama. Kennedy's much-hoped-for peaceful revolution had swept the globe. Yet along with this peaceful revolution there were the lingering problems of global poverty, militarism, ecological degradation, and growing disparities of wealth both within and between nations. As for the last remaining superpower, US hegemony and its global dominance in global relations from the period between 1945 and 1968 continued its inexorable decline. The power of the American empire has been dramatically diminished in the aftermath of the Vietnam War, the Iraq War and, in the year 2008, by the greatest US financial collapse since the Great Depression of the 1930s.

Reacting to the events of the 2008 financial meltdown, Ikeda specifically addressed the meaning and ramifications of this most recent phenomenon in his 2009 peace proposal, entitled "Toward Humanitarian Competition: A New Current in History." In response to the financial crisis of 2008 and the human meaning of these unfolding events, Ikeda wrote, "If we remember that the Great Depression only fully set in two years after the 1929 stock market crash, the gravity of the current situation becomes even more apparent. People have the right to live in peace and humane conditions, and to that end, they exert themselves assiduously day after day. It is unacceptable that the foundations of people's livelihoods should be disrupted and devastated by the effects of 'tsunami' that they could not foresee and which originated in realms far beyond their control" (Ikeda 2009-PP, 1).

Clearly, Ikeda has invoked his altruistic view of how human beings should be treated and found that the existing system is devoid of ethics, humane practices, a sense of justice, and an understanding of what constitutes human rights. In his personal assessment, Ikeda writes the following:

> Currency itself—the scraps of paper and metal and, most recently, bits of electronic information that rule market economies—has, of course, virtually no use value; it has only exchange value. And exchange value stands on the foundation of understanding and agreement among people; *in essence, currency is both abstract and anonymous.* The financial markets divest it of any meaningful connection to concrete (and therefore finite) goods and services; thus as an object of human desire, it has no real or inherent limits. Herein lies the particular characteristic, *the fateful pathology,* of our fixation on currency. (Ikeda 2009-PP, 2)

From this analysis, Ikeda addresses what he identifies as *the spirit of abstraction* and notes, ". . . the spirit of abstraction is not value-neutral" (Ikeda 2009-PP, 3). He argues that the spirit of abstraction is "the essentially destructive process by which our conceptions of things are alienated from concrete realities" (Ikeda 2009-PP, 2). Because we have been caught up in this spirit of abstraction, we have been "losing our essential human capacity to see through the fact that . . . currency is nothing other than a convention, a kind of virtual reality. . . . *Ensnared by the spirit of abstraction, we have lost sight of the fact that our genuine humanity exists only in the totality of our personhood.* To a greater or lesser degree, we have all become *Homo economicus*, incapable of recognizing any value other than the monetary" (Ikeda 2009-PP, 3; italics added). As a direct consequence of these historical trends, Ikeda notes, "The predominance of monetary interests has accentuated the negative aspects of capitalism such as global income disparity, unstable labor markets and environmental destruction" (Ikeda 2009-PP, 4). The legacy of these trends is now more than clear: "It is now apparent that the faith in free competition and markets to resolve all problems was misplaced; nothing in the world is so neatly preordained" (Ikeda 2009-PP, 4).

Fritjof Capra addressed the foundations of this problem in his 1982 book, *The Turning Point: Science, Society, and the Rising Culture.* Like Ikeda, his central thesis is the idea that the major problems of our time are all different facets of one and the same crisis, which is essentially a crisis of perception. Like the crisis in physics in the 1920s, it derives from the fact that we are trying to apply the concepts of an outdated worldview—the mechanistic worldview of Cartesian–Newtonian science—to a reality that can no longer be understood in terms of these concepts. Specifically, with regard to the impasses of economics, Capra asserts the following:

The nature of large corporations is profoundly inhuman. Competition, coercion, and exploitation are essential aspects of their activities, all motivated by the desire for indefinite expansion. Continuing growth is built into the corporate structure. For example, corporate executives who knowingly bypass an opportunity for increasing the corporation's profits, for whatever reason, are liable to lawsuit." Thus, the resulting human tragedy is that ". . . the maximization of profits becomes the ultimate goal, to the exclusion of all other considerations" (Capra 1982, 221).

In conjunction with Capra's analysis, we should juxtapose the content of a dialogic exchange between Ikeda and Majid Tehranian about the value of the *"three freedoms"*—freedom from dogma, illusion, and greed. From the standpoint of Buddhism, insofar as these particular qualities are concerned, they are understood as emanating from the realm of illusion. With this in mind, Tehranian notes the importance of Ikeda's reference in the early part of their dialogue as to why Shakyamuni had abandoned the secular world. The reason was because "[h]e had discovered that the causes of human suffering are not just 'tragic situations' like poverty and sickness, but more fundamentally troubles rooted in the heart—egoistic preoccupation with self–other distinctions, as between the health and sick or between young and old." Ikeda responds by noting that "Buddhism is a practical philosophy aimed at seeking liberation from the iron chains of such perversions of the heart." Ikeda reminds us that in the Buddhist tradition, dogma, illusion, and greed are three traits, which are referred to as *ton* (greed), *jin* (anger), and *chi* (stupidity). The last one is most interesting. We find that "*[c]hi* can be translated as either stupidity or ignorance. It means the inability to correctly perceive things as they are, which in turn gives rise to distorted or twisted understanding. Rather than lack of comprehension, *chi* should be taken as misunderstanding, illusion, or misperception" (Ikeda and Tehranian 2003, 99).

Chi can be seen at work in the mental maps that we have constructed for our social relations, as well as our political, economic, and cultural endeavors. If our mental maps and worldviews are infused with dogmatic certainties that act to block out our ability to form an objective assessment as to what is or is not the case, then it logically follows that our misunderstandings and misperceptions can lead to everything from "market failures" to wars. Therefore, Ikeda's discussion about *chi* provides us with an important insight. That is because it constitutes an explanatory linkage between the constructs forged by individuals with regard to their personal identity, values, and mental maps and, in turn, how those constructs serve to forge a similar image and set of perceptions with regard to interpreting the larger social world. *If* we understand that there is an objective nexus that can be identified between the human mind—as a form of self-organization—and see that it can be extended to the larger world of social and ecological systems, *then* we can understand the linkage between individual transformation and global transformation in an entirely new and compelling way.

For example, Capra states thus:

> The human mind is a multi-leveled and integrated pattern of processes that represent the dynamics of human self-organization. Mind is a pattern of organization. . . . The totality of the human mind, with its conscious and unconscious realms, I shall call, with Jung, the psyche. Because the system view of mind is not limited to individuals but can be extended to social and ecological systems, we may say that groups of people, societies and cultures have a collective mind, and therefore also possess a collective consciousness . . . As individuals we participate in these collective mental patterns, are influenced by them, and shape them in turn. (Capra 1982, 296)

In light of this assessment, we can attach Ikeda's diagnosis of the problems faced in the aftermath of the 2008 financial collapse, wherein he notes, "*People everywhere seem to be in the grip of a sense of claustrophobic powerlessness—a sense that depends in direct proportion to the advance of globalization. This is, in my view, an inevitable outcome of the arrogance and egotism that pursues profit blindly, imagining that human society can continue to exist even as it destroys the natural and cultural environment*" (Ikeda 2009-PP, 3–4; italics added). Again, we are returned to the fundamental recognition, formulated by Capra, that "[a]s individuals we participate in these collective mental patterns, are influenced by them, and shape them in turn" (Capra 1982, 296). There is a real dialectic at work here. That is because "[m]ore than any other species we engage in collective thinking and in so doing we create a world of culture and values that becomes an integral part of our natural environment. Thus, biological and cultural characteristics of human nature cannot be separated. Humankind emerged through the very process of creating culture and needs this culture for survival and further evolution" (Capra 1982, 298).

Ikeda has addressed this very point when he analyzes the relationship between legal and structural reforms, on the one hand, along with the need for a corresponding revolution in consciousness. He argues that it is only when individuals recognize their common humanity throughout their society and culture that true equality between people can be realized. For Ikeda, like Capra, we need to be aware of the power of a dynamic synergy between the internal world of individuals and the external world of the culture and society in which they live. Therefore, Ikeda notes, "To be maximally effective, legal and structural reforms must be supported by a corresponding revolution in consciousness—the development of the kind of universal humanity that transcends differences from within. It is only when a renewed awareness of our common humanity takes root in individuals throughout society that the dream of genuine equality will be realized. There must, in other words, be a creative synergy between internal—spiritual, introspective—reforms within individuals, and external—legal and institutional—reforms in society" (Ikeda 2001a, 113). Similarly, Capra argues that *"[h]uman evolution, then, progresses through an interplay of inner and outer worlds, individuals and societies, nature and culture.* All these realms are living systems in mutual interaction that display similar patterns of self-organization. Social institutions evolve toward increasing complexity and differentiation, not unlike organic structures, and mental patterns exhibit the creativity and urge for self-transcendence that is characteristic of all life" (Capra 1982, 298; italics added).

In their analysis, Ikeda and Capra have supplied the broad and general outlines for understanding the linkages between individual transformation and the nature of societal change. The matrix of our reality and our world— however short-lived and provisional it may turn out to be—is the result of the interplay between internal and introspective reforms, on the one hand, with external legal and institutional reforms, on the other. The problem that confronts us in building a more just society—at both the national and global levels—reveals itself in the form of the failure of individuals who enjoy power to also act in a manner that is consistent with and complementary to the exercise of self-control. As Rajni Kothari explains, "A proper concept of justice . . . should foster respect for and preserve diversities in human propensities and preferred social arrangement, creating an awareness that whatever one does, individually or socially, is bound to be imperfect and that those who enjoy power must also exercise self-control and act with humility toward others." Therefore, Kothari argues, we are confronted with a dilemma: "The passion for justice is reverberating in the hearts and souls of large sections of humanity *alongside* a sociopolitical–ecological–ethical thrust toward injustice that seems to be growing apace, *the two coexisting almost in the fashion of an organic tie, not just following some dialectic of history*" (Kothari 2000, 99; italics added).

The problem and the challenge that Kothari has identified apply equally to democratic states and to nondemocratic states. It is a problem that afflicts the United States as much as it troubles people throughout the nations of the global South. In other words, it is a universal problem. Within the context of the twentieth-century history of the United States, the problem was perhaps most objectively addressed by Robert Kennedy. In 1966, Kennedy's call for rebuilding a sense of community came closest to addressing the heart of the matter. His call for reflection and readjustment stood in stark contrast to prevailing ideologies of both the political right (who saw no useful role for government outside of guaranteeing public safety) and the left (who had come to regard large-scale federal intervention as the preferred remedy for any domestic ill). Kennedy stood outside these extremes by concentrating his contempt and criticism on the celebration of "*the big*"—the drive toward bigness in business, corporate finance, and all economic and social forces that denied importance to the dignity of the person and the integrity and culture of the community to which they belonged. Kennedy noted, "Even as the drive toward bigness [and] concentration . . . has reached heights never before dreamt of in the past, we have come suddenly to realize how heavy a price we have paid: in overcrowding and pollution of the atmosphere, and impersonality; in growth of organizations, particularly government, so large and powerful that individual effort and importance seem lost . . . Bigness, loss of community, organizations and society grown far past the human scale—these are the besetting sins of the twentieth century, which threaten to paralyze our very capacity to act, or our ability to preserve the traditions and values of our past in a time of swirling, constant change" (Kennedy 1993, 211–12).

The powerlessness of the poor relative to big institutions and organizations and the need to provide the poor with institutional channels to voice their concerns and affect decisions that affected their very lives were major themes to which Kennedy returned many times throughout his career. Beginning with his testimony before a Senate Committee in his role of attorney general of the United States, Kennedy stated the following:

> The institutions which affect the poor—education, welfare, recreation, business, labor—are huge, complex structures, operating from

outside their control. *They plan programs for the poor, not with them.* Part of the sense of helplessness and futility comes from the feeling of powerlessness to affect the operation of these organizations. The community action programs must basically change these organizations by building into the program real representation for the poor. This bill calls for maximum feasible participation of residents. This means the involvement of the poor in planning and implementing programs: *giving them a real voice in their institutions.* (Donovan 1967, 35; italics added)

In keeping with the spirit of Kennedy's diagnosis, Kothari observed that "[w]hile old hegemonies might be crumbling, new ones are being formed and perpetuated. There is also a slow but seductive crystallization of doctrines— about security, of stability, of unity—that are all being used to legitimize patterns of governance that are clearly antidemocratic. Even less clearly recognized is the fact that the very structures that had been conceived for promoting the democratic process and providing liberation from traditional constraints—political parties, representative institutions, the judiciary—are producing conditions not just of political instability but of incipient break-downs of social order" (Kothari 2000, 100). The antidemocratic trends, to which Kothari refers, have been over a century in the making. One could make the argument that these trends date back to the nineteenth century when corporate power in the West began the process of ongoing deregulation of the marketplace ". . . combined with the simultaneous and continuous expansion of corporate rights" (Wettstein 2009, 184).

The crux of the battle had been one between government, on the one hand, and the marketplace, on the other. In this context, the question was whether the government or the marketplace would control the *"commanding heights"* of the economy. The actual term (the *commanding heights*) goes back to 1922 when Lenin addressed the Fourth Congress of the Communist International in St. Petersburg, then called Petrograd. He declared that the state would control *the commanding heights*—the most important elements of the economy. Throughout the twentieth century the question as to where the frontier be-tween the state and the market is to be drawn has never been a matter that could be settled, once and for all. The importance of this question is found in the realization that "[t]his frontier defines not the boundaries of nations but the division of roles within them. What are the realm and responsibility of the state in the economy, and what kind of protection is the state to afford its citizens? What is the preserve of private decision-making, and what are the responsibilities of the individual?" (Yergin and Stanislaw 1998, 11). The state's victories were solidified in the early half of the twentieth century by revolution, two world wars, and the Great Depression. Additionally, it was ". . . also powered by the demands of the public in the industrial democracies for greater security, by the drive for progress and improved living conditions in developing countries—and by the quest for justice and fairness. Behind all this was the conviction that markets went to excesses, that they could readily fail, that there were too many needs and services they could not deliver, that the risks and the human and social costs were too high and the potential for abuse too great" (Yergin and Stanislaw 1998, 11).

Tragically, with the ascendancy of the ideology of Reaganism in the United States and Thatcherism in Great Britain, the great Western democracies had now committed their governments to the dismantling of the welfare state and endorsing the headlong rush to privatization, thereby surrendering the commanding heights to the markets. By the decade of the 1990s, in response to the high costs of control and the disillusionment with its effectiveness, governments were privatizing at so fast a rate that the selling-off of government assets and responsibilities to corporations and markets resulted in "... the greatest sale in the history of the world." It was a situation that resulted in a process where history would record the phenomena of "[g]overnments getting out of businesses by disposing of what amounts to trillions of dollars of assets" (Yergin and Stanislaw 1998, 13). All this took place around the world from the former Soviet Union to Eastern Europe, from China to Western Europe, from Asia to Latin America and Africa, so that "[t]he world over, governments have come to plan less, to own less, and to regulate less, allowing instead the frontiers of the market to expand" (Yergin and Stanislaw 1998, 13). What will be the new role of government? Since the 1980s and through the US financial collapse and concomitant global recession of 2008, we find that "[t]he state accepts the discipline of the market; government moves away from being the producer, controller, and intervenor, whether through state ownership or heavy-handed regulation. The state as manager is an increasing laggard in the competitive, mobile economy" (Yergin and Stanislaw 1998, 373).

As a consequence of these trends, Kothari tabulates the cost of removing humane and inclusive governmental intervention from the commanding heights with the observation that *"[p]roblems of the world are no longer seen in terms of the possibility of bridging chasms between rich and poor. Instead, the new vision seeks to provide—to the exclusion of all humanist considerations— for the unhindered advance of technology that would integrate the world into a single unified world political economy*. Large segments of the powerless and backward, comprising a variety of emerging nations, traditional communities, and cultures, are incapable of keeping pace with or finding a place in this rapidly transforming world" (Kothari 2000, 100; italics added). The effects of these trends are to isolate individuals and communities from their bonds of human solidarity. The neoliberal economic and political model has been especially harsh in its proclivity to punish the poor and people of color. This is most evident in the "prison-industrial-complex" that operates on a for-profit basis throughout the United States. For example, "In the 1980s, the United States added an average of 20,000 African-Americans to its total prisoner stock *every year*.... And, for the first time in the twentieth century, the country's penitentiaries held more blacks than whites: African Americans made up 12 percent of the national population but supplied 53 percent of the prison inmates in 1995, as against 38 percent a quarter-century earlier. The rate of incarceration for blacks *tripled in only a dozen years* to reach 1,895 per 100,000 in 1993—amounting to nearly seven times the rate for whites (293 per 100,000) and twenty times the rates recorded in the main European countries at that time" (Wacquant 2009, 61; italics in original). The failure to even address the growing inequalities and disparities both within and between nations has served to create a twenty-first-century global crisis. The resolution of this global crisis, according to Ikeda, is to recognize that "*[p]eople—communities, nations—cannot exist in isolation; they depend on one another for help. The building of a world community, a global civilization of justice, compassion and hope must begin by turning away from the 'eat or be eaten' ethos of competition and cultivating in its place a shared ethos of cooperation and interdependence*" (Ikeda 2001a, 76; italics added).

Humanitarian Competition as a Defining Concept of the Twenty-First Century

It may well be that Ikeda's prescription and vision for the building of "*a global civilization of justice*" may arrive through his resurrection of Tsunesaburo Makiguchi's idea of humanitarian competition, which, unlike the neoliberal economic model that sacrifices people and communities on the altar of the market, seeks to "achieve goals that would otherwise be pursued by military or political force through the intangible power that naturally exerts a moral influence; in other words, to be respected rather than feared" (Ikeda 2009-PP, 7). It is for this reason that Ikeda states thus:

> *I am fully convinced that the time has now arrived, a hundred years after it was originally proposed, for us to turn our attention to humanitarian competition as a guiding principle for a new era.* One reason is that social justice and equality, proposed by socialism as an antidote to the ills of capitalism, are indeed rooted in humanistic principles ... Free competition drive by the unrestrained impulses of selfishness can descend into the kind of social Darwinism in which the strong prey on the weak. But competition conducted within an appropriate framework of rules and conventions brings forth the energies of individuals and revitalizes society. (Ikeda 2009-PP, 8; italics added)

It is at this point that we see, once again, the nexus between the individual and the society. The interplay between the two is not deterministic; it is dynamic. It is defined by the presence and influence of humanistic values transforming the internal character of people, who, in turn, transform their societies and the direction of global culture and civilization in the process. This configuration of the evolutionary process of change is predicated upon the energy of individuals impacting upon their fellows and society in such a way that the society itself is revitalized and given a new meaning and direction. Out of this synergistic nexus we find that place in which human historical possibilities are unleashed. If the approach taken involves what Ikeda terms humanitarian competition, then history itself is transformed in accordance with that dynamic which can not only resolve the many aspects of our global crisis but also move beyond crisis in creating a more peaceful global civilization. Given this understanding, Ikeda concludes, "Herein lies the value of *humanitarian competition*. As a concept, it compels us to confront the reality of competition while ensuring that it is conducted firmly on the basis of *humane values*, thus bringing forth *a synergistic reaction between humanitarian concerns and competitive energies. It is this that qualifies humanitarian competition to be a key paradigm for the twenty-first century*" (Ikeda 2009-PP, 8; italics added).

Having failed to embrace the values and principles that make up humanitarian competition, America continued down the path of unregulated markets and a culture of greed. America's substantial and intimate linkages to both the WTO and Wall Street as its organizing principals, for its guiding policies and financial profits, had begun to create the economic conditions for a perfect storm. This danger was already clearly evident a full three years before the 2008 financial crash. Given his reading of trends, Prof. Walden Bello made a prescient prediction when I noted, "*America will continue to decline economically because the global framework for transnational cooperation to which the WTO is central is eroding*." In fact, in light of these ominous trends, "[r]egional economic collaborations among Third World countries—or, in the parlance of development economics, '*South–South cooperation*'—are the wave of the future" (Bello 2005, 212; italics added).

I expanded upon Bello's analysis in 2009 when he presented a new thesis in the field of international relations on the future direction of global relations. My thesis was based on both the decline of US hegemony and, juxtaposed to that trend, the nature of *South–South cooperation* in an emerging pos-thegemonic world. Having previously written, witnessed, and commented upon the growth of social movements for justice and human rights across the global South, as well as the trends linking many of these states in a "counter-hegemonic alliance" (Paupp 2007) against US interventionism throughout the world, I observed that "[t]he juxtaposition of the crumbling walls of American hegemony with the image of the rising regions of China, India, South and East Asia, Latin America, the Middle East, and the European Union has allowed me to frame a unified thesis about this newly evolving twenty-first-century world order that transcends the nature of previous discussions about world order." The central and most predominant reason for the conceptual inadequacy of past discussions on the nature of world order can be traced back, I argue, to the limited and myopic focus upon

> . . . geopolitical paradigms that have been habitually centered on assumptions about the enduring nature of American hegemony and unipolarity [which] are in the process of being swept away with the debris of history. These geopolitical paradigms are being either fundamentally altered or entirely replaced by the concept of a 'polycentric' world order. What makes this polycentric world order so different from the configurations of the past? It is that the idea of a polycentric, multipolar, and/or multicentric world order is currently being reconstructed around newly maturing regional arrangements and security communities. (Paupp 2009, 1–2)

I shall argue that these emerging forms of South–South cooperation represent an emerging global incarnation of the idea of humanitarian competition. As such it is a phenomenon that may serve as a template for the evolution of global relations in the twenty-first century. For example, in the context of Asia, international history records the facts that attempts to unify Asia date back about 2,500 years to a period of hierarchically organized state relations. However, the human reality is that

> Despite geographic and historical diversity, the peoples of Asia share a common culture in regard to international relations. One aspect of culture is the set of shared beliefs and sentiments that serve to orient leaders of states to their roles as international actors. The similar roles of leaders of Asian states reflect shared cultural orientations regarding pre-colonial, colonial, and postcolonial development. The reason for this convergence is that historical conditions shaped a common interest in peaceful modes of state behavior. Interlopers from outside the region further underscored the virtues of peaceful statecraft, and the destiny of the countries of Asia has come to depend more and more upon efforts to forge a common identity and a compatible operational code in foreign policy. The Asian Way developed in the years after World War II, as Asian leaders began to deal directly with one another; it is not an indigenous pre-historical cultural concept. The Asian Way arose because it was gradually realized that many so-called principles in international relations observed in Western political experience could not be applied satisfactorily in an Asian context. (Haas 1989, 2–3)

In this same vein, Prof. Andre Gunder Frank astutely observed that "[t]he implications . . . are that the 'Rise' of East Asia need come as no surprise just because it does not fit into the Western scheme of things. . . . *'Leadership' of the world system—more than 'hegemony'—has been temporarily 'centered' in one sector and region (or a few), only to shift again to one or more others. That happened in the nineteenth century, and it appears to be happening again at the beginning of the twenty-first, as the 'center' of the world economy seems to be shifting back to the 'East'"* (Frank 1998, 7; italics added). On this matter, there seems to be a gathering consensus among progressive scholars on this trend. For example, Richard Falk has argued that since 1991 it has become evident that *"the unipolar moment"* was only a brief interregnum (Falk 1994). Similarly, Kothari has argued that "[i]f this reading of the situation is correct, the democratic impulse that lies at the bottom of the upsurges of civil society could also join the battle against global hegemonic forces, though the outcome may still be uncertain" (Kothari 2000, 107).

While the final outcome of this struggle lies in the future and for that reason may still be "uncertain," what can be claimed with certainty is that the nature of this global struggle between the "global hegemony of the industrialized powers" and the nations of the global South has been evident to progressive scholars for decades. In 1984, Prof. R. B. J. Walker acknowledged the fact that "[t]heories of 'development' . . . are said to be a mere mask for the realities of 'underdevelopment.' The universalization of parochial social and political concepts thereby appears as part of a system of stratification, one in which poorer states are integrated into a global division of labor organized by, and to the advantage of, the dominant powers" (Walker 1984a, 7). What critics of the Western approach to "development" have exposed is nothing less than the presence of *"cultural imperialism."* That is why "[i]nternational law, for all that it embodies the universalist hopes of Western liberals, appears as merely a consecration of the will of the great powers. *Invocations of human rights lean more toward the specifically Western version that emphasizes individual freedom rather than socioeconomic well-being"* (Walker 1984a, 15; italics added).

Socioeconomic Well-Being and the Unfulfilled Promises of Human Rights

Hence, as far as the cause of Third World "development" is concerned, as far as the cause of "human rights" is concerned, the truth of the matter is that the critics of Western imperialism and the anticolonial struggles (that begin in earnest in 1919)—as well as the persistent work of nonviolent social and political movements—have actually accomplished more for the cause of advancing human rights than all of the proclamations of Western elites. In this critical regard, Richard Falk notes, the historical record reveals one striking truth:

> The achievement of human rights by shrinking circles of exclusion nationally and globally occurred not mainly because of ethical clarification and moral reflection, but as a result of stones thrown

by critics and initiatives by and on behalf of victims. The spread of rights has depended almost completely on the dedicated work of nonviolent social and political movements that have challenged the established orders of power and privilege all over the world *before their demands were finally translated into legally protected rights.* The remarkable forward global momentum of the last half century is mostly due to the success of the *anti-colonial and anti-apartheid struggles* that liberated millions from oppressive conditions, but also to those developmental success stories that have lifted hundreds of millions more from the crushing burdens of extreme poverty. (Falk 2009, 2–3; italics added)

The historical record that supports this view has, however, been questioned by some scholars who want to challenge the widespread belief that Western countries have been antagonistic to economic and social human rights. One example is that of Daniel Whelan and Jack Donnelly, in their article entitled "The West, Economic and Social Rights, and the Global Human Rights Regime: Setting the Record Straight" (Whelan and Donnelly 2007, 908–49). Based on their particular reading of the Universal Declaration and the Covenants, the development of functional regimes for money, trade, and workers' rights, they set out to "prove" their case that Western advocacy of economic and social rights was strong and essential to creating the postwar international order. They attack as "revisionist history" and as "an almost complete inversion of the truth" the assertion that there has been a *"Western opposition"* to the attainment of these rights (Whelan and Donnelly 2007, 910). Specifically, they state, "While *the myth of Western opposition* has many dimensions, here we take on perhaps the most perverse aspect of the myth, namely, the claim that the West resisted or opposed including economic and social rights in the postwar global human rights regime" (Whelan and Donnelly 2007, 910; italics added). Yet, as will be revealed herein, such an opposition was put in place by the dominant Western powers—both ideologically and structurally. Great Britain's self-imposed mandate to "rule the waves" and ensure that "the sun never set on the British Empire" served to lay the foundations for the continuation of colonial policies and an imperial ideology that could only be maintained through the violation of human rights. By the time the United States assumed its imperial role in 1945 as Great Britain's power had receded, the allure of hegemony and the demands of empire eclipsed America's fidelity to the practice of implementing human rights in its foreign policy and in its hierarchy of economic priorities (Blum 2000, 2004; Chomsky and Herman 1979a,b).

In response to the views of Whelan and Donnelly, Alex Kirkup and Tony Evans have offered the following reply: "From our perspective, what is missing from Whelan and Donnelly is any sense of politics. Their article frames questions of power and interests within conventionally conceived concepts of the state, sovereignty, and natural rights, in the tradition of international society. Therefore, *their framework does not involve an analysis of questions concerning the role of human rights in legitimating the dominant socioeconomic global order which the state inhabits, or the exclusionary practices that arise from adopting particular human rights procedures*" (Kirkup and Evans 2009, 223; italics added). In other words, they have ignored the role of US hegemony and empire which ". . . promoted the construction of global market dominated by US interests. In this sense, the central role of human rights discourse in the post-war order was to legitimize the expansion of global market through universal and inclusive claims of individual freedom" (Kirkup and Evans 2009, 225). So we find the actual content of "*human rights discourse*" has been essentially and effectively bifurcated by dominant Western financial interests who allowed civil and political rights alone to emerge as universal and inalienable rights, while at the same time "[e]conomic and social rights, in contrast, have existed as no more than 'entitlement' won either in the marketplace or by political struggle over the welfare state" (Kirkup and Evans 2009, 225). They maintain that the truth that lies behind this bifurcation of political and civil rights from the realm of social and economic rights can be explained by the fact that "*'positive' economic and social rights place a constraint upon the freedom of market actors. They can only be aspirations because their fulfillment must come at another's expense*" (Kirkup and Evans 2009, 225; italics added).

Similarly, Prof. Susan Kang's response to the Whelan and Donnelly article addresses "*[t]he Unsettled Relationship of Economic and Social Rights and the West: A Response to Whelan and Donnelly*" (Kang 2009, 1006–54). Kang critically notes, "Whelan and Donnelly notably claim that no countries have embraced social and economic rights 'with more genuine commitment or greater actual impact than the United States and Great Britain.' This statement claims that the United States and the United Kingdom had a greater 'commitment' than other states and that they were more influential than other states within negotiations" (Kang 2009, 1008–09). Yet this claim is not accurate insofar as there are ". . . problems with their conception of 'centrality' and claims about the primacy of economic and social rights in the West" (Kang 2009, 1009). As evidence, she points to the fact that ". . . the obligations and extent of economic and social rights remain contested, and social movements and workers' organizations both inside and outside the West continue to make claims for their rights against elites who may not be amenable to such claims" (Kang 2009, 1029). Ironically, Kang also notes that "Whelan and Donnelly recognize that the United States and the West have had a mixed record in terms of promoting economic and social rights internationally" (Kang 2009, 1025). Part of this failure is attributable to the fact that "[t]he US government refuses to ratify many of the basic international labor conventions, citing fears that this might create a 'back door' means to change domestic labor laws"

(Kang 2009, 1016). Hence, it becomes easier to refute the historical illusion that Whelan and Donnelly seek to project when we can acknowledge that "Whelan and Donnelly's claim that by the time of the Universal Declaration *no* Western state had 'any serious theoretical or practical opposition, domestically or internationally, to economic and social rights' is historically difficult to support" (Kang 2009, 1015; italics in original).

After conducting a more thorough review of twentieth-century history, the historical reality is that "*[t]he affirmation of abstract rights managed to endow the modern state with a façade of legitimacy that successfully concealed its deep structures of injustice, abuse, and exploitation*" (Falk 2009, 2; italics added). These deep structural arrangements that allowed for the continuation of injustice, abuse, and exploitation were allowed to remain under the rubric of "sovereignty." After all, the world order since the end of World War II has been built on the guiding principle of "*sovereignty first.*" In truth, however, it was "... not sovereignty as such that presented difficulties, but rather *the prevalence of authoritarianism and colonialism,* as well as the persistence of illiberal elements in even the most democratic of states" (Falk 2009, 3; italics added).

In a groundbreaking chapter entitled "Counter-hegemonic International Law: Rethinking Human Rights and Development as a Third World Strategy," Balakrishnan Rajagopal has noted the following:

> The idea that human rights can be hegemonic can strike its core believers as nothing less than sacrilege. The self-image of human rights discourse is that of a post-imperial discourse, unsullied by the ugly colonial politics of pre-1948, when the Universal Declaration of Human Rights (UDHR) initiated the modern human rights movement. In this self-image the new international law of human rights effectively superseded the old international law of colonialism. To the contrary, one could argue that a true historical reading of the role played by the international human rights corpus in anti-imperial struggles (a task that is yet to be performed thoroughly) may reveal several uncomfortable facts. These include the following: (1) the UDHR did not apply directly to the colonial areas and was subjected to intense maneuvering by Britain at the drafting stage to prevent its application to its colonies despite Soviet pressure; (2) anti-colonial struggles were hardly ever taken up for scrutiny at the UN Commission on Human Rights before many Third World states came on board in 1967, when membership was enlarged, and even then remained tangential on the agenda formally; (3) anti-colonial nationalist revolts in places such as Kenya and Malaya were successfully characterized by the British as 'emergencies' to be dealt with as law and order issues, thereby avoiding the application of either human rights or humanitarian law to these violent encounters; (4) the main anti-imperialist

strand of the human rights discourse—the critique of apartheid in South Africa and of Israeli policies in the Palestinian territories using human rights terms by the Third World during the 1960s to 1980s—remained tangential to the mainstream human rights discourse coming from the West; and (5) very little of the mainstream human rights scholarship acknowledges that human rights discourse influenced or was influenced in any significant way by anti-colonial struggles after World War II, although as Ignatieff notes, the core beliefs of our time, such as the idea of human equality and self-determination, are the result of the anti-colonial revolt against empire. (Rajagopal 2008, 65–66)

What these above-cited points reveal for us (in the task of interpreting the history of human rights) is that there is a huge gap between the *codifications* of human rights versus the actual *implementation* of those rights. In the final analysis,

> [t]he tragic irony . . . is that the enforcement of these rights was left to utterly dysfunctional national law enforcement institutions. Most public justice systems in the developing world have their roots in the *colonial era*, when their core function was to serve those in power—usually the *colonial state*. As the colonial powers departed, authoritarian governments frequently took their place. They inherited the public justice systems of the *colonial past*, which they proceeded to use to protect their own interests and power, in much the same way that their *colonial predecessors* had. Rather than fulfill the *post-colonial mandate* of broad public service, the police and judiciaries of the developing world often serve a narrow set of elite interests. *The public justice systems of this part of the world were never designed to serve the poor, which means that there is often no credible deterrent to restrain those who commit crimes against them.* (Haugen and Boutros 2010, 55; italics added)

So, on the one hand, we find that in the post–World War II era, when a number of scholars and diplomats began to codify international standards on fundamental rights (*such as the Universal Declaration of Human Rights; the International Covenant on Economic, Social, and Cultural Rights; the International Covenant on Civil and Political Rights*), the human rights movement worked to embed the growing body of international norms into national law. However, on the other hand, we also find that "[t]wo generations of global human rights efforts have been predicated—consciously or unconsciously—on assumptions about the effectiveness of the public justice systems in the developing world. But those systems clearly lack effective enforcement tools; as a result, *the great legal reforms of the modern human rights movement often deliver only empty parchment promises to the poor*" (Haugen and Boutros 2010, 55–56; italics added).

The grim prospects for social justice in the twenty-first century have been a long time in the making. The realization of global social justice has been blocked over just the last two centuries[2] by the forces of rampant racial discrimination, militarism, colonialism and neocolonialism, imperialism and neoimperialism, Great Power interventionism, the influence of hegemony and hegemonic preferences, fascist client-states, and the negative effects of the neoliberal economic model supported by the Washington Consensus— just to name a few. Reflecting on where these trends have left humanity in real time, Rajni Kothari observes, "Problems of the world are no longer seen in terms of the possibility of bridging chasms between rich and poor. Instead, the new vision seeks to provide—*to the exclusion of all humanist considerations*—for the unhindered advance of technology that would integrate the world into a single unified world political economy. Large segments of the powerless and backward, comprising a variety of emerging nations, traditional communities, and cultures, are incapable of keeping pace with or finding a place in this rapidly transforming world" (Kothari 2000, 100).

In other words, we are discovering in the first decade of the twenty-first century a heightening of global inequality both within and between nations. The Western democracies are not immune from this phenomenon because they are suffering from the effects of this transformation of civilization into barbarism as well. An inequality that is born of a politics of division, isolation, and social separation is now resulting in a loss of empathy, which is being replaced with the imposition of harsh and draconian measures to "keep the rabble in line." As a result of these trends, it seems that

> Those engaged in a systematic onslaught on the poor and deprived sections of society do not seem to realize the costs of what they are doing. As the sense of insecurity among the people grows alongside persisting poverty, unemployment, and increasing injustice and discrimination, the poor and the unemployed are pushed into a culture of protest and anger, and desperation, contributing further to an overall condition of insecurity that is then exploited by sectarian politicians and is sought to be put down by a criminalized police and paramilitary establishment. Slowly and without their knowing it, the poor are being pushed into a world of crime and criminality, of interethnic violence and militancy against the state. It is this wanton criminalization of poverty spurred on by the politics of the elite that poses the most fundamental crisis of survival. It also poses a crisis in the system and its stability. (Kothari 2000, 101)

These trends expose the soft underbelly of a system of injustice that is eating itself alive. By failing to see life as a totality and the interconnectedness of life in that totality, we are witnessing humanity turn inward and against that which makes us truly human. The transformative vision of which Ikeda and his contemporaries have spoken and been the advocates for is a vision that is at risk as long as individuals fail to engage in a process of inner transformation and as long as elites continue to rule by a philosophy of "divide and conquer," for the reality is that as long as people engage in a politics of division and ignore the totality of their own being and the need to see that same kind of totality reflected in the social, economic, and political systems, the harsh inequalities born of a politics of division and discrimination, injustice and inequality, will simply lead to greater levels of criminality and the denial of human rights. The antidote to these very destructive trends has been set forth by Ikeda, who notes the following:

> The French philosopher and diplomat, Jacques Maritain said that, in order to fulfill the responsibility of ensuring observation of human rights, humanity must become a single, open totality. This means that each individual must be such a totality and participate in a universal totality. Furthermore, *all individuals must be open to contact with all others*. Enlightenment to the Buddhist Law Dharma merges us all into universal totality. The Dharma exists only within human beings and their environment. But all humans are equally endowed with it and therefore equal among themselves and worthy of respect. Awareness of this equality . . . eliminates discrimination and the violations of human rights they cause. (Ikeda and de Athayde 2009, 77)

On this matter, I have argued that it will be necessary to move beyond all exclusionary structures and institutions that continue to deny human rights and replace them with what I call the policies, practices, and priorities of the *"Inclusionary State"* (Paupp 2000). Such a radical and fundamental altering of the current power structure of exclusion was articulated by Martin Luther King and Robert F. Kennedy. It was an approach that finally experienced success with the fall of the apartheid regime in South Africa and the ascension to that nation's presidency by Nelson Mandela.

In order to implement Ikeda's vision, it will be necessary to acknowledge that "all individuals must be open to contact with all others." In the absence of this spirit of openness it will be impossible for the Buddhist law dharma to be made operative and thereby effectuate the merger of all people into a universal totality that makes possible the recognition of our equality within and between ourselves as people who are worthy of respect. Today, instead of a vibrant universal totality we find that people are still trapped within oppressive and exploitative institutional structures and channels that work to deny them the exercise of this consciousness of our equality and entitlement to mutual respect, thereby denying the actualization of our human rights. For Kothari, this situation means that "[i]f the poor have no recognized institutional channels through which to take up their grievances against the continuous injustices that they face, and if the elite no longer considers it necessary to act through the same institutions and their systems of accountability—they already seem to be acting more and more outside the institutional framework, thereby reducing their legitimacy—there seems to be less and less scope for improving the condition of the people through the operation of the existing order" (Kothari 2000, 101). In point of fact, it has become quite clear that the "existing order" is probably not worth preserving. In this regard, Ikeda has recognized the historical truth that

> once acquired, liberty alone proved insufficient to the protection of the weak and the disabled. Unbridled liberty was a mixed blessing. *Western laissez-faire policies in the eighteenth and nineteenth century widened the gap between the rich and the poor and condoned serious social injustices. A ruthlessly competitive society ignored the weak, disabled and unsuccessful. To rectify the situation, it became necessary to formulate new human rights to guard the victims of unrestrained economic and social license.* (Ikeda and de Athayde 2009, 104; italics added)

On a global scale, in terms of North–South disparities, Ikeda has quoted from the 1996 Human Development Report of the UN development program, which noted that the problems of poverty, population growth, and environmental problems are directly attributable to the North–South disparities that have resulted from the structure of the international economy. Therefore, not only have the United States and Europe failed to advance human rights and equality within their own sovereign borders, but their own policies have engendered *a global crisis* which has resulted in the global denial of human rights, the global failure of humanity to be able to protect human dignity and equality, and has created a global legitimacy crisis for the current system. In this regard, "The report describes the distortions of economic growth under five patterns: (1) *jobless growth* (growth without an increase in job opportunities); (2) *ruthless growth* (growth that does nothing to redress the disparity between rich and poor); (3) *voiceless growth* (growth not accompanied by democratization or the advance of individuals in society); (4) *rootless growth* (growth that infringes on the ethnic identity of individuals); and (5) *futureless growth* (growth through wasteful consumption of resources needed by future generations). *In sum, the report says 'development that perpetuates today's inequalities is neither sustainable nor worth sustaining'*" (Ikeda 2001a, 163–64; italics added). Again, it is not just my opinion, or just the opinion of the authors of the UN development program report, but Ikeda's own opinion as well that maintains that this present system, which perpetuates today's inequalities, is *"neither sustainable nor worth sustaining."*

In summary, the current national and global system of neoliberal capitalism has created social conditions that are dehumanizing for all concerned.

These realities represent a worsening of conditions for all humanity, at every level. In the words and analysis of Kothari, we find that

> It is not just the poor that are pitched against the rich and the rich against the poor. The poor also fight against other poor, faced as they are by an overall climate of deprivation and a growing sense of insecurity among various subgroups. But such a combination of deprivation and a sense of insecurity—getting worse because of inflation and unemployment—is also hurting the less poor sections of society. It is producing divisions among the middle classes and even sections of the rich. (Kothari 2000, 101)

Yet at the same time there are reasons for hope. As we begin to witness the inexorable and inevitable "crumbling walls" of US hegemony give way to a new posthegemonic era of "rising regions," we shall witness the phenomenon of the *process of regionalization* and the *ideology of regionalism* begin to create a multicentric world of governing structures that are infinitely more humane and inclusive than the old capitalistically centered ones of the neoliberal order and variety (Paupp 2009).

Similarly, Kothari maintains that

> Despite the growth of atomizing tendencies there exists a wide arena of plural identities and structures, and these are likely to grow, giving rise to both new possibilities and new vulnerabilities. Globally, the inherent multilateralism provides a broad arena of pluralism despite recent deformities based on various modes of centralization and globalization. To this is being added, by leading exponents of word order, *a 'regional alternative.' Within individual nations . . . there exist—and these are growing—the various federal and federating (and confederating) structures and, within these, diverse regional and social units, communities, castes, and ethnically and ecologically based habitats, all of them seeking a place under the sun as part of a larger, more inclusive and plural structure.* (Kothari 2000, 105; italics added)

Kothari's description perfectly matches my view of an emerging world order of global relations that will be mainly defined by the *processes of regionalization* and the *ideology of regionalism* (Paupp 2009). Kothari's description of this emerging world order also perfectly matches Ikeda's discussions about the global movement toward a universal totality that respects the rights, dignity, and equality of individuals. The clear articulation of this view and vision is strongly reminiscent of *The Geography of Human Life*, published at the beginning of the twentieth century by Tsunesaburo Makiguchi. The relevance, beauty, and prescience of this work can be found in the way that it accomplishes an intertwining of both descriptive and predictive elements.

Responding to the book's message and meaning, Ikeda states, "Moving from the descriptive to the predictive, he set out a vision of what he termed 'humanitarian competition,' which represents a profound qualitative transformation of competition itself, toward a model that recognizes our interrelatedness and emphasized the cooperative aspects of living. He envisaged a time in which people and countries would compete—in the original sense of the words *striving together*—to make the greatest contribution to human happiness and well-being" (Ikeda 2001a, 71–72; italics in original). In light of the emerging trends in the first decade of the twenty-first century, it would seem that Makiguchi's vision is in the process of being incarnated into human history. If that is the case, then the promise contained in the vision of an era of humanitarian competition is emerging in our midst.

Conclusion: The Power of Character and the Concept of "Universal Humanity"

This chapter has examined the dynamic interplay of individual character as a transformative force in juxtaposition to the emergence of a global civilization of peace as the external manifestation of that internal achievement. Therefore, it is appropriate to conclude our thoughts with that dynamic in mind. Ikeda's reflections on this subject inspired him to write this: "Jose Marti, during the struggle for the independence of his homeland, Cuba, declared his true homeland to be all of humanity. He also asserted that there can be no hatred between races because 'there are no races'—that is, race is an artificially constructed concept. I firmly believe that the key to resolving all forms of conflict among ethnic groups lies in discovering and revealing the kind of universal humanity so powerfully embodied in Dr. King, America's conscience, and Jose Marti, Cuba's conscience" (Ikeda 2001a, 114).

This same worldview or "frame of reference" is also characteristic of what has been described as the "Asian Way" insofar as it constitutes an approach to domestic and international relations that stresses the idea that there is an equality of cultures and each should be accorded equal status. In this sense, the Asian Way is a conceptual paradigm that is quite complementary to the idea of "*universal*" because, "[a]s Thanat Khoman stated, the *Asian Way* comprises a 'spirit of tolerance and partnership' that contrasts sharply with the 'concept of domination and subjugation' that typified the imperialist powers in their dealings with Asian peoples. *Given ethnic divisions and national rivalries, international relations should not be likened to fights, to games, or to debates but instead to informal discussions in which each party is accorded equal status*" (Haas 1989, 6; italics added). According to Michael Haas, "The theory of the Asian way . . . is *a cultural theory of international cooperation*. . . . The net result of collaborative efforts of the Asian Way has been a fuller respect for the integrity of other countries, a spirit of solidarity and sharing, a belief that intense conflict is unacceptably fratricidal and unprofitable, and thus the development of a peaceful community among Asian countries. Countries outside the web of interrelationships forged by the Asian Way continue to be plagued with economic, political, and technical difficulties in their efforts to achieve economic development" (Hass 1989, 21; italics in original). In this regard, the theory of the Asian Way can help us to propel our global thinking, policies, and developmental paradigm in a new direction as far as the idea of the *"right to development"* is treated in the context of international law and political practice.

As defined by the UN-approved "Declaration on the Right to Development" in 1986, every human being and *all peoples have the right to development*, to participate in, contribute to, and enjoy economic, social, cultural, and political development. Yet despite the intent of this statement, a debate has continued to take place concerning the extent of this right. On one side, there are those who maintain that this right remains on the level of political rhetoric. On the other side of the debate are those who rely on Article 28 of the UN Universal Declaration to argue that respect for human rights involves obligations not only to states but to individuals as well (Felice 1996, 70). What can be said with some degree of certainty is that, as far as definitions are concerned, there is a collective, social dimension to what it means to be a human being that must be included in any discussion of human rights (Felice 1996, 70). Therefore, we are left to contemplate what this right means when we juxtapose its claims to universality up against the idea that "[h]uman rights apply at the local, national, and international levels" (Felice 1996, 70).

Emerging from discussions about this principle, we must then confront the objective fact that there is a severe global maldistribution of wealth. While one-third of the world is rich, the vast majority remain poor. It is an objective reality that is reinforced by the structural realities of hierarchy and hegemony—structural realities that have led to great unevenness throughout the world economy. Given the human suffering and injustices that have emerged in conjunction with these structural realities in the global economy, William Felice argues, "*This notion of the right to development as a collective human right and a principle of international law challenges all of us to side with the poor.... It rejects the elite bias found in legal positivism*" (Felice 1996, 89; italics added).

On this very point Felice finds common ground with another scholar of international law, Balakrishnan Rajagopal, who has been critical of the historical failure of the Bretton Woods Institutions (BWIs)—the World Bank and IMF—to take into account the voices and the real needs of the poor throughout the global South (Third World). According to Rajagopal, "Ignoring the role of the local as an agent of institutional transformation is, I maintain, inseparable from the hegemonic nature of international law as an elitist discipline" (Rajagopal 2000, 530). After all, if the universal claim of human rights is ever to be recognized, then the excluded individuals and groups of the world need to be made a part of this inclusive enterprise. Only in that way can the universal claims and needs of humanity be given a voice and a direction in the shaping of their own history, not to mention in the struggle to achieve social justice.

The functionalist explanation of international institutions stands for the proposition that institutions are "born and expand due to top-down policy decisions that correlate with the functional needs of international society. This theory does not recognize grassroots groups, individuals, or social movements as agents of institutional transformation or international legal history" (Rajagopal 2000, 530–31). The clearly exclusionary focus of this theory is perfectly designed to maintain an elite hierarchy while, at the same time, serves as an ideological force for the purpose of protecting an international status quo that is supportive of hegemonic practices. Therefore, in order to be truthful about history, change, as well as the transformative power of individuals, we need to rescue the theory of institutional change in the BWIs from the elites who want to continue to dominate and perpetuate an unjust global hierarchy and hegemony for the rich. That is why Rajagopal states, "It is my argument that the expansion and renewal of international institutions cannot be understood in isolation from Third World resistance. Indeed, I claim that social movements from the Third World such as peasant rebellions, environmental movements, and human rights movements, have propelled the expansion of international institutions since the late 1960s. In other words, the very architecture of contemporary international law has been constituted by its continuous evocation of and interaction with the category '*Third World*,' which has included not only states, but also these social movements" (Rajagopal 2000, 532). These social movements constitute what he calls "*subaltern groups*" (subordinated groups). They have been largely made up of protest groups and social movements dedicated to human rights and social justice issues and demands. Unfortunately, ". . . international law has never been concerned primarily with mass protest or social movements, except in the context of self-determination and the formation of states" (Rajagopal 2000, 534). Again, this concern for this one exception goes back to the primacy concern of Western elites to maintain the status quo in international affairs—especially as it related to the support of hegemonic practices, interests, and power.

Insofar as the BWIs were born in the aftermath of World War II and the product of the United States, as leader of the "Free World," the BWIs were born into the mentality of the Cold War—a confrontational paradigm that viewed the West's financial predominance in global affairs as a "national security" concern. Hence, an examination of this period reveals that "[t]his marriage of security and development was reflected in the academic discourse as well as in the practice of the BWIs" (Rajagopal 2000, 544). It was a situation further complicated by the fact that in the practices and policies of the World Bank, the security dimensions of development began to have a major impact, in addition to the fact that the World Bank was "... dependent upon Wall Street for its financing" (Rajagopal 2000, 546). It was only with pressure from social movements and human rights advocates that the World Bank would evolve toward "discovering" poverty as part of its discourse and begin to engage the "poor, dark, and hungry masses of the Third World."

This movement of the BWIs toward the recognition of what Ikeda has called our universal humanity would only come gradually, in a series of steps. Each step that was taken reflected the influence of Third World social movements, comprised of persons of conscience, who used the power of the "human revolution" to engage in "altruistic living" by engaging in these movements for social justice. The recalcitrance of the West and its hegemonic machinations with respect to ideas about national security and the sanctity of international capital and finance was a constant source of frustration and challenge for those who sought a newer world.

Yet steps were taken in response to these Third World pressures and the social movements driving them. In this regard,

> First, there was the realization that in the Cold War–driven competition for allegiance of regimes, it was essential to promote intra-country redistribution to pacify the masses that were becoming restive due to rising anti-colonialism and nationalism . . . Second, there was also an awareness that traditional foreign lending was too focused on accumulation of capital (mainly through infrastructure and power projects) and too little on so-called social lending . . . Third—and connected to the first two—the World Bank itself was clearly realizing the politically quiescent effect that its loans were having on Third World peoples . . . Fourth, the discovery of so-called underdevelopment as a domain of intervention in the 1950s had put poverty squarely on the international agenda. (Rajagopal 2000, 548–49)

In fact, the discovery of poverty emerged as a working principle of the process whereby the domain of interaction between the West and the non-West was defined. However, this turn in perspective was not fully realized until the 1970s. Hence, it may be surmised that "the BWIs were neither benevolent do-gooders nor mechanistic tools in the hands of global capital opposed to social justice and equity. Rather, they constituted a complex space in which power, justice, security, and humanitarianism functioned in contradictory and complementary ways" (Rajagopal 2000, 551). In the final analysis, what the historical record demonstrates is that "the evolution of the BWIs is the result of an ambivalent urge to engage and contain the popular energy unleashed by social movements of various kinds emanating from the Third World, and not the result of functionalist imperatives of the geniuses of international institutional design" (Rajagopal 2000, 577).

What a review of the historical record of development from the mid-twentieth century to the dawn of the twenty-first century makes clear is that "[i]t challenges us to move the rights to development out of the realm of charity and into the realm of entitlement under international law. It rejects the elite bias found in legal positivism. It begins with the developmental needs of the bottom half of the world's population as a compelling moral framework to locate rights" (Felice 1996, 89). This same perspective is, as we have already seen in this chapter, reflective of Latin American liberation theology, the Buddhist emphasis on altruistic living, and Ikeda's reinvigoration of the concept of humanitarian competition. In all of these endeavors, avenues, and channels for the human revolution, we discover that when we look to the poor, the excluded, the victims of injustice, we discover that meeting their needs and hearing their voices constitute the necessary first steps toward the realization of our common and universal humanity. We also discover that "[f]rom these needs it is possible to determine rights and duties for both individuals and governments to meet the right to development. In today's maldeveloped world, it is hard to imagine a more pressing and urgent legal and moral priority" (Felice 1996, 89). What is even more revelatory about the problem of poverty is that it has been a decades-old reality in which the real solutions have been known and acknowledged since the 1960s. For example, between 1967 and 1968, Martin King spoke out against the Vietnam War because he understood that the bombs that were dropped in Vietnam "exploded in American cities" as the funds to fight poverty dried up to pay for the war. In this environment, as historian Thomas Jackson notes, "King had spoken of America as a world house of international people. But now, amid collapsing domestic dreams, King thought it all the more important to put America's house in order and *shift resources from militarism to the domestic and global conquest of poverty*" (Jackson 2007, 328; italics added). This insight is especially relevant because, "[i]n more graphic terms, poverty becomes a crucible in which social discrimination, including the degradation of institutions such as health care and education, and the arbitrariness of power fester and become self-sustaining. 'Growth' often presented as a cure-all in dominant policies of poverty alleviation, appears a faint solution to this deeper political condition" (Mittelman and Tambe 2000, 79). The ideology of "growth" has been the mantra of neoliberal economists and their advocates since the early 1980s. Yet it is little more than an ideological fig leaf that attempts to cover the negative effects of corporate globalization, privatization, and unabated militarism.

Today, the global crisis of the early twenty-first century reveals itself as an inflated version of the crisis of 1967 and 1968 which Martin King attempted to redress. The conditions that now exist are characterized by growing inequalities at every level of global society. Some scholars have specifically blamed global corporate power for making these conditions worse. For example, Robin Broad and John Cavanagh argue that

> [r]ather than create an integrated global village, these corporations
> are weaving webs of production, consumption, finance, and culture
> that incorporate billions of people but leave out billions more.....
> For example, researchers at the Institute for Policy Studies cal-
> culate that the combined wealth of the world's 447 billionaires is
> greater than the income of the poorest half of the world's people....
> These and similar calculations show that at least two-thirds of
> the world's people are left out, hurt, or marginalized by global-
> ization. . . . The inequalities are growing within nations as well
> as between blocks of nations. (Broad and Cavanagh 2000, 193;
> italics added)

What will be the final result of these trends? It has been suggested that "*[s]uch greed and hubris may well be the final straw which causes the American empire to unravel and the entire system to fall apart.* The growth of militarism, as Martin King prophesied, may finally cause the end of democracy in America, with the unraveling ultimately resulting from an economic collapse spurred on by *the exploitative hegemony called globalization* by which America seeks to impose its model on the major economies of the world—a model in which unbridled, non-value-producing speculators thrive and consumerism is a sacred activity" (Pepper 2003, 171; italics added). It is a prediction made by many scholars over the last decade for these reasons—and a few more (Paupp 2007, 2009).

Throughout the course of this chapter we have identified and quoted Ikeda on these issues and cited his positions. We have cited other authorities and commentators either from earlier times or his contemporaries. In so doing, we have presented a case against the current order of privilege and power and, at the same time, articulated both solutions and alternatives that have the capacity to birth into existence a more peaceful global order—a global civilization wherein all humanity could benefit. At some point in the not too distant future it will come into being. In the meantime, the main challenge and greatest problem is that the global current order will not disappear or go quietly into the night of history. Given its addictions to profits above people, militarism above diplomacy and dialogue, environmental degradation above environmental sustainability, it is doubtful that it will admit to the errors of its ways, the folly of its judgments, or admit to the cruelty it has imposed on the poor, the vulnerable, and the defenseless. Yet it is also true that it will probably just come crashing down one day under the weight of its own contradictions, misplaced values, and crimes against humanity. These are its sins. And as the Old and New Testament scriptures have declared, "The wages of sin are death." Out of its death the hope of a new and more humane world may yet be born. In fact, humanity may be in the midst of witnessing the final birth pangs of a new era in the first decades of the twenty-first century.

Notes

1. As Urbain (2010) has clarified, in Ikeda's texts, the term *human revolution* mostly designates a specific form of inner transformation that can be accomplished by the practice of a form of Buddhism called Nichiren Buddhism. Throughout this volume, however, it is used not only in the specific meaning mentioned above but as a metonymy for any type of inner transformation, accomplished by any spiritual or nonspiritual means.
2. Kant and the Enlightenment thinkers, in the way they expressed the vision for global social justice, are considered as having formulated "what should have been" by the authors.

5

Dialogue and Dialogic Mechanisms: Creating a Global Framework for Deliberative Democracy, Human Rights, and Cultural Pluralism

"The splitting of the world into antagonistic groups is essentially attributable to a lack of mutual understanding among peoples . . . I believe that the most crucial key to world peace is the promotion of understanding among peoples. When this understanding becomes a reality, Americans and Russians alike will see that they are similar in many respects and that each belongs to the same human race. When an overflowing stream of common feeling underlies the speech and actions of all people, the hostility of governments will become absurd . . . To build mutual understanding as a sound foundation for international relations is the first prerequisite for lasting world peace."

—Daisaku Ikeda
(Ikeda and Toynbee [1976] 2007, 237)

"The awakening of selfhood, brought on by the differentiation process, is crucial to the development and extension of empathy. The more individualized and developed the self is, the greater is our sense of our own unique, mortal existence, as well as our existential aloneness and the many challenges we face in the struggle to be and to flourish. It is these very feelings in ourselves that allow us to empathize with similar existential feelings in others . . . This is the process that characterizes what we call civilization. Civilization is the detribalization of blood ties and the resocialization of distinct individuals based on associational ties. Empathetic extension is the psychological mechanism that

> *makes the conversion and the transition possible. When we*
> *say to civilize, we mean to empathize."*
>
> —Jeremy Rifkin
> (Rifkin 2009, 24)

> *"... the seeds of human community are sown the moment human*
> *beings enter into intercourse with each other, not the moment they*
> *decide to settle down together within the same territory. Rather than*
> *being necessary, boundaries are therefore arbitrary restrictions on*
> *such intercourse, and on those very practices of sharing*
> *that are constitutive of the possibility of human*
> *community."*
>
> —Jens Bartelson
> (Bartelson 2009, 178)

The role of dialogue in human affairs is of the most profound significance in the thought and philosophy of Ikeda. Dialogue is foundational with respect to human affairs and the human prospect. If human history is to have a future, then that future will be the product of effective, transformative, and truthful dialogues between not only individuals and groups, but also between nations and between different cultures. Emerging out of these dialogic processes humans will create their future. In Ikeda's words we find the strongest articulation of what the transformative power of dialogue can accomplish when we realize that "[t]he future fate of our planet depends in large measure on the extent to which we can strengthen and expand human abilities to engage in dialogue. If, as the Spanish philosopher Ortega y Gasset said, violence is the Magna Carta of barbarism, dialogue can be called the Magna Carta of civilization" (Ikeda and Yalman 2009, 117). Ikeda sees the role of dialogue as essential in making a more peaceful global civilization possible because the dialogic method is not meant to "impose" a particular point of view or political arrangement upon the world. Rather, dialogue is understood to be dedicated to furthering the evolution of a more peaceful global civilization as it seeks the voluntary participation of all people in a democratized dialogue about all of those issues which impact upon the human future. Herein lies both the genius and the dynamic of dialogue in the service of civilization. In the words of Prof. Majid Tehranian, "Both empires and civilization have a dream in common: social order and harmony. They part company in their methods: empires impose; civilizations seek voluntary participation" (Tehranian 2007, 15).

The Role of Dialogue in an Age of Interdependence

As a contemporary of Ikeda and as one who has engaged in dialogue with him, we find in the words of Majid Tehranian an insightful and thoughtful contribution to our reflections and continuing investigation into the role of dialogue in conjunction with an explication of the true meaning of the word "civilization." From the perspective of Tehranian, it is vitally important to avoid the ideological uses of the term "civilization." Rather, he strongly advocates that we work to ". . . reconstruct it as a normative concept aiming at the pacific methods of settling human conflicts" (Tehranian 2007, 8). He argues that

> [t]he need for this re-conceptualization is compelling. The human family stands at a crucial juncture. The technological advances of the past ten thousand years have created a global village, but the village is in a deepening state of terror. *Unless civilized methods of governance are pursued and perfected, terrorism as a method of warfare between states and oppositions will continue.* Prejudice and hatred rather than compassion and love will rule the world (Tehranian 2007, 8; italics added).

In other words, the phenomenon of globalization has created a more integrated world in the realms of economics, trade, and communications, but in so doing it has exacerbated old fears, ethnic rivalries, and has situated privileged economic minorities in positions of power while the vast majority of people have been excluded from the fruits of progress. Governance on the global level has largely been left at the mercy of the markets. The result is that markets remain largely devoid of concern for the dignity and rights of the person because they are focused on obtaining economic profits and maintaining elite and privileged positions for the few. As a result, we are now starting to discover that there is an incompatibility between markets and democracy. On this matter, Amy Chua notes that

> [a]lthough rarely acknowledged by international policymakers, the conflict between markets and democracy in the developing world is real, combustible, and sometimes lethal. The mediating devices found in the developed world are generally absent from developing societies—an absence made especially problematic given the extent of poverty and the rapidity of democratization in the developing world. Moreover, in some developing countries, free market democracy faces an additional, formidable structural problem: the problem of market-dominant ethnic minorities. This distinctive mapping of ethnicity onto class—generally not seen in the developed world today—pits an impoverished 'indigenous' majority against an economically dominant "outsider" minority, converting the paradox of free market democracy into an engine of potentially catastrophic ethnonationalism (Chua 2000, 378–79).

In light of all of these problems and contradictions, Chua correctly observes that "[a]s we enter the new millennium, some of the optimism about the immediate prospects of markets and democracy in the developing world has worn off . . . But rather than facing up to the painful, often awkward realities of the developing world, the international community has tended instead to grasp for new cure-alls and buzzwords" (Chua 2000, 379).

In contrast to cure-alls and buzzwords, Ikeda has specifically advocated the concrete need to give greater attention to meeting the requirements for the actualization of a "philosophy of coexistence that will permit us to build a world of human harmony" (Ikeda 2001a, 67). This means that we must disband with stereotypes which only work to obscure the truth of people and situations. Therefore, Ikeda concludes that "[t]his is why person-to-person dialogue—always the basis of dialogue among civilizations—is more than ever in demand. I am convinced that we can solve any problem as long as we keep our minds open and stand firm in our belief in our common humanity" (Ikeda 2001a, 67).

By centralizing the significance of dialogue, Ikeda has taken us out of the realm of abstractions and cultural constructs, as well as discourses and ideologies that so often impede human communication and the search for truth. After all, we cannot really depend on a conceptual construct called "world order" to organize the world. From Ikeda's perspective, we need to recognize our own power to order the world in a more peaceful and harmonious direction by embracing an attitude of tolerance toward the plurality and diversity of peoples and cultures that exist in this one world. Hence, Ikeda reminds us that "[t]olerance is more than just a mental attitude; it must grow out of a sense of larger order and coexistence, a cosmic sensibility that issues up from the deepest wellsprings of life . . . Tolerance rooted in a world view of dynamic interdependence can, I believe, be instrumental in enabling us *to transcend the clash of civilizations* and to realize a philosophy of coexistence that will permit us to build a world of human harmony" (Ikeda 2001a, 67; italics added). However, that is not an approach or viewpoint embodied within the Western/capitalist view of world order—the most dominant and dominating perspective on "world order."

Transcending Western Dominance by Embracing Cultural Pluralism

Insofar as our very idea of *world order* or *world politics* has been predominantly the product of an essentially European or Western tradition of thought—with particular historical, geographical, economic and ideological interests—it is an idea that ". . . seeks to understand, explain and guide events which have long ceased to be only European or even Western in their scope" (Walker 1984b, 182). In other words, the Western produced model or paradigm of world order is transfixed upon its own time, place, and situation in the historical continuum. By failing to see that Western conceptions of world order remain trapped within the temporal boundaries of the Western experience, it has allowed its concepts and perspectives on the true nature of "world order" to be trapped within the delimiting boundaries of particular and historically-conditioned categories of thought, discourse, and interpretation. It is this narrow and limited lens of interpretation and conceptualization that renders it a less than truthful picture of the world—a world which is comprised of a plurality of civilizations, traditions, and cultures. Given this assessment of the dominant Western paradigm for world order, we can say of this particular version of world order, derived as it is from a history of Western dominance in world affairs, that "[w]hile grasping at a global or universal phenomenon, it does so almost entirely within one culturally and intellectually circumscribed perspective" (Walker 1984b, 182).

The direct consequence of this condition is a form of reasoning that remains locked into the fabric of the past, a past wherein conflict is inevitable because categories of thought and action really do not change that much. Hence, Samuel Huntington argues in his now classic book, *The Clash of Civilizations and the Remaking of World Order* (1996), that ". . . the post-Cold War world is a world of seven or eight major civilizations. Cultural commonalities and differences shape the interests, antagonisms, and associations of states. The most important countries in the world come overwhelmingly from different civilizations. The local conflicts most likely to escalate into broader war are those between groups and states from different civilizations" (Huntington 1996, 29). Huntington's thesis, as expressed in the above-cited quote from his book, derives its power from the assumption that we can neatly place civilizations within boundaries and then extrapolate from the differences between these bounded cultural regions that such differences will lead to conflict and war. Huntington begins his analysis of conflict in the contemporary world through the prism of the idea that "identity wars" emerge out of these bounded cultural regions when previously multiple identities "become focused and hardened." This process leads to increases in violence wherein a "hate dynamic" emerges which is fed by mutual fears and distrust. Under these conditions, he argues that "[e]ach side dramatizes and magnifies the distinction between the forces of virtue and the forces of evil and eventually attempts to transform this distinction into the ultimate distinction between the quick and the dead" (Huntington 1996, 266).

However, what if our moral values and civilizational experiences are not circumscribed by artificial boundaries? What if we can argue that our moral values actually arise from our ability to share meaningful experiences in common with other people? In this regard, Jens Bartelson has noted that ". . . if our moral values do not derive from the particular communities we happen to inhabit, but rather from our ability to share meaningful experiences in common with other people, then such values would stand an equal chance of evolving irrespective of the existence of boundaries. So, even if we agreed that some sense of community is indeed necessary in order for any morality to evolve, there is no reason to assume that this sense of community requires the prior existence of bounded societies in order to emerge and spread" (Bartelson 2009, 178). The same point is made by Ikeda: "As explained by the Buddhist doctrine of 'dependent origination,' no phenomenon in either the human or natural domains arises independently of all others. The cosmos is created through the interrelation and interdependence of all things" (Ikeda 2001a, 67).

It is precisely this point that is missed by Huntington's "clash thesis." Huntington simply fails to see or to acknowledge the possibility of intercivilizational sharing, commonality, dialogue, culture, and discourse as the means to create a common value structure. By failing to see the dynamics that have historically arisen out of numerous global examples of interrelatedness and interdependence, Huntington's thesis is automatically thrown into a world of artificial boundaries in which differences are so conflated that people from the same geographically-bounded area are pigeonholed and categorized into neat compartments while, on the other hand, cultures and traditions that are geographically and culturally located in other parts of the world are automatically set at odds against the West. This simplistic framework is articulated by Huntington in his rather short depiction of the dominant division in the world order of the twenty-first century as "the West and the rest." He frames intercivilizational issues in the starkest and most artificial terms when he asserts that

> [i]n the emerging world, the relations between states and groups from different civilizations will not be close and will often be antagonistic ... At the micro level, the most violent fault lines are between Islam and its Orthodox, Hindu, African, and Western Christian neighbors. At the macro level, the dominant division is between "the West and the rest," with the most intense conflicts occurring between Muslim and Asian societies on the one hand, and the West on the other. The dangerous clashes of the future are likely to arise from the interaction of Western arrogance, Islamic intolerance, and Sinic assertiveness (Huntington 1996, 183).

Always seeking out differences and never searching for clear commonalities that would point toward the interaction and interconnectedness of the world's various cultures and civilizations, Huntington increasingly continues his effort to fortify the walls of one civilization against the walls of another. He does so by his incessant efforts to draw out differentiations between Western and non-Western civilizations. We can see this most clearly in Huntington's argument about the source of the world's leading political ideologies and the world's leading religions. On this point, Huntington maintains that

> [t]he great political ideologies of the twentieth century include liberalism, socialism, anarchism, corporatism, Marxism, communism,

social democracy, conservatism, nationalism, fascism, and Christian democracy. They all share one thing in common: they are products of Western civilization. No other civilization has generated a significant political ideology. The West, however, has never generated a major religion. The great religions of the world are all products of non-Western civilizations and, in most cases, antedate Western civilization. As the world moves out of its Western phase, the ideologies which typified late Western civilization decline, and their place is taken by religions and other culturally based forms of identity and commitment . . . The intracivilizational clash of political ideas spawned by the West is being supplanted by an intracivilizational clash of culture and religion" (Huntington 1996, 53–54).

In assessing the historical validity of this statement we have to ask ourselves whether Huntington is describing actual historical divisions between civilizations or, in the alternative, whether he is trying to create divisions. From a more historically-oriented perspective, it has been argued that "[i]n the past as today, many who preached about a 'clash of civilizations' were trying to create divisions, not describe them. Islamic and Christian religions drew upon common cultural materials, and both were shaped at the intersection of the Mediterranean Sea and its adjacent landmasses, extending into Europe, Africa, and southwest Asia. The clashes were real enough, but they had more to do with similarity than difference, with overlapping ideas, resources, and territorial ambitions" (Burbank and Cooper 2010, 70).

In large measure, it can be argued that Huntington's "clash thesis" is representative of a culturally and intellectually constrained perspective which has made possible the West's historical drive for cultural, military, economic, and political dominance. At the same time, it embodies an imperialistic perspective which is guilty of failing to respect or to acknowledge the plurality of the world's varied cultural traditions. The centralization of the West's role in the history of human civilizations only serves to circumscribe the truth of humankind's historical unfolding. By masking this historical truth, it has the effect of turning the writing of history into an ideological project that is more dedicated to the explication of an ideological and/or imperialistic agenda than being an explication of the human experience that can lead to seeing commonalities and a shared experience which may open the door to dialogue and greater understanding. In so doing, it is a perspective on world history that fails to recognize that there exists a genuine plurality of cultural traditions.

By acknowledging this fundamental limitation in Huntington's thesis, we are now free to come to terms with the fact that these Western-dominated concepts and abstract constructions of "world order" have misconceived other civilizations—as well as its own. We can make this argument for a number of reasons. First, because "[c]ivilizations exist in the plural. They coexist with each other within one civilization of modernity, or what we often call today a global world. Civilizations are pluralist. Their internal pluralism results from multiple traditions and vigorous debates and disagreements" (Katzenstein 2010, 1). From the vantage point of cultural pluralism and the recognition of multiple traditions, various scholars have noted that "[c]ivilizations are better understood as ongoing processes, and in particular, as ongoing processes through which boundaries are continually produced and reproduced" (Hall and Jackson 2007, 6). Second, the shifting boundaries between civilizations point to not only patterns of differentiation, but also to the foundations of a united humankind. The various communities and the variety of civilizations that have arisen throughout history cannot be adequately understood in isolation from one another. Rather, it is the case that "[s]ince human communities have all been formed on the basis of the common capacities of their members, particular communities cannot be understood in isolation from the concerns of mankind as a whole. Since each particular community derives its existence from such a universal community, relations between such lesser communities must be understood as fundamentally embedded within this larger whole" (Bartelson 2009, 140). A similar view has been expressed by Prof. Terry Nardin: "Both the idea of a society of states and that of a world society of individuals are abstractions according to which the complex and mutable reality of world affairs has been interpreted. Neither offers a completely accurate description of world order, although at different historical moments one has seemed more plausible than the other" (Nardin 1983, 44).

Given these critiques of "world order" we can better appreciate the inadequacy of the three major accounts of modern world politics or world order—the liberal realists, the liberal functionalists/technocrats/utopians, and the neo-Marxian structuralists. All three accounts suffer from the fact that they are "excessively reductionist and deterministic" (Walker 1984b, 197). All three of these constructions about "world order" are actually discourses which have both descriptive and prescriptive categories of contemporary political life. Therefore, what is required in assessing the category of "world order" and "civilization" is an appreciation of what these various accounts and discourses about the nature of world order actually embody and how they function. On this very point, one scholar has noted that ". . . discourse is, in a fundamental sense, a colonization of our understanding by the society in which we live and, because of its constitutive relation to social practices, implies a uniformization of our lives" (Blasius 1984, 246).

To embark upon an attempt to bring uniformity to our discourse is to work, at the same time, to undermine the integrity of our dialogue—within and between nations. The attempt to bring such uniformity usually serves a political function—to solidify the power of the status quo, as well as the concepts, ideologies, and patterns of thought that support it and give it legitimacy. Such an effort does a disservice to the integrity of dialogue as a truth-finding function. The attempt to impose uniformity on consciousness and discourse also incapacitates and neuters the power of deliberative democracy to transcend the narrow interests of the powerful and those forces that support the current arrangements of economic, social, and political privilege. In order to overcome this situation, Ikeda argues that dialogue itself must transcend the temptation to automatically and uncritically adopt the conventions and assumptions of the moment. The danger to the integrity of dialogue which is posed by the imposition of the dominant conventions and assumptions of the moment is that it will have the effect of abrogating both the integrity of culture and the dignity of the individual at the same time. Ikeda notes that "[a]s you know, the English word 'culture' derives from the Latin verb *colere*, to till or cultivate. We cultivate the individual human being by filling the fields of intellect, emotions, and thought. On a larger scale, we improve culture by cultivating society. The idea of culture inspires expectations for seeking and manifesting inner psychological and spiritual values" (Ikeda and Diez-Hochleitner 2008, 98; italics in original).

From Ikeda's perspective, we learn that the ultimate purpose of dialogue is not merely to defend or promote a position, but rather to discover truth. In this regard, Ikeda emphatically asserts that "[w]hen dialogue is pursued in the spirit or with the intention of influencing others, it is impossible to proceed without discussing issues of right and wrong, good and evil. This is because, as Montaigne says, the ultimate purpose of dialogue is to search for the truth, and the mutual critique developed by the participants thereby represents the sublime manifestation of the human spirit" (Ikeda 2001a, 61). By centering our attention on seeking out the truth of a situation or elaborating on the objective elements of an issue in the format of an open dialogue, Ikeda believes that it then becomes possible to avoid conflict, transcend enmity between people, and instead open the door to truth and tolerance.

Unlike the "clash thesis" promoted by Huntington, we find that Ikeda does not choose to recognize the presence of supposedly immutable boundaries between people, civilizations, or cultures. Rather, Ikeda embraces the idea that there are many communities from which human morality may emerge and that it is not helpful to artificially narrow the range of possible sources of morality or truth to an unnecessary minimum. In this regard, Ikeda is also able to look beyond the differences between the world's major religions and argues that "[t]he inherent role of religion can be defined as taking human hearts that are divided and connecting them through a universal human spirit" (Ikeda 2001a, 96). Hence, he sees the ". . . true role of faith" as "providing the profound spiritual energy that will support a mutually beneficial globalism" (Ikeda 2001a, 96). Specifically, Ikeda sees the achievement of global unity as the product of educational and cultural exchanges, as well as competition— in its most constructive sense—as being the ingredients for world unity and peace. This is an approach that moves us well beyond the "clash thesis" and beyond global crisis insofar as "[i]nstead of competing to achieve the greatest military strength . . . countries could vie in the production of strong global citizens. Our goal should be nothing less than to instil an ethos of worldwide citizenry" (Ikeda 2001a, 98).

Similarly, Prof. Jens Bartelson affirms the importance of engaging in a competition or "contest" between value and norms "that aspire to universal validity within a world community." In a world of human diversity and a plurality of cultures, what matters most, Bartelson argues, is that we pay attention to the necessity of mutual respect. Juxtaposed against the "clash thesis" and its presumptions, Bartelson states,

> To insist that communities have to be bounded in order for morality to be possible is . . . to narrow down the range of possible sources of morality to an unnecessary minimum. Therefore, the only moral precept that follows from the social ontology of the world community is the requirement of mutual respect in the face of human diversity. What matters from the vantage point of mankind is not the actual content of all those norms and values that aspire to universal validity within a world community, but the very *contest* that inevitably arises as a consequence of these claims. Since this contest cannot be judged with reference to any higher principles, it can only be mitigated by an acceptance that such diversity is an inescapable part of the human condition (Bartelson 2009, 178).

Precisely because we cannot frame the importance of norms or values in reference to some preordained hierarchy of principles, it then becomes possible to both appreciate the plurality and diversity of civilizations as a "given." In the spirit of Ikeda, it becomes necessary to recognize the need for the increased attention we should give to the role of dialogue. In this regard, Peter Katzenstein has observed that "[p]luralism and plurality are the concepts that best encapsulate contemporary civilizational politics. *Civilizations are not what they are often thought to be—internally coherent arrays of values. They acquire such coherence only when established discursively as primordial constructions with dispositional capacity*" (Katzenstein 2010, 36; italics added).

Hence, the role of discourse and dialogue in creating and attaining a more peaceful and humane global civilization cannot be ignored. Rather, dialogue needs to be centralized in all fields of human endeavor, between all civilizations, and within and between all nations. The importance of people sharing with one another is what creates the conditions for a true global community. It is the human activities of sharing, dialogue, and discourse that enable us to move beyond global crisis and share in a common global community—a global commons. This is the actual environment in which the moral values of a peaceful global civilization will be forged. As Bartelson notes, ". . . if our moral values do not derive from the particular communities we happen to inhabit, but rather form our ability to share meaningful experiences in common with other people, then such values would stand an equal chance of evolving irrespective of the existence of boundaries between the people doing the sharing. So even if we agreed that some sense of community is indeed necessary in order for any morality to evolve, there is no reason to assume that this sense of community requires the prior existence of bounded societies in order to emerge and spread" (Bartelson 2009, 178). A concrete historical example of a community that did not require the prior existence of a bounded society in order to emerge and spread is found in the regional organization of the Association of Southeast Asian Nations (ASEAN). It is to this organization and the cultural milieu from which it emerged that we now turn.

ASEAN's Regional Example for Creating a Peaceful Global Community

So where do we find world unity? How will we define the dimensions, quality, and membership of world unity? Is the achievement of world unity impossible in a world of pluralistic cultures and widespread diversity? What do all civilizations share in common with one another? In answer to these questions, Katzenstein concludes that "[c]ivilizations are most similar not in their cultural coherence and isolation or tendency toward clash but in their pluralist differences, in their plurality, and in their encounters and engagements" (Katzenstein 2010, 38). In a globalized world, there will invariably be an increase in encounters and engagements between civilizations. This translates into increasing the importance we ascribe to dialogue in world affairs at every level—from state, to regional and to international. Hence, Prof. Amitav Acharya notes that

> [n]either power politics nor functional imperatives adequately explain the institutional trajectory and outcomes of Asian regionalism . . . the diffusion of idea and normative change in world politics is not produced by universal norm entrepreneurs where local actors remain 'passive targets.' Local actors also condition the reception of global norms by acting out of a historically constructed normative base. The constitutive localization dynamic explains the success, limitations, and prospects for Asian regionalism. Instead of expecting it to replicate the European institutional purpose and design, normative change and institution-building in Asia are better viewed as evolutionary processes contingent upon prior regional norms and processes" (Acharya 2009b, 7).

This means that in our examination of Asian regionalism, we need to employ an understanding of human communication and dialogue that travels not only with a "top-down" perspective, but also in a "bottom-up" direction. More precisely, the phenomenon of Asian regionalism should be evaluated and assessed from the perspective that the dialogic process and the force of norms, as well as the shaping force of normative concerns, should have their trajectories understood as going from the local level to the national level, from the regional level to the international level, while not forgetting that—in the dynamic interplay—the power of dialogue and norms travel both ways as constitutive forces.

At the international level we can identify "outside" norms traveling down the avenue of hierarchical relations to the local level. But, at the local level, these norms are not automatically incorporated "whole" into the life of the community. Rather, these outside norms may meet resistance, or undergo alterations, changes, and transformations in correspondence with local and regional normative and value structures. In this process, it has been suggested that the localization of such ideas and norms by elites can be understood ". . . as being motivated by a desire to achieve an incremental and progressive promotion of universal ideas and norms (whether it be Gandhi's localization of nationalism and passive resistance in India or more recent efforts to introduce cooperative security and collective intervention norms in Asia)" (Acharya 2009b, 7). This is a contrary perspective to the "clash thesis" wherein Huntington ". . . sees the tendency of elites in developing countries to retreat into their local religious or cultural values (a phenomenon he calls 'de-Westernization and indigenization of elites') as a major reason behind the clash of civilizations . . ." (Acharya 2009b, 7). Therefore, it would seem that a more plausible explanation for the recent evolution of human history in the direction of regionalism and a greater reliance on dialogue in the pacific settlement of disputes is found in the words of Majid Tehranian, who notes that "[h]uman history may be viewed as a dialectical process of globalization from the top and democratization from the bottom, while civilization as the pacific settlement of human disputes lays the foundation for democratic conflict management" (Tehranian 2007, 17).

In the late twentieth and early twenty-first century, there is, perhaps, no better arena in which to evaluate the dynamics of an intra-civilizational project for the pacific settlement of human disputes than in Asia and the embrace of the ASEAN Way as it has emerged in the context of regionalism (as an ideology) and the phenomenon of regionalization (as a process). The ASEAN provides an important and rich area of investigation into the study of regional order and the development of "security communities." Since its formation in 1967, ASEAN has played a representative role in providing humankind with a model for peaceful relations between nation-states and civilizations that is unequaled in human history. ASEAN was established at Bangkok on August 8, 1967. It brought together five countries—Indonesia, Malaysia, Thailand, Singapore, and the Philippines. It represented a truly divergent group of states. In this respect, "[n]ot only were its members very dissimilar in terms of their physical size, ethnic composition, sociocultural heritage and identity, and in the colonial experience and postcolonial policies, they also lacked any significant previous experience in multilateral cooperation. Since cultural and political homogeneity could not serve as an adequate basis for regionalism, the latter had to be constructed through interaction. Such interactions could only be purposeful if they were consistent and rule-based, employing those rules which would ensure peaceful conduct among member states. To this end, ASEAN's founders over a period of a decade from its inception adopted a set of norms for intra-regional relations" (Acharya 2009a, 54).

Obviously, the adoption of a set of norms for intra-regional relations required engagement in dialogue. In the search for the proper construction of a regional security community among these ASEAN member states, dialogue was the primary channel through which the process of regionalization would either succeed or fail. In particular, in the case of ASEAN, it was a form of dialogue that was made accountable to shared norms based on respect for certain guiding principles: avoiding war and conflict, refraining from the threat of force or its use, and nonintervention into the sovereign affairs of member states. Specifically, the evolution of ASEAN's norms and principles can be divided into four categories: "... those dealing with the nonuse of force and the pacific settlement of disputes; those concerning regional autonomy and collective self-reliance; the doctrine of non-interference in the internal affairs of states; and, last but not least, the rejection of an ASEAN military pact and the preference for bilateral defense cooperation" (Archarya 2009a, 55). These principles are contained within and subsumed under the *Treaty of Amity and Cooperation* (TAC), adopted by ASEAN at its Bali summit in 1976. Contained in the TAC are six very specific principles that embrace those outlined in the UN Charter. The treaty's overarching goal is "to promote perpetual peace, everlasting amity and cooperation." In reaching these goals the treaty stipulates that relations between members should be guided by six basic principles: (1) Mutual respect for the independence, sovereignty, equality, territorial integrity, and national identity of all nations; (2) The right of every state to lead its national existence free from external interference, subversion, or coercion; (3) Noninterference in the affairs of one another; (4) Settlement of differences or disputes by peaceful means; (5) Renunciation of the threat or use of force; and (6) Effective cooperation among themselves (Hong 2005, 162–63).

So returning to Ikeda's comprehensive formulation of the role of dialogue and discourse in creating the foundation for a peaceful global civilization, we can identify three essential components that are present in Ikeda's philosophy and also present in ASEAN's founding documents, normative structure, and announced values as a regional organization:

1. The self-realization of individuals under the combined forces of one's own enlightenment and the contributions of one's own culture—as well as the larger global culture—to that enlightenment;
2. From the values embodied in that individual through these combined processes we find a spiritual and intellectual maturation process at work that creates the possibility for a shared dialogue with other persons from different backgrounds, yet also possessing commonly held beliefs and core values;
3. As a global dialogue evolves between individuals and cultures, we reach a point of possibility for cultural convergence (not a "clash of civilizations") wherein it becomes possible to address not only common existential and spiritual needs, but common economic, political, and social concerns about equality, human welfare, and human rights. This formulation is what leads to the possibility of actually achieving a peaceful global civilization.

Having identified these three central components for the building and long-term sustainability of a peaceful global civilization, it is necessary to address the specific institutional forms which would be most appropriate for this effort to be undertaken within. History has already provided us with working models from nation-states to empire, from dictatorships to democracies, from federations to experiments with regional arrangements. For Ikeda, while it is true that ". . . politically successful regimes like the Chinese Empire or the Tokugawa shogunate in Japan have brought peace to their nations," the fact is also that ". . . under such systems the creativity and freedom of the people have been subjected to considerable restraint, and the regimes themselves have tended to be closed and fixed. Systems that suppressed individual creativity allowed Japan and China to stagnate" (Ikeda and Toynbee [1976] 2007, 228).

In order to strike a more appropriate balance that honors deliberative democracy, human rights, and cultural pluralism, Ikeda states, "I feel that a precedent for future world unity may be found in the current European attempt to achieve an intercontinental federation of nations. This suggestion reflects my thought that the European formula (in which local sovereign states with varied historical backgrounds and characteristics form a federation maintaining independence and unique characteristics on equal terms) ought to be adopted as a basic way to achieve world unity" (Ikeda and Toynbee [1976] 2007, 239). Still, it is important to note that when Ikeda speaks of the value of "the European formula" he does not mean that we should blindly or automatically adopt and imitate every element of the European model. Rather, we should pay attention to what is appropriate in each and every cultural context. For example, "The ASEAN Way is usually described as a decision-making process that features a high degree of consultation and consensus. It is a claim about the *process* of regional interactions and cooperation based on discreteness, informality, consensus building and non-confrontational bargaining styles which are often contrasted with the adversarial posturing, majority vote and other legalistic decision-making procedures in Western multilateral negotiations" (Acharya 2009a, 79; italics in original).

Within his analysis of the European formula, we discover that Ikeda seems to have linked his central notions about the value of dialogue with the idea of a federation of cultures that protects their values and cultural uniqueness but, at the same time, makes them more democratically accountable to a larger social, economic, and political unity that can eventually move in the direction of greater world unity—a peaceful global civilization that is not monolithic or hegemonic, but rather is pluralistic, democratic, and cosmopolitan. Therefore, in this sense, Ikeda's proposal for moving toward the larger goals of establishing global unity has much in common with David Held's formulation of a cosmopolitan model of democracy. In defining this model, Held maintains that "[p]eople can enjoy membership in the diverse communities which significantly affect them and accordingly, access to a variety of forms of political participation. Citizenship would be extended, in principle, to membership in all cross-cutting political communities, from the local to the global" (Held 1995, 272). This process is already under way throughout Asia within the broad context of Asian regionalism under the banner of ASEAN and the norms and principles which guide it. Commenting on this process and its implications for humanity's being able to move toward building a more peaceful global civilization, Ikeda notes that

> . . . the undercurrent of Buddhist philosophy common to all the peoples of Eastern Asia deserves attention because its future influence can be great. Though its visible influence today is small, Buddhist thought has cultivated and enriched the spiritual life of East Asian peoples for centuries and has enveloped their histories in an aura of peace. East Asian culture, which was reared under the influence of Buddhist philosophy and which inspires repose and a sense of wonderful harmony between man and nature, has inspired in the peoples of this part of the world a mighty urge to live. It seems to me that philosophy and religion, especially Buddhism, will be the fields in which the peoples of Eastern Asia can make the greatest contributions to peace and civilization (Ikeda and Toynbee [1976] 2007, 225–26).

The traditional cultures of Buddhism, Confucianism, Hinduism, and Islam provided Asia with a complex set of norms for international relations in which peace was considered more normal than war. What is remarkable about the "Asian Way" in general is its approach to conflict resolution. We find that "[t]he main principle underlying the growth of new international organizations in Asia is that peace may be achieved through the cultural affinity cultivated by the Asian Way. This is perhaps an indirect approach to peace, for it rests on the assumption that [the] causes of war in Asia can be attacked by bringing about a common culture, which in turn can spill over into economic and political cooperation" (Haas 1989, 19). One of the strategies employed by practitioners of the Asian Way is the way in which they have chosen to highlight the primacy of economics over politics. They have made this choice because "[i]n choosing to control their own destinies together, Asian countries have gradually come to the realization that they must work together economically on a truly multilateral basis if they are ever to make progress separately" (Haas 1989, 19).

The ASEAN version of multilateralism differs significantly with that of the West with its legalistic apparatus. This is primarily due to the fact that ASEAN's construction and conceptualization of multilateralism was viewed by its members ". . . not as a legal or formal framework for interactions, but as creating a conducive socio-psychological setting for intra-mural problem solving" (Acharya 2009a, 84–85). As to the evolution of this framework and the cultural milieu from which it arose, Acharya notes that "[o]f the many attributes and elements of the ASEAN Way, two are of particular importance. The first is the preference for informality and a related aversion to institutionalization of cooperation" (Acharya 2009a, 79). In addition, "[n]ext to informality and aversion to formal institutions, the ASEAN Way is characterized by the concept and practice of consensus building" (Acharya 2009a, 82). This is an important value to recognize insofar as

> [t]he idea of consensus is not an abstract notion, but was conceived as a pragmatic way of advancing regional economic and political cooperation in Southeast Asia . . . the concept was initially applied to overcome hesitancy and indifference among the ASEAN members toward intra-ASEAN economic cooperation, including ASEAN industrial joint ventures and tariff reductions. As Lee Kuan Yew observed in the context of ASEAN economic cooperation (at a time when ASEAN consisted of only five members: Indonesia, Malaysia, Thailand, the Philippines and Singapore): *'When four agree [to a certain scheme] and one does not, this can still be considered as consensus and the five-minus-one scheme can benefit the participating four without damaging the remaining one.'* In this context, consensus building was seen as a way of advancing regional cooperation schemes despite the reluctance of some of the members to participate in them (Acharya 2009a, 83; italics added).

ASEAN's experience with multilateralism and consensus building also serves as a commentary on identity politics under the auspices of regional arrangements, norms, and rule-making. Its experience reveals the fact that international relations in the twenty-first century has matured beyond the neatly configured paradigm of a stable pluralist order. From the perspective of Prof. Andrew Hurrell, "[t]he globalization and the deterritorialization of identity politics is one of the most important reasons why a neat pluralist global order has been rendered obsolete, and this is true at the regional as well as the national level" (Hurrell 2007, 248). Similarly, James Tully notes that ". . . cultures are not internally homogeneous. They are continually contested, imagined, and re-imagined, transformed and negotiated, both by their members and through their interaction with others." Hence, in the final analysis, "Cultural diversity is a tangled labyrinth of intertwining cultural differences and similarities, not a panopticon of fixed, independent and incommensurable worldviews in which we are either prisoners or cosmopolitan spectators in the central tower" (Tully 1995, 11).

Because cultures are not internally homogeneous, there are serious questions about the degree to which we can realistically speak of "universalism" in the context of building a global civilization. Insofar as the political strengths of the universalist position lies in its appeal to the solidarity of the human race, and economically, in the current trends towards an integrated world market under the auspices of globalization, there are needed intermediary steps available under the rubric of "regionalism" that better protect the realities associated with cultural diversity and the normative concerns which are advanced under the banner of a regional organization, such as ASEAN. Hence, ". . . the regionalist position may be reconciled with the universalist position by stressing the usefulness of regionalism as a stepping stone or intermediary stage in cooperation toward universalism. In this view, regional agencies are not seen as substitutes for a world organization but as laboratories for developing a habit of collaboration and gradually building up areas of consensus, to eventually achieve global coordination and integration" (van Staden 2007, 44).

From Ikeda's perspective, another way of pointing to the phenomenon of globalization, the deterritorialization of identity politics and the goals associated with universalism is by employing the term *"transnationalism."* According to Ikeda, we find that the idea of "transnationalism" had already been formulated by his mentor Josei Toda as early as 1952, when he used the term *chikyu minzoku shugi* (global nationalism, also translated as one-worldism) (Urbain 2010, 63). This was Toda's way of advocating for the idea of the "global family at a time when the tensions of the Cold War were intensifying, and few paid attention to his ideas. [O]At best, they were dismissed as unrealistic reveries. But today, this idea has finally entered the public consciousness as 'transnationalism,' which has become a key concept in explaining and predicting the future direction of global affairs" (Ikeda 2001a, 65). In this regard, we would argue that regionalism and regionalization are expressions of this notion of transnationalism. As suggested by van Staden (above), it is clear that regional organizations (such as ASEAN) can be identified as "laboratories for developing a habit of collaboration." This has been especially important for

Asian cultures in the twentieth century as they have embarked upon their version of regionalism through a process of what Acharya calls "constitutive localization." In Acharya's historical analysis, "[t]he normative explanation of Asian regionalism . . . can be traced through two stages of *constitutive localization* . . . During the first phase . . . covering the immediate post-World War II period, Asia's leaders faced two ideas about how to promote regional security and order: non-intervention and collective defense. These ideas interacted with their prior beliefs about anti-colonialism and aversion to great power sphere of influences. After a period of contestation and compromises, non-intervention found broad acceptance. It was even enhanced to include an injunction against superpower-led military pacts. In contrast, collective defense, promoted by the United States and represented by the South East Asian Treaty Organization, failed" (Acharya 2009b, 6; italics added).

In this first phase of "constitutive localization," it is clear that the member states of ASEAN did not want to be placed under the geopolitical umbrella of the United States in its drive for world hegemony (Paupp 2009). Further, the pressures of the Cold War exacerbated this hegemonic dynamic insofar as the United States and the Soviet Union viewed the entire Third World as a battleground for spheres of influence. They sought to extend their respective empires into the Third World for the sake of obtaining alliances and strategic advantage in the search for markets and in order to exploit natural resources either through aggrandizement of unequal trade advantages. By resisting these pressures and dangers to Asia's regional sovereignty, many Asian states and cultures built a framework which Acharya has called "soft institutionalism" and also developed "mechanisms of cooperative security." The net effect of these trends was to create what Acharya has termed a "regionalist cognitive prior." We find that

> [t]his cognitive prior not only diffused through subsequent institu-
> tion-building processes (especially through the ASEAN established
> in 1967), but also shaped post-Cold War era institutional change.
> Then, it became the receptacle for new international norms
> through a second post-Cold War phase of constitutive localization.
> During this phase . . . Asia's leaders considering a new regional
> security architecture were faced with two sets of norms: common
> security and collective intervention. The outcome of this second
> phase was the acceptance and institutionalization of the former,
> and the rejection (at least for the immediate future) of the latter
> (Acharya 2009b, 7).

From this review of recent history, we find that the importance of reflecting on these two phases of constitutive localization is threefold. First, the way in which the problems of security choices were resolved, in conjunction with the region's guiding norms, reveal the power of dialogue in bridging the gap between universal ideas and values, on the one hand, and in enabling actors to make regional adaptations to the mandates and prerequisites of a regional order with moral purpose on the other. Second, as social, cultural, and civilizational entities, we have discovered (contrary to Huntington) that regions do not always clash. Rather, states and peoples within regions can learn to adapt, dialogue, and come to a mutually beneficial set of agreements as long as they believe in the existence of a common consensus on values, morals, and shared purpose. Third, the evolution of global relations and world politics is best viewed as a continuous process which need not result in instant or comprehensive wins and defeats of one set of ideas (or peoples) over another. Hence, what the regional experience of ASEAN reveals is that there can be a progressive blending of both local and universal norms.[1]

Insofar as the early twenty-first century represents a time of radical shifts and transitions affecting not only previous patterns of power, but identities as well, the dangers of such a time encompass the question of whether humanity will continue to play a game called "winners" and "losers" or, in the alternative, move toward more consensual patterns of behavior, communication, and policies that avoid the threat of civil strife due to the numbers of "defeated" people who are treated as "losers." The norms and politics of ASEAN is a model for how such an outcome may be mitigated, if not altogether eliminated. From Ikeda's perspective, "[t]his determination not to create losers is crucial if we are to resolve the widespread civil strife that plagues our world today. So long as there are even a few losers, people who know the bitter taste of defeat, we can neither hope for a truly stable society nor expect to eliminate completely the seeds of future conflict" (Ikeda 2001a, 89).

From Ikeda's analysis of the dynamics leading to civil strife and future conflicts, we can appreciate the strategic value of the ASEAN experience in a new light. It is not only a normative and constitutive strategy for consensus building, but it is also a way to construct a security community that is potent enough to assure its members that there is a viable means to effectuate peaceful change. In this regard, employing Ikeda's concept of *"transnationalism,"* Acharya has discovered that "[a] pluralistic security community may be defined as a *'transnational region'* comprised of sovereign states whose people maintain dependable expectations of peaceful change. Such a community could be identified in terms of several features. The first is the absence of war, and the second is the absence of significant organized preparations for war *vis-à-vis* any other members" (Acharya 2009a, 18; italics added).

Further, another benefit of ruling out war or planning and preparation for war is that "[s]ecurity communities are also marked by the absence of a competitive military build-up or arms race involving their members . . . A security community . . . must be based on a fundamental, unambiguous and long term *convergence* of interests among the actors in the avoidance of war" (Acharya 2009a, 19; italics in the original). These are the significant differences and qualities which separate the idea of a security community from an *alliance* or a *defense community*. On this matter, Acharya notes that "[a]n alliance is usually conceived and directed against a pre-recognized and commonly perceived external threat. Security communities, on the other hand, identify no such threat or may have no function of organizing a joint defense against it. A security community implies a relationship of peace and stability among a group of states without any sense of how they might collectively relate to external actors" (Acharya 2009a, 21). This distinction is also what separates the "peace" and "security" role of regional organizations from that of a "defense community." Whereas the "peace" role, ". . . central to a security community, refers to the 'potential of a regional organization, through its peace-keeping machinery and diplomatic techniques, for controlling the settlement of conflict among its own members'" we find that the security role which is ". . . integral to a defense community, denotes 'the potential of the organization to present a common military front against an outside actor or actors" (Acharya 2009a, 21).

In addressing the adequacy of these linkages, we turn to Prof. Andrew Hurrell, an international relations scholar who is also ". . . concerned with the ability of the inherited anarchical society of sovereign states to provide a practically viable and normatively acceptable framework for global political order in an era of globalization" (Hurrell 2007, 1–2). Hurrell argues that the nature of the challenge facing international society is threefold: ". . . the need to capture shared and common interests, to manage unequal power, and to mediate cultural diversity and value conflict" (Hurrell 2007, 2). In the case of ASEAN regionalism, we are finding that all three elements of Hurrell's test for assessing the challenges facing international society are being met with sufficient capacity by the membership of ASEAN and their plans for integrating the rest of Asia under their umbrella or, at the very least, acting in concert with their aims and aspirations. Hence, in ASEAN we have found that its approach incorporates both the "regulatory" and "constitutive" aspects of norms which has, in turn, had an effect on state behavior. In this critical respect, Acharya notes that "[n]orms not only prescribe and regulate behavior (the regulatory effect), they also define and constitute identities (the constitutive effect). To put it differently, norms not only establish expectations about how particular actors will behave, they also 'teach' states, which are exposed to norms, new interests and identities" (Acharya 2009a, 26). The dynamic interplay of norms in the context of ASEAN provides us with substantive evidence of the value of Ikeda's formulations and proposals about the uses and significance of dialogue in advancing civilizational identities which can be supportive of peace processes at both the regional and global levels. Further, insofar as this purposeful use of dialogue also has the effect of shaping identities and new interests, it becomes even clearer that the role of dialogue can make up for the absence of explicit regional institutional structures. Donald Weatherbee characterized ASEAN regionalism as a phenomenon in which the "... absence of explicit organizational arrangements and formally articulated regional structures becomes less important than the attitudinal underpinnings that support a recognized pattern of practice around which expectations converge" (Weatherbee 1984, 259–68).

Given this dynamic, we shall proceed to argue that norms and the expectations which they engender are part of a dialogic process that can have an inclusive effect on people's perceptions and their commitment to the cause of peace at the local, regional, national, and international levels. By virtue of their capacity to advance peaceful pursuits and war avoidance, it seems that they can advance practices of war avoidance between states and also serve as instigators for an ongoing dialogue dedicated to the creation of a new global civilization which is reflective of these norms. From Ikeda's perspective it is necessary to recognize that "[d]ialogue must be pivotal in our endeavors, reaching out to all people everywhere as we seek to forge a new global civilization" (Ikeda 2001a, 57). In this task, "[n]orms help to coordinate values among states and societies. By making similar behavioral claims on different states, norms create parallel patterns of behavior among states over wide areas. This helps ensure that the principles and practice of peaceful conduct and war avoidance are shared among states and contribute to the development of a sense of community" (Acharya 2009a, 26).

In summary, we can assert (as we have previously suggested that the norms and values which we put forth to guide our path toward a more inclusive and humane global civilization do not have to come from one nation or one cultural tradition that occupies a bounded and well-defined geographical territory. Rather, the shared values and common ethos of people who are dedicated to the cause of peace know no physical boundaries. In fact, these shared values and the common ethos or milieu out of which they arise have a constitutive effect "... by transforming the identity of states form being that of egoistic and sovereignty-bound actors to members of a social group sharing a common habit of peaceful conduct" (Acharya 2009a, 26). This seems to be the greatest achievement of ASEAN to date.

Now, at the dawn of the twenty-first century, ASEAN states have found themselves "... confronted with parallel concerns about major power roles, intra-ASEAN unity, and indeed the future of Southeast Asia as a meaningful region and organizing principle" (Ba 2009, 159). Efforts have been underway to extend ASEAN's TAC, as well as ASEAN processes beyond Asia. These efforts have already begun to focus attention "... on the appropriateness of ASEAN principles, processes, and modes of engagement beyond Southeast Asia. The products of these debates will be a refined US–ASEAN security relationship, a new Southeast Asian Nuclear Weapons Free Zone (SEANWFZ)—only ASEAN's second treaty—an expanded regional purview, and most significantly, the creation of an ASEAN Regional Forum (ARF), *the Asia-Pacific's first official security dialogue* and states' first ASEAN-led institutional foray into ASEAN-plus regionalism" (Ba 2009, 159–60; italics added). At the heart of all of these regional efforts has been the use of dialogue as the most effective way in building a new security community for Asia. The various global implications of this particular strategy are genuinely staggering. That is because the power of dialogic engagement to advance the process of engaging people in a consensus over shared values has, at the same time, advanced a normative framework which is increasingly reflective of people's growing aspirations for peace and community. This, in turn, has had a fundamental effect on issues such as the nonuse of nuclear weapons which has, until recently, been an issue held hostage by recalcitrant governments and their national security establishments.

Commenting on this emerging trend in world affairs toward the expansion of regional frameworks for the nonuse of nuclear weapons, Ikeda wrote in his 2010 peace proposal, entitled *"Toward a New Era of Value Creation,"* about the fact that

> [t]o date, the establishment of nuclear weapons–free zones (NWFZ) has represented an effort to fill the gap in the legal framework left by the absence of any treaty or convention providing a blanket prohibition against the use of nuclear weapons. In 2009, NWFZ treaties were entered into force in Central Asia and Africa. These followed similar agreements covering Latin America and the Caribbean, the South Pacific and Southeast Asia. The decision by so many governments to eliminate nuclear weapons from so many regions around the world is truly significant (Ikeda 2010-PP, 4).

It is especially significant in light of the tragic reality that "[a]lthough the preamble to the NPT, which entered into force forty years ago, calls on signatories to 'make every effort to avert the danger of such a war and to take measures to safeguard the security of peoples,' *it is clear that the nuclear-weapon states have not fulfilled that obligation*" (Ikeda 2010-PP, 4; italics added). The blatant failure of leaders and elites in governments around the world to undertake their sworn obligations under the treaty structure of international law and in the furtherance of the articulated aspirations of the majority of humankind reminds us, in the words of Ikeda, that ". . . we cannot afford to forget that the majority must assume basic initiative in all systems. If the people do not take the initiative, no matter how ideal the system may appear to be, it will degenerate into a regime of evil and oppression" (Ikeda 2007-PP, 215). In the case of Asian regionalism, however, we find that the people did take the initiative in advancing the Southeast Asian Nuclear Weapons Free Zone (SEANWFZ). The same may be said of the initiative called the Zone of Peace, Freedom, and Neutrality (ZOPFAN) in addition to efforts to extend the reach of the TAC. In all of these endeavors, the effect of these three major initiatives has been that they have ". . . assumed new relevance and significance as developments continued to blur the lines between Southeast Asia and Northeast Asia. In particular, the late 1980s and early 1990s saw new proposals to extend principles that had been explicitly and exclusively Southeast Asian beyond Southeast Asia" (Ba 2009, 185).

These trends were especially salient with respect to questions concerning the extension of TAC to non-Southeast Asian powers. If the extension of TAC was to be sought after, the question then arose to whether there should be separate protocols for Southeast and non-Southeast Asian states. While that question remains to be answered and resolved, the primary point to be emphasized is that by extending ASEAN's norms, values, and practices this became a proposal that raised ASEAN's regional and international profile. In so doing, it also served to provide the global community with new ideas and insights about how the principles, shared values, and norms which have characterized ASEAN might be replicated elsewhere in the world. In attempting to assess the possibilities for the ASEAN model on the global stage, it should be noted that "Asian regionalism has been viewed as an inclusive, open and informal regionalism . . . It was based, in general, on a commitment to non-discrimination and a willingness to include new members or partners who could contribute to the Asian growth story" (Mukherji 2008, 163).

ASEAN's normative structure which emphasized the shared values of inclusion and openness was central to India finally becoming a member. Its inclusive nature also opened the door in December 1995 for India, China, and Russia being given the status of full dialogue partners. In addition, India and Singapore signed the Comprehensive Economic Cooperation Agreement, which became operational from August 1, 2005 (Mukherji 2008, 173). The implications of this signing are great insofar as "[t]he agreement could serve as a model for other economic partnerships in the future" (Mukherji 2008, 176). Given the way in which outside or "universal norms" can be reinterpreted at the "local level" this approach also serves to reemphasize the importance that Ikeda has ascribed to the role of dialogue in moving individuals and nations forward in their historical evolution. In attempting to fully comprehend the dynamic nature of this process, it has been suggested that the methodology of *"constructivism"* be employed insofar as

> . . . *constructivism* does not regard norms and identities as a given, or as something that is prior to the process of socialization. *Constructivism* allows for outside or "universal" norms to be modified or reinterpreted (and sometimes their meaning and scope either expanded or constricted) at the recipient's end through a process of localization, or to evolve from *local discourses and practices.* Moreover, some entirely new norms may appear in the local milieu through the early stages of interaction of a social group without necessarily being borrowed and adapted from outside. International (regional) institutions act

as the agents of diffusion of norms, including the localization of outside norms and indigenous construction of new norms. Hence *the effectiveness of norms ... also depends on the ability of a social group to modify international norms and create entirely new ones to meet local challenges and suit its local cultural, economic, and political circumstances* (Acharya 2009a, 27–28; italics added).

The approach of constructivism represents the kind of interpersonal dynamics and discourse that Ikeda would approve of. It is an approach which values human dignity, guarantees freedom of conscience and the fulfillment of human needs, protecting them against structures of behavior and action artificially imposed on individuals and groups. It is an approach that extends the realm of human creativity and innovation so that particular needs can be met through a rearticulation of universal norms. This approach stands in stark contrast to the dynamics of globalization and US hegemony. In order to explicate these differences, it is necessary that we make clear what is at stake. Therefore, it is a subject to which we now turn.

Reflections on creating a new Paradigm in International Relations—Beyond US Hegemony and toward a Multi-centric World of Regions

Reflecting on this historical approach to regional development and global relations, we rediscover a fundamental insight. That insight centers on the realization that (1) inclusive forms of regional governance and (2) the employment of consensual norms in the international arena, stand in sharp contrast to the history and performance of both empires and nation-states. As the two most dominant historical embodiments of international political, economic, and social organization, empires and nation-states have been the preeminent political paradigms in creating and shaping global order for the past centuries. In that period of time, they have proved to be very effective in seeking and creating hierarchical arrangements which have served to reinforce unequal power, as well as suppress cultural diversity and identities. However, these two dominant paradigms have done little to advance the articulation of shared and common interests among people. In short, both empires and nation-states have rarely moved beyond a narrow focus upon (and preoccupation with) maintaining power for power's sake. The result of this myopic preoccupation with the accumulation of power for the sake of power—whether it is the idea of establishing a "balance of power," or the idea of overcoming international anarchy under the auspices of "hegemonic stability theory"—has been to create a history of wars, violence, and endless conflict (Paupp 2007, 2009).

The historical record reveals that the various theories used to legitimize the pursuit of empire (or the national interest of the nation-state) have usually been dedicated to maintaining a particular status quo of elite power arrangements. This has transpired throughout the history of global society and has served to channel a great deal of energy and effort into maintaining systems of dominance and hierarchy in international affairs. These particular manifestations of centralized power have often been coupled with the proclivity of empires to project and extend their global influence into territories beyond their own borders with the rather tragic and predictable result that they have failed to create any kind of sustainable consensus and, instead, made conflicts, wars and/or ethnic strife inevitable. To a large degree, we find that conflicts, wars, and revolts throughout the history of empires and nation-states may be attributable to the amount of resistance they engender among the excluded, the oppressed, and the marginalized who they have sought to lord over—despite the heavy toll that their dominance has extracted in terms of the costs to human dignity, human rights, and cultural plurality.

In light of this history we have, in short, a record of conduct wherein the dominant political arrangements of both empires and nation-states have usually resulted in situations under which limited and very narrow interests have been sought, unequal power enforced, and cultural diversity subordinated. On this matter, Burbank and Cooper ask,

> What, then, is an empire, and how do we distinguish empire from other political entities? Empires are large political units, expansionist or with a memory of power extended over space, polities that maintain distinction and hierarchy as they incorporate new people. The nation-state, in contrast, is based on the idea of a single people in a single territory constituting itself as a unique political community. The nation-state proclaims the commonality of its people—even if the reality is more complicated—while the empire-state declares the non-equivalence of multiple populations. Both kinds of states are incorporative—they insist that people be ruled by their institutions— but the nation-state tends to homogenize those inside its borders and exclude those who do not belong, while the empire reaches outward and draws, usually coercively, peoples whose difference it made explicit under its rule. The concept of empire presumes that different peoples within the polity will be governed differently (Burbank and Cooper 2010, 8).

In contrast to both empires and nation-states, we find that the regional experiment known as ASEAN is emblematic of a new day in global affairs. This is predominantly the case insofar as the dialogue, shared values, and norms which have historically defined ASEAN are now being pursued in an ASEAN Charter which truly centralizes the role of "*the people*" and not solely a "*power elite.*" Adopted in November 2007 at ASEAN's thirteenth summit and entered into force in December 2008, the Charter specifically seeks to create an ASEAN Community by 2015. It will be based primarily on security, economic, and sociocultural pillars. What is of particular importance in this undertaking is ". . . the Charter's recognition of societal groups and transnational networks [which] is reflective of a growing awareness that ASEAN's longevity will ultimately depend not just on elites, but also on the 'people'" (Ba 2009, 245). This approach certainly complements the views of Ikeda, especially when he offered the admonition, "If the people do not take the initiative, no matter how ideal the system may appear to be, it will degenerate into a regime of evil and oppression" (Ikeda 2007-PP, 215).

In large measure, both nation-states and empires came to embody regimes that degenerated into embodiments of evil and oppression insofar as they worked at excluding so many people from having a voice in how they were to be governed and the course of their own destiny. At least with Asian regionalism there is now a principled and successful experiment with governing tactics, values, and approaches opposite to those of empires and individual nation-states. With gathering success at the regional level, there is now even greater hope for building a peaceful global civilization at the international level. In the words of Ikeda, we now have arrived at a situation where "Eastern Asia preserves a number of historical assets that may enable it to become the geographical and cultural axis for the unification of the whole world" (Ikeda 2007-PP, 227). After making this statement, Ikeda then proceeds to enumerate eight different assets that he identifies as being central in the task of writing "the next chapter of mankind's history" and thereby engaging in "the constructive enterprise of helping mankind to put its affairs in order peacefully."[2]

In delineating these assets Ikeda emphasizes an idea that is in the background of each of them—the central idea that humankind's aim should be to live in harmony with nature and with other human beings. In order to effectuate this aim, Ikeda praises the ecumenical spirit of the Chinese for having produced the humanism contained in Confucianism's worldview (as well as the rationalism of both Confucianism and Buddhism). Yet, behind his idea about the need to effectuate harmony in the affairs and worldview of humankind, there is something about Ikeda's conception of harmony that necessitates making a differentiation between the meaning that he ascribes and intends for the term versus that of the West. Specifically, ". . . harmonization usually suggests a search for common behavior rules. Harmonization as integration takes many forms, from voluntary and noncoercive, to mandatory and specific. Much modern integration is implemented through law making—as political communities today tend to hold most of the power to coerce behavior from their members" (Backer 2007, xiv). Clearly, the kind of harmonization that ASEAN has embarked upon (and that Ikeda has endorsed) is neither mandatory nor overly specific. Rather, the kind of regional community that ASEAN represents—including China—is one that centralizes the values of voluntary and noncoercive integration. This is necessary to build both a peaceful regional community as well as a peaceful global community.

In keeping with Ikeda's previously discussed concepts of inner transformation and human revolution, we find that what remains central is the value of a choice that individuals freely make (without coercion) so that when an external consensus is reached with other people, it can be sustained based on the pure motivation and intention of the parties. This is what differentiates Ikeda's approach from the more legalistic and coercive approaches of the West, and what differentiates his vision for peaceful regional and global communities from that of nation-states and empires. In short, there is a great difference between conformity, on the one hand, and consensus on the other. Therefore, it can be argued that "[f]or all their power, neither globalization, as a set of influential conduct norms, nor harmonization, as a collection of methodologies of integration, have ever been able to assert dominance over all individuals and communities. As a historical matter, every form of globalization, and every attempt to integrate behavior within a single set of norms, has met with resistance. World history does not reveal a time in which everyone has embraced one single set of norms" (Backer 2007, xiv).

Rather than attempting to impose norms upon people and polities, the writings of Ikeda stress the practices of assimilation and inclusion as better approaches to building a long-term and sustainable consensus between peoples. In a world of diverse cultures, political systems, and values, Ikeda points to a historical record wherein he reminds us that "in the past, the Japanese people have shown a great talent for absorbing and assimilating alien civilizations and cultures. During the first ancient period of unification, Japan modeled her political and social order on that of China and learned production techniques and arts from both China and Korea . . . Until the nineteenth century, Japan's history was one of comparatively brief, widely spaced periods of cultural borrowing followed by long periods of assimilation and creativity" (Ikeda and Toynbee [1976] 2007, 232). Similarly, long periods of assimilation and creativity have shaped the regional experience of ASEAN.

The global significance of these practices and the insights that can be derived from them serve to address the question of what is necessary for war-avoidance in the twenty-first century. Ikeda has emphatically stated, "War now threatens our civilization and our continued existence on this globe. We must do something to alter the basic nature of economics so that it no longer stimulates warfare. There are a number of factors aside from war that can promote economic growth. For instance, expanding and improving our social security and educational systems, providing better housing for our people, and giving massive foreign aid to underdeveloped countries would demand sums sufficiently vast to support the economies of most nations" (Ikeda and Toynbee [1976] 2007, 181).

The contemporary global crisis which humankind confronts has now reached unprecedented proportions not only because of the threat of war, but also because the economic paradigm of neoliberal capitalism has proven itself to be exploitative, unsustainable, and nonproductive. As a direct consequence of this breakdown of the system of Western dominance, we have discovered that both economic practices and the Western-based system of international law that has guided and regulated the relations between states can no longer be sustained. It is untenable. On this point, Richard Falk has observed that "[i]nternational law during most of the Westphalian era was preoccupied with regulating relations among sovereign states. In this period, law was shaped according to the priorities of a Eurocentric world, including the legalization of diplomatic and economic relationships, and based on a statist logic that accepted force, war and hierarchy as rational instruments of statecraft" (Falk 2008a, 31).

Now, at the close of the first decade of the twenty-first century, we see that Ikeda is correct about the need to reject war as an acceptable paradigm for the conduct of statecraft and switch, instead, to a new economic paradigm that transcends the use of force, war, and hierarchy as legitimate tools of statecraft in the international forum of our global community. A gathering body of evidence demonstrates that the reign of US hegemony is coming to an end as the "crumbling walls" of its global financial and military empire are being eclipsed by a world of "rising regions" (Paupp 2009). Some assessment of recent trends in global relations point to the phenomenon of what happens when "*the East moves West*" (Kemp 2010). Not only India and China, but also Pakistan, Japan, and South Korea are in the process of engaging the Middle East and starting to eclipse the previous dominance of US hegemony in the region. These emerging trends are revealing the twenty-first century's new dynamic—a dynamic which signals the strength of rising economies and political outreach gathering from the rising regions of Asia as the new international embodiment of what is fast becoming a multi-centric world.

While the traditionally powerful Western economies are barely treading water, beset by crises in banking, housing, and employment, industrial growth and economic development are exploding in India and China. In this new era, the world's two most populous nations are the main reason for Asia's growing influence and footprint on other global regions. This is especially the case in the Middle East. In the search for new sources of energy, new questions are being raised about whether the emergence of these Asian giants strengthens the case for cooperative security, particularly in the maritime arena. After all, safe and open sea-lanes remain an essential component of mutually beneficial intercontinental trade, thereby making China and India increasingly dependent on safe passage of oil tankers. Or, in the alternative, will the future give us a reversion to more traditional competition and even conflict?

What is becoming an unfolding realization with respect to these questions is that some old forms of traditional competition and conflict have been mitigated, but never fully resolved, by an imperial logic that is now in decline (Wallerstein 2003). Hence, we are confronted with the reality that the danger of conflict remains active just underneath the foundations of this order which suffers from an inherent instability. Contrary to the arguments put forth by the proponents of *"Hegemonic Stability Theory,"* the reality is that hegemony is always a precarious foundation on which to attempt to sustain peace within this current formulation of global order (Paupp 2009). Part of the reason for the rather precarious nature of a system that orbits around the concept of hegemony is that "[e]ven though all states may share an interest in free trade as economic theory implies, there are strong distributional implications from alternative economic regimes" (Lake 2009, 153). Therefore, while this previously entrenched set of US-led set of practices has directed the course of global relations and effectively worked to mitigate an unraveling of status quo practices and arrangements, social movements throughout the global South in opposition to US hegemony have been forming a counterhegemonic alliance to any continued US control over the international order (Paupp 2007, 2009).

According to Stokes and Raphael, a review of recent history reveals that "... the national logic of the US Empire remains at the heart of Washington's strategic thinking, and the positive-sum order has been constructed specifically in order to sustain American hegemony over other powers ... By promoting and maintaining an order wherein all major powers are content, the United States works to integrate *and thereby pacify* any potential challenges to its privileged position ... Eager to maintain a status quo, potential rivals to the US mantle of global hegemony in fact delegate to Washington the task of 'system maintenance.' US hegemony is in turn reinforced and the set of asymmetric relations are consolidated as the American state gets to play a guiding, managerial role over others" (Stokes and Raphael 2010, 14; italics in original). However, this set of global relations cannot continue for much longer insofar as "... a more active resistance to the US-led neo-liberal agenda and wider American hegemony has emerged at many points across the South throughout the postwar era. Such counterhegemonic forces present an especially grave threat to US interests, since they often seek to pursue an alternative path of economic and political development outside of Washington's orbit" (Stokes and Raphael 2010, 54).

The global South has embarked on the pursuit of an alternative path because the peoples of the global South have not been able to engage in a constructive dialogue with the US Empire. Rather, the global South has historically been threatened by the US Empire through the combined mechanisms of coercion, the threat of force, and the reality of intervention. According to David Lake, "... the construction and maintenance of political authority necessarily involves a degree of coercion to enforce rules and sustain compliance in the face of individual incentives to defect from that order ... Subordinates can be expected to defect when possible in ways large and small, and a failure to enforce the rules will lead to a fraying and possible disintegration of the order" (Lake 2009, 113). Similarly, I have offered an expanded version of this argument in light of the growth of social movements in opposition to the US Empire, the overextension of US military power into the Middle East and elsewhere, the meltdown of the US financial system, and a lack of global legitimacy and/or consensus over US policies from dissenting European allies to the "rising regions" of the global South (Paupp 2007, 2009). A broad overview of these trends reveals that "[s]ince the early 1940s, the United States has pursued a grand strategy of extra-regional hegemony . . . The historical record shows that hegemonic grand strategies invariably have proved self-defeating, because they result in counterhegemonic balancing and/or imperial overstretch" (Layne 2006, 193).

Even beyond these considerations of hegemony as a political and economic grand strategy for a dominant power like the United States, there are broader considerations that must now be taken into account in the twenty-first century given the reality of rising regional powers in the global South, climate change, competition over dwindling resources, and energy shortages. Michael Klare notes that "[i]f we continue to extract and consume the planet's vital resources in the same improvident fashion as in the past, we will, sooner rather than later, transform the earth into a barely habitable scene of desolation. And if the leaders of today's Great Powers behave like those of previous epochs—relying on military instruments to achieve their primary objectives—we will witness unending crisis and conflict over what remains of value on our barren wasteland" (Klare 2008, 261). Yet, despite these trends, we find that the decision-makers among the elite of the US Empire have continued to pursue their version and vision of American hegemony irrespective of these realities. Hence, this is the fundamental reality which remains at the center of our twenty-first century global crisis. It is also at this point that Ikeda's strategy of peace and the example of ASEAN retain their most profound relevance. For what is at stake is whether dialogue and consensus will ultimately triumph in human affairs or, in the alternative, whether the old and familiar paths of domination and coercion will continue to be the prevailing strategies that define the direction of global governance.

Understanding that these considerations frame the central issues which reside at the tipping point of our contemporary dilemma within the matrix of this global crisis, we should come to appreciate the larger reality articulated by Prof. Backer that "[n]ot every autonomous community encountering any given framework for globalization would invariably choose to embrace those universal behavior norms, irrespective of the manner in which the community is confronted by that framework. Not every autonomous community reacts positively to inducements to modify rules and law to implement (or induce) greater integration with global standards. Such inducements can as easily be interpreted as attempts to shift the power to govern from within a political community to groups outside of, and not subject to the control of, the members of the political community now subject to its rule making power" (Backer 2007, xiv).

Backer's analysis of the global crisis is borne out in any objective review of recent history. For example, it is possible to identify a backlash to Western-led globalization and US hegemony in three principal forms:

> First, a more militant ideology of neo-liberal global economic policy which frustrated Third World efforts to achieve a fairer, more equal world economy. Second, the revival of interventionist diplomacy under the guise of humanitarianism. Third, the double standards in the administration of the non-proliferation regime. In effect, the Kennan imperative of sustaining the disparities between wealth, resource use and population were re-established as the basis of geopolitics, creating a crisis of world order parallel to the crisis of global governance (Falk 2008a, 31).

Irrespective of the claims, rights, and priorities of the people of the global South, the historical record of the last fifty years of the twentieth century and the first decade of the twenty-first century demonstrate the utter arrogance of the managers of US hegemony and American-styled globalization toward the autonomous communities of the global South. The true nature of the situation that has been created is one where

> [t]he managers of globalization have decided on the order of treatment of those wounded and maimed by the negative impact of globalization, and many millions have simply been condemned to die. This is not just a challenge to social theory but also to the moral and ethical principles raised by today's global polity. The reality is that this polity has taken a negative turn since 2001 with the eclipse of the "pure" neo-liberal pro-globalizers and the emergence of a new breed of "regressive globalizers" who, according to *Global Civil Society 2003 "see the world as a zero-sum game, in which they seek to maximize the benefit of the few, which they represent, at the expense of the welfare of the many, about which they are indifferent at best"* . . . Against this gloomy scenario we can posit the continued mobilization of reformist and radical counter-globalization and antiwar movements that are conscious of the risks for global order if the present tendencies toward ever-greater social exclusion continue to prevail (Munck 2005, 165; italics added).

Summary: The Future as Global Exclusion or Inclusion

Currently, global order may be seen as being forged in the dynamic interplay between the dominant paradigm and practice of a globalized capitalist-led assault of global exclusion against the welfare, human rights, and dignity of the majority of the world's peoples *versus* the moral claims of a humanistic discourse of global inclusion. Given the realities of a declining US hegemony, the expansion of regionalism and regionalization, a growing consciousness of global problems from climate change to nuclear disarmament to, more generally, issues of world peace versus the dangers of world war, there are sufficient grounds and subjects for a global dialogue. From trade and patent laws to global health, from educational provisions to ecological restraint, from debt to development there is a need for these subjects to be addressed—within a broad and inclusive framework that includes the views of peoples who have been historically marginalized and excluded from even participation in forums that address their very concerns and lives.[3]

The overriding problem with Western-led approaches to global economic governance is that they fail to take into account the realities of social, economic, and political exclusion—which are themselves products of the logic of the capitalist order itself. Western-led approaches to the task of economic growth are approaches that virtually mandate the exclusion of developing countries from the profits derived from investments and even the value of their own natural resources. The incessant drive of wealthy elites—both in the West and within Third World countries—constitutes a group of people who are the exemplars of an unenlightened constituency (from a social justice viewpoint) because they do not care about the ramifications and consequences of their actions or the policies that they endorse and impose upon the powerless, the poor, and the excluded. That is why the problem ". . . lies deeper than just the uneasy mix between economic-liberalism and social-welfare approaches. The World Bank and development agencies throughout the world today promote social capital as the new paradigm that will lead to poverty reduction . . . However, it is unclear precisely how social capital will be developed, or civil society empowered in a worldwide system based essentially on economic concentration and marginalization of the losers in the competitiveness race, whether people or countries" (Munck 2005, 57). Recognizing the true nature of the current situation many social movements ". . . are seeking in diverse ways to promote social regulation and the reembedding of the economy within communities. They are social movements that contest the 'commodification' of labor, knowledge, and human beings. Across the world there are diverse movements or processes of economic democratization seeking to re-embed the economy within society . . . *In different but complementary ways all these counter-movements offer an alternative social logic and refuse social exclusion*" (Munck 2005, 160; italics added).

It is unfortunate that the US primacy coalition which has been promoting another century of US hegemony cannot see that the decline of the US Empire is inevitable and inexorable (Paupp 2009). This is especially evident insofar as the three pillars which sustain a viable hegemony are all weakened or hopelessly dissipated. The first pillar is that of military strength.

Despite its much-vaunted imperial power as displayed across the globe by over seven hundred military bases on every continent there is the problem of "imperial overstretch." The US Empire has spread itself too thin (as the long enduring war and occupation of Iraq has shown). The costs of the Iraq war have been estimated to exceed $3 trillion. This leads to the second pillar of what is required for sustainable hegemony—financial strength. The US financial crisis of 2008 has turned into a long recession that borders on depression. Its problems have negatively affected its allies in Europe and the European Union, as of 2010, is on the brink of fragmentation. The third and final pillar of what is required for sustainable hegemony is global consensus. Over the eight years of the Bush II presidency, the United States lost the world's support due to its unilateral economic and military blunders. In response to what is perceived to be its illegitimate and illegal rule, we are witnessing an increase of social movements being formed across every continent that are encouraging their governments to join in a counterhegemonic alliance against US hegemony. Further, in addition to social movements in opposition, there is a world of "rising regions" that are pushing global relations in the direction of greater regionalization and the birth of a multicentric and posthegemonic world order. For all of these reasons, it seems evident that

> [t]he fall is likely because the leading states of the West are prisoners of the developmental paths that have made their fortunes, both political and economic. The paths are yielding decreasing returns in terms of rates of accumulation relative to the East Asian regional path, but they cannot be abandoned in favor of the more dynamic path without causing social strains so unbearable that they would result in chaos rather than "competitiveness." A similar situation arose in past hegemonic transitions. At the time of their respective hegemonic crises, both the Dutch and the British got themselves ever more deeply into the particular path of development that had made their fortunes, despite the fact that more dynamic paths were being opened up at the margins of their radius of action. And neither got out of the established path until the world system centered on them broke down (Arrighi 1999, 288).

So we have to ask ourselves, *What exactly is the nature of the logic of the capitalist order?* The central logic has to do with profit-making and continuing to manifest it through endless growth in a global process called "capital accumulation" which, in turn, leads to tremendous concentration of wealth for an elite while producing widening circles of inequality, poverty, and sociopolitical exclusion for the majority. Recognizing this reality in the 1970s, the developing countries of the Third World responded by calling for the inauguration of a New International Economic Order (NIEO). The history of this period reveals that "[u]nder the NIEO approach, Third World countries proceed from the premise that the market does not always allocate resources toward fulfilling their most important needs such as addressing poverty. Third World countries therefore argue in favor of enacting interventions to address the blind spots and narrow focus of market governance on issues such as efficiency to the exclusion of values such as distributive equity and fairness" (Gathii 2008, 255). In the final analysis, it is the issue of equity and equality that becomes centralized in the social justice perspective embodied by the NIEO advocates. In the 1970s they had majorities in the United Nations General Assembly. Acting together as the "Group of 77," the developing countries drafted and campaigned for the adoption of the *Charter of Economic Rights and Duties of States*. In this effort, the NIEO advocates represented a constituency that sought to restructure international economic relations so that a balance could be established between the predominantly raw materials producing economies of the global South (Third World) and the Western industrial economies. Their undertaking involved a frontal challenge to unfair terms of trade, investment, and finance rules, as well as strong advocacy for the concept of a "right to development."

In all of these endeavors, the NIEO advocates were consistently opposed by the United States. The United States targeted the entire United Nations development system from the Economic and Social Council (ECOSOC) to the General Assembly. Additionally, US pressure resulted in the dismantling of the UN Center on Transnational Corporations that monitored the activities of transnational corporations (TNCs) throughout the global South (Bello 2005, 136). The driving force behind the American government's effort to dismantle the NIEO has been a wealthy class of elite capitalists who have been referred to in the academic literature of international relations as the "Capitalist Security Community" (CSC). To define this group more precisely it has been suggested that "[t]he CSC refers to that group of capitalists, along with their intellectual and political supporters, who equate their own safety and well-being with effective management of a global market system, which they are confident can generate economic growth, widespread prosperity and peace. Despite (or in pursuit of) those benign objectives, the CSC has proven willing to use violence to protect its interests, and it is implicated in much of the warfare of the past century" (Goldfischer 2005, 200).

The CSC has influenced and directed the US military and national security structures of the US government so as to create "the flexible architecture of America's global military reach" and laid the foundation for "... the *hegemony strategy*," whereby the United States sought 'to extend unilateral protection over as many states as possible' in order to maximize US security and protect American interests. Such a strategy mimicked, on a grand scale, the protectorate regime strategy introduced in the Bidlack-Mallarino Treaty with Columbia in 1846. Protective imperialism in the Western Hemisphere had

193

been transformed into a planetary grand strategy accompanied by a national security doctrine and force structure to implement it" (Loveman 2010, 355; italics added). This is the structure which has served to create accelerating rates of inequality and poverty throughout the global South from the early 1970s up to the present. The dominance of the CSC has remained uncontested insofar as CSC hegemony is entrenched within the US government—which operates and functions as the world's dominant hegemonic state (Goldfischer 2005, 211). Because of this intertwined set of arrangements, it can be objectively argued that "... for the CSC, whose members have benefited most from capitalism's historical conquests over rival social orders, the pursuit of national security *and* further globalization have long been indistinguishable objectives" (Goldfischer 2005, 200; italics added). Hence, the accumulated economic data and evidence demonstrates that, under the guidance and directives of the CSC, as globalization has evolved over recent decades it has brought with it a logic that has sanctioned increased global inequality. This trend has been allowed to continue despite the fact that these policies have generated global resentment, widening wealth gaps between social classes and nations, and increased levels of poverty in both First and Third World nations (Paupp 2000).

In the intervening years between the 1970s and 2010, massive amounts of data have been accumulated which clearly demonstrates that international inequality is not declining as a result of globalization and "... neither is intra-national income distribution improving, according to a detailed World Bank study" (Munck 2005, 44). What we do find, however, is that in the period from 1988 to 1993 "... the poorest 5 percent of the world's population lost almost one-quarter of its income while the top 5 percent gained by 12 percent" (Munck 2005, 44). Additionally, a 2001-United Nations University study that surveyed seventy-three countries found that while nine countries (accounting for 5 percent of the total population) had seen decreasing levels of income inequality when comparing the 1960s with the 1990s, forty-eight countries (accounting for 59 percent of the population) saw increasing levels of income inequality over the same period, with the balance (sixteen countries and 36 percent of the population) having seen stable levels of inequality (Munck 2005, 44–45).

On the issue of equality, Ikeda's perspective is best summed up in his account of the Bodhisattva Never Disparaging. His account of the Bodhisattva emphasizes the role of "*compassionate dialogue*" as the most appropriate means through which to realize equality between people and nations. That is because employing compassionate dialogue will help to reawaken the inner knowledge of our universal dignity—thereby awakening a sense of empathy toward others and a desire to enact justice through the realization of equality between individuals and nations. In short, it is an approach to the problem of evil that avoids violent action by seeking to undertake nonviolent compassionate dialogue so as to extirpate anger, greed, and foolishness. Of the Bodhisattva Never Disparaging, Ikeda notes that

> [h]is attitude convinced even his revilers to join him in working to relieve suffering. His behavior—a model for human rights advocates of the future—may be summarized as follows: (1) Firm belief in absolute equality; (2) Unwavering reliance on nonviolent, *compassionate dialogue*; (3) Earnest, courageous challenge to achieving the self-realization of oneself and others. Firm belief in absolute equality means to believe that all living beings are equally endowed with buddhahood, which is universal dignity. Unwavering reliance on nonviolent *compassionate dialogue* is the battle to extirpate evils such as anger, greed and foolishness and to evoke the spirit of compassion and justice, *by means of dialogue* without resorting to violent means (Ikeda and de Athayde 2009, 110–11; italics added).

Unfortunately, the fact remains that the kind of compassionate dialogue which Ikeda is advocating is not the focus of either the "progressive globalizers" or the "regressive globalizers." Therefore, the call to dialogue on the issue of global inequalities becomes the responsibility of those who have been able to transcend the narrowness of vision, the lack of empathy, the dominance of greed. In this undertaking, Ikeda reminds us that ". . . the characteristics motivating egoism are found in what is called the seventh, or *mano*-consciousness. The great Buddhist scholar Vasubandhu says that the *mano*-consciousness is always accompanied by the Four Great Delusions:

(One)   The delusion arising from obsession with the small, exclusive self and ignorance of the larger universally accessible self.

(Two)   The delusion that the small self is the true self; this delusion generates biased views and comparisons between the self and others.

(Three) The conceited delusion that the small self is equal, superior, or not greatly inferior to others. Envy and hunger for control, wealth, and power always accompany such conceit. People swept away by it lose sight of justice and act unfairly.

(Four)   Obsession with the self obscured by the other three delusions. In Japanese, this fourth delusion is called *gai-ai* or self-love. The word love in this context expresses desire and all kinds of greed. Discrimination rooted in such greed leads to unjust domination over others through power or authority" (Ikeda and de Athayde 2009, 24; italics in original).

From the above discussion, it is clear that the massive global inequalities which characterize our global history during the first decade of the twenty-first century are the product of a mind-set rooted in discrimination toward others by those who participate in the kind of egoism which is exemplified by the "progressive globalizers" and the "regressive globalizers." The fruits of their efforts, in combination with a single-minded drive for the accumulation of wealth for wealth's own sake, has created an entire global system wherein the excluded, the marginalized, and the poor are all subject to an "unjust domination" by virtue of having been placed under the economic model of neo-liberal globalization. The power and authority exercised by the managers of this system, in combination with the power elites of the political and financial establishments, supported by uninvolved and uncaring publics who pay the taxes that support this system of global exploitation, are all fundamentally complicit in producing and reproducing a system of global suffering for many millions of people. By virtue of being trapped within the confines, intellectual constructs and economic ghettos of this capitalist-dominated system, the claims of universal equality remain not only unrealized, but forcefully denied.

In order to change this situation and overcome its dire consequences, we will have to argue, in the spirit of Ikeda's philosophy, that the rich and powerful—as well as the publics who support their form of governance and the system that they have created for wealth-creation—must come to an enlightened recognition of the essential equality of all people. This is the case because to actually see and to comprehend the essential equality of all people then makes it impossible to support a system that is dedicated to maintaining the inequality of all people. In this regard, from Ikeda's perspective, we discover the reality that "[u]niversal observation of the human rights of all peoples can be achieved only when we have triumphed over the small self and, motivated by enlightenment to our inherent Buddha natures, learn to follow the nonviolent, compassionate way of the greater self. Lives enlightened to the greater self are free of the Four Delusions and fully embody the essential quality (called *byodo-sho-chi* in Japanese) of all peoples. Once this equality is understood and respected, all peoples can live in a symbiosis free of discrimination" (Ikeda and de Athayde 2009, 25; italics in original).

In elaborating upon this distinction between the "small self" and the "greater self," Ikeda has made an important definitional distinction between two kinds or varieties of universalism and then proceeds to explain why this is important for the achievement of equality. Ikeda states,

> ... I propose a methodological concept to help guide our search for a new globalism. This is the concept of inner universalism. Let us first see how this concept can be applied to the individual human being. In his writings, Nichiren said that the inherent dignity of one person serves as an example of all, meaning that all human beings should be regarded as equal. The idea of absolute equality and the sanctity of all human beings expressed here is the product of the unrelenting inward exploration of life itself as manifested in the individual. Because this view of the human being is internally generated, it leaves

no room for distinctions based on such factors as nationality and race. By contrast, the kind of universalism that has characterized the confrontational ideologies of the United States and the former Soviet Union is external and transcends the individual. Both liberal democracy and communism are by and large institutional concepts in that they seek to control human beings from outside and/or from above. So while both ideologies go beyond the framework of the nation or the state, they do so in a manner external to the individual (Ikeda 2001a, 168).

Ikeda's above-referenced perspective has tremendous implications for global governance, international relations theory, and aspirations for the building of a peaceful global civilization. Put more precisely, we are confronted with the age-old problem of how power and morality could be combined in the design of a peaceful world order. This exact issue was specifically addressed in the conclusion of E. H. Carr's (1961) *Twenty Years' Crisis* entitled, "*The Prospects of a New International Order.*" It is worth recalling E. H. Carr's depiction of the fundamental prerequisite for maintaining power: "Those who profit most" from a peaceful international order "can in the long run only hope to maintain it by making sufficient concessions to make it tolerable to those who profit by it the least; and the responsibility for seeing that these changes take place as far as possible in an orderly way rests as much on the defenders as on the challengers" (Carr 1961, 169).

In a subsequent commentary on Carr's thought entitled, "*The End of the Old Order?—Globalization and the Prospects for World Order,*" David Held and Anthony McGrew stated, "In a world where *powerful states make decisions not just for their peoples but for others as well*, and where transnational actors and forces cut across the boundaries of national communities in diverse ways, the questions of who should be accountable to whom, and on what basis, do not easily resolve themselves. Political space for the development and pursuit of effective government and the accountability of power is no longer coterminous with a delimited political territory. Contemporary forms of political globalization involve a complex deterritorialization and re-territorialization of political authority" (Held and McGrew 1998, 235; italics added).

Given these developments it is all the more clear that the accountability of power is enforced by some kind of democratic accountability that transcends the individual nation-states. Because "*powerful states make decisions not just for their peoples but for others as well*" it can be argued that this fact is what creates the nexus for the need to combine power and morality together in the construction and design of a peaceful world order that is also characterized by democratic accountability. This is necessarily the case insofar as the late twentieth century world has bequeathed us with a series of new types of "boundary problems." In order to effectively deal with the "boundary problems," Robert Johansen has argued that it is vital to recognize the new reality:

"Traditional thinking about democracy has been severely limited by national blinders that in practice encourage us to ignore the rights of people outside our own nation. Any decision to go to war is an extreme denial of democracy, because the lives of the targeted people are deliberately taken by a government that has not represented them in a decision to bomb, burn, and destroy them. The democratic accountability suggested by global constitutionalism and required by truly effective efforts at war prevention means that *more responsible and principled governing authority must be developed not only 'vertically' within domestic societies from the local to the national level, but also 'horizontally' across national borders and 'vertically' to encompass world society at the global level*" (Johansen 1993, 41; italics added).

As mentioned earlier in this chapter, along with the new types of "boundary problems," there are new challenges and opportunities for change with regard to emerging global trends toward regionalism and regionalization. According to Richard Falk, "From a world order perspective the role of regionalism is to help create a new equilibrium in politics that balances the protection of the vulnerable and the interests of humanity as a whole (including future generations) against the integrative, technological dynamic associated with globalism. One kind of balance is being promoted by transnational social forces connected with human rights and the environment, but regionalism could be another" (Falk 1999, 80). Within the dynamic interplay of our emerging global civilization, we are both observers and participants in an emerging world where "[p]atterns of regional and global change are transforming the nature and context of political action, creating *a system of multiple power centers and overlapping spheres of authority*" (Held and McGrew 1998, 236; italics added). In response to these global transformations, we can acknowledge that "[t]oday, in Carr's words, *'the old order cannot be restored, and drastic change of outlook is unavoidable.'* Such changes of outlook are clearly delineated in the contest between neo-liberalism, liberal-reformism, radicalism and cosmopolitanism. Globalization is not, as some suggest, narrowing or foreclosing political discussion; on the contrary, it is re-illuminating and reinvigorating the contemporary political terrain" (Held and McGrew 1998, 243; italics added).

A clear case of how globalization is changing the contemporary political terrain is found within the context of the recent history of South Africa's transformation. South Africa's experience with establishing a new constitution in a post-apartheid era has implications for the transnational future of democracy and a possibly emerging transnational constitutional order. That is of particular importance for not only the traditional nation-state, but also the entire international order. Because the relationships of constitutions to democracy are complex, it is important to get the constitution "right." Specifically, it matters because "[c]onstitutions facilitate democracy by establishing fixed ground rules for basic structures and elections and by protecting the preconditions for democratic decision-making, such as free speech; constitutions are designed to respect outcomes of democratic decision-making when they do not threaten constitutional values; and constitutions are intended to constrain democratic outputs when they do cross constitutional lines" (Jackson 2010, 266).

In terms of this chapter's discussions about equality, norms, and values, we find that South Africa's successful completion of the constitution-making process represents a new blend of constitutionalism ". . . which rests *not only on* the formality of prior legitimate consent, *but on* transnational substantive norms—democracy, the protection of minority rights, and respect for human equality and dignity—that draw their legitimacy from both substantive political morality and the clear approval of a majority of South Africans. South Africa both drew on and contributed to these *transnational norms*, not merely of human rights protection, but of the broader organization of a structure of governance designed to secure their protection" (Jackson 2010, 267; italics added).

Apart from the national security apparatus of the US government, there is still a legal structure in place that holds American political action accountable to agreed upon and established constitutional norms. So even in the domestic political context of the United States—despite its imperial foreign policy—we discover that "[l]ooking to foreign and international law . . . has been a legitimate feature of the US interpretative canon . . . and because the legitimacy of national states depends more than in the past on their respect for transnational values of democracy, human rights, and the rule of law. *Constitutional law does not always coincide with international law, or with transnational consensus on particular points, but respectful consideration of those transnational sources can help dispel the appearance of disregard for what are properly viewed as shared legal concerns*" (Jackson 2010, 255; italics added).

Therefore, as the US Empire crumbles and we hopefully are able to witness the rebirth of American democracy in a post-imperial America, there remains the future promise that *the transnational consensus* about the rule of law, international norms regarding human rights, and *transnational sources of law* (which serve to maintain the claims of morality with respect to the use of power) may yet allow for power to combine with morality in order to reshape and reconfigure America's place in the world and, at the same time, combine to help design a peaceful global civilization. In this crucial regard, the promise of the future is that the exercise of power—at the national and international levels—will become consciously accountable to a transnational moral standard that both safeguards and advances the evolution of a peaceful global civilization.

As such, it would be a global civilization that embraces nuclear disarmament, norms of mutual respect and consensus, renounces force or the threat of force, and respects the sovereignty of nations and regions. At the center of this process is the role of dialogue. As Ikeda makes clear, the path toward a more peaceful global civilization is intimately linked to the nature of the dialogic process that shapes that civilization. In the give and take of dialogue, there emerges a cross-cultural clarification of meaning. And, in this regard, it is the achievement of a shared meaning that makes possible a shared consensus. There is nothing more important than this at every level of our emerging global civilization. Dialogue is ultimately a process which is dedicated to the establishment of shared truth, a consensus that has been developed over shared values and norms, and a reflection of the desire of peoples from different cultures to participate in a shared unity that respects the motivations and plurality of others who do not inhabit our particular territorial boundaries.

Therefore, because dialogue knows no limitations, it has the capacity to engender a respect for the unity that exists beyond territorial boundaries. In this regard, dialogue helps us to transcend the boundaries of our own partial knowledge and the delimiting boundaries of our prejudices and ignorance. Hence, dialogue allows us to expand our knowledge, empathy, and awareness of others so that we can grasp the true nature of our global unity. In the midst of this plurality and diversity, we find, as Ikeda has argued, that a global civilization exists not despite the reality of plurality and diversity but because of it. Therefore, we have come to a point in history where we can finally recognize that a truly peaceful global civilization will have to reflect and embody the full spectrum of our plurality and diversity. In the final analysis, it is the power of dialogue that makes this possible as a human/historical achievement.

Notes

1. Amitav Acharya notes that "[a] broader implication is that contestations over seemingly incompatible 'universal' values and ideas on the one hand, and local ones on the other hand, often result in compromises imbued with moral purpose and defined by mutual adaptations. As ideational or civilizational entities, regions do not always clash, but learn and borrow from each other. The ideational foundation of world politics is formed by a continuous process of constitutive localization, which does not result in instant or comprehensive wins or defeats of one set of ideas over another. Rather, it rests on gradual, evolutionary, and everyday forms of normative and institutional change and a progressive blending of local and universal norms and values" (Amitav Acharya 2009b. Whose Ideas Matter?—Agency and Power in Asian Regionalism. Ithaca: Cornell University Press, pp. 7–8).

2. Ikeda writes, "These assets are, as I see them (1) the Chinese people's experience, during the last twenty-one centuries, of maintaining an empire that is a regional model for a literally worldwide state; (2) the ecumenical spirit with which the Chinese have been imbued during this long chapter of Chinese history; (3) the humanism of the Confucian Weltanschauung;

(4) the rationalism of both Confucianism and Buddhism; (5) the sense of the mystery of the universe and the recognition that human attempts to dominate the universe are self-defeating (to me, the most precious intuitions of Taoism); (6) the conviction (shared with Buddhism and Shinto by Chinese philosophy of all schools, except perhaps the now extinct Legalist school) that, far from trying to dominate nonhuman nature, man's aim should be to live in harmony with it; (7) the demonstration, by the Japanese people, that it is possible for East Asian peoples to beat the Westerners' own modern game of applying science to both civilian and military technology; and (8) the courage shown by both the Japanese and the Vietnamese in daring to challenge the West. This courage will, I hope, survive to be dedicated, in the next chapter of mankind's history, to the constructive enterprise of helping mankind to put its affairs in order peacefully" (Ikeda and Toynbee [1976] 2007. Choose Life: A Dialogue—Arnold Toynbee and Daisaku Ikeda, edited by Richard Gage. London: I.B. Tauris, p. 227).

3.   Amartya Sen has noted that "[t]he distribution of the benefits of global relations depends not only on domestic policies, but also on a variety of international social arrangements, including trade agreements, patent laws, global health initiatives, international educational provisions, facilities for technological dissemination, ecological and environmental restraint, treatment of accumulated debts (often incurred by irresponsible military rulers of the past), and the restraining of conflicts and local wars. These are all eminently discussable issues which could be fruitful subjects for global dialogue, including criticisms coming from far as well as near" (Amartya Sen, The Idea of Justice. Cambridge: Harvard University Press, 2009, p. 409; italics added).

Part III

Visualizing a Global Civilization of Harmony and Interdependence in Concrete Terms

6

The Converging Theoretical and Empirical Elements of Global Civilization: International Relations, Inclusive/ Humane Governance, and Cosmopolitan Democracy

"I agree that collective human power, whether local or worldwide, is the basis on which rests the awareness of nation and of antagonism between nation and nation. I further agree that this power and the concept of the national state are not suitable objects of worship. As civilization has advanced, the life basis of modern man has expanded to worldwide limits; that is to say, the land in which one lives today is the entire world. Consequently, the feeling that the earth is one's homeland and a love of all mankind must take the place of the narrow patriotism of the past. When world-embracing patriotism gains precedence, national patriotism will sink to the level of loyalty to a locality."

—Daisaku Ikeda
(Ikeda 2007-PP, 179)

"Beginning sometime after World War II the overall structure of world politics began to undergo change, to bifurcate, with the flourishing of innumerable actors other than states clambering up on to the world stage and undertaking actions with consequence for the course of events. As a result, what I call a 'multi-centric' world evolved that consists of a great variety of collectivities and that has come to rival the long-standing, anarchical state-centric system . . . Consequently, the multi-centric world now provides avenues for local groups to articulate their needs and goals as they join with each other in persuading governments in the state-centric world to heed—or at least to hear—their claims . . . It is hard to imagine any future gathering of leaders of the state-centric world that is not accompanied by a

204

simultaneous and adjacent gathering of organizations and individuals from the multi-centric world, a reality that is profoundly and thoroughly expressive of the dynamics of fragmentation."

—James N. Rosenau
(Rosenau 2005, 141)

"A great power is great by virtue of superior military force and economic wealth. A hegemon is a great power which exercises remarkable command over international public opinion. There is more to political power than the ability to punish and reward. The power of a state is not reckoned by mere counting of heads. Command over public opinion is as essential for political purposes as command of force and control of riches . . . A hegemonic world order exists when the major members of an international system agree on a code of norms, rules and laws which helps govern the behavior of all."

—Torbjorn L. Knutsen
(Knutsen 1999, 49)

The subject of world order demands an interdisciplinary approach. A proper understanding of world order can no longer be confined to the fields of history, political science, or international relations. In other words, there must be a dialogue between the disciplines. This is necessarily the case insofar as the passage of time and the flow of historical events has allowed for the evolution of human societies, human organizations, and the idea of humanity itself. Therefore, to predicate our current conceptions of world order and/or international society on the nation-state system will do a disservice to our present understandings as well as our future undertakings in global affairs. After all, the nation-state system was not even inaugurated until the year 1648, which marked the signing of the Peace of Westphalia. The Westphalian perspective which centers on the relations between states has largely governed international relations and international law for about four hundred years of the West's history. At the dawn of the twenty-first century, however, we have entered into a post-Westphalian world. In part, this dynamic transition is directly attributable to the nature of capitalism's current rebirth. In previous cycles of changing balances of power, capitalism's rebirth within the nation-state system was characterized by the destruction of existing institutions and the creation of new ones by one hegemonic city or nation-state.

Today, in capitalism's rebirth under the process of globalization ". . . that task has fallen upon the United States. The striking feature of the US response is a decisive shift from seeking order through consensus between nation-states to imposing order through coercion upon states" (Jha 2006, 174). This process has gone on since the 1970s because the leaders of the US primacy coalition have effectively alienated both allies and adversaries throughout the state system, coupled with the fact that "[a] hegemonic world order exists when the major members of an international system agree on a code of norms, rules and law which helps govern the behavior of all" (Knutsen 1999, 49; Paupp 2009). The Bush administration's illegal invasion of Iraq in 2003 changed all of that. As a result of the series of US-led interventions in Afghanistan and Iraq, coupled with an illegal occupation of these nations, the lack of an official sanction for these actions by the UN Security Council as a guarantor of global order under the terms of the UN Charter, we find that American hegemony was now opposed by social movements, states, and regions who saw the global future in terms of a world without US hegemony (Paupp 2007, 2009). A global trend has been progressing since 2003 wherein a global counter-hegemonic alliance against US hegemony has been spreading between states and social movements throughout Latin America, Asia, and the Middle East. Further, it is evident that US hegemonic decline has been spurred by its own imperial overreach in terms of wars and over 730 military bases around the world coupled with a severe financial collapse in 2008 from which it has yet to recover. Now, lacking consensus, suffering from imperial overreach, and trapped in a lingering financial recession, we find that the "crumbling walls" of US hegemony are exposing the reality of a multi-centric world of "rising regions" (Paupp 2009). This emerging world is the product of both a new normative focus on social justice issues and growing opposition to US-led globalization, militarism, and US-led dominance over the World Bank, the International Monetary Fund (IMF), and the World Trade Organization (WTO) as global rule-makers without a true global consensus (Aaronson and Zimmerman 2008; Abouharb and Cingranelli 2007; Bhala 2003; Jackson 2006; Toussaint 2005, 2008).

As the twentieth century came to a close, the reconstruction of world order under the rubric of the nation-state (supplied by the Westphalian system) was in the process of being reshaped and redesigned by the forces of globalization, US hegemony, and the intertwined and attendant processes of fragmentation as well as the growing role and influence of nongovernmental organizations (NGOs). The dynamic forces of global disaggregation were combining to trigger major realignment of nations, regions, and emerging centers of power in a truly multi-centric world. As a result of these trends, while the processes associated with globalization moved global relations toward greater integration, there were countervailing responses coming into focus, which pointed in the direction of resistance and fragmentation (Rosenau 2005, 136). Given these trends, it was clear that resistance to US hegemony coupled with the fragmentation of the global consensus was developing a new global dynamic for international relations and the possibilities for building a more peaceful global civilization. James Rosenau has posited the suggestion that ". . . by viewing the world through fragmentative lenses one can discern the underlying dynamics of our epoch with a clarity that is not otherwise available" (Rosenau 2005, 136).

In the midst of great uncertainty about the nature of this newly emerging order, what is certain is that economic advances had finally superseded the nation-state system of fixed territorial boundaries that had been established in 1648. To be sure, the future nature and direction of international relations would not be business as usual. The reason for this global transformation seems to center, in large measure, around the following observation: "What is contested is why so many countries and people are left behind or harmed in a process which is presented as benefiting all" (Tabb 2004, 21). In other words, the growth of inequality both within and between nations has exposed the fact that globalization has not produced what it supposedly promised. With this in mind, Robert Wade has cautioned: "If global inequality is widening by plausible measures and the number of people in extreme poverty probably not falling, we cannot conclude that globalization—or the spread of free-market relations—is moving the world in the right direction . . . The balance of probability is that—like global warming—the world is moving in the wrong direction—in terms of poverty and income inequality, which strengthens the case for applying *the precautionary principle* and revisiting development prescriptions and the design of the international economic regime" (Wade 2003, 42; italics added).

The full scope of the resulting global crisis that has emerged out of this conundrum is yet to be fully appreciated. Applying the precautionary principle points us in the direction of having to reassess the nature of interstate law, the need to revisit international human rights law, and the *law of humanity*. Now, at the dawn of the twenty-first century, according to Richard Falk, "The notion of world order is situated between interstate law and the law of humanity, although not necessarily at all in the middle . . . The law of humanity is associated with the future; it is more a matter of potentiality than of history or experience" (Falk 1998, 33). What is meant by *interstate law* are the formal international law categories of sovereignty and all of those practices associated with maintaining the territorial supremacy of the nation-state. What is meant by the law of humanity is ". . . prefigured, and to some extent embodied, in the substance and theory of the international law of human rights" (Falk 1998, 33). Therefore, we need to recognize that "[t]here exists in the corpus of interstate law *latent* recognition of important ingredients of the law of humanity, making the latter function as a normative catalyst, and not necessarily as an innovative and idealistic alternative" (Falk 1998, 39; italics in original). To rediscover the law of humanity within the broader context of interstate law is to recover the missing normative component of what constitutes genuine national and international security—*human security.* In this regard, Ramesh Thakur notes as follows:

> [A]s the sun rises on the new century and illumines some of the darker legacies of the last one, we should engage in sober reflection

and sober introspection. It is simply not acceptable that (1) at a time of unprecedented economic prosperity and stock market booms in some parts of the world, millions of people should continue to be condemned to a life of poverty, illiteracy, and ill health; (2) the combined GDP of the forty-eight least developed countries should be less than the assets of the world's three richest people; and (3) the annual income of 2.5 billion people—47 percent—of the world's poorest people should be less than that of the richest 225. (Thakur 2002, 284)

These are concerns which have not defined the traditional focus of international relations. Yet because of the gravity of these aforementioned global trends and conditions, even the subject area of international relations is being rethought so as to incorporate normative considerations and theoretical concepts into its analysis with as much dedication as it has shown in the past to undertaking a strictly empirical approach. Its historical preoccupation with the sovereignty of the nation-state and interstate relations has largely relegated attention given to human rights concerns to the backburner. As a consequence of the global crisis of the late twentieth century and early twenty-first century this lack of attention to human rights issues is about to change. In so doing, we are forced to confront historical failures to realize human rights and now begin the practical task of implementing policies and institutions that can finally translate the realization of these rights into practice at every level.

Before the modern advent of a universal and truly international human rights law in the post-1945 era, "Governmental engagement with this affirmation of human rights was understood from the beginning as never intended to be more than a gesture, and was carefully phrased so as not to challenge the sanctity of the sovereign state" (Falk 2009, 3). Therefore, when we examine debates about the global human rights regime from the perspective of those who adopt an empirical and positivist approach we discover that "... their methodology does not question the role of politics in the regime's construction and day-to-day existence ... They obscure the all-too-obvious discrepancy between the formal human rights regime and actual human rights practice, which can only be understood when human rights are, in the broader perspective of power and interests, contextualized within the global political economy, the post-1945 political institutionalization of market relations on a global scale" (Kirkup and Evans 2009, 222). However, when human rights are taken seriously and actually affect sociopolitical and socioeconomic practice, we then find that "[t]he impulse to acknowledge the universal scope of the rights of men and women directly contradicted the operational and doctrinal primacy accorded sovereignty, nationalism, and territorial supremacy" (Falk 2009, 3). This contradiction between the claims of human rights, on the one hand, and the traditional centrality of sovereignty and territorial supremacy on the other, has cracked open the door of human historical possibility for humanity to move beyond the old paradigms and divisions of the past. The recognition of this contradiction has provided us with a strong enough rationale to both critique and negate the realities of a status quo, which has sanctioned both unnecessarily high levels of human suffering and the denial of human rights. As such, it is a recognition that has also made possible the affirmation of a vision that reflects a qualitatively different global order—one governed not so much by a profit-driven fixation for elites in a national and global hierarchy of privilege as one governed by greater equality, a more comprehensive respect and enforcement of human rights and one which exemplifies a greater emphasis upon humane governance and inclusive governance (Falk 1995; Paupp 2000).

The Theory and Practice of Human Rights in World Order and Politics

Both empirically and practically, with the mid-twentieth century success of movements dedicated to decolonization and imperialism and the subsequent rise in the importance of the concept of self-determination, the global stage was set for the rise of the Third World from its colonial bondage. The theory of self-determination and its legitimate claim on the emerging human rights consciousness of global civilization was in the process of taking hold over both the socioeconomic and sociopolitical realms of international life. However, the Universal Declaration of Human Rights adopted by the United Nations in 1948 avoided any reference to the right of self-determination so as not to challenge, even obliquely, the legitimacy of colonial rule. So what made the "gift" of universal human rights an actual possibility was to be found in the ". . . accompanying dispiriting assurances that the norms of human rights would never be implemented by force. The promise of non-enforcement was signaled in many ways, but most clearly by placing the norms, standards, and principles constituting the substance of human rights in a text named the Universal *Declaration* of Human Rights. By modestly labeling the framework document establishing the content of human rights as a 'declaration' it was acknowledged that these norms were never meant to be obligatory, but were intended only to express aspirational goals the fulfillment of which depended on voluntary political reforms undertaken *within* individual states" (Falk 2009, 3; italics in original). Hence, the record actually does show that there was a Western opposition to the realization of human rights and this opposition was not a myth. However, by failing to take this historical context and the matter of human "intention" into account, we find that those who embrace an empirical and positivist approach have been too easily allowed to present a wealth of empirical examples, references to international law, speeches, and regional human rights regimes as evidence to demonstrate what they call the *myth of Western opposition* to the realization of human rights as a preposterous lie.

Yet when we discover the problematic discrepancy between legal rules, on the one hand, and actual practice on the other, it finally becomes clear that the positivist and empirical approach ". . . frames questions of power and interests within conventionally conceived concepts of the state, sovereignty, and natural rights, in the tradition of international society. They then define interests as the interests of all people in security, including economic security, for which the state is responsible. Therefore, their framework does not involve an analysis of questions concerning the role of human rights in legitimating the dominant socioeconomic global order which the state inhabits, or the exclusionary practices that arise from adopting particular human rights procedures" (Kirkup and Evans 2009, 223). On this precise point, Susan Kang notes thus:

> Economic and social rights remain controversial in many liberal Western countries. This unsettled status of economic and social rights in the West is perhaps most evident in the contemporary United States. Despite record levels of unemployment, home foreclosures, and widespread economic vulnerability during the current economic downturn, many US politicians have rejected resources for social provisions because of ideological commitments. Entitlements to basic economic and social provisions are not central to the dominant US political discourse, but rather remain politically contested." (Kang 2009, 1008)

Therefore, we discover at the national and the international level a proclivity both within and between nation-states to deny the sweeping and universal claims of human rights (Sunstein 2004). By invoking exclusionary practices these states have become what I call "exclusionary states" (ES) because they fail to incorporate all of their citizens in having their rights fully realized or even having a voice in deliberations that affect their very lives (Paupp 2000). Additionally, as already noted above, Falk has written about the vital importance of the law of humanity as a legal means through which we may come to actualize what have previously been merely "aspirational goals."

Specifically, in reference to Kang's just-cited description of the contemporary United States as excluding millions of its citizens from entitlements to basic economic and social provisions, it is interesting to recall Falk's discussion regarding the normative value and importance of Articles 25 and 28 of the Universal Declaration of Human Rights. Falk notes, "There exists agreement among international law specialists that the Universal Declaration has been incorporated into positive international law, but many provisions are simply ignored by human rights organizations as well as by others. Article 25 confers the right upon every person to an adequate standard of living, while Article 28 confers an even more far-reaching right: '*Everyone is entitled to a social and international order in which the rights and freedoms set forth in this Declaration can be fully* realized"' (Falk 1998, 39; italics added). Hence, we can argue that "[i]t seems desirable to break the silence, to speculate as to the shape of such '*a social and international order*' and to insist that market forces be held accountable for upholding such standards within their sphere of operations and that states undertake to full such legal expectations" (Falk 1998, 39–40; italics added).

I would argue that this is especially true in light of the combined pressures of globalization and the post-2008 global economic downturn. From the perspective of Ikeda, the factors leading to the underlying pathology of contemporary civilization can be found in an inordinate subordination of human rights and human well-being to profit for the few in an unregulated capitalist casino of global proportions. In his 2009 peace proposal, Ikeda writes thus:

> *The main cause of the crisis* can be traced to the rampant dominance of speculative financial assets, whose scale has been variously estimated at four times the cumulative value of world GDP. The financial markets, whose function is to support and facilitate other economic activities, have thrust themselves to center stage; dealers and traders who single-mindedly pursue earnings and profit, often with no thought for the impact on others, have become celebrated stars of the era. The runaway avarice of present-day capitalism is a widely documented phenomenon. As I have pointed out in these proposals on a number of occasions, *the deepest root of the crisis* is an unhealthy fixation on the abstract and ultimately insubstantial signifier of wealth—currency. This is the underlying pathology of contemporary civilization. (Ikeda 2009-PP, 1)

Just as Falk has written of the law of humanity as a means to change the shape of our global social and international order into one that provides a decent standard of living for every person, so too Ikeda has written of the need to move "*Toward a New Era of Value Creation.*" In his 2010 peace proposal, Ikeda writes, "Even when a sheer rock face looms before us, we should refuse to be disheartened, but instead continue the patient search for a way forward. In this sense, *what is most strongly required of us is the imagination that can appreciate the present crises as an opportunity to fundamentally transform the direction of history*" (Ikeda 2010-PP, 2; italics added).

The kind of imagination of which Ikeda writes is especially needed not only in the task of moving beyond global crisis, but also in dealing with the realities of a world of declining nation-states in juxtaposition to the forces of both globalization and fragmentation. In other words, the nation-state system of creating international law through the long and arduous process of state practice, custom, and diplomacy—all organized around the statist paradigm of sovereign territorial units—has just recently started to give way to a process of global fragmentation.[1] From the perspective of international relations scholar, James Rosenau, this fragmentation involves "the confluence of two major and contrary dynamics. One involves all those forces that press for centralization, integration, and globalization, and the other consists of those forces that press for decentralization, fragmentation, and localization" (Rosenau 2005, 135).

Whereas political authority had been more or less centralized in the individual nation-state since 1648, we now find that there has been a dispersal and fragmentation of that authority ever since the end of World War II. In fact, the birth of the United Nations in 1945 signaled the beginning of such an organizational dispersal of political authority by virtue of the fact that individual nation-states, through their representatives, became signatories to the UN Charter—a constitution for the international community.

Understood as such, the UN Charter was (at least in part) designed to overcome the inherent problems of the nation-state system. The specific defects of the nation-state system have been brilliantly summarized by Richard Falk: ". . . the state as the outer limit of nationalist identity and as the highest source of political authority decisively weakened the case for *human* solidarity. The pursuit of national interest in the name of 'realism' became the highest expression of ethical commitment in the external affairs of states . . . To this day, international law and foreign economic assistance have been unable to ensure either world peace or an end to poverty. At most, such efforts to regulate and help the economically disadvantaged are mainly selfishly justified by reference to the national interest in a stable and peaceful world . . . Cosmopolitan and species identifications are marginalized in modernity, derided as vague, vacant, abstract, and utopian" (Falk 2009, 194; italics in original).

Historically, a central problem of the nation-state system was articulated by Thomas Hobbes in the thirteenth chapter of his political treatise, *Leviathan*. "Sovereigns," wrote Hobbes, "are perpetually 'in the state and posture of gladiators,' which is 'a posture of war.'" This condition of war "consists not in actual fighting but in the known disposition thereto during all the time there is no assurance to the contrary" and lasts as long as sovereigns are without a common power "to keep them in awe." In this situation, whatever may be the circumstances of the outbreak of particular wars, "the fundamental cause is the absence of international government; in other words, the anarchy of sovereign states." Thus, we discover that, according to Terry Nardin: "Anarchy is a condition of war because of the fertile ground it offers for the germination of mutual fear. Each power, unable to count on the amity of others, must take steps to protect its own security. It must seek power. But by doing so it necessarily threatens the security of others. The consequence is perpetuation of what has come to be labeled 'Hobbesian fear' or, more commonly, the 'security dilemma', a predicament so exasperating as to invite resort to desperate measures to escape it" (Nardin 1983, 38).

Given this predicament, it can be argued that the formation of the United Nations and the UN Charter serves to provide humanity with a foundational agreement upon the basis of which individual nation-states should be expected to abstain from aggression against one another because there is the beginning of a global order based on common rules. The central problem with the UN system, however, has been one of enforceability. Insofar as the UN is not a world government with its own standing army, it must rely on nation-states to adhere to the rules, practices, and values of the UN Charter that are held out as guidelines for global governance. The only other alternative for truly effectuating a rule-governed order in human affairs is one where rules and government are united. However, it can be argued that "between the extremes of anarchy as a situation lacking either government or rules and the order of the state, there exists the possibility of life according to common rules ('society') even in the absence of common government ('anarchy')" (Nardin 1983, 40). In this sense, "International society, understood as an association of states in terms of common rules but without a common government, is thus at least a logically possible form of international order, however unstable or otherwise unsatisfactory it may turn out to be" (Nardin 1983, 40). It is this conceptualization of international society to which Ikeda turns in making his case that "[a]s civilization has advanced, the life basis of modern man has expanded to worldwide limits; that is to say, the land in which one lives today is the entire world" (Ikeda and Toynbee [1976] 2007, 179). By embracing the idea that humanity now has the capacity to see the human condition as one that exists beyond the traditional boundaries of the nation-states, one can see that humanity now stands at the threshold of a commonly understood and appreciated global unity. This is what makes possible the realization that "the earth is one's homeland and a love of all mankind must take the place of the narrow patriotism of the past" (Ikeda and Toynbee [1976] 2007, 179).

To see the "life basis of modern man" as one that has "expanded to worldwide limits" is, at the same time, to acknowledge that the international system (as presently constituted) as both the cause and perpetrator of injustice. The structural impediments to the full realization of human rights are part of the current international order to the extent that the dominant and dominating institutions of the international system have been placed in the service of international capital and the undemocratic interests and powers which lurk behind it. The insidious nature of the current international system is such that both First and Third World nations suffer from a common affliction—that of injustice for the majority of the citizenry. Under the exploitative dynamics of neoliberal capitalist globalization, the quality of life for all of the globe's citizens has become more unequal and more unjust—thereby leading toward a raising of global consciousness among First and Third World citizens about the need to confront, engage, and challenge the dominant hierarchy of privilege that is now in place. By challenging this system, it is also clear that a concomitant ethical responsibility has been revealed, which brings to bear the power of a new consciousness of responsibility to right the wrongs and injustices that such an order creates.

The abrogation of this current order has been evolving into a moral mandate for global transformation in the direction of affirming the desirability to create a more peaceful and universal global civilization while, at the same time, negating the systematic production of injustices of the current system of global power relations that transcends national boundaries. According to Thomas M. Franck, we discover that a review of contemporary history reveals the fact that

> [i]n more recent times, beginning with the 1970s campaign for a New International Economic Order, attention has been shifted to the international system, both as the cause and perpetrator of injustice and as the locus of appropriate remedial measures. This shift has occurred at a time when the globalization of so much that affects the quality of life has begun to impinge on the consciousness of even the most fortunate of citizenries. The convergence of these historic tendencies has laid the foundation for a widening communitarian consensus that in the world, as in the state, the happenstance of affluence carries a responsibility to alleviate the condition of the less fortunate: *a responsibility which transcends the historic accident of national boundaries.* (Franck 1995, 415; italics added)

Human Solidarity and the Quest for "Moral Globalization"

In harmony with Ikeda's formulation about the new nature of our emerging global civilization, Richard Falk maintains that "[f]or an ethically acceptable solution to the crisis of global governance . . . a sense of human solidarity *of global scope,* with allowance for plural identities, is indispensable. Putting realistic alternatives on the horizon by reference to humanity rather than to nation-states carries the quest for moral globalization to a new domain of post-Westphalian realities" (Falk 2009, 200; italics in original). Falk's reading of the global situation is complemented by Rosenau's depiction of the current global crisis as one of transition when he notes, "As technologies shrink the world, as people become increasingly skillful, as organizations proliferate, as the multi-centric world expands, and as the mobility upheaval sustains vast movements of people, the meaning of territory becomes less compelling and states and their sovereignty become weaker" (Rosenau 2005, 142).

In this post-Westphalian environment, we discover that it is more accurate to speak not so much of the weakening of the nation-state as its displacement from its previous position of centrality in the tasks of governance.

The state is now augmented by other international institutions that have come into being as a consequence of globalization and with increased levels of transnational exchange and communication. We find that "[i]nstitutions are needed to deal with the evermore complex dilemmas of collective action that emerge in a globalized world. Norms, rules, and institutions are generated because they help states and other actors to deal with common problems and because they enhance welfare" (Hurrell 2007, 68). Hence, the normative ambitions of international society have been expanded in response to an evolving global environment that is demanding a redefinition of what constitutes genuine security. According to Hurrell, we discover, "The normative ambitions of international society in relation to security have therefore come to include: progressively tighter limits on legitimate justifications for the use of force by states, more effective control over the development and proliferation of weapons of mass destruction, and increased concern for the security of an expanded range of social groups against an expanded range of threats" (Hurrell 2007, 191).

Given these current historical trends, we can argue that the doors of our collective perception have once again been widened enough for us to see and conceive a different future. The conception of a new and more humane global civilization emerges out from under the rubble of a broken nation-state system, unregulated capitalism, and rampant globalization.[2] Beyond the old security dilemmas of the nation-state system, we can now speak of human security in such a way that unites humankind. We are now positioned so as to take advantage of the processes of globalization, the decline of the nation-state, and the crumbling walls of US hegemony by virtue of the fact that we can rediscover the reality that human beings are profoundly sociable. On this precise point, Jens Bartelson has observed that "[w]hile Grotius, Hobbes, and Locke accepted the division of mankind into distinct communities as an inescapable part of the human condition, authors like Shaftesbury, Vico, Turgot, and Diderot sought to recover the patterns underlying this differentiation, and hence also the foundations of a united mankind. These authors tried to formulate an alternative to the particularistic social ontology of Hobbes and Locke by arguing that human beings are profoundly sociable, and that all human communities must be understood as expressions of such sociability" (Bartelson 2009, 139).

Now, at the dawn of the twenty-first century, the idea of "humanity" as a global reality takes on a new and redefining significance for us as we confront the sweeping multidimensionality of our global crisis. As Falk notes, "Humanity as a principal organizing idea in political and ethical discourse is being used as a polemical tool, as a descriptive category, and as the embodiment in social reality of essential ethical and spiritual ideals" (Falk 2009, 192). But there is an attendant problem with this new role for the idea of humanity insofar as: "Ambiguity and confusion results from this multiple usage, which limits the potential contributions of the idea of humanity to what I have called *'moral globalization'"* (Falk 2009, 192; italics added). In his 2009 peace proposal, Ikeda presents a concrete corrective to this problem of "ambiguity and confusion" that has been identified by Falk. Ikeda states thus:

> Soon after the end of World War II, the French philosopher Gabriel Marcel (1889–1973) offered a penetrating analysis in an essay entitled *"The Spirit of Abstraction, as a Factor Making for War."* While the ability to develop and manipulate abstract concepts is indispensable to human intellectual activity, the resulting abstractions are ultimately without substance. The idea of the *"human being,"* for example, must be understood in some sense to be a fiction. The reality is that we are women or men, Japanese or Americans, older or younger, originating from some particular place. The greater the care with which we observe people, the more we come to recognize them as distinct and unique. This is the world of concrete reality. Any discussion of *"human beings"* or *"humanity"* that fails to take these differences fully into account will generate abstract concepts that take on a life of their own. (Ikeda 2009-PP, 2; Italics added)

Despite Falk's misgivings about the ultimate trajectory of the idea of humanity as a "principal organizing idea in political and ethical discourse," Rosenau—like Ikeda—firmly believes that structural constraints and conceptual blocks that currently prevail in the global system can be undone. Rosenau's optimism is vetted in three aspects of "an upbeat answer that may prove operative if one is willing to look beyond the immediate present." He cites them as follows: "In the first place, more than a little truth attaches to the aphorism that there is safety in numbers . . . Every rule system . . . will be hemmed in by all the others, thus conducing to a growing awareness of the *virtues of cooperation* and the need to contain the worst effects of deleterious fragmentation. Second, there is a consciousness of and intelligence about the processes of globalization that is spreading to every corner of the earth" so that "people in all walks of life have begun to appreciate their *interdependence with others* as time and distance shrink . . . Third, the advent of networks and the flow of horizontal communications have brought many more people into one or another *aspects of the ongoing dialogue.* The conditions for *the emergence of a series of global consensuses* never existed to quite the extent they do today. The skills of individuals and the organizations they support are increasingly conducive to *convergence around shared values*" (Rosenau 2005, 150–51; italics added).

Like Ikeda, Rosenau writes of similar trends and qualitative changes that are transpiring in the midst of the current global crisis which open the doors of possibility rather widely for the birth of a more peaceful, humane, and inclusive global civilization. Specifically, we find that both Ikeda and Rosenau concur on the following: (1) the virtues of cooperation; (2) an emerging recognition of our interdependence with others; and (3) the dynamics of an ongoing dialogue, which is making possible the emergence of a series of global consensuses that are conducive to convergence around shared values. Taken together, we can now see how the ingredients of our shared humanity have the potential to emerge in concrete form. Further, we would suggest that this perspective offers a compelling reply to Gabriel Marcel's concern over "the spirit of abstraction."

Insofar as our conceptions of "humanity" and "human being" are not alienated from concrete realities, we are now empowered to move from concrete realities toward the attainment of a peaceful global civilization. From the virtues of cooperation to an emerging recognition of our interdependence with others, Ikeda, Falk, Paupp, and Rosenau have reminded us of the need to embark upon radically different paths toward our collective future. Fueled by the dynamics of inner transformation combined with engagement in dialogue, the emergence of a more peaceful global civilization can be seen as possible from participation in and fidelity to shared values. The good news is that there is an objective and empirical basis for making this normative claim. At the dawn of the twenty-first century, the empirical basis for this assertion is found in the fact that

> The normative structure of international society has evolved in ways which help to undercut the arguments of those who deny the existence of a global justice community . . . The meaning of many moral principles might not be universal, but it is certainly widely diffused across the world and embedded in many institutions and practices. There is now a denser and more integrated network of shared institutions and practices within which social expectations of global justice and injustice have become more securely established. There are good reasons for believing that the density of international society provides a meaningful basis for debate over our responsibilities to the most vulnerable and most deprived of distant strangers. Thus we have seen the emergence of an international and transnational culture of human rights that involves a widely shared common language, an inclusive moral vocabulary, and an authoritative and well-developed normative structure from which very few groups are prepared to try to exempt themselves. This shared discourse implies a general acceptance of certain general principles and processes and of a particular kind of rationality and argumentation. (Hurrell 2007, 304–05)

It is with Hurrell's interpretation of the emergence of an international and transnational culture of human rights in mind that we now turn to a discussion of the current state of affairs in the academic field of international relations (IR).

The New Emphasis on Norms in International
Relations Scholarship

This shared discourse on human rights has emerged not from just a few decades but many centuries of dialogue within and between nations, cultures, and philosophical positions concerning the true nature and character of international relations. As such, the human rights legal regime, as well as the emerging global discourse on human rights, has been the consequence of a creative global enterprise of human self-understanding that has resulted in an ongoing process of communication over the nature and character of global society and the workings of its component parts. In analyzing the historical, political, and economic dynamics of the unfolding of global society, we find that the nature of academic analysis on this subject has led to new understandings and points of emphasis, which have served to significantly transform the explanatory power and focus of the scholarly field of international relations (IR).

The growing recognition of the centrality of theoretical inquiry, norms, and values in the shaping of both the explanations and conceptualizations of how we view international relations has, in turn, revealed the presence of densely constructed networks and institutions, which are dedicated to the eventual transformation of world politics as well as the evolution of humankind's social, cultural, political, and economic organization toward a more unified and peaceful global civilization. In that process, there has been a gradual evolution in the academic field of international relations (IR) from its historical preoccupation with the conduct of individual nation-states—and relations between states—to a field of global inquiry that has increasingly seen the creative, analytical, and historical importance of theoretical inquiry and normative concerns as the driving force behind empirical inquiry.

In that regard, Christian Reus-Smit and Duncan Snidal address this change of emphasis in IR within their introduction (to *The Oxford Handbook of International Relations*) on the current state of IR studies (Reus-Smit and Snidal, 2008). They begin their introduction by discussing the rationale behind their emphasis on theory, on conceptions of international relations as a discipline, on contending ideas of theoretical progress, on different theoretical perspectives, and methodological ideas that drive and ultimately define the study of world politics. After enumerating these considerations, they proceed to note thus:

> We have adopted this emphasis not because we value theoretical over empirical inquiry or the pursuit of abstract ideas over more "practical" forms of scholarship. We have done so because we believe that theoretical assumptions (and debates surrounding them) determine the contours of the field and inform even the most empirical research. An inquiry into the field of international relation ought,

first and foremost, to be an inquiry into the ideas that animate it—the ideas that distinguish international relations (or global politics) as a domain of social and political life, the ideas that determine what constitutes knowledge of this political realm, the ideas that dictate the questions that merit answers, and the ideas that shape the field's relations with other disciplines. Without these ideas, international relations would have neither identity, skeleton, nor pulse. (Reus-Smit and Snidal 2008, 5)

The authors proceed to further define exactly what they mean by "theory" when they state, "The most distinctive feature of the *Handbook* is not its focus on theory but on our reading of theory as *both* empirical a*nd* normative" (Reus-Smit and Snidal 2008, 6; italics in original).
The authors acknowledge that

[m]ost surveys of international relations theory concentrate on empirical (and/or positive) theory; if normative theory receives any attention, it is left for a final chapter or two on 'ethics and international affairs'. . . The assumptions appear to be that empirical and normative inquiry can be segregated and that international relations theory is almost exclusively an empirical or positive project. Although it is acknowledged (in some limited fashion) that there is another body of theory—normative theory—that treats the international as its subject, this is the preserve of philosophers or political theorists. Thus the default position is that international relations is an explanatory endeavor, concerned with the 'is' of world politics not the 'ought.' We find this segregation both unsustainable and unhelpful. All theories of international relations and global politics have important empirical *and* normative dimensions, and their deep interconnection is unavoidable. (Reus-Smit and Snidal 2008, 6)

Hence, both realist scholars and post-modernist scholars ultimately arrive at their criticisms and critiques of world order in a way that can be defended only normatively.[3]
On this point, it should be noted that Reus-Smit's and Snidal's clearly stated linkage on theory—as *both* empirical *and* normative—has great implications for our own explication of Ikeda's proposals and vision for building a more peaceful global civilization. The significance of this assertion should be evident. It is found in numerous examples where the normative goal and value of "peace" is then linked to an empirical problem such as nuclear disarmament and the associated problem of war as a continuing means of statecraft. Ikeda, throughout his writings and speeches, has consistently stated what the empirical problem "is" and then references our focus to a solution that is found in peace movements that articulate an ethical "ought." For example, Ikeda notes thus:

> At enormous cost to humankind, we have finally learned that nothing is more tragic and cruel than war. Yet wars keep on coming as before, with no sign of letting up. We have become entangled in a cycle from which *there is no way out without first shifting from a system of state-centered security to one of human-centered security.* The stimulus and drive to accomplish that are going to come out of the popular, grass-roots peace movements. (Ikeda and Tehranian 2003, 130; italics added)

What we have in this statement is Ikeda's answer to the problem of war and nuclear weapons through a *paradigm shift*. By shifting the old paradigm of state-centered security to a paradigm of human-centered security, Ikeda has allowed the "ethical ought" in his theory of human-centered security to trump the rationale of what "is"—and has been the foundational norm of international affairs—the historical persistence of a state-centered security paradigm (Haslam 2002; Jackson and Sorensen 1999; Knutsen 1997; Little 2007). Now, insofar as the achievement of peace (as a normative goal) is interconnected to a variety of related concerns (such as the idea of human security, as opposed to national security or state-centered security) Ikeda has realized that the goal of achieving peace must be empirically connected to the empirical means of how to precisely formulate concrete policies and strategies that will facilitate reaching the goal of a sustainable peace (universally conceived).

Hence, as in the field of IR itself, we are necessarily concerned with both the "is" of world politics (as an empirical reality) and the ethical "ought" (the normative vision and means of how to change what "is"—that which is antithetical to the realization of peace). We find Ikeda accomplishes this through *a paradigmatic shift* that not only replaces state-centered notions of security with a peace-oriented paradigm of human security but also introduces a normative theoretical element into the equation for peace that removes the central obstacles and blockages to the achievement of such a peace. Ikeda is advocating the removal of all of the old assumptions that have guided humanity to war, time and again, by reliance on a paradigm of state-centered security thinking, strategies centered upon "balance of power" considerations, and state-centric policies, which have ignored the larger human interest by maintaining a narrow focus on perceptions of what constitutes the "national interest" (Kaufmann et al. 2007).

In bringing his paradigm shift to its fullest expression, Ikeda articulates what he believes are the most concrete channels through which "human security demands" can be effectuated and finally realized. Ikeda's proposals for expanding the arsenal of peaceful channels that would advance human security include, a rearticulation of international law premises about what constitutes genuine security, assuring that the premises around the concept of human security are advanced to the foreground of consciousness and action, and advancing efforts aimed at strengthening the role of the United

Nations in the task of effectuating the shift to a paradigm of human security. In explaining the various interconnections between these aforementioned components, Ikeda asserts, "I believe human security demands broadening international law, extending its premises to foreground the interests of humanity, supporting and strengthening the United Nations. *International law was formed over the centuries-long tenure of the Westphalia system, developing as a set of rules that prioritized the adjustment of inter-state interests and privileged the traditional exclusive sovereignty of the state.* So it is difficult to build consensus on the basis of the interests of humanity, or even if some agreement is reached, it is usually short-lived and hobbled by constraints that erode its practical effectiveness" (Ikeda and Tehranian 2003, 131; italics added). So to reach a historical tipping point where we can achieve a sustainable consensus about human security, we will need to achieve a paradigm shift that permanently replaces the state-centered paradigm of our Westphalian heritage with a human-security centered paradigm that places humanity on a new historical trajectory.

What this points to is a convergence of the three central tenets of Ikeda's philosophy of peace becoming fully operational: (1) an inner transformation of the consciousness of individuals that makes possible a human revolution in thought, in spirit, and in action; (2) the employment of dialogue and dialogic processes that help to unleash new insights and new forms of communication and understanding that can help to build a sustainable consensus around shared values; and (3) a paradigm shift toward understanding and appreciating our global citizenship as world citizens who have a greater moral, ethical, and political obligation to humanity as a whole, rather than the claims of a particular nation-state.

In reconnecting these ideas of Ikeda with newly articulated approaches in the field of international relations, we return to Christian Reus-Smit and Duncan Snidal who note. "From the outset, international relations theory has been a practical discourse . . . we mean that all international relations theories, in one form or another, have at some level been concerned with the question, *how should we act?*" (Reus-Smit and Snidal 2008, 7; italics added). In reviewing the three aforementioned tenets and/or components of Ikeda's philosophy of peace, we can assert that all three components are designed in such a way that they also address the question, *how should we act?* That question requires a normative answer which, in turn, presents us with an empirical challenge. Again, the central point to be made is that from the evolving perspective of IR theorists, as well as from the perspective of Ikeda, what is required for a proper assessment of world politics is a deep appreciation of both the empirical and normative dimensions of world politics. Such an interconnection is unavoidable.

In conjunction with the question, *how should we act*, there is a related question which has tremendous implications for both IR scholarship and the implementation of Ikeda's idea of global civilization. That question is, "*Will the future be like the past?*" Once again, we are confronted by a question that has both normative and empirical features. In terms of a traditional IR perspective on this question, the usual components of an answer would involve an analysis of nation-states and their material capabilities, their relationship to one another, and the governing influence of the idea of the "balance of power" existing between them. On this matter, Robert W. Cox notes, "This basic approach is devised to explain what happens among the state entities as levels of military and economic capability among them change. Change in material capabilities takes place *within* the system, but the nature or basic structure *of* the system never changes" (Cox 2008, 84 italics in original). So if the basic structure *of* the system never changes, then history is transfixed upon a pattern of violent and hierarchical arrangements that are simply doomed to replicate a history of exploitation, war, and sociopolitical and socioeconomic exclusion long into the future (Paupp 2000, 2007, 2009).

This analytical approach sums up the basic approach of neorealist IR scholars who have regarded history as ". . . a quarry for mining data to test the system. *The point of 'neo-realism' was to explain shifting power relations in a world that did not change in its basic character*" (Cox 2008, 85; italics added). In terms of neorealism's approach to the study of IR, with its proclivity to interrogate the past as a key indicator for future global trends, the past is indeed prologue. In the neorealist vision, the future was largely predetermined by history, thereby providing an affirmative answer to the question, *will the future be like the past?* Therefore, the inevitable challenge that neorealists would eventually face was not one of explanation but that of change in the structure of world power and global relations. The nature of neorealist inquiry has been content to view the history of humanity as a history devoid of purpose, especially since neorealists have refused to incorporate into their discipline and appreciation of the subjective notion of an inherent purpose unfolding in human history. Given this orientation, "Historical actors, individual or collective (that is, states), can have purposes, but for the positivist observer, there can be no cosmic purpose inherent in the process of interaction itself" (Cox 2008, 85).

The effect of neutering our understanding of international relations under the rubric of the neorealist paradigm limits the range of our attention so that we focus on an event-driven view of history that cannot fully comprehend the entirety of systemic realities or hope to comprehend a general perspective. According to two other IR scholars, Barry Buzan and Richard Little, such an approach is worse than inadequate. They assert, "Our view is that international relations represents a subject of such immense size and complexity that it is best approached from a systemic or general perspective rather than an event-driven or particularistic one . . . *To understand international relations, therefore, we need to start looking at systems as a whole, rather than by opening with an examination of their component parts . . . The failure of history and theory to join forces has led to an impoverished understanding of international relations.* We see the idea of the international system as providing the best possible location where history and theory can meet" (Buzan and Little 2000, 33; italics added).

It is with this critique in mind, as well as the critique of IR presented by Reus-Smit and Snidal (as discussed above), that Steve Smith has offered six "wishes" or proposals designed to make the discipline of IR more relevant to the demands of the twenty-first century. They are as follows:

(1) "All approaches should be seen has having normative commitments." That is because "international relations is unavoidably normative for two related reasons: first there can be no simple separation between 'fact' and 'values;' second, international relations is a practical discipline, concerned with how we should act" (Smith 2008, 727).

(2) "International relations has to become less of an American discipline." That is because "[a]ny academic discipline will take particular interest in the policy concerns of its major subjects, but in international relations, the US policy agenda, and its dominant methodology, has been so influential that other voices have been either ignored or placed in a position whereby they are of interest or relevance only insofar as they relate to the dominant agenda . . . If international relations remains a narrow American social science, the dangers are that it will be irrelevant to the concerns of large parts of the world's population, and more problematically it may become increasingly part of the process of US hegemony" (Smith 2008, 727–28).

(3) "International relations has to reject its current, and historic, privileging of a specific, and culturally entailed, social scientific approach." This is because "International relations has been overwhelmingly focused on one version of social science for the last fifty years. Positivism has legitimated international relations, and has served as the benchmark for what counts as acceptable work... Unless the discipline accepts that there is a wide set of legitimate approaches to studying world politics, then it will become more and more restricted in its ability to relate to other disciplines and it will become a besieged academic fortress validated and legitimated only internally" (Smith 2008, 728).

(4) "International relations academics need to reflect on their relation to power and on their social location." This is because ". . . what we research and teach are choices we make as academics; these choices can be explained as simply studying the 'main features' of world politics, but this merely covers up what are at base political and ethical choices . . . Unless we question the assumptions we make when we teach and research, then we will simply be reinforcing the existing distribution of power, and reinforcing the agenda of the powerful" (Smith 2008. 728–29).

(5) "International relations needs to focus on the relationship between the material and the ideational." This is because "Marxism has been much

missed in international relations over the last twenty years; it was a theoretical position that had a clear, if contested, view of how material and
ideational worlds interrelated" (Smith 2008, 729).

(6) "International relations should not take core concerns of the most
powerful as the dominant issues for the discipline." This is because "International relations has historically ignored large sections of humanity
. . . Unless international relations is able to deal with agendas outside
those of the dominant powers, then it will be completely unable to
account for the motivations of all those who fundamentally reject
the Western models of development, human rights, and civil society"
(Smith 2008, 729–30).

Similarly, a review of Ikeda's writings show that he agrees with all six points
of Smith's critique of international relations, especially the suggestion that
history and theory (and the normative forces behind it) need to join forces in
order to overcome our present historical predicament and move beyond global
crisis. After all, Ikeda centralizes the importance of inner transformation as
the starting point for the kind of change which makes possible an intelligent
answer to the question, how shall we act? In confronting that question, every
person must undergo a process of self-interrogation in order that a transformative change in both consciousness and action becomes possible and then
becomes probable. Emerging from such a process of inner transformation
allows each person who has undertaken this inner journey to then undertake
the challenges of the dialogic process. After all, a changed consciousness
leads to new questions about where one needs to go from that point. It is the
beginning of the inquiry that asks "will the future be like the past?" As the
responses to these questions begin to converge, we find, according to Ikeda,
that history itself begins to be transformed by virtue of the fact that we have
(a) courageously undertaken the task of accepting responsibility for our lives
and, as a consequence of accepting this responsibility have (b) channeled our
energy into living a "contributive way of life" that cares about the suffering of
others and seeks to rectify the situation that has created such suffering. This
means that with a renewed and transformed perspective, we can start to take
responsibility for our history, instead of falling into the trap of assuming that
we are merely victims of it.

In other words, history can be recreated by us so that the future need not
be a mere repetition of the past. On this matter, Ikeda is quite explicit. He
notes, for example, that

> [w]hen the Soka Gakkai was founded in 1930, Japan and the world
> were shuddering under the impact of the financial panic of the
> previous year. People were afflicted by a—deepening sense of dread
> and unease. Writing at that time, the founder of the organization,
> Tsunesaburo Makiguchi (1871–1944), called for a transition from
> a dependent or even an independent way of life to what he called a

contributive way of life. He rejected a passive, dependent way of life in which one is swayed by and at the mercy of one's surroundings and the conditions of the times. He likewise rejected a way of life in which we are capable of looking out for our own needs but remain indifferent to *the sufferings of others*. (Ikeda 2010-PP, 2; italics added)

Addressing the *sufferings of others* is also at the heart of Ikeda's 2009 peace proposal where, once again, he quoted from the written works of his mentor's mentor, Makiguchi, "What is important is to set aside egotistical motives, striving to protect and improve not only one's own life but also the lives of others because by benefiting others, we benefit ourselves" (Makiguchi 1981–88, 2:399). Following from this quote, Ikeda states, "I am now fully convinced that the time has now arrived, a hundred years after it was originally proposed, for us to turn our attention to humanitarian competition as a guiding principle for the new era" (Ikeda 2009-PP, 8). In his discussion of humanitarian competition, Ikeda is equally critical of capitalism and socialism insofar as capitalism has largely abandoned the search for social justice and equality while socialism's failure "can be attributed to the failure to adequately take into account the value of competition as a source of energy and vitality . . . Free competition driven by the unrestrained impulses of selfishness can descend into the kind of social Darwinism in which the strong prey on the weak. But competition conducted within an appropriate framework of rules and conventions brings forth the energies of individuals and revitalizes society" (Ikeda 2009-PP, 8).

Clearly, unregulated capitalism (as advanced and advocated in the neoliberal model) is antithetical to the proper orientation of the individual because it merely feeds the Darwinian hunger to conquer and exploit others regardless of the suffering it creates in their lives. It also explains why under the rubric of social Darwinism, the future is little more than a mere repetition of the past. Insofar as the practice of social Darwinism fails to call for the evolution of a higher consciousness toward the treatment of others and is largely only concerned with self-aggrandizement for the sake of profit and gain, it leaves little room for the future to become anything other than a continuation of history's record of human brutality and human suffering. It is for this reason that society—nationally and globally—is not revitalized but is rather trapped in a cauldron of greed, suffering, and endless exploitation. However, if humanity were to adopt humane values instead of the Darwinian mandate (the "law of the jungle"), then we could appreciate the true value of humanitarian competition. This is the case because, as Ikeda notes, "As a concept, it compels us to confront the reality of competition while ensuring that it is conducted firmly on the basis of *humane values*, thus bringing forth *a synergistic reaction between humanitarian concerns and competitive energies*. It is this that qualifies humanitarian competition to be a key paradigm for the twenty-first century" (Ikeda 2009-PP, 8; italics added).

For Ikeda, humanitarian competition becomes the corrective for a long history of human suffering that has left humankind in a state of cultural disintegration, moral paralysis, and psychological collapse. Such an antidote is desperately needed for the transformation of human history for, as Ashis Nandy has observed, "Continuous suffering inflicted by fellow human beings, centuries of inequity and deprivation of basic human dignity, generations of poverty, long experiences of authoritarian political rule or imperialism—these distort the cultures and minds, especially the values and the self-concepts, of the sufferers and those involved in the manufacturing of suffering. Long-term suffering also generally means the establishment of powerful justifications for the suffering in the minds of both the oppressors and the oppressed . . . In sum, no vision of the future can ignore the way that institutional suffering touches the deepest core of human beings and that societies must work through the culture and psychology of such suffering, in addition to its politics and economics" (Nandy 1984, 153).

Also contained in his 2009 peace proposal, we discover that Ikeda explicitly notes, "[I]f the current crisis is indeed a crisis of the modern Western social system with capitalism and democracy at its heart, it becomes all the more imperative to discover *alternative universal perspectives and principles*" (Ikeda 2009-PP, 7; italics added). In Ikeda's dialogue with Majid Tehranian, we find an articulation of the perceived need to redefine globalization itself in light of a more universal perspective so that we can better comprehend its true direction and, thereby, make a course correction, which will allow us to more effectively deal with newly emerging destabilizing forces. This then opens up a consideration of which values and norms shall be chosen and emphasized as we work toward the construction of a more peaceful global civilization. The exchange between Ikeda and Tehranian is as follows:

> Ikeda: With growing globalization in recent decades, the term "a global civilization" is certainly taking on a realistic meaning. But the current trend toward globalization seems to lack direction, which in turn has given rise to new destabilizing factors. *Insofar as globalization is an irreversible trend, we need a solid vision of philosophy that provides a clear direction in which globalization should proceed.*

> Tehranian: Right. *Since every civilization maximizes certain values and norms, sometimes at the expense of others, we also need to have some clarity on what constitutes a desirable norm for the global civilization that is in the process of formation.* My proposal is to consider dialogue and the movement from cultural narcissism to cultural altruism as a basis for such a civilizational development (Ikeda and Tehranian 2003, 73–74; italics added).

The ideas expressed in the Ikeda/Tehranian exchange are ideas widely held and expressed by Ikeda's contemporaries. Analysts, scholars, and intellectual leaders such as Richard Falk, George Soros, Paul Streeten, Joseph Stiglitiz, David Held, Mathias Koenig-Archibugi, Robert Hunter Wade, John H. Dunning, Hans Kung, Terrence Paupp, Thomas W. Pogge, Alan Gewirth, and Depak Lal have all expressed similar concerns and developed complementary perspectives. In what follows some examples from a few of these scholars/analysts would suffice to illustrate the continuity, balance, and a common consensus around shared norms, which are held by both Ikeda and his contemporaries. For the sake of brevity and to avoid unnecessary duplication, we shall concentrate on the specific contributions of Richard Falk (1975, 1985, 1995, 1998, 2000a, 2003, 2008c, 2009), Joseph Stiglitz (2005), Thomas Pogge (2007), Alan Gewirth (1996), David Held (1989, 1995, 1999, 2003, 2004, 2007), and Terrence Paupp (2000, 2007, 2009). When viewed in juxtaposition to each other, their combined efforts all may be described as having converged in what Ikeda has called alternative universal perspectives and principles. It is to this concept and its leading proponents that we now turn.

Alternative Universal Perspectives and Principles

Richard Falk's academic career is particularly distinguished by his decades-long focus on global norms and values that could lead to what he has termed "humane governance." Falk has recounted this history when he notes, "The World Order Models Project (WOMP), which started its work in the late 1960s, is illustrative of a somewhat more far-reaching and comprehensive effort to challenge the existing world order and find alternatives, through the medium of diagnosis and prescription by a transnational group of independent academicians" (Falk 2003, 290). In later decades, he continued to discuss the "normative vacuum" created by neoliberal capitalism without the challenge of socialism. Falk has been rather explicit on this matter noting, "Neo-liberalism, without the challenge of socialism, dispensed with pretensions that economic policy should take explicit account of the needs of people to the extent politically possible, and world capitalism showed its cruel face. Despite sustained economic growth and some national success stories in Asia, income inequalities within and between countries greatly increased, and mass poverty persisted. This global setting of reduced concern about traditional war/peace issues and *the rise of predatory globalization created a normative vacuum on the world stage*" (Falk 2009, 5 italics added).

In order to offset this trend, Falk has placed great hope on the political relevance of global civil society. To that end, he cites the power of the anti-globalization movement since the 1990s and its demands in juxtaposition to the managers of the global business world. By virtue of having adopted a perspective on civilizational development that mirrors that of Ikeda and Tehranian, Falk makes the following observation:

227

[The] interplay between demands for reform from civil society and accommodation and response by global business world marked a new point of departure for world politics in that it was no longer merely a sequel to the Cold War, but rather represented the beginning of contestation in an era of economic globalization. The common need for *normative* (moral, legal, and regulative) adjustment in the actual and perceived workings of the world economy, so that economic growth was seen as contributing a greater share of the return on investment and trade revenue to *public goods* (domestically, regionally, and globally); and by so doing, to insulate fragile economies from sharp decline . . . The humanizing of capitalism is not a self-generating force, but must be achieved by the constant exertion of pressure. These include both challenges from those that allege victimization and responses by those that control economic policy. (Falk 2003, 282–83; italics in original)

In outlining a strategy through which the "humanizing of capital" can be realized, Falk invokes the idea of the constant exertion of pressure by "the elements of normative democracy." The eight elements that he identifies are as follows: (1) consent of the citizenry; (2) rule of law; (3) human rights; (4) participation; (5) accountability; (6) public goods; (7) transparency; and (8) nonviolence (Falk 2003, 294–95). To avoid a mistaken perception of the purpose of such a list, Falk states, "It is not an enumeration that is a wish list, but rather descriptive and explanatory of an *embedded consensus* with respect to political reform" (Falk 2003, 294; italics added).

The articulation of such an *embedded consensus* is necessary not only for the pure sake of political reform but also its flipside, which is an ethical framework because, according to Hans Kung in the long run, global capitalism will only be sustainable if it is socially acceptable. After all, in a democratic society the majority of the electorate has to be repeatedly convinced on at least three issues: (1) that the economic system is rewarding for themselves and for those whom they feel responsible in any way; (2) that economic participation, inclusiveness and social justice are integral parts of the objectives of this economic system; and (3) that a strong ethical framework supports both the operation and effects of the global markets and the extra market institutions and that this framework influences the behavior and the decisions of those who are directly involved in the process of production and distribution. (Kung 2003, 147–48)

These ethical and democratic concerns are even more important as an established global consensus, given the economic failures of global capitalism. This insight is vital because, as Kung admits, ". . . it is already evident that if any one of the three elements, whether it be economics, politics, or morality, does not work, it can cause serious difficulties for the capitalist system" (Kung 2003, 145).

Insofar as all of the concerns of normative democracy and, correspondingly, the elements of a strong ethical framework to support it are ultimately dedicated to the welfare of people, not only in individual societies but throughout the entire global society, it is vital to ensure that global capitalism is made accountable to the people of the entire earth. This inclusive vision is at the heart of Ikeda's own ethical stance and his conceptualization of a peaceful global civilization. In his 2010 peace proposal, Ikeda addresses this theme and notes, "Surveying the challenges that confront contemporary global society, I am convinced that nothing is more crucial than an essential reorientation of our way of life based on a commitment to the welfare of all of humankind and the entire planet, such as Makiguchi and Toda called for. Rather than stand to one side and ponder how the future might develop, we must focus on what each of us can do at this critical moment, *the role each of us can choose to play in changing the direction of history. We must strive to make a proactive, contributive way of life the prevailing spirit of the new era*" (Ikeda 2010-PP, 2; italics added). Ikeda's call is directed to every individual to participate "in changing the direction of history." This is a practical necessity so that humanity will be empowered collectively (and in solidarity) to embark upon a normative revolution, which centralizes the value of a "contributive way of life" which can become "the prevailing spirit of the new era."

In short, this is a call which strongly resonates with Falk's own emphasis on the need to take advantage of the complexities and uncertainties of the moment by advocating for the realization of a set of particular normative values that can effectively challenge the powerful political forces that are blocking these normative claims for a fundamentally different future. Because ". . . the future remains open to a wide spectrum of possibilities, including those directly associated with humane global governance" (Falk 2000a, 38). With this perspective, Falk argues that we can overcome "a sense of resignation or cynicism."[4] Falk's admonition is important for it helps to explicate what makes his conception of humane governance so radically unique. Falk has previously written, "Humane governance is not a structure to be blueprinted, but *a process of engagement* that is guided by an ethos of nonviolence. While ecumenical in spirit, humane governance is sensitive to and responsive to claims based on locale and difference. In this regard, a crucial early test of the clarity and integrity of adherents of humane governance is their attitude towards those who are vulnerable or in circumstances of acute distress" (Falk 1995, 171; italics added). And precisely because humane governance is best characterized as "a process of engagement" that is "guided by an ethos of nonviolence," it comports well with Ikeda's prescription about how best to advance "several concrete policy proposals focused on two main challenges. The first is nuclear weapons, which continue to threaten humankind as the ultimate embodiment of a cruel and blatant dismissal of the needs and welfare of others. The second is the structural distortions of global society where poverty and other threats continue to undermine the human dignity of vast numbers of people" (Ikeda 2010-PP, 3).

The common denominator in both of Ikeda's proposals is the requirement that we take into account the needs and welfare of all people throughout the entire global society, but especially those who suffer under the structural distortions of global society and the unremitting and unrelenting torture of poverty, which deprives the individual of their dignity. This brings us full circle and returns us back to a consideration of the nature and structural problem of unregulated global capitalism and its proclivity to lead to increased levels of global instability. Insofar as the violence of the global war system and a nuclear weapons culture serves to exacerbate the related problems of global poverty, Ikeda has pointed out that there is a strong nexus between the violence of a nuclear weapons culture and the violence of poverty—both disregard the sanctity of life and the dignity of the individual. Hence, a weapons culture correlates to a culture of poverty. Aside from the obvious fact that huge sums of wealth and capital are taken to feed a weapons culture, there is the corresponding reality that basic human needs, human welfare, and the cause of peace itself are all treated as expendable or part of "the-cost-of-doing-business" under this paradigm of global militarism and profit.[5]

Further, the multinational corporate drive for profit over people is protected and advanced by investments in the procurement of arms and weapons insofar as the wealthy and powerful global elite can intervene in other countries with the purpose of exploiting and stealing their natural resources and threaten others who would dare question the status quo and the hierarchical arrangement of privilege that it is dedicated to serve. Hence, after researching the dynamics of the global system with regard to armaments versus social development, Tamas Szentes, in his essay "The Economic Impact of Global Militarization," was compelled to write, "The competition for resources between development needs and the international arms race has long been recognized for many years. Both in literature and at international forums, *disarmament has been consistently and vigorously recommended as a means of releasing resources for economic and social development*" (Szentes 1984, 45; italics added).

In stark and unconditional terms, Szentes has condemned the global status quo because

> [m]ilitarization on a global scale limits the development of pro-
> ductive forces, just as it does in national economies, but in a more
> specific way. By affecting the weaker underdeveloped economies
> more adversely, militarization contributes to the internationally
> uneven character of development and to the marginalization of the
> productive forces of certain peoples and social strata. By the dam-
> age it inflicts on the global environment, public health, education,
> and the human culture and spirit, militarization contributes to the

increasing deterioration of conditions necessary for the reproduction of the human labor force. *Militarization makes the global allocation of the productive forces of humankind and their direction of development even less rational.* (Szentes 1984, 64; italics added)

More recently, this analysis has been expanded upon by Elizabeth Ashford, who also notes thus:

> The arms trade is another factor that significantly affects the capacity of non-democratic rulers to drain their country's resources and to hold onto power through internal repression, while bringing huge revenue to affluent countries. There is therefore a cogent case for the claim that a predictable result of the conjunction of all these kinds of factors is that the chronically poor are largely forcibly deprived of their fair share of the benefits of natural resources and of fair opportunities to make a living, while a grossly disproportionate share of those benefits is funneled to Third World elites, oppressive governments, and affluent countries and corporations. Another predictable result is that the chronically poor are deprived of their democratic rights that would enable them to effectively demand a subsistence income. Furthermore, while the affluent get most of the benefits of exploiting natural resources, the chronically poor who are largely excluded from those benefits often suffer the worst effects of the resulting pollution. (Ashford 2007, 194)

Without a global paradigm shift toward a normative orientation that is supportive of humane governance, humanitarian competition, and inclusionary governance (Paupp 2000), we find that there is an inevitable increase in global instability at every level of governance and human experience. This becomes even more evident in the interplay between the processes of militarization and globalization. Both processes are responsible for stifling human development and contributing to the problem of global poverty and inequality in every nation and continent around the globe. As Ikeda observed in his 2009 peace proposal, "The bottom billion—the poorest of the poor in fifty-eight countries who have long been left behind by global economic growth—were one focus of debate at the UN last year. The stark disparity in the value of human life and dignity, virtually predetermined by where one is born, is an unconscionable injustice in global society that must be corrected" (Ikeda 2009-PP, 17).

Ikeda's prescription that such "an unconscionable injustice in global society" is one that "must be corrected" should not be seen as a simplistic solution. For when we factor in all of the elements that have made poverty so rampant throughout the global South, it becomes clear that many things can be corrected by going directly to the sources of the problem. Examples abound in a long line of interrelated phenomena that includes the fact that the rich countries have been engaged in dominating an unjust global rule structure, which brings them the lion's share of trade and resource benefits while starving the poor. It is this struggle for the control of resources, which fuels the conflicts and ethnic strife that often erupt as a direct consequence of competition for limited resources and the demands and desires of Western consumers—such as the diamond trade in Africa or the unbridled scramble for oil riches in Sudan. Sudan is an oil-producing country; however, it has been said that the oil can be considered "conflict oil" because most of the proven reserves are in the South and control over this resource remains in the domain of the central government, which has been using the revenues to strengthen its power and authority in relation to all the other sections of the country (Ahmed 2008, 74). On a global scale, Zeleza has noted that "[s] ince the end of the Cold War and the onset of the twenty-first century new forms of imperialism, often cloaked in the giddy rhetoric of globalization, are engendering new contexts and excuses for imperialist adventures that are stoking local and regional conflicts across the world" (Zeleza 2008, 23).

So how do these trends worsen the global problem of poverty? The answer is that these trends toward greater conflict worsen global poverty insofar as ".conflict is a cause of food insecurity and exacerbates poverty in Africa because it destroys or damages the human and physical capital that undermines production, leads to economic disruption and distortion of state expenditures, and encourages capital flight and diversion . . . In some cases the destruction of physical capital and the resultant food shortages or even famines are not merely unfortunate byproducts of war, but are deliberately deployed as instruments of war. Food aid provided in times of conflict often contributes to conflict when it is used as a weapon by the warring factions, and threatens local production in the long term, thereby contributing to the perpetuation of poverty" (Zaleza 2008, 23–24). Given these examples, it is clear that Ikeda's call to confront poverty as "an unconscionable injustice in global society" and demand that it "must be corrected" is far from a simplistic statement—it is a profound indictment of our current global system, which allows for the interplay between war, capitalism, and poverty.

The focus on the "unconscionable injustice" of poverty in the current structure of global society serves to underscore Ikeda's dedication to mandate action on the problem before we even dare to speak of achieving a peaceful global civilization. For, in the final analysis, a peaceful global civilization is going to be ultimately predicated upon removing the problem of poverty as a source of conflict. Indeed, critical studies have concluded that

> The world's weakest states are typically poor states that lack the capacity to fulfill essential governmental functions, chiefly (1) to secure their population from violent conflict, (2) to completely meet the basic human needs of their population (that is, food, health, education),

(3) to govern legitimately and effectively with the acceptance of a majority of their population, and (4) to foster sustainable and equitable economic growth. (Rice 2007, 33–34)

Further, to realize this dynamic is also to realize that poverty and state weakness is a two-way street. This dynamic is best summed up by the realization that "[p]overty fundamentally erodes state capacity—by fueling conflict, sapping human capital, by hollowing out or impeding the development of effective state institutions and markets, and by creating especially conducive environments for corrupt governance. Though poverty underlies state weakness, weakness is also a consequence of other capacity deficits: a lack of political legitimacy, a lack of competence in economic governance and in the adequate provision of essential services to the population, and a lack of security as evidenced by conflict and instability. Each of these capacity gaps can, in turn, exacerbate poverty" (Rice 2007, 34).

Therefore, to deal with the challenge of reducing and eliminating poverty from the global village also means that it will be necessary to undertake a transformation of the apparatus of the state itself. This requirement will, in turn, mean giving substantive credence and credibility to genuine democratic transformations that lead state and institutional and market practices away from tendencies that reinforce *exclusionary governance* toward those state and institutional and market practices that promote the practice of *inclusionary governance* (Paupp 2000). Under the rubric of current practices throughout global society, there exists an international system of transnational capitalist system that is responsible for the creation of nothing less than a vicious cycle of violence that obfuscates, blocks, and acts to move against all efforts to transform the current world system into a peaceful global civilization. The reason for this is found in the realization that "[p]overty and state weakness often interact in a vicious, destructive cycle, further entrenching poverty and in turn compromising the capacity of states to provide for their citizens and uphold their responsibilities to the international community" (Rice 2010, 23).

In other words, the international community suffers when state weakness and conditions of unmitigated poverty feed off each other in a vicious and unending cycle. However, the real problem goes even deeper than that because the real problem resides in the rules which structure the world economy itself and those rules are written for and by the earth's most wealthy societies, which in their rule-making practices and procedures actually discriminate against the global poor (Pogge 2002, 116–17).

What Susan Rice's analysis fails to do is to take the analysis of poverty and state weakness to the next level—that is, to the international level where the "rules of the game" are "fixed" and largely determined by a small set of wealthy and elite power brokers. Their often undemocratic and unaccountable decisions create conditions for a continuation of past practices in an uncritical acceptance of rules which have outlived their usefulness and have always been at odds with the global human interest. In other words, as Thomas Pogge reminds us, "[T]he rules structuring the world economy have a profound impact on the global economic distribution just as the economic order of a national society has a profound impact on its domestic economic distribution" (Pogge 2002, 116). Therefore, we have to come to acknowledge the most fundamental fact of our current global crisis, which is that "if national and global economic regimes are comparable in their workings and impact, then we are after all employing a double standard when we count avoidable extremes of poverty and inequality against national economic regimes only" (Pogge 2002, 117). We must, in sort, begin to critique the entire global order and the way in which it is unfairly structured. This is absolutely essential because "[b]y continuing to support the current global order and the national policies that shape and sustain it without taking compensating action toward institutional reform or shielding its victims, we share a negative responsibility for the undue harms they forseeably produce" (Pogge 2002, 144).

This is patently true throughout the continent of Latin America where servicing the debt, in order to comply with World Bank and IMF criteria, simply serves to exacerbate poverty, financial crisis, and higher levels of social instability. In this regard, "If servicing the debt and assuring an attractive environment for global finance markets has had deleterious effects on the living conditions of popular classes and placed Latin America in ever increasing hock to transnational finance capital, it also cemented the power of the emergent transnational bloc in the region. But once debt-repayment pressures reach the point at which default becomes a possibility or a government can no longer contain pressure for it to meet even minimal social obligations, the spiral of crisis begins. Local states are caught between the withdrawal of transnational investors and mounting unrest from poor majorities who can no longer bear any further austerity" (Robinson 2008, 269).

Like Pogge, Ikeda is a strong advocate for dealing effectively with foreseeable harm by working toward developing ". . . international safety nets to safeguard the lives and dignity of people and to make human security a robust reality" (Ikeda 2010-PP, 13). Still, the fact remains that in light of a global history of inequality, which reaches back to the colonial era, there is a concomitant requirement to remake and to revolutionize the entire international order so that it reflects the interests of the entire human race and not just privileged elements of it. Such a global revolution in institutions, structures, and policies is necessary insofar as the affluent countries ". . . have been using their power to shape the rules of the world economy according to their own interests and thereby have deprived the poorest populations of a fair share of global economic growth . . ." (Pogge 2002, 201).

Given the intractable nature of these long-term realities, it is time to bring back into the "growth equation" a moral assessment of our collective guilt and responsibility for the continuation of these conditions and the structural inequalities that allow for such grave injustices to exist without adequate remedies to remove them. Ultimately, what this means is that once we finally acknowledge our complicity in an unjust system, it then becomes possible to call for a dismantling of a global institutional order "... that regularly produces severe poverty and/or by effectively excluding them from a fair share of the value of exploited natural resources and/or by upholding a radical inequality that evolved through a historical process pervaded by horrendous crimes" (Pogge 2002, 211).

Hence, given the nature of this history, the only legitimate conclusion that can be reached on these facts is that "[t]he continuing imposition of this global order, essentially unmodified, constitutes a massive violation of the human right to basic necessities—a violation for which the governments and electorates of the most powerful countries bear primary responsibility" (Pogge 2007a,b, 53). The implications that flow from this assessment are enormous insofar as they bear on the question of whether or not the twenty-first century will move in the direction of becoming an era which protects and extends protections to human dignity or, in the alternative, records of the destruction of human dignity, human rights, and human security.

From the viewpoint of Ikeda, writing in his 2009 peace proposal, we come to realize that

> [i]f we are to lay any claim to human dignity—to manifest the feel-ings of compassion that Jean-Jacques Rousseau (1712–78) assures us were at the heart of even the earliest human communities—we must take steps to remedy this situation. Nobel laureate in eco-nomics Amartya Sen has astutely pointed out that "[P]overty must be seen as the deprivation of basic capabilities rather than merely as lowness of incomes." For people in the bottom billion, what is urgently needed is the kind of support from the international community that will empower them to take steps out of difficult and often degrading circumstances. Japan was able to make a rapid and remarkable recovery from the devastation of defeat in World War II. It is my earnest hope that Japan will put this experience to good use, demonstrating active leadership in the effort to es-tablish, as a global common good for the twenty-first century, the right of all people to live in peace and humane conditions. (Ikeda 2009-PP, 17–18)

In short, Ikeda recommends that we begin to think of moving out of our current global system insofar as it is a nonsynergic system. Therefore, we must move instead toward developing a global culture and civilization that adopts a synergistic system which is truly conducive to sustaining a peaceful global civilization. On this precise point, Ashis Nandy reminds us that

Gandhi acted as if he was aware that non-synergic systems, driven by zero-sum competition and search for power, control, and masculinity, force the victims of oppression to internalize the norms of the systems, so that when they displace their exploiters, they build a system in which the older norms covertly prevail. So, his concept of non-cooperation set a different goal for the victims; he stressed that the aim of the oppressed should be, not to become a first-class citizen in the world of oppression instead of a second- or third-class one, but to become the citizen of an alternative world where he can hope to win back his human authenticity. (Nandy 1984, 159)

As humanity now moves toward a global effort to build the kind of peaceful global civilization that Ikeda envisions, it is important to remember the cautionary words of Nandy. It is vital to avoid "build[ing] a system in which the older norms covertly prevail." Rather, as Nandy suggests, each of us needs to transcend the past and "become the citizen of an alternative world" where all human beings can hope to win back their authenticity. Speaking on this subject in a speech delivered at Ankara University, Turkey, June 24, 1992, Ikeda stated thus:

> The concerns of people in the contemporary world increasingly are transnational and global, and they demand moderation and restraint. *We can no longer afford to let dogmatic or parochial views inform our actions; we must develop the ability to see ourselves objectively with respect to the rest of the world.* Only those with far-sighted open-mindedness can aspire to globalism. *The ability to strike a balance between one's own interests and those of other nations—or, at a deeper level, between the individual and the universal—is the mark of a world citizen.* In the long run, these are the qualities that must become the spiritual foundation for the rules and structures of a just international order. (Ikeda 2009a,b, 134–35; italics added)

Insofar as we are predominantly concerned with the task of how to go about building a more peaceful global civilization, it is important to stop here in order to underscore the critical nexus that exists between (1) the individual, on the one hand, and (2) the larger national and global community, on the other. In his book, *The Community of Rights*, Alan Gewirth, a professor of philosophy, extended his fundamental principle of equal and universal human rights, the *Principle of Generic Consistency*, into the arena of social and political philosophy, exploring its implications for both social and economic rights. He argues that the ethical requirements logically imposed on individual action hold equally for communal institutions and, in particular, for the supportive state, whose chief function should be to maintain and promote the universal human rights to freedom and well-being. Such contemporary afflictions as poverty, unemployment, and homelessness constitute basic violations of these rights, which the supportive state is obliged to overcome. Succinctly put, he states that the two chief aims of his book are (1) to show that rights and community, far from being antithetical to one another, have a relation of mutual support, and (2) to show how this relation can serve to fulfill the economic and other rights of the most deprived members of society and thereby lead to greater economic and political equality. Therefore, taken together these two arguments are ultimately "... concerned with the moral justification of economic and social policies and institutions, especially as they help to relieve human suffering. Such policies and institutions, when they are embodied in the state or political society, constitute what I call *the community of rights*" (Gewirth 1996, 1; italics added).

In similar fashion, Ikeda is also concerned with the nexus that exists between rights afforded an individual and how they find expression on both the national and global level. According to Ikeda, we find that "in Japanese there is a word *kosei*, which may be translated as 'the spirit of fairness.' It also means equality and impartiality as well as justice. A person with the spirit of fairness recognizes the inherent contradiction in economic activity that makes the rich richer and the poor poorer, both on the individual and national levels" (Ikeda 2001a, 76–77; italics in original). The fundamentally radical and transformative nature of Ikeda's viewpoint on this matter stands in sharp contrast to the policies of the World Bank and its fundamental adherence to Cold War liberalism and the maintenance of a nation-state system under the direct control of US hegemony.[6] Ikeda states, "The spirit of fairness or justice is not an a priori condition. Through tough challenges, the spirit of fairness is transformed from the ethos of a people into a universal principle endowed with the strength of steel, the warmth of the sun, and the vastness of the sky. *A true sense of fairness must be derived from a universal spirit manifested on this higher plane.* In the world of business, such a universal spirit would not be preoccupied with the good of one's own venture or nation. It would always consider the greater, holistic interest of the entire planet and of all humankind and thereby inspire one to make impartial judgments, even if at times it meant self-sacrifice" (Ikeda 2001a, 77; italics added).

As Ikeda notes, because a *"true sense of fairness must be derived from a universal spirit manifested on this higher plane,"* it follows that the current nature and policies of both governments and international institutions must change or be swept away with the debris of history. The current global crisis is of truly planetary proportions given the widespread discontent that current structures, practices, and dominant forces have engendered to deprive the majority of humankind their rights and dignity in the name of "making a financial profit" irrespective of the human cost. Hence, as Thomas Franck has astutely observed, "Governments with vision must confront the unpleasant realization that essential international institutions are facing imminent breakdown caused by widespread dissatisfaction with both what they do and

237

how they do it. The increasingly heard charges of illegitimacy, injustice, and unfairness must be addressed. The discontent can be addressed in various ways, but none will suffice unless the process itself is rethought and opened up" (Franck 1995, 483).

Meeting this challenge will entail nothing less than a reframing of world order. All elements of this challenge will require a radical reframing and reordering of the status quo. As such, the nature and scope of this global transformation will necessitate the articulation of fundamentally different legal, moral, political, economic, cultural, and philosophical discourses that will be capable of sustaining a truly universal principle of human coopera-tion, mutual respect, and human rights that is authoritatively supportive of this concept of human solidarity and is committed to the maintenance of a genuinely peaceful global civilization. Maintaining such a global civilization will also require a distinctive and authoritative legal framework that supplies a rubric underneath which convergent perspectives can find a common voice around shared values that are ultimately dedicated to ensuring the primacy of those values.

In this common endeavor, what is required is nothing less than a shared global consciousness, which centralizes the importance of peace, inclusion, and humane behaviors. The universal nature and scope of this consciousness will have to be dedicated to the institutionalization of actions, behaviors, and structures that create the historical space for the success of this undertaking. By engaging in this process, it can be posited that humanity will finally be allowed to discover that "[i]n effect, the international legal order is a socio-historical product of convergent perspectives of formal authority and actual behavior" (Falk 1985, 117). Richard Falk has argued that this undertaking involves a "transition problem," which means that we have to appreciate the fact that what we are contemplating is "... the problem of system-change on the macro level of international society" and this means dealing with what "... is entailed in moving from an existing system to a preferred system" (Falk 1985, 118). To do this, we will have to ".postulate five highly abstract preferences so as to make an explanation of priorities necessary in each setting of decision:

1. The minimization of violence;
2. The promotion of human rights of individuals and groups, especially national autonomy and racial equality;
3. The transfer of wealth and income from rich states to poor states;
4. The equitable participation of diverse cultures, regions, and ideologies in a composite system of global order;
5. The growth of supranational and international institutions" (Falk 1985, 118).

Following from this philosophical perspective and normative approach, Richard Falk has also proposed a specific legal strategy for how to

238

construct a more peaceful global civilization. In Falk's view, "It would seem quite appropriate to frame a future world order by two different, although complementary, legal directives," which involves *both* (1) the right to a standard of living that can meet basic human needs *and* (2) a new globalist ethos of human solidarity (Falk 2008c, 28). In more precise detail, Falk first highlights the centrality of *"(1) the affirmations in Articles 25 and 28 of the Universal Declaration of Human Rights that everyone enjoys 'the right to a standard of living' adequate to meet basic human needs and that 'everyone is entitled to a social and international order' that realizes all of the specific enumerated human rights in the document"* (Falk 2008c, 25; italics added).

In emphasizing the content of Articles 25 and 28, Falk suggests an approach, which is very close to what both Gewirth and Ikeda recommend (as referenced above). In fact, what becomes manifestly clear is that Gewirth, Ikeda, and Falk all share a common belief in the proposition that the individuals (who make up civil society) are legally and ethically empowered to make moral, political, and economic claims upon their respective national communities as well as the international community as a whole. They possess a moral mandate as responsible global citizens which enables them to act in true human solidarity, irrespective of the claims of the powerful interests that currently dominant global society and have contributed so much to the current global crisis.

These claims and demands from global civil society—which arise out of the commonly held vision of a truly peaceful global civilization—reflect an aspirational movement toward the final achievement of truly universal global justice, universal humane global governance, and more inclusive forms of national and global governance. As such, these claims have the practical capacity to lead humanity toward the ending of poverty, the end of war as a legitimate means of statecraft, and toward the embrace of an uncontested respect for human rights. In so doing, this historical movement of peoples and their rights-claims constitutes the basis of the second prong of Falk's legal directive for a future world order. Its purpose is *"(2) to articulate and act upon a new globalist ethos of human solidarity that informs a concept of responsible global citizenship, mindful of specific overlapping, national and regional identities, but dedicated to the whole rather than to its parts, whereby 'global law' come to anchor world order rather than Westphalian international law"* (Falk 2008c, 25; italics added).

Hence, the nation-state system and its attendant proclivities to reinforce a world of hierarchical privilege, dominance, and hegemony can finally be swept aside by virtue of this new global ethos. The adoption of such a global ethos can also clear the way for the realization of Ikeda's vision of a more peaceful global civilization. In large measure, a move in this direction is made possible by virtue of the fact that Ikeda's vision for a more peaceful global civilization has the strength to discard those values which have been supportive of exploitative institutions, structures, and policies. The power of Ikeda's vision is such that it both negates the worst and most exploitative practices of the past while, at the same time, affirms alternative values, which are supportive of a distinctively new and more humane future. In this way, the mantra of the past can be progressively replaced by an alternative vision of a future global order, which is inherently more conducive to the practice, embodiment, and institutionalization of those transformative elements and shared values that Ikeda, Falk, and Gewirth have articulated. From this perspective, as Ikeda has expressed it, "As globalization proceeds, conflicts and abuses turn people's minds inward, resulting in significant divisions and social friction. For this reason, *we have an unprecedented need for mutual understanding, founded on amity and solidarity, and the willingness to transcend ideologies to cope with the global problem*" (Ikeda and Yalman 2009, 128; italics added).

According to Joseph Stiglitz, over the past three decades the phenomenon of globalization has led to serious economic crises in close to one hundred countries while, at the same time, the suffering of the global poor has dramatically risen and become more acute because

> globalization has been accompanied by increased instability: close to a hundred countries have had crises in the past three decades. Globalization created economic volatility, and *those at the bottom of the income distribution in poor countries often suffer the most*. They have no reserves to shield them from economic shocks, and the social safety nets in most developing countries are anemic. With inadequate safety nets, the suffering in these crises of those who lost their jobs is enormous. (Stiglitz 2005, 240; italics added)

The importance and uniqueness of the observations offered by Stiglitz are found in the fact that he has combined three different evaluative frameworks in assessing the global crises that have been unleashed by globalization (resource-based, income-based, and the capability-approach). Usually, the most dominant and familiar account and/or evaluative framework for assessing globalization is that of a resource or income-based evaluation. However, such an approach that focuses purely on income-based indicators of poverty and inequality proves to be unable to capture other key dimensions, which play into the creation of poverty and inequality. Therefore, a more comprehensive evaluative framework needs to be invoked to offer a fuller explanation of the globalization dynamic. That evaluative framework or account is known as a capability account or capability approach because it gives particular attention to democratic capabilities rather than being predominantly preoccupied with resource-based or income-based evaluations. In this regard, Ingrid Robeyns asserts, "If we endorse the conceptual arguments of the capability approach to well-being assessment, we would need to look at a wider range of issues, among them those that include people's agency" (Robeyns 2005, 44). By taking such an approach, we find that "[p]eople's agency to take their lives into their own hands and to make collective decisions about how to organize their communities and manage their commons can be as important for them as to secure minimal material or financial welfare. While the quantifiable functionings and capabilities may well be limited in capturing these dimensions, the overall framework of the capabilities approach gives a clear rationale for why we should pay due attention to nonmaterial dimensions, such as family time together, emotional well-being, and democratic agency" (Robeyns 2005, 45).

In extrapolating upon the significance of the varied concerns that are addressed in the "capabilities approach," we find that Ikeda is more than sympathetic to this approach in light of its capacity to address the comprehensive and multidimensional nature of the globalization challenge and all of the attendant considerations which range from spiritual health to the role of democracy and human agency. Because of Ikeda's Buddhist-oriented focus on the necessity for both individual and collective transformation, we discover that Ikeda's prescription for building a global culture of peace is predicated upon the interplay of agency, democratic capabilities, and a consensus on shared values, which are supportive of humane and inclusive forms of global governance. Ikeda states, "The human spirit is endowed with the ability to transform even the most difficult circumstances, creating value and ever richer meaning. When each person brings this limitless spiritual capacity to full flower, and when ordinary citizens unite in a commitment to positive change, a culture of peace—a century of life—will come into being" (Ikeda 2001a, 212).

The various critiques of Stiglitz, Robeyns, and Ikeda all converge to demonstrate the necessity to combine normative considerations with empirical assessments. A similar conclusion was reached earlier in this chapter in the context of our review of international relations scholarship and approaches. Both normative and empirical considerations need to be constructively combined to inform one another, thereby leading us to a more truthful and comprehensive understanding of the challenges that lie before us in a host of issue areas. Take, for example, the challenge of understanding how China was able to economically progress in a world subject to the pressures of globalization, yet did not succumb to the economic collapses that characterized Russia, Latin America, and other parts of Asia in the decade of the 1990s. In large measure, China avoided the pitfalls of these other nations and regions because it rejected the West's neoliberal economic model and managed globalization on its own terms. On this point, Stiglitz notes, "The success of China and other countries which managed globalization on their own terms is even more impressive, because it took place in the context of globalization where the rules of the game have, for the most part, been set by the advanced industrial countries in their own interests, or more precisely, in the interests of special interests within these countries. It is the inequities in global trade agreements, the lack of balance with which the global agenda has been pursued and the economic policies that have often accompanied globalization that are the problem, not globalization itself" (Stiglitz 2005, 256).

Once again, we find in Stiglitz's critique an empirical and normative realization that resonates with Ikeda, Falk, Gewirth, Robeyns, and many members of the school of International Relations—the realization that the presence of *both* human agency *and* democratic accountability through strengthened democratic institutions are required for achieving a broad-based and universal human development agenda that will be capable of effectively leading to a genuine respect for human rights, human dignity, and human autonomy from the negative impacts of those international institutions that engage in the promotion of dehumanizing policies, exclusionary institutions, and structures, which reinforce inequality and poverty both within and between nations. Clear and convincing evidence of these allegations can be found by examining the economic policies of the WTO. In so doing, we come to the harsh realization that "[t]he WTO's failure to eliminate developed-world protectionism against underdeveloped countries is a clear case of injustice. Multilateral reduction of protectionist policies that do not allow provision for less-developed countries to protect vulnerable producers and infant industries are also unjust if the harms that result are not compensated. At the level of policy, the failure of the WTO to subsidize the participation of underdeveloped countries casts serious doubts on its procedural fairness; and if the WTO does not allow for policies to protect the environment, workers, and public health, its practices will be further at fault" (Moellendorf 2005, 154).

In this national and international environment, it becomes clear that Multinational Corporations (MNCs) have been set free in a virtually unregulated business world of power-grabbing and influence peddling to set a developmental course whereby "[t]he essence of the MNC effort is to concentrate power beyond national control and to assure itself a stable set of market situations within which to operate. Its short-run effects are to—(1) transfer technology and knowledge to poor sectors; (2) standardize global consumptive patterns and preferences; (3) provide some employment and training opportunities in the Third World; (4) encourage counterinsurgency postures and counterrevolutionary outlooks throughout the Third World; (5) create a post-statist kind of global ideology" (Falk 1975, 395). Ever since the decade of the 1970s, this MNC-sanctioned global ideology has led to an historical process of economic evolution in which

> [t]he poor countries were regarded merely as late comers to the development process; the sooner they started on that process,

the sooner the removal of their terrible curse of poverty. The rich countries could speed up the process somewhat by a combination of charity (foreign aid, international assistance) and self-interest (foreign investment) . . . [But] this development utopia, even on its own terms, has always lacked substance: the GNP increases are siphoned off to benefit the higher strata of poor societies; the underdevelopment of Third World countries plays a functional role within the world economic structure; *the charity of the rich, when carefully considered, represents a further extension of hegemony and exploitation rather than a contribution to self-reliance and genuine development.* (Falk 1975, 397; italics added)

More recently, I have expanded upon this analysis by looking at the true nature of the US Empire and its efforts to extend the reach of American hegemony throughout the world (Paupp 2009). As a direct consequence of this effort by the American primacy coalition and its elite, there has been a growing complicity among rich nations to deepen global poverty for the sake of profit for profit's sake. The effect of this policy throughout the global South (formerly referred to as the "Third World") has been to worsen the problems associated with "exclusionary governance"—the dimensions of which are "(1) weak states; (2) fragmented civil society; (3) shifting political coalitions; (4) short-terms policies; (5) elite-led pacts; (6) 'rule by law' in place of 'rule of law'" (Paupp 2000, 404). Hence, the so-called failed state syndrome is actually a structural consequence of a skewed global order that has structurally reinforced social injustice, economic exploitation, and done so through either indirect coercion or direct military subjugation and occupation, as in the cases of Iraq and Afghanistan (Davies 2007, 49–54; Herman 2007, 41–44). By continuing to follow a foreign policy course predicated on the maintenance of US hegemony at any cost, Noam Chomsky has astutely noted thus:

> The world has not renounced war. Quite the contrary. By now, the world's hegemonic power accords itself the right to wage war at will, under a doctrine of 'anticipatory self-defense' with unstated bounds. International law, treaties, and rules of world order are sternly imposed on others with much self-righteous posturing, but dismissed as irrelevant for the United States—a long-standing practice, driven to new depths by the Reagan and Bush II administrations. (Chomsky 2006, 3)

The nature of the current global crisis, while multifaceted and complex is still interconnected in many ways to the use and misuse of power by the US Empire and its desire to continue to dominate the world through its hegemonic power. Despite its predominant power in terms of military capacities, the fact remains that ". . . because of the current construction of global politics, the

243

specific identity of the United States, and new understandings of the means of creation of customary international law, the US hegemon is precluded from effective dominance even in areas central to its perceived interests, and despite its overwhelming material power" (Toope 2003, 291). In this respect, the good news is that as humanity continues to develop its international legal system in a more just and equitable direction for the majority of people on the planet, the reality is that "[c]ustomary international law, like all law, is relatively autonomous from material power" (Toope 2003, 315). Therefore, the conclusion that can be reached is that

> [t]o shape customary law, the United States cannot rely on its raw material power to exert brute force because such practice will simply fail to partake of a legitimate process of law creation. Increasingly, the United States must *persuade* other States of the need for normative consolidation or change. Legal power lies in the capacity to persuade. If the United States withdraws into that part of its identity preoccupied with the sovereign self, it will likely become less persuasive in the evolution and application of customary international law, despite its preponderant material power. (Toope 2003, 316; italics in original)

If we were to juxtapose this legal analysis against the moral/normative standard followed by Ikeda, we would discover that—from Ikeda's perspective—the way out of the current global crisis is to reject all that divides people ("evil") and instead embrace the aspiration toward unity ("goodness"). What such a normative shift would mean empirically and practically in the lives of people would be radical and revolutionary—the very basis of what is required to move beyond global crisis. This is because—in Ikeda's words— *"I believe that the essence of goodness is the aspiration toward unity, while evil directs toward division and sundering.* The function of evil is ever to create divisions; to cause fissures in the human heart; to sever the bonds among family members, colleagues, friends, and acquaintances; to engender enmity between countries as well as ethnic groups; and to destroy the human sense of unity with nature and the universe. Where divisiveness reigns, human beings become isolated and victims of unhappiness and misery" (Ikeda 2001a, 87; italics added). This is the choice that the United States faces with respect to its relationships with the rest of world. Will it move in the direction of more war in order to attempt to hold onto its collapsing hegemony, its ebbing economy, and the remnants of what was once a global consensus? Or, in the alternative, will it see the value of Ikeda's prescription for global peace in the service of a global civilization? In large measure, the answer to these questions rests on the combination of individual transformation, the power of dialogue, and social action dedicated to the realization and creation of democratic institutions of global governance that can resolve issues of global inequality and international conflict peaceably.[7]

Even more fundamentally, Ikeda's emphasis upon "the aspiration toward unity," when juxtaposed against "division and sundering" as the source of "unhappiness and misery," supplies us with a strong normative critique from which we can posit an empirical solution to the current global crisis and move beyond it. This can largely be accomplished by recognizing that the "aspiration toward unity" is—in the most practical of terms—a call for a global civilization based on real equality. The achievement of such a goal can be realized through a multilateral system that is based on equality. To move in this direction means that we must, at the same time, negate the practice and maintenance of hegemony as a viable option. That is because hegemony is antithetical to equality insofar as hegemony is predicated on hierarchy—a society of unequal nations subject to the vicissitudes of the hegemon's preferences which, most often, result in all kind of inequalities, disparities, and injustices. Further, while a multilateral system predicated on the value of equality is most likely to produce higher levels of genuine consensus on issues of common concern, it also follows that there will be a greater perception of justice and a greater realization of justice by virtue of the fact we have an equal treatment of equals by equals. Hence, Nico Krisch has a valid point to make when he notes, "[I]f order does not require hegemonic power, neither does justice: the mere fact that some goals that appear desirable under a substantive conception of justice might be achieved faster and more easily within a hegemonic order does not justify the existence of such an order instead of a multilateral system based on equality" (Krisch 2003, 174).

Out of this analysis, we can, once more, acknowledge that the true value of current international relations (IR) scholarship is to expose the fact that every empirical theory has, at its center, a normative core. Hence, in advocating that Ikeda is correct in positing the central importance of "the aspiration toward unity" as a call to acknowledge the equality, dignity, and rights of all nations and peoples, constitutes an empirical basis from which we may begin to restructure the entire international order. In so doing, we can arguably achieve a more peaceful global civilization in a way that cannot be dismissed as being "utopian" but is, rather, the rational choice of rational people. In making this choice, we have clearly chosen to supplant purely Western values and Western answers with responses and solutions that are emerging from a global twenty-first century consciousness. In so doing, the irony is that we are also calling on Western States to honor their proclaimed fidelity to equality by endorsing an international order and a global civilization that honors the ideal of equality in practice. Therefore, we may conclude that "[h]istory should remind Western States that for centuries their ideas of what was good for the rest of the world turned out to be mistaken. Moreover, respect for the equality of others has long been one of the central tenets of their own, liberal conceptions of society, and this respect should find at least some reflection in the international sphere as well. Seen in this light, reaffirming equality is both prudent and necessary" (Kirsch 2003, 175).

To reaffirm the centrality of equality in the global context is even more vital in light of what the unrestrained policies and practices of globalization have created. In the view of David Held, we are in the midst of a global crisis because "Globalization has not just integrated peoples and nations, but created new forms of antagonism and conflict. The globalization of communications does not just make it easier to establish mutual understandings, but often highlights what it is that people do not have in common and how and why differences matter" (Held 2003, 182). Ikeda himself has addressed this problem when he noted: "There is no doubt that nationalism, ethnic identity and other much used and abused slogans today have been perfect objects of this easy credulity and fanaticism. This is because concepts like 'race' and 'ethnicity' are in large part fictitious and ethnic identifications have typically been artificially constructed by one means or another. This may sound rather extreme, but I believe the circumstances warrant candid words; in a world where ethnic and national identities have become the source of brutal violence, a definitive revision of our understanding of the concepts is critical" (Ikeda 2001a, 88).

For David Held, undertaking this challenge means a number of things. This would include the necessity to recognize the new reality of our times—which is that we all share multiple citizenships because we simultaneously inhabit many different communities. In other words, we are no longer trapped in one locality, one community, with only one frozen identity that remains unalterable until our last day. Rather, what Held's vision of the *cosmopolitan project* reveals is that at every level of global existence we need to (a) be democratically regulated and (b) have access to membership in diverse political communities. With these two elements in place, Held contends that we come to recognize that we share a common fate under the rubric of a common global civilization. In his own words, Held clearly notes, "[T]he cosmopolitan project contends that, if many contemporary forms of power are to become accountable and if many of the complex issues that affect us all—locally, nationally, regionally and globally—are to be democratically regulated, people will have to have access to, and membership in, *diverse* political communities. Put differently, a democratic political community for the new millennium necessarily describes a world where citizens enjoy multiple citizenships. Faced with overlapping communities of fate they need to be not only citizens of their own communities, but also of the wider regions in which they live, and the wider global order" (Held et al. 1999, 449; italics in original).

As articulated here, Held's approach seems to constitute the kind of definitive revision of our understanding of concepts that Ikeda has called for. To the extent that Held is able to theoretically, normatively, and empirically integrate the idea of membership in diverse political communities, it would seem that he has provided a critical agenda for taking for first steps toward the realization of a peaceful global civilization. Held's vision of the "cosmopolitan project" perfectly conjoins with the essential elements of Ikeda's vision for a peaceful globalization, Falk's conceptualization of the basic features of "human governance," and my articulation of the central features of "inclusionary governance." Held has enumerated no less than eight essential features for the "cosmopolitan model of democracy." The central features of the cosmopolitan project include propositions listed in Table 6.1 at the end of this chapter.

The greatest value of the cosmopolitan project is that it is able to conceptually transcend the present world order, which is primarily a product of US global hegemony. This is important because it is doubtful ". . . without a profound change in US policy or a fundamental challenge to US hegemony, international governance will ever be in a position to tame globalization or to advance global social justice" (Held and McGrew 2007, 143). Yet, as I have demonstrated, an international counter-hegemonic alliance to US hegemony has been maturing over the period of 2001 to the present (Paupp 2007, 2009). Given the dynamics involved in this new historical opening, Held is more than justified in arguing that "[t]he cosmopolitan principles set out above can be thought of as the guiding ethical basis of global social democracy" (Held 2004, 178). Due to the fact that "[e]conomic processes have become progressively internationalized in a number of key spheres: communications, production, trade, finance and in many matters of coordination," we are discovering that these phenomena have created the suspicion that the very idea of a national economy has been superseded and, as such, that these trends have been "eroding the capacity of the state to control its own economic future. *At the very least, there appears to be a diminution of state autonomy and a disjuncture between the premises of the theory of the sovereign state and the conditions of modern economies*" (Held 1989, 229–30; italics added).

As the traditional state disintegrates in terms of its reach and power in controlling and directing the economic realm, there is a corresponding need to develop more inclusive policies, practices, and goals for national and international governance that will protect the democratic rights, decision-making capacity, and the legitimate distributional justice concerns of the world's citizens. In all of these arenas, however, the most contested element or issue is that of citizen and group participation. While this is not a new challenge, it has certainly grown more complex. Therefore, the need to develop specific policies, practices, and goals in order to advance *inclusionary governance* has become even more critical. To that end, I have developed an approach to governance, which contemplates reregulating the market for more just outcomes, changing political structures and practices by mandating greater inclusion of all major groups and parties in decision-making processes and policymaking practices, and by proposing strategies to remove the root causes of categorical inequality (Paupp 2000, 386–87). To address these

Table 6.1   The Cosmopolitan Model of Democracy

1. The global order consists of multiple and overlapping networks of power involving the body, welfare, culture, civic associations, the economy, coercive relations and organized violence, and regulatory and legal relations. The case for cosmopolitan democracy arises from these diverse networks—the different power systems which constitute the interconnectedness of different peoples and nations.

2. All groups and associations are assumed to have a capacity for self-determination which can be specified by a commitment to the principle of autonomy and specific clusters of rights and obligations. These clusters cut across each network of power and are subsumed under the following categories: health, social, cultural, civic, economic, pacific, and political. Together, they form the basis of an empowering legal order—a cosmopolitan democratic law.

3. Legal principles are adopted which delimit the form and scope of individual and collective action within the organizations and associations of the state, economy, and civil society. Certain standards are specified for the treatment of all, which no political regime or association can legitimately violate.

4. Lawmaking and law enforcement can be developed within this framework at a variety of levels along with an expansion of the influence of regional and international courts to monitor and check political and social authority.

5. The defense of self-determination, the creation of a common structure of political action and the preservation of the democratic good are the overall collective priorities; the commitment to democratic autonomy creates both an agenda of long-term change and a program of urgent priorities, focused on transforming the conditions of those whose circumstances fall radically short of equal membership in the public realm.

6. Determinate principles of social justice follow: the *modus operandi* of the production, distribution, and the exploitation of resources must be conducive to, and compatible with, the democratic process and a common structure of political action.

7. The principle of noncoercive relations governs the settlement of disputes, though the use of force must remain a collective option of last resort in the face of clear attacks to eradicate cosmopolitan democratic law. Cosmopolitan democracy might justify the deployment of force, after all other forms of negotiation and sanction have been exhausted in the context of a threat to international democracy and a denial of democratic rights and obligations by tyrannical regimes or by circumstances which spiral beyond the control of particular peoples and agents (such as the disintegration of a state).

8. People can enjoy membership in the diverse communities which significantly affect them and accordingly access to a variety of forms of political participations. Citizenship would be extended, in principle, to membership in all cross-cutting political communities, from the local to the global.

Source: David Held, *Democracy and the Global Order: From the Modern State to Cosmopolitan Governance.* Stanford: Stanford University Press, 1995, pp. 271–72.

aforementioned challenges to governance at both the national and international levels, the policies, practices, and goals listed in Table 6.2 are useful.

Conclusion: The Promise of Realizing the Converging Theoretical and Empirical Elements of a Peaceful Global Civilization

The evolution of global human history in the twenty-first century has been moving in the direction of the realization of a more cooperative and generous global civilization. In fact, evolving regional experiments, such as the ASEAN and the European Union, have begun to teach us is that the essential nature of this new global civilization will have to be ultimately grounded on a strong ethical and normative basis, which is consciously reflective of our commonly shared existence—an existence which incorporates the shared aspirations of all civilizations. Such a global civilization will have to exhibit qualities that include a commitment that supports the building and maintenance of social spaces for communication, dialogue, and respect for the inherent dignity and rights of the person, the principle of self-determination, and a shared determination to move past the destructive nature of power games, geopolitical calculations, and the antiquated temptation to accentuate the possibilities for clashes between civilizations in place of identifying the many areas of human interaction and dialogue that create opportunities for convergence.

Hence, the proper characterization what is meant by the term *shared existence* involves infinitely more than the limited connotation that is usually ascribed to it—which is mere survival. Rather, the nature and kind of shared existence, which Ikeda and his contemporaries ascribe to the idea is one that is ultimately defined by the capacity of individuals, groups, and organizations—public and private—to work together for the peaceful resolutions to issues, to engage in the forging of close bonds of mutual cooperation, and to embrace the recognition of the value and dignity of each person without reservation. In combination, these shared approaches to experiencing our global existence and interaction with one another leads to a condition of hope—hope in the name of harmonious coexistence. In fact, these shared approaches give substance to an idea and concept of global civilization, which has previously been relegated to the realm of mere utopian thought and aspiration. That this new perspective is now increasingly viewed as viable, achievable, and self-evident has been articulated in a dialogic exchange between Diez-Hochleitner and Ikeda:

> Diez-Hochleitner: Fulfilling my duties as a representative of private groups or as an envoy of international and inter-government organizations, I have visited China and India on several occasions. That is why I have various reasons for respecting and lauding both countries. We must never forget that the total population of both

Table 6.2   The Policies, Practices, and Goals of the Inclusionary State

Policies:

1. Advance the "rule of law" and condemn the practice of "rule by law".

2. Engage in the protection and extension of human rights in all realms.

3. Promote tolerance, mutuality, and cooperation between all social classes by removing the roots of categorical inequality and the connections that preserve and reinforce it.

4. Encourage the members of civil society to increase popular participation in social movements that place claims upon the state to promote an agenda which reflects the claims of distributive justice and democratic inclusion.

5. Maintain state integrity in decision-making by removing practices that advance exploitation and opportunity hoarding.

6. Advance an inclusionary agenda for inclusionary development that emphasizes material equalization by weakening the links and connections among the categories of exploitation and opportunity hoarding.

7. Construct mediating institutions between the state and civil society which allow for greater reliance upon a variety of forms for negotiation, mediation, and the arbitration of conflicting policy choices so as to expand the range of opportunities and resources for previously excluded individuals, groups, and classes.

Practices:

1. Create, establish, and maintain an independent and impartial judiciary.

2. Establish constitutionally protected human rights categories and channels for redress of grievances.

3. Build state-society linkages which promote negotiation, mediation, and arbitration in accord with the principles of an IS and inclusionary development.

4. Make economic decisions in accord with the claims of distributive justice and advanced practices of equitable distribution so that growth is not left isolated from distributional considerations.

5. Remove categories that protect and preserve exploitation and opportunity hoarding.

(Continued)

Table 6.2 (Continued)

Policies:

6. Bring the state back in to selectively regulate market mechanisms and remedy market failures that negatively affect the poor and excluded under the rubric of an IS and the criteria of an inclusionary developmental agenda.

7. Incorporate the poor and excluded into a participatory framework of institution-building through mediating institutions that give voice, political empowerment, and legal force to their inclusionary and equitable claims.

Goals:

1. Remove the threat of the exercise of arbitrary state power from old categories that reflect the values and priorities associated with class exploitation and opportunity hoarding.

2. Enforce and expand human rights protections through domestic and international bills of rights.

3. Strengthen state and civil society linkages and bonds for accommodating the articulation of new claims which advance inclusionary development and an IS.

4. Maintain a policy orientation and state practice which is directed toward the realization of the values, norms, and priorities that are embodied in the concept and practice of distributive justice.

5. Preserve the legitimacy of the IS through maintaining the integrity of its decision-making and policymaking practices.

6. Eliminate absolute poverty by ensuring the meeting of basic human needs while, at the same time, working to expand the social, economic, and political space that is required for participatory inclusion and to eliminate the growth/equity trade-off.

7. Realize and institutionalize the newly gained rights of previously excluded groups.

Source: Terrence E. Paupp, *Achieving Inclusionary Governance: Advancing Peace and Development in First and Third World Nations.* New York: Transnational Publishers, 2000, pp. 386–87.

countries is about half that of the earth as a whole. *Like the rest of the world, Japan, China and India must overcome past animosities and work together for peaceful resolutions to issues. They must form close bonds of mutual cooperation; individually and together, these three countries can create a basis for world hope. In addition, the West must address the East face-to-face on an equal footing.*

Ikeda: Exactly. *We must avoid so-called clashes of civilizations: humanity living on an ailing Earth can no longer afford to engage in imperialism or power games.* You from the West and I from the East must never stop urging the leaders of the world to engage in dialogue and cooperate in the name of harmonious coexistence (Ikeda and Diez-Hochleitner 2008, 71; italics added).

What is clearly evident in this dialogic exchange between Ikeda and Diez-Hochleitner is a deep commitment and trust in the capacity of people to reinvent global cooperation. Reinventing global cooperation will necessitate a series of steps: (1) a renunciation of imperialism, hegemony, and power games; (2) avoiding clashes between civilizations; (3) affirm and copy the strategies employed by Japan, China, and India that have been successfully used to overcome past animosities; (4) form close bonds of mutual cooperation between peoples and cultures that reveal the fact we all share multiple identities in multiple communities; and (5) stress and address the need for East and West to communicate with one another face-to-face and on an equal footing.

In this regard, a somewhat similar articulation of this very strategy has been proposed by Prof. Jeffrey Sachs, Director of The Earth Institute at Columbia University. In his 2008 book, *Common Wealth: Economics for a Crowded Planet*, Sachs wrote of the need to reinvent global cooperation when he noted: "At the core of our problems today is the collapse of faith in global problem solving, and a widespread cynical disbelief in global cooperation itself. Opinion leaders dismiss global objectives such as the Millennium Development Goals or the mitigation of greenhouse gas emissions as unrealistic or even utopian . . . The achievement of global goals can no longer depend on US leadership alone but requires robust global cooperation. That cooperation depends on an active network of governments, international organization, the private sector, and academic and non-governmental organizations" (Sachs 2008, 295).

In summary, Ikeda's philosophy for achieving a peaceful global civilization transcends the cynical disbelief in global cooperation by virtue of his faith in the capacity of individual's to transform themselves through the power of the human revolution. Additionally, Ikeda's faith in the power of dialogue as a means to transcend clashes between peoples and civilizations provides a practical avenue along which humanity may travel toward cooperation in the name of harmonious coexistence. This harmony can be retained through the practice of humanitarian competition—which allows people to channel their creative energies toward mutually beneficial enterprises. Such enterprises will include the building of new global institutions to replace the defective ones that have been in the service of either Western imperialism or corporate greed and profit-maximization as ends in themselves. Hence, Ikeda points us toward to new historical trajectory for humanity's future, which envisions robust global cooperation among many interrelated networks of people and institutions, thereby revealing the fact that we all possess memberships in a variety of communities. In this interconnected world, a consciousness of our interrelatedness and interdependence provides us with the power to remake the world and redefine the scope and power of global civilization itself.

Notes

1. According to Prof. Terry Nardin, "[I]nternational society as such, that inclusive society of states, or community of communities, within which all international association takes place—is not a purposive association constituted by a joint wish on the part of all states to pursue certain ends in concert. It is, rather, an association of independent and diverse political communities, each devoted to its own ends and its own conception of the good, often related to one another by nothing more than the fragile ties of a common tradition of diplomacy. The common good of this inclusive community resides not in the ends that some, or at times even most, of its members may wish collectively to pursue but in the values of justice, peace, security, and coexistence, which can only be enjoyed through participation in a common body of authoritative practices" (Terry Nardin, Law, Morality, and the Relations of States. Princeton, NJ: Princeton University Press, 1983, pp. 18–19).

2. Nobel-Prize-winning economist Joseph E. Stiglitz notes, "For the past two centuries or so, the center of political power in most successful countries has been at the level of the nation state. Globalization has entailed a loss of national sovereignty. International organizations, imposing international agreements, have seized power. So have international capital markets as they have been deregulated. And there are a variety of indirect ways in which globalization has impaired the effectiveness of the nation state, including the erosion of national cultures . . . So, though globalization may not be the cause of failed states, it has in some instances contributed to them" (Joseph E. Stiglitz, "The Overselling of Globalization," in Globalization: What's New, edited by Michael M. Weinstein. New York: Columbia University Press, 2005, p. 235).

3. Christian Reus-Smit and Duncan Snidal note, "When realists criticize national governments for acting in ways inconsistent with the national interest, or for acting in ways that destabilize international order, they base their criticisms on values of interest and order that can be defended only normatively. When postmodernists recommend a scholarly stance of relentless critique and deconstruction, they do so not for interpretative reasons (though this is in part their motive) but because this constitutes a practice of resistance against structures of power and domination" (Christian Reus-Smit and Duncan Snidal, "Between Utopia and Reality:

The Practical Discourses of International Relations," in *The Oxford Handbook of International Relations*, edited by Christian Reus-Smit and Duncan Snidal. New York: Oxford University Press, 2008, p. 6).

4. Richard Falk notes, "[I]n commenting on global trends and future arrangements, the context is too complex to yield the sort of understandings that could support meaningful predictions as to what will happen. This uncertainty is an encouragement for those in favor of the normative ideas being advocated. The current perception that overwhelmingly powerful political forces and countervailing ideas block their realization should not be converted into a sense of resignation or cynicism. The future remains open to a wide spectrum of possibilities, including those directly associated with humane global governance" (Richard Falk, "Humane Governance for the World: Reviving the Quest," in *Global Futures: Shaping Globalization*, edited by Jan Nederveen Pieterse. New York: Zed Books).

5. Tamas Szentes notes, "Global militarization, the arms race, and arms transfers exacerbate the tension-laden inequities in the world's social relations of production, i.e., in the international distribution of ownership and control of development resources, the global division of labor, and world income distribution. Notwithstanding the existence of armed forces 'organized primarily to liberate the country from colonial rule and to resist foreign economic dominance', militarization on the world scale contributes to an increasing concentration of power and a deepening of asymmetrical dependence relations" (Tamas Szentes, "The Economic Impact of Global Militarization," in *Alternatives: A Journal of World Policy*, Vol. X, No. 1, Summer 1984, pp. 64–65).

6. Mark Berger and Mark Beeson have noted that "[f]rom its inception . . . the World Bank was grounded in the wider power relations of the Cold War." Because of this primary focus, we find that the 1997 crisis in East Asia was the result of capitalist development policies offered by the World Bank to the detriment of the people of East Asia. Hence, it can be argued that "[u]ltimately . . . in the context of the shifting contours of the global political economy and the nation-state system, the World Bank played a crucial role in domesticating the East Asian miracle to the dominant liberal narrative of modernization and in facilitating the wider reinvention of liberalism in the post-1945 period" (Mark Berger and Mark Beeson, "Miracles of Modernization and Crises of Capitalism: The World Bank, East Asian Development and Liberal Hegemony," in *The World Bank: Development, Poverty, and Hegemony*, edited by David Moore. South Africa: University of KwaZulu-Natal Press, 2007, pp. 319, 340).

7. Terry Boswell has noted, "While a future global war is a possibility as the United States continues to decline, I think that the world-system cycles and trends that have produced violent hegemonic rivalry in the past can be changed by social action. Such a world revolution would create democratic institutions of global governance that can resolve issues of global inequality and international conflict peaceably" (Terry Boswell, "Hegemonic Decline and Revolution: When the World is Up for Grabs," in Globalization, Hegemony and Power: Anti-systemic Movements and the Global System, edited by Thomas E. Reifer. Boulder: Paradigm Publishers, 2004, p. 160).

7

Emerging Pillars of a Peaceful Global Civilization: Nuclear Disarmament, United Nations Reform, and the International Criminal Court

"Humanitarian issues are not restricted to the scope of any single country. The awareness is finally emerging that they must be dealt with through coordinated international efforts. Attempts to create new systems capable of responding effectively to this need have been viewed by states as attempts to limit . . . the prerogatives of national sovereignty— which to some extent they inevitably are—and this has prompted protracted resistance to the idea of an international criminal court."

—Daisaku Ikeda
(Ikeda 2001a, 210)

"Certainly the road to disarmament is long and rocky. Nor does the far-from-successful course of past arms negotiations inspire unmitigated optimism. Nonetheless, the road must be followed. Human hands produced nuclear weapons and weaponry systems, and human hands should be able to reduce and eliminate them. If we stand idle and fail in this, we will rob future generations of their dreams. But even more horrendous, given the total-destruction capabilities of contemporary weapons, we could rob future generations not only of their dreams but also of their very existence."

—Daisaku Ikeda
(Ikeda 2001a, 199–200)

"Some people say that human history is a history of war and violence. This may be true, but at the same time, one could also say that it is a history of assiduous efforts and challenges to eliminate the horrors of war. Throughout the war-and-violence-ravaged twentieth century, a system was created based on a consensus that called for a shift away from an

ethos of 'might makes right' to the 'rule of law', thanks especially to the sacrifices and heroic efforts of many who brought justice to international society. The United Nations, needless to say, has been central to this effort. Today, however, both the rule of law as well as the United Nations itself are facing serious crises . . . Personally, I am extremely alarmed about the continued efforts, even into the twenty-first century, to legitimize the philosophy of 'might makes right' rather than the rule of law."

—Daisaku Ikeda
(Ikeda 2007-PP, 111)

"Democratizing global governance raises a variety of issues, including greater degrees of accountability, transparency, and equity throughout the United Nations system, as well as establishing spaces for non-state participation. The most promising and practical way to acknowledge the challenge and organize a response is to establish in some form *a global parliament with the mandate to incorporate transnational and futurist non-state civil societal priorities."*

—Richard Falk
(Falk 2009, 22; italics in original)

The entire range and scope of humanitarian issues that have preoccupied the thoughts and efforts of peacemakers since the start of the twentieth century have expanded exponentially in the twenty-first century. Take, for example, the concept of "security," as well as the issue of what actually constitutes "security." It is now a transitioning concept that has moved beyond the traditional boundaries of "military security" as a central focus of international law and state practice toward the more global idea and concept of "human security." While the twentieth century laid the groundwork for this more expansive concept, the historical record shows that any real progress made in this direction was, in some very critical respects, directly related to the consequences that stemmed from horrific wars—which have only been magnified in their destructive potential by technological advances. Therefore, in this chapter we will be discussing more expansive ways of how to begin the task of reconceptualizing humanitarian issues, the enduring problem of the largely unregulated use of force in the service of hegemonic geopolitics, and search for solutions on how best to rebuild the role of the United Nations as a vehicle for collective security. To that end, we shall be specifically addressing the challenge of what can be done to offset the declining effectiveness of the United Nations in the global domain of peace and security issues. In that regard, according to Richard Falk, we find that the increasing effectiveness of the UN can be seen most predominantly in two areas: "standard-setting (*especially with respect to human rights and self-determination*) and (2) consciousness-raising (*especially in relation to emergent problems of global concern*)" (Falk 2000b, 140; italics added).

The Purpose of the United Nations versus the Hegemonic State

The United Nations was created in the aftermath of two world wars in the hope that the use of military force, aggression, or intervention by any nation could be either halted or significantly constrained by the mandates of the UN Charter and the active role of the UN Security Council, as both normative and institutional safeguards against those remaining proclivities of power-politics and their inherently aggressive tendencies which are attendant throughout the nation-state system. Herein lies the problem. According to Falk, we find that ". . . the UN approach to power and law has far more operational significance given the centrality of the Security Council on matters of peace and security, and considering the use of the veto, and its threatened use, by permanent members whenever controversial decisions are being made, thereby often gridlocking the UN at times of greatest urgency. In effect, this veto power institutionalizes 'hegemonic international law' by formalizing sovereign *inequality* as a basic ordering principle of pervasive operational significance" (Falk 2009, 32; italics in original). The same defect arises with respect to the principle of *"sovereign equality"* in international law itself. In some constellations and conceptualizations of international law, there is a tendency to accord what Falk calls "hegemonic status power *within* the law, creating a tension between the political–juridical myth that international relations and world order are based on norms of 'sovereign equality' and assertions that inequalities of status and power deserve to be acknowledged as having a 'desirable' lawmaking effect" (Falk 2009, 32; italics in original).

Hence, both the UN and international law itself are built on a fundamental contradiction—the contradiction between the announced *"sovereign equality of states"* versus the practical reality of *"hegemonic status power"* within world order. Both the UN and international law allow for inequalities and contradictions to persist. One need only recall the fact that this stratification emerges rather explicitly and prominently in the form of a veto power given to the five permanent members of the UN Security Council. Hence, we discover that "in effect, the veto assures the five permanent members (United States, Russia, China, France, United Kingdom) an exemption from legal accountability with respect to the obligations of the charter, including the core commitment to refrain from non-defensive uses of force to resolve international disputes" (Falk 2009, 47).

It is this contradiction which best serves to reveal the hidden truth that "[i]nternational law is used by dominant political actors to lend an aura of legitimacy to the geopolitical stratification of relations among sovereign states" (Falk 2009, 47). This contradiction has opened up a moral, ethical, and political chasm in global relations insofar as such stratification is in direct conflict with the norm of the juridical equality of states, which is affirmed in the UN Charter, Article 2 (1): "The United Nations is based on the sovereign equality of all its members."

In this chapter, I submit that the failure of the UN and international law to fully honor this principle in practice has contributed a great deal of turmoil to the current global crisis. Therefore, I maintain that in order to effectively move beyond the current global crisis, it is essential that this contradiction be removed. To begin with, it should be removed from the institutional structure of the UN by virtue of making fundamental changes to the UN Security Council itself. Further, this contradiction should be removed from international law, which speaks of "sovereign equality" on the one hand, while granting global space for the virtually unfettered use of "hegemonic status power" on the other. I believe that for the sake of the integrity of the UN, adherence to its charter, the Nuremberg Principles and all related areas of international law, that genuine sovereign equality should be enjoyed by all nations and the final determination of this principle—in practice—needs to be resolved in favor of all humanity. It is for this reason that we should have the intellectual courage and integrity to confront and remove the hypocrisy of this double standard by invoking what I call the *"Principle of Hegemonic State Accountability"* (PHSA) (Paupp 2009).

The purpose of the PHSA is dedicated to expanding our focus on the activities, behaviors, foreign policy practices, and actual conduct of hegemonic states to include and encompass "the hegemonic practices of any nation or group of nations that engage in formulating policies or actions undertaken in furtherance of (unlawful) acts that are undertaken for the sole purpose of achieving hegemonic dominance in world affairs. Additionally, if the primacy purpose of the State's conduct (and behavior) is specifically undertaken in furtherance of a Hegemonic State's national and/or geopolitical agenda to the exclusion of all other standards of international law and it subsequently undertakes actions that may be considered acts of aggression that violate established principles, practices, and obligations governing State action in world affairs, then the Hegemonic State shall be deemed to have engaged in unlawful acts against the international community and must be held accountable for those acts under the applicable standards of what constitutes the boundaries of acceptable State conduct in international law" (Paupp 2009, 195).

In explicating the legal and normative basis behind the wording of the PHSA, Paupp states, "With this formulation, it is my primary intention to design and to apply an international legal standard that is aligned with a clear and internationally accepted normative framework—as embodied in the UN Charter, the ruling of the International Court of Justice (ICJ), the rulings of the International Criminal Court (ICC), and the Nuremberg Charter (Nuremberg

Principles)—that is capable of addressing and assessing the 'purpose' of Hegemonic State action in relationship to its conduct and obligations in international affairs" (Paupp 2009, 196).

The practical importance of this formulation is found in the recognition that ". . . if a state's 'policies or actions' are 'undertaken for the sole purpose of achieving hegemonic dominance in world affairs,' then its policies and actions should automatically be considered (presumed to be) unlawful and potentially criminal (*in the sense that its policies and/or actions render the established principles of self-determination, sovereignty, human rights, humanitarian intervention, and restraints on the use of force, virtually null and void*)" (Paupp 2009, 197; italics in the original).

It should be noted that the PHSA was written in the aftermath of the 2003 invasion of Iraq by the United States and in response to both the illegality of the invasion and the continuing occupation. Additionally, it should also be noted that the wording, concepts, and inspiration for the PHSA is derived predominantly from the Nuremberg Charter and Nuremberg Principles. Hence, in the spirit of the Nuremberg Charter and Principles, the PHSA seeks to make the preservation of peace and accountability of State action in international affairs throughout the global commonwealth its central concern. To that end, the PHSA represents both a call and a demand that the United Nations, the International Criminal Court, and the nuclear weapons states remain, at all times, accountable to the line which divides legitimate self-defense from aggression. Yet, even beyond that central focus (which is well established in the UN Charter and international law) there is a broader concern with finally acknowledging and respecting the principle of the "*sovereign equality*" of all nations and the rights of the people within them. For, in the final analysis, every nation (even a hegemonic state) remains ultimately accountable and subject to international law, treaties, and covenants which all explicitly advance the recognition of the dignity, rights, and worth of each person. It is in this light and from this perspective that the PHSA stands as a condemnation of our global nuclear weapons culture and the violence associated with it. To that end, it should be noted that within Chapter 1, Article 1, of the UN Charter states that the very purpose of the United Nations is "[t]o maintain peace and security, and to that end: to take effective collective measures for the preservation and removal of threats to peace . . . and to being about by peaceful means, and in conformity with the principles of justice and international law, adjustment or settlement of international disputes or situations which might lead to a breach of the peace." Further, in the spirit of the Nuremberg Charter and Principles, the PHSA holds all nations not only accountable for unauthorized uses of military force, but also seeks to evaluate, condemn, and outlaw the geopolitical intentions, behaviors, and actions of states which not only sustain exploitative and oppressive geopolitical structures of stratification, but also seek to pursue a hegemonic agenda that is at odds with the purpose and intent of the UN Charter, the bulk of international law, and the aspirations of all who seek a more just international order.

The Imperative of Nuclear Abolition and the Nuremberg Principles

The Nuremberg Principles arose out of the 1946 trial of the Nazi leadership in Germany for war crimes committed in the planning and execution of World War II. In the summer of 1945, representatives of France, Great Britain, the Soviet Union, and the United States met in London to formulate plans for the trial of the major Nazi war criminals. It was decided that there would be a single multinational trial and that the tribunal would be composed of the four states represented at the planning conference. The head of the tribunal, Justice Robert H. Jackson, "was intent on penalizing the Germans for their war of aggression, and suggested that the United States might refuse to participate in the trial unless the crime of aggressive war was included within the Nuremberg Charter" (Lippman 2008, 511). The central reason for Jackson's insistence on that issue was the belief that it was "vital to clearly establish that the launching of a war of aggression which threatened world order would be regarded as an international crime" (Lippman 2008, 511). With the matter finally resolved, on August 8, 1945, the United States, France, the United Kingdom, and the Soviet Union signed the Agreement for the Prosecution and Punishment of the Major War Criminals of the European Axis Power.[1]

The tribunal initially turned its attention to the substantive offenses punishable under the charter. The three substantive offenses are as follows: Article 6(a)—Crimes Against Peace; Article 6(b)—War Crimes, and; Article 6(c)—Crimes Against Humanity. In Table 7.1, we find a detailed explication of the substantive prohibitions found in the Nuremberg Charter. Contained in Table 7.1, we find a detailed list of substantive prohibitions found within the Nuremberg Charter as a consequence of their having been acts declared to be criminal and, therefore, acts which mean that they entail not only charges against a particular regime, but also entail individual responsibility. Their contemporary significance is found with respect to humanity's twenty-first century predicament with regard to the illegality of nuclear weapons and the threat they pose to our planetary existence. In that regard, "[s]ince the Nazi preparations to commit unquestionably illegal actions is conceptually similar to the plans and threats of the US government to use nuclear weapons, there seems little question that threatening the use of nuclear weapons is criminal under the legally binding principles of the Nuremberg Charter" (Kauzlarich and Kramer 1998, 33).

A review of these substantive offenses makes clear that "[w]hat is unusual about the prohibitions found in the Nuremberg Charter is not only the outlawing of malign conduct of belligerents in war, but also the significant amount of

Table 7.1   Substantive Prohibitions Found in the Nuremberg Charter

The following acts are crimes falling within the jurisdiction of the tribunal for which there shall be individual responsibility.

1. Crimes against Peace: namely, planning, preparation, initiation, or waging a war of aggression, or a war in violation of international treaties, agreements, or assurances, or participation in a common plan or conspiracy for the accomplishment of any of the foregoing.

2. War Crimes: namely, violations of the laws or customs of war. Such violations shall include, but not be limited to, murder, ill-treatment, or deportation to slave labor or for any other purpose of civilian population or in occupied territory, murder, or ill-treatment of prisoners of war or persons on seas, killing of hostages, plunder of public or private property, wanton destruction of cities, towns, or villages, or devastation no justified by military necessity.

3. Crimes against Humanity: namely, murder, extermination, enslavement, deportation, and other inhumane acts committed against any civilian population, before or during war, prosecutions on political, racial, or religious grounds in execution of or in connection with any crime within the jurisdiction of the tribunal, whether or not in violation of the domestic law of the country where perpetrated.

Source: Roberts and Guelff, 1982. Also, reprinted in Terrence E. Paupp, 2000; and in Terrence E. Paupp, 2005, p. 85.

attention paid to the crimes of conspiracy, planning, and threatening to commit the crimes of murder and other inhumane acts. In its deliberations, the tribunal convicted many individuals, as well as organizations such as the German Gestapo, of conspiracy to violate the principles of humanity and peace" (Kauzlarich and Kramer 1998, 31–33). In light of the thematic, normative, and moral turn toward focusing on all of humanity and not just a select few nations and their interests, we discover that the UN Charter and the Nuremberg Charter and Principle combine to reshape human consciousness, actions, and priorities from the delimiting boundaries of the nation-state and a single-minded focus on the pursuit of the "national interest" to the well-being of all peoples—the peace, security, and promise of an emerging global civilization.

Hence, in light of this history, the thematic, moral, and normative turn of moral inquiry, international law, and global justice concerns all points toward the need to begin to more consciously focus on the entire global community and the needs of an emerging global civilization. It is a consciousness that effectively and demonstrably points to a new and alternative reality:

> Allegiance to the state must be replaced by a loyalty to the human community and by a respect for international law. It is not the rebel

who threatens civilization, but the compliant conformist who mechanically suppresses her moral qualms when confronted with the dictates of authority. The German philosopher Karl Jaspers some forty years ago also reflected on the subject of German guilt: 'The essential point is whether the Nuremberg trial comes to be a link in a chain of meaningful constructive political acts, or whether by the yardstick there applied to mankind the very power now erecting this Nuremberg trail will in the end be found wanting.' Richard Falk writes it is imperative that Jasper's '*Nuremberg Promise*' should be fulfilled (Lippman 2008, 543; italics added).

Similarly, in conjunction with the problems of unauthorized, illegitimate, and legally unsanctioned state power, we also discover that the very existence of nuclear weapons has been a central source of concern and consternation for nation-states, the United Nations and UN Security Council, international courts and international law since the dawning of the atomic age in 1945. The continued reliance by the nuclear states on nuclear weapons as a means of statecraft has contributed to the dangers of nuclear proliferation and the violation of emerging international norms that have called for their abolition. On this very point, Scott Ritter, former Chief Weapons Inspector for the United Nations Special Commission in Iraq from 1991 to 1998, has noted that

> [t]he United States, President Obama will come to discover, is a nation addicted to nuclear weapons and the power and prestige, both real and illusory, that these weapons bring. Breaking this addiction will prove extremely difficult. This is especially true given the lack of having any real nuclear disarmament policy in place since the dawn of the nuclear age. The failure of the United States to formulate or to implement effective nuclear disarmament policy has placed America and the world in a very dangerous place. The longer America and the world continue to possess nuclear weapons, the greater the likelihood of nuclear weapons being used. The only way to prevent such a dire outcome is through the abolition, and not the reduction or control, of all nuclear weapons (Ritter 2010, xxiii).

Upon reflection, the fact that the United States has never embarked upon creating an effective nuclear disarmament policy is difficult to accept. The absence of such a policy is not only reckless and arrogant—it represents the victory of technology and "technique" over moral discourse. The advent of the nuclear age has virtually erased the moral boundaries that have historically acted as a constraint on decisions to make, threaten, and wage war. In this regard, "technology has been transformed into a new theology with autonomy of its own, and theology and moral argument have been subsumed under the umbrella of technological discourse" (Paupp 2005, 73). The challenge to undertake the quest for nuclear abolition is caught in between the technology of a nuclear weapons culture (that is supported by the ideological justifica-tions of the leading nuclear weapons states), on the one hand, against those moral obligations, global justice concerns, and ethical claims of humanity which argue for revitalizing personal responsibility to resolve this situation, on the other. I have called this situation *"the nuclear crucible"* insofar as "[t]he nuclear crucible continues to sacrifice both the individual and the well-being of collective humanity vis-à-vis a Nazi/nuclear narrative, which induces a psychological sense of denial and inoculates those who adopt it against feel-ing the full weight of personal moral responsibility for a potential nuclear holocaust" (Paupp 2005, 76).

Hence, we may conclude that the most fundamental reasons for explain-ing why the successive US governments have never embarked upon creating an effective nuclear disarmament policy are an unwillingness to take moral responsibility for the technological advance of nuclear weaponry and the adoption of ideological justifications for this choice.[2] The abdication of criti-cal choices on nuclear weapons and issues of war and peace to the guardians of the nuclear arsenals represents a combination of the failure of moral re-sponsibility with the empowerment of the guardians of the nuclear arsenals, thereby strengthening the practices of exclusionary governance under the auspices of an exclusionary state (Paupp 2000, 51–112).

Given the nature of this historical trajectory since the end of World War II, it is increasingly evident that global resistance to threats from a US weap-ons culture, augmented by over 750 US-military bases spanning the globe, in combination with immense suffering, poverty, and humiliation perceived as the result of US-led policies replete with structural violence, has invited a growth in terrorism and terrorist activity against the US Empire and its at-tempt to maintain its hegemonic domination of the earth's peoples. In light of post-1945 global history, it becomes evident what happens when policies depend on violence. In a dialogic exchange between Ikeda and Joseph Rot-blat, we find an explication of how a mind-set rooted in a weapons culture nurtures a mind-set of violence. The pivotal point of this dialogic exchange reads as follows:

> Rotblat: That terrorism is spreading to such an extent throughout the world is the direct result of policies that are dependent on violence. *If we are to combat terrorism, we must begin to nurture a culture of peace, not the strategy followed by the United States.* We often tell young people not to choose violence. However, young people can see that we are attempting to achieve peace through the most evil weaponry ever invented by man. This mind-set ultimately nurtures a culture of violence.

> Ikeda: I agree. We really must think more seriously about how we have created a culture of war. For many years in the Third World,

we trampled on people's dignity with violence that is both direct, as in the violence perpetrated by colonial rule, as well as indirect and structural, through the debilitating impact of poverty and inequality. *Resentment and dissatisfaction are the root cause of terrorism in today's world. If we continually focus on religious conflict and the clash of cultures, we may misinterpret the problem.* Of course, terrorism should never be excused, and an international framework to prevent terrorism should be put in place. This alone, however, is only a partial solution and not a way to reach a fundamental resolution. The other half of *the solution should be to address the conditions that give rise to terrorism in the first place. This would involve creating a world founded on principles of equality and coexistence. As a first step toward achieving such a world, the danger of nuclear weapons and the associated potential for human extinction should be eliminated* (Ikeda and Rotblat 2007, 79; italics added).

The Conflicting Agendas of the United Nations and of a Global *Pax Americana*

The enduring problem and danger of being a hegemonic state committed to predominantly geopolitical calculations reflects a larger global reality. That larger reality is that unresolved dangers associated with a hierarchical international order cannot and will not provide the basis for true "human security." Seeking to recreate "another American century," and to do so through a global *Pax Americana*, can only ultimately stand for a policy that is designed to impose another century of US hegemony on global arrangements through the combined threat of nuclear weapons use coupled with military interventionism and a long string of preemptive wars (Calder 2007). The consequence of taking such a course is found in the realization that Washington's power elite have actually invited an unintended response of greater nuclear weapons proliferation and the heightened danger of nuclear terrorism (Krieger 2006, 381–96; Morgan 2008, 31–50).

Chossudovsky (2003), among others, asserts that the American primacy coalition has found that sovereign inequality leads to greater private profits for its multinational corporations, for Wall Street, and the US Treasury/IMF/World Bank/WTO complex. In so doing, it has abrogated the human rights approach to development and, in its place, substituted a "race to the bottom" (Osmani 2006, 255–73). Abouharb and Cingranelli (2007) add the following: "Since the passage of the United Nations Universal Declaration of Human Rights in 1948, the promotion of better human rights practices by governments around the world has been one of the most important functions of the United Nations. It is morally wrong for agencies of the United Nations, which include both the World Bank and the International Monetary Fund, to undermine one of their parent organization's most important goals, the promotion of good human rights practices . . . The practical implication . . . is that structural adjustment programs are not producing good economic outcomes mainly because they combine relatively ineffective policies with the undermining of a necessary precondition for economic growth—respect for human rights" (227). Walden Bello has outlined at least five critical areas where, almost invariably, both World Bank and IMF structural adjustment loans and programs exhibited abuses and/or denials of human rights ranging from cutting spending on health, education, and welfare to removing restrictions on foreign investment; from privatizing state enterprises to devaluing the nation's currency, from cutting wages to weakening labor protections in general.[3]

In this regard, the West's predominant role in organizing the structure of international financial institutions, deciding the rules and policies which select winners and losers in the processes of globalization, and still clinging to the tendency of the powerful to suppress and ignore the legitimate claims and rights of the weak, has only served to create an untenable global crisis. In large measure, therefore, I argue that the current global crisis is a product of this recent history. From my perspective, I see the response of nations and regions throughout the entire global South to this outcome in the form of not only social movements in opposition to US hegemony and US policies, but also regional efforts to build counterhegemonic alliances against the United States and any further attempted imposition of these aforementioned draconian policies emanating from the IMF, World Bank, and WTO (Paupp 2007, 2009). On this matter, I concur with the analysis of these events presented by Walden Bello who notes, "[t]he democracy movement, East Asian countries and Islamic revivalist movements are not going to make comfortable bedfellows, but a strategic alliance can be forged on the common platform of opposition to Northern reconcentration of economic power and corporate-driven globalization; for an end to a free-market global framework for trade and investment, for the abolition of the multilateral trinity of the World Bank, IMF, and the WTO; and for a 'New Deal' for the South embodied in trade, investment, aid, and technology policies" (Bello 1998, 225). These contending interests and forces are continuing to drive the global crisis of the early twenty-first century (Bush 2007; Cavanagh et al. 1994; DeMartino 2000; Gould 2005; Peet 2003; Saad-Filho and Johnston 2005; Soederberg 2006).

Further, it is a crisis which will not and cannot be resolved successfully by the United States through its military power alone. On this matter, historian Gabriel Kolko has astutely noted that

> [t]here has now been a qualitative leap in technology that makes all inherited conventional wisdom, and was as an instrument of political policy, utterly irrelevant, not just to the United States but to any other nation that embarks on this course . . . The Pentagon in

August 2000, at a cost of $250 million, held a simulated war against Iran and lost it. Most of the American fleet was sunk. All attempts to devise defenses against speedboats armed with explosives and rockets failed. Technological devises to stop even the most primitive attacks has been expensive failures, and anti-missile technology everywhere has remained unreliable, even after decades of effort and billions of dollars spent (Kolko 2009, 149).

These new realities serve to underscore the difficulty that the US Empire and the American primacy coalition face in taking their project for hegemonic domination into the future (Paupp 2009). Further, these new realities raise the following question: *"Is a consensual Empire even possible?"* In answer, Prof. Carl Boggs notes that "[o]ne possible answer is that American power will sooner or later disintegrate from the weight of its own contradictions—so long as in decline or defeat it does not initiate a nuclear holocaust that would render discussion of future Empire meaningless. The US imperial domain, despite appearances of insurmountable strength, is in many ways fragile and vulnerable" (Boggs 2005, 201).

The Doctrine of "Humanitarian Intervention": Truly Humane?

We now find that the problems of ethnic cleansing and genocide have been exacerbated since the end of the Cold War. The new version of the doctrine of "humanitarian intervention" is especially troubling given the reality that in ". . . the long history of Western intervention throughout the world, intervention of an unprecedented scope and scale, has resulted in the destruction of hundreds of millions of lives by slaughter, hunger, disease, and poverty" (Williams 2010, 63). The question then becomes *"Why would such tragic consequences result from an enterprise that sounds as morally viable as 'humanitarian intervention'?"* The answer is that in the aftermath of an "intervention," often guided by the hidden motivations of an imperialistic agenda, the status quo which has served the wealthy and powerful interests so well is basically left in place—but at a very high human cost. Western interventionism has usually led to greater levels of human destruction rather than genuine social transformation. In turn, social transformation is usually predicated upon bringing about radical change in the structures of the status quo, not further "adjustments" to the status quo and the privileged classes which have a vested interest in its preservation. Hence, the real challenge for those committed to human development is not making a series of "adjustments" to the world as it is, but rather to engage in a program of "readjustment" that places human history on an entirely new trajectory—more humane, more inclusive, more just.

Writing in 1981 at the beginning of the Reagan presidency, on the subject of developing a common vision for humanity that replaced the geopolitical and hegemonic paradigms that had dominated international relations in theory and practice, historian L.S. Stavrianos noted that

> [t]he key Third World problem today is how to realize the basic *"social transformation"* called for by Prebisch. In essence it requires readjustment of power relationships, and the readjustment, if it is to be effective, must be across the board. It must be implemented not only within Third World countries but also in the relations between developed and underdeveloped countries. And this, in turn, requires that the readjustment be extended to power relationships within the developed countries of the First and Second Worlds (Stavrianos 1981, 806; italics added).

What Stavrianos has proposed is a theoretical and normative change in how we perceive the possibilities for building a more peaceful global civilization and, at the same time, laid out the objective and empirical requirements associated with its attainment. To that end, we find that the First, Second, and Third Worlds need to move toward policies that bring an end to the artificial limitations imposed by global hierarchical structures and the hegemony of a few elite states over the well-being, democratic aspirations, and human rights of the vast majority. In short, the global North needs to recognize that its fate is also contingent on the fate of the peoples of the global South. By finding common cause and common purpose between these nations and regions, it then becomes possible to reach a turning point where the argument can be made that we will find our own advancement in the search for the advancement of all.

In his analysis of the essential nature of the global crisis that characterized the early 1980s, Stavrianos quoted some of the central findings which emerged out of a symposium organized under UN auspices by the International Foundation for Development Alternatives in July 1979. The symposium emphasized the need for *"structural remedies"* to resolve the problems of environmental degradation, the persistence of poverty, the waste of resources, and a deep crisis of values and cultural identity. It was asserted that "[t]here is a crisis in the North, which is no less basic than that in the South. Therefore *the new development strategy should be a global strategy which is addressed to the South, the North, and the institutions and processes that relate to the two. The strategy should encompass what is basically wrong with the North, as with the South, as well as the relationship between maldevelopment in the North and the inadequate, unjust, and unbalanced development patterns in the South*— phenomena which incidentally provide the context for the universal revolt of the younger generation and its alienation, cutting across both North and South. The new development strategy must relate itself to this large global context of structural and cultural change" (Stavrianos 1981, 810; italics added).

All of these concerns are essential to moving beyond global crisis. Yet all of these concerns are eliminated from consideration and virtually ignored by the modern trend to engage in debates about the need for "humanitarian intervention" by the North in the affairs of the global South.

Despite a long record of good intentions that reveals that the idea of humanitarian intervention dates back more than two hundred years, there is compelling evidence that it remains necessary to question and to challenge a morally motivated foreign policy (Bass 2008). In an incisive book review of Gary Bass's study entitled Freedom's Battle: The Origins of Humanitarian Intervention, Prof. Samuel Moyn notes that "[t]he most troubling fact about international politics in the nineteenth century is not that moral appeals to save suffering humanity were absent but that they were commonplace. The British, who led the international campaign to end the slave trade, and then slavery, abused that credential by tirelessly *citing their national and moral superiority as justification for imperial rule—including invasion and expansion.* The crimes of savage peoples and backward states had to be stopped, and the British—self-styled agents of humane values—were the ones to do it" (Moyn 2008, 30; italics added). The 2003 invasion and occupation of Iraq by the United States under the presidency of George W. Bush certainly reflected this same hubris (Isikoff and Corn 2006). Under Bush's rule, however, it was a motivation that was further contaminated by his version of *"democracy promotion"*—a dubious endeavor given the history of US relations and foreign policy with Middle Eastern countries that were authoritarian, but were nonetheless compliant regimes when it came to selling their oil resources to an oil-addicted United States and Europe (Gardner 2009; Khalidi 2004). If we examine the entire historical record of US interventions, ". . . it becomes clear that the role of the United States with respect to genocide includes all of the following forms of activity: (1) precipitating, participating in, and helping carry out genocide; (2) acting in such ways as to escalate genocide; (3) blocking attempts to mitigate genocide; (4) doing nothing; (5) facilitating attempts to mitigate genocide" (Williams 2010, 65).

In fact, in the aftermath of the US/NATO intervention in Kosovo, it has been observed that "[t]here is another reason, apart from the problem of pretextual abuses of human rights, that international law has thus far rejected the doctrine of humanitarian intervention. The primacy goal of the United Nations is to 'save succeeding generations from the scourge of war.' The charter thus requires that war be viewed as a last resort, taken only after all peaceful alternatives have failed. The procedural mechanism that the charter employs is to further that substantive goal requires that decisions to go to war be made only by a deliberative body of states representing a broad range of constituents: the Security Council" (Lobel and Ratner 2000, 114). Hence, we may conclude that what recent history demonstrates, in this instance, is that "[t]he Kosovo crisis illustrates the danger of bypassing that procedural restraint. It is possible that the settlement that ended the air war could have been achieved without the use of force . . . Moreover, the greater destructiveness of war that led to charter's framers to choose peace as its central tenet was illustrated by the Kosovo events: many more Kosovars and Serbs were killed and wounded after the air war started than during the prior two years of civil strife and human rights abuses in Kosovo" (Lobel and Ratner 2000, 114).

Recent history also serves to demonstrate what was discussed earlier in this chapter regarding the relevance of the UN Charter, the Nuremberg Principles, and the PHSA with respect to waging what has been euphemistically termed "discretionary wars." Richard Falk has criticized Prof. Anne-Marie Slaughter for suggesting a scenario where ". . . if approval by the Security Council is thwarted by an actual or anticipated veto that is politically motivated, then recourse to force would be justified, even without UN approval" (Falk 2008c, 142). But were this course of action to be adopted in practice, Falk cautions, we would invariably find that "[s]o long as the power of exception is a matter of decision by a hegemonic government, the limitations associated with the constraining guidelines are not likely to inhibit discretionary wars" (Falk 2008c, 142). Hence, we are returned to consider the necessary and unavoidable need to revitalize the Nuremberg Principles and to apply the PHSA to the workings of the UN in the Security Council. To fail to apply these two sets of principles would be tantamount to allowing Slaughter's argument to rule the day by introducing what Falk has termed *"the possibility of retrospective legitimation"* (Falk 2008c, 142). The legal reality of the situation is that "[t] here is no customary rule that construes military intervention as the way to 'enforce' human rights. There is only the imprecise and ad hoc expansion of the definition of threats to peace and security from interstate to internal civil disturbances, and the generalized moral discourse of human rights, which enable the Security Council and others to justify violations of state sovereignty in the name of humanitarianism" (Cohen 2005, 183). Therefore, in stating a contrary opinion, with due deference to the human rights fundamentalists, Cohen asserts ". . . that *one cannot simply postulate a human right to protection, to rescue, to security, or to civilian inviolability and then assert that any state or collective body able to do so has the moral duty to enforce such rights through military intervention.* Indeed, the argument, via analogy with civil disobedience, that it is necessary to update international law by such illegal military means is deeply unconvincing and counterintuitive" (Cohen 2005, 183; italics added).

The US/NATO war in Kosovo (1990s), as well as the subsequent invasion and occupation of Iraq and Afghanistan (2003–present), are all examples of recent events which have brought into the question the efficacy of the UN as a means of constraining superpower efforts to engage in "wars of choice." At the same time, the issue of war crimes and the reappearance of war criminals has brought renewed focus and attention on the role of and necessity for an active International Criminal Court (ICC) as a legitimate and necessary means of bringing accountability to the practice of international law and justice for those who engage in genocide—as well as those powers who remain addicted to engaging in preemptive wars, wars of choice, and the practice of geopolitical excesses by hegemonic states in their conduct of global relations. The problems and challenges associated with these twenty-first century realities are best summed up in Falk's observation that "[t]he Nuremberg approach continues to lack credibility whenever it collides with the stubborn realities of geopolitics. The state system is still beholden to dominant states that insist on their prerogative to wage illegal and aggressive 'wars of choice,' thereby dangerously and often imprudently subordinating legality to a warped logic of political expediency" (Falk 2008c, 165).

In the final analysis, Falk concludes that "[i]t is not just a matter of upgrading the relevance of law, but of downgrading the utility and acceptability of war as a policy option" (Falk 2008c, 170). To that end, the empowerment of and adherence to the ideas contained in the PHSA offers a series of concrete strategies through which the UN Security Council can be remade while, at the same time, an emerging multicentric world of *"rising regions"* can effectively guide the evolution of global relations in conjunction with a *"counter-hegemonic alliance"* in opposition to the continued application of US power, force, and militarism (Paupp 2009).

Related and complementary perspectives on these issues have been set forth by Prof. Jean Cohen who astutely notes that ". . . today the re-articulation and democratization of sovereignty (internal and external), configured within a multilayered world order with effective international institutions and an updated international law, is the *sine qua non* for the emergence of a global 'rule of law' and constitutes an important part of the counter-project to empire. Without a global rule of law that protects sovereignty as well as human rights, any talk of 'cosmopolitan' right, especially and above all the alleged right to intervene militarily to enforce human rights, is inherently suspect. Cosmopolitan right can supplement—but not replace—sovereignty-based public international law" (Cohen 2005, 162; italics in original). In harmony with Falk and Paupp, Cohen disagrees with Slaughter's attempt to engage in *"the possibility of retrospective legitimation"* in the case of the US/NATO war on Kosovo. In fact, Cohen explicitly argues that it is necessary and essential for a global rule of law ". . . to stop the trend toward the deformalization of international law that began in the 1990s with the invasion of Kosovo and that has been fostered by every subsequent 'humanitarian intervention' . . . For *there is at present no 'law of humanitarian intervention,' and, strictly speaking, the Security Council is authorized to approve military interventions only when international peace and security are threatened"* (Cohen 2005, 183; italics added). In similar fashion, C. G. Weeramantry, judge of the International Court of Justice from

1991 to 2000, has reexamined the UN Charter with respect to the Bush II administration's invasion of Iraq in 2003 and concluded that

> Articles 42 and 51 are the only articles that deal with the actual use of armed force. Nowhere in the scheme of the charter is any member state permitted to resort to force unilaterally except in the extremely limited case provided for by Article 51, when an armed attack actually occurs against a member State. This too is extremely circumscribed for such actions may only be unilaterally taken until the Security Council has taken necessary measures to maintain peace and security. It would be true to say therefore that by its very structure, by its express provisions, and by its underlying intent the UN Charter completely outlaws unilateral resort to armed force. *That is the hard-won advance in civilizational progress already referred to, which it is the compelling duty of every Member State to preserve. Any negation of this principle sets back the advancement of the human condition, and more particularly where that negation is by a power which wields special influence and authority in community of nations.* In that event the damage done may well be incalculable (Weeramantry 2005, 21–22; italics added).

Hence, because the United States negated these principles governing the use of force in the UN Charter, the damage done by the illegal US invasion and occupation of Iraq created even greater harm within the international system given its capacity to wield *"special influence and authority in the community of nations."* Therefore, my advocacy for the need to invoke the PHSA in conjunction with the Nuremberg Principles and the UN Charter is even more urgent (Paupp 2009). This is not only so that humanity may begin to rectify the damage wrought by this ill-conceived and illegal invasion of the nation of Iraq, but also to foreclose upon the possibility of this history and course of action being used as a precedent in the future for any such repetition of this kind of action (as would be the case if there were to be a US or Israeli attack on the sovereign state of Iran).

The unfortunate truth is that the unilateral foreign policy of the United States has defined the use and limits of employing military force from the presidency of Clinton through that of Bush II. Instead of downgrading the role of force and military interventionism, the United States has actively embraced its imperial role with increasing carelessness and frequency since the end of the Cold War. Using the guise of an ad hoc concept called "humanitarian intervention," the United States has undertaken illegal actions around the globe in the name of enforcing human rights (as both law and principle). From 1992 through the presidency of Bush II, this policy was embraced despite the fact that "[t]here is no customary rule that construes military intervention as the way to 'enforce' human rights law" (Cohen 2005, 183). In fact, what we find is that virtually all of these interventions (*especially with respect to Iraq*) had one overarching common denominator—a deployment of US forces to protect the interests of US elites against any potential enemy or rival that threatened to "... possess the kinds of weapons of mass destruction the United States first developed and still wished to monopolize" (Johnson 2004, 22).

The primary concern about weapons of mass destruction is a determinative preoccupation among US elites because of their overwhelming desire to figure out how best to project American military power so that it will not only secure the interests of US corporate investors, but also be capable of being able to secure ready access to oil and energy resources in oil-producing regions. The holy trinity of corporate profits, the capacity to project US military forces around the globe to ensure access to resources, investments, and vital regions, along with the continuing need for a ready supply of oil and energy resources to keep the imperial project on the move has largely defined the contours of current US foreign policy and its central purposes (Bacevich 2010; Chomsky 2003; Clark 1992; Engelhardt 2010; Johnson 2004, 2010; Klare 1995, 2001, 2004, 2008; Loveman 2010; Singer 2003).

In this regard, Prof. Michael Klare has explicitly analyzed the Pentagon's 2001 report of the Quadrennial Defense Review (QDR), noting that "... the QDR devotes particular attention to the enhancement of American power-projection capacity: 'The United States must retain the capability to send well-armed and logistically supported forces to critical points around the globe, even in the face of enemy opposition.' It also explicitly identifies *overseas oil-producing regions as 'critical points' that American military forces may conceivably have to invade*, going on to assert that because the Middle East, in particular, includes several states with formidable conventional capacities as well as the capacity to manufacture weapons of mass destruction (WMD), American forces must be strong enough to overpower them and eliminate WMD stockpiles" (Klare 2004, 71; italics added). Hence, in its nuclear policies, as well as its energy policies, the United States has ignored the "rule of law" and endorsed the "rule of might" as the ultimate superpower "right" in exercising its hegemonic prerogatives. In short, the preservation of the US monopoly of power—in all of its dimensions—is seen by Republicans and Democrats alike as the ultimate purpose to which US military and economic power should be dedicated.[4] This is the central reason why the Bush doctrine not only reigned supreme from 2001 to 2008, but explains why it continues on into the foreign policy plans of the Obama administration, largely unencumbered (Lowenthal et al. 2009; Prevost and Campos 2007; Renshon 2010; Rosen 2008).

As a corollary benefit to its duplicitous use of the concept of "humanitarian intervention," it is also arguable that the United States has sought to maintain and spread its influence through its various hegemonic and geopolitical advantages as a globally-oriented economic superpower. Peter Gowan commenting on the ramifications of this matter from both a philosophical and historical perspective astutely notes that

[w]orld politics is not enclosed within a constitutional state order with a fully fledged legal regime and law-enforcement agency. Legal thought and practices are no doubt a significant element in inter-national affairs . . . but international public law remains a rather half-formed, perhaps only embryonic force . . . Furthermore, when powers like the US or UK go to war they do so for reasons of national interest, in pursuit of state objectives. As for the idea that attacking a country is equal to enforcing a law, the greatest of classical liberal rights-based philosophers, Immanuel Kant, long ago taught us that war is inherently anti-law (Gowan 1999, 143).

The proposition that "war is inherently anti-law" is evident in all of those enterprises, wars, and US interventions since 1992 that have been essentially dedicated and committed to the spread and integration of American-style "market democracy" via globalization. Since 1992, the net effect of these polices has been to corrupt international law and to weaken the mandates of the UN Charter, a charter that was originally designed to facilitate the en-forcement of global peace by relying on the UN Security Council to control and circumscribe the unilateral capacity of states to wage wars or conduct interventions. On this point, C. G. Weeramantry, a judge of the International Court of Justice from 1991 to 2000, has noted that

[w]ith even rudimentary knowledge of international law at least a dozen legal principles would immediately spring to mind which are violated and mangled by the use of force against Iraq . . . Chapter VII of the UN Charter is a tightly structured framework within which alone force can be used in the new world order that emerged from the chaos of World War II. It gives to the Security Council the exclusive authority to determine the existence of any threat to the peace, breach of the peace or act of aggression. Once so determined it is the Security Council alone that can make recommendations and decide what action should be taken to restore international peace and security (Weeramantry 2005, 21).

Yet, despite the clear mandate of the UN Charter and the well-established responsibility of the UN Security Council with respect to matters of war and peace, it is clear that the imperial agenda of Anglo-American corporate interests has been substituted for the governing force and authority of the UN Charter and the clearly articulated mandates of international law. In this situation, we discover the reality that the unipolar power of the United States, as a hegemonic state, has been substituted for the governing authority of the UN Charter and the role of the UN Security Council in matters of war and peace with regard to the Iraq War. As such, there has been not even been a semblance of hegemonic state accountability for the crimes against peace and against humanity, in the case of the US assertion of its decision to unilaterally embark upon the Iraq war and occupation.

Tragically, it is also true that the United Nation's oversight of the IMF and World Bank has been corrupted and weakened by the imperial agenda of Anglo-American corporate interests that have corrupted the US and UK governments by what essentially amounts to what the business community would call a "hostile takeover." Hence, the net effect of these efforts have been to engage in the practice of "exclusionary governance" and to remove democratic accountability, transparency, and regulatory oversight capacities from governing functions and policies that were theoretically supposed to remain in the hands of "We the People." What we find in place of democratic controls in the United States, for example, is that the corporate globalization agenda—as pursued by Bechtel, Lockheed-Martin, Chevron, and Halliburton—has roots in the IMF, World Bank, and WTO. The primary goal of these various groups and interests has been to promote so-called "free-trade" policies, which allow the world's largest corporations to earn vast wealth for a few elite players at the expense of entire populations (Juhasz 2006). Hence, these actions work at cross purposes with the United Nation's own developmental agenda and goals, which are designed to eliminate global poverty and are normatively supposed to be ultimately and primarily dedicated to the protection of human rights.

Chalmers Johnson has traced the trajectory of this process and concluded that "[p]erhaps the most deceptive aspect of globalization was its claim to embody fundamental and inevitable technological developments rather than the conscious policies of Anglo-American political elites trying to advance the interests of their own countries at the expense of others" (Johnson 2004, 260). It is a problem that has grown with tragic frequency since 1945. On this matter, Peter Gowan notes that "[b]efore 1945 different capitalist centers had different geographic zones of political and economic dominance. The United States ended that arrangement, making the whole capitalist world its geographic sphere of political dominance. On this basis it shaped and reshaped the conditions and forms of international capital accumulation throughout the capitalist world" (Gowan 2004, 57).

It is because of this history and the current threat that this sociopolitical and socioeconomic set of arrangements poses to world law, the UN Charter, and to world peace, that I have reiterated the immediate need to employ and enact all of the provisions of his PHSA—in conjunction with the Nuremberg Principles and UN Charter—so that a concerted effort can be finally undertaken to counteract this geopolitical nightmare (Paupp 2009). The necessity and urgency of this proposal is further underscored by Samir Amin in his essay "*Confronting Empire*" (Amin 2004, 104–11). Reflecting on the Bush II administration's invasion of Iraq, Amin has asserted that "[t]he idea of 'preventive war,' now claimed as a right by Washington, does away with any notion of international law" (Amin 2004, 104). Hence, without taking responsive actions to counteract Washington's imperial prerogatives to engage in "preemptive wars" for geopolitical advantage, the result is that "[t]he abolition of the common rights of all peoples is already underway" (Amin 2004, 105).

What has already transpired as a result of this doctrine and policy of aggressive war-making is a domino effect of tragic proportions for humanity. It has been a policy that began with "... the single-minded focus on maximizing the financial profitability of dominant capital in the short term, putting the military at the disposal of this capital, and delinking this capital from any system of human values" (Amin 2004, 105). As this delinking of capital took place with support by the military forces of the US Empire, the collateral damage to global relations between states has been enormous. Before the US invasion of Iraq, both France and Germany led an effort to make sure that the United States and Iraq were engaged in dialogue and, further, that the UN weapons inspectors would be given a chance to prove that no weapons of mass destruction (WMD) were left in Iraq—thereby removing the formal justification for an invasion by US forces. There were several interrelated reasons for this approach: "Lead by France and Germany, most states followed suit to press for more stringent weapons inspections in Iraq and to engage the United States in dialogue, not from a position of weakness or in an effort to revive an outdated institution, as the Bush administration argued, but because they understood that bypassing the United Nations meant that all countries could become vulnerable to the whims of US hegemonic power" (Ehrenberg et al. 2010, xxiii). The urgency to enact and employ the PHSA emerges from this need to curtail any further aggressive wars or interventions by the United States as a hegemonic power (Paupp 2009).

Given this history, we are left to ask fundamental questions about the future of international law in the shaping of a more peaceful twenty-first century global civilization. In the effort to understand and contemplate the possibilities for building such a civilization with a vibrant and effective legal basis to sustain it remains a huge challenge. What realistic prospects can we hold out for a revival and application of the Nuremberg Principles? Also, can we expect any further progress in the field of international law or the general effectiveness of the United Nations if the PHSA is taken seriously and applied to real-world problems? In short, can we have any real hope that war criminals will be brought to justice or that war crimes will be effectively addressed by the International Criminal Court and/or some UN sanctioned tribunal on the subject? Samir Amin has asked, "Will the dominant class in the United States be able to carry forward the criminal program behind which it has rallied?" (Amin 2004, 110). His answer is that, "... this coalition can only govern if other segments of capital accept it. Clearly, political, diplomatic, and even military setbacks could encourage the minority in the US establishment who are ready to renounce the military adventures the country is engaged in." (Amin 2004, 111).

In light of the Nuremberg Principles and their application to the US-waged wars of aggression in both Vietnam and Iraq, Amin's challenge for the world's peoples—especially the American people—is not a new challenge. It is a challenge that goes to the heart of the integrity of the UN, international law, US Constitutional law, and the rules and principles that have governed the entire structure of international security right up until the 2003 invasion of Iraq by the Bush II administration. Yet, it is the Nuremberg Principles in particular that have the greatest salience on this matter, given their explicit concern with "planning and preparation for aggressive war." The United States and allied war crimes trial in Nuremberg actually hanged members of the Nazi regime for crimes that the United States later engaged in committing in both the Vietnam and Iraq War. Hence, the issue of principle and fundamental values in the conduct of global affairs is what is really at stake in this discussion. Writing on this issue in his 1971 book, *Nuremberg and Vietnam: An American Tragedy*, Telford Taylor, the US Chief Counsel at Nuremberg, noted that "[h]owever history may ultimately assess the wisdom or un-wisdom of the war crimes trials, one thing is indisputable: At their conclusion, the United States Government stood legally, politically, and morally committed to the principles enunciated in the charters and judgments of the tribunals . . . Thus, the integrity of the nation is staked on those principles, and today the questions is how they apply to our conduct of the war in Vietnam, and whether the United States Government is prepared to face the consequences of their application" (Taylor 1971, 94).

Now, in the second decade of the twenty-first century, the same question can be applied with equal force to the situation the US hegemonic state now finds itself in throughout the Middle East in particular, and the rest of the world general. In assessing the meaning of this situation for international order in the twenty-first century, Falk has asserted that "[t]he Iraq War, more than any foreign policy concern since Vietnam, has raised crucial issues about whether the United States government is prepared to comply with the core rules of international law governing the use of force" (Falk 2005, 107). At the most basic level of analysis, Falk concludes that

> [t]he Iraq War showcases the consequences of abandoning a law-oriented approach to foreign policy and world order. It represents for the United States a complete inversion of its earlier role in the aftermath of World War II as champion of the Nuremberg approach to international accountability for those who act on behalf of sovereign states and of the unconditional repudiation of aggressive war. The experience in Iraq would tend to confirm the *practical* wisdom of these earlier *normative* views as to the limits of legal discretion

given to states with respect to recourse to war. The United States, the world, and the future would all benefit from the voluntary acceptance of the constraints of international law as the foundation for a global security system (Falk 2005, 117–18; italics in original).

In reflecting on the war crimes of the Bush II administration with regard to its wars of aggression and crimes against peace in Iraq and Afghanistan, Prof. Michael Haas notes that

> [t]he real complaining party is Civilization. International law, a struggling and imperfect force, points to the sequence of aggressions and war crimes and to the greater potentialities for destruction elsewhere in the days to come. It is not necessary to argue the proposition that to start or wage an aggressive war has the moral qualities of the worse of crimes. The refuge of the defendants can be only in their hope that international law will lag so far behind the moral sense of mankind that conduct that is crime in the moral sense must be regarded as innocent in law. Civilization asks whether law is so laggard as to be utterly helpless to deal with crimes by criminals of this order of importance. It does not expect that war can be made impossible. It does expect that juridical action will put the forces of international law, its precepts, its prohibitions, and, most of all, its sanctions, on the side of peace, so that men and women of good will, in all countries, may have "leave to live by no one's leave, underneath the law" (Haas 2009, 219–20).

Expanding the Circle of Human Solidarity

In combination, by examining the issues of UN reform, nuclear abolition, and accountability for war crimes and crimes against humanity through the ICC, it is hoped that we shall finally discover, throughout the course of this chapter, how the power of egocentrism can be transformed into altruistic traits—such as compassion, trust, and nonviolence. Following Ikeda's lead in this area, we can blend principle with practice as we recognize the salience and relevance of why Nichiren spoke of earthly desires being used as fuel for the flame of wisdom. In large measure it is because "[t]he underlying delusions that drive our desires—including the desire for the development of science and civilizations—can be essentially transformed in a way that changes selfishness into altruism, violence into nonviolence, and suspicion into trust" (Ikeda and Krieger 2002, 108).

Ikeda identifies two intertwined realities that have defined human history up to this point: delusions, on the one hand, and the power of transformation, on the other. The central delusions of both human history and our current global crisis may be described in terms of a loss of moral ends or goals in both our individual and collective lives. The overcoming of delusion has been discussed in previous chapters as we have reviewed the central elements of Ikeda's philosophy. The basis and starting point of Ikeda's approach to change is with the inner transformation of one's deepest tendencies and motivations, which describes the essential nature of the human revolution. In turn, Ikeda's focus upon the necessity for undertaking one's inner transformation is testimony to the challenge that confronts not only each and every individual, but ultimately all nations, cultures, and the promise of an emerging global civilization. That is because, as Martin Luther King, Jr. noted, *"[o]ur hope for creative living in this world house that we have inherited lies in our ability to re-establish the moral ends of our lives in personal character and social justice.* Without this spiritual and moral reawakening we shall destroy ourselves in the misuse of our own instruments"* (King 1968, 201–02; italics added). In no other endeavor of the human arena is this more manifestly true that than of nuclear weapons and the danger they pose to planetary extinction. This reality returns our attention to how we define ourselves and how we define the nature of "human security."

For Ikeda and his contemporaries, the challenge presented to us for redefining global security as human security entails a sense of responsibility among all global citizens to insist on a more sustainable concept of human security. This is hardly a new idea, but it has become a more urgent one. As C. Wright Mills put it in 1960, at the height of Cold War tensions, "As war now means the universal annihilation of man, so peace now is to the universal interests of man . . . War is now total; therefore, peace must now be total" (Mills 1960, 135–36). Hence, the delusions of war and its false premises about reliance on force—as a way in which we can magically extend the "blessings" of national security—must be replaced by the powerful insight that inner transformation, dialogue, and a visionary transformation of our concept of what constitutes a sustainable peace, requires that we build a global "human security" structure which benefits all of humanity. As Martin Luther King, Jr. acknowledged in 1968, *"In a real sense, all life is interrelated. The agony of the poor impoverishes the rich; the betterment of the poor enriches the rich.* We are inevitably our brother's keeper because we are our brother's brother. *Whatever affects one directly affects all indirectly"* (King 1968, 211; italics added).

Ikeda has maintained that "Buddhism teaches that the altruistic way of life glows with the flame of wisdom. *The bodhisattva way is to let wisdom put knowledge to use and to couple compassion with compassionate action"* (Ikeda and Krieger 2002, 108; italics added). We have already seen this process evolving at the regional level—as with ASEAN and the European Union (see chapter 5). Throughout the course of this chapter, we shall expand upon growing meaning, promise, and potential of these regional developments by also examining the dynamic and transformative role of *"confidence building measures"* (CBMs), which have already played such an essential role in the improvement of East–West relations during the Cold War (Krepon 1999,

1). Previously, these confidence building measures were briefly addressed in our case study about the inner transformations of President John F. Kennedy and Nikita Khrushchev during the 1962 Cuban missile crisis, followed by the signing of the 1963 Limited Test Ban Treaty (see chapter 3). We now seek to expand upon CBMs in this chapter in order to show how they can be used in building a more peaceful global civilization and be employed in the task of fundamentally transforming a global nuclear weapons culture into a global culture characterized by *nuclear weapons free zones* (NWFZ) that ultimately leads to the abolition of all nuclear weapons.

This chapter also undertakes the task of addressing the dynamic inter-relationships that exist between the UN, the ICC, and the abolition of nuclear weapons. To that end, we shall examine the promise of UN reform in combination with addressing the attendant interplay between the realms of global civil society, governments, and the rulings of international courts that have served to demand the abolition of nuclear weapons and have thereby created the possibility of achieving the abolition of nuclear weapons. As a consequence of this recent history, we shall engage in an analysis of these legal rulings and the actions which they mandate. In so doing, peace movements and global social movements for nuclear abolition shall be examined in conjunction with a complementary discussion of reasons which support the strengthening of the International Criminal Court (ICC). After all, the ICC represents and embodies an internationally-sanctioned and ratified institutional means through which the Nuremberg Principles can finally find a voice and through which criminal liability can be assessed for crimes against humanity, crimes against peace, and war crimes. Obviously, this can come to include planning and preparation for war using or threatening to use outlawed nuclear weapons, (based on the 1996 Advisory Opinion by the International Court of Justice on the *Legality of the Threat or Use of Nuclear Weapons*). In this same juridical setting, humanity can begin to realize the full potential of the PHSA and, in so doing, global citizens can be inspired to work more effectively for the ultimate realization of a just and peaceful global civilization. In short, humanity has reached a critical juncture where we shall *either* remain locked in self-defeating discourses about what the boundaries and limitations are with respect to the national interest, national defense, and the prerogatives of the hegemonic state *or*, in the alternative, find that it will be more beneficial to move in the direction of a global "*human republic*" in which all peoples can be victors.

With regard to these choices and issues, Ikeda presents us with a twenty-first century challenge and a dynamic proposition:

> Whether we can make the new century one of symbiosis and hope depends on the extent to which citizens awaken to the needs of the whole human race, expand the circle of global solidarity, and work

actively within that circle. *What's important is the wisdom of each individual living by a firm philosophy rooted in respect for life. Such wise, ordinary people have the power to halt war and the abuse of authority.* Instead of continuing a society dominated by war and violence, our struggle is to build *a human republic* in which everyone is happy and all are victors. Rather than giving into fate or circumstances, let us prove our humanity and show its true power as we write a new history of peace. Resolutely and courageously striving to that end indicates that we have chosen hope (Ikeda and Krieger 2002, 180; italics added).

To that end, as we next turn an examination of the specifics of what is involved in both UN reform and nuclear abolition, we will be primarily considering the challenge of how best to begin building a human security structure which benefits all humanity.

Building a "Human Security" Structure which Benefits all Humanity

In previous chapters, I have referenced the importance that Ikeda assigns to the idea of "humanitarian competition." It is the concept of a "win-win world" that begins with the premise that what is important is to set aside egotistical motives. By so doing, we are then free to strive to protect and improve not only our own lives, but also the lives of others. The time has now arrived for this principle to guide both the tasks of UN reform and the abolition of nuclear weapons. To do so will mean that *humanitarian competition* should be the guiding principle for the new era. What this involves from Ikeda's perspective, in the words of Olivier Urbain, is the following: "Combining the concept of a flexible framework allowing different cultures to cooperate, the concept of human security and idea of humanitarian competition, one can list the following elements as constitutive of a global civilization of peace: building a flexible framework for world global governance, keeping a reasonable amount of sovereignty for national governments, placing the emphasis on human security, and ensuring the participation of all individuals and groups" (Urbain 2010, 165).

I have previously addressed how Ikeda's contemporaries have presented proposals and made various suggestions as to how this undertaking may be designed and accomplished. First, creating a flexible framework that allows different cultures to cooperate involves overcoming the "clash of civilizations" and substituting the power of dialogue as a means to reach a consensus on how to engage in humanitarian competition. Second, the retention of a reasonable amount of sovereignty for national governments is essential for the practice of democracy at the national, regional, and international levels. The maintenance of this kind of sovereignty should be able to better balance a narrowly defined national interest against the broader and more inclusive conception of the human interest. Third, by centralizing the importance of human security throughout the entire framework and structures of global governance, we maintain that humanity is better positioned to practice the normative and practical strategies that have been articulated by Falk with respect to "*humane governance*" and by me with respect to "*inclusionary governance.*" By joining the theoretical, empirical, and normative components of these governing strategies together, in the service of humanitarian competition, we believe that genuine human security can be achieved and sustained. After all, for Ikeda, the starting point of the process towards such an inclusive global civilization is predicated upon our capacity to engage in personal relations and dialogue as we also exhibit a willingness to "build tolerant and enduring links" (Ikeda 2001a, 132).

Twenty years ago, Robert Johansen published an essay entitled "Toward an Alternative Security System" (Johansen 1991, 252–75). He proposed seven policy models which illustrate the range of options relevant to establishing a more secure global system. The first four options depict the nature of the status quo. The remaining three options, however, point beyond the limitations of the status quo and the logic behind it. The first four options are as follows: (1) "Current US national security policy illustrates the first policy model: a nuclear war-fighting capability" (Johansen 1991, 252); (2) "Mutual assured destruction was a policy designed more to deter war than to carry out nuclear battles" (Johansen 1991, 254); (3) "A minimum deterrent posture differs from mutual assured destruction in that it would deliberately stop the nuclear arms race by resisting political and economic pressures for overkill and by claiming the need for no more than the minimum number of weapons required to destroy one's opponent" (Johansen 1991, 256); (4) "A defensive weapons system, based on conventional arms, has received surprisingly little attention, especially given its special relevance to Europe" (Johansen 1991, 257).

The remaining three options are more progressive with respect to undertaking Ikeda's principles about the values of coexistence, the use of limited force for self-defense, a concept of global security informed by a worldview that while human beings are responsible for having created the current war-system, the fact remains that human beings have the capacity to change it. So Johansen's fifth option: (5) "A policy to establish a peacekeeping federation seeks to strengthen regional and global international organizations so they can verify and eventually enforce multilateral arms reductions. Advocates of this approach believe that a decentralized balance of power system can never provide lasting peace and, therefore, should be replaced. *No mystery surrounds the type of system that can keep peace. After all, most disputes inside national societies are resolved without violence.* Domestic conflicts often involve millions of people with different languages, religious traditions, races, and lifestyles. *If such numbers can co-exist peacefully, then the appropriate conditions and political institutions, if established, could also provide peace for all of the planet's citizens"* (Johansen 1991, 259; italics added).

Between the years 2002 and 2008, Ikeda renewed his call for organized global solidarity concerning environmental problems, human rights, and nuclear disarmament—among other issues. In this regard, Ikeda has regarded a consciousness of our global citizenship as the basis for acknowledging our shared global solidarity, thereby leading to the creation of political institutions which promote dialogue and problem-solving with the human interest uppermost in mind (Urbain 2010, 167). Clearly, the greatest benefit of such solidarity in changing the international system and previous conceptions of global relations governing it are that the "balance of power" system is removed from the lexicon of international affairs and statecraft because its pursuit has never provided lasting peace and because it reinforces geopolitical tendencies that are supportive of hegemony and hierarchy. Therefore, to undertake the removal of the "balance of power" concept and practice from international statecraft is a precondition for realizing the PHSA insofar as it forces hegemonic states to restrain their aggressive tendencies and, instead, adopt a more mutually cooperative set of policies that augment the functioning of a peaceful global civilization.

Johansen's sixth option notes that "[a] security policy based on civilian resistance for national defense is rooted in an understanding, common to all five preceding policies, that the use of power is necessary to defend one's country against external attack" (Johansen 1991, 260). The implementation of such a security policy could, however, become a moot issue if Ikeda's proposal for a Universal Declaration for the Renunciation of War (UDRW) were to be adopted. In 1984 and 1988, Ikeda proposed the UDRW after having been inspired by the Universal Declaration of Human Rights (UDHR). In the 1984 peace proposal, he wrote as follows: "I propose that the United Nations adopt a *Universal Declaration Renouncing War.* Consensus among nations on such a declaration would be an important breakthrough in actualizing peace." Ikeda then concluded, "Lest I be criticized for overoptimistically believing the goals can be attained at once, I further propose that, as a first step, nongovernmental organizations (NGOs) begin the process by building up a foundation for the ultimate adoption of a *Universal Declaration Renouncing War* in the United Nations" (Ikeda 1984-PP, 35; Urbain 2010, 171; italics added).

Clearly, by placing his faith in the capacity of the United Nations to garner a global constituency to support his proposed UDRW, we discover Ikeda's strategy of peace is predicated upon building up a sense of global solidarity between individuals, groups, nations, and regions that can finally culminate in a global consensus within the venue of an international association of States, as we have with the United Nations. Under this rubric, concerns with self-defense become a concern involving the defense of all.

Hence, human security moves from being an ideal to be attained toward a practical reality in which every nation and peoples want to invest in and be supportive of because it represents their own best interest while, at the same time, guaranteeing compliance. In this regard, it might also be argued that instead of merely subscribing to a "declaration" that Ikeda's proposed UDRW be made into a treaty in which all nations become signatories.

The reason for this alternative suggestion as to legal form is that, according to John Burroughs, "[t]reaties by their very nature involved some sacrifice of sovereignty. In exchange, treaty regimes contribute to national and global security in important ways, including by: (1) articulating global norms; (2) promoting and recognizing compliance with norms; (3) building monitoring and enforcement mechanisms; (4) increasing the likelihood of detecting violations and effectively addressing them; (5) providing a benchmark for measurement of progress; (6) establishing a foundation of confidence, trust, experience, and expertise for further progress; (7) providing criteria to guide states' activities and legislation, and focal points for discussion of policy issues." Hence, Burroughs concludes: "Over the long term, treaty regimes are a far more reliable basis for achieving global policy objectives and compliance with norms than 'do as we say, not as we do' directives from an overwhelmingly powerful state" (Burroughs 2003, xiii). Also, insofar as treaty regimes are more effective in achieving global policy directives, it follows that a treaty which embodies the language and objectives of Ikeda's UDRW is a more effective way to enact, advance, and employ the PHSA because it would bring the full force of measures of compliance and oversight to bear upon the narrowly defined geopolitical priorities and calculations of a hegemonic power.

In conjunction with Ikeda's UDRW, my PHSA, and Burrough's advocacy of treaty regimes, we should also include a reference to Ronald McCoy's case for a *"Nuclear Weapons Convention."* According to McCoy,

> [a] Nuclear Weapons Convention is an international treaty that would prohibit the development, production, testing, deployment, stockpiling, transfer, threat, or use of nuclear weapons. It would provide for the elimination of nuclear weapons in much the same way comparable treaties have banned landmines and chemical and biological weapons. In a wider sense, a Nuclear Weapons Convention would embody the universal condemnation of nuclear weapons by society and the codification of the customary norm against all weapons of mass destruction. It would embrace national and international measures that prohibit and delegitimize nuclear weapons. Such a treaty would engender a wider social and political movement away from reliance on nuclear weapons and the use of military force to resolve conflict, and would reflect the desires and responsibilities of the international community for a less militarized world. It would

accomplish the long-standing objective of advancing nuclear disarmament to the point of abolition, thus freeing present and future generations and ecosystems from the unparalleled threat of total destruction" (McCoy 2009, 189).

The case for enacting a *"Nuclear Weapons Convention"* leads us to a consideration of Johansen's seventh and final option.

Johansen's seventh and final option notes that

> [w]e can imagine yet another policy, one that aims at achieving global security. For reasons of prudence and ethics, its purpose is to provide security equally for all people. In practice, security for one is connected with security for all. In ethics, it is not right that security for one nation should be purchased at the price of insecurity for another. This worldview is informed by an appreciation of diplomatic history and scientific studies of war. It is realism without dogma. Given humanity's . . . knowledge of the technology of destruction and willingness to use it, this approach finds lasting security possible only with effective efforts to abolish war itself. According to this view, the current international system is, at its base, a war system. Although this system persists with such resilience that it *seems* to be a part of nature, in fact human beings created it. *Human beings can transform it"* (Johansen 1991, 261; italics added).

This option is most congruent with the arguments advanced throughout this book. In fact, at the beginning of this chapter we discussed the necessity for the international system to recognize the mandate in the UN Charter itself to honor the sovereign equality of all nations.

Global human security is predicated upon the practical observance of the norm honoring the "sovereign equality" of all nations—both as a rule and as a practical guide to statecraft and the conduct of international relations. When actualized in practice, the norm of sovereign equality has the practical effect of enforcing the mandates for state behavior which are contained in the PHSA. This mandate, in turn, has the capacity to force even a hegemonic state to restrain itself in its conduct throughout the world as it seeks to pursue its geopolitical objectives. By virtue of having had to remove the threat of force or the actual use of force from its arsenal of influence and statecraft options, the hegemonic state—and all other States—remain bound and accountable to the PHSA (Paupp 2009, 184–88, 193–211). This is necessarily the case because the war-system itself is, due to being made accountable for criminal acts in the geopolitical realm, being slowly abolished and replaced by practices that legitimate and protect global human security as a global public good and as a matter of international concern with which all nations are invested. This approach has particular salience with respect to the possession of nuclear weapons. According to David Krieger, we can argue that "[t]he possession of nuclear weapons can be viewed as a crime of state, and this crime would apply to the nine states in possession of nuclear weapons. But beyond state criminal activity, there should also be culpability for the crime against the future by the leading state and military officials that support and promote nuclear weapons possession, as well as policies that make nuclear war more likely and total nuclear disarmament less likely. In addition, corporations, corporate executives, and scientists who contribute to the maintenance and improvement of nuclear weapons should also be considered culpable for committing a crime against future generations" (Krieger 2009, 113).

Establishing culpability for the crimes of aggressive states and also establishing accountability for the individuals who support them and carry out their orders in violation of international law is at the heart of both the Nuremberg Principles and the PHSA. History reminds us that "[a]t the Nuremberg Tribunals following World War II, the principle was upheld that all individuals who commit crimes under international law are responsible for such acts, and this is true even if they are high government officials and domestic law does not hold such acts to be crimes" (Krieger 2009, 113). Pursuant to the Nuremberg Principles, the culpability of individuals for the commission of crimes in the name of the state has been a long-established principle since 1946. In his 1988 presidential address to the American Society of Criminology, William Chambliss defined state crime as *"acts defined by law as criminal and committed by state officials in pursuit of their job as representatives of the state."* Despite the fidelity that his wording exhibited toward the spirit and letter of the Nuremberg Principles, a few years after Chambliss provided this definition, he chose to update it with a caveat in 1995, in which he revised his definition of state crime to include *"behavior that violates international agreements and principles established in the courts and treaties of international bodies"* (Paupp 2009, 194). The caveat is important because it expands the principle of accountability for state crimes beyond the Nuremberg Principles per se. It does so by reminding his audience that international law—as embodied in international agreements established in the courts and treaties of international bodies—expands the scope of the Nuremberg Principles so that the force of these principles can be understood as having accessed acceptance in a variety of legal forums and instruments.

In being able to understand that the force of the Nuremberg Principles transcends a particular historical moment, it becomes clear that these principles can attain a universal meaning and protective force throughout the global community. This is especially relevant when we look at the role of international protection mechanisms that exist under the auspices of the United Nations. The United Nation's human rights and humanitarian enforcement mechanisms are either UN-treaty or UN Charter-based. Within the UN enforcement system, there are diverse organs, such as courts/tribunals, committees, special procedural mechanisms, working groups, rapporteurs, experts, and representatives (Martin et al. 2006, 6). The only true courts/ tribunals at present are the following: (1) International Court of Justice ("The Hague" or ICJ); (2) International Criminal Court (ICC); (3) International Criminal Tribunals for the Former Yugoslavia (ICTY); and (4) International Criminal Tribunal for Rwanda (ICTR). These human rights and humanitarian enforcement mechanisms of the United Nations represent a strengthening and application of the Nuremberg Principles in late twentieth century and early twenty-first century global society. As such, they also represent key legal components of a global security policy that has evolved to meet the needs of persons who have been unable to elicit either justice or protection from the States in which they reside.

Yet, even beyond their focus on the individual victims of State abuses, we can recognize a new reality—a reality that stands for the proposition that these courts and tribunals also embody an attempt to build a dependable global security order that involves not only war prevention, but also reflects the sincere commitment of the entire international community to support a worldview in which normative boundaries are at least as important as territorial boundaries. Therefore, our evolving global consciousness speaks to the realization that, in the final analysis, any truly meaningful and effective conceptualization of human security must embody a sense of species solidarity. Such a worldview contains the normative force to make universal claims upon all states so that they will attain to a level of accountability for their actions and will, thereby, be forced into a position of responsibility in which they shall finally be obligated (in theory and practice) to abide by the principles of the UN Charter and the Nuremberg Charter. By recognizing that all members of the human race (and not just some segments of it) are deserving of protection, this worldview—in combination with the aforementioned UN human rights and humanitarian enforcement mechanisms—will be empowered to create a more peaceful, just, and sustainable global civilization.

In looking toward to realization of that end, Robert Johansen has argued that a truly effective global security policy must invariably seek to include the following five central and distinguishing features: "First, it tries to prevent the desire for short-range advantage from dominating decisions at the expense of long-run interests" (Johansen 1991, 261). "Second, the global security approach must emphasize the importance of providing greatly expanded positive incentives rather than relying largely on negative military threats as the means to influence other nations' security policies and to establish a dependable security order" (Johansen 1991, 262). "Third, a global security policy emphasizes a positive image of peace which includes much more than war prevention" (Johansen 1991, 263). "Fourth, this approach moves beyond the familiar, singular focus on security for one nation-state. All people of the human race, not one national segment of it, consciously become the beneficiaries of security policies. A sense of species solidarity and global citizenship becomes more equitable" (Johansen 1991, 263). "Fifth, in this worldview normative boundaries are at least as important as territorial boundaries" (Johansen 1991, 264; italics added). Having outlined these principles and features for building an effective global security policy, we now turn to a discussion of contemporary trends toward the practice of "*Confidence-and Security-Building Measures*" (CSBMs), the historical evolution and development of *Nuclear Weapons Free Zones* (NWFZs), and the promise of a *Nuclear Weapons Free World* (NWFW).

Global Confidence Building and Nuclear Weapons Free Zones

The above-referenced discussion about the need to pursue long-term interests for the sake of global human security brings us to the transformative role and importance of CSBMs. CSBMs include ". . . formal and informal measures, whether unilateral, bilateral, or multilateral, that address, prevent, or resolve uncertainties among states, including military and political elements" (Cossa 1999, 27). In keeping with Ikeda's emphasis upon the central importance of dialogue in human affairs, as well seeking "win-win solutions," respect for cultural differences in and among peoples and regions, achieving a shared consensus around global norms, the need for institution-building to facilitate a sustainable global peace, appreciation of the value of accommodation, the importance of long-term approaches as opposed to short-term fixes, and the need to instil habits of cooperation, we find that the strategies associated with CSBMs are conducive to building the kind of peaceful global civilization that Ikeda has been an advocate on behalf of. Therefore, Table 7.2 is dedicated to outlining and summarizing the key elements of CSBMs.

As already discussed in chapter 6, the regional arrangements designed under ASEAN, pursuant to the *Treaty of Amity and Cooperation* is a concrete embodiment of the above-referenced principles guiding CSBMs. Article 2 of the Treaty of Amity and Cooperation, adopted by ASEAN at its Bali summit in 1976, also contained a statement of the principle of "noninterference in the international affairs of one another." The Declaration of ASEAN Concord, also adopted at Bali, stipulated that "member states shall vigorously develop . . . a strong ASEAN community . . . in accordance with the principles of self-determination, sovereign equality, and noninterference in the internal affairs of other nations" (Acharya 2009a, 71). As such, ASEAN represents the embodiment of a security community, which ". . . must be based on a fundamental, unambiguous and long-term *convergence* of interests among the actors in the avoidance of war" (Acharya 2009a, 19; italics in original). In fact, a major difference between a security community (such as ASEAN) and a collective security arrangement (such as NATO) ". . . relates to the means employed to ensure war avoidance" (Acharya 2009a, 22). In this regard, we find that "[s]ecurity communities . . . inhibit war through the development of reasonably strong and enduring institutions and practices and a sense of 'collective identity'" (Acharya 2009a, 22). Therefore, security communities have a greater advantage in advancing the cause of peace and being in compliance with the UN Charter because "[a] security community . . . seeks to ensure conflict prevention through integrative processes and formal or

Table 7.2   An Outline of Key Confidence and Security-Building Measures

1. CSBMs cannot work in the absence of a desire on the part of the participants to cooperate. There must be a general awareness among participants that the benefits to be gained outweigh both the risks associated with cooperation or the unilateral advantages to be gained by not cooperating. CSBMs must be viewed in "win-win," not "win-lose" terms.

2. CSBMs are most effective if they build upon or are guided by regional (and global) norms. They must be suited to prevailing strategic realities and cultures, in tune with the underlying political, economic, and cultural dynamism of the region in which they are being applied.

3. Foreign models do not necessarily apply. Most measures are highly situation-dependent and require extensive tailoring. Even widely test "universal" models may prove unworkable if an attempt is made to impose them from the outside.

4. CSBMs are stepping stones or building blocks, not institutions. They represent means toward an end. By helping lay the groundwork, however, they may serve as useful preconditions for effective institution building.

5. CSBMs have realistic paradigmatic, clearly defined objectives. Objectives should be measurable, and there should be common agreement as to what constitutes compliance and progress. Measures that overreach the political willingness of the states to implement them can become sources of contention rather than accommodation.

6. Gradual, methodical, incremental approaches seem to work best. Long-term approaches provide greater opportunity for consensus building. Attempts to leapfrog over interim steps are generally ill-advised.

7. The process, in many instances, may be as (or more) important than the product. Nonetheless, while the process of installing habits of cooperation, in and of itself, may initially result in greater levels of trust and understanding over time, some progress on substantive issues must ultimately occur. Dialogue without a defined purpose can be difficult to sustain.

Source: Ralph A. Cossa, "Asia-Pacific Confidence-Building Measures for Regional Security," in *Global Confidence Building: New Tools for Troubled Regions*, edited by Michael Krepon, et al. New York: St. Martin's Press, 1999, p. 28.

informal mechanisms for conflict resolution . . . [Hence] a security community completely delegitimizes the use of force within it. In other words, the use of force has no place in the management of relations among the members of a security community" (Acharya 2009a, 22).

At this point in our discussion, it is worth underscoring the fact that ". . . the United States has not played a leading role in the development of regional cooperative arrangements in East or Southeast Asia. Even during the period 1990–2000—a period when global multilateralism seemed to take center stage in US foreign policy—the United States was often described as being, at most, 'lukewarm' toward new regional arrangements. While the United States did turn to a more multilaterally supportive rhetoric, its support for regional arrangements extended only so far as it did not challenge the primacy or US-centrism of existing bilateral security arrangements" (Ba 2009, 237). These hostile policies of the United States to any efforts that it perceives of as an intrusion on its global hegemony are also indicative of the general contempt exhibited by US foreign policymakers toward the United Nations itself. Insofar as ASEAN and other neighboring states have been moving toward the establishment of NWFZs, in compliance with UN mandates, it is obscene to watch the United States act in such a single-minded fashion with regard to protecting what it perceives to be its declining hegemony.

The global trend toward embracing NWFZs is dramatic and important. It has been noted that "[r]egional nuclear weapons-free zones (NWFZs) have now successfully denuclearized more than half the globe's surface, including almost all of the Southern Hemisphere, at least in relation to regional acquisition of nuclear weapons and land-based stationing by nuclear weapon powers. The recently signed NWFZ treaties in Southeast Asia (SEANFZ Treaty, Bangkok, December 1995) and Africa (Pelindaba Treaty, Cairo, April 1996), together with the already established zones in Antarctica (1959), Latin America (Tlatelolco Treaty 1967) and the South Pacific (Rarotonga Treaty 1985), have effectively created a new legally binding regime of denuclearization, which extends across all the significant land territories of the Southern Hemisphere" (Hamel-Green 1998, 118).

To its credit, the United Nations and its agencies have been at the center of efforts designed to advance, promote, and support the regional nuclear-free zone concept. By the late 1990s, the UN began to revise its original 1975 concepts of NWFZs, as well as strategies to establish them. In this regard, the UN had begun to view the effort to advance ". . . NWFZ establishment as one rung in the regional confidence-building ladder that needs to be erected in the remaining crisis regions of the world, with zone establishment integrated into a wider agenda of arms control, nonproliferation, disarmament, security and political measures that need to be negotiated at both regional and global levels" ((Hamel-Green 1998, 123–24). Looking at the potential long-term significance of this current progress toward denuclearization gives hope to those who seek to build a more peaceful global civilization. In fact, to move beyond the global crisis, it is certain that the increased UN role in ". . . facilitating regional denuclearization will be vital if the nonproliferation regime is to be consolidated, catastrophic use of nuclear or other weapons of mass destruction in future regional conflict averted and the long-term goal of complete nuclear weapons elimination achieved" (Hamel-Green 1998, 133).

The importance of UN success in advancing the regional nuclear-free zone concept can be appreciated even more when we take into account the fact ". . . *if the security of all people is to increase, then the importance of territorial boundaries must diminish and that of political, legal, and ethical boundaries of human behavior must increase.* This rationale deems it better to strengthen a norm against all use of nuclear weapons than to bolster through nuclear deterrence one's defense of disputed territory" (Johansen 1991, 265–66; italics added). The implementation of this rationale not only represents a normative choice, but reflects a practical and empirical choice insofar as "[t]he motivating force for emphasizing the 'human interest' more and narrow national interest less stems not form sentimental globalism, but from prudent calculations of security needs" (Johansen 1991, 266).

In his 1999 peace proposal, Ikeda wrote this: "To make the new millennium an age of peace and hope, we must explore means of deinstitutionalizing war" (Ikeda 1999-PP, 28). Following this statement, Ikeda then makes three concrete proposals in order to effectuate that result: (1) the establishment of a *"Northeast Asia Peace Community"*; (2) the creation of a treaty that would expand the arms trade reporting system so that it can cover more kinds of armament and be more effective; and (3) the creation of an "Ottawa Process" for the abolition of nuclear weapons (Urbain 2010, 172). Ikeda's proposals are mutually supportive initiatives that represent an imaginative approach to bringing an end to a previously unregulated global arms industry. In particular, his proposal for the establishment of a Northeast Asia Peace Community should be understood as an initiative that is designed to work in conjunction with an appreciation of regional efforts to put an end to war-making capacities. Such regional efforts include *"confidence building measures"* (CBMs) which are designed to enhance the role of dialogue in the resolution of disputes. Further, these proposals represent a subtle challenge to the continuing problems and menace to human security posed by the policies pursued by unconstrained US hegemony—including those capacities and practices that have allowed a dangerous global nuclear weapons regime to remain in force and functioning without serious demands for its abolition being made by the United Nations or by the five leading nuclear weapons states who hold permanent membership positions on the UN Security Council.

Ikeda's three-pronged proposal reflects a thought process which centralizes the power of ideas as the best means to change the behavior of human collectivities. This involves moving beyond the cognitive constructs, most of which are trapped within the intellectual matrix of military solutions when addressing security concerns. Ikeda's call to explore means of *"deinstitutionalizing war"* shatters the dialogic structures of paradigms caught up in a militarized context and supplies us with a new forum for debate on all of those issues bound up with the maintenance of a global nuclear weapons regime. For those who remain dedicated to finding peaceful solutions to global problems and concerned about the task of framing a new paradigm for dialogue, who can envision the power of ideas as unleashing alternatives to the status quo, we find a fresh perspective in the words of MacFarlane and Khong who note that

> [w]e start from the assumption that the behavior of states and organizations of states—like the behavior of other human collectivities—is informed by ideas. Policymakers interpret the world around them and the problems it generates in terms of cognitive constructs. These constructs allow them to separate data that are important from data that can be ignored and allow them to prioritize among significant bodies of information and focus on those deemed most important. These structures are constructed in particular social contexts. They supply the parameters within which debate on action occurs and beyond which it generally does not. Cognitive constructs may in turn be strongly informed by normative assumptions or logics of appropriate behavior. They may be accompanied by specific value preferences (what is right and what is wrong), which again are the product of shared historical experience and interpretation of that experience. In other words, behavioral outcomes are not merely the product of external stimuli. They also reflect subjectivity—how these stimuli are interpreted, what significance is attributed to them, and what might be seen to be an appropriate response to them (MacFarlane and Khong 2006, 5).

The recalcitrance of the United States to be supportive of regional efforts aimed at guaranteeing the peace and slowing the escalation of potential arms races—including nuclear arms races (*as between India and Pakistan*)—is nothing short of reckless, irresponsible, and basically lawless (*in the sense that United States' actions in this area directly violate the spirit and intent of the UN Charter and UN policies on how to proceed toward the goal of nuclear disarmament*). This allegation is underscored by the recognition of the fact that "[a]mong the states that perceived existential threats, Pakistan relies more immediately and substantially on its nuclear weapon capability to mitigate the negative effects of the imbalance in conventional military capability and deter large-scale and conventional nuclear attack by India" (Alagappa 2008a,b, 485). In fact, United States' recalcitrance to be supportive of regional efforts aimed at guaranteeing the peace also demonstrates a clear disregard for working toward global security in the nuclear age. By remaining cognitively trapped in a militaristic paradigm, US foreign policymakers have sealed themselves off from the power of ideas that do not correspond to their ultimate concern—which remains the uncritical acceptance and maintenance of US hegemony. As such, US policies which are hostile to ASEAN and other regional efforts and enterprises represent a failure to recognize the new global realities. Hence, it has been argued that ". . . whether there is war or peace will be decided far more often in Washington than any other place. Ultimately, there will not be peace in the world unless all nations relinquish war as an instrument of policy, not only because of ethical or moral reasoning but because wars have become deadlier and more destructive of social institutions. A precondition of peace is for nations not to attempt to impose their vision on others, adjudicate their differences, and never to assume that their need for the economic or strategic resources of another country warrants interference of any sort in its internal affairs" (Kolko 2006, 176).

A year after President Barack Obama set very high expectations with an April 2009 speech in Prague outlining his vision of a world without nuclear weapons, his administration released its Nuclear Posture Review (NPR), which goes some distances toward meeting the president's stated goal of reducing the United States' reliance on nuclear weapons, but is still disappointing. According to Morton H. Halperin, "[t]he most disappointing part of the NPR is the section dealing with decisions about the size of the deployed force and the continued reliance on a version of mutually assured destruction as the basis for determining force size and posture" (Halperin 2010, 18). The inevitability of such a disappointment was apparent shortly after the speech to former Soviet President Mikhail Gorbachev, who noted on April 16, 2009, that the huge US defense budget may prove an "insurmountable obstacle" to reaching that goal (Hanley 2009). Gorbachev, who once bargained with President Reagan over the possibility of eliminating nuclear arsenals, said that the major nuclear powers only recently have recognized that "the current situation is untenable"—a world with more than twenty-three thousand atomic warheads, 95 percent of them in the United States and Russian hands. But a "militarized" world without nuclear weapons would also be untenable, he suggested, since it would leave other nations potentially vulnerable to US military power (Hanley 2009). In fact, as early as 2002, it was apparent to some scholars and commentators that "[w]ith the US retaining and modernizing thousands of nuclear weapons, building missile defenses, and drastically expanding its spending for a wide variety of other high-tech armaments, while issuing military threats against a number of countries almost on a daily basis, any state that sees the possibility of conflict with the US will likely maintain or expand its weapons spending" (Lichterman and Cabasso 2002, 84).

Such is the nature of the current global crisis when the United States fails to relinquish its hegemonic practices and its proclivity to make threats against other nations. By refusing to accept a degree of control by other nations over US actions—as envisioned within the PHSA—the United States is left without restraint to simply proceed with its past practice of seeking imperial domination over other nations, instead of honoring the sovereign equality of all nations, the mandates of the UN Charter, and the Nuremberg Principles, as well as the rules contained in its own US Constitution with respect to the exercise of the "war power" (Paupp 1987, 47–71). The refusal of the US primacy coalition to renounce its practice of giving primary force and attention to its geopolitical concerns, at the expense of the common interests of all humanity, has reinforced the nature and power of the global war system, the proclivity of the United States to engage in threatening to use even its nuclear forces in pursuit of its self-stated objectives, and led to an escalation of international tensions in which threatened states feel obligated to obtain a nuclear strike force in their own defense.[5]

In contrast to this US-centric approach, a genuine "global security policy" would move nuclear disarmament efforts in an entirely different direction. In this regard, as Robert Johansen has astutely noted, "[a] global security policy acknowledges that in the nuclear age nations cannot be secure and still be fully sovereign. This is a dramatic reversal of the time-honored truth, now an untruth, that to be secure a nation must be sovereign . . . For the United States to reject a degree of control by other nations over United States' actions means in turn that the United States cannot obtain control over the behavior of others—except through imperial domination, which is no longer a reasonable possibility. In short, to gain limits on the military behavior of others requires willingness to accept limits on oneself. *To achieve fair and dependable restraints on the use of force should be the overriding purpose of diplomacy. To achieve such limits is worth a price at least as high as now is paid to continue the arms buildup, which decreases our security over time and speeds the decay of human civilization*" (Johansen 1991, 265; italics added).

Clearly, Ikeda's perspective on how to achieve global human security can be neatly conjoined with Johansen's analysis on how best to avoid the "decay of human civilization" and work instead toward the realization of a peaceful global civilization. To that end, if we return to the example of CSBMs, discussed above, we have the capacity to discover an approach to human security that can be employed not only at the regional level, but also applied at the global level. This is a possibility because, as far as the conduct of global governance is concerned, it is equally affected by challenges associated with the need to engage people in the process of moving toward genuine consensus-building in a world of diverse states, cultures, and religions. So, returning to the Asian context, we discover that "[w]ithin the Asia-Pacific region, preference is generally given to measures that address specific security problems, that take into account the unique geo-strategic character and cultures of the region and subregions, that are relevant to the prevailing stage of political accommodation among all participating states, and that build upon historical and institutional experiences in the region" (Cossa 1999, 28–29). This dynamic is outlined below in Table 7.3, which contains some general observations about "confidence building measures" (CBMs) in the Asia-Pacific context.

In viewing the success of this approach over the past four decades, especially since the ratification of the Southeast Asian Nuclear Weapons Free Zone (SEANWFZ) Treaty in 1997, we find that ". . . despite the proliferation trends characterizing Northeast and South Asia, the countries of Southeast Asia have made clear that acquiring nuclear weapons is not important to their security interests at this juncture. Its deficiencies notwithstanding, SEANWEZ Treaty stands as a firm expression of self-renunciation of such weapons by all Southeast Asian states" (Seng 2008, 468). These emerging regional realities point toward a pathway wherein which humanity can forge the foundation for the realization of a new global nuclear order. After all, the Cold War nuclear order emerged in the context of a largely Eurocentric Soviet-American confrontation which meant that "Asia was a sideshow in that order. Policies, strategies, and agreements reached in a Eurocentric context were

Table 7.3   Asia-Pacific CBMs—General Observations

1. CBMs cannot work in the absence of a desire to cooperate.
2. CBMs must be viewed in "win-win," not "win-lose" terms.
3. CBMs are most effective if they build upon regional/global norms.
4. Foreign models do not necessarily apply.
5. CBMs are stepping stone or building blocks, not institutions.
6. CBMs should have realistic, pragmatic, clearly defined objectives.
7. Gradual, methodological, incremental approaches work best.
8. Unilateral and bilateral approaches can serve as useful models.
9. The process may be as (or more) important than the product.
10. As regards Asia-Pacific CBMs in particular, remember that
    —the Asia-Pacific region is not homogeneous
    —there is a preference for informal structures
    —consensus building is a key prerequisite
    —there is a general distrust of outside "solutions"
    —there is a genuine commitment to the principle of noninterference in one another's internal affairs.

Source: Ralph A. Cossa, "Asia-Pacific Confidence-Building Measures for Regional Security," in *Global Confidence Building: New Tools for Troubled Regions*, edited by Michael Krepon, et al. New York: St. Martin's Press, 1999, p. 29.

imposed on Asia. The implications for Asia were often an afterthought. The Cold War is out of sync with present realities . . . A new nuclear order must center on the Asian security region, which has six nuclear weapon states (six including Israel; even if North Korea is included) and which has become a core world region with potential to emerge as the central region of the world in the twenty-first century" (Alagappa 2008a,b, 535).

When viewed in the newly emerging context of a *"multicentric world of rising regions"*—a world that is increasingly being driven by the ideology of regionalism and the processes of regionalization—we are better equipped to appreciate the fact that in ASEAN, and across the region of Southeast Asia in general, there is an emerging new dynamic for peace, for dialogue, for progress on nuclear disarmament. These trends are transpiring at a time when major efforts are also being made toward regional economic integration (Paupp 2009). In this regard, some scholars have already concurred with the assessment that "[t]he ASEAN Charter will clearly be an important step toward rule-based regionalism, although its current emphasis is on regional economic integration, not security cooperation, much less cooperation on nonproliferation" (Seng 2008, 469). In short, the phenomena of regionalism and regionalization are forces which are unleashing a number of complementary trends that have global implications. These trends include the following: (1) demilitarization; (2) depolarization; (3) denationalization, and finally; (4) transnationalization. In combination, the greatest benefit of these trends is that they are converging to accomplish something in human history that has not yet been achieved, which is the realization of the sovereign equality of all nations (the UN's original dream) and the building of a global culture of reciprocity.

At this point, I need to pause in order to more clearly define what is meant by these aforementioned terms and how they relate to one another. Robert Johansen has supplied us with such a formula, which is as follows: "Whereas *demilitarization* pertains to military affairs, *depolarization* applies to political and economic conditions, *denationalization* to social, cultural, and psychological factors, and *transnationalization* to institutions. More specifically, *depolarization* reflects political and economic efforts to soften rigid bloc and alliance boundaries, to diminish East-West and North-South conflicts, and to reduce antagonism between adversaries wherever possible. Hegemonic states, for example, should tailor their political and economic policies to achieve greater equity for all societies. *Reciprocity* in economic and political relations, regardless of a state's ideology, is the touchstone of depolarization" (Johansen 1991, 267; italics added). All of these terms may be subsumed under Ikeda's definition of *"humanitarian competition,"* while the legal concept of the sovereign equality of all states and the need to hold hegemonic states accountable for their "exceptionalism" has been addressed by my PHSA (Paupp 2009).

What we are left with is an agenda that addresses the current global crisis and helps us to envision how we may yet move beyond it. In the alternative, if we allow the current global system to remain in place, based as it is on an interstate imbalance of military power, then such a result will allow the current global crisis to cascade over the entire planet because the current world system is designed to inhibit the denationalization of human affairs and to discourage the growth of human solidarity across national boundaries. Such a result will not only damage the well-being of people of the planet, but will ultimately destroy US hegemony and the imperial project on which it has embarked. This is necessarily the case insofar as "[d]emocratic societies bent on high military expenditures and the projection of power globally *need* a national enemy to help divert money from social programs to military production. Wasting scarce resources hurts almost everyone globally, but the burden falls most heavily on the poor. To justify inequity, a rich nation will frequently discriminate unfairly against other nationalities through its trade, aid, and immigration policies" (Johansen 1991, 273; italics in original).

These dangers to the world, in general, and the US Empire, in particular, have been evident for decades. Ever since the 1980s, scholars and commentators have written of how the militarization of the United States had distorted the entire economy into an "armament culture" (Luckham 1984, 1–44). In 1970, Seymour Melman warned about the dangers of "Pentagon capitalism" (Melman 1970) and how America's "permanent war economy" had placed American capitalism itself on the road to decline (Melman 1974). More recently, Prof. Gar Alperovitz reminded his readers that ". . . ultimately democracy in a nation depends upon the development of democracy in its communities" and that ". . . America is unlikely to play a different role in the world until it is a different America—until it finds ways once again to realize values of equality, liberty, democracy, and, one day, perhaps even of community in our own land" (Alperovitz 2005, 239).

More recently, Walden Bello has observed that "[u]nder imperialism, the rules favoring one group of countries at the expense of the majority breed instability and resentment. A weakened imperial center would create the conditions for the phasing out of global double standards. Such hypocrisy—for instance, the tacit understanding that it is legitimate for the United States and the other big powers to maintain nuclear arsenals but illegitimate for others to do so—is a fundamental cause of international conflict . . . But the crisis of the empire bodes well not only for the rest of the world. It may also benefit the people of the United States. It opens up the possibility of Americans relating to other peoples as equals and not as masters. Failure of the empire is, moreover, a precondition for the reemergence of a democratic republic. That was the American promise before it was hijacked by imperial democracy" (Bello 2005, 217).

Similarly, professor emeritus of politics at Princeton University, Sheldon Wolin, has astutely noted in his critique of *"democracy incorporated"* that

> ... empire and Superpower undermine and implicitly oppose two presumable fundamental principles of American political ideology: that the Constitution provides the standard for a government of limited powers, and that American governance and politics are democratic. Despite the incongruity and inherent tensions between unlimited global hegemony and constitutionally limited domestic power, between arbitrary power projected abroad (unilateralism, preemptive war) and democratic power responsible to the citizenry at home, the implications of Superpower, imperial power, and globalizing capital for democracy and constitutionalism have not been publicly confronted ... On the contrary, the defenders and practitioners of these extraordinary forms of power profess to be employing Superpower to force the values of American democracy and the institutions of the free market upon the world. For their part, American citizens are expected to support the project of imposing democracy while remaining in denial of their own complicity in ravaging foreign populations and economies (Wolin 2008, 237).

As long as these contradictions remain unresolved and unaddressed in the consciousness of American citizens, we will be faced with an unending global crisis until the US Empire and its hegemonic aspirations finally collapse under their own weight. Yet, for those who are aware and consciously engaged in the struggles against injustice in our time, there is the responsibility and hope that a commitment to the values of inner transformation, the power of dialogue, and the aspirations for a more peaceful, humane, and inclusive global civilization will tear down off the mask of official illusion. To that end, we now turn to a discussion of how the rest of the world, region to region, is trying to reengage with the United Nations in order to demand that there be international accountability for meeting human needs in the midst of the current global crisis. Important ingredients of that discussion return us to the need to embark upon serious structural and institutional reform at United Nations, the ability of the world's people to expand the mandate of the International Criminal Court in order to bring an end to preemptive wars and the unaccountable actions of hegemonic states and their leaders, and the necessity of restructuring the UN Security Council so that preemptive wars are made unacceptable and the abolition of nuclear weapons becomes viable and attainable.

Toward a Renewed General Assembly and Reformed Security Council

The employment of CBMs, the worldwide mandate to bring about a demilitarized and depolarized world, and the success of implementing NWFZs throughout Southeast Asia, are not only signs of a successful effort in forging a set of trends toward rule-based regionalism, but are also important global developmental trajectories toward peace in light of the limitations of the United Nations Charter itself. For example, "[t]he United Nations Charter makes no mention of the term 'proliferation' and makes no distinction in the language of its provisions as between conventional and nonconventional weapons. Making such a distinction based upon particular weapons technologies only evolved as customary practice after the advent of the nuclear weapons age in August 1945, only two months after the signing of the UN Charter in June of that year . . ." (Joyner 2009, 159).

Further, it can be argued that we should lend even greater significance to progress made in the arena of rule-based regionalism, especially given the fact that, as far as the United Nations is concerned, ". . . both the General Assembly and the Security Council have largely failed to fulfil the roles and mandates given them under the Charter in the area of nonproliferation law creation" (Joyner 2009, 167). This is despite the fact that in 1978, working in alliance with the United Nations, the Conference on Disarmament (CD) was given a broad and ambitious mandate by the General Assembly to ". . . undertake the elaboration of a comprehensive program of disarmament encompassing all measures thought to be advisable in order to ensure that the goal of general and complete disarmament under effective international control becomes a reality in a world in which international peace and security prevail and in which the new international economic order is strengthened and consolidated" (Joyner 2009, 170).

In 1978, the CD was composed of forty member states, including all of the five acknowledged nuclear weapons states and thirty-five other states representing geographical regions. In 1996, the CD decided to admit twenty-three more states to membership, and in 1999 five more states were added (from twenty states requesting membership). Further, the CD adopts its own rules of procedure and its own agenda, ". . . usually influenced by recommendations from the UN General Assembly. The CD reports to the General Assembly at least annually. The budget of the CD is included in the budget of the United Nations" (Joyner 2009, 171). Over the course of its four decades of operation, the CD has served as both the negotiating and drafting forum for a number of multinational arms controls treaties, including the 1968 Nonproliferation Treaty, the 1972 Biological Weapons Convention, the 1993 Chemical Weapons Convention, and the 1996 Comprehensive Test Ban Treaty. In short, the CD has been instrumental to the UN General Assembly in facilitating the negotiation and establishment of the aforementioned multilateral treaties. However, when viewed in light of the fact that the General Assembly has been working on these particular issues since the passage of its very first resolution in 1946, the conclusion to be drawn is that ". . . the results actually produced through the General Assembly's sixty years of efforts to fulfil its Article II (1) mandate have been relatively modest" (Joyner 2009, 172).

As disappointing as the record of the General Assembly is with regard to Article II (1) on the issue of arms control and nonproliferation, it is even worse for the Security Council. The historical record reveals that ". . . the Security Council's record of efforts to fulfil its role under Article 26 of the charter has been virtually nonexistent, at least since 1949" (Joyner 2009, 173). As far as arms control, nuclear proliferation, and the threat of war are concerned, this is especially pathetic insofar as "[w]hether viewed as a socio-legal project gently civilizing states away from an older politics of diplomacy, deterrence, self-help, and legitimate warfare, or as an institutional project establishing a collective security system premised on the rule of law, the primary purpose of the United Nations today remains the maintenance of international peace and security and the abolition of the 'scourge of war'" (Danchin and Fischer 2010, 1). In pertinent part, Article 26 specifies the Security Council's responsibilities regarding the regulation of armaments thus: "In order to promote the establishment and maintenance of international peace and security with the least diversion for armaments of the world's human and economic resources, the Security Council shall be responsible for formulating, with the assistance of the Military Staff Committee referred to in Article 47, plans to be submitted to the members of the United Nations for the establishment of a system for the regulation of armaments" (Lowe et al. 2008b, 5).

In assessing why the Security Council has been so ineffectual to meet its Article 26 mandate it would be helpful to recall the fact that "[t]he Security Council is like no other body in history. It gives permanent members—China, France, Russia, the United Kingdom, and the United States—account for nearly 30 percent of the world's population and more than 40 percent of global economic output. In military affairs, their dominance is even more overwhelming. They control more than twenty-six thousand nuclear warheads, 99 percent of all those in existence. They have a combined 5.5 million men and women in arms. When the Council is united, its members can wage war, impose blockades, unseat governments, and levy sanctions, all in the name of the international community, There are almost no limits to the body's authority" (Bosco 2009, 3).

Given these facts, which expose great imbalances in the economic and military powers of the individual members of the Security Council, the choice for reform seems to be limited to one of two possibilities. First, it is argued that "[o]ne can opt for a world order dominated by a hegemonic United States, audacious but foolhardy, idealistic yet classically realist . . ." or, second, ". . . one can throw one's lot in with the United Nations, an organization struggling to balance efficacy against autocracy and an organization paralyzed by a paradox at its core: that in an age of democracy it is run by an oligarchy" (Malksoo 2010, 113). Having said this, we may yet discover a third choice or option. That third option would be realized in the fact that "[a] 'democracy' (in terms of an international normative order) that takes into account the interests of both Great Powers and small states has not become an outdated normative ideal. In that sense, 'democracy' is preferable to the rule of an aristocracy" (Malksoo 2010, 113). Therefore, giving greater representative weight to the General Assembly may, in terms of advancing the cause of genuine UN reform, be one of the most positive and dramatic moves possible. After all, as one commentator notes, "[t]here are compelling reasons to remain skeptical about the fantasy of increasing the power of the Security Council at the cost of the General Assembly, especially under conditions that do not reform the veto power of the permanent members" (Malksoo 2010, 113).

Regarding the problems associated with an undemocratic veto power, Ikeda has called for the UN to become a place where the interests of the people, and not just the member states, are represented (Urbain 2010, 174). To that end, Ikeda has recognized the fact that "[o]ne of the main obstacles preventing the UN from becoming a true parliament of humanity is the veto power of the five permanent members of the UN Security Council. Ikeda has repeatedly criticized this flaw (1982, 1987, 1991), and in 1992, he mentioned Galtung's proposal for dividing the United Nations General Assembly (UNGA) into lower and upper houses" (Urbain 2010, 174). In 1995, Ikeda wrote this: ". . . we must conclude that the current state of the United Nations—with the Security Council in a position of preeminence and the General Assembly playing a subordinate role—is undesirable. If we are to enhance the qualities of what *should become a parliament of humanity*, I believe we should do all we can to strengthen and further empower the General Assembly" (Ikeda 1995-PP, 24; italics added).

As valid as these proposals and recommendations appear, the fact remains that both the Security Council and the General Assembly are constantly undermined by the recalcitrance of the United States when it chooses to act as a hegemonic state and assumes it right to do so by virtue of its hegemonic status. This was made abundantly clear by the actions of the Bush II administration's run up to its invasion and occupation of Iraq in 2003. As far as the UN was concerned,

> [i]n the 'hierarchy of decision-making' revealed by the United States's treatment of the Council in 2002 and 2003, the Security Council was not at the apex. The question for the Bush administration was not whether the Security Council would allow a return to military action in Iraq, but whether military action in Iraq would allow a return to the Security Council. *Why accept a world powered by rules when it could have a world ruled by power?* That the United States views the UN instrumentally is only natural. All countries do to a large extent, but the United States does so with more import—not

the least because it now tends to view the whole globe as its natural 'sphere of influence.' Given that Washington's attention span can be very short, and then only on a few issues at any given time, it is hardly surprising that the UN often recedes from view in the US capital" (Malone 2006, 275–76; italics added).

Given this history, we now turn to the role of the International Criminal Court as a new forum wherein the actions of individuals and states that are in violation of the Nuremberg Principles, the UN Charter, and the PHSA, may be brought to the bar of international accountability.

The International Criminal Court and Hegemonic State Accountability

Despite its hegemonic propensities to proceed on its own with regard to the use of force, in violation of the UN Charter's prohibitions, as demonstrated by its having launched the 2003 war against Iraq, the fact remains that the United States is still constrained in global affairs by its need for some degree of domestic and global consensus with regard to its conduct. On this matter, Torbjorn Knutsen notes that "[a] hegemonic world order exists when the major members of an international system agree on a code of norms, rules, and laws which helps govern the behavior of all" (Knutsen 1999, 49). In the case of the Iraq invasion of 2003, the United States squandered its global consensus as it evaporated with its clear contempt for the noncompliant Security Council to grant its imprimatur. This reality has clearly defined implications for the United States as it moves into the future insofar as all members of the UN have agreed to allow the Security Council to carry out its duties in such a way that the Security Council itself is obliged to act on behalf of all members. Therefore, for the United States to have acted unilaterally and absolved itself of the requirements of Article 24 of the UN Charter, by its invasion of Iraq without UN approval, it effectively undermined the very purposes for which the UN Charter was originally drafted, which was to "save succeeding generations from the scourge of war."

On this matter, Joyner has noted that "[t]he UN Charter in Article 24 confers upon the Security Council *primary responsibility for the maintenance of international peace and security.* In the same paragraph the members of the United Nations *agree that in carrying out its duties under this responsibility, the Security Council acts on their behalf.* This statement is the closest the charter comes to attempting to remedy the nondemocratic reality, made requisite by geopolitical circumstances in 1945, that the most powerful organ of the United Nations and the only organ capable of issuing decisions binding upon all UN members, is composed of only 15 of those members (who now total 191), five of whom are given permanent status and have an effective veto power over every decision of the Council" (Joyner 2009, 186–87; italics added). In light of this history, Ikeda's suggestion about the need to turn the UNGA into a true parliament of mankind acquires a new sense of urgency, insofar as its addresses a central concern with the need to democratize the UN and, in so doing, make viable some means to hold the geopolitical actions of hegemonic states accountable to the rule of international law.

Further, it is a recommendation underscored by the old dilemma concerning the difference between legality and legitimacy offered by Carl Schmitt, the great Nazi legal scholar of the 1930s. According to Falk, we find that "[t]he ongoing preoccupation in political theory [that is] generated by Carl Schmitt's conceptualizations of legality and legitimacy have seldom explicitly influenced the application of such terminology to the *international* behavior and status of a sovereign state. The Schmitt perspective, arising in the context of emergent Nazi dictatorial rule, was supportive of the view that 'legitimacy' was essentially an expression of political will that was inherently rooted in sovereignty, and took precedence over deference to 'legality' in the internal and international operations of government. The sovereign should not be constrained by illusions about the primacy of law, which for Schmitt was the fatal flaw of liberal democracy" (Falk 2008c, 148; italics in original).

In the US government's Department of Justice, during the Bush II administration, a lawyer and law professor by the name of John Yoo took up Schmitt's argument to justify the invasion of Iraq by relying on a nonmainstream and constitutionally suspect redefinition of the "*Commander-in-Chief*" clause of the US Constitution, in combination with a suspect theory of the "*unitary executive*" (Johnson 2006, 251–54; Moss 2008, 178; Paupp 2007, 9–10). The same degree of legal deviation from international norms and the Geneva Conventions was exhibited by Yoo and the Bush administration on the issue of torture as one more means to conduct the US version of its "war on terrorism." On this subject, President Bush ". . . seems to have authorized torture largely for symbolic value—the desire of his administration and its neoconservative backers to show the world that the United States was indeed a new Rome, that could act with impunity unchecked by any established norms of international law" (Johnson 2006, 37–38).

Hence, by declaring that the United States was "*a new Rome*," the Bush administration allowed itself the flexibility that such an interpretation brought, but, at the same time, by claiming that *new geopolitical circumstances* had transformed it into a "*a new Rome,*" it weakened the clarity of the inhibiting texts of the Geneva Conventions, international law, and the text of the eighth Amendment of its own constitution. The central problem with this Schmitt-inspired perspective, as well as the Bush II administration adoption of the approach which it endorses, is that it exhibits such an ambivalence about international law that it fails to recognize the fact that ". . . the gap between legality and legitimacy is not a matter of substantive standard, but interpretative clarity . . . By incorporating through interpretation changing circumstances, flexibility is achieved, but the clarity of an inhibiting text is definitely weakened" (Falk 2008c, 149).

Extending this logic out beyond the realm of endorsing torture to finding justification for the illegal United States invasion of Iraq, it becomes possible to see the common-denominator beneath all of these United States violations of international law and its contempt for the UN Security Council. All of these actions by the United States reflected a motivation and intent to argue that its geopolitical clout justified the insertion of its own hegemonic judgments about what would be appropriate or inappropriate in the conduct of the affairs of State. This failure to restrain its actions in light of a greater international accountability to inflexible standards meant that the United States was freed in making judgments about the use of international force—thereby opening the door to unsanctioned war with Iraq, violations of norms involving the use of torture, and a failure to abide by its own democratic principles and constitutional mandates. As Falk notes, "A motive for inflexibility in formulating constraints on the use of force is to minimize the ambit of discretion available to governments, and thereby contribute to the basic undertaking of the United Nations 'to save succeeding generations from the scourge of war'" (Falk 2008c, 149).

As a consequence of these choices, by introducing its version of what we could characterize as *"hegemonic flexibility"* into global relations, there has been a counter-hegemonic effect with regard to an increase in terrorist actions directed against the US Empire and its hegemonic pretensions. In large measure, this is because the Bush II administration opened the door to international lawlessness by its unilateral invocation of the doctrine of "preemption", thereby inviting the international community to respond to it with its own version of preemptive force—terrorism. Yet as has been pointed out by Prof. George Fletcher, who disagrees with the logic of preemption, "[t]he Bush administration likes to argue that a shift in the balance of power justifies our use of preemption, but we do not extend the same privilege to rogue states. Rogue states are on the *receiving* end of this argument, just as they are on the receiving end of our bombs. But one again this opens up a nonreciprocal treatment of states within the international system, which is intolerable. Just as your use of legitimate defense on the street does not depend on your station in life, so too, a nation's use of legitimate defense in the international sphere should not depend on its status within the international community" (Fletcher and Ohlin 2008, 176).

This result provides the central reason why the PHSA condemns the practice of pursing geopolitical agendas that violate the inflexible standards of international law. Insofar as a peaceful world of global relations is ultimately predicated upon adherence to principles and norms that are supportive of reciprocity between states, it follows that any real deviation from those principles and norms violates the central organizing principle of the system—which is the "sovereign equality of states." By negating this principle, there is a corresponding negation of the principle and practice of reciprocity. With such a negation, the result is that there is a collapse of the hope of realizing a shared sense of justice and fairness in dealing with other states, and there is also an end to realizing any real semblance of what constitutes a peaceful global civilization.

In July 2002, the *Rome Statute* of the International Criminal Court entered into force, ushering in an era of accountability for "the most serious crimes of concern to the international community as a whole" (Rome Statute 1998, Preamble). Within a year, the Court was fully operational. In June 2005, its first arrest warrants were issued, and in January 2009, its first trial began. Benjamin Schiff has described the preamble to the *Rome Statute* as ". . . captur[ing] the idealism of the ICC project and mirror[ing] the tensions between a universalistic image of humanity and a global society riven by national loyalties" (Schiff 2008, 73). Adopted and opened for ratification by an overwhelming majority of countries in July 1998, the ratifications have since logged in at an astounding rate given the complexities of the treaty that endows the world's first permanent criminal court with jurisdiction to try individuals for genocide, war crimes, and crimes against humanity, and eventually aggression (Burroughs 2003, 113). In many ways, the true significance of the ICC, from a historical perspective, is found in the realization that it is dedicated to fulfilling the legacy and promise of the Nuremberg Charter and Nuremberg Principles (Schabas 2010, 1–27). In this connection, it has recently been observed that, in the most profound way, ". . . Nuremberg has contributed to eroding the idea that mass atrocities would necessarily go unpunished. The Nuremberg proceedings have also supplied many of the rules and principles that now form the core of international criminal law and it laid down the cornerstone of a still fragile construction: a system of international criminal law and international criminal justice that functions beside and complements domestic judicial systems where those are incapable of sanctioning serious violations of international humanitarian law" (Mettraux 2008, xii).

Standing in the tradition of the Nuremberg Principles, the Rome Statute sets out the contours of a Court that will prosecute individuals for genocide, war crimes, and crimes against humanity because, most importantly, "[t]he Statue recognizes no immunities for crimes within the Court's jurisdiction, even if those crimes are deemed official acts or are committed by a head of state. Thus, the ICC is intended to help '*end the culture of impunity*,' the assumption that atrocities can be committed without fear of legal consequences. It is expected that when combined with associated improvement capabilities in national legal system, the ICC will bolster global security by deterring the commission of serious human rights violations and atrocities" (Burroughs 2003, 115; italics added). However, the ICC does not enjoy unfettered universal jurisdiction. One of two conditions must be met for the Court to exercise jurisdiction in most cases: (1) the state where the crimes occurred ("territorial state") is a party to the Rome Statute or consents to the jurisdiction of the Court; *or* (2) the state of nationality of the accused is party to the Statute or consents to the jurisdiction of the Court. These preconditions do not apply when the UN Security Council refers a case to the ICC acting under Chapter VII of the UN Charter (Burroughs 2003, 115).

The net effect of these preconditions have largely protected the United States—as a global hegemonic state—from being made accountable with regard to the Iraq War (Mandel 2004, 3–28). By refusing to be a party to the Rome Statue and by refusing to consent to the jurisdiction of the Court, the United States has absented itself from the claims of international justice, jurisprudence, and accountability for its illegal conduct (Mandel 2004, 207–53). Part of the reason for this result is that while the Rome Statute was in the process of being drafted, "[t]he Americans won some . . . very important concessions at Rome, even while staying out of the statute" (Mandel 2004, 209). What remains amazing about this process is that "[d]espite all these successes, the Americans have steadfastly refused to ratify the statute" (Mandel 2004, 211). In this regard, "[w]hen 120 countries voted to adopt the Rome Statute of the International Criminal Court on July 17, 1998, the United States was not among them. Rather than being part of the rising global tide toward a fair and effective system of international justice, the United States joined with China, Libya, Iraq, Israel, Qatar, and Yemen to reject the treaty" (Burroughs 2003, 117).

The clear insincerity of the United States' objections to the ICC was highlighted by its defiance of the Security Council in March 2003 when it invaded Iraq. In retrospect, we can further argue that US hypocrisy with regard to its objections of the ICC is made transparent by the central claim made by the Bush administration when it "*unsigned*" the Rome Treaty in 2002: "[W]e believe the International Criminal Court undermines the role of the United Nations Security Council in maintaining international peace and security . . . the treaty dilutes the authority of the UN Security Council and departs from the system that the framers of the UN Charter envisioned."[6] Responding to this chain of events, Michael Mandel notes that

> [p]seudo-legal arguments apart, the United States's objection to the ICC boiled down to a claim that the Court, free of the discipline of the Security Council (with an American veto), *might actually prosecute Americans*. This was apart altogether from the question of whether the Americans charged might be guilty. In other words, it was not about "wrongful convictions," in the sense of convicting an innocent person. The Bush administration put the arguments in terms of pure sovereignty: "While sovereign nations have the authority to try noncitizens who have committed crimes against their citizens or in their territory, the United States has never recognized the right of an

international organization to do so absent consent or a UN Security Council mandate" (Mandel 2004, 212–13; italics in original).

Speaking to this point, John Burroughs notes that "[t]he United Sates had long hoped that the Court would be made dependent on the UN Security Council for the cases that could come before it. However, the role of the Security Council was greatly circumscribed in the final text of the Rome Statute. It is this aspect—the degree of independence of the Council—that led the United States to oppose the permanent Court at the same time that it fully supported the creation and maintenance of the *ad hoc* tribunals" (Burroughs 2003, 118; italics in original). It was only when it became clear that the ICC would not be dependent on the Security Council for authority to prosecute that the United States then pursued the possibility of explicit exemptions for nationals of nonstates parties.[7]

The independence of the ICC from the Security Council is perhaps the most important point to take note of when arguing that the ICC has legal, political, and structural integrity to advance the ideals and purposes of the UN Charter, in particular, and international law in general. In drafting its provisions, the authors of the *Rome Statute* made sure that the ICC will be an independent institution and not an arm of the United Nations (Rome Statute preamble and Article 2). Hence, the ICC will be largely independent of the Security Council. This doctrinal reality frees the ICC from the veto power of the United States as a hegemonic state which has proven by its actions and policies that its ultimate fidelity is to its own imperial project at the expense of the rest of the peoples and nations on earth.

In his commentary on the ICC, William Schabas notes that "Article 2 sets out the general principle of the relationship agreement, but other provisions of the *Rome Statute* address specific matters about the interaction between the Court and the United Nations, notably where the authority of the Security Council is involved . . . More generally, the Court fits within an international system whose center of gravity is the United Nations and whose primacy legal instrument is the Charter of the United Nations . . . The preamble of the *Rome Statute* '[r]eaffirm[s]' the Purposes and Principles of the Charter of the United Nations, and in particular that all States shall refrain from the threat or use of force against the territorial integrity or political independence of any State, or in any other manner inconsistent with the Purposes of the United Nations" (Schabas 2010, 65). This outcome reflects the concerns of the Preparatory Committee at the time the *Rome Statute* was being drafted. The Preparatory Committee noted that "[a] close relationship between the Court and the United Nations was considered essential and a necessary to link the universality and standing of the Court, *though such a relationship should in no way jeopardize the independence of the Court*" (Schabas 2010, 69; italics added).

The implications that flow from this juridical arrangement between the ICC and the United Nations are enormous and potentially transformative for the future of world order and the realization of a peaceful global civilization. As discussed above, the Preamble of the Rome Statute and Article 2 serve to provide the ICC with the power to end the impunity of war crimes and war criminals—even when they are committed by the heads of a hegemonic state. In this regard, the ICC is the closest institutional and legal embodiment of a means for actualizing and implementing the PHSA. The ICC has had this power specified for it insofar as the Rome Statute has articulated a carefully crafted *complementarity scheme* which situates the ICC as a court of last resort which would come into play only when the national system has been unwilling or unable to act. (Rome Statute, 1998, Article 17; italics added). While there are still present certain preconditions of territoriality and nationality that were built into the statute as a curb on triggering outright jurisdiction, the fact remains that the ICC is intended to complement national systems rather than impinge upon them while—at the same time—narrowing the jurisdictional gaps, practical and substantive, that have long allowed for impunity (Rome Statute 1998, Article 13).

Given these parameters, the ICC has the capacity and potential to bring the United States and United Kingdom administrations to the bar of justice for the assumption that they had some kind of global mandate to wage an aggressive war against Iraq—and then proceed with an illegal occupation of Iraq—without the benefit of any kind of Security Council endorsement or authorization for such actions.[8] If these nuclear states are to still enjoy impunity for this war and not be subject to accountability in an international legal forum, then any real hope of constraining international aggression by a hegemonic state is virtually dead. However, the ICC does have the capacity and the authority to bring these war crimes and war criminals into account (Brecher et al. 2005; Falk et al. 2006). In this regard, as Denis Halliday stated in a testimony given to the World Tribunal on Iraq, in Istanbul on June 25, 2005, "[t]he world has witnessed in Iraq the most serious of international crimes—the crime of aggression on a sovereign member state by US and UK force . . . The world waits for the UN to act in keeping with the provisions of international law, including the application of International Criminal Court provisions to Bush, Blair and their henchmen and women who have violated the core tenets of the UN Charter, the Universal Declaration of Human Rights and the Geneva Conventions and Protocols" (Halliday 2006, 85).

Conclusion: The Interconnections between the UN, ICC, and Nuclear Weapons Abolition

The UN and ICC are both the legal and institutional means through which the entire global community can be empowered to address the challenge of nuclear weapons abolition. In the case of the Rome Statute which established the ICC, it is clear that it ". . . strongly reinforces the existing taboo against the use of weapons of mass destruction" (Burroughs 2003, 116). In fact, the Statute expressly bans the use of chemical weapons (Rome Statute 1998, Article 8(2) (b) (xvii) and (xviii)). Additionally, use of biological, nuclear, and other weapons of mass or indiscriminate destruction is generally prohibited by several provisions—including those criminalizing attacks upon civilians and attacks which disproportionately kill or injure civilians and damage the environment (Rome Statute 1998, Article 8 (2) (b) (iv) and 8 (2) (b) (xx); *see also*, Austin and Bruch 2000).

As positive as these ICC directives are for advancing the cause of peace, they are potentially offset by the undemocratic nature of the UN Security Council with its "veto power" acting as an encumbrance on holding the hegemonic state accountable for waging preemptive wars *or* wars of aggression under the rubric of "humanitarian intervention." In this connection, Thomas Nichols has powerfully argued that "[u]nless the iron tautology of the veto is broken and the composition of the Security Council changed in a way that reflects the growing wave of global democratization, the United Nations will be doomed, at least as any kind of recognized arbiter of the use of force. If states are going to act on notions of rights and justice in going to war, whether to alleviate suffering or to prevent aggression, terrorism, or other disasters, international organizations must be constituted by members who believe that each has at least some moral standing to levy judgment on the other or they will reject community action in favor of unilateral solutions" (Nichols 2008, 143). Hence, the threat and danger of unilateral solutions continue to haunt the present and the future because, as James Steinberg has suggested, "[a]lthough expanding the scope of Security Council action is certainly a valuable step, recent history powerfully suggests that this will not obviate the use of force when the council fails to act" (Steinberg 2007, 31).

Given these constraints, we are forced to look at some other strategy by which nuclear weapons abolition can be undertaken that will be respected by all States and adhered to by all States. In that connection, C. G. Weeramantry, a sitting judge on the International Court of Justice (ICJ) at the time an *Advisory Opinion on Legality of the Threat or Use of Nuclear Weapons* was issued, on July 8, 1996, has recently reminded the world that the Opinion underscores the reality that ". . . this weapon, incapable of being contained in space and time, has the potential to destroy all civilization and the entire ecosystem of the planet . . . The conclusion so clearly stated in international jurisprudence demands urgent action at every level, through every discipline and by every nation, for the elimination of this peril" (Weeramantry 2009, iii). To that end, he has endorsed the idea of a Nuclear Weapons Convention (NWC), pursuant to the Treaty on the Non-Proliferation of Nuclear Weapons, in order to meet its Article VI obligation to achieve complete nuclear disarmament. In addition, it should be noted that this proposal is linked to the ICJ Advisory Opinion and has received widespread and high-level support. At the center of this proposal is the express obligation, contained in Article VI, which mandates that States "pursue negotiations in *good faith* on effective measures relating to . . . nuclear disarmament" (Italics added). The issue of "good faith" is the operative wording.

On this point, Falk has observed that ". . . the most comprehensive international treaty on the subject, the Non-Proliferation of Nuclear Weapons (1968) commits nuclear weapon stated in Article VI to end 'the nuclear arms race at an early date' and 'pursue negotiations in good faith' to achieve 'nuclear disarmament.' Such clear legal admonitions have been ignored by nuclear weapon states, most pointedly by the United States, without causing any notable criticism either in diplomatic circles or within domestic politics" (Falk 2008b, 225). In response to these failures of the US hegemonic state and other nuclear weapons states, I have noted that "[t]he Delhi Declaration of 1978 called for the entire world to be made into a nuclear weapons-free zone. The declaration proposes the immediate negotiation of a Nuclear Disarmament Treaty, outlining its principal features and insisting that serious negotiations to make it happen be held" (Paupp 2005, 91).

More recently, the approach outlined in the Delhi Declaration of 1978 has been renamed as a "Nuclear Weapon-Free World" (NWFW). In fact, "[o]ne of the ideas of how to achieve a NWFW is the concept of a Nuclear Weapons Convention (NWC). Such a comprehensive convention would effectively prohibit and eliminate all nuclear weapons and their infrastructure. It would supplement a Biological Weapons Convention and a Chemical Weapons Convention, completing the ban on all Weapons of Mass Destruction (WMD). The NWC has been suggested since its foundation in 1993 by the International Network of Engineers and Scientists Against Proliferation (INESAP) . . . An INESAP Study Group, comprising of more than fifty experts from seventeen countries, presented its report '*Beyond the NPT: A Nuclear Weapon-Free World*' during the NPT review and extension conference in New York in April 1995, which outlines the transformation process of the traditional nonproliferation regime into a NWFW, represented by a Nuclear Weapons Convention" (Scheffran 2008, 188). The substance of the NWC is summarized as follows:

> The NWC would have to ban not only the possession and production of nuclear weapons; it would also prohibit all kinds of acquisition (including research), transfer, deployment (or any preparations for re-deployment), use and threat of use. The convention would call for the elimination of the whole infrastructure serving the manufacture and possession of nuclear warheads and their means of delivery. It would provide a system of international control for guarding and accounting for all remaining weapon-usable fissile material. The convention would incorporate, and

thus replace, other existing relevant treaties as bans on nuclear weapons tests, and on the production of weapon-grade fissile material—it would make these bans universal. The convention would replace the NPT itself.[9]

Such an approach needs to be resurrected in the aftermath of the US Senate's 1999 defeat of the Comprehensive Test Ban Treaty and the 2003 Iraq War. The value and necessity of such an approach also needs to be advanced in light of the continuing problems discussed above, ranging from the tendency of hegemonic states to engage in wars of preemption, the veto problem on the Security Council, and the failure of the major nuclear weapons states to follow the global democratic imperative to disarm. To that end, I maintain that the goal of a NWFW should be advanced in conjunction with both the PHSA (Paupp 2009) and the seven principles of *"inclusionary governance"*— which have the capacity to impact the direction, course, and success of global efforts aimed at nuclear weapons abolition. The seven conditions associated with the realization of inclusionary governance are contained in Table 7.4.

The above-cited proposals and rationales for a NWC are absolutely critical if the goal of nuclear abolition is to be achieved. For, in the alternative, we are left with the policies and perspectives of those who guide and lead the major nuclear weapon state—the US hegemonic state—to dictate to the rest of the world whether its future will be one of peace, a future that is left to the mercy and discretion of the American primacy coalition. Take, for example, the following statements and definition of issues presented by authors associated with the Brookings Institution: "As the sole current superpower, the United States has immense influence on global affairs. In many respects, it is also the *'norm leader',* which means that its decisions may lead other governments to reconsider their own policies" (Chyba and Sasikumar 2006, 20; italics added). As the "norm leader" with regard to waging wars of aggression and preemptive wars, the United States has certainly led North Korea and Iran to consider their own policies with regard to protecting themselves against the kind of invasion that Iraq was subjected to in 2003. Hence, whether acknowledging this phenomenon and the dilemmas resulting from it (or not), these authors proceed to make the assertion that "*[t]here is no general rule for weighing the potential drawbacks of the one course against the other.* Nevertheless, certain issues are crucial for the formulation of US nuclear weapons policy" (Chyba and Sasikumar 2006, 20; italics added). The various issues they have chosen to highlight are outlined in Table 7.5.

The contrast between the policy choices, issues, and standards employed by the authors of Table 7.5 versus those employed by the advocates and authors of the NWC could not be more graphic, stark, or radically divergent. It is evident from a review of the six proposed policy choices provided by the authors of Table 7.5 that they reflect the policy parameters and

Table 7.4 Invoking the Principles of Inclusionary Governance as a Means to Effectuate the Process of Nuclear Weapons Abolition

1. Structures and policies that allow for the continued investment in and expansion of both nuclear and nonnuclear assets shall be dismantled and replaced with peacekeeping and monitoring institutions. Actions not specifically mandated by Article 2 of the UN Charter must be clearly prohibited.

2. In recognition of the fact that spending on nuclear and nonnuclear assets depletes First and Third World economies, it shall be the task of inclusionary governments and inclusionary regimes to embark upon the deepening of democratic norms, practices, and policies so as to alter current spending priorities. These norms are not to be enforced by any one coalition of nations without the support of the UN Security Council.

3. The necessity to embark upon a path toward inclusionary governance and demilitarization is supported by accumulated scientific evidence, which provides sufficient proof that the exchange and/or detonation of just a few nuclear bombs will have the capacity to create a global condition known as "nuclear winter" that could lead to climatic catastrophe, agricultural collapse, and world famine.

4. The history and evolution of international law is moving in the direction of disarmament and has the capacity to build a global institutional structure that supports an alternative security system.

5. The historical and recent experience of war and conflict has proven that a failure to recognize the influence of preexisting beliefs has implications for decision-making and must become more inclusionary so as to overcome a history and practice of concealment, secrecy, and distortion through propaganda as well as bureaucratic and media manipulation.

6. Genuine security and a peaceful world order cannot be premised upon notions of "deterrence" and "balance of power" because a spiral of violence is created by these concepts so that the exercise of power becomes self-defeating.

7. The recognized need for a global security policy that places emphasis upon nonmilitary incentives to channel government's behavior empowers the international system to give added support to an expanded role for international organizations or security regimes to facilitate cooperation and to regulate inter-group conflict.

Source: Terrence E. Paupp, *Achieving Inclusionary Governance: Advancing Peace and Development in First and Third World Nations.* New York: Transnational Publishers, 2000, pp. 84–104.

preferences established by US policymaking elites who reside at the center of the US hegemonic state. The self-laudatory references to the United States as the *"sole current superpower"* is presented as the primacy justification for determining the parameters of US nuclear weapons policy, as well as its self-definition as a *"norm leader"* in global affairs. Now, contrast this set of nuclear weapons policy choices (Table 7.5) with the above-cited proposal (in summary and in bold type in the text and cited as footnote no. 9) from the INEASP Study Group authors who wrote *Beyond the NPT: A Nuclear Weapon-Free World.*

Whereas the NWC proposal bans the possession and production of nuclear weapons, the authors of the Table 7.5 policy choices authorize "the role of potential new nuclear weapons and choices to be made regarding nuclear use". Whereas the NWC proposal advocates the idea that the convention would replace the NPT itself, the authors of the Table 7.5 policy choices want to retain the NPT regime and further mold it to fit with US geopolitical strategies. Whereas the NWC proposal seeks to prohibit the use or threat of use of nuclear weapons, the authors of the Table 7.5 policy choices want to allow the United States the option of retaining such nuclear weapons use or threat of use vis-à-vis preemptive attack or preventive war. In this case, such a choice would also be augmented by US ballistic missile defense systems (BMD), formerly

Table 7.5   Issues for the Formulation of US Nuclear Weapons Policy

1. The interactions and changing balance among strategies of dissuasion, deterrence, preemptive attack, and preventive war.

2. The nuclear nonproliferation regime, its historical successes and failure, and the lessons to be drawn from history.

3. New challenges to the nonproliferation regime, especially those posed by the spread of weapons-related technologies, latent proliferation, and nuclear smuggling networks.

4. Appropriate responses to these challenges, including to current "hard cases," particularly those of Iran and North Korea, and for very different reasons India, Israel, and Pakistan.

5. The interdiction of the delivery of nuclear weapons, including the role of ballistic missile defense.

6. The role of potential new nuclear weapons and choices to be made regarding nuclear use.

Source: Christopher F. Chyba and Karthika Sasikumar, "A World of Risk: The Current Environment for US Nuclear Weapons Policy," in *US Nuclear Weapons Policy: Confronting Today's Threats*, edited by George Bunn and Christopher F. Chyba. Washington, DC: Brookings Institution Press, 2006, p. 20.

referred to as national missile defense (NMD), theater missile defense (TMD), or more euphemistically referred to as "Star Wars" technology. Whereas the NWC proposal seeks to replace other relevant treaties which bans nuclear weapons technologies by making the NWC universal and global, the authors of the Table 7.5 policy choices want to enable the US hegemonic state to retain its unilateral power to decide for itself what will be involved in "[t]he role of potential new nuclear weapons and choices to be made regarding nuclear use." In short, the authors of Table 7.5 have not only refused to challenge the status quo of US hegemony and the global military–industrial complex, they have actively devised policy-options to maintain these forces and the powerful interests behind them. By being advocates for the status quo of US hegemony, the authors of Table 7.5 have embarked upon endorsing a course of action that allows for a continuous subversion of the Nuremberg Principles, ignoring the condemnation of nuclear weapons by the 1996-Advisory Opinion of the International Court of Justice, and contempt for the mandates of the UN Charter with respect to the threat and use of force.

The post-1945 foreign policy tragedies of the twentieth century center around the historical reality that ". . . the US has done everything possible to subvert the Nuremberg Principles, which makes its ringing endorsement of human rights meaningless and the rule of law abstract, hypocritical, and meaningless. Indeed, the horrific legacy of war crimes and human rights abuses stemming from unfettered US global power has its roots in historical *continuity*, the result of a deliberate, planned, and systematic pattern of imperial aggrandizement" (Boggs 2003, 224; italics in original). The precise nature of "imperial aggrandizement is captured in a statement by the Bush II administration's US Undersecretary of Defense, Douglas Feith, who told the Senate Armed services committee that ". . . because we know something about technology and we know something about capabilities of potential adversaries, we can anticipate that we're going to have to confront certain capabilities and then we need the capabilities to respond to the capabilities that our enemies might have."[10] In response to this testimony, both the Program Director and Executive Director of the Western States Legal Foundation have warned thus: "Imagine the shape of the future if every government that sees the US as a 'potential adversary' seeks to counter the military capabilities the United States 'might have.' *This is the kind of thinking that creates and sustains arms races*" (Lichterman and Cabasso 2002, 85; italics added).

The reform of the UN Security Council becomes all the more vital because in order to avoid the illegal use of force by states, as well as the kind of thinking that creates and sustains arms races, it is important to acknowledge the flawed forms of thought and thinking patterns which have led us into the current predicament. As forcefully argued by Prof. Brian Foley, we find that "[a] characteristic of competent problem-solving (as well as critical thinking) is asking the right questions. For example, in generating solutions, one might repeatedly ask, '*What else might we do here?*' To guide that inquiry, one might also ask, '*How can we see this problem as an opportunity to address the needs of a wide spectrum of people and constituencies?*' To generate answers, one would use an array of thinking techniques and methods, both traditional and innovative, all of which can be taught and learned" (Foley 2003, 155; italics added). Prof. Foley proceeds to offer a series of examples of questions that decision-makers could be required to ask and answer when they are considering whether the use of force is necessary. He begins with the need to engage in, "**Defining the problem:** (1) What is the threat or harm to be limited? (2) What is/are the precise goal(s), and what value(s) are sought to be achieved and vindicated?" Then, "**Process:** (3) What cognitive techniques or methods can we use to find possible solutions? (4) Who outside the decision-making group should be involved in this search for alternatives? (5) What facts are needed? (6) What are some possible solutions? Will they work? Why/why not?" Finally, we arrive at the issue of "**Effectiveness:** (7) What are the best ways to achieve the goal and vindicate the value? Attitude is important. For example, the question is not, 'Can we use force? But, '*Must* we resort to force, and how can we avoid using force?" (Foley 2003, 156).

From Ikeda's perspective, the essence of the matter is found in the realization that "[t]he right to a fulfilled life lived in peace that Toda proclaimed transcends nation-state boundaries. He condemned the would-be users of nuclear weapons as the worst criminals because, in our mad age of hydrogen bombs, they threaten the entire human race . . . From Mr. Toda's standpoint, the right to a fulfilled life lived in peace takes precedence over everything. No national interests or theories of deterrence can compete with it" (Ikeda and De Athayde 2009, 105). The choices represented by the advocates and proponents of a NWC, on the one hand, versus the choices offered by the American primacy coalition (as expressed in Table 7.5), present humanity with a basic decision. Either adopt life-affirming paths to global peace or, in the alternative, perish in the flames of unconstrained ego, greed, and the holocaust of a nuclear war. The approach to nuclear weapons abolition offered by the proponents of a NWC, versus the choices outlined by the authors of Table 7.5, offers a fundamental choice between historical continuity (*with an unending reliance on nuclear weapons*) or, in the alternative, a viable and sustainable path to a unified and peaceful global civilization. On the nature of this choice, Ikeda has written this: "Bertrand Russell, too, called nuclear weapons the absolute evil—and I fully concur. The evil lies not only in their overwhelming power to cause destruction and death but also in the profound distrust emanating from their possession. This distrust has created the so-called cult of deterrence, the belief that nuclear weapons are necessary for protection against nuclear weapons. Trust in nuclear arms is a negation of trust in humanity. The more people trust in arms, the less they trust one another. *Ceasing to put their trust in arms is the only way to cultivate mutual trust among peoples"* (Ikeda 2001a, 187; italics added).

In order to confront the "imperial hubris" we need to realize that this constitutes not only a political task that needs to be assigned to mass movements for peace, but rather, it also involves changing the character, perceptions, and behaviors of the individual. On this matter, in a dialogue with Ikeda, Toynbee stated, "It is hard to see how, in the atomic age, mankind can avoid committing mass suicide if it does not raise the average level of its behavior to the level actually attained by the Buddha and by Saint Francis of Assisi . . . But these higher standards of behavior have been actually achieved in practice only by a tiny minority. The majority has recognized the validity of the standards, but it has treated them as 'counsels of perfection,' which ordinary people cannot reasonably be expected to follow" (Ikeda and Toynbee [1976] 2007, 305). In response, Ikeda answers that

> [w]hile it is true that complete self-mastery is too difficult a goal for the majority, it seems unfair to say that it is the reason for the human inability to master the self is lack of will, since the obstruction to this mastery lies on a level deeper than desire or consciousness. In other words, *in order to attain self-mastery one must devise a way of tapping power that lies deeper than consciousness. I am convinced that the power to make the effort to perform this admittedly difficult task is inherent in all people.* The problem is finding ways to bring that power to light (Ikeda and Toynbee [1976] 2007, 305–06; italics added).

Ikeda concludes this part of the dialogue with Toynbee by observing that

> [a] total reformation of the individual from below the depths of consciousness is essential. *Of course, this reformation cannot be imposed from without. Instead, the individual, in striving to better his own personality, must consciously strive to effect his own reformation. At the least, a philosophy propounding the need for such a reformation must give its followers strength sufficient to the task. It is this kind of reformation that I mean by the human revolution* (Ikeda and Toynbee [1976] 2007, 306; italics added).

Elsewhere in his dialogues, Ikeda has made this same point about the centrality of the "human revolution" in the task of realizing a peaceful global civilization. In more succinct terms, Ikeda has noted that "[w]hereas science begins with a reformation of the external world, Buddhism starts with reforming the inner human world—what we call the *human revolution*—and moves on to society. If we want to halt the excesses of science and technology and save humanity from the crises confronting contemporary civilization, we can no longer merely treat the symptoms" (Ikeda and Krieger 2002, 107; italics in original). In the case of nuclear weapons, what Ikeda exposes about the *"excesses of science"* is actually an indictment of the *misuses* of science which have lead to a political doctrine of mutually assured destruction, reliance on "deterrence" as opposed to trust between peoples, and the proclivity of the US hegemonic states to launch wars of aggression in the name of "preemption." Perhaps that diagnosis of our current global crisis—especially with respect to the problems posed by nuclear weapons—underscores the human reality that in order to have a *"nuclear revolution"* (nuclear abolition) we must first experience the *"human revolution."*

Notes

1. Agreement for the Prosecution and Punishment of the Major War Criminals of the European Axis, 59 Stat. 1544, 82 U.N.T.S. 284 reprinted in 39 AM.J.INT'LL. 257 (Suppl. 1945).
2. I note, "The psychological surrender is tantamount to a surrender of moral responsibility. The effect of this process is twofold: on the one hand, it frees the individual from making choices and decisions that are then abdicated to the guardians of the nuclear arsenals and, on the other hand, it empowers the guardians of the nuclear arsenals to effectively ignore democratic demands for disarmament and nuclear abolition, thereby ensuring the maintenance of patterns of exclusionary governance through an exclusionary state" (Terrence E. Paupp, "The Nuclear Crucible: The Moral and International Law Implications of Weapons of Mass Destruction," in *In Democracy's Shadow: The Secret World of National Security*, edited by Marcus Raskin and A. Carl LeVan. Nation Books: New York, 2005, p. 76).
3. Walden Bello, "The Bretton Woods Institutions and the Demise of the UN Development System," in *Between Sovereignty and Global Governance: The United Nations, the State, and Civil Society*, edited by Albert Paolini, Anthony Jarvis, and Christian Reus-Smit, St. Martin's Press, 1998, p. 217.
4. Tony Smith argues, "Blinded by its will-to-power; by organized interests from oil to the Israel lobby to conservative Christians; by its self-righteous liberal conviction that it has found the key to the worldwide promotion of freedom, prosperity, and peace; and by a realistic concern that defeat in Iraq could lead to reversals elsewhere, a good part of the political elites in this country, Democrats and Republicans alike, appeared wedded to a self-perpetuating and self-defeating framework for action more dangerous than any other initiative ever undertaken in the history of American foreign policy" (Tony Smith, "Wilsonianism after Iraq: The End of Liberal Internationalism?" in *The Crisis of American Foreign Policy: Wilsonianism in the Twenty-first Century*, edited by G. John Ikenberry, et al. Princeton University Press, 2009, p. 85).
5. Richard Falk notes, "We are unfortunately living in a world where the primacy of geopolitics often suppresses the relevance of international law in those settings where the political actors who are in a situation to exert

this kind of overbearing influence can shape the way in which conflicts are perceived, and either resolved or perpetuated. Whether in relation to nuclear weaponry or the rights of self-determination of a people, this vulnerability to geopolitics is responsible for much of the injustice and danger in the world" (Richard Falk, "Non-Proliferation Treaty Illusions and International Lawlessness," in *At the Nuclear Precipice: Catastrophe or Transformation?*, edited by Richard Falk and David Krieger. New York: Palgrave-Macmillan, 2008, p. 42).

6. Marc Grossman, Under Secretary for Political Affairs, "American Foreign Policy and the International Criminal Court," Remarks to the Center for Strategic and International Studies, Washington, DC, May 6, 2002, www.state.gove/p/9949.htm.

7. John Burroughs notes, "In the quest for special treatment in the new scheme of international justice, US officials argued that, as the sole remaining superpower, the US was expected to deploy its military to 'hot spots' more often than other countries. That would make it more vulnerable to politically motivated accusations and prosecutions. This concern was addressed by other delegations in the negotiations and was the reason for several articles in the Statute intended to provide a series of checks and balances with respect to the prosecutor's authority to self-start cases" (John Burroughs, "The Rome Statute of the International Criminal Court," in *Rule of Power or Rule of Law?—An Assessment of US Policies and Actions Regarding Security-Related Treaties*, edited by Nicole Deller, et al. New York: Apex Press, 2003, p. 118).

8. Richard Falk notes, "Recourse to war against Iraq in 2003 and the persisting buildup of tensions in relation to Iran are both aggressive undertaking predicated on the notion that the existing nuclear weapons states, led by the United States, have some kind of global mandate to wage aggressive war in order to prevent others from possessing these kinds of weapons, or even from acquiring the knowledge, materials, and technology that might at some future time be dedicated to the production of such weaponry . . .. Back in 2002 and early 2003, feverish American diplomacy was relied upon to persuade other governments, the UN, and public opinion that it was necessary for the United States (and Britain) to wage a war in defiance of international law, in defiance of the of the UN, because our country, itself a nuclear weapons superpower, believed it was entitled to wage war to prevent another country from acting to acquire these weapons. Even if the factual allegations had turned out to be true, which they were not, it would still not have provided an acceptable basis for recourse to war" (Richard Falk, "Nuclear Weapons, War, and the Discipline of International Law," in *At the Nuclear Precipice: Catastrophe or Transformation?*, edited by Richard Falk and David Krieger. Palgrave-Macmillan, 2008, p. 230).

9. Beyond the NPT—A Nuclear Weapons Free World, INESAP Study Group Report (Darmstadt/New York, 1995), p. 9. The Executive Summary has been published as a supplement in INESAP Bulletin, July 6, 1995.

10. Douglas J. Feith, "Statement of the Honorable Douglas J. Feith, Undersecretary of Defense for the Policy Senate Armed Services hearing on the Nuclear Posture Review," February 14, 2002, p. 28.

8

The Challenge of Climate Change: Searching for Human Solidarity in a Divided World

Economic growth and prosperity brought about by technological advancement have so captured people's imaginations that the progress and spread of the civilization of science and technology has known no limits and no barriers. But now we find the triumph to be marred, with damage to the earth's environment inflicted by the side effects of that civilization, telling us that progress may in fact turn out to be our downfall. Air, water and soil pollution, indiscriminate cutting of vast forests, desertification, damage to the earth's protective ozone layer and the resultant effects of global warming; none of these issues can simply be left to resolve themselves."

–Daisaku Ikeda (Ikeda 2001a, 9–10)

"Geopolitics has always been based on the assumption that the environment is a giant battleground—a war of all against all—where we fight with one another to secure resources to ensure our individual survival. Biosphere politics, by contrast, is based on the idea that the Earth is like a living organism made up of interdependent relationships and that we each survive by stewarding the larger communities of which we are a part."

–Jeremy Rifkin (Rifkin 2009, 615)

"Climate change will be one of the definitive forces shaping prospects for human development during the 21st century. Through its impact on ecology, rainfall, temperature and weather systems, global warming will directly affect all countries. Nobody will be immune to its consequences. However, some countries and peoples are more vulnerable than others. In the long term, the whole of humanity faces risks, but

more immediately, the risks and vulnerabilities are skewed toward the
world's poorest people."
–United Nations Development Program
(Human Development Report 2007, 24)

"There is no doubt that the Earth is warming and the climate is
changing. A consensus exists among scientists that these changes are
human induced, or anthropogenic. Anthropogenic climate change
is the greatest of all environmental risks, since large-scale climate
change would disrupt every ecosystem and impose catastrophic hard-
ships on many parts of the world."
–Jeffrey D. Sachs (Sachs 2008, 83)

Ikeda's approach to interpreting the global dimensions of humanity's global environmental crisis can be seen throughout his body of writings. His UN peace proposals, UN Decade education proposal, as well as his numerous dialogues with leaders in the fields of politics, science, culture, education, and ethics all reflect his preoccupation with the need to embark upon a global revolution to save the environment which, of necessity, starts with the individual. From Ikeda's perspective, *"Saving the environment requires a global revolution that must start with individual human revolutions. That is the road to the solution of the complex of worldwide problems"* (Ikeda and Diez-Hochleitner 2008, 39; italics added).

The *"Spirit of Abstraction"* and the Exploitation of the Environment

As was already suggested in the concluding sentences of chapter 7, Ikeda has maintained that the most fundamental way to bring about a "nuclear revolution" that results in nuclear abolition is to begin with the "human revolution." This is also relevant with respect to the environmental issues of the twenty-first century. In this profound observation resides a deeper truth. It is a truth which also serves as a common denominator that connects the task of saving the earth's environment with the challenge of abolishing the threat of nuclear weapons. Prof. Samuel Kim has made the point that "[i]n a broader sense the development of nuclear weapons systems entails (1) the mining of uranium and plutonium, (2) transporting nuclear materials, (3) releasing anthropogenic radiation into the oceans, air, and soil, and (4) dumping deadly nuclear wastes. *All raise the levels of environmental and epidemiological hazards"* (Kim 1984, 269; italics added). Hence, when we juxtapose the environmental challenge with that of nuclear weapons aboli-tion, we discover, at the most fundamental level, the reality that ". . . *human behavior never functions in a social vacuum.* It is bounded and guided by social values and structures" (Kim 1984, 293; italics added).

The root cause of both the environmental and nuclear weapons crises can be traced back to what the French existentialist philosopher Gabriel Marcel (1889–1973) called the *"spirit of abstraction."* The *"spirit of abstraction"* involves the act of reducing the humanity of *"the Other"* into little more than an abstract concept, thereby reducing both human persons and the natural environment into things. The *"spirit of abstraction"* turns people and the resources of the environment into little more than mere commodities that can be manipulated, dominated, exploited, and sold for the sake of financial profit and personal gain. Under capitalism, the worker sells his/her labor while, at the same time, the integrity of the environment is compromised by the selling off of resources to either make a profit or to pay off a debt. The historical antecedents of this developmental trajectory took off with a vengeance during the industrial revolution of the nineteenth century; therefore, "[i]n a fundamental sense, most ecological problems are outgrowths of pre-ecological (industrial) social structures. Inevitably, eco-developmental self-correction and self-steering are constrained by these anachronistic social structures" (Kim 1984, 296). In short, this entire process is an economic path that leads to the objectification of person and planet. In this way, both the value of persons and reverence for the environment have been debased and rendered devoid of their inherent worth, dignity, and value.

From this perspective, Ikeda argues that while it is undeniable that ". . . the planet is in a pathological condition symptomized by poverty and the environmental problem," it is equally true that ". . . the fundamental issue is the pathological condition of humanity itself" (Ikeda and Diez-Hochleitner 2008, 42). What makes this situation "pathological" is in the fact that "[w]hat emerges is a notion of man's perpetual progress exempt from the laws of ecology. In short, *the anthropocentric world view has created the illusion of man's independence from nature, fostering an exceptionalist [and] exemptionalist mentality in human development"* (Kim 1984, 246–47; italics added). In response to the global environmental crisis born of this mentality, Theodore Roszak argues that ". . . if there is any hope of saving the rights of the person and planet in the years ahead, we—by which I mean the ordinary, chronically powerless people who live in the belly of the urban-industrial leviathan—*we* are going to have to find our way back to a comparable sense of mutual aid, a comparable capacity to live self-reliantly within more local and domestic economies, a comparable appreciation of the wealth that lies in modest means and simplicity of need. We are going to have to rethink some of our most firmly held assumptions about property and privacy, security and success, recognizing that there is simply no livable future for the competitive, self-regarding, high-consumption, middle-class way of life which we have been taught to regard as the culmination of industrial progress" (Roszak 1978, 287; italics in original).

In tracing the ramifications of this analysis, Ikeda makes the connection between the consequences of millions of people being denied their right to bequeath a livable global environment to posterity, on the one hand, with the inevitability and tragedy of environmental degradation, on the other. In his 1992 peace proposal, Ikeda maintained that

> [i]t goes without saying that the essence of our environmental problem is how we should go about creating a society that can exit in harmony with the natural ecosystem. For this reason, it is a compound problem that transcends the boundaries of politics, economics, science and technology . . . This is *an issue that cannot be successfully solved only from the political or economic viewpoint of individual nations.* We must instead proceed with *a reformation of the consciousness of all the Earth's people,* a task that renders the need for internal spirituality all the more acute. In the course of my earlier discussion of the *"abstract spirit"* the issue of environmental destruction was on my mind constantly. Regardless of the system that embodies it, the *"abstract spirit"* has continued to wield the same deadly sword over the environment as it has over humanity itself . . . Surely, the reformation of our internal consciousness, as citizens of the Earth who share a sense of crisis, is an issue that bears on the entire course of human history (Goulah 2010, 4; Ikeda 1992-PP; italics added).

The central value and ultimate significance of Ikeda's perspective is contained in his proposition that what is required to solve this global environmental crisis is the realization that this is *"an issue that cannot be successfully solved from only the political or economic viewpoint of individual nations,"* but that it will require *"a reformation of the consciousness of all the Earth's people."* What this means, as a practical matter, is that we have to revisit, change, and transform the nature of the North–South dialogue and—in particular—Northern and Southern perspectives on the global environment. This is necessary and essential because "[h]istorically, the developing countries' views on global environmental issues have been shaped to a considerable extent by their preoccupation with economic growth, their fears of high costs of environmental protection, and their general distrust of the policies of the industrialized states. Developing countries have generally regarded the negotiation of global regimes on ozone depletion, climate change, biodiversity loss, and conservation of endangered species as a Northern agenda" (Porter et al. 2000, 178). In this regard, a recent 2007 study on global inequality, North–South politics, and climate policy has astutely observed that

> . . . many climate policy analysts dismiss the claims of *"environmental imperialism," "ecological debt," "ecologically unequal exchange,"* and *"climate injustice"* made by developing country negotiators as empty

and distracting rhetoric used as a negotiating tactic. But, however irrational and uncooperative these claims may seem . . . these are real perceptions and these perceptions shape the way governments view their interests. And, importantly, a growing body of empirical evidence suggests that Southern worldviews and casual beliefs in some cases cannot be dismissed as false constructs or erroneous mental models used to justify poor performance. By almost any measure . . . we can say with confidence that ecologically unequal exchange is not just a perception; it is a social reality . . . (Roberts and Parks 2007, 29; italics added).

Again, in reference to some arguments previously made in chapter 7, Ikeda's assessment of the environmental crisis needs to be connected to the crisis of nuclear weapons. In his 2010 peace proposal, Ikeda once again took up the theme of humanity's need to come together in a spirit of solidarity—so as to become more effectively equipped to confront the reality of the world's limited human and economic resources. After all, the *"spirit of abstraction"* has become so widespread that it has affected humanity's thinking about basic "human security" issues—to such a great extent—that an acknowledgement of the linkage which exists between poverty and environmental destruction has often been lost. It has been lost along with the recognition that military spending, in general, and nuclear weapons, in particular, cannot resolve the complex of global issues. In Ikeda's formulation, he notes that "[i]n an era when all societies must come together to respond to the common challenges facing humankind, such as poverty and environmental destruction, *military spending has absorbed far too much of the world's limited human and economic resources.* Nuclear weapons, in particular, are a fundamental evil that cannot resolve in any way the complex of global issues, but only exacerbate them" (Ikeda 2010-PP, 12; italics added).

What this analysis of our global crisis points toward is the realization that the dominant nuclear weapons states are also the same states that consume the majority of the planet's resources (relatively speaking) and—at the same time—endanger the human security of all humankind with nuclear destruction as well. In combination, the nuclear weapons concerns coupled with environmental concerns dovetail and converge to form a double-edged sword of threat for humanity's future. This problem is not only a product of the hierarchical structure of global relations and the inequality of nation-states, it also reveals the fundamental problem that "[i]n many ways, both North and South have failed to understand the imperatives of the growing interdependence of mankind" (Ul Haq 1982, 330). Similarly, Samuel Kim has noted that "[d]eforestation, desertification, and degradation of cropland not only threaten the stability of terrestrial ecosystems, but also directly affect the societal capacity to meet basic human needs. If conventional economics and ecology seem mutually incompatible, the same cannot be said of the relationship between two world order values—basic human needs and human ecology" (Kim 1984, 294). From Ikeda's perspective, the division between conventional (traditional) economic theory and ecology is representative of the deadly effects of the *"spirit of abstraction."* After all, conventional economics places stress on the concepts of "comparative advantage" and "competitive drive" whereas, in the alternative, a more holistic worldview would emphasize the harmony of "mutuality" and "indivisibility." Given this assessment of the inadequacies of our past paradigms, concepts, and dominant values in the realm of economics and ecology, we ought to be better positioned to adopt a new strategy that refuses to start with any preconceived proposals. To that end, it has been suggested that we should ask four concrete questions:

(1) What are the premises on which the old order was based?
(2) Are these premises still valid?
(3) If not, what are the new premises which should replace them?
(4) Will the new global order meet the legitimate interests of all sides? (Ul Haq 1982, 331).

In his 2009 peace proposal, Ikeda revisited the relevance and role of the *"spirit of abstraction"* as the primary driving force behind the 2008 global economic meltdown. From Ikeda's perspective, this was useful in order to identify and acknowledge. Insofar as the 2008 economic meltdown and ensuing global recession was largely the product of the rampages of an unbridled capitalism (which denigrated and oppressed "the Other" vis-à-vis an abstract valuation of money), it became evident that an over-reliance on concepts which only furthered the *"spirit of abstraction"* could seriously harm the entire global community. Ikeda concluded that "... currency is both abstract and anonymous," because "[t]he financial markets divest it of any meaningful connection to concrete (and therefore finite) goods and services; thus, as an object of human desire, it has no real or inherent limits. Herein lies the particular characteristic, *the fateful pathology*, of our fixation on currency" (Ikeda 2009-PP, 2; italics added).

The exact same process of valuation and reductionism has reduced the natural environment—on a global scale—to something that capitalism has historically treated as infinite (even though its resources are finite). In so doing, the European and American approach to both the environment and to the people of the global South has been to "colonize" them, to seek to "control" them, and to "exploit" them. In this process, the economic, political, and cultural means chosen to effectuate various forms of exploitation (in the name of capitalism and profit) has led to resource depletion, as well as resource wars. As both a guiding paradigm and policy, the employment of and reliance upon the *"spirit of abstraction"* has simultaneously led to a world of less and less fairness, less and less equitable distribution of the earth's "common-wealth," and a diminished quality of life for the majority of the earth's peoples who have been subjected to these practices. These results are all the ultimate manifestation of anti-ecological tendencies inherent to capitalism as long as it comes to organize social product. According to Joel Kovel, the consequence of this organization is threefold:

1. Capital tends to degrade the conditions of its own production.
2. Capital must expand without end in order to exist.
3. Capital leads to a chaotic world-system increasingly polarized between rich and poor, which cannot adequately address the ecological crisis (Kovel 2007, 38).

The Ideology of Growth, Global Inequality, and the Environment

In 1974, long before the terms "climate change" or "global warming" entered into the mainstream of global consciousness, Richard Barnett and Ronald Muller published what was to become a classic book entitled, *Global Reach: The Power of Multinational Corporations*. In their discussion of the role of capitalist corporations in the global economy, they questioned the right of a self-selected corporate-elite, without clearly defined social responsibility, to act as social planners for all of humankind. In their critique of these self-proclaimed "world managers," Barnett and Muller noted that "[d]riven by the ideology of infinite growth, a religion rooted in the existential terrors of oligopolistic competition, global corporations act as if they must grow or die, and in the process they have remade thrift into a liability and waste into a virtue. The rapid growth of the global corporate economy requires ever-increasing consumption of energy. The corporate vision depends upon converting ever-greater portions of the earth into throwaway societies: ever-greater quantities of unusable waste produced with each ton of increasingly scarce mineral resources; ever-greater consumption of non-disposable and non-returnable packaging; ever-greater consumption of energy to produce a unit of energy; and ever more heat in our water and our air—in short, ever more ecological imbalance" (Barnett and Muller 1974, 364–65).

By the late-1990s it had become evident how prescient Barnett and Muller were in their assessments and predictions about the capitalist paradigm that had been designed by the world's multinational corporate leadership. According to findings contained in UNDP's 1998 Human Development Report, the 20 percent of the world's people in the highest-income countries account for 86 percent of total private consumption expenditures—the poorest 20 percent for a minuscule 1.3 percent. More specifically, the richest fifth

1. consume 45 percent of all meat and fish; the poorest fifth, 5 percent;
2. consume 58 percent of total energy; the poorest fifth less than 4 percent;
3. have 74 percent of all telephone lines; the poorest fifth, 1.5 percent;
4. consume 84 percent of all paper; the poorest fifth, 1.1 percent;

5. own 87 percent of the world's vehicle fleet; the poorest fifth, less than 1 percent (UNDP 1998; Porter et al. 2000, 180).

The trajectory of these trends toward greater levels of global inequality is not a new phenomenon. Rather, these trends have been in place since the nineteenth century and have merely accelerated in dimensionality and scope during the course of the twentieth century. In this regard, Samuel Kim has noted that "[i]nequality has always been a part of international life, but neither conservatives nor liberals can or want to explain contemporary contradictions of this age-old problem. Why has the per capita income gap between the richest and poorest country widened from 2:1 at the beginning of the nineteenth century (the century of colonialism) to its current ratio of 80–100:1 (the century of decolonization)?" (Kim 1984, 191). Similarly, Joseph Camilleri has observed that once every two or three years, we are told, ". . . the developed economies generate additional wealth equal to or greater than the total wealth of the underdeveloped economies, and this additional wealth accrues to those societies which are already consuming twelve times as much as the other two-thirds of humanity" (Camilleri 1976, 69).

As staggering as these financial assessments are it should be remembered that they reflect the global situation as it existed in the year of 1976. Now, fast forward to 2007, and we discover that ". . . increasing consumption in Europe and the United States sets an aspirational model for the rest of the world to follow. However, for everyone on Earth to live at the current European average level of consumption, more than double the bio-capacity actually available would be required—the equivalent of 2.1 planets the size of our Earth; for everyone to consume at the United States' rate, five would be required" (Woodward and Simms 2007, 134). This factual reality brings us into the nexus of global inequality and its relationship to the global environmental crisis, at which point resides the problem of climate change at the epicenter. Understanding this reality invariably and inexorably leads to the conclusion that "[g]lobal inequality plays a determining role in who suffers most immediately and profoundly from the impacts of climate change, who is most responsible for climate change, and who is most willing and able to seriously address the problem" (Roberts and Parks 2007, 31). In assessing the harms suffered by both planet Earth and those trapped in poverty on the earth we can realistically discern a "cause and effect" relationship with regard to how the rich countries are in a position within the global hierarchy of actually *causing* environmental problems in radically disproportionate manner.

According to the research results obtained by two experts in the Department of Economic and Social Affairs (DESA) of the United Secretariat, it is now an established fact that"

[w]hile rich countries are disproportionately *causing* environmental problems . . . it is the poor countries—and especially the poorer people within them—who suffer the most serious consequences. The problem is one of inverse dynamics: while the poorest receive very little of the benefit of global growth . . . they bear a disproportionate share of its costs—for example, the consequences of global warming. *As a result, the pursuit of poverty reduction through a strategy based primarily on global economic growth quickly becomes perverse: the already wealthy become both relatively and absolutely wealthier, while the poorest both slip further behind economically and have their well-being and prospects further undermined by environmental degradation* (Woodward and Simms 2007, 134–35; italics added).

In short, environmental degradation and global warming are intimately linked in important ways to the global reality of economic and social inequality as well as the failed policies of growth.

In the final analysis, from a purely economic perspective, we have reached a point where it is beyond dispute that "[m]aximizing economic growth, and hoping that we will make some progress towards our ultimate objectives as a by-product, has not, will not, and cannot work" (Woodward and Simms 2007, 156). It is for this reason, as well as others, that Oswaldo de Rivero has concluded that "[c]apitalism's triumph is an obstacle to the rise of a new planetary ethic and of a global society with less social exclusion and more environmental protection. The economy is being globalized, but ethics is not" (De Rivero 2001, 141). On this point, Ikeda would completely agree with de Rivero's assessment, which is precisely the reason why Ikeda has identified not only the "*spirit of abstraction*" as an obstacle to achieving social justice and environmental protection, but has also sought to point a way out of the entire debacle by emphasizing the benefits to be derived through the pursuit of "*humanitarian competition*," a crucial concept already mentioned in a previous chapter.

According to Ikeda, in order to escape the numerous limits which are constantly being imposed upon humankind by political, economic, and militaristic competition, we would be better off if we were to adopt a new paradigm which is supportive of a new planetary ethics and set of behaviors. Through a sincere commitment to "*humanitarian competition*," he argues, we can fundamentally begin to alter global trends that have led to our multidimensional global crisis because "[a]s a concept, it compels us to confront the reality of competition while ensuring that it is conducted firmly on the basis of humane values, thus bringing forth a synergistic reaction between humanitarian concerns and competitive energies. It is this that qualifies humanitarian competition to be a key paradigm for the twenty-first century. It is crucial here that we heed Gabriel Marcel's warning always to keep concrete realities in view" (Ikeda 2009-PP, 8).

Given this analysis, it should now be clear as to why Ikeda's condemnation of the "*spirit of abstraction*," as well as his prescription of "*humanitarian competition*," is a prescient alternative to the status quo. Ikeda's views and presentation of an alternative are prescient insofar as "[t]oday, the fashion is the quick profit, instantaneous material gratification and the obsession to participate in the material consumption banquet, at any price and no matter how. These are the components of a Darwinian, competitive, predatory behavior. *All science, technology and economic theory are at the service of this frenzy for quick profits and material gratification that is devouring social rights, as well as the environment*" (De Rivero 2001, 141; italics added).

If we are to seriously address the environmental challenge, then such an effort needs to be predicated upon an alternative set of values and behaviors that are capable of replacing those embodied in and exemplified by that which is "economic Darwinism," a single-minded competitive drive for profit (the winner–loser dichotomy), and vicissitudes of predatory globalization. Insofar as Ikeda's conception of *"humanitarian competition"* looks toward implementing a strategy of endorsing and applying forms of ethical norms and behaviors which are humane, mutually advantageous for the citizens of the North as well as the global South (win-win), and predicated upon cooperation through dialogue, then we would argue that the promise of a peaceful global civilization becomes more likely and, therefore, more attainable.

Humanitarian Competition and Overcoming the North–South Divide

The history of Northern relations with the global South is one which is largely comprised of a two-centuries-old project of the nations of the rich North imposing colonialism, neo-colonialism, imperialism, neo-imperialism, neo-liberalism upon the poor countries of the global South. As a consequence of these experiences, it should come as no shock that deeply embedded resentments have made a fruitful dialogue between North and South next to impossible as the cascading effects of these strategies of domination have served to create widening circles of socioeconomic and sociopolitical inequality within and between the two regions. In the language of "dependency theory" or "world-systems" analysis, the "center" (the North) has been engaged in furthering the "development of under-development" throughout the "periphery" of the world capitalist system (the global South).

Ikeda has argued that the best way to advance harmony, coexistence, and coprosperity among the nations of the world—especially between those of the North and South—would be through applying the Buddhist principle of "*esho funi*"—that sees the self and "the Other" (the self and the environment) as being inseparably and cooperatively interconnected. *Esho funi* is based on the view that everything is fundamentally interconnected based on the principle of *"engi,"* or dependent origination. But, before this strategy becomes a real possibility, it will be necessary to overcome the resentment, distrust, and anger of the people of the global South ("Third World") who have become the victims of tremendous economic discrepancies between themselves and the rich North through a trading system (GATT and WTO) that has subordinated most of them to a status quo of poverty in the international hierarchy of nations. It is a situation that has been compounded by the financial activities and policies of those in leadership positions at the IMF and World Bank who have encouraged the people of the Third World to go down the same path of industrialization that was pursued by the West in its rise to global preeminence. It is in this context, given this long-term experiential trajectory of Western industrialization and dominance in international affairs, that in his dialogue with French philosopher René Huyghe, we discover Ikeda having to acknowledge the historical reality that

> [t]hese peoples [of the Third World nations] are deeply dissatisfied with the excessively wide gap separating them from the industrialized nations, at whose hands they have endured deeply resented tyranny and selfishness. Far from being confined to North Africa, emotions of this kind are general and very widespread. Resentment greatly aggravates the difficulty of convincing the peoples of the Third World of the dangers they face if they fail to avoid the errors and mistakes already made by the industrialized West. *No amount of preaching about harmony and cooperation with nature can be effective in the face of mistrust and existing differences in living standards.* We must first strive to eliminate distrust by rectifying discrepancies between the Third World nations and the industrialized ones. Then, we must act sincerely to offer words of caution about the crisis (Ikeda and Huyghe 2007, 71–72).

In short, the global dimensions of international economic inequality and the growing problems associated with environmental degradation and climate change have converged with a vengeance in the early twenty-first century. Even though the North and global South attempted to engage in dialogue in the early 1970s during UN-centered debates about the need to construct a New International Economic Order (NIEO), those attempts to make the dialogue transformative and instructive fell apart. The fragmentation of these dialogues and the ensuing stalemate to deal with either the problem of global inequality or the problem of environmental degradation has led Mahbub ul Haq to note that "[t]he North tried to sell the old relationships of dependency to the South under the newly dusted slogan of interdependence; unfortunately, it did not recognize the practical implications of its own growing dependence on the South, or the fact that *genuine interdependence is impossible without greater equality of opportunity.* The South bargained for greater equality, without paying attention to the Northern interests or to the costs of sudden adjustment. The result has been a stalemate" (Ul Haq 1982, 330; italics added). Hence, just as Ikeda has suggested that *"[n]o amount of preaching about harmony and cooperation with nature can be effective in the face of mistrust and existing differences in living standards"* (Ikeda and Huyghe 2007, 71–72; italics added).

The issue of trust and the quality of dialogue are now being seen and appreciated in the task of making progress in the areas of both global inequalities and the problems posed by climate change and environmental degradation. In 2007, some scholars who had been studying the social roots of environmental damage for over twelve years embarked upon writing a book that employs a world-system analysis of global warming. Inspired by scholars from Latin America and Africa, these scholars sought to understand the global economy in a holistic way. In combination, they employed an interdisciplinary approach to the problems posed by climate change through an investigation of not only international relations, but also economics, development studies, and international negotiations. This led to many new discoveries. Not only did this approach open the door to better understanding the theoretical complementarities in international relations that might provide a complex explanation for patterns in the ratification of environmental treaties, but also led to a second bridge-building effort to marry the proximate causes and deeper social and historical determinants of vulnerability to climate disasters. This effort then allowed for an assessment of the causal significance of the role of trust, worldviews, causal beliefs, and principled understandings in North–South politics and their relationship to climate policy (Roberts and Parks 2007, x). In developing an explanation for what Roberts and Parks have called *"a model of North-South (Non-) Cooperation,"* they found that "[a]mong the many causal pathways through which global inequality influences international environmental cooperation, perhaps the most important and understudied factor is the level of trust among developed and developing nations . . . The irony is that commentators and policy makers have repeatedly emphasized that the 'climate of mistrust' surrounding international negotiations has become a tremendous obstacle to cooperation" (Robert and Parks 2007, 40).

In many critical respects, the *"climate of mistrust"* that has surrounded North–South discussions and dialogues about the necessity to deal with the continuing problems of environmental degradation and climate change has its roots in the decade of the 1970s when the South made its demands for a New International Economic Order (NIEO). It is, therefore, worth a brief examination of this period because its meaning, ramifications, and problems have direct relevance to our current dilemmas in achieving a global consensus as to what to do about climate change and the environmental crisis of the twenty-first century. To begin with, it was evident, as early as 1982, that both North and South had ". . . made major mistakes in their approach to the negotiations for a new International Economic Order (NIEO)" (Ul Haq 1982, 328). These mistakes included a catalogue of about five major mistakes by the South. These mistakes included

1. the fact that the objectives of the dialogue were not clearly perceived;
2. many developing countries did not adequately realize that internal reforms were even more important than international reforms for the welfare of their people;
3. the fact that the Third World did little service to its own cause by presenting the NIEO as a "demand" of the South when, in fact, it should have presented its case as "a global need" because the existing economic order had not been working well for any side, as evidenced by everything from the energy crisis to a host of environmental concerns;
4. the fact that the South entered the dialogue without adequate preparation and, in light of its diverse membership, that it required more frequent South–South dialogues to shape a package of negotiations that could satisfy the different interests of its various constituencies; and
5. the South made the fatal mistake of assuming that a NIEO would be "given" to it by the North, without realizing that such an order would primarily evolve through its own efforts and actions (Ul Haq 1982, 328–29).

Correspondingly, the mistakes of the South were more than matched by those of the North. These mistakes included the following three core ones:

1. The North had only assumed that the NIEO was essentially a demand of the Third World and, as such, represented no real concerns of its own. By pursuing a strategy of filibuster in various UN negotiating forums, the North engaged in finding numerous problems for every solution that the South offered, rather than trying to honestly explore a number of policy options for each problem presented,
2. Because the North was preoccupied with the more immediate problems of recession, inflation, and unemployment, it made the mistake of assuming that the answers and solutions to these short-term challenges could be found without the cooperation of the South. The energy issue by itself should have made clear the folly of such an assumption,
3. Even when the North recognized the pressure for long-term structural change, there was a natural temptation to delay adjustment. Hence, confronted with radically altered prospects for oil pricing and supply, the North merely postponed the more difficult conservation policies and deregulation of oil prices. In such an environment, long-term changes were often mortgaged to short-term expediency (Ul Haq 1982, 329–30).

Out of the ashes of these mistakes and the disappointments which followed, it became clear that only by thinking *collectively* about our global future and the contours of a preferred global civilization could humanity transcend its seemingly permanent global crisis. This ideational emphasis upon our *"collective life"* was prefigured in the writings of Tsunesaburo Makiguchi (1871–1944), the original author of the concept of "humanitarian competition."

Ikeda has refined the concept of humanitarian competition in two critical respects. First, Ikeda argues that humanitarian competition provides a means for fostering environmental sustainability, social justice, and peace. In his 2008 peace proposal, Ikeda asserted that "Tsunesaburo Makiguchi called for 'humanitarian competition' among states. *This was a vision of an international order in which the world's diverse states strive to positively influence each other, to coexist and flourish together rather than pursuing narrowly defined national interests at each other's expense. I feel that the work of solving the global environmental crisis provides a unique opportunity to move toward such a world"* (Ikeda 2008-PP, 31; italics added). Second, Ikeda also envisions humanitarian competition as being complementary to not only working out environmental issues between nation-states, but also impacting upon the responsibilities that individuals must assume as well. In this critical regard, Ikeda has maintained that *"[e]cological integrity is the shared interest and concern of all humankind, an issue that transcends national borders and priorities.* Any solution to the problems we face will require a strong sense of individual responsibility and commitment by each of us as inhabitants sharing the same planet" (Ikeda 2008-PP, 6; italics added). To that end, Ikeda has strongly reiterated this conviction in his 2009 peace proposal, when he notes that "[i]n my peace proposal last year I called for humanitarian competition to be at the heart of efforts to solve the global environmental crisis, urging the promotion of renewable energy measures and energy efficiency initiatives as a way to realize a transition from dependence on fossil fuels to a low-carbon no-waste society. Recent developments suggest movement in this direction" (Ikeda 2009-PP, 29).

Taken in combination, it can be argued that Ikeda's refinement of the concept of humanitarian competition serves to address several interrelated global problems at once. First, without directly saying it, Ikeda acknowledges the fact that the environmental crisis and related global crises are not temporary in nature. Rather, they are deeply rooted in our present international structures and institutions. Hence, unilateral national action will not resolve these problems because their ultimate resolution is dependent upon a global dialogue which takes into account the long-term interests of all nations. Second, what is ultimately at stake and at issue is a sharing of economic and political power, both within and between nations. Hence, under the banner of humanitarian competition, Ikeda is actually calling for all nations to engage in an orderly change so that humanity can more easily minimize the costs of transition to a new international order—an order conducive to peaceful change, mutual cooperation, and shared responsibility.

Such a new global order was envisioned by the leaders and grassroots social movements of the global South during the decade of the 1970s as they struggled to realize a New International Economic Order (NIEO). However, given the dialogic failures (as cited above) for rich North and poor countries of the global South to move beyond their entrenched positions, the status quo was preserved. By the start of the decade of the 1980s, there were those who still sought to accomplish such a global change in humanity's collective restructuring. Such a new global order was envisioned and articulated in 1982 by Mahbub ul Haq, who argued that "[w]hat is urgently needed is for the global community to finally show its readiness to assume certain global responsibilities in key areas of policy and to set in motion certain mechanisms and processes through which these responsibilities can be implemented" (Ul Haq 1982, 341). To that end, Ul Haq identified seven key measures, which are outlined in Table 8.1. He maintained that such a political compact of

Table 8.1   A Political Compact of Global Responsibilities

1. An internationally accepted floor below absolute poverty all over the globe and a concrete framework through which this objective can be reached over the next two decades.

2. An agreed system of international food security, based on additional investment for less-developed countries' national production, adequate food reserves, and emergency assistance in times of crisis.

3. A global responsibility for putting in place a new international energy security system, including global understanding on energy conservation, vastly increased investment resources for energy development, and mechanisms for more predictable increases in real prices.

4. Acceptance of the principle of greater automaticity in mobilization of resources to be channeled through international institutions under genuine international control.

5. Acceptance of the principle that any international reserve currency should be created only under international jurisdiction and for the benefit of all nations.

6. Acceptance of the global responsibility for creating adequate recycling mechanisms, particularly to ensure that adjustment in the next few years is not at the cost of either economic growth or social programs, or political survival of developing countries.

7. Clear recognition of the contradictions between present levels of armaments spending, global population increase and global environment deterioration for the evolution of a new order.

Source: Mahbub ul Haq, "Negotiating the Future," in, *Studies on a Just World Order—Volume 1—Toward a Just World Order*, edited by Richard Falk, Samuel S. Kim, and Saul H. Mendlovitz. Boulder, CO: Westview Press, 1982, p. 341.

global responsibilities should include an agreement in at least the following essential areas:

The articulation of the above-cited concerns in this global political compact of responsibilities serves as an illustration of a larger matrix of interlocking concerns when it comes to addressing the planetary challenges of the environmental crisis. The value of this template of global governance concerns is also found in its capacity to outline the nexus between normative concerns and concrete proposals for planetary action. Further, it is also valuable as a blueprint for the task of reimagining our approach to twenty-first century environmental challenges. In the most basic of terms, its value is found in the way in which it serves to lay bare the complexities involved in forging a global political compact of responsibilities which is inclusive of all nations while being international in scope. By virtue of the fact that this compact sets out a series of interconnected and complementary principles for reorganizing the value-structure by which we evaluate and choose certain policies over other policy choices it returns us to the most fundamental task of all—what Robert Johansen has called "value clarification."

On this matter, Johansen asserts that

> no profess of value clarification can eliminate arbitrariness or subjectivity in selecting preferred values. But this approach underscores the need to make deliberate choices and tradeoffs in the interaction of different values. In the short run at least, some preferred values may conflict with others; all cannot be grasped without the right hand knowing what the left hand is doing. To maximize food production, for example, one may need to use chemical fertilizers or pesticides that pollute. *An approach that does not emphasize values obscures the choice among conflicting goals* (Johansen 1982, 206; italics added).

Also, in correspondence with the above-cited principles and values of this global political compact of responsibilities, it becomes manifestly clear that

> [a] value-centered approach also helps overcome the level-of-analysis problem. That is, *by adopting a value-framework that can be deliberately constructed so as to reflect planetary rather than strictly national concerns, it is easier to avoid the trap of looking at international relations from a parochial nation-state view.* Officials can then give adequate attention to both the total world system and the subsystems within it. Sensitivity to double standards is enhanced by this approach because explicit norms can be universally applied" (Johansen 1982, 206; italics added).

Johansen's assessment of the problems and challenges associated with value-clarification is shared by Samuel Kim, who notes that "the most problematic feature of the value-shaping process is its limited normative parameters. Operating as it does within the state-centric framework, the process allows the shaping or reshaping of values in a deliberately restrained and incremental fashion that never challenges the basic premises of the existing social order in domestic and international societies" (Kim 1984, 286).

Aware of the problems posed by the state-centric framework of global relations that distorts value-clarification processes that attempt to make universal and planetary claims, Ikeda has charted a different path out of the quagmire of this problem through his reliance on the concept of *humanitarian competition* and the principle of *esho funi* when addressing the environmental crisis. The genius of Ikeda was evident in 2006 when he ". . . articulated environmental issues as a raison d'etre of *humanitarian competition,* again referring to his proposal for the UN Decade of Education for Sustainable Development and considering *esho funi* as a principle that can help resolve the environmental crisis" (Goulah 2010, 14). By virtue of taking this approach to the environmental crisis, Ikeda has effectively removed the resolution of this crisis from the traditional normative domain of state-centric logics and excuses for either taking no action, or limited action. Instead, he placed the issue of the environmental crisis on the global agenda, within the institutional body of the UN which, by virtue of its Charter, has a formally agreed-upon mandate to undertake international action on this crisis in such a manner that it can force governments to be more receptive not only to their own citizens, but also to the citizens of the world.

By undertaking this plan of action, Ikeda has also reintroduced the dynamic process of the *human revolution,* which leads to a more complete recomposition of the individual subject and the world. Insofar as the principle of *esho funi* demands that we put an end to the separation of the person from their environment and instead becomes enabled to see the self and *"the Other"* as inseparable and cooperatively connected, there is a new historical opening in human consciousness and action where "[w]e can no longer accept modes of thought and action based on binary oppositions, obliging us to protect culture from nature, reason from emotion, men from women, and civilization from savages. *We endeavor to bring together what has been sundered, to replace conquest with dialogue and a quest for new combinations"* (Touraine 1997, 143; italics added). This is the great challenge of the twenty-first century with respect to global warming and climate change, insofar as "[t]oday, the transition to a globalized world is progressing rapidly, but the transition to a sustainable one is not" (Speth 2003, 2). As we examine the historical record of who has done the most to move the global environmental agenda forward since the 1970s, it can be attributed to a small, international leadership community in science, governments, the UN, and NGOs (Speth 2003, 7). It is to the subject of this leadership group and their work over the last four decades that we now turn.

From 1970 to 2001: The Great Global Environmental Accomplishments

The decade of the 1960s witnessed the growth of a predominantly domestic environmental agenda that matured in the decade of the 1970s. During the 1970s, a steady stream of publications began to adopt a planetary perspective on global-scale problems. Although most were authored by scientists, many nonscientists from the fields of law, history, and political science added their voices. Some of the most prominent of these publications included the following: (1) *Man's Impact on the Global Environment* (1970), Report of the Study of Critical Environmental Problems (the work-product of a scientific group assembled at MIT); (2) *This Endangered Planet* (1971), Richard Falk; (3) *Exploring New Ethics for Survival* (1972), Garrett Hardin; (4) *The Limits to Growth* (1972), Dennis Meadows, et al; (5) *Only One Earth* (1972), Barbara Ward and Rene Dubos; (6) *The Human Future Revisited* (1978), Harrison Brown; (7) *The Twenty-Ninth Day* (1978), Lester Brown. Yet, the bulk of work being done in the 1970s was by scientific groups, especially panels and commissions organized by the International Council of Scientific Unions, the US National Academy of Sciences, the International Union for the Conservation of Nature (IUCN), and the UN Environment Program (UNEP). Among all of these report, the "Charney Report" of 1970 represented the first effort of the US National Academy of Sciences on the problem of global climate change.

By the early 1980s, a second generation of report appeared which attempted to gather together the major issues into a more coherent agenda for international action. According to Gustave Speth, "[t]hese syntheses, predominantly scientific efforts, were designed to being global-scale challenges forcefully to the attention of governments" (Speth 2003, 5). Collectively, these reports stressed ten principal concerns, as outlined in Table 8.2.

The decade of the 1980s saw the emergence of a truly global agenda. It was in the 1980s that, for the first time in history, governments and other organizations really did start to take notice of the environmental crisis as a global one. They also began to take responsibility for planetary management. Hence, over the course of the last two decades (1990–2010), the international community embarked upon humanity's tepid efforts to engage in the task of global environmental governance. In assessing the progress made thus far, it is important to note what has been accomplished to date in the area of environmental global governance (as outlined in Table 8.3).

The progress noted in the above-cited chronology of progress toward global environmental governance has been contemporaneous with the work and writings of Ikeda. In 1978, Ikeda proposed the creation of an "Environmental United Nations" for the precise reason that he knew governance issues with regard to the emerging climate crisis would have to be at the heart and center of global action, governance, and consciousness. Therefore, Ikeda's

Table 8.2   Ten Principal Environmental Challenges from the 1980s

1. Depletion of the stratospheric Ozone layers by CFCs and other gases.

2. Loss of crop and grazing land due to desertification, erosion, conversation of land to nonfarm uses, and other factors.

3. Depletion of the world's tropical forests, leading to loss of forest resources, serious watershed damage (erosion, flooding, and siltation, and other adverse consequences).

4. Mass extinction of species, principally from the global loss of wildlife habitat, and the associated loss of genetic resources.

5. Rapid population growth, burgeoning Third World cities, and ecological refugees.

6. Mismanagement and shortages of freshwater resources.

7. Over-fishing, habitat destruction, and pollution in the marine environment.

8. Threats to human health from mismanagement of pesticides and persistent organic pollutants.

9. Climate change due to the increase in "greenhouse gases" in the atmosphere.

10. Acid rain and, more generally, the effects of a complex mix of air pollutants on fisheries, forests, and crops.

Source: James Gustave Speth, "Two Perspectives on Globalization and the Environment," in, *Worlds Apart: Globalization and the Environment*, edited by James Gustave Speth. Washington, DC: Island Press, 2003, pp. 5–6.

emphasis upon the need to establish an Environmental United Nations has been predicated upon involving all nations in the task of pooling their brain power in the study, research, and investment needed in order to formulate and effectuate the development of concrete policies that would be capable of solving these ecological difficulties. Ikeda's proposals, however, were not limited to study and research. He simultaneously argued that the promise of harmony, coexistence, and coprosperity of nations could be predicated upon healing the divisions and rift between the rich North and the poor global South.

Within this framework of understanding, Ikeda's various proposals in the area of environmental protection, global governance, sustainable development, as well as the growth of environmental consciousness, have been ultimately predicated upon his keen acknowledgment of the necessity to place all of these efforts in the service of an actualized humanitarian competition. Only in this way would it be possible to craft a global plan of action which

Table 8.3 Progress toward Global Environmental Governance

1. An agenda has been defined—an agenda of the principal large-scale environmental concerns of the international community.

2. In response to this agenda, a huge upsurge of international conferences, negotiations, action plans, treaties, and other initiatives has occurred. New fields of international environmental law and diplomacy have been born. There are now over 250 international environmental treaties, two thirds of them signed in recent decades.

3. There has been a vast outpouring of impressive and relevant scientific research and policy analysis.

4. An ever-stronger international community of environmental and other nongovernmental organizations (NGOs) has launched increasingly sophisticated campaigns. Initiatives have spanned from global to local, from civil disobedience to restrained think-tank publications.

5. National governments as well as multilateral institutions from the United Nations to the international development banks have recognized these concerns and have created major units to address global-scale issues.

6. While many multinational corporations are still in denial, many others have moved ahead with impressive steps, often ahead of their governments.

7. In the academy, international environmental affairs have become a major subject of academic inquiry and teaching in political science, economics, and other departments. A large body of scholarly analysis now exists.

8. The United Nations has sponsored an extraordinary series of milestone events: The 1972 Stockholm Conference on the Human Environment was followed by the 1992 Rio Earth Summit and the 2002 World Summit for Sustainable Development in Johannesburg.

Source: James Gustave Speth, "Two Perspectives on Globalization and the Environment," in, *World's Apart: Globalization and the Environment*, edited by James Gustave Speth. Washington, DC: Island Press, 2003, pp. 3–4.

could serve as an antidote to the spirit of abstraction. Hence, Ikeda's proposals have also envisioned the application of these plans to the articulation of focused educational programs that would have the power to engage people at the grassroots in such a way that the power of humanity's collective voice would be heard.

Ikeda's prescription for the working out of this strategy involves the articulation of an approach to global change wherein "[i]n addition to 'top down' reform through institutional reframing, it is crucial to encourage 'bottom-up' change by broadening grassroots engagement and empowering people toward collective action." To this end, Ikeda added that "[t]his conviction underpinned my call for a *Decade of Education for Sustainable Development . . .*

Empowerment through learning brings out the unlimited potentials of individuals and consequently creates current, first within the respective regions, and eventually globally across borders, that can fundamentally transform the world in which we live" (Ikeda 2008-PP, 32; italics added). Ikeda's views on this matter correspond well with the thirty-year update of *Limits to Growth* (Meadows et al. 2004). The authors of the thirty-year update emphatically state, "Humanity cannot triumph in the adventure of reducing the human footprint to a sustainable level if that adventure is not undertaken in a spirit of global partnership. Collapse cannot be avoided if people do not learn to view themselves and others as part of one integrated global society. Both will require compassion, not only with the here and now, but with the . . . future as well. Humanity must learn to love the idea of leaving future generations a living planet" (Meadows et al. 2004, 282–83).

This set of values and views is also a perspective which radiates out from the pages of the UNDP's Human Development Report 2007/2008. The various authors of the UNDP document unequivocally state, "*The human fact of climate change cannot be captured and packaged in statistics.* Many of the current impacts are impossible to separate from wider pressures. Others will happen in the future. There is uncertainty about the location, timing and magnitude of these impacts. However, uncertainty is not a cause for complacency. We know that climate-related risks are a major cause of human suffering, poverty and diminished opportunity. We know that climate change is implicated. And we know that the threat will intensify over time" (UNDP 2009, 73–74; italics added). Yet, as James Speth has noted, ". . . the global environmental agenda emerged and moved forward due primarily to a relatively small, international leadership community in science, government, the UN, and the NGOs. These groups took available opportunities to put the issues forward—indeed, they created such opportunities—so that governments had little choice but to take some action. The game that many governments played was to respond but not to respond forcefully" (Speth 2003, 7).

The Unfinished Global Agenda for Environmental Transformation

In light of the recalcitrance of governments to move further than they actually did, Speth postulates that we should consider some of the contrasts between governmental action (inaction) and the proposals advanced by the global environmental community. He begins with the observation that "[t]he issues on the US domestic environmental agenda of the 1970s . . . tended to be acute, immediate, and understandable by the public. Those on the global agenda tend to be more chronic, more remote (at least in the North), and more technically complicated and thus more difficult to understand and appreciate. Over time these differences have translated into major differences in the degree of public awareness and support" (Speth 2003, 8).

Alternatively, in contrast to Seth, Prof. Samuel Kim argues that

> [t]he common language of the knowledge-expanding, norm-making, and programmatic activities in the domain of global eco-politics belies the invisible constraints imposed by the heavy hand of the dominant states. Global eco-politics tries hard but seldom succeeds in escaping from the strategic and economic imperatives of international politics ... the very existence of states in an anarchical/hierarchical system can only generate the will to compete, conquer, and control. The hegemonic structure of global geopolitics is in absolute conflict with the politics of a planetary eco-order ... [T]he quest to bring the social environment into harmony with the natural environment does not seem too promising without normative, structural, and behavioral transformations in both domestic and international societies (Kim 1984, 296–97).

This is precisely the challenge that makes the climate change issue so daunting at the dawn of the twenty-first century. As discussed previously in chapter 7, the problems associated with hegemonic states are directly attributable to their nonaccountability to the global commonwealth and their preoccupation with a narrowly defined national interest and geopolitical narrative which disrupts the introduction of a more humane, inclusive, and normative discourse from having any real effect on state practices and policies (Paupp 2009). Hence, the challenge with which we are confronted is largely one that centers on a question of priorities as to whether the forces working on behalf of a new approach to economics and politics—that is accountable to environmental values—will be able to overcome past centuries of practices and policies which have automatically rewarded the destructive enterprises and policies of those who were guided by a normative structure in their endeavors to dominate, control, and exploit (regardless of the cost and irrespective of the long-term consequences). From the perspective of Samuel Kim, "The ecological crisis is a crisis of priorities in human development. The perspective of the victims deserves more attention than it has received in ecological literature. The poor in both rich and poor countries suffer most as they live in the most polluted areas. Even the holistic world order approach faces the clear and continuing danger of losing touch with the voices of the oppressed by abstracting—and diluting—the consequences of ecological transgressions in terms of the 'tragedy of the commons' or escaping from the *present* plight of the wretched of the earth into the holistic ecological obligations to *future* generations" (Kim 1984, 297; italics in original).

Along these same lines, other scholars have argued that an overemphasis upon the market and the neo-liberal model of economics has sacrificed both people and the environment upon the altar of profit "for the few." Therefore, if we are to remake the world and rescue the environment, then we must abandon the old creeds of capitalist practice and embrace an alternative society with alternative practices, norms, and values at both the domestic and international levels. Hence, it has been argued that we should invert our economic thinking. In so doing, the argument goes, we are freed to see that

> "[t]he alternative historical project proposes inverting the relationship between private interests and the common good, ultimately favoring the whole. Totality-based project are centered on the citizenry in its natural surroundings. *Social rights and the right to life are derived from membership in the human community and not limited by participation in the market or to its confines.* This project would not abolish the market, but would gradually subordinate its rationality to that of the citizenry. In other words, it would intercede between private interests and the common good in favor of the latter. It essentially aims to invert economic rationality to favor the citizenry instead of private interests. It is *highly inclusive* and does not *a priori* exclude any sector (Dierckxsens 2000, 153–54; italics added).

In the spirit of Ikeda, one scholar has concluded that "inverting the global economic rationality is a political, not economic issue. This same economic globalization also provides the possibility and even the historical need to subordinate micro-level efficiency to macro-level vitality. *By reclaiming the Common Good it becomes possible to transcend the nationalism of the past and, for the first time in history, to function on behalf of humanity as a whole*" (Dierckxsens 2000, 155; italics added). This process is already underway in the Asia-Pacific region. It is a trend that has been close to Ikeda's own heart and aspirations when he called for the creation of an East Asian environment and development organization as a pilot model of regional cooperation and the kernel for the eventual creation of an East Asian Union (Goulah 2010, 14).

According to Richard Falk, we find this vision currently unfolding under the rubric of regionalism and under the auspices of ASEAN. Falk has observed that

> [i]n the Asia-Pacific region, the internal dimension of regionalism is to take early, mainly informal, and ad hoc steps toward economic cooperation and coordination, viewing especially ASEAN as possessing potential for expansion and further institutionalization in the post-Cold War era. These steps are reinforced by a new Asian cultural assertiveness, which both moves toward the affirmation of a regional identity but also represents a deepening of the decolonization process by its implicit repudiation of Eurocentrism. In this regard, *Asia-Pacific regionalism* resists any renewal of Western hegemonic projects and helps explain Asian unity with respect to opposing doctrines of humanitarian intervention to correct several abuses of human rights or to remove military rulers from power. As

such, Asian/Pacific regionalism, even more than its European counterpart, may be moving toward limiting the Western role, especially
the United States, thereby encouraging a *defensive* dimension of
regionalism (Falk 2004a, 62; italics in original).

Falk's view is in keeping with the historical perspective regarding the role
of global corporations throughout the underdeveloped as depicted in the
1974 classic work on the subject, *Global Reach* (Barnett and Muller 1974).
The authors noted that

> [t]he finance capital generated by the natural wealth of many coun-
> tries of the underdeveloped world was not used to develop local fac-
> tories, schools, and other structures for generating more wealth but
> was siphoned off to the developed world—first as plunder, then in the
> more respectable form of dividends, royalties, and technical fees . . .
> Thus, the power over national wealth was largely in the hands of
> foreigners, the finance-capital generated by past wealth-producing
> activities was not used to maintain, much less to expand, the local
> economy. The result was a process of wealth depletion which has
> resulted inevitably in lower consumption for the local population.
> The net outflow of finance capital from the underdeveloped societ-
> ies weakened their capacity to develop the knowledge to produce
> wealth, and this further decreased their bargaining power (Barnett
> and Muller 1974, 135).

Taken in combination, these views are in keeping with Ikeda's perspective
on the need to protect and advance regionalism in East Asia and Southeast
Asia. As we have already commented upon in previous chapters, the ASEAN
experiment in regionalism has been a success in promoting peace and the
processes associated with demilitarization. To that list of accomplishments
we may also include environmental management successes at the regional
level. The ASEAN experience in environmental management illustrates
the strengths and limitations of environmental governance at the regional
level, with important lessons for the global level. In this regard, the role and
functions of ASEAN in the environmental domain is one model for regional
governance with implications for the global level (Lian and Robinson 2002,
101–20). When ASEAN's environmental policies are considered in light of
the region's environmental needs, several key strengths become apparent,
as shown in Table 8.4.

The above-cited strengths of ASEAN's environmental policies and approach
represents a number of new and innovative approaches to the design of global
governance, especially with respect to dealing with the challenge of climate
change and global warming. First, the "ASEAN Way" is widely regarded as ". . .
a defined approach, distinct from the more formalistic parliamentary decision-
making systems of Europe and North America, [which] is evidence of the

Table 8.4   Some Key Strengths of ASEAN's Environmental Policies

1. *Adaptation capacity.* In many instances, ASEAN has demonstrated an ability to adapt to new circumstances. ASEAN overcame the reunification of Vietnam in 1975, Vietnam's invasion of Cambodia in 1979, and the end of the Cold War in the early 1990s, when the organization was expected to disband.

2. *Effective regional policy formulation.* ASEAN has been remarkably successful in shaping a common regional environment policy framework. By respecting each country's internal procedures, ASEAN has facilitated cooperation.

3. *Stable relationships among members.* The noninterventionist approach has contributed to building relatively stable relations among member states. The community building process has facilitated social and political interaction, rather than interference, and has reduced intra-ASEAN tensions.

4. *Sound foundation for implementation.* ASEAN's consensus building process has created a sound foundation for implementation. For instance, the Working Group on Nature Conservation and Biodiversity has drafted an ASEAN framework agreement on access to genetic resources, which may be effective in shaping a common approach among the administrations and parliaments of the ASEAN states, or may form the basis for new regional hard law instrument. It is also likely to minimize—in advance—possible regional trade disputes on the subject.

Source: Koh Kheng Lian and Nicholas A. Robinson, "Regional Environmental Governance: Examining the Association of Southeast Asian Nations (ASEAN) Model," in, *Global Environmental Governance: Options and Opportunities*, edited by Daniel C. Etsy and Maria H. Ivanova. Yale Center for Environmental Law and Policy, 2002, pp. 110–11.

proposition that ASEAN bears close study by those interested in strengthening regional and global environmental governance" (Lian and Robinson 2002, 107). Second, ASEAN has been very effective in its effort to manage biodiversity and in the way in which it addresses transboundary air pollution from forest fires. Third, ASEAN has been effective as an example of how regions can not only promote economic and cultural cooperation, but also how every region across the globe can benefit from its capacity to engage in "confidence-building" (as discussed in chapter 5).

In combination, these three points make the case that *"[r]egional environmental governance represents an indispensable link between, and complement to, national and global initiatives.* As illustrated by the ASEAN case, to be more effective, regional systems for environmental governance need to supplement cooperative policy formulation with effective mechanisms to facilitate implementation of policies at both the subregional and national levels"

(Lian and Robinson 2002, 118; italics added). In support of this perspective, Richard Falk notes that "[i]nstitutional and normative expressions of regional and global solidarity will be needed to address such issues as climate change, regulation of the world economy, establishment of security, maintenance of human rights, and implementation of the ethos of a responsibility to protect peoples confronting an imminent human catastrophe. As well, sustainability will depend on taking into present account the needs of future generations, with respect to resources and the foundations of life supportive of individual and collective human dignity" (Falk 2009, 58). These insights have increased relevance given the weaknesses of the UN system with respect to the tasks associated with effective environmental global governance. The weaknesses of the UN system are addressed in Table 8.5.

The above-cited criticisms of the current UN system serve to underscore Ikeda's wisdom in his 1992 peace proposal which sought to reorganize the UN to address the great environmental issues that were not considered at its inception. This involved the need to revisit the idea of an environmental UN, as well as his 1991 peace proposal which advocated the establishment of an Environmental Security Council. By 1992, this idea had been endorsed by Japan and other nations. The proposal for the establishment of an Environmental Security Council involved dividing the UN into two strengthened

Table 8.5 The Weakness of the UN System of Global Environmental Governance

1. There is no global institution with adequate authority to mobilize the financial resources to protect the global commons. Such actions could include the creation of financial incentives for responsible environmental behavior and fines and taxes for irresponsible behavior.

2. There is no independently powerful global authority able to operate with impartiality and even-handedness and to name and publicize nation-states in violation of the norms and rules codified in international environmental law.

3. There is no global authority in charge of coordinating and integrating all programs and agencies engaged in global environmental governance.

4. There is a lack of integration of environmental and development concerns in policy planning at the global level. The powerful international agencies (World Bank/IMF) pursue an agenda of economic liberalization with environmental concerns often an afterthought. The environmental intergovernmental organizations (IGOs) lack the resources and power to balance the developmental agenda. A full integration must be a priority.

Source: William F. Felice, *The Global New Deal: Economic and Social Human Rights in World Politics*. Lanham, MD: Rowman & Littlefield Publishers, Inc., 2003, p. 117.

and independent bodies—one concerned with peacekeeping and the other concerned with problems such as environmental global governance and human rights (Goulah 2010, 11). From Ikeda's perspective, such an institutional reformulation of the UN would have the double benefit of removing our governing values, priorities, and policies form the effects of the *"abstract spirit,"* as well as helping in the task of readjusting each nation's self-chosen priorities to more perfectly mirror the ideas behind the concept of *"humanitarian competition"*—thereby empowering countries to see the wisdom of abandoning the idea of the primacy of sovereignty so that each country could transfer part of its authority to an international body that could more effectively coordinate the diverse components of our global environmental governance regime. Hence, the final realization of a UN of Environment and Development would signal the demise of *"the myth of development"* which ". . . is so deeply rooted in the collective subconscious of the political class that they think that they only have to set in motion the economic and financial policy that is in fashion, and has been dictated by the great economic powers, the transnationals and the international economic and financial organizations" (De Rivero 2001, 186).

Conclusion

By refusing to fall in lockstep behind the current masters of the status quo, humanity will finally discover that, especially in the less industrialized world of the global South,

> it would be folly for them to pursue the resource intensive industrial one previously followed by the countries of the Global North. Of course, it is also clear that the countries of the Global North bear considerable responsibility for creating this development dilemma because of their own excessive resource consumption and cumulative pollution. Nearly half of the population of the Global South is now living in China and India. The developmental choices made by these countries will have an enormous impact on future ecological security. Envisioning the environmental impact of a fully industrialized India and China in 2025, based on current US consumption patterns, highlights the need to find a more ecologically sound model for future development (Pirages and DeGeest 2004, 200).

Correspondingly, Peter Evans notes that

> the poor cities of the developing world are often vibrant hubs of economic and cultural activity, but they are also ecologically unsustainable and, for ordinary citizens, increasingly unlivable. Three-fourths of those joining the world's population during the next century will live in Third World cities. Unless these cities are

able to provide decent livelihoods for ordinary people and become ecologically sustainable, the future is bleak. The politics of livelihood and sustainability in these cities has become the archetypal challenge of twenty-first century governance (Evans 2002, 1).

Unless radical alterations are made to the status quo of a market-driven economics and a culturally-driven consumerism, we will continue to witness the emergence of a global environment that is more undemocratic, more unsustainable, and more unjust. Therefore, the conclusion that logically follows is best expressed by Paul and Anne Ehrlich, who maintain that "[w]e are convinced that the prudent course for the United States and other developed nations that wish to reduce terrorism in the short term, and avoid collision with the natural world in the medium term, is not to attempt to rule the world by brute force. A much better approach, and one more likely to succeed, is to work to ameliorate conditions for the poorest people around the world" (Ehrlich and Ehrlich 2004, 137). I have made the same argument with regard to the need of the United States to renounce its informal empire, its pursuit of hegemony, and its continued reliance on military force to advance its geopolitical agenda as a hegemonic state (Paupp 2007, 2009). Rather, it is better to embrace the fact the walls of empire and hegemony are crumbling and, in its place, we are witnessing the emergence of a twenty-first century multicentric world of "rising regions" (Paupp 2009).

A little over eight years ago, in December 1928, Gandhi wrote, "God forbid that India should ever take to industrialization after the manner of the West. The economic imperialism of a single tiny island kingdom [England] is today keeping the world in chains. If an entire nation of three hundred million [India's population at the time] took to similar economic exploitation, it would strip the world like locusts" (quoted in: Guha 2000, 22). On this point, Prof. Giovanni Arrighi observed that "Gandhi already knew then what many leaders of Southern emancipation have yet to learn or have forgotten: *Western success along the extroverted, Industrial Revolution path was based upon the exclusion of the vast majority of the world's population from access to the natural and human resources needed to benefit rather than bear the costs of global industrialization.* As such, it never was an option for the majority" (Arrighi 2007, 386; italics added). Similarly, Kamla Chowdhry reminds us that "[t]he environmentalists, like Gandhi, share the idea of austerity, of not having affluent lifestyles, of equitably sharing resources, of bearing in mind the limited resources of the planet. The ancients in India recognized that one should take from the earth only as much as one can put back. In the *Atharva Veda*, in the hymn to the earth, they chanted: '*What of thee I dig out, let that quickly grow over. Let me not hit thy vitals or thy heart*'" (Chowdhry 1989, 153; italics added).

This insight is not confined to either the culture of India or the personage of Gandhi. Rather, it is also a central part of what Ken Jones has called "*the new social face of Buddhism*" which asserts that "... engaged Buddhism is a radical conservatism. On the one hand, it has a revolutionary vision originating in its insight into human potential. On the other, it remains grounded in the stubborn realities of our ecological and social predicament and rooted in the deep tangled texture of history" (Jones 2003, 233). In the context of the global environmental crisis (which all humans must now confront), we are also forced to confront our collective and individual delusions, our ever changing forms of identity, and what we identify with—whether it be the market-driven capitalism of neo-liberalism, or a more progressive, nuanced, and socially-conscious quest to improve the human condition. In either case, we "... are assemblages of dynamic yet wholly conditioned structures (*samskara*) forged through the crucible of past actions and experience" (Waldron 2003, 153).

As we progress through this crucible, we are struggling with the task of finding common ground and common cause with one another, as well as within our own self-understanding. This task is complicated by what Buddhism has referred to as the "*affliction of identity*." In coming to terms with the most relevant meaning of this concept, professor of South Asian Buddhism, William Waldron has observed that "...

> identity is inherently unstable, its instability grounded in the social and cultural nature of its origins, and any cultural symbol system is similarly and necessarily fragile and vulnerable. We are always changing our minds, our feelings, our modes of expression, our established patterns of interaction, and our complex symbolizations of reality. Identities, meanings, and shared symbols proliferate and disperse with distressing regularity, ever prone to differentiation, dissolution, and decay. And it is precisely this tension between the sheer necessity for such overlapping levels of identity and inherent fragility of all such constructions that drives the underlying compulsions behind humanity's massive, engineered inhumanity. "Identities," the Buddhists remind us, are constructs designed to counteract the impermanent, restless, and identity-less nature of things, to, in short, turn reality on its head (Waldron 2003, 164).

Imagine applying the above-referenced discussion on the "affliction of identity" to the multifaceted problems twenty-first century humanity faces with regard to the energy crisis, competition over limited energy resources, and the "resource wars" that have been undertaken from Iraq to Afghanistan. Imagine if we were to take all of the proposals presented in this chapter—especially those by Ikeda—and cast them into a new mold of human identity in which cooperation, rather than conflict, was the central organizing principle of our actions and policies? What if global cooperation, instead of global conflict, became our most principal principle? From the perspective of one scholar who has undertaken this challenge, we find, in the words of Michael Klare,

It seems reasonable to ask whether a resource-acquisition strategy based on global cooperation rather than recurring conflict might not prove more effective in guaranteeing access to critical supplies over the long run. Such a strategy would call for the equitable distribution of the world's existing resource stockpiles in times of acute scarcity, as well as an accelerated, global program of research on alternative energy sources and industrial processes. Coordinated international efforts would be inaugurated to conserve scarce commodities and employ material-saving technologies. The key to making this strategy work effectively would be the establishment of robust international institutions that could address major resource problems while retaining the confidence of global leaders and the public . . . In return for their support of these efforts, member states would be assured of emergency deliveries of vital materials and would be guaranteed access to any new technologies generated by the common research effort (Klare 2001, 223).

Clearly, the adoption of such a strategy would invariably lead to a shifting of identities and behaviors—individually, nationally, and internationally. In many ways, it would also begin to point toward environmental sanity and away from war and conflict as the primary means of solving human problems. In short, such a strategy of cooperation based on the pursuit of peace and the peaceful resolution of problems might, at the last, produce the greatest climate change of all—a shifting away from a *"climate of mistrust"* toward a *"climate of human solidarity,"* as we collectively embark upon the resolution of our global problems from a stance of mutual cooperation, shared values, and common purpose.

9

Conclusion: Contextualizing Ikeda in the Struggle to Restructure International Politics

A human right to peace, if it is to be more than an empty phrase, would require a radical restructuring of international politics. That might, in some abstract moral sense, be desirable. But I see no evidence that it is in fact widely desired by the citizenry of most states, let alone by governments. And exactly how we would get from here to there remains a mystery."
—Jack Donnelly (2006, 154)

[W]e should bear in mind that positive peace is multidimensional. It involves, among other things, equitable, participatory, and stable political institutions, as well as economic, social, and cultural conditions that guarantee diversity and minimal standards of well-being and protection for the vulnerable. The human rights covenants are themselves the widely acknowledged source for such norms and standards. Still . . . human rights are also a source of controversy and therefore in their contemporary forms are neither an accurate reflection of international practice nor a fully adequate articulation of positive peace."
—Said and Lerche (2006, 134)

[E]ven before the adoption of the Universal Declaration of Human Rights, 82 percent of the national constitutions that had been drafted between 1788 and 1948 contained some kind of protection for human rights. Thereafter, the percentage increased further so that 93 percent of the constitutions drafted between 1949 and 1975 included human rights provisions."
—Alston (1999, 3)

Whether 'universal' human rights exist at any given moment is rarely self-evident and always open to debate. What cannot be disputed is that there is no such thing as universal human rights whose validity has been accepted at all times, by all peoples, and in all places. Much like the closely connected concepts of justice, freedom, and equality, the concept of human rights has both evolutionary and revolutionary potential."

—Kim (1991, 357)

Human rights, as much as any domain of societal endeavor, is always in motion as values change and social movements emerge."

—Falk (2009, 8)

[I]t is only in the course of the 17th and 18th centuries that the fatalistic acceptance of war as a natural and inevitable element in human affairs comes under sustained challenge, that peace becomes an imaginable political reality, and that religious and political movements come to be organized around this idea. Peace and a pacific theory of international relations had to be invented."

—Hurrell (2007, 69)

Throughout this book, I have sought to chronicle the great breadth of issues that make up and constitute our current global crisis. Yet beyond engaging in a mere recital of the various crises, I have sought to set forth the ideas of Ikeda and his contemporaries in order to provide the reader with a series of possible solutions, road maps and remedies in order to help transcend the magnitude and scope of what the global crisis entails. We find in Ikeda's various works a series of road maps and remedies for humanity that might help to ensure a more efficient and comprehensive exit from the causes and consequences of the current global crisis. In so doing, I have juxtaposed his works and perspectives with those of various leading Western scholars and "Third World" voices from across the entire global South. In order to do this effectively, I have referenced the writings of both Eastern and Western thinkers in an attempt to demonstrate how both Ikeda and his other contemporaries have chosen to address issues of global concern through a more holistic approach that centralizes preferred world-order values such as justice, human rights, peace, and environmental sustainability.

The answers and insights that Ikeda and his contemporaries have all coalesced around provide us with new analytical tools and concepts that we can use to reframe our own perceptions. In fact, this is largely the challenge posed by Ikeda's concepts of inner transformation (human revolution), dialogue, and global citizenship. By having engaged in an examination of these categories, we have been able to extrapolate on the dynamic interchange between these three major categories of Ikeda's philosophy. We are now further enabled to challenge our old assumptions and revive a centuries-old hope for finding a way out of the trap of war and even transcend the definition of peace as being little more than the absence of war ("negative peace"). We are at the threshold of an even greater historical opportunity at the dawn of the twenty-first century. By seeking to achieve a more peaceful global civilization we are forced to examine the multidimensional nature of peace and the totality of its meaning because—in order to capture and maintain the benefits of a "positive peace"—we must be engaged in seeking a comprehensive peace that allows us the possibility of realistically working toward the achievement of a peaceful global civilization. In this regard, we have now arrived at a *human needs/human rights nexus*. While it is true that a "human rights/human needs nexus does not mean that the two categories are the same concepts," such a nexus does imply that we can and must seek "a closer relationship between indispensable need and actual rights" (Kim 1991, 369). To put the matter another way, it has been argued that "either we as human beings have to accept the oppression, violence, and injustice in the world as fundamental to the human condition and therefore irremediable, or we accept the premise of human needs theory that there are basic norms and needs that, when reflected in our institutions and processes of governance, should foster social peace, stability, and progress" (Said and Lerche 2006, 142).

Such a reframing of our thoughts and definitions about human rights and human needs would have profound effects on the possibilities inherent in restructuring our global order and the very nature of global relations. At its heart, the essential and core nature of this paradigmatic shift in focus would be transformational because it moves us away from a statist-orientation and a statist set of assumptions about international relations (IR) theory which sees human rights as principally a matter of sovereign national jurisdiction. Instead of remaining trapped in this Westphalian worldview, the adoption of a *human needs/human rights nexus* allows for the chance to move us toward a cosmopolitan perspective on IR where we start with individuals who are seen more as members of a single global political community (Said and Lerche 2006, 135). Hence, the adoption of a *human needs/human rights nexus* constitutes a transformational shift in our thinking because it would point us in the direction of seeking to create a global civilization in which human dignity and respect for the rights of the person serve to redefine our policies, reprioritize our values, and challenge the very institutions of the status quo. In this regard, both Ikeda and his contemporaries are arguing that change is essential so that we can create new and more humane global institutional arrangements, as well as more inclusive forms of global governance, which are supportive of both the human right to peace and the human right to development.

Historically, the diverse literature on human rights largely agrees on one point—*Human rights are concerned with the dignity of the individual*. However, this particular formulation is not as straightforward as it looks at first glance. While the pursuit of human dignity is universal, it is defined by the culture of a people (Said and Lerche 2006, 134). At the dawn of the twenty-first century, the defining force of the "culture of a people" is no longer just a matter of local, national, or regional concern and influence—it is a global concern and it emanates from an emerging global culture. Yet the historical fact remains that many of the roots of our globalizing world culture have their source and origination in the religious traditions of the world's major religions. Our human rights culture has been largely derived from the Judeo-Christian tradition of the West as its predominant source. The problem is that this emphasis on the West's human rights culture as a common denominator for the world has been characterized as a parochial view of human rights, ". . . neglecting the traditional and present conditions of the global South" (Said and Lerche 2006, 135). Therefore, if we are to move in a new direction that is capable of achieving a global and universal human rights perspective, then we must answer the question: *what are the human values and standards which, in our contemporary and globalizing world, can be regarded as universally valid and acceptable?*

The answer to this question provides us with a vital and important task not only for the cause of human rights and dignity, the human right to peace and to development, but also in light of the massive crisis engendered by the crisis and breakdown of the entire world-capitalist system. According to a number of authors, we can distinguish between three types of failures of the capitalist system: (1) a failure of markets, (2) a failure of institutions, and (3) a deficiency of moral virtues (Kung 2003, 145–46). All three areas have affected and will continue to affect the realization of human rights. Yet it is also important to realize the centrality of moral virtues in this global crisis. The global crisis of human rights and the global crisis of the world capitalist system have an overlap of concerns in the area of moral virtues.

If we are to find a cross-cultural set of ethical values and standards that provide guidance for an emerging global civilization, then both Ikeda and various Western-Christian theologians, such as Hans Kung, would argue that all the world's great religions must be involved in a global dialogue on the subject so that a clearly delineated set of basic values could be enumerated. In this regard, Hans Kung has published a table of values from the "*Declaration Toward a Global Ethic*," produced by the Parliament of the World's Religions, Chicago (1993). The significance of this declaration is discovered in the realization that it helps us to contextualize the work of Ikeda—and that of his contemporaries—on the subject of reaching a consensus on the content of a viable global ethical standard. It also provides an excellent example of what a human rights standard of ethics (which is global in scope) should look like. In this regard, it has the additional virtue of going beyond the narrow confines of a Western legalistic formulation of human rights. Finally, this declaration also has great value insofar as it shows that there is a significant correspondence between the writings and philosophy of Ikeda with the central tenets and values articulated in this Declaration Toward a Global Ethic. Therefore, the list of values from this declaration, produced by the Parliament of the World's Religions, is presented next, in Table 9.1.

The above-referenced values are all supportive of a human right to peace. Given this assertion, if we accept it at face value, it allows us to make the idea and claims of a human right to peace much more than an empty phrase. That is because the acceptance of a definition of a human right to peace necessitates the adoption of these values, which, in turn, can be understood as being desired by the vast majority of the world's citizens. While governments may resist the claims associated with a human right to peace, the fact remains that these particular values possess a cross-cultural power and consensus that can sweep down the mightiest walls of oppression and resistance. Therefore, the question of exactly how we would get "from here to there" no longer has to remain a true mystery. According to Prof. Samuel Kim, we discover that "[t]he establishment of a world order/human rights interface calls for the following tasks: (1) clarifying core assumption and principles; (2) redefining 'human rights'; (3) formulating the human rights/human needs nexus; and (4) establishing a world order hierarchy of human rights" (Kim 1991, 367). With regard to the task of clarifying core assumptions and principles, Professor Kim further argues that "[t]he starting point for establishing a world order/ human rights interface is a holistic and humanistic affirmation of the supreme value of human life and development" (Kim 1991, 367). The aforementioned principles accomplish that task. In point of fact, we find an amazing congruence between those principles and Kim's own articulation of what he calls "world order values" insofar as the "quality of world order and the quality of 'human rights' are mutually enhancing or corrupting. Human rights when properly defined and effectively implemented become living norms of a just world order" (Kim 1991, 367). More specifically, Professor Kim (1991, 367) provides his own list of what a world order/human rights interface would look like. It is based on the following assumptions and principles:

1. Every human life, regardless of its location in social, territorial, and ethnic space, is of equal value and therefore entitled to equal protection.
2. Each human life is an end in itself and as such it cannot be devalued as a means to the rights of others.
3. Each human person or group is entitled to democratic participation in the shaping and reshaping of human rights values.
4. Each human person or group is entitled to equal benefit in the sharing of human rights values.
5. Human rights are mutually interdependent and indivisible, but some rights are more basic and essential than others in human development.
6. The affirmation of the supreme value of human life and dignity is the only way to reconcile the conflicts between cultural relativism and universal human rights norms.

Table 9.1 Table of Values, with Arguments from the "Declaration Toward a Global Ethic" by the Parliament of the World's Religions, Chicago 1993

Basic Values

• *Humanity*

In the face of all inhumanity, it should be a shared basic ethical principle that every human being must be treated humanely! This means that every human being without distinction of age, sex, race, skin color, physical or mental ability, language, religion, political view, or national or social origin possesses an inalienable and untouchable dignity, and everyone, the individual as well as the state, is therefore obliged to honor this dignity and protect it. Political and economic power must be utilized for service to humanity instead of misusing it in ruthless battles for domination.

• *Reciprocity*

There is a principle which is found and has persisted in many religious and ethical traditions of humankind for thousands of years: What you do not wish to be done to yourself, do not do to others. Or in positive terms: What you wish done for yourself, do to others! This should be the irrevocable, unconditional norm for all areas of life, for families and communities, for races, nations, and religions.

Core Values

• *Respect for life*

A human person is infinitely precious and must be unconditionally respected. But likewise, the lives of animals and plants which inhabit this planet with us deserve protection, preservation, and care. As human beings we have a special responsibility—especially with a view to future generations—for earth and the cosmos, for the air, water, and soil. We are all intertwined together in this cosmos and we are all dependent on each other. Each one of us depends on the welfare of all. All people have a right to life, safety, and the free development of personality insofar as they do not injure the rights of others. No one has the right physically or psychically to torture, injure, much less kill, any other human being.

- *Nonviolence*

Wherever there are humans there will be conflicts. Such conflicts, however, should be resolved without violence and within a framework of justice. This is true for states as well as for individuals. Persons who hold political power must work within the framework of a just order and commit themselves to the most nonviolent, peaceful solutions possible. And they should work for this within an international order of peace which itself has need for protection and defense against perpetrators of violence.

- *Solidarity*

No one has the right to use her or his possessions without concern for the needs of society and earth. Property, limited though it may be, carries with it an obligation, and its use should at the same time serve the common good. Humankind must develop a spirit of compassion with those who suffer, with special care for the children, the aged, the disabled, the refugees, and the lonely.

- *Justice*

The world economy must be structured more justly. Individual good deeds, and assistance projects, indispensable though they be, are insufficient. The participation of all states and the authority of international organizations are needed to build just economic institutions. A distinction must be made between necessary and limitless consumption, between socially beneficial and nonbeneficial uses of property, between justified and unjustified use of natural resources, and between a profit-only and a socially beneficial and ecologically oriented market economy.

- *Tolerance*

No people, no state, no race, no religion has the right to hate, to discriminate against, to "cleanse," to exile, much less to liquidate a "foreign" minority which is different in behavior or holds different beliefs. Every people, every race, every religion must show tolerance and respect—indeed high appreciation—for every other. Minorities need protection and support, whether they be racial, ethnic, or religious.

(Continued)

Table 9.1 *(Continued)*

• *Truthfulness*

Everybody should think, speak, and act truthfully. All people have a right to information to be able to make the decisions that will form their lives. Without an ethical formation they will hardly be able to distinguish the important from the unimportant. Freedom should not be confused with arbitrariness or pluralism with indifference to truth. Truthfulness should be cultivated in our relationships instead of dishonesty, dissembling, and opportunism. Truth should be constantly sought and incorruptible sincerity instead of spreading ideological or partisan half-truths.

• *Equality*

The relationship between women and men should be characterized not by patronizing behavior or exploitation but by love, partnership, and trustworthiness. All over the world there are condemnable forms of patriarchy, domination of one sex over the other, exploitation of women, sexual misuse of children, and forced prostitution. No one has the right to degrade others to mere sex objects, to force them into or hold them in sexual dependency.

• *Partnership*

Partnership is expressed through mutual respect and understanding, mutual concern, tolerance, readiness for reconciliation, and love. Only what has already been experienced in personal and family relationships can be practiced on the level of nations and religions.

Source: Published in German in Hans Kung (editor) (2001), *Globale Unternehmen—Globales Ethos* (Frankfurt: FAZ-Verlag), pp. 154–56. Published in English in Hans Kung (2003) "An Ethical Framework for the Global Market Economy," in *Making Globalization Good: The Moral Challenges of Global Capitalism*, edited by John H. Dunning. New York: Oxford University Press, 2003, pp. 152–53.

Despite this growing consensus on the human needs/human rights nexus, there is still vigorous debate between those who want to affirm a human right to peace and development and those who want to dispute it. Simply put, there are some people who continue to refuse to recognize either the right to peace or the human right to development. They often take this adversarial position because of their reliance of a narrow and legalistic reading of our current legal instruments—whether they are declarations or covenants or charters. This narrow branding of what human rights can or cannot be not only reflects a self-limiting textual analysis but also points toward an orientation toward values and global affairs that are radically disassociated from the goals of humane governance, inclusionary governance, and cosmopolitan governance.

In his *commentary* in opposition to the idea that there exists a human right to peace or a human right to development, Jack Donnelly asserts, "The struggles for peace and for human rights may often intersect and even reinforce one another, but they are fundamentally different. . . . Nothing is to be gained, and much may be lost, conceptually and perhaps even practically, by conflating peace and human rights" (Donnelly 2006, 155). In dramatic contradistinction to this narrow view of human rights, Julie Mertus and Jeffrey Helsing note, "Where there is peace, human rights are more likely to be enforced. Where human rights are upheld, peace is more likely to be achieved . . . the achievement of peace will make the enforcement of human rights easier, more likely to last, and stronger. Incorporating human rights into peace processes will greatly increase the likelihood that an agreed-on peace is sustainable and that conflict is resolved and transformed rather than simply managed or contained" (Mertus and Helsing 2006, 517). So why do Donnelly and others like him find it necessary to oppose the implementation of the human right to peace and to development? Part of the answer lies in the reality that he represents the establishment view of many in the developed states. According to Daniel Aguirre, a large part of the opposition to the human right to peace, as well as the human right to development, is centered in the matrix of power wherein "[d]eveloped [s]tates make rhetorical promises concerning human rights. Yet when economic interests are at stake, states prioritize national interests by abstaining or voting against binding rules. As a result, despite near universal acceptance on paper, the right to development has not been realized in practice for the majority of the people . . . The international community has instead focused cooperation on promoting globalization that may circumvent human rights" (Aguirre 2008, 69). This problem is further exacerbated by the fact that "[a] legalistic approach tends to encumber *universal* human rights with Western middle-class, conservative norms and biases" (Kim 1991, 368; italics in original).

In short, to brand human rights in such a way that it negates the claims of a human right to peace and to development is to simply endorse the current order as a given state of affairs in which there is little or no room for change, regardless of the presence of social movements for change and regardless of the aspirational nature of human rights as fundamental to the realization of human dignity in every sphere of human decision-making—economic, social, cultural, and/or political. In point of fact, Donnelly asserts that "[t]o establish a human right to peace ... would require major changes in our moral, legal, and political practices, and when it comes right down to it, most people—and certainly virtually all states—seem unwilling to do what would be necessary to make such changes" (Donnelly 2006, 153).

Such a cramped view of human rights and its historical potential to alter the consciousness and course of our global civilization is also representative of a style of branding that seeks to effectively limit our interpretations of what is possible in human affairs to the confines of a particular schema of IR that is more ideological in nature. I would argue that it reflects an uncritical embrace of Western triumphalism that has declared an "end of history." Further, it exemplifies an all too easy embrace of structures of dominance and domination that oppress millions around the globe through the debt peonage inflicted on the peoples of the global South by the World Bank, the IMF, and the various appendages of US hegemony. It relegates the problems associated with the persistence of poverty to that of an unfortunate set of historical circumstances, rather than as the product of an inhumane international order of privilege and power that employs the policies of a neoliberal economic model in order to exploit those who have not yet found the means to effectively resist the mechanisms of structural violence and injustice through which the current global system operates. It is a view that allows the ideology of militarism to continue unabashed as the world's military–industrial complex spews forth more armaments to fuel more wars and civil wars while, at the same time, it allows for a continuous increase in the profits of the armament producers and bankers who invest in these enterprises.

Hence, Donnelly's viewpoint is more representative of an apologist of the international status quo by virtue of his disavowal of the human right to peace to come to the surface of current global discourse on the possibilities for the creation of a more peaceful global civilization. His conscripted view is further flawed by the fact that it is less than faithful to a tradition of open scholarly inquiry or critical investigation into the foundational sources, origins, and myths of a historical bias against those forms of social transformation and social movements that come to the aid and rescue of the poor, the vulnerable, and the nonwhite majority of the world's peoples. After all, if we were to uncritically adopt his line of thought and analysis, then we would be hard-pressed to explain the overthrow of the apartheid government of South Africa and the subsequent rise of Nelson Mandela from a prison cell on Robben Island to the presidency of his country.

The Lessons of History

If we simply review the history of the twentieth century beginning with the end of World War I and the ensuing Paris Peace Conference at Versailles, it is possible to further eviscerate the faulty line of argumentation that Donnelly has chosen to pursue. Even before the "right to peace" and the "right to development" became objects of contention by conservative IR scholars, historians have marveled at the recalcitrance of the Western European nations to even entertain the demands and aspirations of non-Western peoples seeking acknowledgment of and acquiescence to their struggles for sovereignty, equality, and dignity under the rubric of self-determination. For example, Erez Manela, associate professor of history at Harvard, noted that in 1919 "[t]he Western powers in Paris ignored the demands and aspirations of non-Western peoples, but their struggles for sovereignty, equality, and dignity as independent actors in international society continued. The Wilsonian moment marked the beginning of the end of the imperial order in international affairs, precipitating the crisis of empire that followed the war and laying the foundations for the eventual triumph of an international order in which the model of the sovereign, self-determining nation-state spread over the entire globe" (Manela 2007, 225).

It would seem that it is this purposive and aspirational quality for human rights and dignity throughout the history of the twentieth-century struggles of non-Western peoples that completely escapes Donnelly's comprehension when he undertakes to degrade the meaning of *"positive peace"*—especially as the late twentieth and early twenty-first centuries point to rising tides of popular commitment to both the right to peace and development. Perhaps this failure to recognize the driving force of history (*and international law's own evolution*) stems from not being able to comprehend the significance of what another historian, Vijay Prashad, has argued regarding the concept and term *Third World*. Prashad notes, "*The Third World was not a place. It was a project.* During the seemingly interminable battles against colonialism, the peoples of Africa, Asia, and Latin America dreamed of a new world. They longed for dignity above all else, but also the basic necessities of life" (Prashad 2007a, xv; italics added). In the anticolonial struggle, the 1955 Bandung Conference witnessed the representatives of the formerly colonized countries signal their refusal to take orders from their formal colonial masters. To memorialize this position, the final communiqué at Bandung demanded that the United Nations admit all those formerly colonized states, such as Libya and Vietnam, and then denied admission into its body. It was the historical beginning of what would become the creation of a UN bloc which, alongside a socialist bloc, would become the bulwark against "dollar imperialism" and offer *an alternative model for development* (Prashad 2007a, 41; italics added). In this regard, Bandung launched a global perspective on the human right to development that transcended the view of the dominant

359

Western powers. As such, Bandung truly inspired an alternative model for development.

As we embark upon the twenty-first century, Daniel Aguirre notes the following:

> The right to development outlines a rights-based process which can help to reduce the problems of globalization. It provides a solid foundation for development from which human rights can be realized. The right to development articulates the entitlement of the developing world. The international community has confirmed it as an inalienable and universal human right. (Aguirre 2008, 67)

In fact, the confirmation of the right to development as an inalienable and universal right was announced at the World Conference on Human Rights, Vienna, 1993, and is unequivocally declared to be a universal right within the document that has come to be known as the Vienna Declaration of 1993.[1] Further, it was not the first time that such a right had been pronounced on behalf of all humanity. Article 1 of *The Declaration on the Right to Development* states that "[t]he right to development is an inalienable human right by virtue of which every human person and all peoples are entitled to participate in, contribute to, and enjoy economic, social, cultural and political development, in which all human rights and fundamental freedoms can be fully realized."[2] The year in which The Declaration on the Right to Development was promulgated was 1986.

The Bandung conference also addressed the racist disregard for human life which was often exhibited by Europe's colonial powers. In addressing this problem, the representatives at Bandung raised the issue of nuclear disarmament. One of the twentieth century's first moves toward articulating a human right to peace had been made. In the conference communiqué, the delegates argued that

> the Third World had to seize the reins of the horses of the apocalypse. The Third World had a *"duty toward humanity and civilization to proclaim their support for disarmament."* As the nuclear powers dithered over talks, the Third World called on the United Nations to insist on dialogue and the creation of a regime to monitor arms control. The Disarmament Sub-Committee of the United Nations had been formed as a result of Indian (and Third World) initiative in the General Assembly in 1953, to *"lift from the peoples of the world [the] burden and [the] fear [of annihilation], and thus to liberate new energies and resources for positive programs of reconstruction and development."* (Prashad 2007a, 42; italics added)

This initiative was followed in 1957 by the United Nation's creation of the International Atomic Energy Agency (IAEA). Significantly, the charter of the

IAEA followed the language and intent of the final communiqué at Bandung, ". . . which asked the powers to *'bring about the regulation, limitation, control and reduction of all armed forces and armaments, including the prohibition of the production, experimentation and use of all weapons of mass destruction, and to establish effective international controls to this end.'* The IAEA, in other words, is a child of Bandung" (Prashad 2007a, 42; italics added). The Bandung conference and its enduring legacy can be characterized, at least in part, as being an example of a "cosmopolitan" model of international human rights, and, as such, I would argue it is a model in which its members see themselves as part of a single global political community. In this regard, it is probably one of the closest approximations to what Ikeda has in mind when he advocates about the need for dialogue, enhancing the role of the UN in the cause of nuclear abolition, and the promise of building a peaceful global civilization in the twenty-first century.

So far in our discussion, given the achievements and claims outlined in the above-referenced conferences from Versailles to Bandung and Vienna, it is increasingly clear from this overview that these various historic milestones—in the cause of human liberation, human rights, and in the struggle for global peace and the control of armaments—have been limited in their implementation. This limitation serves to reveal the hard fact that "[s]tates are responsible for defining the public interest for their national communities and a global public interest can only be defined as the overlap among their various national interests" (Said and Lerche 2006, 136). Therein lies the practical dilemma for those seeking to actualize and implement both the human right to peace and development.

The most wealthy and powerful nation-states, especially the leading nuclear weapons states, refuse to follow what UN covenants and declarations command when it comes to realizing the universal claims of a human right to peace and development. Hence, we discover that "despite the fact that human rights are by definition universal, the regime through which they are given effect will always remain piecemeal and uneven in the context of the state system" (Said and Lerche 2006, 136). Therefore, as I have argued throughout the course of this book (*especially in the chapter on UN reform, the ICC, and nuclear abolition*), it is necessary for humanity to set aside the particularities of any one nation's narrow "national interest" and embrace the evolution of a new set of international institutions and structures that place the "human interest" first. The universal claims, needs, and rights of humankind must take precedence over the narrow, selfish, and greedy agendas of national elites. That is certainly the perspective of Ikeda and the majority of his contemporaries who are quoted throughout this book.

Unfortunately, Donnelly would disagree with my assessment, based on his reading of the current set of power relations within a US-dominated hegemonic order. Donnelly has already stated that "the international society of states is our principal mechanism for assuring international order, however fragile and incomplete that order might be. Before we start talking about dismantling this society, we should be confident not only that the alternative is practically realizable, but also that we understand and are willing to hear the costs and unintended consequences of establishing it" (Donnelly 2006, 154). I could not disagree more.

My dissent from Donnelly's view is predicated on several grounds. To begin with, my strong disagreement and dissent with his position center on his endorsement of the current condition of "the international society of states" as being "our principal mechanism for assuring international order." Connected to this my dissent with an assertion that logically follows from his endorsement of the current condition of global relations—he warns us not to even have a dialogue about "dismantling this society" until that point in time when "we are willing to hear the costs and unintended consequences of establishing it." It is unfortunate that he has not applied the same standard of care to his own assessment of the current order of global relations and the high costs that it is exacting upon millions, if not billions, of the world's peoples. Insofar as the current system is largely under the financial domination of a transnational capitalist elite that continues to derive the bulk of its profits from unfair trade advantages and unequal terms of exchange, from industries involved in supplying armaments for war and benefits from an ongoing process of global militarization, and from oil companies who continue to rely on the sale of fossil fuels that contribute to the crisis of global warming and climate change, I find it difficult not to follow Ikeda's lead and demand a dialogue about these realities— as well as set forth an indictment of those practices by those socioeconomic and sociopolitical classes and forces that have created the global crisis of the late twentieth and early twenty-first centuries. Therefore, my specific points of dissent with Donnelly's perspective are as follows:

First, he dismisses the massive poverty and injustices of the current international order by simply adopting the international society of states, in its current form of institutionalization, as the be all and end all in IR. He endorses this system despite its "fragile" and "incomplete" nature. In contradistinction to this view, throughout this book, I have provided substantial evidence demonstrating that this current order of nation-states and IR is based on militarization, war, and the maintenance of economic privilege for a global oligarchy of transnational capitalist elites, banks, industries, and corporations to the exclusion of the rights and well-being of the majority of people on this planet (Pogge 2007a,b, 2010; Robinson 1996, 2008).

Second, in terms of the longevity of this system, I have argued that its own contradictions have become so manifest that its decline, imminent ruin, and final collapse are manifestly evident (Paupp 2000, 2007, 2009). My view is largely shared by Charles Doran, who writes, "if important action is to be taken in the present international system, the United States must take that action. The United States must not just resort to vetoing the actions of others. It must take a positive lead. But taking the lead, and attempting to act like a hegemon, are two very different kinds of roles" (Doran 2009, 95). What this means is that leadership is not hegemony. In fact, along these same lines of analysis, Stephen Toope has argued that ". . . because of the current construction of global politics, the specific complex identity of the United States, and new understandings of the means of creation of customary international law, the US hegemon is precluded from effective dominance even in areas central to its perceived interests, and despite its overwhelming material power" (Toope 2003, 291).

Third, it is in the very nature of this current international order that the United States has to constantly try to hide the fact that it has been engaged in carrying out massive human rights violations (Boggs 2010; Herman and Peterson 2010). A brilliant critique of this global system of human rights violations was set out by Richard Falk in 1981, when he observed the following:

> There seems to be little doubt that the domestic component of "the growth dividend" in capitalist Third World countries goes predominantly to the upper ten to twenty percent of the population (as well as to external elites), widening the rich/poor gaps, and in most cases deteriorating the real income of the bottom forty percent at least for a period of some decades. In effect, the mass of the population suffers as a result of a capitalist orientation toward development. This orientation can no longer be successfully legitimated by resting the claim of the rich and powerful on some traditional ground of privilege (e.g., caste, vested property rights), or by invoking "trickle down," "expanded pie" imagery. Only repression works. It is functional for a capitalist Third World country, and it generally assumes an acute form because of the depth of poverty, as well as the high ratio of poor to rich in the overall stratification of the population. For this reason, the extent of coercive authority and its duration and severity do not seem as integral for a socialist approach as for a capitalist approach in a Third World country. (Falk 1981, 135)

Fourth, in the midst of this current manifestation of global crisis, neither the withering splendor of US hegemony nor a rising multipolar and multicentric world of regions can navigate the waters of global problems without adopting a more universal perspective (Chossudovsky and Marshall 2010). This is what Ikeda and his contemporaries have provided. They have provided remedies and road maps for the achievement of a "positive peace" that is universal, practical, and foundational to the construction of a peaceful global civilization. Their view of the world involves a rejection of the "negative peace" and who think that the mere absence of war is enough to "declare peace," thereby making the human right to peace and development superfluous. After all, it is Donnelly himself that declares, "By 'peace,' I mean the absence of inter-state war" (Donnelly 2006, 151). Rather, Ikeda and his like-minded contemporaries have embraced a perspective that seeks to advance positive peace as the embodiment of a more cosmopolitan worldview wherein the full and more complete realization of human rights embraces socioeconomic rights and not merely the delimited Western version of sociopolitical rights in isolation from the other categories of rights. Therefore, Ikeda and his contemporaries who are advocates of a positive peace perspective see the radical restructuring of the current international order as essential.

In other words, we can no longer afford a global military–industrial complex that opposes nuclear abolition, drains national wealth from the majority of peoples throughout the nations of the world, and allows climate change to continue unabated because of a selfish refusal of a few elite classes to "rock the boat" of current energy practices and investments because it might diminish "their profits." In short, Ikeda's admonitions about the dangers associated with the "spirit of abstraction" do have practical policy and program consequences for the real world. If we take Ikeda seriously on these matters, then the whole global order needs to be changed and become reoriented toward patterns of restructuring that truly protect and enhance the aspirational requirements of the human right to peace and the human right to development.

In quoting Ikeda throughout this book, I have often referred to his use of the term "*the spirit of abstraction*" as he has employed it against a mind-set that prioritizes the value of money, material things, and possessions over and above the value, dignity, and worth of the individual person. After all, isn't the individual person supposed to be the object of concern in the discourse of human rights—as well as the teaching of the great religions and international law when it contemplates the law of peoples? Yet all too often, we discover that the primacy of human worth and the centrality of human dignity are routinely lost and compromised when we finally arrive at a serious decision-making point involving the implementation of the human right to peace and to development. Various authors have taken this issue quite seriously—for example, Michael Ignatieff, who has astutely observed, "American exceptionalism lays bare the relation between the national and the universal in the rights cultures of all states that have constitutional regimes of liberty. The question is what margin of interpretation should be allowed these nations in their human rights performance, and what margin shades into a permissive surrender of those values that should be universal for all nations" (Ignatieff 2005, 26).

As far as the proclivity of the United States itself to exempt itself from the claims of United Nations declarations and covenants, the demands of international law, compliance with the UN Charter, and the specific requirements of the Universal Declaration of Human Rights (UDHR), I would agree with Harold Koh that the United States has exempted itself ". . . from certain international law rules and agreements, even ones that it may have played a critical role in framing, through such techniques as non-compliance; non-ratification; ratification with reservations, understandings, and declarations; the non-self-executing treaty doctrine; or the latest US gambit, un-signing the Rome Statute of the International Criminal Court (ICC)" (Koh 2005, 113). For all of these reasons, we find that Koh has now referred to this course of US conduct as not only one of "*exceptionalism*" but also one of "*exemptionalism*" (Koh 2005, 113). Insofar as these policies of obfuscation with regard to the universal claims of human rights, in general, and the human right to peace, in particular, they are antithetical to building a peaceful global civilization. In fact, it would seem that, in the words of Professor Kim, "[h]uman rights, instead of limiting state power, are constantly being limited by state power" (Kim 1991, 376).

In response to those who continue to deny the existence of a human right to peace or the human right to development, Ikeda has specifically identified the personages of Einstein, Russell, Schweitzer, Pauling, Rotblat, Camus, Toda, and Norman Cousins as primary examples of people who spoke out coura-geously against war and were involved in leading the fight for the elimination of nuclear arms and an end to warfare. Reflecting on their respective efforts, Ikeda concludes, "*The truly courageous person rejects violence and stands up for the future and the advantage of all humanity. Armed might symbolizes human cowardice and spiritual defeat*" (Ikeda and Krieger 2002, 72; italics added). Standing up for the "the future and the advantage of all humanity" requires and necessitates standing up for the human right to peace and de-velopment. These two rights are now at the fulcrum of what Ikeda and his contemporaries have advocated throughout this book. It is to the legal, moral, and ethical components of these two set of rights that we now turn.

The Future and the Advantage of all Humanity

The various challenges that confront humanity in the twenty-first century are all products of a historical course of evolution and human choice. In fact, the very act of instituting human rights as a normative force in world affairs and global relations was the product of human choice in the aftermath of two world wars. Those responsible for shaping the post-1945 global order were forced to acknowledge and to enact a radically different set of values and in-stitutions on the world stage than what had been present at the dawn of the twentieth century. On closer examination, a review of history from the early nineteenth century to the close of the twentieth century reveals the power of ideas in shaping attitudes, consciousness, and practical outcomes. In no domain of human endeavor is this more evident than in the realm of ideolo-gies regarding war and peace. On this matter, Andrew Hurrell has observed, "The idea of progressive change is itself a historical development. Take war: it is no doubt the case that human beings have always longed for, and dreamt of, the possibility of a true peace that goes beyond mere coexistence and that promises an end to violence, strife, and conflict. However, the notion that war and violence can be, and should be, eradicated as an element of social and political life is comparatively modern—certainly within European thought" (Hurrell 2007, 69).

Perhaps the best historical study available, which Hurrell cites in reference to his assertion, is Martin Ceadel's book, *The Origins of War Prevention: The British Peace Movement and International Relations, 1730–1854.* Ceadel makes the argument that the fatalistic acceptance of war as a natural and inevitable element in human affairs had finally come under scrutiny and sustained challenge from the middle of the eighteenth century to the middle of the nineteenth century. In Ceadel's introduction to *The Origins of War Prevention*, he states, "In . . . drawing attention to the fading of fatalism and the emergence, particularly in Britain, of peace thinking, I shall argue that ideas—including ideologies and political cultures in which they become embedded—are important. This is in harmony with a recent trend in international-relations scholarship. It also supports Paul W. Schroeder's claim, in his important historical study of the decline in the incidence of European war after 1815, that the transformation 'occurred first and above all in the fields of ideas, collective mentalities, and outlooks'" (Ceadel 1996, 15).

This same perspective also provides the thematic emphasis for the concluding paragraph of *The Origins of War Prevention*, wherein Ceadel notes the following:

> [T]he fading of fatalism, which began as early as the 1730s in response to Enlightenment thinking, evangelicalism, and changes in the international system, gave rise in Britain to a peace-or-war debate in which a pacific theory of international relations became more deeply entrenched than in any other country, and therefore better able to survive the setbacks caused by the unfavorable world context of the late nineteenth century and remain an influential viewpoint. This unusual receptiveness to peace thinking can largely be attributed to a political culture with the right degree of liberalism and a strategic situation with the right degree of security. But, although Britain's pioneering peace movement was itself a product of these cultural and strategic factors, it also deserves recognition as a factor in its own right. Indeed, for two centuries now it has kept the flame of hope alive during periods of adversity and dramatized favorable trends of opinion during periods of opportunity. (Ceadel 1996, 517)

In Ceadel's account of the last two hundred and some years of European history we are able to discern the echoes of Britain's peace movement in our own day and generation. Those echoes reverberate in Ikeda's writings, speeches, and peace proposals, as well as those of his like-minded contemporaries. This book has borne witness to the power of their voices and has begun the task of chronicling not only their words and deeds but also the implications, ramifications, and future possibilities of their pronouncements. For example, on the theme of "taking risks for humanity," let us consider a fragment of the following dialogic interchange between David Krieger and Ikeda:

> Krieger: Our development as a species has reached the point where it is required that we take some risks for humanity. One such risk is to take a change on finding better ways than violence to resolve our differences. Another is to risk sharing in the belief that what we do for others will make our own lives richer.

> Ikeda: Risky adventures like those are of primary importance. They represent *altering our ways of thinking about human life and society and the struggle against selfish desire.* (Ikeda and Krieger 2002, 110; italics added)

In this dialogic exchange we are once again provided with an explanation of how the power of ideas can inspire actions that lead to a greater realization of human rights to peace and to development by virtue of the fact that these ideas expose our spirits, minds, and political will to the possibilities inherent in a restructured world. In this regard, what Ikeda reminds us of is the essential and foundational need to engage in a process of *inner transformation* (human revolution) so that we will be equipped for a higher level of *dialogic interchange* with others, thereby making possible a global consensus on the need to achieve a transcendent ideal by concretizing its achievement in our daily lives as individuals, as well as in our collective efforts with one another as *global citizens*, acting in solidarity with one another. Only in this way can we move beyond a failed and dying nation-state system of contending and contentious national interests. Only in this way can we assert the power of new ideas and right-claims so as to finally change human behaviors, state practices, and international modes of governance in order to bring into existence a more peaceful global civilization. The logical ordering and sequencing of these elements actually bring us to a point in our global and legal history where we can effectively address what has been an ongoing debate: *How can we overcome the objection that the right to development is incompatible with the philosophy underlying human rights law—that is, that human rights are individual rights, and the right to development is a collective right of some sort?*

In the years between 1981 and 1986 an extensive literature developed on the right to development. In 1980, the UNGA adopted Resolution 35–174, which emphasized the right to development as a human right. The General Assembly asked the Commission on Human Rights to take the necessary measures to promote development as a human right and ". . . asked the Secretary General to hold a seminar to examine the relationship between human rights, peace, and development, and to present the results to the Commission on

Human Rights" (Whelan 2010, 168). These two reports led the commission to adopt Resolution 36 (XXXVII) in 1981, establishing a Working Group on the Right to Development under the auspices of the commission. The following year, the General Assembly declared in paragraph 8 of its Resolution 36/133 that the right to development was now an *inalienable* human right (Whelan 2010, 168).

In defense of this right, Philip Alston, who was chairperson of the Committee on Economic, Social and Cultural Rights at the time, noted the appeal of declaring such a right: "It is now widely accepted that the characterization of a specific goal as a human right elevates it above the rank and file of competing societal goals, gives it a degree of immunity from challenge and generally endows it with an aura of timelessness, absoluteness and universal validity" (Whelan 2010, 171). Even more importantly, Alston identified the right to development as a *"solidarity right"*—alongside the right to "a clean environment," the "right of peoples to peace," and the right to humanitarian assistance. In this regard, Alston also pointed out that the right to development could be viewed as a synthesis of strands of already existing international law and policy "which have been hitherto artificially compartmentalized into the separate domains of human rights on the one hand and development on the other" (Whelan 2010, 171). In short, Alston favored the idea of a right to development as taking human rights outside of the realm of "myopic and incestuous" legal debates constituted by "regurgitated principles" and bad research (Whelan 2010, 171).

Clearly, Alston would reject Donnelly's objections to the human right to peace and development because these objections fit perfectly the situation he described with respect to "myopic and incestuous" legal debates. In Donnelly's own words, we find him exposed of committing such an offense when he asserts, "For purposes of this commentary I will take the 1948 Universal Declaration of Human Rights and the 1966 International Human Rights Covenants as an authoritative list" (Donnelly 2006, 151). By having promulgated his "authoritative list," he should have just admitted to his readers that it was really an artificially delimited list that was designed to automatically exclude all relevant debate, dialogue, and discourse at the outset of any discussion on the topic of the human right to peace and development. Perhaps he had to take such a delimited and myopic position in light of the fact that, as Professor Kim has pointed out, "[a]lthough there is no clear and concise definition of *'right to development,'* it has been contended that *'almost all of the elements that constitute the right to development are the subject of existing declarations, resolutions, conventions or covenants'*" (Kim 1991, 372; italics added).

The same analysis can be applied to the human right to peace. Prof. Cancado Trindade has acknowledged this reality in his book, *International Law for Humankind: Towards a New* Jus Gentium (*an updated and revised version of the General Course on Public International Law delivered by him at The Hague Academy of International Law in 2005*). Trindade expands on Professor Kim's just-cited observations when he notes, "Elements provided by Public International Law of relevance for the acknowledgment of the right to peace can be found in the 1928 General Treaty for the Renunciation of War (the so-called Briand-Kellog Pact); in Articles 1 and 2(4) of the United Nations Charter; complemented by the 1970 UN Declaration on Principles of International Law Concerning Friendly Relations and Cooperation among States; the 1970 Declaration on the Strengthening of International Security; and the 1974 Definition of Aggression; in the Code of Offenses against the Peace and Security of Mankind, drafted by the UN International Law Commission; and in resolutions of the UN General Assembly pertaining to the right of peace, relating it to disarmament" (Trindade 2010, 353–54).

In more recent developments in the formulation of the right to peace, Trindade also notes the following:

> The antecedents of the right to peace also comprise the long-standing tradition of UNESCO of sponsoring studies to foster a culture of peace. Within the framework of such a tradition, UNESCO launched the initiative, in 1997, of the formulation of the *human right to peace*. To that end, the then Director-General of UNESCO (F. Mayor) convened a Group of Legal Experts (acting in their individual capacity) which, at the end of their meetings of Las Palmas Island (February 1997) and Oslo (June 1997), produced the *Draft Declaration on the Human Right to Peace*. Its preamble read that: *"Peace, a common good of humanity, is a universal and fundamental value to which all individuals and all peoples, and in particular the youth of the world, aspire."* The right to peace was duly inserted into a framework of human rights, which was taken into account to assert peace as a right and a duty. It was asserted as a right inherent in all human beings, embodying demands of the human person and of peoples to the ultimate benefit of humankind. (Trindade 2010, 355; italics added)

When viewed in combination, these advances in the international law of the human right to peace and the human right to development are evidence of the reason why, according to Falk, "[i]t has always been important to distinguish the discourse of law from complementary discourses of politics, culture, ethics, and religion. The legal structure of international human rights has been established by formal legal texts negotiated and ratified by governments of sovereign states, as well as by the institutions and procedures for implementation that have been given an intergovernmental role either within the United Nations or elsewhere. Politics and culture play a large role in exerting pressure for and against implementing particular norms contained in these texts, as do ethical standards and religious attitudes" (Falk 2009, 8).

What has been described here by Falk is recognizable not only with respect to international struggles to implement the human right to peace and development but also with respect to widening the traditional view of what constitutes "human security" in general, especially with regard to the protection of the environment. For example, it can be acknowledged that "[h]istorically, a new concept of 'security' emerged only in the wake of a major, catastrophic war, during which established patterns of social values and behavior suffered profound disruption. Eco-disasters of rare, unexpected kinds in the 1950s and 1960s cried out for new concepts of 'ecological aggression' and 'ecological security'" (Kim 1984, 293; italics added). In the 1970s the issue of ecocide was raised for the first time at a Congressional Conference on War and National Responsibility. At that time, biologist Arthur Galston said that ". . . the willful and permanent destruction of environment in which a people can live in a manner of their own choosing" is no less a crime than genocide and hence "ought similarly to be considered a crime against humanity, to be designated by the term *ecocide*" (Knoll and McFadden 1970, 71; italics in the original). In the immediate aftermath of this testimony, we discover that

> In 1973, Richard Falk proposed several draft legal instruments including a *Proposed International Convention of the Crime of Ecocide.* In 1974, Norman Cousins broadened the concept of "crimes against humanity" by extending it to the human transgression of the life-protecting ozone in the stratosphere. Yet the concept of ecological security seems to have been virtually ignored, if not downright repudiated. *One major difficulty lies in the inherent conflict between traditional economic principles and new ecological concepts.* (Kim 1984, 293; italics added)

Despite the obstacles encountered by the concept of "ecological security," it is possible to see a more hopeful trajectory for the implementation of the human right to peace and to development. As demonstrated by the above-cited legal references offered by Professor Trindade, we find that there has been progress on realizing the human right to peace. In large measure, this has been possible because there have been several major advances to incorporate and implement the right into the cannon of international law and state practice. In this regard, perhaps a large measure of success for the global desire to implement the human right to peace and development is found in the realization that, according to Margot Salomon, "[w]idespread deprivation of economic, social, and cultural human rights today is largely a consequence of a global system that structurally disadvantages half the world's population. In the area of international law aimed at the protection and promotion of human rights, we are witnessing a trend towards responding to this massive failure of the international community of states to allow for minimum essential levels of human rights to be secured globally, a shift that requires revisiting the ways in which responsibility is determined" (Salomon 2006, 96).

In a subsequent publication, just one year later, Salomon observed that

> Some commentators have referred to the Declaration on the Right to Development as providing a suitable example in law of "what ought to be" as opposed to "what is." These authors emphasized the need to distinguish between moral claims and legal assertions, and concluded that the DRD provides "a broad framework yet to crystallize into substantive law." The vast majority of commentators nonetheless agree that certain General Assembly resolutions or declarations may indeed set in motion, influence, or become part of the process of custom-building, that they play a pivotal role in the international law-making process, and that by embodying the convictions of adopting states, they may create expectations on the part of other states. Thus it has been noted that "the mere recognition of a rule and the conditions for its execution in a resolution give it the beginning of legal force." Taken together, these views suggest that General Assembly resolutions can become a critical means of standard-setting. (Salomon 2007, 88–89)

This process of "custom-building" has great significance for the future course and realization of the human right to peace and development. Commenting on this connection, but especially with respect to the interaction of fundamental ethical principles with customary international law, Prof. Brian Lepard has argued that "[w]e can infer from a principle of equal human dignity that all individuals must enjoy certain fundamental human rights, and indeed both the UN Charter and the Universal Declaration of Human Rights proclaim the existence of these universal rights. For example, according to the UN Charter, the 'peoples of the United Nations . . . reaffirm faith in fundamental human rights, in the dignity and worth of the human person, [and] in the equal rights of men and women.' The Universal Declaration upholds the 'equal and inalienable rights of all members of the human family,' declaring . . . that all people are born free and equal in rights" (Lepard 2010, 82). It is worth noting that in Professor Lepard's schema he centralizes the preeminent ethical principle of "unity in diversity." He argues that all ethical principles endorsed by contemporary international law are ultimately related to the principle of *unity in diversity* and that in his classification of ethical principles we can discern that "'[e]ssential ethical principles' are those compelling ethical principles that deserve the highest weight, and in most circumstances cannot be trumped by other ethical principles, because they bear such a close relationship to the principle of unity in diversity" (Lepard 2010, 82). In explicating this proposed classification of ethical principles, he differentiates between fundamental, compelling, and essential ethical principles in an ascending manner, as outlined in Table 9.2.

Table 9.2 A Proposed Classification of Ethical Principles

1. Fundamental ethical principles are those ethical principles endorsed by contemporary international law, including the UN Charter and international human rights and humanitarian law, which are deserving of significant weight in relation to other ethical principles because they bear some logical relationship to the preeminent ethical principle of unity in diversity.

2. Compelling ethical principles are those fundamental ethical principles which are deserving of especially high weight in relation to other ethical principles because of their direct and immediate logical relationship to the preeminent principle of unity in diversity.

3. Essential ethical principles are those compelling ethical principles which are so closely related to the preeminent principle of unity in diversity that they deserve the highest weight and therefore cannot normally be overridden by other ethical principles.

Source: Brian D. Lepard, *Customary International Law: A New Theory with Practical Applications*. New York: Cambridge University Press, 2010, p. 83.

The value of Professor Lepard's approach to customary law has direct bearing on the question of whether or not there exists a human right to peace and to development. To begin with, his analysis of ethical principles, which impinge on the law-making process itself, exposes the central role played by the concept of unity in diversity. It is a concept that has been used throughout Ikeda's own works, especially under the rubric of *humanitarian competition* because it asks of us that we undertake a path of peace, nonviolence, and tolerance for the purpose of developing a shared ethos throughout our global commons as we strive to build a peaceful global civilization. Hence, out of our unity in diversity, Ikeda would argue, we partake in an indivisible unity as the human race strives to recognize and to implement obligations, duties, and responsibilities for the well-being, advancement, and care for others in the midst of that diversity.

From the standpoint of customary international law, the fact remains: "The principle of unity in diversity directly implies that all individuals and government form part of global human and state communities, along with smaller regional, national, or local communities, all of which should strive to achieve peace, nonviolence, and unity among their members and the realization of all fundamental ethical principles. It highlights the ideal of establishing *unity* among states, not mere coexistence or mutual toleration. It also suggests that states should endeavor to strengthen international law as a means of achieving peaceful and unified relations among them, and, in fact, that respect for international law is ethically meritorious" (Lepard

2010, 91; italics in the original). In this regard, Lepard's sentiments about the concept of unity in diversity as an ethically supportive foundation for new forms of human actions toward building a more peaceful global civilization resonate with the concepts advanced by Ikeda and his like-minded contemporaries.

Not only does Lepard's concept of unity in diversity provide us with an analytical and clearly articulated legal foundation for claiming a human right to peace and to development, but it also places a great stress on the universal nature of this claim. In so doing, the concept of unity in diversity allows us to transcend the narrow confines of those who engage in legal "textualism" and law's own version of literalism through an all too comprehensive practice of being overly attached to the limitations imposed by black-letter law, irrespective of the evolving standards and consciousness of humankind. In this regard, Professor Kim has been quite prescient in asserting that "[t]he right to development as a universal human right is . . . designed to seek a more humane interface between individual and national development so as to bring about the realization of the potentialities of the human person in harmony with the social process of his/her community. *This redefines development in terms of a hierarchical expansion of human and social potentialities in a mutually complementary way.* In short, development becomes a dynamic process of creating conditions conducive to the material, moral, and spiritual advancement of the whole human being in both individual and social capacities" (Kim 1991, 372; italics added).

This intellectual recognition of the indivisible nature of the human right to development, by virtue of it having application and relevance in *both* individual *and* social capacities, is critically important. It is important because, as Professor Trindade has noted, "The 1986 UN Declaration on the Right to development saw fit to underline that, in order to promote development, equal and urgent attention should be given to the implementation of civil, political, economic, social and cultural rights (*given their indivisibility and interdependence*), and the observance of certain human rights cannot thus justify the denial of others; likewise, all aspects of the right to development are indivisible and interdependent and each of them is to be considered in the context of that right as a whole" (Trindade 2010, 359; italics added).

The clearly indivisible and interdependent nature of the UN Declaration on the Right to Development is articulated in Articles 6(2) and 9(1), as well as in the Preamble. While the historical record of the second half of the twentieth century records a debate on a distinction that emanates between the international law *"of"* development and the right *"to"* development, in the early twenty-first century it should be admitted and acknowledged that "the right to development, addressed the matter from the perspective of human beings and peoples, without excluding States from its construction. It appeared, as propounded by the 1986 Declaration, as a subjective human right, embodying demands of the human person and of peoples which ought to be respected, to the benefit, ultimately, of humankind" (Trindade 2010, 358).

Similarly, with regard to interpreting the human right to peace, as it was outlined and expressed in the aforementioned UNESCO (United Nations Educational, Scientific and Cultural Organization) initiative—which produced the *Draft Declaration on the Human Right to Peace*—we find that "[i]n recent years the recognition of the right to peace has been fostered by the advent and evolution of the International Law of Human Rights and of International Environmental Law; the conception of sustainable development, as endorsed by the 1992 UN Conference on Environment and Development, e.g., *points to the ineluctable relationship between the rights to peace and to development*" (Trindade 2010, 356–57; italics added). Historically speaking, when we trace back the evolution of the idea of the relationship between the observance of human rights in connection with the maintenance of peace, it is evident that as early as 1968 such a relationship was articulated in the Final Act of the World Conference on Human Rights of the United Nations, held in Tehran.[3]

The Indivisibility of Human Rights as Pointing to Solidarity Rights

Given normative phenomenon that Trindade has referred to as *"the ineluctable relationship"* that exists between the human right to peace and the human right to development, we should ask ourselves why it has taken so long and involved so many different struggles just to arrive at this point in law, in politics, and in our global culture where we can finally speak of the ineluctable relationship between human right to peace and to development. The most basic answer is to be found in the fact that throughout the history of modern IR there have been "three generations of human rights" emanating from three competing schools of thought: (1) the first generation of civil and political rights; (2) the second generation of social, economic, and cultural rights; and (3) the third generation of solidarity rights.

In the final analysis, what this demarcation of rights into "generations" really represents is a simplified abstraction of the complex and confusing picture of what can be referred to as "human rights politics" (Kim 1991, 357). This framework for understanding the history of human rights emerged in the late 1970s. Its author was Karel Vasak, then a lawyer at the UNESCO. In 1977 he put forth a formulaic model for explaining the way in which the historical development of human rights unfolded. It remains the preeminent model for tracing the historical trajectory of human rights to this day. Vasak's model presents four different dimensions of each of the three generations of rights. In turn, each right is based on one of the philosophical ideals and/ or principles of the French Revolution: liberty, equality, and fraternity.[4] According to Prof. Daniel Whelan, "The categories of rights that reflect these historically bound ideals are civil and political rights (from classical liberalism), economic and social rights (from socialism/Marxism), and finally, solidarity or group rights, such as the right to self-determination, sovereignty over natural resources and the right to development. Table 9.3 reflects Whelan's reading of Vasak's formula.

First-generation rights view the state as the primary violator of rights. Second-generation rights seek to combat the power of the market. Third-generation rights are anticolonial. As such, third-generation rights are linked to second-generation rights in terms of the globalization of markets. According to Whelan, "[E]ach generation can be attached neatly to the priorities of the other three worlds we commonly associate with Western capitalism, state-socialism, and developing states" (Whelan 2010, 210). The most significant problem with this framework is that it is hampered by the fact that each of the generations of rights is ". . . based on normative assumptions built into the model" (Whelan 2010, 210). Hence, according to Whelan, "The problem with the generations approach is that it permanently categorizes rights, not only by fixing the categories in history, but also by finding within each generation incompatible philosophical sources of inspiration" (Whelan 2010, 210). Hence, the problems created by the generational approach to human rights leave both the definitions of human rights and human rights practitioners virtually fixated on a particular tradition's philosophical judgments and priorities to the exclusion of the other competing philosophical judgments and priorities. This creates some serious confusion and contradictions. For example, Donnelly has argued against the idea that there is a human right to peace because, in his view, "states do have a duty to protect their citizens from foreign invasion and international violence, and this ultimately may require war. International law recognizes the rights to states to self-defense, not the right of states (let alone individuals) to peace" (Donnelly 2006, 153).

Table 9.3 Three Generations of Human Rights

	First generation	Second generation	Third generation
Principle reflected	Liberty	Equality	Fraternity
Types of rights	Civil/political	Economic/social	Solidarity/group
Target of claims	Antistate	Antimarket	Anticolonial
Prioritized by	First World	Second World	Third World

Source: Daniel J. Whelan, *Indivisible Human Rights: A History*. Philadelphia: University of Pennsylvania Press, 2010, p. 209.

In contradistinction to Donnelly's assertions, Falk contends that international challenges on the issues of war and peace still have to pass through the United Nations Security Council, pursuant to the UN Charter—to which the United States is a signatory and retains a permanent seat on the Security Council. Therefore, the unilateral invasion of Iraq by the United States in 2003 was outside the scope of the UN Chanter and international law by virtue of the fact that the US invasion was a unilateral undertaking. Rather, it was an example of how geopolitical calculations in the hands of a superpower can effectively circumvent international law and institutions, thereby rendering a conception of an international order predicated on the rule of law rather moot—if not altogether irrelevant. Hence, Falk has correctly observed that "[b]ringing humanity to bear on global policy is a tricky matter and is inevitably intertwined with geopolitical ambitions. . . . The normative tension between upholding human rights in circumstances of extreme abuse collides with the struggle to prohibit reliance on war as a discretionary means for projecting power by sovereign states" (Falk 2009, 199). Trapped in the middle between these contending trends are both the human right to development and to peace. Both are intimately implicated by neoliberal globalization and the structural arrangements of the existing world order system.[5]

In summary, we live in a global war-system which endangers not only the human right to peace but the right to life itself. In this regard, C. G. Weeramantry has argued that

> *the manufacture of nuclear weapons must always be with a knowledge of their possible use* and with real or reasonably imputable knowledge that, once used, an all-out nuclear war is extremely probable. It must also be with real or reasonably imputable knowledge of those various other considerations, only too well known today, which render manufacture a source of increased risk and *which make manufacture inherently illegal and destructive of human rights.* Intention and knowledge of consequences are key factors in determining legal responsibilities for the consequences of one's action. Concerning nuclear weapons, it is submitted that there can be no justification for placing responsibility for manufacture in a different legal category from responsibility for use. The only difference is the difference between commission of a crime and preparation to commit a crime. (Weeramantry 2004, 520; italics added)

Along these same lines, I have argued in chapter 7, and throughout this book, that the Nuremberg Principles (Charter), the UN Charter, and the Principle of Hegemonic State Accountability (PHSA) stand against the proposition that a state can engage in the unauthorized use of force or threat of force, wars of aggression, or attempt to justify an attack on another state without UN Security Council authorization by relying on the dubious doctrine of "preemption."[6] In this regard, we should add the universal problem posed by nuclear weapons and the call of Ikeda, as well as others, for a nuclear weapons convention and nuclear weapons abolition (see chapter 7).

Throughout this book, Ikeda and his like-minded contemporaries have stressed that the universal risk and potential for planetary suicide resulting from the use of nuclear weapons present the strongest argument on behalf of claiming a universal human right to peace and, correspondingly, invoking the claims for a human right to development. Ikeda has recognized, along with many other individuals involved in the struggle for peace, that "[i]t is social injustice, economic malaise, and environmental decline that lead, *independently and interdependently,* to frustration, conflict, and oftentimes, ultimately violence" (Weston 1990, 97; italics added). Therefore, "it also bears emphasis that *it is not, on final analysis, treaties and charters prescribing specific norms, procedures, and institutions that will guarantee an enduring condition of peace among nations.* It is, rather, the ingrained assumption and habits of men and women everywhere, above all men and women in government and other arenas of social responsibility, that ultimately will be determinative in this regard" (Weston 1990, 97; italics added). Ikeda could probably not agree more with the ideas and sentiments behind this statement. That is primarily because it sets forth an acknowledgement of the need for an inner transformation in individual persons, which can ultimately lead to a practical application of what Ikeda has called humanitarian competition.

Similarly, voices speaking on behalf of the global South have acknowledged the current reality that

> The prospects for the transformation of international law into a purely counter-hegemonic tool, capable of aiding the weak and the victims, and of holding the powerful accountable, are bleak on its own. On the other hand, I would argue that international law is only a small (though important) part of counter-hegemonic power in the world today. The future of the world—its ability to deal with problems of peace, war, survival, prosperity, planetary health and pluralism—depends on a range of factors, including the politics of the "multitude," as Hardt and Negri call the governed. The stakes in legal reform between an agenda dictated by elite politics alone and an agenda shaped by mass politics have never been higher. (Rajagopal 2006, 780)

This is because "[t]he gap between what is and what ought to be is greater in the field of human rights than in any other domain of global politics. . . . Yet much of the prevailing approach has been preoccupied with surface symptoms rather than with structural causes. . . . The human rights [problem] cannot be overcome to any significant degree without transforming the existing world order system" (Kim 1991, 373). To that end, Ikeda and his like-minded contemporaries have supplied the road maps and remedies on how to bring about global transformation—a transformation leading to a more peaceful global civilization.

Notes

1. Vienna Declaration and Programme for Action, World Conference on Human Rights, Vienna, June 14–25, 1993, UN Doc. A.CONF.157/24 (Part I) at 20 (Vienna Declaration and Programme for Action), Part 1, para 10.
2. Declaration on the Right to Development (4 Dec. 1986), UNGA Res. 41/128, annex 41, Suppl. no. 53 at 186, UN Doc. A/41/53 (DRD).
3. In fact, as early as in 1968 the *Final Act* of the I World Conference on Human Rights of the United Nations (held in Teheran) contained several references to the relationship between the observance of human rights and the maintenance of peace; cf. UN, *Final Act of the International Conference on Human Rights* (1968), UN doc.A/CONF.32/41,NY,UN,1968, pp. 4, 6, 9, 14, and 36. And the UN General Assembly, on its turn, has constantly been attentive to address the requirements of *survival* of humankind as a whole.
4. On this matter, see Antonio Cassese, *The Human Dimension of International Law: Selected Papers*. New York: Oxford University Press, 2008, pp. 70–98.
5. On this matter, Richard Falk has noted the following:
    To the extent that neo-liberal perspectives are anti-authoritarian, they tend to encourage implementation of human rights in state/society relations, especially through the argument that an economistic approach to development will be frustrated if such rights are not upheld. However, the neo-liberal outlook ruptures a sense of human solidarity within a given political community by effectively rejecting any commitment of responsibility for those members who are economically and socially disadvantaged. And in times of difficulty this weakening of community bonds tends to impose the most difficult burdens of adjustment on those who are least able to bear them, including those with marginal jobs or unemployed. As such, it represents a *de facto* repeal of the broad scope of human rights as initially specified by the UDHR and carried forward in the International Covenant on Economic, Social and Cultural Rights. (Richard Falk, "A Half Century of Human Rights: Geopolitics and Values," in *The Future of International Human Rights*, edited by Burns H. Weston and Stephen P. Marks. New York: Transnational Publishers, p. 15.)
6. On this matter, see Philip Alston and Euan MacDonald, editors, *Human Rights, Intervention, and the Use of Force*. New York: Oxford University Press, 2008.

Afterword

After reading and reflecting on *Beyond Global Crisis*, I am struck by how important this work is, not only for what it says but for what it *does*. Terrence Paupp brilliantly brings many things together that normally are not considered together. For one, he brings together Western and Eastern thinking. I write this from Seoul, Republic of Korea, a vibrant city in a vibrant nation whose people are bringing together Eastern and Western thought. I am jealous of the people here who speak Korean and English. My own language learning has been Western (English and French, with some stabs at German and Danish). Language reflects, helps, shapes, but also limits thought. People who speak English and Korean bridge two worlds. It is as if they are bringing the left and right hemispheres of the big brain of Earth together, finally. Or perhaps reuniting these two spheres after they've been severed by accidents of geography, weather, war—whatever separated the first group of people's descendants from each other.

This unification, this unity of thought, this intermarriage of ideas, brings great promise for humanity's future. There is a risk of conflict, of course, but I am an optimist—we must engage in this "risky adventure," as Ikeda would call it (*see* BGC 301). This adventure will be aided and speeded through works such as *Beyond Global Crisis*. Indeed, a central theme of *Beyond Global Crisis* is that humanity must move toward cooperation and away from competition, from mistrust to trust (*see* BGC 285).

Beyond Global Crisis also represents a pairing of victor and vanquished: the thinkers representative of international relations and international law scholarship hail, for the most part, from the United States, which mercilessly fire- and atomic-bombed Japan into an unconditional surrender in 1945. Out of those radioactive ashes grew some reconciliation. But for Ikeda, who saw firsthand the ravages of that war, something further grew: a commitment to peace and the peaceful resolution of crises. For the United States, unfortunately, a commitment to militarism took root, and, unfortunately, some international relations and international law scholars are apologists for this militarism.

Beyond Global Crisis also, more broadly, and perhaps most importantly for me, intelligently and courageously pairs two different kinds of work and approaches. There is what I call the hard-headed (and hard-hearted) approach of international relations and international law scholarship, where military violence is still accepted in some contexts as a legitimate aspect of international relations. Much of the work in this area mimics the polite, drawing room language and tone of international diplomacy and similarly (and offensively) speaks casually and euphemistically of using such force. But Ikeda's work is different. It is unapologetically Buddhist. It is visionary. It is optimistic. It is full-hearted, human. It is not state-centric but human-centered. Such work by Ikeda and his like-minded contemporaries is seldom included in international relations and international law scholarship. Rather, it is often relegated to Peace Studies (which is not taken seriously by "serious people") or even relegated to the Religious/Spiritual or New Age sections of bookstores. The irony, of course, is that Ikeda *in general* has not been ignored. The man has received at least three hundred honorary degrees from universities around the world. But the international relations and international law scholars who march at those graduations have not acknowledged his work in their own. A search for "Daisaku Ikeda" in the law journals database on Westlaw, which includes international law journals, yields just seven articles. (I do not work in IR and have not made a comparable search in the literature of that field.) Contemplating such visionary work, apparently, is not the way to tenure, appointments to the State Department, or publication in *Foreign Affairs* or in the op-ed pages of the *New York Times, Washington Post,* or *Wall Street Journal.*

But it is crucial that the work of Ikeda and his like-minded contemporaries be considered in international relations and international law scholarship. At the end of the day, when we think about creating and maintaining peace, we are talking about human beings, and changes of mind and spirit. These changes will change the behavior of states, and not vice versa. To think otherwise is unserious. As Ikeda has said, "World peace is not something that can be realized simply by politicians signing treaties, or by business leaders creating economic cooperation. True and lasting peace will be realized only by forging bonds of trust between people at the deepest level, in the depths of their very lives." And more ominously, regarding nuclear weapons, Ikeda has stated, "Trust in nuclear arms is a negation of trust in humanity. The more people trust in arms, the less they trust one another. Ceasing to put their trust in arms is the only way to cultivate mutual trust among peoples" (*see* BGC 40). Paupp, in *Beyond Global Crisis* and in his other works, is pioneering this sort of holistic, realistic, intellectually rigorous scholarship.

The sort of visionary work that *Beyond Global Crisis* represents and engages with is work that has informed and inspired much of my scholarship—but I have not highlighted it, in what I see now as my less-than-fully-conscious effort to have my work taken "seriously." (One of my first scholarly articles was rejected by a student-run international law journal at a leading US law school in 2002; an editor explained that my article was "inflammatory." I had merely written honestly about the human, economic, political, and environmental costs of military force.) What *Beyond Global Crisis* shows, however, is that if we are truly serious about what I see as the ultimate goal of international relations and international law, friendly and trusting and productive relations between states and people, then we must consider the work of Ikeda and his like-minded contemporaries.

One of the aspects of *Beyond Global Crisis* that I most admire is that it takes on and (in *jujitsu* fashion) "flips" current dialogue in international relations and international law scholarship. Paupp quotes L. S. Stavrianos: "The world of the late twentieth century can ill afford superpower *realpolitik* that ends up as crackpot realism" (*see* BGC 75). Paupp later writes, "We are re-learning the truth that self-interest must be tempered by the general interest. Coexistence and tolerance must be rediscovered in our own time as governing principles for the planet. In short, embarking upon Ikeda's "*third path*" represents the ends of illusions and a radically demystified understanding of power" (*see* BGC 75). This statement and other such statements throughout the book— and Paupp's rigorous challenging of conventional scholarship—expose the intellectual paucity of many current preconceptions and point up the truth that Ikeda is highly relevant and necessary to current international relations and international law thinking. Indeed, it may be the mystification of power (and politics) that holds back international relations and international law scholars from even considering the work of visionaries such as Ikeda. If that is the case, then *Beyond Global Crisis* could help lead to a rethinking of many of these self-limiting preconceptions.

Two examples from toward the end of *Beyond Global Crisis* illustrate this point. One is where Paupp discusses some of my work proposing that the UN Security Council procedure be more "judicialized" when it comes to determining whether military violence should be used in a given situation (*see* BGC 287). I have argued that the Security Council's process, at least in this context, has to be reformed to become somewhat "judicialized"; that is, there needs to be a formal opportunity for cross-examination and rebuttal to presentations of evidence. (For example, I read better refutations of US Secretary of State Colin Powell's infamous February 5, 2003 Security Council presentation in the "alternative press" than any made inside the Security Council.) As a matter of intellect, the need for such improved process seems clear, and the lack of it seems indefensible. But I am coming to think that the only way this point can be reached intellectually is if there is first a heart-centered revulsion at and rejection of war, and if people take what Ikeda might call a "leap of trust" toward other people of different nations, cultures, religions, and regions.

The other example is where Paupp argues that we must acknowledge a human right to peace. Given the dislocation and destruction caused by war and military violence (no matter how "surgical"), this proposal seems incontrovertible. As US Supreme Court Justice Robert Jackson famously argued as chief prosecutor at Nuremberg, "To initiate a war of aggression, therefore, is not only an international crime; it is the supreme international crime differing only from other war crimes in that it contains within itself the accumulated evil of the whole." But, again, we will likely come to this understanding intellectually only after we have thought more deeply and more rigorously and with a more Ikeda-informed vision about what war and human rights really mean.

Beyond Global Crisis is a valuable resource. I hope that it is seen as the start of meaningful consideration of the work of Daisaku Ikeda and his like-minded contemporaries by those who work in international relations and international law. Embracing these visionaries is a "risky adventure" that should make our work and our future richer and more compassionate.

Brian J. Foley
Seoul, Republic of Korea
August 2011

Appendix

Preamble of the Rome Statute of the International Criminal Court

The State Parties to this Statute

Conscious that all peoples are united by common bonds, their cultures pieced together in a shared heritage, and concerned that this delicate mosaic may be shattered at any time,

Mindful, that during this century millions of children, women and men have been victims of unimaginable atrocities that deeply shock the conscience of humanity,

Recognizing that such grave crimes threaten the peace, security and well-being of the world,

Affirming that the most serious crimes of concern to the international community as a whole must not go unpunished and that their effective prosecution must be ensured by taking measures at the national level and by enhancing international cooperation,

Determined to put an end to immunity for the perpetrators of these crimes and thus to contribute to the prevention of such crimes,

Recalling that it is the duty of every State to exercise its criminal jurisdiction over those responsible for international crimes,

Reaffirming the Purpose and Principles of the Charter of the United Nations, and in particular that all States shall refrain from the threat or use of force against the territorial integrity or political independence of any State, or in any other manner inconsistent with the Purposes of the United Nations,

Emphasizing in this connection that nothing in this Statute shall be taken as authorizing any State Party to intervene in an armed conflict or in the internal affairs of any State,

Determined to these ends and for the sake of the present and future generations, to establish an independent permanent International Criminal Court in relationship with the United Nations system, with jurisdiction over the most serious crimes of concern to the international community as a whole,

Emphasizing that the International Criminal Court established under this Statute shall be complementary to national criminal jurisdictions,

Resolved to guarantee lasting respect for and the enforcement of international justice,

Have agreed as follows:

Bibliography

A

Aaronson, Susan A. and Zimmerman, Jamie M. 2008. *Trade Imbalance: The Struggle to Weigh Human Rights Concerns in Trade Policymaking*. New York, NY: Cambridge University Press.

Abegunrin, Olayiwola. 2009. *Africa in Global Politics in the Twenty-First Century: A Pan-African Perspective*. New York, NY: Palgrave Macmillan.

Abernethy, David B. 2000. *The Dynamics of Global Dominance: European Overseas Empires, 1415–1980*. New Haven, CT: Yale University Press.

Abouharb, M. Rodwan and Cingranelli, David. 2007. *Human Rights and Structural Adjustment*. Cambridge, UK: Cambridge University Press.

Acharya, Amitav. 2009a. *Constructing a Security Community in Southeast Asia: ASEAN and the Problem of Regional Order—Second Edition*. New York, NY: Routledge.

Acharya, Amitav. 2009b. *Whose Ideas Matter?—Agency and Power in Asia's Regionalism*. Ithaca, NY: Cornell University Press.

Adebajo, Adekeye. 2008. "From Bandung to Durban: Whither the Afro-Asian Coalition?" in *Bandung Revisited: The Legacy of the 1955 Asian-African Conference for International Order*, edited by See Seng Tan and Amitav Acharya. Singapore: National University of Singapore Press.

Aguirre, Daniel. 2008. *The Human Rights to Development in a Globalized World*. London: Ashgate.

Ahmed, Abdel, G.M. 2008. "Multiple Complexity and Prospects for Reconciliation and Unity: The Sudan Conundrum," in *The Roots of African Conflicts: The Causes and Costs*, edited by Alfred Nhema and Paul T. Zeleza. Athens, OH: Ohio University Press.

Alagappa, Muthiah. 2008a. "Nuclear Weapons and National Security: Far-Reaching Influence and Deterrence Dominance," in *The Long Shadow: Nuclear Weapons and Security in 21st Century Asia*, edited by Muthiah Alagappa. Stanford, CA: Stanford University Press.

Alagappa, Muthiah. 2008b. "Reinforcing National Security and Regional Stability: The Implications of Nuclear Weapons and Strategies," in *The Long Shadow: Nuclear Weapons and Security in 21st Century Asia*, edited by Muthiah Alagappa. Stanford, CA: Stanford University Press.

Allott, Philip. 2002. *The Health of Nations: Society and Law Beyond the State*. Cambridge: Cambridge University Press.

Alperovitz, Gar. 2005. *America Beyond Capitalism: Reclaiming Our Wealth, Our Liberty, and Our Democracy.* Hoboken, NJ: John Wiley & Sons.

Alston, Philip. 1999. "A Framework for the Comparative Analysis of Bills of Rights," in *Promoting Human Rights Through Bills of Rights: Comparative Perspectives,* edited by Philip Alston. New York, NY: Oxford University Press.

Amin, Samir. 2003. *Obsolescent Capitalism: Contemporary Politics and Global Disorder,* translated by Patrick Camiller. New York, NY: Zed Books.

Amin, Samir. 2004. "Confronting the Empire," in *Pox Americana: Exposing the American Empire,* edited by John Bellamy Foster and Robert W. McChesney. New York, NY: Monthly Review Press.

Amin, Samir. 2008. *The World We Wish to See: Revolutionary Objectives in the Twenty-First Century,* translated by James Membrez. New York, NY: Monthly Review Press.

Arnold, Guy. 2006. *Historical Dictionary of the Non-Aligned Movement and Third World.* Lanham, MD: Scarecrow Press.

Arrighi, Giovanni. 1999. *Chaos and Governance in the Modern World System.* Minneapolis, MN: University of Minnesota Press.

Arrighi, Giovanni. 2007. *Adam Smith in Beijing: Lineages of the Twenty-First Century.* London: Verso.

Ashford, Elizabeth. 2007. "The Duties Imposed by the Human Right to Basic Necessities," in *Freedom from Poverty as a Human Right: Who Owes What to the Very Poor?,* edited by Thomas Pogge. New York, NY: Oxford University Press.

Austin, Jay E. and Bruch, Carl E. (editors). 2000. *The Environmental Consequences of War: Legal, Economic, and Scientific Perspectives.* New York, NY: Cambridge University Press.

B

Ba, Alice D. 2009. *[Re]Negotiating East and Southeast Asia: Region, Regionalism, and the Association of Southeast Asian Nations.* Stanford, CA: Stanford University Press.

Bacevich, Andrew. 2010. *Washington Rules: America's Path to Permanent War.* New York, NY: Metropolitan Books.

Backer, Larry Cata. 2007. *Harmonizing Law in an Era of Globalization: Convergence, Divergence, and Resistance,* edited by Larry Cata Backer. Durham, NC: Carolina Academic Press.

Baker, Dean. 2009. *Plunder and Blunder: The Rise and Fall of the Bubble Economy.* Sausalito, CA: PoliPointPress.

Ball, Howard. 2007. *Bush, the Detainees and the Constitution: The Battle over Presidential Power in the War on Terror.* Lawrence, KS: University of Kansas Press.

Barnett, Richard J. 1965. "Preparations for Progress." *The Strategy of World Order—(Volume 1)—Toward a Theory of War Prevention,* edited by Richard A. Falk and Saul H. Medlovitz. New York, NY: World Law Fund.

Barnett, Richard J., and Muller, Ronald E. 1974. *Global Reach: The Power of the Multinational Corporations*. New York, NY: Simon and Schuster.

Bartelson, Jens. 2009. *Visions of World Community*. New York, NY: Cambridge University Press.

Bartholomew, Amy. 2006. *Empire's Law: The American Imperial Project and the "War to Remake the World"*. London: Pluto Press.

Bass, Gary J. 2008. *Freedom's Battle: The Origins of Humanitarian Intervention*. New York, NY: Alfred A. Knopf.

Bello, Walden. 1998. "The Bretton Woods Institutions and the Demise of the UN Development System," in *Between Sovereignty and Global Governance: The United Nations, the State and Civil Society*, edited by Albert Paolini, Anthony Jarvis, and Christian Reus-Smit. New York, NY: St. Martin's Press.

Bello, Walden. 2005. *Dilemmas of Domination: The Unmaking of the American Empire*. New York, NY: Metropolitan Books.

Berger, Mark and Beeson, Mark. 2007. "Miracles of Modernization and Crises of Capitalism: The World Bank, East Asian Development and Liberal Hegemony," in *The World Bank: Development, Poverty, and Hegemony*, edited by David Moore. South Africa: University of KwaZulu-Natal Press.

Beschloss, Michael R. 1991. *The Crisis Years: Kennedy and Khrushchev, 1960–1963*. New York, NY: Harper Collins Publishers.

Bethel, Dayle. 2000. "The Legacy of Tsunesaburo Makiguci: Value-Creating Education and Global Citizenship," in *Global Citizens: The Soka Gakkai Buddhist Movement in the World*, edited by David Machacek and Bryan Wilson. Oxford: Oxford University Press.

Bhala, Raj. 2003. *Trade, Development, and Social Justice*. Durham, NC: Carolina Academic Press.

Bix, Herbert P. 2000. *Hirohito and the Making of Modern Japan*, New York, NY: Harper-Collins Publishers.

Bjola, Corneliu. 2009. *Legitimizing the Use of Force in International Politics: Kosovo, Iraq and the Ethics of Intervention*. New York, NY: Routledge.

Blasius, Mark. 1984. "The Discourse of World Order," in *Culture, Ideology, and World Order*, edited by R.B.J. Walker. Boulder, CO: Westview Press.

Blum, William. 2000. *Rogue State: A Guide to the World's Only Superpower*. Monroe, ME: Common Courage Press.

Blum, William. 2004. *Killing Hope: US Military and CIA Interventions Since World War II—The Updated Edition*. Monroe, ME: Common Courage Press.

Boggs, Carl. 2000. *The End of Politics: Corporate Power and Decline of the Public Sphere*. New York and London: Guilford Press.

Boggs, Carl. 2003. "Outlaw Nation: The Legacy of US War Crimes," in *Masters of War: Militarism and Blowback in the Era of American Empire*, edited by Carl Boggs. New York, NY: Routledge.

Boggs, Carl. 2005. *Imperial Delusions: American Militarism and Endless War*. Lanham, MD: Rowman & Littlefield Publishers.

Boggs, Carl. 2010. *The Crimes of Empire: Rogue Superpower and World Domination*. London: Pluto Press.

Bosco, David L. 2009. *Five To Rule Them All: The UN Security Council and the Making of the Modern World*. New York, NY: Oxford University Press.

Boswell, Terry. 2004. "Hegemonic Decline and Revolution: When the World is Up for Grabs," in *Globalization, Hegemony and Power: Anti-systemic Movements and the Global System*, edited by Thomas E. Reifer. Boulder, CO: Paradigm Publishers.

Boulding, Kenneth. 1978. *Stable Peace*. Austin, TX: University of Texas Press.

Bowden, Brett. 2009. *The Empire of Civilization: The Evolution of an Imperial Idea*. Chicago, IL: University of Chicago Press.

Bowles, Paul and Veltmeyer, Henry. 2007. "The Lexicon of Globalization: Comparative National Perspectives," in *National Perspectives on Globalization*, edited by Paul Bowles and Henry Veltmeyer. New York, NY: Palgrave Macmillan.

Brecher, Jeremy; Cutler, Jill, and Smith, Brandan (editors). 2005. *In the Name of Democracy: American War Crimes in Iraq and Beyond*. New York, NY: Metropolitan Books.

Broad, Robin and Cavanagh, John. 2000. "Global Backlash: Citizen Initiatives to Counter Corporate-Led Globalization," in *Principled World Politics: The Challenge of Normative International Relations*, edited by Paul Wapner and Lester Edwin J. Ruiz. Lanham, MD: Rowman & Littlefield Publishers.

Brocheux, Pierre and Hemery, Daniel. 2009. *Indochina: An Ambiguous Colonization, 1858–1954*. Berkeley, CA: University of California Press.

Bunn, George and Chyba, Christopher F. (editors). 2006. *US Nuclear Weapons Policy: Confronting Today's Threats*. Stanford, CA: Center for International Security and Cooperation, Stanford University and Washington, DC: Brookings Institution Press.

Burbank, Jane and Cooper, Frederick. 2010. *Empires in World History: Power and the Politics of Difference*. Princeton, NJ: Princeton University Press.

Burleigh, Michael. 2005. *Earthly Powers: The Clash of Religion and Politics in Europe, from the French Revolution to the Great War*. New York, Harper-Collins Publishers.

Burleigh, Michael. 2007. *Sacred Causes: The Clash of Religion and Politics from the Great War to the War on Terror*. New York, NY: Harper-Collins Publishers.

Burroughs, John. 2003. "Preface," in *Rule of Power or Rule of Law: An Assessment of US Policies and Actions Regarding Security-Related Treaties*, edited by John Burroughs, et al. New York, NY: Apex Press.

Burroughs, John. 2007. "Understanding U.S. Policy," in *Nuclear Disorder or Cooperative Security?: US Weapons of Terror, the Global Proliferation Crisis, and Paths to Peace—An Assessment of the Final Report of the Weapons of Mass Destruction Commission and Its Implications for US Policy*, edited by John Burroughs, et al. New York, NY: Lawyers' Committee on Nuclear Policy.

Bush, Ray. 2007. *Poverty and Neo-Liberalism: Persistence and Reproduction in the Global South*. London: Pluto Press.

Buzan, Barry and Little, Richard. 2000. *International Systems in World History: Remaking the Study of International Relations*. New York, NY: Oxford University Press.

C

Calder, Kent. 2007. *Embattled Garrisons: Comparative Base Politics and American Globalism*. Princeton, NJ: Princeton University Press.

Camilleri, Joseph A. 1976. *Civilization in Crisis: Human Prospects in a Changing World*. New York, NY: Cambridge University Press.

Capra, Fritjof. 1982. *The Turning Point: Science, Society, and the Rising Culture*. New York, NY: Simon and Schuster.

Carr, Edward H. 1961. *The Twenty Years Crisis, 1919–1930: An Introduction to the Study of International Relations*. London: Macmillan.

Castells, Manuel. 2004. *The Power of Identity—Second Edition*. Malden, MA: Blackwell Publishing.

Castro, Fidel and Ramonet, Ignacio. 2007. *Fidel Castro: My Life—A Spoken Autobiography*, edited by Ignacio Ramonet and translated by Andrew Hurley. New York, NY: Scribner.

Cavanagh, John, Wysham, Daphne, and Arruda, Marcos (editors). 1994. *Beyond Bretton Woods: Alternatives to the Global Economic Order*. London: Pluto Press.

Ceadel, Martin. 1996. *The Origins of War Prevention: The British Peace Movement and International Relations, 1730–1854*. New York, NY: Oxford University Press.

Chomsky, Noam and Herman, Edward S. 1979a. *The Washington Connection and Third World Fascism—The Political Economy of Human Rights (Volume I)*. Boston, MA: South End Press.

Chomsky, Noam and Herman, Edward S. 1979b. *After the Cataclysm: Postwar Indochina and the Reconstruction of Imperial Ideology—The Political Economy of Human Rights (Volume II)*. Boston, MA: South End Press.

Chomsky, Noam. 1991. *Deterring Democracy*. London and New York, NY: Verso.

Chomsky, Noam. 2003. *Hegemony or Survival: America's Quest for Global Dominance*. New York, NY: Metropolitan Books.

Chomsky, Noam. 2006. *Failed States: The Abuse of Power and the Assault on Democracy*. New York, NY: Metropolitan Books.

Chossudovsky, Michel. 2003. *The Globalization of Poverty and the New World Order—Second Edition*. Montreal, QC: Global Research.

Chossudovsky, Michel. 2005. *America's 'War on Terrorism'—Second Edition*. Canada: Global Research.

Chossudovsky, Michel and Marshall, Andrew Gavin. 2010. *The Global Economic Crisis: The Great Depression of the XXI Century*. Canada: Global Research.

Chowdhry, Kamla. 1989. "Poverty, Environment, Development," *Daedalus: Journal of the American Academy of Arts and Sciences—"A World to Make: Development in Perspective,"* Vol. 118, No. 1.

Chua, Amy L. 2000. "The Paradox of Free Market Democracy: Rethinking Development Policy," *Harvard International Law Journal*, Vol. 41, No. 2.

Chyba, Christopher F. and Sasikumar, Karthika. 2006. "A World of Risk: The Current Environment for US Nuclear Weapons Policy," in *US Nuclear*

Weapons Policy: Confronting Today's Threats, edited by George Bunn and Christopher F. Chyba. Washington, DC: Brookings Institution Press.

Clark, Ramsey. 1992. *The Fire This Time: US War Crimes in the Gulf.* New York, NY: Thunder's Mouth Press.

Cohen, Jean L. 2005. "Whose Sovereignty?: Empire versus International Law," in *Global Institutions and Responsibilities: Achieving Global Justice*, edited by Christian Barry and Thomas W. Pogge. Malden, MA: Blackwell Publishing.

Cossa, Ralph A. 1999. "Asia-Pacific Confidence-Building Measures for Regional Security," in *Global Confidence Building: New Tools for Troubled Regions*, edited by Michael Krepon, et al. New York, NY: St. Martin's Press.

Cousins, Norman. 1987. *The Pathology of Power.* New York, NY: W.W. Norton & Company.

Cox, Harvey G. and Daisaku Ikeda. 2009. *The Persistence of Religion: Comparative Perspectives on Modern Spirituality.* London and New York, NY: I.B. Tauris.

Cox, Robert W. 1979. "Ideologies and the New International Economic Order: Reflections on Some Recent Literature," *International Organization*, Vol. 33, No. 2.

Cox, Robert W. 2008. "The Point is Not Just to Explain the World but to Change It," in *The Oxford Handbook of International Relations.* New York, NY: Oxford University Press.

Crenson, Matthew and Ginsberg, Benjamin. 2007. *Presidential Power: Unchecked and Unbalanced.* New York and London: W.W. Norton & Company.

D

Dallek, Robert. 2003. *An Unfinished Life: John F. Kennedy (1917–1963).* Boston, MA: Little, Brown and Company.

Danchin, Peter G. and Fischer, Horst. 2010. "Introduction: The New Collective Security," in *United Nations Reform and the New Collective Security.* Cambridge, UK: Cambridge University Press.

Davies, Nicholas J.S. 2007. "From Aggression to Genocide: Setting the Record Straight on the US Invasion and Destruction of Iraq," *Z-Magazine*, September 2007, pp. 49–54.

De Rivero, Oswaldo. 2001. *The Myth of Development: Non-Viable Economies of the 21st Century*, translated by Claudia Encinas and Janet Herrick Encinas. London: Zed Books.

Deller, Nicole, Makhijani, Arjun, and Burroughs, John (editors). 2003. *Rule of Power or Rule of Law?—An Assessment of US Policies and Actions Regarding Security-Related Treaties.* New York, NY: Apex Press.

DeMartino, George F. 2000. *Global Economy, Global Justice: Theoretical Objections and Policy Alternatives to Neo-Liberalism.* London: Routledge.

Dierckxsens, Wim. 2000. *The Limits of Capitalism: An Approach to Globalization without Neo-Liberalism*, translated by Jayne Hutchcroft. London: Zed Books.

Dittmer Lowell. 2010. "China's Rise, Global Identity, and the Developing World," in *China, the Developing World, and the New Global Dynamic,* edited by Lowell Dittmer and George T. Yu. Boulder, CO: Lynne Rienner Publishers.

Donnelly, Jack. 2006. "Peace as a Human Right—Commentary," in *Human Rights and Conflict: Exploring the Links between Rights, Law, and Peace-building,* edited by Julie A. Mertus and Jeffrey W. Helsing. Washington, DC: United States Institute of Peace Press.

Donovan, John C. 1967. *The Politics of Poverty.* New York, NY: Western Publishing Company.

Doran, Charles F. 2009. "Statecraft Today: Regional Predicaments, Global Conundrums," in *Imbalance of Power: US Hegemony and International Order,* edited by I. William Zartman. Boulder, CO: Lynne Rienner Publishers.

Douglass, James W. 2008. *JFK and the Unspeakable: Why He Died and Why It Matters.* New York, NY: Orbis Books.

Dower, John W. 1986. *War Without Mercy: Race and Power in the Pacific War.* New York, NY: Pantheon Books.

Dower, John W. 1999. *Embracing Defeat: Japan in the Wake of World War II.* New York, NY: W.W. Norton & Company/The New Press.

Doyle, Michael W. 2008. *Striking First: Preemption and Prevention in International Conflict.* Princeton, NJ: Princeton University Press.

Dunoff, Jeffrey L. and Trachtman, Joel P. (editors) 2009. *Ruling the World? Constitutionalism, International Law, and Global Governance.* New York, NY: Cambridge University Press.

E

Ehrenberg, John, et al. (editors). 2010. *The Iraq Papers.* New York, NY: Oxford University Press.

Ehrlich, Paul and Ehrlich, Anne. 2004. One with Nineveh: Politics, Consumption, and the Human Future. Washington, DC: Island Press.

Eide, Asbjorn. 2006. "Human Rights-Based Development in the Age of Economic Globalization: Background and Prospects," in *Development as a Human Right: Legal, Political, and Economic Dimensions,* edited by Bard A. Andreassen and Stephen P. Marks. Cambridge, MA: Harvard University Press.

Ellsberg, Daniel. 2009. "Roots of the Upcoming Nuclear Crisis," in *The Challenge of Abolishing Nuclear Weapons,* edited by David Krieger, New Brunswick, NJ: Transaction Publishers.

Ellul, Jacques. 1964. *The Technological Society,* translated from the French by John Wilkinson. New York, NY: Vintage Books.

Engelhardt, Tom. 2010. *The American Way of War: How Bush's Wars Became Obama's.* Chicago, IL: Haymarket Books.

Evans, Peter. 2002. "Introduction: Looking for Agents of Urban Livability in a Globalized Political Economy," in *Livable Cities?—Urban Struggles for Livelihood and Sustainability,* edited by Peter Evans. Berkeley, CA: University of California Press.

F

Falk, Richard A. 1966. "Historical Tendencies, Modernizing and Revolutionary Nations, and the International Legal Order," *The Strategy of World Order—(Volume 2)—International Law*, edited by Richard A. Falk and Saul H. Mendlovitz. New York, NY: World Law Fund.

Falk, Richard. 1975. *A Study of Future Worlds*. New York, NY: Free Press.

Falk, Richard. 1981. *Human Rights and State Sovereignty*. New York, NY: Holmes & Meier Publishers.

Falk, Richard. 1985. "The Interplay of Westphalia and Charter Conceptions of International Legal Order," in *International Law: A Contemporary Perspective*, edited by Richard Falk, Friedrich Kratochwil, and Saul H. Mendlovitz. Boulder, CO: Westview Press.

Falk, Richard. 1994. "Regionalism and World Order after the Cold War," WIDER/IPSA Workshop, Berlin.

Falk, Richard. 1995. *On Humane Governance: Toward a New Global Politics*. University Park, PA: Pennsylvania State University Press.

Falk, Richard. 1998. *Law in an Emerging Global Village: A Post-Westphalian Perspective*. New York, NY: Transnational Publishers.

Falk, Richard. 1999. *Predatory Globalization: A Critique*. London: Polity.

Falk, Richard. 2000a. "Humane Governance for the World: Reviving the Quest," in *Global Futures: Shaping Globalization*, edited by Jan Nederveen Pieterse. New York, NY: Zed Books.

Falk, Richard. 2000b. *Human Rights Horizons: The Pursuit of Justice in a Globalizing World*. New York, NY: Routledge.

Falk, Richard. 2003. "On the Political Relevance of Global Society," in *Making Globalization Good: The Moral Challenges of Global Capitalism*, edited by John H. Dunning. New York, NY: Oxford University Press.

Falk, Richard. 2004a. *The Declining World Order: America's Imperial Geopolitics*. New York, NY: Routledge.

Falk, Richard. 2004b. "State Terror versus Humanitarian Law," *War and State Terrorism: The United States, Japan, and the Asia-Pacific in the Long Twentieth Century*, edited by Mark Selden and Alvin Y. So. Lanham, MD: Roman & Littlefield Publishers.

Falk, Richard. 2005. "The Iraq War and the Future of International Law," in *Democracy's Shadow: The Secret World of National Security*, edited by Marcus Raskin and A. Carl LeVan. New York, NY: Nation Books.

Falk, Richard. 2008a. "International Law and the Future," in *International Law and the Third World: Reshaping Justice*, edited by Richard Falk, Balakrishnan Rajagopal and Jacqueline Stevens. New York, NY: Routledge-Cavendish.

Falk, Richard. 2008b. "Nuclear Weapons, War, and the Discipline of International Law," in *At the Nuclear Precipice: Catastrophe or Transformation?*, edited by Richard Falk and David Krieger. New York, NY: Palgrave Macmillan.

Falk, Richard. 2008c. *The Costs of War: International Law, the UN, and World Order after Iraq*. New York, NY: Routledge.

Falk, Richard. 2009. *Achieving Human Rights*. New York, NY: Routledge.

Falk, Richard, Gendzier, Irene, and Lifton, Robert (editors). 2006. *Crimes of War—Iraq*. New York, NY: Nation Books.

Fanon, Frantz. 1968. *The Wretched of the Earth*. New York, NY: Grove Press.

Farmer, Paul. 2003. *Pathologies of Power: Health, Human Rights, and the New War on the Poor*. Berkeley, CA: University of California Press.

Felice, William F. 1996. *Taking Suffering Seriously: The Importance of Collective Human Rights*. New York, NY: State University of New York Press.

Felice, William F. 2003. *The Global New Deal: Economic and Social Human Rights in World Politics*. Lanham, MD: Rowman & Littlefield Publishers, Inc., p. 117.

Finlay, Brian. 2009. "Cooperating to Prevent Catastrophe." *Courier*, Number 65, Winter, The Stanley Foundation.

Fisher, Louis. 2008. *The Constitution and 9/11: Recurring Threats to America's Freedoms*. Lawrence, KS: University of Kansas Press.

Fletcher, George P. and Ohlin, Jens David. 2008. *Defending Humanity: When Force is Justified and Why*. New York, NY: Oxford University Press.

Foley, Brian. 2003. "Avoiding a Death Dance: Adding Steps to the International Law on the Use of Force to Improve the Search for Alternatives to Force and Prevent Likely Harms," *Brooklyn Journal of International Law*, Vol. 29, No. 1.

Forsythe, David P. 2004. "International Criminal Justice and the United States: Law, Culture, and Power," in *From Sovereign Impunity to International Accountability: The Search for Justice in a World of States*, edited by Ramesh Thakur and Peter Malcontent. Tokyo: United Nations University Press.

Foster, John Bellamy and Fred Magdoff. 2009. *The Great Financial Crisis: Causes and Consequences*. New York, NY: Monthly Review Press.

Frank, Andre Gunder. 1998. *Re-Orient: Global Economy in the Asian Age*. Berkeley, CA: University of California Press.

Franck, Thomas M. 1995. *Fairness in International Law and Institutions*. New York, NY: Oxford University Press.

Franck, Thomas M. 1999. *The Empowered Self: Law and Society in the Age of Individualism*. New York, NY: Oxford University Press.

Franck, Thomas M. 2009. "Preface: International Institutions: Why Constitutionalize?" in *Ruling the World? Constitutionalism, International Law, and Global Governance*, edited by Jeffrey L. Dunoff and Joel P. Trachtman. New York, NY: Cambridge University Press.

Fredrickson, George M. 1995. *Black Liberation: A Comparative History of Black Ideologies in the United States and South Africa*. New York, NY: Oxford University Press.

Freedman, Lawrence. 2000. *Kennedy's Wars: Berlin, Cuba, Laos, and Vietnam*. New York, NY: Oxford University Press.

Fromm, Erich. 1965. *The Sane Society*. New York, NY: Fawcett Premier.

Fromm, Erich. 1975. *The Anatomy of Human Destructiveness*. New York, NY: Fawcett Crest.

Fursenko, Aleksandr and Naftali, Timothy. 1997. *"One Hell of a Gamble"— Khrushchev, Castro, and Kennedy, 1958–1964.* New York, NY: W.W. Norton & Company.

G

Gaddy, Clifford G. 1996. *The Price of the Past: Russia's Struggle with the Legacy of a Militarized Economy.* Washington, DC: Brookings Institution Press.

Gardbaum, Stephen. 2009. "Human Rights and International Constitutionalism," in *Ruling the World?—Constitutionalism, International Law, and Global Government,* edited by Jeff Dunhoff and Joel Tractman. New York, NY: Cambridge University Press.

Gardner, Lloyd C. 2009. *Three Kings: The Rise of an American Empire in the Middle East after World War II.* New York, NY: New Press.

Gathii, James Thuo. 2008. "Third World Approaches to International Economic Governance," in *International Law and the Third World: Reshaping Justice,* edited by Richard Falk. Balakrishnan Rajagopal, and Jacqueline Stevens. London: Routledge-Cavendish.

George, Susan. 2000. "A Short History of Neoliberalism: Twenty Years of Elite Economics and Emerging Opportunities for Structural Change," in *Global Finance: New Thinking on Regulating Speculative Capital Markets,* edited by Walden Bello, et al. London and New York, NY: Zed Books.

Gerson, Joseph. 2007. *Empire and the Bomb: How the US Uses Nuclear Weapons to Dominate the World.* London: Pluto Press.

Gervasi, Tom. 1986. *The Myth of Soviet Military Supremacy.* New York, NY: Harper & Row, Publishers.

Gewirth, Alan. 1996. *The Community of Rights.* Chicago, IL: University of Chicago Press.

Gibson, Donald. 1994. *Battling Wall Street: The Kennedy Presidency.* New York, NY: Sheridan Square Press.

Gills, Barry K. (editor) 2000. *Globalization and the Politics of Resistance,* foreword by John Kenneth Galbraith. New York, NY: Palgrave.

Goldfischer, David. 2005. "Prospects for a New World Order," in *Globalization, Security, and the Nation-State: Paradigms in Transition,* edited by Ersel Aydinli and James N. Rosenau. Albany, NY: State University of New York Press.

Goldsmith, Jack L. and Posner, Eric A. 2005. *The Limits of International Law.* New York, NY: Oxford University Press.

Goulah, Jason. 2010. "Daisaku Ikeda's Environmental Ethics of Humanitarian Competition: A Review of His United Nations Peace and Education Proposals," in *Peace Studies Journal,* Vol. 3, No. 1, April 2010.

Gould, Jeremy (editor) 2005. *The New Conditionality: The Politics of Poverty Reduction Strategies.* London: Zed Books.

Goulet, Denis. 2006. *Development Ethics at Work: Explorations—(1960–2002).* London and New York, NY: Routledge.

Gowan, Peter. 1999. *The Global Gamble: Washington's Faustian Bid for World Dominance.* London: Verso.

Gowan, Peter. 2004. "US Hegemony Today," in *Pox Americana: Exposing the American Empire*, edited by John Bellamy Foster and Robert W. McChesney. New York, NY: Monthly Review Press.

Groden, Robert J. and Livingstone, Harrison Edward. 1989. *High Treason: The Assassination of John F. Kennedy—What Really Happened*. New York, NY: Conservatory Press.

Guha, Ramachandra. 2000. *Environmentalism: A Global History*. New York, NY: Longman.

Gutierrez, Gustavo. 1973. *A Theology of Liberation: History, Politics, and Salvation*, translated and edited by Caridad Inda and John Eagleson. New York, NY: Orbis Books.

H

Haas, Michael. 1989. *The Asian Way to Peace: A Story of Regional Cooperation*. New York, NY: Praeger.

Haas, Michael. 2009. *George W. Bush, War Criminal?: The Bush Administration's Liability for 269 War Crimes*. Westport, CT: Praeger.

Habermas, Jurgen. [1980] 2007. "Modernity: An Unfinished Project," in *Contemporary Sociological Theory—Second Edition*, edited by Craig Calhoun et al. London: Blackwell, 2007.

Habermas, Jurgen 1984. *The Theory of Communicative Action, Volume (I): Reason and the Rationalization of Society*. Boston, MA: Beacon Press.

Hall, Martin and Jackson, Patrick Thaddeus. 2007. "Introduction: Civilizations and International Relations Theory," in *Civilizational Identity: The Production and Reproduction of 'Civilizations' in International Relations*, edited by Martin Hall and Patrick Thaddeus Jackson. New York, NY: Palgrave.

Halliday, Denis. 2006. "The UN and Its Conduct During the Invasion and Occupation of Iraq," in *Empire's Law: The American Imperial Project and the "War to Remake the World"*, edited by Amy Bartholomew. London: Pluto Press.

Halperin, Morton H. 2010. "A New Nuclear Posture," in *Arms Control Today*, Vol. 40, No. 4, May 2010. Washington, DC: Arms Control Association.

Hamel-Green, Michael. 1998. "The UN Role in Facilitating Nuclear-Free and Weapons of Mass Destruction-Free Zones," in *Between Sovereignty and Global Governance: The United Nations, the State and Civil Society*, edited by Albert J. Paolini, Anthony P. Jarvis, and Christian Reus-Smit. New York, NY: St. Martin's Press.

Hanley, Charles J. 2009. "Gorbachev: US Military Power Blocks 'No Nukes,'" *Antiwar Newswire*, AP-News, April 16, 2009. Available at: http://wire.antiwar.com/2009/04/16/gorbachev-us-military-power-blocks-no-nukes/.

Hasegawa, Tsuyoshi. 2005. *Racing the Enemy: Stalin, Truman, and the Surrender of Japan*. Cambridge, MA: Harvard University Press.

Haslam, Jonathan. 2002. *No Virtue Like Necessity: Realist Thought in International Relations since Machiavelli*. New Haven, CT: Yale University Press.

Haugen, Gary and Boutros, Victor. 2010. "And Justice for All: Enforcing Human Rights for the World's Poor," in *Foreign Affairs*, Vol. 89, No. 3, May/June 2010. New York, NY: Council on Foreign Relations.

Held, David. 1989. *Political Theory and the Modern State: Essays on State, Power, and Democracy*. Stanford, CA: Stanford University Press.

Held, David. 1995. *Democracy and the Global Order: From Modern State to Cosmopolitan Governance*. Stanford, CA: Stanford University Press.

Held, David. 2003. "From Executive to Cosmopolitan Multilateralism," in *Taming Globalization: Frontiers of Governance*, edited by David Held and Mathias Koenig-Archibugi. Cambridge, UK: Polity.

Held, David. 2004. *Global Covenant: The Social Democratic Alternative to the Washington Consensus*. Cambridge, UK: Polity.

Held, David and McGrew, Anthony. 1998. "The End of the Old Order?—Globalization and the Prospects for World Order," in *The Eighty Years' Crisis: International Relations, 1919–1999*, edited by Tim Dunne, Michael Cox and Ken Booth. Cambridge, UK: Cambridge University Press.

Held, David and McGrew, Anthony. 2007. *Globalization/Anti-Globalization: Beyond the Great Divide—Second Edition*. Cambridge, UK: Polity.

Held, David and McGrew, Anthony, et al. 1999. *Global Transformations: Politics, Economics and Culture*. Stanford, CA: Stanford University Press.

Hepburn, James. 2002. *Farewell America: The Plot to Kill JFK*. New York, NY: Penmarin Books.

Herman, Edward S. 2007. "Western Elite's War Against the Third World: An Urgent Global Problem is Containment of the United States and its Principal Client State in the Middle East," *Z-Magazine*, September 2007, pp. 41–44.

Herman, Edward S. and Peterson, David. 2010. *The Politics of Genocide*. New York, NY: Monthly Review Press.

Hixson, Walter L. 2008. *The Myth of American Diplomacy: National Identity and U.S. Foreign Policy*. New Haven, CT: Yale University Press.

Hobsbawm, Eric J. 1987. *The Age of Empire (1875–1914)*. New York, NY: Pantheon Books.

Hong, Cai Peng. 2005. "Non-Traditional Security and China-ASEAN Relations: Cooperation, Commitments and Challenges," in *China and Southeast Asia: Global Changes and Regional Challenges*, edited by Ho Khai Leong and Samuel C.Y. Ku. Singapore: Institute of Southeast Asian Studies and the Center for Southeast Asian Studies.

Hudson, Michael. 2005. *Global Fracture: The New International Economic Order—New Edition*. London: Pluto Press.

Huntington, Samuel P. 1996. *The Clash of Civilizations and the Remaking of World Order*. New York, NY: Simon & Schuster.

Hurrell, Andrew. 2007. *On Global Order: Power, Values, and the Constitution of International Society*. New York, NY: Oxford University Press.

Hymans, Jacques E.C. 2006. *The Psychology of Nuclear Proliferation: Identity, Emotions, and Foreign Policy*. New York, NY: Cambridge University Press.

I

Ignatieff, Michael. 2005. "Introduction: American Exceptionalism and Human Rights," in *American Exceptionalism and Human Rights*, edited by Michael Ignatieff. Princeton, NJ: Princeton University Press.
Ikeda, Daisaku. 1984-PP. *"A World without War"* (1984 peace proposal). Tokyo: Soka Gakkai.
Ikeda, Daisaku. 1989-PP. *"Towards a New Globalism"* (1989 peace proposal). Tokyo: Soka Gakkai.
Ikeda, Daisaku. 1991. *Dawn of the Century of Humanity.* Tokyo: Soka Gakkai.
Ikeda, Daisaku. 1992-PP. *"A Renaissance of Hope and Harmony"* (1992 peace proposal). Tokyo: Soka Gakkai.
Ikeda, Daisaku. 1995-PP. *"Creating a Century Without War Through Human Solidarity"* (1995 peace proposal). Tokyo: Soka Gakkai.
Ikeda, Daisaku. 1999-PP. *"Toward a Culture of Peace: A Cosmic View"* (1999 peace proposal). Tokyo: Soka Gakkai.
Ikeda, Daisaku. 2001a. *For the Sake of Peace: Seven Paths to Global Harmony—A Buddhist Perspective.* Santa Monica, CA: Middleway Press.
Ikeda, Daisaku. 2001b. Speech delivered at Teachers College, Columbia University, on June 13, 1996: "Education for Global Citizenship," in *Soka Education: a Buddhist Vision for Teachers, Students and Parents.* Santa Monica, CA: Middleway Press.
Ikeda, Daisaku. 2001c. "The Evil over which we Must Triumph," in *From the Ashes: A Spiritual Response to the Attack on America.* Emmaus, PA: Rodale Press.
Ikeda, Daisaku. 2001–7. *The New Human Revolution*, Vol. 7. Santa Monica, CA: World Tribune Press.
Ikeda, Daisaku. 2004a. *The Human Revolution.* Santa Monica, CA: World Tribune Press.
Ikeda, Daisaku. 2004b. *Fighting for Peace: Poems by Daisaku Ikeda.* Tokyo: Soka Gakkai.
Ikeda, Daisaku. 2005-PP. *"Toward a New Era of Dialogue: Humanism Explored"* (2005 peace proposal). Tokyo: Soka Gakkai.
Ikeda, Daisaku. [2007] 2008. "Moving Beyond the Use of Military Force," editorial in *The Japan Times*, January 11, 2007. In *Embracing the Future.* Tokyo: The Japan Times.
Ikeda, Daisaku. 2007-PP. *"Restoring the Human Connection: The First Step to Global Peace"* (2007 peace proposal). Tokyo: Soka Gakkai.
Ikeda, Daisaku. 2008-PP. *"Humanizing Religion, Creating Peace"* (2008 peace proposal). Tokyo: Soka Gakkai.
Ikeda, Daisaku. 2009a. *Building Global Solidarity Toward Nuclear Abolition.* Retrieved on 12 September 2009 from http://www.daisakuikeda.org/sub/resources/works/props/disarm_proposal.html.
Ikeda, Daisaku. 2009b. "A Life Dedicated to Dialogue," in *Monthly SGI Newsletter*, No. 314, August/September 2009. Tokyo: Soka Gakkai.

Ikeda, Daisaku. 2009-PP. *"Toward Humanitarian Competition: A New Current in History"* (2009 peace proposal). Tokyo: Soka Gakkai.

Ikeda, Daisaku. 2010-PP. *"Toward a New Era of Value Creation"* (2010 peace proposal). Tokyo: Soka Gakkai.

Ikeda, Daisaku, and Lokesh Chandra. 2009. *Buddhism: a Way of Values.* New Delhi: Eternal Ganges Press.

Ikeda, Daisaku and de Athayde, Austregesilo. 2009. *Human Rights in the Twenty-First Century: A Dialogue—Austregesilo de Athayde and Daisaku Ikeda.* London: I.B. Tauris.

Ikeda, Daisaku and Diez-Hochleitner, Ricardo. 2008. *A Dialogue Between East and West: Looking to a Human Revolution.* London and New York, NY: I.B. Tauris.

Ikeda, Daisaku and Johan Galtung. 1995. *Choose Peace.* London: Pluto Press.

Ikeda, Daisaku, and Hazel Henderson. 2004. *Planetary Citizenship: Your Values, Beliefs and Actions Can Shape a Sustainable World.* Santa Monica, CA: Middleway Press.

Ikeda, Daisaku and Huyghe, Rene. 2007. *Dawn after Dark: A Dialogue, Echoes and Reflections—The Selected Works of Daisaku Ikeda.* London: I.B. Tauris.

Ikeda, Daisaku and Krieger, David. 2002. *Choose Hope: Your Role in Waging Peace in the Nuclear Age.* Santa Monica, CA: Middleway Press.

Ikeda, Daisaku and Pauling, Linus. 2009. *A Lifelong Quest for Peace,* edited and translated by Richard L. Gage. London and New York, NY: I.B. Tauris.

Ikeda, Daisaku and Rotblat, Joseph. 2007. *A Quest for Global Peace: Rotblat and Ikeda on War, Ethics and the Nuclear Threat.* London: I.B. Tauris.

Ikeda, Daisaku and Tehranian, Majid. 2003. *Global Civilization: A Buddhist–Islamic Dialogue.* New York, NY: British Academic Press.

Ikeda, Daisaku and Toynbee, Arnold. [1976] 2007. *Choose Life: A Dialogue—Arnold Toynbee and Daisaku Ikeda,* edited by Richard L. Gage. London: I.B. Tauris.

Ikeda, Daisaku. and Nur Yalman. 2009. *A Passage to Peace: Global Solutions from East and West.* London: I.B.Tauris.

Irons, Peter. 2005. *War Powers: How the Imperial Presidency Hijacked the Constitution.* New York, NY: Metropolitan Books.

Isikoff, Michael and Corn, David. 2006. *Hubris: The Inside Story of Spin, Scandal, and the Selling of the Iraq War.* New York, NY: Crown Publishers.

J

Jackson, John. 2006. *Sovereignty, the WTO and Changing Fundamentals of International Law.* New York, NY: Cambridge University Press.

Jackson, Richard L. 1983. *The Non-Aligned, the UN, and the Superpowers.* New York, NY: Praeger.

Jackson, Robert and Sorensen, Georg. 1999. *Introduction to International Relations.* New York, NY: Oxford University Press.

Jackson, Thomas F. 2007. *From Civil Rights to Human Rights: Martin Luther King Jr., and the Struggle for Economic Justice.* Philadelphia, PA: University of Pennsylvania Press.

Jackson, Vicki C. 2010. *Constitutional Engagement in a Transnational Era.* New York, NY: Oxford University Press.

Janis, Irving L. 1983. *Groupthink: Psychological Studies of Policy Decisions and Fiascoes—Second Edition, Revised.* Boston, MA: Houghton Mifflin Company.

Jha, Prem Shankar. 2006. *The Twilight of the Nation State: Globalization, Chaos and War.* London: Pluto Press.

Johansen, Robert C. 1980. *The National Interest and the Human Interest: An Analysis of US Foreign Policy,* Princeton, NJ: Princeton University Press.

Johansen, Robert. 1982. "The Elusiveness of a Humane World Community," in *Studies on a Just World Order—Vol. 1—Toward a Just World Order,* edited by Richard Falk, Samuel S. Kim, and Saul Mendlovitz. Boulder, CO: Westview Press.

Johansen, Robert. 1991. "Toward an Alternative Security System," in *The United Nations and a Just World Order,* edited by Richard Falk, Samuel Kim, and Saul Mendlovitz. Boulder, CO: Westview Press.

Johansen, Robert C. 1993. "Toward a New Code of International Conduct: War, Peacekeeping, and Global Constitutionalism," in *The Constitutional Foundations of World Peace,* edited by Richard Falk, Robert C. Johansen, and Samuel S. Kim. Albany, NY: State University of New York Press.

Johnson, Chalmers. 2004. *The Sorrows of Empire: Militarism, Secrecy, and the End of the Republic.* New York, NY: Metropolitan Books.

Johnson, Chalmers. 2006. *Nemesis: The Last Days of the American Republic.* New York, NY: Metropolitan Books.

Johnson, Chalmers. 2010. *Dismantling the Empire: America's Last Best Hope.* New York, NY: Metropolitan Books.

Johnson, Simon and Kwak, James. 2010. *13 Bankers: The Wall Street Takeover and the Next Financial Meltdown.* New York, NY: Pantheon Books.

Johnston, Andrew M. 2005. *Hegemony and Culture in the Origins of NATO Nuclear First-Use, 1945–1955.* New York, NY: Palgrave Macmillan.

Jones, Adam (editor). 2004. *Genocide, War Crimes and the West: History and Complicity.* New York, NY: Zed Books.

Jones, Ken. 2003. *The New Social Face of Buddhism: A Call to Action.* Boston, MA: Wisdom Publications.

Jones, Matthew. 2010. *After Hiroshima: The United States, Race and Nuclear Weapons in Asia, 1945–1965.* New York, NY: Cambridge University Press.

Joseph, Paul. 1981. *Cracks in the Empire: State Politics in the Vietnam War.* Boston, MA: South End Press.

Joyner, Daniel H. 2009. *International Law and the Proliferation of Weapons of Mass Destruction.* New York, NY: Oxford University Press.

Juhasz, Antonia. 2006. *The Bush Agenda: Invading the World One Economy at a Time.* New York, NY: Regan Books.

K

Kaiser, David. 2000. *American Tragedy: Kennedy, Johnson, and the Origins of the Vietnam War.* Cambridge, MA and London, England: Belknap Press of Harvard University Press.

Kang, Susan L. 2009. "The Unsettled Relationship of Economic and Social Rights and the West: A Response to Whelan and Donnelly," in *Human Rights Quarterly,* Vol. 31, No. 4, November 2009. Cincinnati, OH: John Hopkins University Press.

Kaplan, Fred. 1983. *The Wizards of Armageddon.* New York, NY: Simon & Schuster.

Katzenstein, Peter J. 2010. "A World of Plural and Pluralist Civilizations: Multiple Actors, Traditions, and Practices," in *Civilizations in World Politics: Plural and Pluralist Perspectives,* edited by Peter J. Katzenstein. London and New York, NY: Routledge.

Kaufmann, Stuart, J., Little, Richard, and Wohlforth, William C. (editors) 2007. *The Balance of Power in World History.* New York, NY: Palgrave Macmillan.

Kauzlarich, David and Kramer, Ronald C. 1998. *Crimes of the American Nuclear State: At Home and Abroad.* Boston, MA: Northeastern University Press.

Keal, Paul. 2003. *European Conquest and the Rights of Indigenous Peoples: The Moral Backwardness of International Society.* New York, NY: Cambridge University Press.

Keller, William W. and Mitchell, Gordon R. (editors). 2006. *Hitting First: Preventive Force in US Security Strategy.* Pittsburgh, PA: University of Pittsburgh Press.

Kellner, Douglas. 1991. *Introduction to the Second Edition of One-Dimensional Man.* Boston, MA: Beacon Press.

Kemp, Geoffrey. 2010. *The East Moves West: India, China, and Asia's Growing Presence in the Middle East.* Washington, DC: Brookings Institution Press.

Kennedy, John F. 1961. *The Strategy of Peace,* edited by Allan Nevins. New York, NY: Popular Library.

Kennedy, John F. 1964. *Public Papers of the Presidents of the United States— John F. Kennedy: Containing the Public Messages, Speeches, and Statements of the President (January 1 to November 22, 1963).* Washington, DC: United States Government Printing Office.

Kennedy, Robert F. 1968a. *Robert F. Kennedy: Apostle of Change—A Review of His Public Record with Analysis by Douglas Ross.* New York, NY: Pocket Books.

Kennedy, Robert F. 1968b. "Speech on the Occasion of Martin Luther King's Assassination [as quoted in: Jack Newfield," *Robert Kennedy: A Memoir.* New York, NY: Bantam Books].

Kennedy, Robert F. 1993. *RFK: Collected Speeches,* edited and introduced by Edwin O. Guthman and C. Richard Allen. New York, NY: Viking.

Khalidi, Rashid. 2004. *Resurrecting Empire: Western Footprints and America's Perilous Path in the Middle East.* Boston, MA: Beacon Press.

Khalidi, Rashid. 2009. *Sowing Crisis: The Cold War and American Dominance in the Middle East.* Boston, MA: Beacon Press.

Khrushchev, Nikita. 2007. *Memoirs of Nikita Khrushchev—Volume 3—Statesman [1953–1964],* edited by Sergei Khrushchev, Memoirs translated by George Shriver, University Park, PA: Pennsylvania State University Press.

Kim, Samuel S. 1984. *The Quest for a Just World Order.* Boulder, CO: Westview Press.

Kim, Samuel S. 1991. "Global Human Rights and World Order," in *The United Nations and a Just World Order,* edited by Richard A. Falk, Samuel S. Kim, and Saul H. Mendlovitz. Boulder, CO: Westview Press.

King, Martin Luther. 1968. *Where Do We Go From Here: Chaos or Community?* New York, NY: Bantam Books.

Kirkup, Alex and Evans, Tony. 2009. "The Myth of Western Opposition to Economic, Social, and Cultural Rights?—A Reply to Whelan and Donnelly," in *Human Rights Quarterly,* Vol. 31, No. 1, February 2009. Cincinnati, OH: John Hopkins University Press.

Klare, Michael. 1995. *Rogue States and Nuclear Outlaws: America's Search for a New Foreign Policy.* New York, NY: Hill and Wang.

Klare, Michael. 2001. *Resource Wars: The New Landscape of Global Conflict.* New York, NY: Metropolitan Books.

Klare, Michael. 2004. *Blood and Oil: The Dangers and Consequences of America's Growing Dependency on Imported Petroleum.* New York, NY: Metropolitan Books.

Klare. Michael T. 2008. *Rising Powers, Shrinking Planet: The New Geopolitics of Energy.* New York, NY: Metropolitan Books.

Knoll, Erin and McFadden, Judith N. (editors). 1970. *War Crimes and the American Conscience.* New York, NY: Holt, Rinehart and Winston.

Knutsen, Torbjorn, L. 1997. *A History of International Relations Theory—Second Edition.* New York, NY: Manchester University Press.

Knutsen, Torbjorn L. 1999. *The Rise and Fall of World Orders.* New York, NY: Manchester University Press.

Koh, Harold Hongju. 2005. "America's Jekyll-and-Hyde Exceptionalism," in *American Exceptionalism and Human Rights,* edited by Michael Ignatieff. Princeton, NJ: Princeton University Press.

Kolko, Gabriel. 1990. *The Politics of War: The World and United States Foreign Policy, 1943–1945,* New York, NY: Pantheon Books, [1968].

Kolko, Gabriel. 1994. *Century of War: Politics, Conflict, and Society Since 1914.* New York, NY: New Press.

Kolko, Gabriel. 2006. *The Age of War: The United States Confronts the World.* Boulder, CO: Lynne Reinner Publishers.

Kolko, Gabriel. 2009. *World in Crisis: The End of the American Century.* London: Pluto Press.

Kolko, Joyce. 1988. *Restructuring the World Economy.* New York, NY: Pantheon Books.

Kothari, Rajni. 2000. "Social Justice: Growing Consciousness, Receding Prospects," in *Principled World Politics: The Challenge of Normative International Relations,* edited by Paul Wapner and Lester Edwin J. Ruiz. New York, NY: Rowman & Littlefield Publishers.

Kovel, Joel. 2007. *The Enemy of Nature: The End of Capitalism or the End of the World—Second Edition.* London: Zed Books.

Kozul-Wright, Richard and Paul Rayment. 2007. *The Resistible Rise of Market Fundamentalism: Rethinking Development Policy in an Unbalanced World.* New York, NY: Zed Books.

Krepon, Michael. 1999. "Conflict Avoidance, Confidence Building, and Peacemaking," in *Global Confidence Building: New Tools for Troubled Regions,* edited by Michael Krepon, et al. New York, NY: St. Martin's Press.

Krieger, David. 2006. "The War in Iraq as Illegal and Illegitimate," in *The Iraq Crisis and World Order: Structural, Institutional and Normative Challenges,* edited by Ramesh Thakur and Waheguru Pal Singh Sidhu. Tokyo: United Nations University Press.

Krieger, David (editor) 2009. *The Challenge of Abolishing Nuclear Weapons.* New Brunswick, NJ and London: Transaction Publishers.

Krisch, Nico. 2003. "More Equal than the Rest?—Hierarchy, Equality, and US Predominance in International Law," in *United States Hegemony and the Foundations of International Law,* edited by Michael Byers and Georg Nolte. Cambridge, UK: Cambridge University Press.

Kung, Hans. 2003. "An Ethical Framework for the Global Market Economy," in *Making Globalization Good: The Moral Challenges of Global Capitalism,* edited by John H. Dunning. New York, NY: Oxford University Press.

Kupchan, Charles A. 2010. *How Enemies Become Friends: The Sources of Stable Peace.* Princeton, NJ: Princeton University Press.

L

Lagos, Gustavo. 1975. "The Revolution of Being," in *On the Creation of a Just World Order: Preferred Worlds for the 1990s,* edited by Saul H. Mendlovitz. New York, NY: Free Press.

Lagos, Gustavo and Horacio H. Godoy. 1977. *Revolution of Being: A Latin American View of the Future.* New York, NY: Free Press.

Lake, David A. 2009. *Hierarchy in International Relations.* Ithaca, NY and London: Cornell University Press.

Lake, Marilyn and Reynolds, Henry. 2008. *Drawing the Global Color Line: White Men's Countries and the International Challenge of Racial Equality.* New York, NY: Cambridge University Press.

Lawrence, Mark Atwood. 2005. *Assuming the Burden: Europe and the American Commitment to War in Vietnam.* Berkeley, CA: University of California Press.

Layne, Christopher. 2006. *The Peace of Illusions: American Grand Strategy from 1940 to the Present.* Ithaca, NY: Cornell University Press.

Leaming, Barbara. 2006. *Jack Kennedy: The Education of a Statesman*. New York, NY: W.W. Norton & Company.

Lebow, Richard Ned and Stein, Janice Gross. 1994. *We All Lost the Cold War*. Princeton, NJ: Princeton University Press.

Lepard, Brian D. 2010. *Customary International Law: A New Theory with Practical Applications*. New York, NY: Cambridge University Press.

Lian, Koh Kheng and Robinson, Nicholas A. 2002. "Regional Environmental Governance: Examining the Association of Southeast Asian Nations (ASEAN) Model," in *Global Environmental Governance: Options and Opportunities*, edited by Daniel C. Esty and Maria H. Ivanova. New Haven, CT: Yale School of Forestry and Environmental Studies.

Lichterman, Andrew and Cabasso, Jacqueline. 2002. "The End of Disarmament and the Arms Races to Come," in *Social Justice: A Journal of Crime, Conflict & World Order*, Vol. 29, No. 3, 2002.

Lifton, Robert Jay. 2003. *Superpower Syndrome: America's Apocalyptic Confrontation with the World*. New York, NY: Thunder's Mouth Press/ Nation Books.

Lippman, Matthew. 2008. "Nuremberg: Forty Five Years Later," in *Perspectives on the Nuremberg Trial*, edited by Guenael Mettraux. New York, NY: Oxford University Press.

Little, Richard. 2007. *The Balance of Power in International Relations: Metaphors, Myths and Models*. New York, NY: Cambridge University Press.

Lobel, Jules and Ratner, Michael. 2000. "Humanitarian Intervention: A Dangerous Doctrine," in *Global Focus: US Foreign Policy at the Turn of the Millennium*, edited by Martha Honey and Tom Barry. New York, NY: St. Martin's Press.

Loveman, Brian. 2010. *No Higher Law: American Foreign Policy and the Western Hemisphere Since 1776*. Chapel Hill, NC: University of North Carolina Press.

Lowe, Vaughan, et al. 2008a. *The United Nations Security Council and War: The Evolution of Thought and Practice Since 1945*. New York, NY: Oxford University Press.

Lowe, Vaughan, et al. 2008b. "Introduction," in *The United Nations Security Council and War: The Evolution of Thought and Practice Since 1945*, edited by Vaughan Lowe, Adam Roberts, Jennifer Welsh, and Dominik Zaum. New York, NY: Oxford University Press.

Lowenthal, Abraham F., Piccone, Theodore J., and Whitehead, Laurence (editors). 2009. *The Obama Administration and the Americas: Agenda for Change*. Washington, DC: Brookings Institution.

Luckham, Robin. 1984. "Armament Culture," *Alternatives: A Journal of World Policy*. New York, NY: World Policy Institute—Center for the Study of Developing Societies. Vol. X, No. 1.

M

MacFarlane, S. Neil and Khong, Yuen Foong. 2006. *Human Security and the UN: A Critical History*. Bloomington, IN: Indiana University Press.

Maddock, Shane J. 2010. *Nuclear Apartheid: The Quest for American Atomic Supremacy from World War II to the Present*. Chapel Hill, NC: University of North Carolina Press.

Maier, Charles S. 2006. *Among Empires: American Ascendancy and Its Predecessors*. Cambridge, MA: Harvard University Press.

Makiguchi, Tsunesaburo. 1971–80. *Jinsei Chirigaku (The Geography of Human Life)*, 5 Vols. Tokyo: Seikyo Press.

Makiguchi, Tsunesaburo. [1903] 1983. "*Jinsei Chirigaku* (The Geography of Human Life)," in *Makiguchi Tsunesaburo Zenshu (The Complete Works of Tsunesaburo Makiguchi)*, Vols. 1–2 (in Japanese). Tokyo: Daisan Bunmeisha.

Makiguchi, Tsunesaburo. 1981–88. *Makiguchi Tsunesaburo Zenshu (The Complete Works of Tsunesaburo Makiguchi)* (in Japanese). Tokyo: Daisan Bunmeisha.

Malksoo, Lauri. 2010. "Great Powers Then and Now: Security Council Reform and Responses to Threats to Peace and Security," in *United Nations Reform and the New Collective Security*, edited by Peter G. Danchin and Horst Fischer. Cambridge, UK: Cambridge University Press.

Malone, David (editor). 2004. *The UN Security Council: From the Cold War to the 21st Century*. Boulder, CO: Lynne Rienner Publishers.

Malone, David M. 2006. *The International Struggle Over Iraq: Politics at the UN Security Council, 1980–2005*. New York, NY: Oxford University Press.

Manby, Bronwen. 2004. "The African Union, NEPAD, and Human Rights: The Missing Agenda," *Human Rights Quarterly*, Vol. 26, No. 4.

Mandel, Michael. 2004. *How America Gets Away with Murder: Illegal Wars, Collateral Damage and Crimes Against Humanity*. London: Pluto Press.

Manela, Erez. 2007. *The Wilsonian Moment: Self-Determination and the International Origins of Anti-Colonial Nationalism*. New York, NY: Oxford University Press.

Mannheim, Karl. 1936. *Ideology and Utopia: An Introduction to the Sociology of Knowledge*, translated from the German by Louis Wirth and Edward Shils. New York, NY: Harvest Book-Harcourt, Brace & World.

Marcuse, Herbert. 1964 [1991]. *One-Dimensional Man: Studies in the Ideology of Advanced Industrial Society*, with a new Introduction by Douglas Kellner. Boston, MA: Beacon Press.

Marcuse, Herbert. 1972. *Counter-Revolution and Revolt*. Boston, MA: Beacon Press.

Marichal, Carlos. 2008. "The Finances of Hegemony in Latin America: Debt Negotiations and the Role of the US Government, 1945–2005," in *Empire and Dissent: The United States and Latin America*, edited by Fred Rosen. Durham, NC; and London: Duke University Press.

Markusen, Ann and Hall, Peter, et al. 1991. *The Rise of the Gun-Belt: The Military Remapping of Industrial America*. New York, NY: Oxford University Press.

Markusen, Ann and Yudken, Joel. 1992. *Dismantling the Cold War Economy*. New York, NY: Basic Books—A Division of HarperCollins Publishers.

Marshall, Jonathan. 1995. *To Have and Have Not: Southeast Asian Raw Materials and the Origins of the Pacific War*. Berkeley, CA: University of California Press.

Martin, Francisco F., et al. 2006. *International Human Rights and Humanitarian Law: Treaties, Cases and Analysis*. New York, NY: Cambridge University Press.

Massie, Robert K. 1997. *Loosing the Bonds: The United States and South Africa in the Apartheid Era*. New York, NY: Doubleday.

Mazrui, Ali A. 1976. *A World Federation of Cultures: An African Perspective (World Order Models Project)*. New York, NY: Free Press.

McCarthy, Thomas. 2009. *Race, Empire, and Idea of Human Development*. New York, NY: Cambridge University Press.

McCoy, Ronald. 2009. "The Case for a Nuclear Weapons Convention," in *The Challenge of Abolishing Nuclear Weapons*, edited by David Krieger. New Brunswick, NJ: Transaction Publishers.

McMahan, Jeff. 1985. *Reagan and the World: Imperial Policy in the New Cold War*. New York, NY: Monthly Review Press.

Meadows, Donella and Randers, Jorgen, and Meadows, Dennis. 2004. *Limits to Growth: The 30-Year Update*. Vermont: Chelsea Green Publishing Company.

Melman, Seymour. 1970. *Pentagon Capitalism: The Political Economy of War*. New York, NY: McGraw-Hill Book Company.

Melman, Seymour. 1974. *The Permanent War Economy: American Capitalism in Decline*. New York, NY: Simon and Schuster.

Merton, Thomas. 1966. *Raids on the Unspeakable*. New York, NY: New Directions.

Mertus, Julie A. and Helsing, Jeffrey W. 2006. "Toward a More Integrated Approach," in *Human Rights and Conflict: Exploring the Links between Rights, Law, and Peacebuilding*, edited by Julie A. Mertus and Jeffrey W. Helsing. Washington, DC: United States Institute of Peace Press.

Metraux, Daniel. 2000. "The Expansion of the Soka Gakkai into Southeast Asia," in *Global Citizens: The Soka Gakkai Buddhist Movement in the World*, edited by David Machacek and Bryan Wilson. Oxford: Oxford University Press.

Mettraux, Guenael. 2008. "Foreword," in *Perspectives on the Nuremberg Trial*, edited by Guenael Mattraux. New York, NY: Oxford University Press.

Mills, C. Wright. 1956. *The Power Elite*. New York, NY: Oxford University Press.

Mills, C. Wright. 1960. *The Causes of World War Three*. New York, NY: Ballantine Books.

Mittelman, James H. 2000. *The Globalization Syndrome: Transformation and Resistance*. Princeton, NJ: Princeton University Press.

Mittelman, James H. 2010. *Hyperconflict: Globalization and Insecurity*. Stanford, CA: Stanford University Press.

Mittelman, James H. and Tambe, Ashwini. 2000. "Reconceptualizing Global Poverty: Globalization, Marginalization, and Gender," in *Principled World Politics: The Challenge of Normative International Relations*, edited by

Paul Wapner and Lester E. Ruiz. Lanham, MD: Rowman & Littlefield Publishers.

Moellendorf, Darrel. 2005. "The World Trade Organization and Egalitarian Justice," in *Global Institutions and Responsibilities: Achieving Global Justice*, edited by Christian Barry and Thomas W. Pogge. MA: Blackwell Publishing.

Moore, John Norton and Morrison, Alex (editors). 2000. *Strengthening the United Nations and Enhancing War Prevention*. Durham, NC: Carolina Academic Press.

Morgan, Patrick M. 2008. "American Military Power and Challenges to International Security," in *From Superpower to Besieged Global Power: Restoring World Order after the Failure of the Bush Doctrine*, edited by Edward Kolodziej and Roger Kanet. Athens, GA: University of Georgia Press.

Morgan, Ted. 2010. *Valley of Death: The Tragedy at Dien Bien Phu that Led America into the Vietnam War*. New York, NY: Random House.

Moss, Kenneth B. 2008. *Undeclared War and the Future of US Foreign Policy*. Baltimore, MD: Johns Hopkins University Press.

Moyn, Samuel. 2008. "Spectacular Wrongs," *The Nation*, October 13, 2008.

Mukherji, Rahul. 2008. "Appraising the Legacy of Bandung: A View from India," in *Bandung Revisited: The Legacy of the 1955 Asian-African Conference for International Order*, edited by See Seng Tan and Amitav Acharya. Singapore: National University Press of Singapore.

Munck, Ronaldo. 2005. *Globalization and Social Exclusion: A Transformationalist Perspective*. West Hartford, CT: Kumarian Press.

Muthu, Sankar. 2003. *Enlightenment Against Empire*. Princeton, NJ: Princeton University Press.

N

Nandy, Ashis. 1984. "Oppression and Human Liberation: Toward a Third World Utopia," in *Culture, Ideology, and World Order*, edited by R.B.J. Walker. Boulder, CO: Westview Press.

Nardin, Terry. 1983. *Law, Morality, and the Relations of States*. Princeton, NJ: Princeton University Press.

Nash, Philip. 1999. "Bear Any Burden? John F. Kennedy and Nuclear Weapons," in *Cold War Statesmen Confront the Bomb: Nuclear Diplomacy Since 1945*, edited by John Lewis Gaddis, Philip H. Gordon, Ernest R. May, and Jonathan Rosenberg. New York, NY: Oxford University Press.

Nesadurai, Helen E.S. 2008. "Bandung and the Political Economy of North–South Relations: Sowing the Seeds for Re-Visioning International Society," *Bandung Revisited: The Legacy of the 1955 Asian-African Conference for International Order*, edited by See Seng Tan and Amitav Acharya. Singapore: NUS Press.

Nichols, Thomas M. 2008. *Eve of Destruction: The Coming Age of Preventive War*. Philadelphia, PA: University of Pennsylvania Press.

Nolan, Janne E. 1989. *Guardians of the Arsenal: The Politics of Nuclear Strategy*. New York, NY: Basic Books.

O

O'Connell, Mary Ellen. 2008. *The Power and Purpose of International Law: Insights from the Theory and Practice of Enforcement.* New York, NY: Oxford University Press.

Odom, William E. 1998. *The Collapse of the Soviet Military.* New Haven, CT: Yale University Press.

Offner, Arnold A. 2002. *Another Such Victory: President Truman and the Cold War, 1945–1953.* Stanford, CA: Stanford University Press.

Oglesby, Carl. 1976. *The Yankee and Cowboy War: Conspiracies from Dallas TO Watergate.* Kansas City, MO: Sheed Andrews and McMeel.

Oliver, Kendrik. 1998. *Kennedy, Macmillan and the Nuclear Test Ban Debate, 1961–1963.* New York, NY: St. Martin's Press.

Osmani, Siddiq. 2006. "Globalization and the Human Rights Approach to Development," in *Development as a Human Right: Legal, Political, and Economic Dimensions,* edited by Louise Arbour. Cambridge, MA: Harvard University Press.

P

Panitch, Leo and Martijn Konings (editors) 2009. *American Empire and the Political Economy of Global Finance.* New York, NY: Palgrave Macmillan.

Panitch, Leo, et al. 2009. "The Political Economy of the Subprime Crisis," in *American Empire and the Political Economy of Global Finance,* edited by Leo Panitch and Martin Konings. New York, NY: Palgrave Macmillan.

Paupp, Terrence E. 1978. *The Revolutionary Core of Liberation Theology: The Union of Faith and Ideology in the Works of Hugo Assmann and Juan Luis Seguendo.* (An unpublished master's thesis for the degree of Master of Theological Studies, completed at the Lutheran School of Theology at Chicago.)

Paupp, Terrence E. 1987. "Between the Arrows and the Olive Branch: The Tortured Path of the War Powers Resolution in the Reagan Years (1981–1987)," *The Journal of Contemporary Legal Issues,* Vol. 1, No. 1.

Paupp, Terrence E. 1988. *As Legacy, As Vision: Charting the Implications of the Urban-Race-Poverty Nexus in the Thought of Robert F. Kennedy.* (An unpublished manuscript, completed for course work at the University of San Diego School of Law.)

Paupp, Terrence E. 2000. *Achieving Inclusionary Governance: Advancing Peace and Development in First and Third World Nations.* New York, NY: Transnational Publishers.

Paupp, Terrence E. 2005. "The Nuclear Crucible: The Moral and International Law Implications of Weapons of Mass Destruction," in *Democracy's Shadow: The Secret World of National Security,* edited by Marcus Raskin and A. Carl LeVan. New York, NY: Nation Books.

Paupp, Terrence E. 2007. *Exodus from Empire: The Fall of America's Empire and the Rise of the Global Community.* London: Pluto Press.

Paupp, Terrence E. 2009. *The Future of Global Relations: Crumbling Walls, Rising Regions.* New York, NY: Palgrave Macmillan.

Peet, Richard. 2003. *Unholy Trinity: The IMF, World Bank and WTO.* London: Zed Books.

Pepper, William F. 2003. *An Act of State: The Execution of Martin Luther King.* New York, NY: Verso.

Petras, James and Henry Veltmeyer. 2007. *Multinationals on Trial: Foreign Investment Matters.* London: Ashgate.

Pirages, Dennis Clark and DeGeest, Theresa Manley. 2004. *Ecological Security: An Evolutionary Perspective on Globalization.* Lanham, MD: Rowman & Littlefield Publishers.

Pogge, Thomas. 2002. *World Poverty and Human Rights: Cosmopolitan Responsibilities and Reforms.* Massachusetts: Polity.

Pogge, Thomas. 2007a. "Severe Poverty as a Human Rights Violation," in *Freedom from Poverty as a Human Right: Who Owes What to the Very Poor?,* edited by Thomas Pogge. New York, NY: Oxford University Press.

Pogge, Thomas (editor) 2007b. *Freedom from Poverty as a Human Right: Who Owes What to the Very Poor?* New York, NY: Oxford University Press.

Pogge, Thomas. 2010. *Politics as Usual: What Lies Behind the Pro-Poor Rhetoric.* Massachusetts: Polity.

Porter, Gareth, et al. 2000. *Global Environmental Politics—Third Edition.* Boulder, CO: Westview Press.

Porter, Gareth. 2005. *Perils of Dominance: Imbalance of Power and the Road to War in Vietnam.* Berkeley, CA: University of California Press.

Posner, Eric A. 2009. *The Perils of Global Legalism.* Chicago, IL; and London: University of Chicago Press.

Posner, Richard A. 2010. *The Crisis of Capitalist Democracy.* Cambridge, MA: Harvard University Press.

Prashad, Vijay. 2007a. *The Darker Nations: A People's History of the Third World.* New York, NY: New Press.

Prashad, Vijay. 2007b. "The Third World Idea," *The Nation,* June 4, 2007.

Prevost, Gary and Campos, Carlos (editors). 2007. *The Bush Doctrine and Latin America.* New York, NY: Palgrave Macmillan.

Prouty, L. Fletcher. 1992. *JFK: The CIA, Vietnam, and the Plot to Assassinate John F. Kennedy.* New York, NY: Birch Lane Press.

R

Rajagopal, Balakrishnan. 2000. "From Resistance to Renewal: The Third World, Social Movements, and the Expansion of International Institutions," *Harvard International Law Journal,* Vol. 41, No. 2.

Rajagopal, Balakrishnan. 2006. "Counter-Hegemonic International Law: Rethinking Human Rights and Development as a Third World Strategy," *Third World Quarterly,* Vol. 27, No. 5.

Rajagopal, Balakrishnan. 2008. "Counter-Hegemonic International Law: Rethinking Human Rights and Development as a Third World Strategy," in *International Law and the Third World: Reshaping Justice,* edited by,

Richard Falk, Balakrishnan Rajagopal and Jacqueline Stevens. New York, NY: Routledge-Cavendish.

Ramcharan, Bertrand G. 2008. *Preventive Diplomacy at the UN*. Bloomington, IN: Indiana University Press.

Reeves, Richard. 1993. *President Kennedy: Profile of Power*. New York, NY: Simon & Schuster.

Renshon, Stanley A. 2010. *National Security in the Obama Administration: Reassessing the Bush Doctrine*. New York, NY: Routledge.

Reus-Smit, Christian and Snidal, Duncan. 2008. "Between Utopia and Reality: The Practical Discourses of International Relations," in *The Oxford Handbook of International Relations*, edited by Christian Reus-Smit and Duncan Snidal. New York, NY: Oxford University Press.

Rice, Susan E. 2007. "Poverty Breeds Insecurity," in *Too Poor for Peace?— Global Poverty, Conflict, and Security in the 21st Century*, edited by Lael Brainard and Derek Chollet. Washington, DC: Brookings Institution Press.

Rice, Susan E. 2010. "Poverty and State Weakness," in *Confronting Poverty: Weak States and US National Security*, edited by Susan E. Rice, Corinne Graff, and Carlos Pascual. Washington, DC: Brookings Institution Press.

Rifkin, Jeremy. 2009. *The Empathetic Civilization: The Race to Global Consciousness in a World in Crisis*. New York, NY: Jeremy P. Tarcher/Penguin.

Ritter, Scott. 2010. *Dangerous Ground: America's Failed Arms Control Policy, from FDR to Obama*. New York, NY: Nation Books.

Roberts, A. and Guelff, R. 1982. *Documents on the Law of War*. Oxford: Clarendon Press.

Roberts, J. Timmons and Parks, Bradley C. 2007. *A Climate of Injustice: Global Inequality, North-South Politics, and Climate Policy*. Cambridge, MA: MIT Press.

Robeyns, Ingrid. 2005. "Assessing Global Poverty and Inequality: Income, Resources, and Capabilities," in *Global Institutions and Responsibilities: Achieving Global Justice*, edited by Christian Barry and Thomas W. Pogge. MA: Blackwell Publishing.

Robinson, William I. 1996. *Promoting Polyarchy: Globalization, US Intervention, and Hegemony*. New York, NY: Cambridge University Press.

Robinson, William I. 2008. *Latin America and Global Capitalism: A Critical Globalization Perspective*. Baltimore, MD: Johns Hopkins University Press.

Rosen, Fred (editor). 2008. *Empire and Dissent: The United States and Latin America*. Durham, NC: Duke University Press.

Rosenau, James N. 2005. "Global Governance as Disaggregated Complexity," in *Contending Perspectives on Global Governance: Coherence, Contestation and World Order*, edited by Alice D. Ba and Matthew J. Hoffmann. New York, NY: Routledge.

Roszak, Theodore. 1973. *Where the Wasteland Ends: Politics and Transcendence in Postindustrial Society*. New York, NY: Anchor Books/Doubleday.

Roszak, Theodore. 1978. *Person/Planet: The Creative Disintegration of Industrial Society.* New York, NY: Anchor Press/Doubleday.

S

Saad-Filho, Alfredo and Johnston, Deborah (editors). 2005. *Neo-liberalism: A Critical Reader.* London: Pluto Press.

Sachs, Jeffrey D. 2008. *Common Wealth: Economics for a Crowded Planet.* New York, NY: Penguin Press.

Said, Abdul Aziz and Lerche, Charles O. 2006. "Peace as a Human Right: Toward an Integrated Understanding," in *Human Rights and Conflict: Exploring the Links between Rights, Law, and Peacebuilding,* edited by Julie A. Mertus and Jeffrey W. Helsing. Washington, DC: United States Institute of Peace Press.

Sale, Kirkpatrick. 1976. *Power Shift: The Rise of the Southern Rim and Its Challenge to the Eastern Establishment.* New York, NY: Vintage Books.

Salomon, Margot E. 2006. "International Human Rights Obligations in Context: Structural Obstacles and the Demands of Global Justice," in *Development as a Human Right: Legal, Political, and Economic Obligations,* edited by Bard A. Andreassen and Stephen P. Marks. Cambridge, MA: Harvard University Press.

Salomon, Margot E. 2007. *Global Responsibility for Human Rights: World Poverty and the Development of International Law.* New York, NY: Oxford University Press.

Salt, Jeremy. 2008. *The Unmaking of the Middle East: A History of Western Disorder in Arab Lands.* Berkeley, CA: University of California Press.

Sauvant, Karl P. and Hasenpflug, Hajo (editors). 1977. *The New International Economic Order: Confrontation or Cooperation between North and South?* Boulder, CO: Westview Press.

Savage, Charlie. 2007. *Takeover: The Return of the Imperial Presidency and the Subversion of American Democracy.* New York and London: Little, Brown and Company.

Schabas, William A. 2010. *The International Criminal Court: A Commentary on the Rome Statute.* New York, NY: Oxford University Press.

Scheffran, Jurgen. 2008. "Strengthening International Security through International Law," in *At the Nuclear Precipice: Catastrophe or Transformation?,* in Richard Falk and David Krieger. New York, NY: Palgrave Macmillan.

Schiff, Benjamin. 2008. *Building the International Criminal Court.* New York, NY: Cambridge University Press.

Schmitt, Edward R. 2010. *President of the Other America: Robert Kennedy and the Politics of Poverty.* Amherst, MA: University of Massachusetts Press.

Schwarz, Frederick A.O. Jr., and Huq, Aziz Z. 2007. *Unchecked and Unbalanced: Presidential Power in a Time of Terror.* New York and London: New Press.

Scoblic, J. Peter. 2008. *U.S. vs. Them: How a Half Century of Conservatism Has Undermined America's Security.* New York, NY: Viking.

Scott, Peter Dale. 1993. *Deep Politics and the Death of JFK*. Berkeley, CA: University of California Press.

Scott, Peter Dale. 2007. *The Road to 9/11: Wealth, Empire, and the Future of America*. Berkeley, CA: University of California Press.

Seaborg, Glenn T. 1981. *Kennedy, Khrushchev and the Test Ban*. Berkeley, CA: University of California Press.

Sen, Amartya. 2009. *The Idea of Justice*. Cambridge, MA: Harvard University Press.

Seng, Tan See. 2008. "ASEAN: The Road Not Taken," in *The Long Shadow: Nuclear Weapons and Security in 21st Century Asia*, edited by Muthiah Alagappa. Stanford, CA: Stanford University Press.

Shelton, Dinah. 2008. *Regional Protection of Human Rights*. New York, NY: Oxford University Press.

Simpson, Christopher. 1988. *Blowback: America's Recruitment of Nazis and Its Effects on the Cold War*. New York, NY: Weidenfeld & Nicolson.

Singer, P.W. 2003. *Corporate Warriors: The Role of the Privatized Military Industry*. Ithaca, NY: Cornell University Press.

Singham, A.W. (editor). 1977. *The Nonaligned Movement in World Politics*. Westport, CT: Lawrence Hill.

Sisk, Timothy D. 1994. *Democratization in South Africa: The Elusive Social Contract*. Princeton, NJ: Princeton University Press.

Smith, Derek D. 2006. *Deterring America: Rogue States and the Proliferation of Weapons of Mass Destruction*. New York, NY: Cambridge University Press.

Smith, Steve. 2008. "Six Wishes for a More Relevant Discipline of International Relations," in *The Oxford Handbook of International Relations*, edited by Christian Reus-Smit and Duncan Snidal. New York, NY: Oxford University Press.

Smith, Tony. 2009. "Wilsonianism after Iraq: The End of Liberal Internationalism?" in *The Crisis of American Foreign Policy: Wilsonianism in the Twenty-first Century*, edited by G. John Ikenberry, et al. Princeton, NJ: Princeton University Press.

Soederberg, Susanne. 2006. *Global Governance in Question: Empire, Class and the New Common Sense in Managing North/South Relations*. London: Pluto Press.

Solingen, Etel. 2007. *Nuclear Logics: Contrasting Paths in East Asia and the Middle East*. Princeton, NJ: Princeton University Press.

Speth, James Gustave. 2003. "Two Perspectives on Globalization and the Environment," in *Worlds Apart: Globalization and the Environment*, edited by James Gustave Speth, at the Yale School of Forestry and Environmental Studies. Washington, DC: Island Press.

Sriram, Chandra L. and Wermester, Karin (editors). 2003. *From Promise to Practice: Strengthening the UN Capacities for the Prevention of Violent Conflict*. Boulder, CO: Lynne Rienner Publishers.

Stavrianos, L.S. 1981. *Global Rift: The Third World Comes of Age*. New York, NY: William Morrow.

Steinberg, James B. 2007. "Weapons of Mass Destruction and the Use of Force," in *Beyond Preemption: Force and Legitimacy in a Changing World*, edited by Ivo H. Daalder. Washington, DC: Brookings Institution Press.

Stern, Sheldon M. 2003. *Averting "The Final Failure"—John F. Kennedy and the Secret Cuban Missile Crisis Meetings*. Stanford, CA: Stanford University Press.

Stiglitz, Joseph E. 2005. "The Overselling of Globalization," in *Globalization: What's New?*, edited by Michael M. Weinstein. New York, NY: Columbia University Press.

Stiglitz, Joseph E. 2010. *Free Fall: America, Free Markets, and the Sinking of the World Economy*, New York and London: W.W. Norton & Company.

Stokes, Doug and Raphael, Sam. 2010. *Global Energy Security and American Hegemony*. Baltimore, MD: Johns Hopkins University Press.

Sunstein, Cass R. 2004. *The Second Bill of Rights: FDR's Unfinished Revolution and Why We Need It More Than Ever*. New York, NY: Basic Books.

Szentes, Tamas. 1984. "The Economic Impact of Global Militarization," *Alternatives: A Journal of World Policy*, Vol. X, No. 1.

T

Tabb, William K. 2004. *Economic Governance in the Age of Globalization*. New York, NY: Columbia University Press.

Talbot, David. 2007. *Brothers: The Hidden History of the Kennedy Years*. New York, NY: Free Press.

Tamaru, Noriyoshi. 2000. "Soka Gakkai in Historical Perspective," in *Global Citizens: The Soka Gakkai Buddhist Movement in the World*, edited by David Machacek and Bryan Wilson. Oxford: Oxford University Press.

Taylor, Telford. 1971. *Nuremberg and Vietnam: An American Tragedy*. New York, NY: Bantam Books.

Tehranian, Majid. 2007. *Rethinking Civilization: Resolving Conflict in the Human Family*. New York, NY: Routledge.

Thakur, Ramesh. 2002. "Security in the New Millennium," in *Enhancing Global Governance: Towards a new Diplomacy?*, edited by Andrew F. Cooper, John English, and Ramesh Thakur. Tokyo: United Nations University Press.

Thompson, Lisa. 2007. "The Contradictions between Globalization and Development? A Perspective from Southern Africa," in *Regional Perspectives on Globalization*, edited by Paul Bowles and Henry Veltmeyer, New York, NY: Palgrave Macmillan.

Thoreau, Henry David. 1947. "Life without Principle (1861)," in *The Portable Thoreau*, edited by Carl Bode. New York, NY: Viking Press.

Tillich, Paul. 1971. *Political Expectation*. New York, NY: Harper & Row, Publishers.

Timmons, Mark. 2002. *Moral Theory: An Introduction*. Lantham, MD: Rowman and Littlefield.

Tonnesson, Stein. 2010. *Vietnam 1946: How the War Began*. Berkeley, CA: University of California Press.

Toope, Stephen. 2003. "Powerful but Unpersuasive?—The Role of the United States in the Evolution of Customary International Law," in *United States Hegemony and the Foundations of International Law*, edited by Michael Byers and Georg Nolte. Cambridge, UK: Cambridge University Press.

Totani, Yuma. 2008. *The Tokyo War Crimes Trial: The Pursuit of Justice in the Wake of World War II*. Cambridge, MA: Harvard University Asia Center-Harvard University Press.

Touraine, Alain. 1997. *What Is Democracy?*, translated by David Macey. Boulder, CO: Westview Press.

Toussaint, Eric. 2005. *Your Money [or] Your Life: The Tyranny of Global Finance—Updated Edition*, translated by Vicki B. Manus. Chicago, IL: Haymarket Books.

Toussaint, Eric. 2008. *The World Bank: A Critical Primer*, translated by Sylvain Dropsy. London: Pluto Press.

Trindade, Antonio Augusto Cancado. 2010. *International Law for Humankind: Towards a New Jus Gentium*. Lieden, The Netherlands: Martinus Nijoff Publishers.

Tully, James. 1995. *Strange Multiplicity: Constitutionalism in an Age of Diversity*. Cambridge: Cambridge University Press.

U

Ul Haq, Mahbub. 1982. "Negotiating the Future," in *Studies on a Just World Order: Toward a Just World Order*, Vol. 1, edited by Richard Falk, Samuel S. Kim, and Saul H. Mendlovitz. Boulder, CO: Westview Press.

UNDP. 1998. *Human Development Report 1998*. New York, NY: Oxford University Press.

UNDP. 2009. *Human Development Report 2007/2008—Fighting Climate Change: Human Solidarity in a Divided World*. New York, NY: United Nations Development Program.

Urbain, Olivier. 2010. *Daisaku Ikeda's Philosophy of Peace: Transformation, Dialogue and Global Citizenship*. London: I.B. Tauris.

V

van Staden, Alfred. 2007. *Between the Rule of Power and the Power of Rule: In Search of an Effective World Order*. Leiden, The Netherlands: Martinus Nijoff Publishers.

Victoria, Brian Daizen. 2006. *Zen at War—Second Edition*. Lanham, MD: Roman & Littlefield Publishers.

W

Wacquant, Loic. 2009. *Punishing the Poor: The Neo-Liberal Government of Social Insecurity*. Durham, NC: Duke University Press.

Wade, Robert Hunter. 2003. "The Disturbing Rise in Poverty and Inequality: Is it All a 'Big Lie'," in *Taming Globalization: Frontiers of Governance*, edited by David Held and Mathias Koenig-Archibugi. Cambridge, UK: Polity.

Waldron, William S. 2003. "Common Ground, Common Cause: Buddhism and Science on the Affliction of Identity," in *Buddhism and Science: Breaking New Ground*, edited by B. Alan Wallace. New York, NY: Columbia University Press.

Walker, R.B.J. 1984a. "East Wind, West Wind: Civilizations, Hegemonies, and World Orders," in *Culture, Ideology, and World Order*, edited by R.B.J. Walker. Boulder, CO: Westview Press.

Walker, R.B.J. 1984b. "World Politics and Western Reason: Universalism, Pluralism, Hegemony," in *Culture, Ideology, and World Order*, edited by R.B.J. Walker. Boulder, CO: Westview Press.

Wallerstein, Immanuel. 2003. *The Decline of American Power: The US in a Chaotic World*. New York, NY: New Press.

Weatherbee, Donald. 1984. "ASEAN Regionalism: The Salient Dimension," in *ASEAN Security and Economic Development*, edited by Karl D. Jackson and M. Hadi Soesastro. Berkeley, CA: University of California, Institute of East Asian Studies.

Weeramantry, C.G. 2004. *Universalizing International Law*. Lieden, The Netherlands: Martinus Nijhoff Publishers.

Weeramantry, C.G. 2005. *Armageddon or Brave New World?: Reflections on the Hostilities in Iraq—Second Edition*. Sri Lanka: Weeramantry International Center for Peace Education and Research.

Weeramantry, C.G. 2009. "Foreword," in *Good Faith Negotiations Leading to the Total Elimination of Nuclear Weapons: Request for an Advisory Opinion from the International Court of Justice—Legal Memorandum*. International Association of Lawyers Against Nuclear Arms (available at: www.ialana.et), Lawyers Committee on Nuclear Policy (available at: www.lcnp.org), and the International Human Rights Clinic, Human Rights Program, Harvard Law School (available at: www.law.harvard.edu/programs/hrp).

Westad, Odd Arne. 2005. *The Global Cold War: Third World Interventions and the Making of Our Times*. New York, NY: Cambridge University Press.

Weston, Burns. 1990. "Law and Alternative Security: Toward a Just World Peace," in *Alternative Security: Living Without Nuclear Deterrence*, edited by Burns H. Weston. Boulder, CO: Westview Press.

Wettstein, Florian. 2009. *Multinational Corporations and Global Justice: Human Rights Obligations of a Quasi-Governmental Institution*. Stanford, CA: Stanford University Press.

Whelan, Daniel J. 2010. *Indivisible Human Rights: A History*. Philadelphia, PA: University of Pennsylvania Press.

Whelan, Daniel J. and Donnelly, Jack. 2007. "The West. Economic and Social Rights, and the Global Human Rights Regime Setting the Record Straight," *Human Rights Quarterly*, Vol. 29, No. 4.

Williams, Randall. 2010. *The Divided World: Human Rights and its Violence*. Minneapolis, MN: University of Minnesota Press.

Winant, Howard. 2001. *The World is a Ghetto: Race and Democracy since World War II*. New York, NY: Basic Books.

Wolin, Sheldon S. 2008. *Democracy Incorporated: Managed Democracy and the Specter of Inverted Totalitarianism.* Princeton, NJ: Princeton University Press.

Woodward, David and Simms, Andrew. 2007. "Growth is Failing the Poor: The Unbalanced Distribution of the Benefits and Costs of Global Economic Growth," in *Flat World, Big Gaps: Economic Liberalization, Globalization, Poverty and Inequality*, edited by Jomo K.S. and Jacques Baudot. New York, NY: Zed Books.

Y

Yergin, Daniel and Stanislaw, Joseph. 1998. *The Commanding Heights: The Battle Between Government and the Marketplace that is Remaking the Modern World.* New York, NY: Simon & Schuster.

Yoo, John. 2005. *The Powers of War and Peace: The Constitution and Foreign Affairs After 9/11.* Chicago, IL; and London: University of Chicago Press.

Yoo, John. 2006. *War by Other Means: An Insider's Account of the War on Terror.* New York, NY: Atlantic Monthly Press.

Yoo, John. 2009. *Crisis and Command: A History of Executive Power from George Washington to George W. Bush.* New York, NY: Kaplan Publishing.

Z

Zeleza, Paul T. 2008. "Introduction: The Causes and Costs of War in Africa: From Liberation Struggles to the 'War on Terror,'" in *The Roots of African Conflict: The Causes and Costs*, edited by Alfred Nhema and Paul T. Zeleza. Athens, OH: Ohio University Press.

Index